Fodor's 2000

Ireland

W9-BYD-912

CONTENTS

MAPS

Circled letters in text correspond to letters on the photographs. For more information on the sights pictured, turn to the indicated page number ⒶⱭ⟩ on each photograph.

DESTINATION IRELAND

All the talk in Ireland these days is of change: An affluence previously unknown in the nation's history has led to a boom in the creation of luxury hotels, innovative restaurants, first-class golf courses, and stylish nightclubs. But beneath all the excitement and hurly-burly of newness, something essential and magical endures. This quintessence of Irishness is hard to define, but it has something to do with the myriad shades of green coloring a landscape that can shift suddenly from fertile plain to rugged coastal mountains. It's visible in the pace at which the locals live their lives, even in the middle of unprecedented prosperity, always taking time to laugh, sip a pint, and extend a warm welcome to a stranger.

DUBLIN

Ⓐ 47

Dublin is 1,000 years and more of history neatly packaged for your convenience. The port city on a deep bay has long attracted the attention of European invaders, and the fingerprints of her conquerors are everywhere. The gray, majestic Ⓓ**St. Patrick's Cathedral** stands on the site of the earliest Celtic settlement, where the man himself is said to have baptized locals in the 5th century. Nearby is the more austere Christ Church, built by the Viking king Sigtyggr Silkbeard in

Ⓑ 48

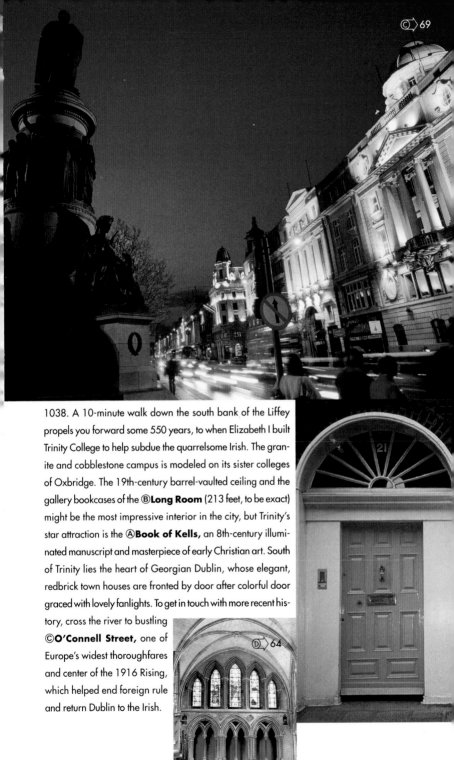

1038. A 10-minute walk down the south bank of the Liffey propels you forward some 550 years, to when Elizabeth I built Trinity College to help subdue the quarrelsome Irish. The granite and cobblestone campus is modeled on its sister colleges of Oxbridge. The 19th-century barrel-vaulted ceiling and the gallery bookcases of the ⑧**Long Room** (213 feet, to be exact) might be the most impressive interior in the city, but Trinity's star attraction is the Ⓐ**Book of Kells,** an 8th-century illuminated manuscript and masterpiece of early Christian art. South of Trinity lies the heart of Georgian Dublin, whose elegant, redbrick town houses are fronted by door after colorful door graced with lovely fanlights. To get in touch with more recent history, cross the river to bustling ©**O'Connell Street,** one of Europe's widest thoroughfares and center of the 1916 Rising, which helped end foreign rule and return Dublin to the Irish.

DUBLIN ENVIRONS

Ⓐ 147

Ⓑ 156

Like the city's great garden, the counties around Dublin—Louth, Meath, Kildare, and Wicklow—draw visitors by the thousand with a concentration of ancient sights, natural wonders, stately homes, and historical towns. The classic, English-style seaside resort town of Ⓔ**Bray** is a favorite of day-trippers. The 85-mile Ⓒ**Wicklow Way,** the nation's premier long-distance footpath—has led generations of more adventurous travelers out of the city and 1,600 feet up into the harsh splendor of the Wicklow Mountains. Nestled in a fecund valley in the middle of those mountains is the serene, early Christian St.

Ⓒ 133

Kevin's Monastery at ⓓ**Glendalough.** Along with the Norman abbey at Mellifont in Louth and the solemn neolithic burial mounds at Newgrange in Meath, Glendalough testifies to the region's role as the cradle and nursery of religion in Ireland. In Louth's historic ⓕ**Drogheda** town, the head of the martyred saint Oliver Plunkett sits preserved for all time in a glass case. Flat, grassy County Kildare is home to three first-class horse-racing tracks: the Curragh, Naas, and ⓑ**Punchestown.** Dublin's 18th-century Protestant Ascendancy had ideas about building their own temples amid the natural splendor that

encircles the capital. Their great houses and adjoining formal gardens rose up in Palladian style to honor Mammon: Russborough, Castletown, and ⓐ**Powerscourt House** are nonpareil monuments to this brash, decorous age.

ⓕ⟩ 141

11

Overlooked and underrated, the Midlands beckon to travelers who like to stray from the beaten path. Although the area lacks a coastline, its waterways are a pleasure; many Irish people refer to the region as the Lakelands. Wild, unpolluted ©**Lough Derg** is the jewel of Ireland's 800 ancient, dark blue lakes and pools and draws all those who love fishing and other water sports. The moisture in the area's rich soil supports the for-

THE MIDLANDS

mation of chocolate-brown peat bogs; ride the ®**Bord na Mona Bog Rail Tour** in County Offaly to gain some insight into the complex ecosystem underlying the mysterious landscape. The bog lands' isolation protected one of early Christian Ireland's foremost monastic settlements, Clonmacnoise. As around Dublin, Protestant landowners in the Midlands built great houses to display their wealth: Strokestown and Belvedere houses are splendid examples, but Ⓐ**Emo Court and Gardens** in County Laois, designed by James Gandon, is the

quintessence of Irish Palladian elegance. The region is home to some of the finest castle towns in Ireland. Castle Leslie, Castlepollard, and Roscommon are all classic examples of villages that grew up in the shadow of a great stronghold. What sets Birr, County Offaly, apart from the rest is the pristine condition of the Gothic Revival Ⓔ**Birr Castle Demesne.** Although the castle itself is not open to the public, you can stroll the 150-acre gardens, including the famous vine-sheltered Ⓓ**Hornbeam Allees.**

Ⓔ 180

Ⓓ 180

THE SOUTHEAST

The Southeast is the warmest, driest part of the country, and its white beaches, like Stradbally and Clonea, have drawn Irish vacationers for many generations. But there's so much more to this place than sand and sun. When Strongbow and his Norman troops landed in Ireland, it was the towns of Waterford, Wexford, and Ⓑ**Kilkenny** that they first conquered and settled. All three towns are large and vibrant; Victorian Kilkenny, with its magnificent 12th-century castle, is a requisite stop. Waterford, of course, is synonymous with fine crystal, and a tour of the ©**Waterford Glass Factory** is an hour well spent. Modern, bustling Wexford is a repository of historic Irish churches, including 12th-century Selskar Abbey. Outside ⒟**Wexford** and the other towns lies some of the most fertile countryside in Ireland—a quiet place dotted with thatched cottages where the sheep often outnumber the people. Numerous fish-rich rivers also wind through this area before spilling into the Irish Sea. On the banks of the Blackwater lies enchanting

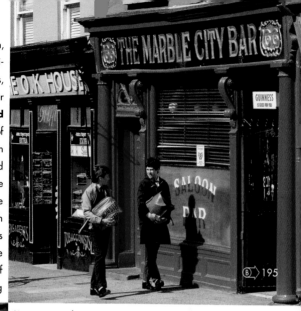

ⒸⒸ〉212

Lismore, population 920. As you cross the bridge to enter the town you'll be struck by a dramatic view of mighty ⒶⒶ**Lismore Castle,** one of many turreted, gray, stone battlements the Normans erected in the Southeast, rebuilt around ruins of its predecessor in the 19th century. Going south from Lismore the land starts to rise at last, and you enter the Knockmealdown Mountains, from which, on a good day, you can see all the way to the mist-shrouded, 200-foot Rock of Cashel.

ⒹⒹ〉202

THE SOUTHWEST

"My Own Lovely Lee," "The Lakes of Killarney," "The Rose of Tralee"— when great tenors sing about Ireland it is usually the glories of the Southwest they are praising. The awesome coast and mountains of west Cork and the three peninsulas of Kerry (the Dingle, Iveragh, and Beara) make for postcard-perfect scenery. On the Iveragh Peninsula, a short drive outside touristy Killarney Town, you can view the sunset from the 12th-century ruined church on the banks of Ⓓ**Lough Leane.** From there a steep climb into the MacGillycuddy's Reeks, Ireland's highest mountains, brings you to the glacially formed Ⓐ**Gap of Dunloe,** in the scenic Ring of Kerry loop drive where five lakes are strung beside skyscraping road. Cars are banned from the Gap, but in summer it's busy with horse and foot traffic. Dingle is the most spectacular of the three peninsulas, and cozy, pub-filled, music-crazy Ⓑ**Dingle Town** is a pleasant alternative to hectic Killarney. Native Irish speakers occupy much of the ancient peninsula, and historic sites range from Dunbeg, the Iron Age promontory fort, to 7th-century Ⓒ**Galarus Oratory,** still watertight after a millennium.

Ⓑ 273

Ⓒ 277

Ⓓ 266

17

Disney himself couldn't have designed a better place for exploring some of the key sights of modern Irish history than "the Rebel County," as County Cork is proud to call itself. Patrick Street in ⒠**Cork City,** now an upscale shopping district, saw some of the worst fighting during the 1919–21 War of Independence. And it was from nearby ⒢**Cobh Harbour,** so picturesque and tranquil today, that many of the infamous "coffin ships" carried a million immigrants to the New World. Cobh was also the last port of call for the doomed *Titanic.* Kinsale, now an affluent tourist town known for its good restaurants, was, in 1601, the site of a decisive battle that pitted the Irish and Spanish against the English and spelled the beginning of the end of Gaelic Ireland. To guard against future foreign intervention, the victorious British built indomitable ⒥**Charles Fort,** one of Europe's best preserved star forts, on top of a cliff looking out to sea. Elizabeth I settled

Ⓗ 247

Ⓘ 258

Cork with her followers, presenting to Sir Walter Raleigh 40,000 acres, including the elegant harbor town of Ⓗ**Youghal,** famed for its beautiful clock tower, in the Blackwater Valley 30 miles east of Cork City. Here as in the rest of Ireland, this new Anglo-Irish Ascendancy proceeded to build for itself some of the finest houses in Europe: few are more spectacular than Ⓘ**Bantry House,** whose fine Italianate gardens overlook the sea. In the rolling, fertile hills between Kinsale and Bantry, Michael Collins, the greatest Irish rebel of them all, was assassinated, only a few miles from Clonakilty, the town of his birth. Cork men and women developed a secret weapon to defy their British rulers, the fabled "gift of the gab." Legend has it that the source of the Irish gift for conversation and wit is the Ⓕ**Blarney Stone,** set into the walls of Blarney Castle. Lie down, throw your head back with abandon, kiss the stone, and never again will you be stuck for a word, be it praise or scorn.

Ⓙ 252

THE WEST

The West is wild—both its landscape and its people. The only part of Ireland never settled by the English, the West seems ancient, untamed, and mysteriously different from the rest of the island. Nature was surely fond of the region, lavishing it with many disparate and spectacular sites. The 710-foot-high, 5-mile-long ©**Cliffs of Moher** rise vertically out of the crashing Atlantic. That same ocean throws some of Europe's most impressive waves against the feral beaches of Ⓓ**Achill Island** and the rest of the coast. The 16-square-mile lunar-like Burren is the nation's fiercest terrain—miraculously, it is transformed into a riotously colored rock garden in summer. Beyond the Burren, the area is dotted with pristine, white-washed villages like Kinvara, Kilkee, and Ⓑ**Ballyvaughan,** where life ambles along in cozy slow mo-

Ⓐ 306

Ⓓ 308

ⓒ 305

D 336

E 320

tion, and a local fish market is the height of excitement. But put your ears up against a door or two and you might be in for a surprise: The West, especially the Gaeltacht—as the Irish-speaking regions of Connemara are known—is the heartland of traditional Irish music and dance. In the tiny coastal village of Doolin, Ⓐ**Gus O'Connor's** pub is known as the high temple of the jig and reel with its free-for-all sessions. In lively Galway City, folks gambol to a different beat, now that foreign residents have introduced an exotic flavor to the ancient city at a slew of new clubs like the salsa-inspired Ⓔ**Cuba Bar.**

THE NORTHWEST

Ⓐ⟩ 380

Like the West, the desolate Northwest of Ireland was pretty much left to its own devices by the land-hungry English settlers. What could they possibly want with Counties Donegal and Sligo—a region of rock and stone typified by Ⓐ**Malin Head,** Ireland's most northerly, most desolate point? The barren moorland surroundings and the great distance from civilization enticed St. Columba and his followers to build a monastery here, at the heart of the region in Ⓑ**Glencolumbkille,** in the 6th century. Driving from village to village through the Derryveagh Mountains, you encounter the savage coastal beauty of the

Ⓑ⟩ 367

Ⓒ⟩ 367

Gweedore Headland and Horn Head. In these relatively unspoiled villages you can still see locals go about their everyday lives, from the pubs of tiny Fal Carrach to the harbor of the fishing town of ©**Killybegs.** Irish is still the first language in many parts of isolated northern Donegal. When fin-de-siècle poets attempted to revive native Irish culture they often sought inspiration in the Northwest. William Butler Yeats was

Ⓓ 360

Ⓔ 352

among the most eloquent to celebrate the lakes, farms, woodland, and dramatic mountains around the now-prosperous market center of Ⓔ**Sligo Town.** "The Lake Isle of Inishfree" is his lament, written from exile, for the island at the center of serene Ⓕ**Lough Gill,** as popular today among fishermen as it once was with writers. In "Under Ben Bulben" the poet talked of where he wanted to be buried and the words he wanted on his gravestone, which you can see today in small Ⓓ**Drumcliff** church, under the shadow of the mountain he loved so well.

Ⓕ 357

NORTHERN IRELAND

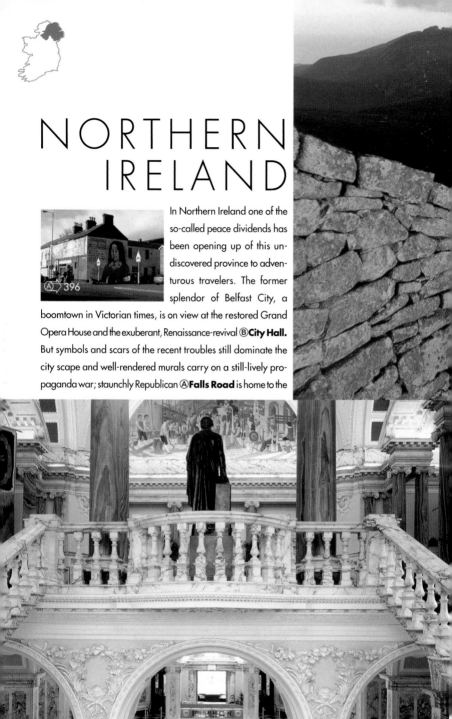

In Northern Ireland one of the so-called peace dividends has been opening up of this undiscovered province to adventurous travelers. The former splendor of Belfast City, a boomtown in Victorian times, is on view at the restored Grand Opera House and the exuberant, Renaissance-revival Ⓑ**City Hall.** But symbols and scars of the recent troubles still dominate the city scape and well-rendered murals carry on a still-lively propaganda war; staunchly Republican Ⓐ**Falls Road** is home to the

Ⓐ 396

Ⓑ 395

© 426

finest examples of this urban art. However disturbing, the tribulations of men can seem somehow temporary when you ponder the beauty of the North's varied landscape. Along the coast of County Antrim, the hazy sea pounds at the base of high, green hills dotted with lush, gently curved glens carved out by glaciers at the end of the Ice Age. Hidden in the glens, small towns like Ballycastle carry on an older, less hurried way of life typified by the ⒟**Oul' Lammas Fair,** a modern version of the ancient harvest festival of Lughnasa. Another wonder, the 37,000 hexagonal basalt pillars known as the ⒠**Giants Causeway,** is the North's premier tourist attraction. Walled Derry and massive Lough Neagh dominate the middle and western sections of the

province, and south of Belfast and scenic Strangford Lough, songwriter Percy French's rolling ©**Mountains of Mourne** "sweep down to the sea"—the most peaceful place in this new province of peace.

⒠ 410

⒟ 410

GREAT ITINERARIES

ATLANTIC OCEAN

Public transportation in rural Ireland is too unreliable and expensive to make it worthwhile. Trains only go to major towns, and bus service is infrequent to many of the more interesting sights and villages off the beaten path. You really need a car to get the most out of your visit.

Highlights of Ireland: The East and the South

5 days

The classical splendor of the great buildings in and around Dublin, the lush Southwest, rugged County Wicklow, and the historic Meath plains are all just a few hours' drive apart. Listen for the variety of accents along the way— proof (if you needed it) that

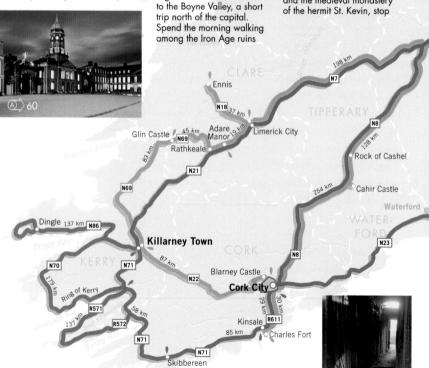

Ⓐ ▷ 60

there is no such thing as a "typical" Irish person.

DUBLIN
1 day. Head straight to Dublin's center. Spend the morning exploring 400-year-old Trinity College. After lunch and a "swift one" in a pub, stroll around the rest of the compact city center, taking in the elegant Georgian architecture around St. Stephen's Green, the austere Ⓐ Dublin Castle, and the national treasures in the museums around Merrion Square and pedestrian Grafton Street. Stop for tea and scones at the Shelbourne Hotel and wind up the day with a show at the Abbey Theatre.
☞ *Exploring Dublin in Chapter 2*

BOYNE VALLEY AND COUNTY WICKLOW
2 days. Rent a car or join an organized tour and head out to the Boyne Valley, a short trip north of the capital. Spend the morning walking among the Iron Age ruins

and rolling Hill of Tara. After a picnic lunch on top of the hill, drive through the old Kells and then to Ⓑ Newgrange, one of Europe's most spectacular prehistoric tombs. One thousand years older than Stonehenge, the great white-quartz structure merits two or three hours. Spend the rest of your day driving through the low hills and valleys of verdant County Meath and on to the Georgian village of Slane. Dominating the town is elegant Slane Castle and 500-ft Slane Hill. The following day, drive through the County Wicklow mountains. You might want to get out of your car in one of the small, quiet towns along the Wicklow Way, Ireland's premier hiking trail, and go for a short hike. Drive on to stately Powerscourt House, whose grounds are perhaps the finest in the country. On the way to Glendalough and the medieval monastery of the hermit St. Kevin, stop

Ⓑ ▷ 139

for a bite in Roundwood, Ireland's highest village.
☞ *North of Dublin in the Boyne Valley, and County Wicklow's Coast and Mountains in Chapter 2*

WEST CORK AND KERRY

2 days. Head south to Cork City, perfect for half a day of walking. Drive directly south to Kinsale, an old fishing town-turned-resort with many good restaurants. A slow three- or four-hour drive along the coast and up through the small towns of west County Cork takes you through the kind of lush landscape that inspired Ireland's nickname, the Emerald Isle. Spend the night in the market town of Skibbereen. Next morning, cross into County Kerry and head

Kells
Slane
Drogheda
26 km
Newgrange
Hill of Tara
63 km
33 km
N3 **N2**
MEATH
Castletown House 20 km
79 km **N7**
Dublin
R117
Russborough House
N7 Powerscourt House
Emo Court and Gardens
54 km
Roundwood
Glendalough
N11
WICKLOW
254 km
WEXFORD
N25
Wexford

straight for popular, bustling Killarney Town, right at the center of a scattering of azure lakes and heather-clad mountains. It's a good base for exploring your pick of three great Atlantic-pounded peninsulas: The Beara Peninsula, the Ring of Kerry, and the Dingle Peninsula. All offer stunning ocean views, hilly landscapes, and welcoming towns with good

B&Bs. The five-hour drive back to Dublin takes you through Limerick City and the lakes of the Midlands.
☞ *Cork City and Environs, Kinsale to Glengarriff via Bantry Bay, the Ring of Kerry, In and Around Killarney, the Dingle Peninsula, and North Kerry and Shannonside in Chapter 5*

Great Irish Houses and Castles

5 to 7 days

If you have an interest in architecture, interior design, and history (including the sinister and macabre kind), then a tour of Ireland's great houses and castles is for you. You might even decide to splurge and stay at one of the grand country-house hotels along the way. It's best to go between June and September, when the maximum number of houses are open. In other months expect to make an appointment a day or so in advance to view a house.

DUBLIN AND ENVIRONS

2 days. Right in the center of Dublin is the historic Dublin Castle and the elegant, 18th-century Royal Hospital Kilmainham. Walk along the inner-city stretch of the River Liffey for excellent views of two of architect James Gandon's Georgian masterpieces, the Custom House and the Four Courts. South of the river, Georgian domestic town architecture is at its best on Merrion Square and Fitzwilliam Street. On day two go west of Dublin to Castletown House, one of Ireland's most magnificent Georgian structures, in Celbridge, County Kildare; it serves as the headquarters of the Irish Georgian Society. From here head south into County Wicklow to visit Russborough House near Blessington.
☞ *Exploring Dublin in Chapter 1 and County Kildare and West Wicklow in Chapter 2*

© 252

THE ROAD TO CORK

1 day. Leave early from Dublin, heading southwest on the road to Cork. Stop on the way at Emo Court and Gardens, another James Gandon design and one of the finest large country houses near Dublin open to the public. You'll pass the Rock of Cashel on your way to Cahir Castle. Continue to Cork City. If you have time, stop at the coastal bulwark, ©Charles Fort, about half an hour south of the city. Spend the night in Cork.
☞ *The Eastern Midlands in Chapter 3; The Nire Valley, The Blackwater Valley, and County Tipperary in Chapter 4; and Cork City and Environs and Kinsale to Glengarriff via Bantry Bay in Chapter 5*

AROUND KILLARNEY

2 days. From Cork City, a short detour off the main road to Killarney leads to ruined 15th-century Blarney Castle, where you can kiss the famed Blarney Stone. Nearby Blarney House was built in 1784 in Scottish baronial style. In Killarney itself, Muckross House, a mid-Victorian manor, is worth seeing for its grounds full of flowers and outstanding rock garden. After a night in Killarney Town, head north to the Shannon estuary, on whose shore looms Glin Castle, ancestral home of the great Anglo-Norman Fitzgeralds. Continue to Rathkeale and Castle Matrix. Stop for tea or dinner at Adare Manor. Stay overnight in or near Limerick City or Ennis.
☞ *Cork City and Environs, In and Around Killarney, and North Kerry and Shannonside in Chapter 5*

Highlights of Ireland: The West and the North

6 to 7 days

"To hell or to Connaught" was the choice given the native population by Cromwell, and indeed the harsh, barren landscape of parts of the west and north might appear cursed to the eye of an uprooted farmer. But there is an appeal in the very wildness of counties

Clare, Galway, Mayo, Sligo, and Donegal—their stunning, steep coastlines hammered and shaped for aeons by the Atlantic. Here, in isolated communities, you'll hear locals speaking Irish as they go about their everyday lives. To the east, in the lusher pastures of long-suffering Northern Ireland, the arrival of peace has opened a treasure trove of gems for travelers.

GALWAY AND CLARE

2 days. A three-hour drive west from Dublin leads straight to the 710-ft ⓓCliffs of Moher,

perhaps the single most impressive sight in Ireland. Using the waterside village of Ballyvaughan as your base, spend a day exploring the lunar landscape of the harsh, limestone Burren. In spring it becomes a mighty rock garden of exotic colors. The next morning head north out of Ballyvaughan toward Galway City. On the way you'll pass 2-million-year-old Ailwee Cave and picture-perfect Kinvara. Galway City, spectacularly overlooking

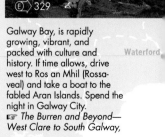

Galway Bay, is rapidly growing, vibrant, and packed with culture and history. If time allows, drive west to Ros an Mhil (Rossaveal) and take a boat to the fabled Aran Islands. Spend the night in Galway City.
☞ *The Burren and Beyond— West Clare to South Galway,*

F > 411

an inlet of Clew Bay, and some of the west coast's finest beaches are nearby. Your drive north leads right through the heart of Yeats Country in Sligo. Just north of cozy Sligo Town is the stark outline of a great hill, Ben Bulben, in whose shadow poet W.B. Yeats wanted to be buried. South of town, follow the signposted Yeats Trail around woody, gorgeously scenic Lough Gill. Continuing north, you pass Yeats's simple grave in unassuming Drumcliff, a 3000 BC tomb in Creevykeel, and small Donegal Town. Head north through Letterkenny on the tight, meandering roads, into the windswept mountains and along the jagged coastline of northern Donegal. A trip on a fishing boat to one of the many islands off the coast is a must, as is a slow drive along the coast from the Gweedore Headland, covered with heather and gorse, to the former plantation village of Dun Fionnachaid (Dunfanaghy), heart of Donegal's Gaelic-speaking Gaeltacht region and a friendly place to spend the night.
☞ *Through Connemara and County Mayo in Chapter 6,*

Yeats Country—Sligo Town and Environs, Around Donegal Bay, and Northern Donegal in Chapter 7

NORTHERN IRELAND
2 days. Begin exploring the province in historic, divided Derry City (called Londonderry by Unionists), Northern Ireland's second city. A few hours is sufficient to take in the views from the old city walls and the fascinating murals of the Catholic Bogside district. Continue on to two of the region's main attractions, the 13th-century Norman fortress of ⒻDunluce Castle and the ⒼGiant's Causeway, shaped from volcanic rock some 60 million years ago. Heading south, sticking to coastal roads for the best scenery, you'll soon pass through the Glens of Antrim, whose green hills roll down into the sea. Tucked away in the Glens are a number of small, unpretentious towns with great hotels. Early in the morning, head straight to Northern Ireland's capital, Belfast. The old port city, gray and usually wet, is a fascinating place recovering from years of war. A morning of driving through its streets will have to suffice before you head west through the rustic, pretty countryside to Lough Neagh, the largest lake in the British Isles. It's time to head back to Dublin, but if you're ahead of schedule, take the longer route that passes though the glorious Mountains of Mourne and around icy blue Carlingford Lough. ☞ *Around Counties Antrim and Derry, and Belfast in Chapter 8*

Galway City and the Aran Islands in Chapter 6

MAYO, SLIGO, AND DONEGAL
2 days. Northwest of Galway City is tiny ⒺClifden, with some of the country's best Atlantic views. From here, head east through one of the most beautiful stretches of road in Connemara—through Kylemore Valley, home of Kylemore Abbey, a huge Gothic Revival castle. After seeing the castle and its grounds, head north through tiny Leenane (the setting of the hit Broadway play *The Beauty Queen of Leenane*) and on to the most attractive town in County Mayo, Westport. It's the perfect spot to spend the night: The 18th-century planned town is on

G > 410

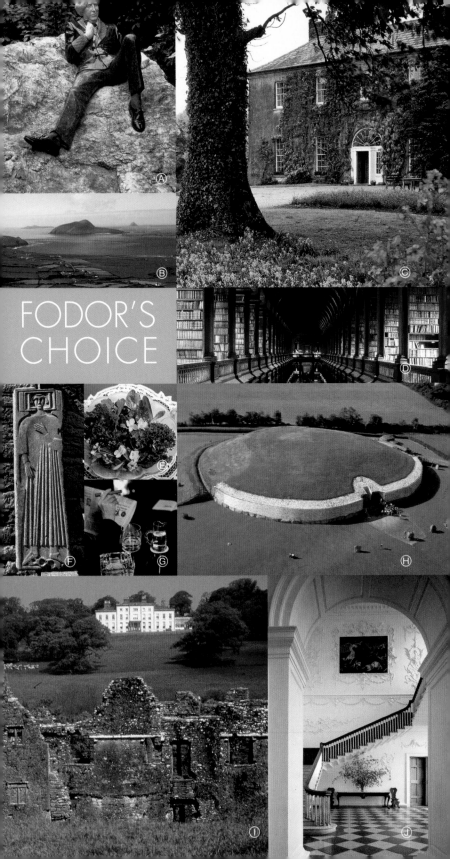

FODOR'S
CHOICE

Even with so many special places in Ireland, Fodor's writers and editors have their favorites. Here are a few that stand out.

QUINTESSENTIAL IRELAND

Ballyhack Village from Passage East, Waterford. The view of the village and its imposing castle at the top of the harbor is inspiring. ☞ p. 209

ⓑ **Blasket Islands from Slea Head, near Dingle.** The view of these rugged—and now uninhabited—islands from the top of these towering cliffs is stunning. ☞ p. 275

Dusk over Killarney's Lower Lake from Aghadoe Heights. Queen Victoria was reputedly overwhelmed by the vista. ☞ p. 266

ⓐ **Georgian squares on a Sunday, Dublin.** St. Stephen's Green and Merrion Square are havens of tranquillity. ☞ p. 52

Glendalough Valley, County Wicklow. This valley with two lakes is home to some of the country's most significant monastic ruins. ☞ p. 149

HISTORIC BUILDINGS AND MONUMENTS

ⓙ **Castletown House, Celbridge.** Begun in 1722, this Palladian-style house is one of the country's architectural glories. ☞ p. 153

Clonmacnoise, County Offaly. One of Ireland's most important monastic settlements, it was famous throughout Europe as a center for learning. ☞ p. 179

Crown Liquor Saloon and the Grand Opera House, Belfast. These two edifices represent the height of the city's Victorian splendor. ☞ p. 397

Glenveagh Castle, County Donegal. This 19th-century house is grand and luxurious, with delightful gardens. ☞ p. 377

ⓗ **Newgrange, County Meath.** A spectacular prehistoric tomb, it dates from the 4th millennium BC. ☞ p. 139

ⓕ **Rock of Cashel, Cashel.** These ruins—cathedral, chapel, and round tower—

are perched dramatically atop a hill. ☞ p. 220

ⓓ **Trinity College, Dublin.** Ireland's oldest university is full of genteel charm. ☞ p. 47

FLAVORS

Deane's, Belfast. Michael Deane trained in Thailand, as you can tell from his innovative cuisine. $$$$ ☞ p. 399

Patrick Guilbaud, Dublin. Guilbaud's chef and staff are French, and the cooking is *magnifique!* $$$$ ☞ p. 77

Peacock Alley, Dublin. Chef-owner Conrad Gallagher cooks with great brio and style. $$$$ ☞ p. 76

Rathsallagh House, Dunlavin, County Wicklow. The culinary talents of owner Kay O'Flynn have become legendary. $$$$ ☞ p. 157

Vintage, Kinsale. Owners Raoul and Seiko de Gendre, a Swiss-Japanese couple, bring sophistication to classical cuisine. $$$$ ☞ p. 252

ⓘ **Longueville House, Mallow.** William O'Callaghan trained with leading European chefs before returning to Ireland to cook in his family's 18th-century country-house hotel. $$$ ☞ p. 250

Shanks, Clandeboye, Bangor, County Down. The Millers run one of Northern Ireland's best restaurants. $$$ ☞ p. 400

ⓒ **Ballymaloe House, Shanagarry, County Cork.** The Allens continue to refine contemporary Irish cooking at their elegant inn. $$$ ☞ p. 248

Casino House, Timoleague. In this stylish farmhouse, the Reljas have brought new standards of casual elegance to Irish country cooking. $$$ ☞ p. 255

Cromleach Lodge, Castlebaldwin. The food is excellent, and every table has panoramic views of Lough Arrow. $$$ ☞ p. 354

Drimcong House, Moycullen, County Galway. One of the elder statesmen of new Irish cuisine, Gerry Galvin creates sublime country-house fare here. $$$ ☞ p. 317

The Wineport, Athlone. The cuisine is wonderfully imaginative in this informal restaurant on the shores of Lough Ree. $$$ ☞ p. 178

COMFORTS

Kildare Hotel and Country Club, Straffan, County Kildare. The lush Arnold Palmer–designed golf course is among many attractions here. $$$$ ☞ p. 155

Merrion, Dublin. Four Georgian town houses make up this luxurious hotel. $$$$ ☞ p. 87

Mount Juliet, Thomastown, County Kilkenny. This Georgian mansion on 1,400 acres has a championship golf course and extensive riding trails. $$$$ ☞ p. 200

ⓖ **Park Hotel, Kenmare.** Formerly a bishop's palace, it's now one of Ireland's premier country-house hotels. $$$$ ☞ p. 260

St. Ernan's House, Donegal Town. On its own wooded island on Donegal Bay, this 19th-century country house is unbeatable. $$$$ ☞ p. 365

Ballynahinch Castle, Recess. This river's-edge hotel has long been a favorite retreat of statesmen and stars. $$$ ☞ p. 329

Ash-Rowan Guest House, Belfast. Every room at this Victorian B&B has its own individual style. $$–$$$ ☞ p. 403

Delphi Lodge, Leenane. This comfortable sporting lodge is surrounded by spectacular mountains-and-lakes scenery. $$ ☞ p. 333

ⓔ **Old Rectory Country House, Wicklow Town.** The comforts at this Greek Revival–style inn prove that you can be treated like royalty without spending a king's ransom. $$ ☞ p. 151

Ballymakeigh House, Youghal. In lush dairy country, this is the sort of creeper-clad Irish farmhouse you dream of finding. $ ☞ p. 247

Number 31, Dublin. This guest house occupies two Georgian mews strikingly renovated in the early '60s. $ ☞ p. 90

1 DUBLIN

Ask any Dubliner what's happening and you may hear echoes of one of W. B. Yeats's most-quoted lines: "All changed, changed utterly." You can practically hear the roar as Western Europe's most intimate capital transforms itself into its fastest-growing urban tourist destination—a boomtown of new construction and restoration. Nowhere are the changes more apparent than in Temple Bar—the cobblestoned arts and culture quarter. But the city's pleasures are uncontainable: historic Georgian buildings, 1,000-odd pubs, buzzing cafés and restaurants, museums of quiet glory, lovely green parks, and, best of all, the easy friendliness of the people.

Updated by
Anto Howard

█ **N HIS INIMITABLE, IRRESISTIBLE WAY,** James Joyce immortalized Dublin in his *Ulysses, Dubliners,* and *A Portrait of the Artist as a Young Man,* filling his works with the people he knew, with their own words, and with not a few of his own. As it turns out, he became one of Dublin's most famous exiles. Disappointed with the city's provincial outlook and small-town manners, he departed in 1902, at the age of 20 (his famed peers Sean O'Casey and Samuel Beckett soon followed). If, however, Joyce was to return to his genteel hometown today and take an extended, quasi-Homeric odyssey through the city (as he does so famously in *Ulysses*), would he even recognize Dublin as his "Dear Dirty Dumpling, foostherfather of fingalls and dotthergills"?

What would he make of Temple Bar—the city's erstwhile down-at-heels neighborhood now crammed with chic restaurants and stylish hotels in its reborn state as Dublin's "Left Bank"? Or the Liffey quays, whose makeover have them standing in for Hollywood backlots? (Not so long ago, he would have found Daniel Day-Lewis acting in Jim Sheridan's film *The Boxer* near the Ha'penny Bridge.) Or of the new Irishness, where every aspect of Celtic culture is hot-hot: Frank McCourt's *Angela's Ashes* dominates American best-seller lists (a movie version was shot in the city and elsewhere around the country); *Riverdance,* the old Irish mass-jig, has gone global; and even patriot Michael Collins has become a movie icon. Plus, the returned Joyce would be soothed by the songs of Sinéad O'Connor, fired up by the films of Neil Jordan, and stirred by the poems of Nobel laureate Seamus Heaney. In short, Irish is way in. As for Ireland's capital, elegant shops and hotels, galleries, art-house cinemas, coffeehouses, and a stunning variety of restaurants are springing up on almost every street in Dublin, transforming the genteel capital that once suffocated Joyce into a city every bit as cosmopolitan as the Paris to which he fled.

Forget the Vikings and the English. Fast-forward to the new Dublin, where the army of invaders landing at the intersection of O'Connell Street and Temple Lane are London lads on a wild bachelor night, Europeans in search of a chic weekend getaway, and representatives from America of the "FBI"—or foreign-born Irish. Thanks to "the Celtic Tiger"—the nickname given to the roaring Irish economy—this most intimate capital city in Western Europe has become a boomtown (with unemployment at an all-time low of 8%, Ireland's per-capita economy is now ranked 19th in the world, higher than that of Great Britain).

No doubt about it: The millennium belongs to Dublin. Yet, a goodly number of its citizens protest that the rapid globalization of the heretofore tranquil capital is forever changing its spirit and character. Some observers view the openings of Planet Hollywood on elegant St. Stephen's Green and the 400-seat Sports Bar in Temple Lane as signs of the corporatization of Ireland's fair city. These skeptics await the outcome of "Dublin: The Sequel"—can the "new Dublin" get beyond the rage stage and sustain its rate of phenomenal growth or will it, like London, have to suffer recession and crisis to rediscover its soul?

Happily, enough of the old Dublin remains to enchant. After all, it's the fundamentals—the Georgian elegance of Merrion Square, the Norman drama of Christ Church Cathedral, a foamy pint at an atmospheric pub—that still gratify. Fittingly, some of the most recent developments hark back to the earliest. Two multimedia shows in the downtown area remind us that Norsemen (various neighborhood names, such as Howth, Leixlip, and Dalkey, echo their historic presence) were responsible for the city's original boom. In ancient days, more than 1,500 years ago, Dublin had been little more than a crossroads—albeit a critical one—of four of the main thoroughfares that traversed the country. Then, it had two names: Baile Atha Cliath, meaning City of the Hurdles, which was bestowed by Celtic traders in the 2nd century AD and which you can still see on buses and billboards throughout the city, and Dubhlinn, or "dark pool" (the murkiness of the water was caused by peat), which is believed to have been where Dublin Castle now stands.

In 837, Norsemen from Scandinavia carried out the first invasion on Dublin, only to be followed by other waves of warriors staking their claim to the city—from the 12th-century Anglo-Normans to Oliver Cromwell in 1651. Not until the 18th century did Dublin reach a period of glory, when a golden age of enlightened patronage by wealthy nobles turned the city into one of Europe's most prepossessing capitals. Streets and squares, such as Merrion and Fitzwilliam squares, were constructed with neoclassic dignity and Palladian grace. If, today, Dublin is still redolent in parts of the elegance of the 18th century, it is due to the imminently refined Georgian style of art and architecture, which flowered in the city between 1714 and 1820 during the English reigns of the three Georges. To satisfy the taste for luxury of the often-titled, unusually wealthy members of society, lemon-color chintz borders, gilded Derbyshire pier tables, and Adamesque boiseries were installed in the salons of town houses. The arts also flourished: Handel, the German-born English composer, wrote much of his great oratorio *Messiah,* here, where it was first performed in 1742. But the aura of "the glorious eighteenth" was short-lived; in 1800, the Act of Union brought Ireland and Britain together in a common United Kingdom, and political power moved from Dublin to London. Dublin quickly lost its cultural and social sparkle, as many members of the nobility moved to the new power center, turning Ireland practically overnight into "the Cinderella of all nations," in historian Maurice Craig's words.

The 19th century proved to be a time of political turmoil and agitation, although Daniel O'Connell, a lord mayor of Dublin, won early success with the introduction of Catholic emancipation in 1829. During the late 1840s, Dublin escaped the worst effects of the famine, caused by potato blight, that ravaged much of southern and western Ireland. As an emerging Victorian middle class introduced an element of genteel snobbery to the city, Dublin began a rapid outward expansion to the new suburban enclaves of Ballsbridge, Rathgar, and Rathmines on the southside and Clontarf and Drumcondra on the northside.

The city entered a period of cultural ferment (☞ Literary Dublin *in* Pleasures and Pastimes, *below*) in the first decade of the 20th century— an era that had its political apotheosis in the Easter Uprising of 1916. A war aimed at winning independence from Britain began in County Tipperary in 1919 and lasted for three years. Dublin remained comparatively unscathed during this period, but during the Civil War, which followed the setting up of the Irish Free State in December 1921, the Four Courts and the Custom House both came under fire and were severely damaged. The capital had to be rebuilt during the 1920s. After the Civil War was over, Dublin entered a new era of political and cultural conservatism, which continued until the late 1970s. Amazingly, the major turning point in Dublin's fortunes occurred in 1972, when Ireland, emerging from 40 years of isolationism, joined the European Economic Community. In the 1980s, while the economy remained in the grasp of recession, Dublin and Ireland once again turned to the cultural sphere to announce itself to the rest of the world. Irish musicians stormed the American and British barricades of rock-and-roll. Bob Geldof and the Boomtown Rats ("I Don't Like Mondays") and Chris de Burgh were among the most prominent of the musicians who found audiences well beyond their native shores, but it was U2, which climbed to the topmost heights of rock-and-roll stardom, that forged a permanent place in international popular culture for Irish musicians. Sinéad O'Connor and the Cranberries have since followed, and more are on the fast track.

If the 1980s saw the ascent of Irish rock stars, the 1990s were truly the boom years—a decade of broadly improved economic fortunes, major capital investment, declining unemployment, and reversing patterns of immigration—all set in motion to a great extent by Ireland's participation in the EEC (now the European Union, or EU). When Ireland overwhelmingly approved the new EU treaty in 1992, it was one of the poorest European nations; it qualified for EU grants of all kinds. Since then, money has, quite simply, *poured* into Ireland—nowhere more so than in Dublin. The International Financial Services Centre, gleaming behind the two-centuries-old Custom House, is one of the most overt signs of the success the city has had in attracting leading multinational corporations, particularly those in telecommunications, software, and service industries. In the spring of 1998, the Irish overwhelmingly voted in favor of membership in the Single European Currency; starting in January 1999, all prices had to be quoted in pounds and Euros, even though the European supercurrency as of press time was not yet in circulation. By the year 2002, Ireland's main currency is to be the Euro and the pound is to be faded out altogether.

Today, roughly half of the Irish Republic's population of 3.6 million people live in Dublin and its suburbs. It's a city of young people—astonishingly so. Students from all over Ireland attend Trinity College and the city's dozen other universities. On weekends, their counterparts from Paris, London, and Rome fly in, swelling the city's youthful contingent, crowding its pubs and clubs to overflowing. After graduating, more and more young people are sticking around rather than emigrating to New York or London, filling the raft of new jobs set up by multinational corporations and contributing to the hubbub that's evident everywhere.

At press time, plans for millennium celebrations were just getting into full swing. They will focus on a new architectural wonder, the Millennium Needle, on O'Connell Street, on the spot where Nelson's Pillar once stood before the IRA blew it up in 1966. A new state-of-the-art Opera House and National Convention Center are both planned along the quays. "Me darlin' Dublin's dead and gone," so goes the old traditional ballad, but the rebirth, at times difficult and a little messy, has been a spectacular success.

Pleasures and Pastimes

Literary Dublin

Dublin packs more literary punch per square foot than practically any other spot on the planet—largely because of the ferment that took hold at the end of the 19th century, when two main cultural movements emerged. In 1893, Douglas Hyde, a Protestant and later the first president of Ireland, founded the Gaelic League (Conradh na Gaelige), whose goal was to preserve the Irish language and Gaelic traditions. At the same time, W. B. Yeats played a pivotal role in the Irish literary renaissance. With the foundation of the **Abbey Theatre** (☞ The Arts, *below*) in 1904 and the growing prominence of such playwrights as

Sean O'Casey and J. M. Synge, Irish literature thrived. The **Dublin Writers Museum** (☞ Exploring Dublin, *below*) gives a terrific introduction to this story and to the more than two dozen major writers Ireland subsequently produced (at least the dead ones—living legends have to wait to be included). To go further back in literary history, head for **Trinity College** (☞ Exploring Dublin, *below*), where you can see a few pages of the legendary 9th-century Book of Kells and stroll through the hallowed campus where Samuel Beckett studied and where a theater now bears his name. If you're an Oscar Wilde fan, you can pay homage at 1 Merrion Square. The **"ReJoyce!"** Close-Up box (☞ *below*) guides you through some key sites connected with Joyce and *Ulysses*. And if you want to stock up on anecdotes about the relationship between the pint and the pen, take the "Dublin Literary Pub Crawl" (☞ Guided Tours *in* Dublin A to Z, *below*).

Musical Dublin

Music fills Dublin's streets (especially **Grafton Street**) and its pubs, where *talk* of music is as popular as the tunes themselves. Dubliners are obsessed with music of every kind and will happily discuss anything from Elvis's earliest recordings (remember Jimmy's father in *The Commitments*?) to U2's latest incarnation. The city has been the stomping ground of so many big-league rock and pop musicians that Dublin Tourism has created a "Rock 'n Stroll" Trail (☞ Guided Tours *in* Dublin A to Z, *below*) that covers 16 sites, most of them in the city center and **Temple Bar**. It includes spots like **Bewley's**, where Bob Geldof and the other members of the Boomtown Rats hung out, and the Bad Ass Café, where Sinéad O'Connor once worked. You're forgiven if you think some connections between the trail sites and the musicians seem hokey, but you're not if you don't seek out Dublin's lively, present-day music scene. A number of small pubs and larger halls host live music, but the best places are midsize venues such as **Olympia Theatre** and the **Temple Bar Music Centre**, where you can hear well-established local acts *and* leading international artists (including world-renowned Irish musicians), playing everything from traditional and folk rock to jazz-funk and "Dubcore," a term coined to describe the city's many noisy alternative bands.

A Thousand Pubs

Even if you only order an Evian, a visit to an Irish pub (or two or three) is a must. The Irish public house is a national institution—down to the spectacle, at some pubs, of patrons standing at closing time to the playing of Ireland's national anthem. Samuel Beckett would often repair to one, believing a glass of Guinness stout was the best way to ward off depression. Indeed, Dublin is for the stout of heart—the city has one pub for every 450 of its 500,000 adults. There are actor's pubs, sports pubs, even pubs for "failed literary types" (Grogan's on South William Street). And any occasion—be it "ordinations, liquidations, cremations," as one storefront puts it—is the right occasion. Today, Irish pubs are being exported at an unprecedented rate all around the world (☞ The Pub *in* Pleasures and Pastimes, but in Dublin, it's a different story altogether. Here, surprisingly, modern, European-style café-bars are fast replacing the capital's traditional drinking spots. The extraordinary prices being offered for the old pubs by new entrepreneurs have proven hard to resist for the long-time owners. The city center is now dotted with high-concept designer pubs with bright, arty facades and a pervasive scent of affluence. To be sure, in the City of 1,000 Pubs, you're still certain of finding a good, old-fashioned watering hole. And if you do find yourself in a new spot, surrounded by the trappings of European chic, you'll soon discover that Dubliners still enjoy good *craic*—quintessentially Irish friendly chat and lively, irony-laced conversation. Wherever you go, remember that when you order a Guinness, the barman first pours it three-quarters of the way, lets it settle, then tops it off and brings it over to the bar. You should then wait again until the top-up has settled, at which point the brew turns a deep black. The mark of a perfect pint? As you drink the glass down, the brew will leave thin rings to mark each mouthful.

EXPLORING DUBLIN

In Dublin's fair city—"where the girls are so pretty" went the centuries-old ditty. Today, parts of the city—particularly the vast, uniform housing projects of the northern suburbs—may not be fair or pretty. But even if you're not conscious of it while you're in the city center, Dublin is in a beautiful setting: It loops around the edge of Dublin Bay and on a plain at the edge of the gorgeous, green, Dublin and Wicklow Mountains, rising softly just to the south. From the famous **Four Courts** building in the heart of town, the sight of the city, the bay, and the mountains will take your breath away. From the city's noted vantage points, such as the **South Wall,** which stretches far out into Dublin Bay, or from choice spots in the suburbs of south and north County Dublin, you can nearly get a full measure of the city. From north to south, Dublin stretches 16 km (10 mi). From its center, immediately adjacent to the port area and the River Liffey, the city spreads westward for an additional 10 km (6 mi); in total, it covers 28,000 acres. But its heart is far more compact than these numbers indicate. As in Paris, London, and Florence, and as in so many other cities throughout the world, a river runs right through Dublin. The River Liffey divides the capital into the "northside" and the "southside," as everyone calls the two principal center-city areas, and almost all the major sights in the area are well within less than an hour's walk of one another.

Coverage is organized into six walks of the city center and the areas immediately surrounding it, and two excursions into County Dublin—the first to the southern suburbs, the latter to the northern. There are also two "rambles" through historic but often overlooked parts of the city. The first two walks—**The Center City: Around Trinity College** and **The Georgian Heart of Dublin**—cover many of the southside's major sites: Trinity College, St. Stephen's Green, Merrion Square, and Grafton Street. It makes sense to do these walks first, as they will quickly orient you to a good portion of the southside. The third walk—**Temple Bar: Dublin's "Left Bank"**—takes you through this revived neighborhood, which is the hottest, hippest zone in the capital. The fourth walk—**Dublin West: From Dublin Castle to the Four Courts**—picks up across the street from Temple Bar and gets you to the Guinness Brewery, the city's most popular attraction. A word about these four walks: Although we've split the southside into four, you'll soon realize that the distance between the areas in all these walks is not very great. The fifth walk—**North of the Liffey**—moves to the northside of the city center and covers all the major cultural sites there, including the James Joyce Cultural Centre, Gate Theatre, Dublin Writers Museum, and Hugh Lane Municipal Gallery of Modern Art. **Phoenix Park and Environs,** at the western fringe of the northside city center, is the main focus of the sixth Dublin walk.

If you're visiting Dublin for more than two or three days, you'll probably want to explore farther afield. There's plenty to see and do a short distance from the center city—in the suburbs of both north and south County Dublin—but since you need either a car or public transportation to reach these destinations, we cover them in our Side Trips section (☞ *below*).

Because of its compact size and traffic congestion (brought on in the last few years by an astronomical increase in the number of new vehicles), *pedestrian* traffic—especially on the city center's busiest streets during commute hours—is astonishing. Watch where you stop to consult your map or you're liable to be swept away by the ceaseless flow of the bustling crowds.

Numbers in the text correspond to numbers in the margin and on the Dublin City Center, Dublin West, County Dublin–Southside, and County Dublin–Northside maps.

Great Itineraries

In a week, you should be able to cover almost all of our Dublin exploring suggestions, including the Side Trips. But in three or even two days, you can see many city-center sites and probably come away with a greater familiarity of the city than you could establish in a similar length of time in any of Europe's other capitals.

IF YOU HAVE 1 DAY

Touring the largest city in Ireland in the space of a single day sounds like an impossible goal, but it can actually—almost—be done in the span of one sunrise to sunset. Think Dublin 101. South of the Liffey are graceful squares and fashionable terraces from Dublin's elegant Georgian heyday; interspersed with some of the city's leading sights, this area is perfect for an introductory city tour. You might begin at **O'-Connell Bridge**—as Dublin has no central focal point, most natives regard it as the city's Piccadilly Circus or Times Square—then head south down Westmoreland Street on your way to view one of Dublin's most spectacular buildings, James Gandon's 18th-century Parliament House, now the **Bank of Ireland** building. To fuel up for the walk ahead, however, first stop at 12 Westmoreland Street and go into **Bewley's Coffee House,** an institution that has been supplying Dubliners with coffee and buns since 1842. After you drink in the grand colonnade of the Bank of Ireland building, head west to the genteel, elegant campus of **Trinity College**—the oldest seat of Irish learning. Your first stop should be the Library, to see the staggering Long Room and Ireland's greatest art treasure, the **Book of Kells,** one of the world's most famous—and most beautiful—illuminated manuscripts.

Leave the campus and take a stroll along **Grafton Street,** Dublin's ritziest shopping street and—"Who will buy my beautiful roses?"—open-air flower market. Appropriately enough, one of the city's favorite relaxation spots, the lovely little park of **St. Stephen's Green,** is nearby. Head over to the northeast corner of the park to find ground zero for the city's cultural institutions. Here, surrounding the four points of Leinster House (built by the Duke of Kildare, Ireland's first patron of Palladianism), are the **National Museum,** replete with artifacts and exhibits dating back to prehistoric times; the **National Gallery of Ireland** (don't miss the Irish collection and the Caravaggio *Taking of Christ*); the **National Library;** and the **Natural History Museum.** Depending on your interests, pick one to explore, and then make a quick detour westward to **Merrion Square**—among Dublin's most famous Georgian landmarks.

For a lovely lunch, head back to Stephen's Green and the Victorian **Shelbourne Hotel**—the lobby salons glow with Waterford chandeliers and blazing fireplaces. From Stephen's Green head west to pay your respects to St. Paddy—**St. Patrick's Cathedral.** If, instead, the Dublin of artists and poets is more your speed, hop a double-decker bus and head north of the Liffey to the **Dublin Writers Museum.** End the day with a performance at the nearby **Gate Theatre,** another Georgian eye-knocker, or spend the evening exploring the cobbled streets, many cafés, and shops of Dublin's bohemian quarter, the compact **Temple Bar** area. Because you couldn't fit in a stop at the Guinness Brewery, top the evening off with a pint at the Norseman pub. By the time the barman says "Finish your pints" to announce closing time at 11 PM, you'll agree that although this day was a lightning tour of the city's main sights, it will have left an indelible impression of what Dublin is all about.

IF YOU HAVE 3 DAYS

The above tour is the grand curtain-raiser for this itinerary. Dedicate your second day to the north and west of the city center. In the morning, cross the Liffey via O'Connell Bridge and walk up **O'Connell Street,** the city's widest thoroughfare, stopping to visit the **General Post Office**—the besieged headquarters of the 1916 rebels—on your way to the **Dublin Writers Museum** and the **Hugh Lane Municipal Gallery of Modern Art.** Be sure to join the thousands of Dubliners strolling down Henry, Moore, and Mary streets, the northside's pedestrian shopping area. In the afternoon, head back to the Liffey for a quayside walk by Dublin's most imposing structure, the **Custom House;** then head west to the **Guinness Brewery.** Hop a bus or catch a cab back into the city and a blow-out dinner at the glamorous Tea Room in the **Temple Bar**'s Clarence hotel. Spend the evening on a **literary pub crawl** to see where the likes of Beckett and Behan held court, perhaps joining a special guided tour. On the third day tour the northern outskirts of Dublin from **Glasnevin Cemetery** and the **National Botanic Gardens** across to the sublime **Marino Casino** in Marino and the quaint fishing village of **Howth.** Back in the city, have tea at Bewley's and catch a musical performance at the **Olympia Theatre** or a play at the **Abbey Theatre.**

IF YOU HAVE 5 DAYS

Start your fourth day at Dublin's dawn—a living history of Dublin can be seen at medieval **Dublinia,** across the street from ancient **Christ Church Cathedral,** whose underground crypt is Dublin's oldest structure. Head north, jumping across the Liffey to the **Four Courts,** James Gandon's Georgian masterpiece and the home of the Irish judiciary. Continue northward to visit the **Royal Kilmainham Hospital**—the home of the Irish Museum of Modern Art—and Kilmainham Gaol, where the leaders of the Easter Rising were executed following their capture. Return via **Dublin Castle,** residence of British power in Ireland for nearly 800 years. On your fifth and final day explore the southern outskirts of the city, accessible by DART train, including the suburban areas of Dalkey and Sandycove (where you can visit the **James Joyce Martello Tower**), and the busy ferry port of **Dun Laoghaire.** Visit the **Chester Beatty Library,** with its many Chinese and Turkish exhibits. Before returning to the city center, take a stroll along the 5-km (3-mi) beach of **Sandymount Strand**—that is, if Irish skies are smiling!

The Center City: Around Trinity College

The River Liffey provides a useful aid to orientation, flowing as it does through the direct middle of Dublin. If you ask a native Dubliner for directions—from under an umbrella, as it will probably be raining in the approved Irish manner—he or she will most likely reply in terms of "up" or "down," up meaning away from the river, and down toward it. Until recently, Dublin's center of gravity was O'Connell Bridge, a diplomatic landmark in that it avoided locating the center to the north or south of the river, as strong local loyalties still prevailed among "northsiders" (who live to the north of the river) and "southsiders," and neither would ever accept that the city's center lay on the other's side of the river. But by the early 1990s, diplomacy had gone by the wayside. Now, Dublin's heart beats loudest southward across the Liffey, due, in part, to a large-scale refurbishment and pedestrianization of Grafton Street, which made this already upscale shopping address *the* street to shop, stop, and be seen. At the foot of Grafton Street is the city's most famous and recognizable landmark, Trinity College; at the top of it is Dublin's most popular strolling retreat, St. Stephen's Green, a 27-acre landscaped park replete with flowers, lakes, bridges, and—most of all—Dubliners enjoying a time-out.

A Good Walk

Numbers in the text correspond to numbers in the margin and on the Dublin City Center map.

Start at **Trinity College** ①, exploring the quadrangle as you head to the Old Library to see the Book of Kells. If you want to see modern art, visit the collection housed in the Douglas Hyde Gallery, just inside the Nassau Street entrance to the college. If you're interested in the Georgian era, try to view the Provost's House and its salon, the grandest in Ireland. Trinity can easily eat up at least an hour or more, so when you come back out the front gate, you can either stop in at the **Bank of Ireland** ②, a neoclassic masterpiece that was once the seat of the Irish Parliament, or make an immediate left and head up **Grafton Street** ③, the pedestrian spine of the southside. The **Dublin Tourism** ④ office is just off Grafton Street, on the corner of Suffolk Street. If Grafton Street's shops whet your appetite for more browsing and shopping, turn right down Wicklow Street, then left up South William Street to **Powerscourt Townhouse Centre** ⑤, where a faux-Georgian atrium (very dubiously set within one of Dublin's greatest 18th-century mansions) houses high-priced shops and pleasant cafés. The **Dublin Civic Museum** ⑥ is next door to Powerscourt, across the alley on its south flank. If you're doing well on time and want to explore the shopping streets farther east, jog via the alley one block east to Drury Street, from which you can access the Victorian **George's Street Arcade** ⑦. Whether or not you make this excursion, you should head back to Grafton Street, where **Bewley's Oriental Café** ⑧, a Dublin institution, is another good place for a break. Grafton Street ends at the northwest corner of **St. Stephen's Green** ⑨, Dublin's most popular public gardens; they absolutely require a stroll-through. **Newman House** ⑩ is on the south side of the green. Amble back across the green, exiting onto the northeast corner, at which sits the grand **Shelbourne Hotel** ⑪, a wonderful place for afternoon tea or a quick pint at one of its two pubs. The **Huguenot Cemetery** ⑫ is just down the street from the hotel, on the same side. If you want to see more art, make a detour to the **RHA Gallagher Gallery** ⑬.

TIMING

Dublin's city center is so compact you could race through this walk in an hour, but in order to gain full advantage of what is on offer, we recommend that you set aside at least half a day—if you can—to explore the treasures of Trinity College and amble up and around Grafton Street to Stephen's Green.

Sights to See

② **Bank of Ireland.** Across the street from the west facade of **Trinity College** (☞ *below*) stands one of Dublin's most striking buildings: now the Bank of Ireland but formerly the original home of the Irish Parliament. The building was begun in 1729 by Sir Edward Lovett Pearce, who designed the central section; three other architects would ultimately be involved in its construction. A pedimented portico fronted by six massive Corinthian columns dominates its grand facade, which follows the curve of Westmoreland Street as it meets College Green, once a Viking

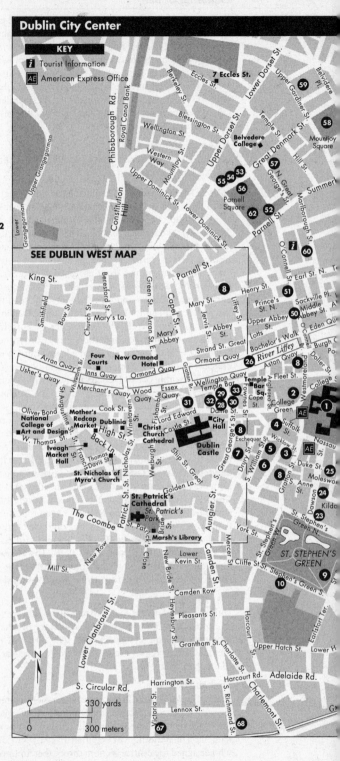

Dublin City Center

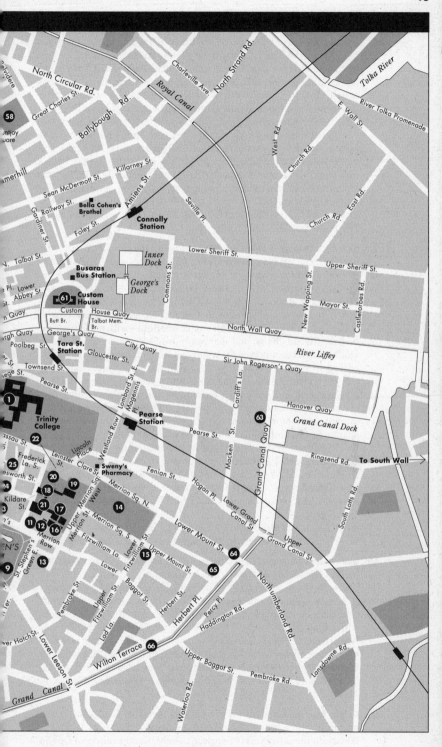

North Circular Rd.

Royal Canal

Charleville Ave.

North Strand Rd.

Tolka River

River Tolka Promenade

58

Great Charles St.

Ballybough Rd.

Killarney St.

West Rd.

E. Wall St.

Church Rd

merhill

Sean McDermott St.

Amiens St.

Church Rd.

Church Rd.

East Rd.

Railway St.

Bella Cohen's Brothel

Seville Pl.

Gardiner St.

Foley St.

Connolly Station

V. Talbot St.

Lower Sheriff St.

Upper Sheriff St.

Pl. Lower Abbey St.

Busaras Bus Station

Inner Dock

New Wapping St.

Mayor St.

Castleforbes Rd.

61 **Custom House**

George's Dock

Commons St.

Custom House Quay

n Quay

Butt Br.

Talbot Mem. Br.

North Wall Quay

rgh Quay

George's Quay

City Quay

Tara St. Station

River Liffey

Poolbeg St.

Gloucester St.

Sir John Rogerson's Quay

Townsend St.

ege St.

Pearse St.

Hanover Quay

1

Lombard St. E.

Magennis

Cardiff's La.

63 *Grand Canal Dock*

Trinity College

Pearse Station

Pearse St.

Macken St.

Ringsend Rd.

To South Wall

22

Lincoln Place

Westland Row

assau St.

Leinster St.

Clare St.

Fenian St.

Hogan Pl.

Lower Grand Canal St.

Grand Canal Quay

South Lotts Rd.

25

Frederick La. S.

Sweny's Pharmacy

esworth St.

20

Merrion Sq. N.

4

18

19

Merrion St. West

Merrion Sq.

14

Kildare St.

21

17

Merrion St.

Merrion Sq. S.

Lower Mount St.

64

3

11

16

Upper Merrion St.

Fitzwilliam La.

Upper Fitzwilliam

Upper Mount St.

Grand Canal St.

Merrion Row

12

Lower Fitzwilliam

15

65

9

13

Lower Fitzwilliam St.

Herbert St.

Northumberland Rd.

N'S

Pembroke St.

Upper Fitzwilliam St.

Baggot St.

Herbert Pl.

Percy Pl.

Haddington Rd.

er Hatch St.

Lower Leeson St.

Fitzwilliam Lad La.

66

Wilton Terrace

Upper Baggot St.

Lansdowne Rd.

Grand Canal

Waterloo Rd.

Pembroke Rd.

meeting place and burial ground. Two years after the Parliament was abolished itself in 1801 under the Act of Union, which brought Ireland under the direct rule of Britain, the building was bought for £40,000 by the Bank of Ireland. Inside, stucco rosettes adorn the coffered ceiling in the pastel-hued, colonnaded, clerestoried **main banking hall,** at one time the Court of Requests, where citizens' petitions were heard. Just down the hall is the original **House of Lords,** with tapestries depicting the Battle of the Boyne and the Siege of Derry, an oak-paneled nave, and a 1,233-piece Waterford glass chandelier; ask a guard to show you in. Visitors are welcome during normal banking hours; a brief guided tour is given every Tuesday at 10:30, 11:30, and 1:45. Accessed via Foster Place South, the small alley on the bank's east flank, the **Bank of Ireland Arts Center** frequently exhibits contemporary Irish art and has a permanent exhibition devoted to "The Story of Banking." ⊠ *2 College Green,* ☎ *01/677–6801; 01/671–1488 arts center.* ⊘ *Mon.–Wed. and Fri. 10–4, Thurs. 10–5; Arts Center Tues.– Fri. 10–4, Sat. 2–5, Sun. 10–1.*

⑧ **Bewley's Oriental Café.** The granddaddies of the capital's cafés, Bewley's has been serving coffee and buns to Dubliners since 1842 and now has four locations. Bewley's trademark stained-glass windows were designed by Harry Clarke (1889–1931), Ireland's most distinguished early 20th-century artist in this medium. They all make fine places in which to observe Dubliners of all ages and occupations; the aroma of coffee is irresistible, and the cafés' dark interiors—with marble-top tables, bentwood chairs, and mahogany trim—evoke a more leisurely Dublin. Until recently even the waitresses look appropriately Victorian, garbed in black dress with white collar, hat, and apron, but sadly they've modernized the uniform to black trousers and T-shirts. The food is overpriced and not particularly good, but people-watching here over a cup of coffee or tea is a quintessential Dublin experience. If you're interested in a more modern cup of coffee, check out the Metro Café, nearby at 43 South William Street—it's one of Dublin's best haunts for the caffeine-addicted and its staff is devoid of the devil-may-care, pseudo-existential inefficiency that seems to plague so many other Dublin cafés. ⊠ *78 Grafton St.,* ☎ *01/677–6761 (for all locations except Great George's St.);* ⊘ *Sun.–Thurs. 7:30 AM–1 AM, Fri.–Sat. 7:30 AM–4 AM.* ⊠ *13 Great George's St.,* ☎ *01/679–2078;* ⊘ *Mon.–Sat. 7:45 AM–6 PM, Fri.–Sat. 7:45 AM–6 PM and 10:30 PM–4 AM.* ⊠ *12 Westmoreland St.;* ⊘ *Mon.–Sat. 7:30 AM–9 PM, Sun. 9:30 AM–9 PM.* ⊠ *40 Mary St.;* ⊘ *Mon.–Wed. and Fri.–Sat. 7 AM–6 PM, Thurs. 7 AM–9 PM.*

⑥ **Dublin Civic Museum.** Built between 1765 and 1771 as an exhibition hall for the Society of Artists, this building later was used as the City Assembly House, precursor of City Hall. The museum's small, esoteric collection includes Stone Age flints, Viking coins, old maps and prints of the city, and the sculpted head of British admiral Horatio Nelson, which used to top Nelson's Pillar, beside the General Post Office (☞ North of the Liffey, *below*) on O'Connell Street; the column was toppled by an explosion in 1966 on the 50th anniversary of the Easter Uprising. The museum often holds exhibitions relating to the city. ⊠ *58 S. William St.,* ☎ *01/679–4260.* ▱ *Free.* ⊘ *Tues.–Sat. 10–6, Sun. 11–2.*

④ **Dublin Tourism.** Churches are not just for prayers, as this deconsecrated medieval church proves. Resurrected as a visitor center, St. Andrew's, fallen into ruin after years of neglect, now houses the offices of Dublin Tourism, a private concern that provides the most complete information on Dublin's sights, restaurants, and hotels; you can even rent a car here. Underneath the elegant roof beams and joists, made all the more pleasant by the stream of natural sunlight, the office provides reservations facilities for all Dublin hotels, as well as guided tours, a plethora of brochures, and a gift shop (beware the exorbitant prices). Upstairs is a pleasant café serving sandwiches and drinks. ⊠ *St. Andrew's Church, Suffolk St.,* ☏ *01/605–7787.* ⊙ *July–Sept., Mon.–Sat. 8:30–6, Sun. 11–5:30; Oct.–June, daily 9–6.*

❼ George's Street Arcade. This Victorian covered market fills the block between Drury Street to the west and South Great George's Street to the east. It's changed little, despite a restoration. You'll find two dozen or so stalls selling books, prints, clothing (mostly secondhand), exotic foodstuffs, and trinkets. ⊠ *S. Great George's St.* ⊙ *Mon.–Sat. 9–6.*

NEED A BREAK?

One of Dublin's most ornate traditional taverns, the **Long Hall Pub** (⊠ 51 S. Great George's St., ☏ 01/475–1590) has Victorian lamps, a mahogany bar, mirrors, chandeliers, and plasterwork ceilings, all more than 100 years old. The pub serves sandwiches and an excellent pint of Guinness.

★ ❸ Grafton Street. It's no more than 200 yards long and about 20 ft wide, but brick-lined Grafton Street, open only to pedestrians, can make a claim to be the most humming street in the city, if not in all of Ireland. It is one of Dublin's vital spines: the most direct route between the front door of Trinity College and Stephen's Green, and the city's premier shopping street, home to Dublin's two most distinguished department stores, **Brown Thomas** and **Marks & Spencer** (☞ Shopping, *below*). Both on Grafton Street itself and on the smaller alleyways that radiate off it, there are also dozens of independent stores, a dozen or so colorful flower sellers, and some of Dublin's most popular watering holes (☞ Pubs *in* Nightlife and the Arts, *below*), including a branch of **Bewley's Oriental Café** (☞ *above*). In summertime buskers from all over the country and the world line both sides of the street, pouring out the sounds of drum, whistle, pipe, and string.

❶❷ Huguenot Cemetery. One of the last such burial grounds in Dublin, this cemetery was used in the late 17th century by French Protestants who had fled persecution in their native land. The gates to the cemetery are rarely open, but you can view its grounds from the street. It stands on the northeast corner across from the square. ⊠ *27 St. Stephen's Green N.*

❶⓪ Newman House. One of the greatest glories of Georgian Dublin, Newman House is actually two imposing town houses joined together. The earliest, No. 85 St. Stephen's Green (1738), was designed by Richard Castle, favored architect of Dublin's rich and famous, and features a winged Palladian window on the Wicklow granite facade. Originally known as Clanwilliam House, it features two landmarks of Irish Georgian style: the Apollo Room, decorated with stucco work depicting the sun god and his muses; and the magnificent Saloon, "the supreme example of Dublin Baroque," according to scholars Jacqueline O'Brien and Desmond Guinness, and crowned with an exuberant ceiling aswirl with cupids and gods, created by the Brothers Lafranchini, the finest *stuccadores* (plasterworkers) of 18th-century Dublin. Next door at No. 86 (1765), the staircase is one of the city's most beautiful rococo examples, with floral swags and musical instruments picked out in cake-frosting white on pastel-color walls. Catholic University (described by James Joyce in *A Portrait of the Artist as a Young Man*) was established in this building in 1850, with Cardinal John Henry Newman as its first rector. At the back of Newman House lie **Iveagh Gardens,** a delightful hideaway with statues and sunken gardens that remains one of Dublin's best-kept secrets (you can enter via Earlsfort Terrace and Harcourt Street). The Commons Restaurant (☞ Dining, *below*) is in the basement. ⊠ *85–86 St. Stephen's Green,* ☎ *01/475–7255.* ☜ *£2.* ☉ *June–Aug., weekdays 9–5.*

❺ Powerscourt Townhouse Centre. Lucky man, this Viscount Powerscourt. In the mid-18th century, not only did he build Ireland's most spectacular country house, in Enniskerry, Country Wicklow (which bears the family name; ☞ Chapter 2), but he also decided to rival that structure's grandeur with one of Dublin's largest stone mansions. Staffed with 22 servants and built of granite from the viscount's own quarry in the Wicklow Hills, Powerscourt House was a major statement in the Palladian style designed by Robert Mack in 1774—a massive, Baroque-style edifice that towers over the little street it sits on (note the top story, framed by massive volutes, that was once intended as an observatory). Inside, the interior decoration runs from rococo salons by James McCullagh to Adamesque plasterwork by Michael Stapleton to—surprise—an imaginative shopping atrium, installed in and around the covered courtyard. The stores here include high-quality Irish crafts shops and numerous food stalls (☞ Shopping, *below*). The mall exit leads to the Carmelite **Church of St. Teresa's** and **Johnson's Court.** Beside the church, a pedestrian lane leads onto Grafton Street. ⊠ *59 S. William St.* ☉ *Mon.–Sat.*

⑬ RHA Gallagher Gallery. The Royal Hibernian Academy, an old Dublin institution, is now housed in one of the city's newer spaces, a large, well-lit building. The gallery holds adventurous exhibitions of the best in contemporary art, both from Ireland and abroad. ⊠ *15 Ely Pl. off St. Stephen's Green,* ☎ *01/661–2558.* ☜ *Free.* ☉ *Mon.–Wed. and Fri.– Sat. 11–5, Thurs. 11–9, Sun. 2–5.*

★ **⑪ Shelbourne Hotel.** The ebullient, redbrick, white wood-trimmed facade of the Shelbourne has commanded "the best address in Dublin" from the north side of St. Stephen's Green since 1824. In 1921 the Irish Free State's constitution was drafted here in a first-floor suite. The most financially painless way to soak up the hotel's old-fashioned luxury and genteel excitement is to step past the entrance—note the statues of Nubian princesses and attendant slaves—for afternoon tea (£9 per person, including sandwiches and cakes) in the elegantly green-wallpapered **Lord Mayor's Lounge** or for a drink in one of its two bars, the **Shelbourne Bar** and the **Horseshoe Bar,** both of which are thronged with businesspeople and politicos after the workday ends (☞ Pubs, *below*). Elizabeth Bowen, famed novelist, wrote her novel *The Hotel* about this very place. ⊠ *St. Stephen's Green,* ☎ *01/676–6471.*

★ **❾ St. Stephen's Green.** Dubliners call it simply Stephen's Green, and green it is (year-round)—a verdant, 27-acre city-center square that was an open common used for the public punishment of criminals until 1664. After a long period of decline, it became a private park in 1814—the first time in its history that it was closed to the general public. Its fortunes changed again in 1880, when Sir Arthur Guinness, later Lord Ardiluan (a member of the Guinness brewery family), paid for it to be laid out anew. Flower gardens, formal lawns, a Victorian bandstand, and an ornamental lake that is home to many waterfowl are all within the park's borders, connected by paths guaranteeing that strolling here or just passing through will offer up unexpected delights (be sure to look out for palm trees). Among the park's many statues are a memorial to Yeats and another to Joyce by Henry Moore, and the *Three Fates,* a dramatic group of bronze female figures watching over man's destiny. In the 18th century the walk on the north side of the green was referred to as the Beaux Walk because most of Dublin's gentlemen's clubs were in town houses here. Today it is dominated by the **Shelbourne Hotel** (☞ *above*). On the south side is another alluring attraction, Georgian-gorgeous Newman House (☞ *above*). ▨ *Free.* ☉ *Daily sunrise–sunset.*

★ ❶ **Trinity College.** Founded in 1592 by Queen Elizabeth I to "civilize" (Her Majesty's word) Dublin, Trinity is Ireland's oldest and most famous college. The memorably atmospheric campus is a must; here you can enjoy tracking the shadows of some of the more noted alumni, such as Jonathan Swift (1667–1745), Oscar Wilde (1854–1900), Bram Stoker (1847–1912), and Samuel Beckett (1906–89). Trinity College, Dublin (familiarly known as TCD) was founded on the site of the confiscated Priory of All Hallows. For centuries Trinity was the preserve of the Protestant church. A free education was offered to Catholics—provided that they accepted the Protestant faith. As a legacy of this condition, until 1966 Catholics who wished to study at Trinity had to obtain a dispensation from their bishop or face excommunication. Today more than 70% of Trinity's students are Catholics, an indication of how far away those days seem to today's generation.

Trinity's grounds cover 40 acres. Most of its buildings were constructed in the 18th and early 19th centuries. The extensive **West Front,** with a classical pedimented portico in the Corinthian style, faces College Green and is directly across from the **Bank of Ireland** (☞ *above*); it was built between 1755 and 1759, possibly the work of Theodore Jacobsen, architect of London's Foundling Hospital. The design is repeated on the interior, so the view is the same both from outside the gates and from the quadrangle inside. On the lawn in front of the inner facade are **statues** of orator Edmund Burke (1729–97) and dramatist Oliver Goldsmith (1728–74), two other alumni. Like the West Front, **Parliament Square** (commonly known as Front Square), the cobblestoned quadrangle that lies just beyond this first patch of lawn, also dates from the 18th century. On the right side of the square is Sir William Chambers's **theater,** or **Examination Hall,** dating from the mid-1780s, which contains the college's most splendid Adamesque interior (designed by Michael Ştapleton). The hall houses an impressive organ retrieved from an 18th-century Spanish ship and a gilded oak chandelier from the old House of Commons; concerts are sometimes held here. The **chapel,** which stands on the left of the quadrangle, has stucco ceilings and fine woodwork. Both the theater and the chapel were designed by Scotsman William Chambers in the late 18th century. The looming **Campanile,** or bell tower, is the symbolic heart of the college; erected in 1853, it dominates the center of the square. To the left of the campanile is the **Graduates Memorial Building,** or GMB. Built in 1892, the slightly Gothic building is now home to both the Philosophical and Historical Societies, Trinity's ancient and fiercely competitive debating groups. At the back of the square stands old redbrick **Rubrics,** looking rather ordinary and out of place among the gray granite and cobblestones. Rubrics, now used as rooms for students and faculty, dates from 1690, making it the oldest building still standing.

★ Ireland's largest collection of books and manuscripts is housed in **Trinity College Library.** Its principal treasure is the **Book of Kells,** generally considered the most striking manuscript ever produced in the Anglo-Saxon world and one of the greatest masterpieces of early Christian art. Once thought to be lost—the Vikings looted the book in 1007 for its jeweled cover but ultimately left the manuscript behind—the book is a splendidly illuminated version of the Gospels. In the 12th century, Guardius Cambensis declared that the book was made by an angel's hand in answer to a prayer of St. Bridget; in the 20th century, scholars decided instead that the book originated on the island of Iona in Scotland, where followers of St. Colomba lived until the island came under siege in the early to mid-9th century. They fled to Kells, County Meath (☞ Chapter 2), bringing the book with them. The 680-page work was rebound in four volumes in 1953, two of which are usually displayed at a time, so you typically see no more than four original pages. (Some wags have taken to calling it the "Page of Kells.") However, such is the incredible workmanship of the Book of Kells that one folio contains the equivalent of many other manuscripts. On some pages, it has been determined that within a quarter inch, no fewer than 158 interlacements of a ribbon pattern of white lines on a black background can be discerned—little wonder some historians feel this book contains all the designs to be found in Celtic art. Note, too, the extraordinary colors, some of which were derived from shellfish, beetles' wings, and crushed pearls. The most famous page shows the "XPI" monogram (symbol of Christ), but if this page is not on display, you can still see a replica of it, and many of the other lavishly illustrated pages, in the adjacent exhibition—dedicated to the history, artistry, and conservation of the book—through which you must pass to see the originals.

Because of the fame and beauty of the Book of Kells, it is all too easy to overlook the other treasures in the library. They include the Book of Armagh, a 9th-century copy of the New Testament that also contains St. Patrick's Confession, and the legendary Book of Durrow, a 7th-century Gospel book from County Offaly. At peak hours you may have to wait in line to enter the library; it's less busy early in the day.

The **Old Library,** aptly known as the **Long Room,** is one of Dublin's most staggering sights, at 213 ft long and 42 ft wide. It contains in its 21 alcoves approximately 200,000 of the 3 million volumes in Trinity's collection. Originally the room had a flat plaster ceiling, but in 1859–60 the perennial need for more shelving resulted in a decision to raise the level of the roof and add the barrel-vaulted ceiling and the gallery bookcases. Since the 1801 Copyright Act, the college has received a copy of every book published in Britain and Ireland, and a great number of these publications must be stored in other parts of the campus and beyond. Of note are the carved Royal Arms of Queen Elizabeth I, above the library entrance—the only surviving relic of the original college buildings—and, lining the Long Room, a grand series of marble busts, of which the most famous is Roubiliac's portrait of Jonathan Swift. The **Trinity College Library Shop** sells books, clothing, jewelry, and postcards. ☎ *01/608–2308.* 🖼 *£3.50.* ⊙ *June–Sept: Mon.–Sat. 9:30–5, Sun. 9:30–4:30; Oct.–May: Mon.–Sat. 9:30–5, Sun. noon–4:30.*

Trinity College's stark, modern Arts and Social Sciences Building, with an entrance on Nassau Street, houses the **Douglas Hyde Gallery of Modern Art,** which concentrates on contemporary art exhibitions and has its own bookstore. Also in the building, down some steps from the gallery, there's a snack bar with coffee, tea, sandwiches, and students willing to talk about life in the old college. ☎ *01/608–1116.* 🖼 *Free.* ⊙ *Mon.–Wed. and Fri. 11–6, Thurs. 11–7, Sat. 11–4:45.*

The **New Berkeley Library,** the main student library at Trinity, was built in 1967 and named after the philosopher and alumnus George Berkeley. The small open space in front of the library contains a spherical brass sculpture designed by Arnaldo Pomodoro. The library is not open to the general public. ⊠ *College Green,* ☎ *01/677–2941.* ⊙ *Grounds daily 8 AM–10 PM.*

In the Thomas Davis Theatre in the arts building, the **"Dublin Experience"** is a 45-minute audiovisual presentation devoted to the history of the city over the last 1,000 years. ☎ *01/608–1688.* ✉ *£2.75; in conjunction with Old Library (☞ above), £5.* ☉ *May–Oct., daily 10–5; shows every hr on the hr.*

The Georgian Heart of Dublin

If there's one travel poster that signifies "Dublin" more than any other, it's the one that pictures 50 or so Georgian doorways—door after colorful door, all graced with lovely fanlights upheld by columns. A building boom began in Dublin in the early 18th century, as the Protestant ascendancy constructed town houses for themselves and civic structures for their city in the style that came to be known as Georgian, for the four successive British Georges who ruled from 1714 through 1830. The Georgian architectural rage owed much to architects like James Gandon and Richard Castle. They and others were influenced by Andrea Palladio (1508–80), whose *Four Books of Architecture* were published in the 1720s in London and helped to precipitate the revival of his style that swept through England and its colonies. Never again would Dublin be so "smart," so filled with decorum and style, nor its visitors' book so full of aristocratic names.(For an introduction to Dublin's Georgian heyday, *see* the Close-Up box "The Age of Elegance: Dublin's Georgian Style," *below.*) Note that while Dublin's southside is a veritable shop window of the Georgian style, there are many other period sights to be found northside—for instance, the august interiors of the Dublin Writers Museum and Belvedere College, or James Gandon's great civic structures, the Custom House and the Four Courts, found quayside. These, and other Georgian goodies, are described in the Exploring sections of West Dublin and the northside, *below.*

A Good Walk

Numbers in the text correspond to numbers in the margin and on the Dublin City Center map.

When Dublin was transformed into a Georgian metropolis, people came from all over to admire the new pillared and corniced city. Today, walking through Fitzwilliam Square or Merrion Street Upper, you can still admire vistas of calm Georgian splendor. Begin your Palladian promenade at the northeast corner of Stephen's Green—here, in front of the men's clubs, was the Beaux Walk, a favorite 18th-century gathering place for fashionable Dublin. Chances are you won't bump into a duke on his way to a Handel concert or an earl on his way to a rout, ball, and supper, but then, you won't have to dodge pigs, which used to dot the cityscape back then. Walk down Merrion Street to **Merrion Square** ⑭—one of Dublin's most attractive squares. The east side of Merrion Square and its continuation, Fitzwilliam Street, form what is known as "the Georgian mile," which, unlike some Irish miles, in fact measures less than a kilometer. On a fine day the Dublin mountains are visible in the distance and the prospect has almost (thanks to the ugly, modern office block of the Electricity Supply Board) been preserved to give an impression of the spacious feel of 18th-century Dublin. Walk down the south side of the square to **Number Twenty-Nine** ⑮. Cut back through the square to visit the refurbished **Government Buildings** ⑯, the **Natural History Museum** ⑰, **Leinster House** ⑱, and/or the **National Gallery of Ireland** ⑲. The last leg of this walk is up Kildare Street to the **National Library** ⑳, passing the back of Leinster House to the **National Museum** ㉑. Stop in at the **Genealogical Office** ㉒ if you're doing research about your ancestors. Walk back to Stephen's Green and down Dawson Street, which runs parallel to Grafton Street. The **Mansion House** ㉓, **Royal Irish Academy** ㉔, and **St.**

Ann's Church ㉕ are on the left as you walk down toward Trinity College's side entrance.

TIMING

Dublin is so compact you could race through this walk in two hours, if you don't linger anywhere or set foot in one of the museums. But there are treasures galore at the National Gallery and the National Museum; the green tranquillity of Merrion Square; and many of Dublin's finest sites along the way (not to mention dozens of the city's most historic pubs)—so if you can, this is a good walk to do over the course of a half day.

Sights to See

㉒ **Genealogical Office.** Are you a Fitzgibbon from Limerick, a Cullen from Waterford, or a McSweeney from Cork? This reference library is a good place to begin your ancestor-tracing efforts. If you're a total novice at genealogical research, you can meet with an advisor (£25 for an hour consultation) who can help get you started. It also houses the **Heraldic Museum,** where displays of flags, coins, stamps, silver, and family crests highlight the uses and development of heraldry in Ireland. Note that a map detailing the geographical origin of the hundred or so most common Irish surnames can be found at the back of this book (☞ Chapter 10). ✉ *2 Kildare St.,* ☎ *01/603–0200. Genealogical Office:* ☉ *Weekdays 10–5, Sat. 10–12:30.* 🎟 *Free. Heraldic Museum:* ☉ *Weekdays 10–8:30, Sat. 10–12:30. Guided tours by appointment.*

⑯ **Government Buildings.** The swan song of British architecture in the capital, this enormous complex was the last neoclassic edifice to be erected by the British government. A landmark of "Edwardian Baroque," it was designed by Sir Aston Webb—who did many of the similarly grand buildings in London's Piccadilly Circus—as the College of Science in the early 1900s. Following a major restoration in the early 1990s, these buildings became the offices of the Department of the *taoiseach* (the prime minister, pronounced *tea*-shuck) and the *tánaiste* (the deputy prime minister, pronounced tawn-*ish*-ta). Fine examples of contemporary Irish furniture and carpets now decorate the offices. A stained-glass window, known as "My Four Green Fields," was originally made by Evie Hone for the 1939 World Trade Fair in New York. It depicts the four ancient provinces of Ireland: Munster, Ulster, Leinster, and Connacht. The government offices are accessible only via 45-minute guided tours given on Saturday (tickets are available on the day of the tour from the National Gallery), though they are dramatically illuminated every night. ✉ *Upper Merrion St.,* ☎ *01/662–4888.* 🎟 *Free.* ☉ *Sat. 10:30–3:30.*

⑱ **Leinster House.** Built in 1745, Leinster House was commissioned by the Duke of Leinster and almost singlehandedly helped to ignite the Georgian style that dominated Dublin for 100 years. It was not only the largest private residence in the city but the first structure in Ireland by Richard Castle, a follower of Palladio, who was to design some of the country's most important Palladian country houses (☞ Powerscourt House and Russborough *in* Chapter 2). Inside, the grand salons were ornamented with coffered ceilings, Rembrandts, and Van Dycks, fitting settings for the parties often given by the duke's wife, Lady Emily Lennox, a celebrated beauty. The building has two facades: The one facing Merrion Square is designed in the style of a country house; the other, on Kildare Street, is a town house. This latter facade—if you ignore the ground-floor level—was a major inspiration for Irishman James Hoban's designs for the White House in Washington, D.C. Built in hard Ardbracan limestone, the house's exterior makes a cold impression, and, in fact, the duke's heirs pronounced the house "melancholy" and

THE AGE OF ELEGANCE: DUBLIN'S GEORGIAN STYLE

EXTRAORDINARY DUBLIN!" sigh art lovers and connoisseurs of the 18th century. It was during the "gorgeous eighteenth" that this duckling of a city was transformed into a preening swan, largely by the Georgian style of art and architecture that flowered between 1714 and 1820 during the reigns of the three English Georges. Today, Dublin remains in good part a sublimely Georgian city, thanks to enduring grace notes: the commodious and uniformly laid out streets, the genteel town squares, the redbrick mansions accented with demilune fan windows. The great 18th-century showpieces are **Merrion, Fitzwilliam, Mountjoy,** and **Parnell squares. Merrion Square East,** the longest Georgian street in town, reveals scenes of decorum, elegance, polish, and charm, all woven into a "tapestry of rosy brick and white enamel," to quote the 18th-century connoisseur Horace Walpole. Setting off the facades are fanlighted doors (often lacquered in black, green, yellow, and red) and the celebrated "patent reveal" window trims, thin plaster linings painted white to catch the light. These demilune fanlights—as iconic of the city as clock towers are of Zurich—are often in neoclassic Adamesque style.

Many exteriors appear severely plain, but don't be fooled: These town houses can be compared to bonbons whose sheaths of hard chocolate conceal deliciously creamy centers. Just behind their stately front doors are entryrooms and stairways aswirl with tinted rococo plasterwork, often the work of *stuccadores,* or plasterworkers imported from Italy (including the talented Franchini brothers). Some of the very finest of these houses are open to the public, such as the **Newman House** (☞ *below*); others are open by appointment, like **Belvedere College** (6 Great Denmark St.).

The Palladian style—as the Georgian style was then called—began to reign supreme in domestic architecture in 1745 when the Croesus-rich Earl of Kildare returned from an Italian Grand Tour and built a gigantic Palladian palace called **Leinster House** in the seedy section of town. "Where I go, fashion will follow," he declared, and indeed it did. By then, the Anglo-Irish elite had given the city London airs by building the **Parliament House, Royal Exchange,** the **Custom House,** and the **Four Courts** (☞ *above* and *below*) in the new style. But this phase of high fashion came to an end with the Act of Union: According to historian Maurice Craig, "On the last stroke of midnight, December 31, 1800, the gaily caparisoned horses turned into mice, the coaches into pumpkins, the silks and brocades into rags, and Ireland was once again the Cinderella among the nations." It was nearly 150 years before the spotlight shone once again on 18th-century Dublin, thanks to the conservation efforts of the **Irish Georgian Society** (✉ 74 Merrion Sq., ☎ 01/676–7073).

ANCESTOR-HUNTING

THE LATE PRESIDENT KENNEDY and, more recently, former President Reagan are only two among many thousands of Americans who have been drawn to Ireland in an attempt to track down their ancestors. So popular has this become that Ireland today has numerous facilities for those in search of their past. However, before you begin some genealogical Sherlock Holmesing, you'll need some detailed information, not just the fact that your last name is Murphy, Kelly, or O'Donnell. The memories of elderly relatives about the place which they or their forebears emigrated, for example, is often a useful starting point. The county name is an aid, but the name of their village or town is even better. It can lead quickly to parish registers, often going back 200 years or more, which the local clergy will usually be very glad to let you see (keep in mind that, recently, many of these parish registers have been moved to regional town halls and government agencies). Best of all, however, is to organize some professional help. The Genealogical Office in Dublin is the best source of information on family names and family crests. Similarly, the Office of the Registrar General in Dublin's Custom House has details of many births, deaths, and marriages after 1864, and some marriages dating back to 1845 (a substantial part of their records were destroyed, however, in the Troubles of 1921). The Public Record Office at the Four Courts and the Registry of the Deeds in Henrietta Street, both in Dublin, are two other potentially useful sources of information. Of course, if your great-grandfather's name was Blarney Killakalarney, you should have an easy time sleuthing your family roots. Chances are, however, your name is one of the more prominent surnames in Ireland (☞ Irish Family Names, *in* Chapter 10), so you'll have a longer time tracking down your ancestors among all the Ahernes.

fled. Today, the house is the seat of Dáil Éireann (the House of Representatives, pronounced dawl *e*rin) and Seanad Éireann (the Senate, pronounced shanad *e*rin), which together constitute the Irish Parliament. When the Dáil is not in session, tours can be arranged weekdays; when the Dáil is in session, tours are available only on Monday and Friday. The Dáil visitors' gallery is included in the tour, although it can be accessed on days when the Dáil is in session and tours are not available. To arrange a visit, contact the public relations office at the phone number provided. ⊠ *Kildare St.*, ☎ *01/618–3000.*

㉓ Mansion House. Home to the mayor of Dublin, the Mansion House dates from 1710, when it was built for Joshua Dawson, who later sold the property to the government on condition that "one loaf of double refined sugar of six pounds weight" be delivered to him every Christmas. In 1919 the Declaration of Irish Independence was adopted here. Dawson Street (named for the house's original tenant) is the site of the annual and popular **August Antiques Fair.** ⊠ *Dawson St.*

★ **⓮ Merrion Square.** Created between 1762 and 1764, this tranquil square a few blocks to the east of St. Stephen's Green is lined on three sides by some of Dublin's best-preserved Georgian town houses, many of which have brightly painted front doors above which sit intricate fan-lights. Leinster House—Dublin's Versailles—along with the Natural History Museum and the National Gallery line the west side of the square, but it is on the other sides that the Georgian terrace streetscape comes into its own, with the finest houses located on the north border. Even when its flower gardens are not in bloom, the vibrant, mostly evergreen grounds, dotted with sculpture and threaded with meandering paths, are worth a walk-through. The square has been the home of several distinguished Dubliners, including Oscar Wilde's parents, Sir William and "Speranza" Wilde (No. 1); Irish national leader Daniel O'Connell (No. 58); and authors W. B. Yeats (Nos. 52 and 82) and Sheridan LeFanu (No. 70). Walk past the houses and read the plaques on the house facades, which identify the former inhabitants. Until 50 years ago, the square was a fashionable residential area, but today most of the houses are offices. At the south end of Merrion Square, on Upper Mount Street, stands **St. Stephen's Church.** Known locally as the "pepper canister" church because of its spire, the structure was inspired in part by Wren's churches in London. ⊠ *Merrion Sq.* ⊘ *Daily sunrise–sunset.*

★ ⑲ **National Gallery of Ireland.** Caravaggio's *The Taking of Christ* (1602), Reynolds's *First Earl of Bellamont* (1773), Vermeer's *Lady Writing a Letter with Her Maid* (ca. 1670) . . . you get the picture. The National Gallery of Ireland—the first in a series of major civic buildings on the west side of Merrion Square—is one of Europe's finest smaller art museums, with more than 3,000 works. Unlike Europe's largest art museums, which are almost guaranteed to induce Stendhal's syndrome, the National Gallery can be thoroughly covered in a morning or afternoon without inducing exhaustion. An 1854 Act of Parliament provided for the establishment of the museum, which was helped along by William Dargan (1799–1867), who was responsible for building much of Ireland's railway network in the 19th century (he is honored by a statue on the front lawn). The 1864 building was designed by Francis Fowke, who was also responsible for London's Victoria & Albert Museum. More art than ever before is on display following the completion in 1996 of a four-year renovation and expansion.

A highlight of the museum is the major collection of paintings by Irish artists from the 17th through 20th centuries, including works by Roderic O'Conor (1860–1940), Sir William Orpen (1878–1931), William Leech (1881–1968), and Jack B. Yeats (1871–1957), the brother of W. B. Yeats and by far the best-known Irish painter of this century. Yeats painted portraits and landscapes in an abstract expressionist style not dissimilar from that of the later Bay Area Figurative painters of the 1950s and 1960s. His *The Liffey Swim* (1923) is particularly worth seeing for its Dublin subject matter (the annual swim is still held, usually on the first weekend in September).

The collection also claims exceptional paintings from the 17th-century French, Dutch, Italian, and Spanish schools. Among the highlights that you should strive to see are the pictures mentioned above (the spectacular Caravaggio made headlines around the world recently when it was found hanging undiscovered in a Jesuit house not far from the museum) and Rembrandt's *Rest on the Flight into Egypt* (1647), Poussin's *The Holy Family* (1649) and *Lamentation over the Dead Christ* (ca. 1655–60), and, somewhat later than these, Goya's *Portrait of Doña Antonia Zárate* (ca. 1810). Don't forget to check out the amazing portrait the *First Earl of Bellamont,* by Reynolds; the earl was among the first to introduce the Georgian fashion to Ireland and this portrait stunningly flaunts the extraordinary style of the man himself. The French

Impressionists are represented with paintings by Monet, Sisley, and Pissarro. The northern wing of the gallery houses the British collection and the Irish National Portrait collection, and the amply stocked **gift shop** is a good place to pick up books on Irish artists. You may see the early stages of construction on nearby Clare Street for an addition slated to be completed in 2000. Free guided tours are available on Saturday at 3 PM and on Sunday at 2:15, 3, and 4. ⊠ *Merrion Sq. W,* ☎ *01/661–5133.* ☜ *Free.* ☉ *Mon.–Wed. and Fri.–Sat. 10–5:30, Thurs. 10–8:30, Sun. 2–5.*

Fitzer's (⊠ Merrion Sq. W, ☎ 01/661–4496), the National Gallery's self-service restaurant, is a find—one of the city's best spots for an inexpensive (all dishes less than £7), top-rate lunch. The 16–20 daily menu items are prepared with an up-to-date take on new European cuisine. It's open Thursday until 8 and Sunday 2–5 in addition to Monday–Saturday lunch.

⑰ Natural History Museum. Dr. Stanley Livingstone inaugurated this museum when it opened in 1857. Today, it is little changed from Victorian times and remains a fascinating repository of mounted mammals, birds, and other flora and fauna. The most famous exhibits are the skeletons of Ireland's extinct, prehistoric giant "Irish elk." The museum is next door to the ☞ **Government Buildings.** ⊠ *Merrion Sq. W,* ☎ *01/677-7444.* ☜ *Free.* ☉ *Tues.–Sat. 10–5, Sun. 2–5.*

⑳ National Library. Ireland is one of the few countries in the world where one can happily admit to being a writer. And few countries as geographically diminutive as Ireland have garnered as many recipients of the Nobel Prize for Literature. Along with works by W. B. Yeats (1923), George Bernard Shaw (1925), Samuel Beckett (1969), and Seamus Heaney (1995), the National Library contains first editions of every major Irish writer, including books by Jonathan Swift, Oliver Goldsmith, and James Joyce (who used the library as the scene of the great literary debate in *Ulysses*). In addition, of course, almost every book ever published in Ireland is kept here, as well as an unequaled selection of old maps and an extensive collection of Irish newspapers and magazines—more than 5 million items in all. The main **Reading Room** opened in 1890 to house the collections of the Royal Dublin Society. Beneath its dramatic domed ceiling, countless authors have researched and written their books over the years. ⊠ *Kildare St.,* ☎ *01/661–8811.* ☜ *Free.* ☉ *Mon. 10–9, Tues.–Wed. 2–9, Thurs.–Fri. 10–5, Sat. 10–1.*

★ ㉑ National Museum. On the other side of Leinster House from the National Library, Ireland's National Museum houses a fabled collection of Irish artifacts, dating from 6000 BC to the present. The museum is organized around a grand rotunda and elaborately decorated, with mosaic floors, marble columns, balustrades, and fancy ironwork. It has the largest collection of Celtic antiquities in the world, including an array of gold jewelry, carved stones, bronze tools, and weapons. The Treasury collection, including some of the museum's most renowned pieces, is open on a permanent basis. Among the priceless relics on display are the 8th-century **Ardagh Chalice,** a two-handle silver cup with gold filigree ornamentation; the bronze-coated, iron **St. Patrick's Bell,** the oldest surviving example (5th–8th centuries) of Irish metalwork; the 8th-century **Tara Brooch,** an intricately decorated piece made of white bronze, amber, and glass; and the 12th-century bejeweled oak **Cross of Cong,** covered with silver and bronze panels. Another room is devoted to the 1916 Easter Uprising and the War of Independence (1919–21); displays here include uniforms, weapons, banners, and a piece of the flag that flew over the General Post Office during Easter

Week, 1916. Upstairs is a permanent exhibit on the Vikings, featuring a full-size Viking skeleton, swords, leather works recovered in Dublin and surrounding areas, and a replica of a small Viking boat. In contrast to the ebullient late-Victorian architecture of the main museum building, the design of the **National Museum Annexe** is purely functional; it houses temporary shows of Irish antiquities. The 18th-century **Collins Barracks,** the most recent addition to the museum, houses the collection of glass, silver, costumes, furniture, and other decorative arts. ⊠ *Kildare St.; Annexe: 7–9 Merrion Row;* ☏ *01/677–7444.* ▣ *Free.* ☉ *Tues.–Sat. 10–5, Sun. 2–5.*

⓯ **Number Twenty-Nine.** Everything in this carefully refurbished 1794 home, known simply as Number Twenty-Nine, is in keeping with the elegant lifestyle of the Dublin middle class between 1790 and 1820, the height of the Georgian period, when the house was owned by a wine merchant's widow. From the basement to the attic, in the kitchen, nursery, servant's quarters, and the formal living areas, the National Museum of Ireland has re-created the period's style with authentic furniture, paintings, carpets, curtains, paint, wallpapers, and even bellpulls. ⊠ *29 Lower Fitzwilliam St.,* ☏ *01/702–6165.* ▣ *£2.50.* ☉ *Tues.–Sat. 10–5, Sun. 2–5.*

㉔ **Royal Irish Academy.** Adjacent to the Mansion House (☞ *above*), the country's leading learned society houses important manuscripts in its 18th-century library, including a large collection of ancient Irish manuscripts such as the 11th–12th century *Book of the Dun Cow* and the library of the 18th-century poet Thomas Moore. ⊠ *19 Dawson St.,* ☏ *01/676–2570.* ▣ *Free.* ☉ *Weekdays 9:30–5:30.*

㉕ **St. Ann's Church** (Church of Ireland). St. Ann's plain, neo-Romanesque, granite exterior, put up in 1868, belies the church's rich Georgian interior, designed in 1720 by Isaac Wills. Among the highlights of the interior are polished-wood balconies, ornate plasterwork, and shelving in the chancel put up in 1723 and still in use for the distribution of bread to the poor of the parish. ⊠ *Dawson St.* ▣ *Free.* ☉ *Weekdays 10–3 and Sun. for services.*

Temple Bar

More than anywhere else in Dublin, it is Temple Bar that represents the dramatic changes (good and bad) and ascending fortunes of Dublin in the 1990s. Named after one of the streets of its central spine, the area was targeted for redevelopment in 1991–92 after a long period of neglect, having survived widely rumored plans to turn it into a massive bus depot and/or a giant parking lot. Temple Bar took off—*fast*—into Dublin's version of New York's SoHo, Paris's Bastille, London's Notting Hill: a thriving mix of high and alternative culture distinct from that in every other part of the city. Dotting the area's narrow cobblestone streets and pedestrian alleyways are award-winning new apartment buildings (inside they tend to be small and uninspired, with sky-high rent), vintage- clothing stores, postage-stamp-size boutiques selling £200 sunglasses and other expensive gewgaws, art galleries galore, a hotel resuscitated by U2, hip restaurants, pubs, clubs, and European-style cafés, and a smattering of cultural venues.

Temple Bar's regeneration was no doubt abetted by that one surefire real estate asset: location, location, location. The area is bordered by Dame Street to the south, the Liffey to the north, Fishamble Street to the west, and Westmoreland Street to the east. In fact, Temple Bar is so perfectly situated between everywhere else in Dublin that it's difficult to believe this neighborhood was once largely forsaken. It's now sometimes called the "playing ground of young Dublin," and for good reason: On weekend evenings and daily in the summer it teems with young people—not only from Dublin but from all over Europe—who fly into the city for the weekend, drawn by its pubs, clubs, and lively *craic*. It has become a favorite of young English men on "stag" weekends, 48-hour bachelor parties heavy on drinking and debauching. Some who have witnessed Temple Bar's rapid gentrification and commercialization complain that it's losing its artistic soul—*Harper's Bazaar* said it was in danger of becoming "a sort of pseudoplace," like London's Covent Garden Piazza or Paris's Les Halles—but there's no denying that this is one of the best places to get a handle on the city right now.

A Good Walk

Numbers in the text correspond to numbers in the margin and on the Dublin City Center map.

Start at O'Connell Bridge and walk down Aston Quay, taking in the terrific view west down the River Liffey. Alleys and narrow roads to your left lead into Temple Bar, but hold off turning in until you get to **Ha'penny Bridge** ㉖, a Liffey landmark. Turn right and walk through Merchant's Arch, the symbolic entry into Temple Bar (see if you can spot the surveillance cameras up on the walls), which leads you onto the area's long spine, named Temple Bar here but also called Fleet Street (to the east) and Essex Street (both east and west, to the west). You're right at Temple Bar Square, one of the two largest plazas in Temple Bar. Just up on the right are two of the area's leading art galleries, the Temple Bar Gallery (at Lower Fownes St.) and, another block up, the Original Print Gallery and Black Church Print Studios (☞ Art Galleries *in* Nightlife and the Arts, *below*). Turn left onto Eustace Street. If you have children, you may want to go to the **Ark** ㉗, a children's cultural center. Across the street from the Ark, stop in at the Temple Bar Information Centre (☞ Visitor Information *in* Dublin A to Z, *below*) and pick up a handy *Temple Bar Guide*. Farther down Eustace Street is the **Irish Film Centre** ㉘, Temple Bar's leading cultural venue and a great place to catch classic or new indie films. In summer, the IFC organizes Saturday-night outdoor screenings on **Meeting House Square** ㉙, behind the Ark, accessed via Curved Street. The street is dominated on one side by the **Arthouse** ㉚ and on the other by the Temple Bar Music Centre (☞ Nightlife and the Arts, *below*). Dublin's leading photography gallery, the **Gallery of Photography** ㉛, is also here. Walk a few steps west to the narrow, cobbled Sycamore Street, and then turn right and walk to Dame Street, where you'll find the **Olympia Theatre** ㉜. Farther down Dame Street, the ultramodern **Central Bank** ㉝ rises above the city. Head for the corner of Parliament Street, where you can stop for a break or begin the next walk.

TIMING

You can easily breeze through Temple Bar in an hour or so, but if you've got the time, plan to spend a morning or afternoon here, drifting in and out of its dozens of stores and galleries, relaxing at a café over a cup of coffee or at a pub over a pint, maybe even seeing a film if you're looking for a change from sightseeing.

Sights to See

㉗ **The Ark.** If you're traveling with children and looking for something fun to do, be sure to stop by the Ark, Ireland's children's cultural center, housed in a former Presbyterian church. Its theater opens onto Meeting House Square for outdoor performances in summer. A gallery and workshop space host ongoing activities. ⊠ *Eustace St.,* ☎ *01/670–7788.* ⊡ *Free.* ☉ *Weekdays 9:30–4, Sat. 10–4.*

③⓪ Arthouse. This is one of the first purpose-built multimedia centers for the arts in the world. Its modern design—all glass, metal, and painted concrete—is the work of award-winning architect Shay Cleary Doyle, who intended the building to reflect the object glorified within: the computer. Inside is a training center, a performance venue, a creative studio, and an exhibition space that plays host to a variety of art exhibitions. Pride of place, however, goes to the Art Information Bureau and the Artifact artist's database, featuring the work of more than 1,000 modern Irish artists working in Ireland and abroad. This useful catalog is open to anyone wishing to buy or admire the work of the listed artists, and it is set up in such a way that you can search for work according to specific criteria; for example, if you want a piece of jewelry in gold from the West of Ireland, just press a few buttons and a list of artists and images of their work fitting your description will appear. ⊠ *Curved St.,* ☎ *01/605–6800.* ⌚ *Free.* ☉ *Weekdays 9:30–6.*

③③ Central Bank. In a recent survey of Dubliners, the ultramodern, glass-and-concrete Central Bank appeared on lists of Dublin's most-loved *and* most-hated buildings in the capital. Designed by Sam Stephenson in 1978, the controversial building suspends huge concrete slabs around a central axis. Skateboarders and in-line skaters have taken up residence on the little plaza in front of the building. ⊠ *Dame St.,* ☎ *01/ 671–6666.* ⌚ *Free.* ☉ *Weekdays 10–6.*

③① Gallery of Photography. Dublin's premier photography gallery has a permanent collection of turn-of-the-century Irish photography and also puts on monthly exhibits of contemporary Irish and international photographers. The bookstore is the best place in the city to browse for photography books and pick up arty postcards. ⊠ *Meeting House Sq. S,* ☎ *01/671–4654.* ⌚ *Free.* ☉ *Varies with exhibitions. Mon.–Sat. 11–6.*

②⑥ Ha'penny Bridge. This heavily trafficked footbridge crosses the Liffey at a prime spot: Temple Bar (☞ *above*) is on the south side, and the bridge provides the fastest route to the thriving Mary and Henry Street shopping areas to the north (☞ Shopping, *below*). Until early in this century, a half-penny toll was charged to cross it. Yeats was one among many Dubliners who found this too high a price to pay—more a matter of principle than of finance—and so made the detour via O'Connell Bridge.

②⑧ Irish Film Centre (IFC). The opening of the IFC in a beautifully restored former Quaker meetinghouse in 1992 helped to launch the revitalization of Temple Bar. It has two comfortable art-house cinemas showing revivals and new independent films, the Irish Film Archive, a bookstore for cineastes, and a bar, all of which make this one of the neighborhood's most vital cultural institutions. ⊠ *6 Eustace St.,* ☎ *01/ 679–5744.* ⌚ *Free.* ☉ *Weekdays 9:30–late, weekends 11–late.*

NEED A BREAK? The creamiest, frothiest coffees in all of Temple Bar can be had at the **Joy of Coffee/Image Gallery Café** (⊠ 25 E. Essex St., Temple Bar, ☎ 01/679–3393); the wall of windows floods light onto the small gallery with original photographs adorning the walls.

②⑨ Meeting House Square. Behind the Ark (☞ *above*) and accessed via Curved Street, Meetinghouse Square has become something of a new gathering place for Dublin's youth and artists. Throughout the summer, seats are erected and a wide variety of events—including classic movies (every Saturday night), theater, games, and family programs—are held here. It's also a favorite site for the continuously changing street sculpture that pops up all over Temple Bar. All year round it's a great spot to sit and relax and engage in a bit of people-watching. The square gets its name from a nearby Quaker meetinghouse.

★ ㉜ **Olympia Theatre.** One of the best places anywhere in Europe to see live musical acts, the Olympia is Dublin's second oldest and one of its busiest theaters. Built in 1879, this classic Victorian music hall has a gorgeous red wrought-iron facade. Conveniently, two pubs are situated through doors directly off the back of the theater's orchestra section. The Olympia's long-standing Friday and Saturday series, "Midnight at the Olympia," has brought a wide array of musical performers to Dublin, and the theater has also seen many notable actors strut its stage, including Alec Guinness, Peggy Ashcroft, Noël Coward, and even Laurel and Hardy. In November 1996, when Van Morrison played Dublin, he chose to perform here rather than in a larger venue. If you have a chance to catch a favorite performer (or to discover someone new), go!— you won't regret it. ⊠ *72 Dame St.,* ☎ *01/677–7744.*

NEED A BREAK?	An old-time oasis in the desert of commercialism, the **Foggy Dew** (⊠ 1 Fownes Street Upper, ☎ 677–9328) has maintained the wood-paneled warmth and top-class pints, which made it a favorite with locals for years. Now it also serves tea and coffee and has a simple but tasty lunch.

From Dublin Castle to the Four Courts

This section of Dublin takes you from the 10th-century crypt at Christ Church Cathedral—the city's oldest surviving structure—to the modern plant of the Guinness Brewery (which sits astride, thanks to all those hops, some of the sweetest-smelling blocks in town). Dublin is so compact, however, that to separate out the following sites from those covered in the two other city-center southside walks is potentially to mislead by suggesting that this area is at some remove from the heart of the city center. In fact, this tour's starting point, City Hall, is just across the street from Thomas Read's, and Christ Church Cathedral is a very short walk farther west. However, the westernmost sites covered here—notably the Royal Hospital and Kilmainham Gaol—*are* at some distance, more so than may be comfortable if you're not an enthusiastic walker, so you may want to drive or catch a cab or a bus out to them.

A Good Walk

Numbers in the text correspond to numbers in the margin and on the Dublin West map.

Begin with a brief visit to **City Hall** ㉞, and then walk up Cork Hill to the Castle Street entrance to **Dublin Castle** ㉟, whose highlights—the grand salons that show off Viceregal Dublin at its most splendid—are only visitable via a guided tour. Leave via the same gate, turn left, and walk up Castle Street to ancient **Christ Church Cathedral** ㊱, picturesquely situated on one of the few hills in the city. At the southeast corner of the cathedral, connected via an utterly beguiling Victorian-era bridge, **Dublinia** ㊲ gives you a chance to experience life in medieval Dublin. Another block farther west, down Back Lane, is the **Mother Redcap's Market** ㊳. And just down Nicholas Street is—begorrah!— **St. Patrick's Cathedral** ㊴. If you're eager to venture back to the 17th century or love old books, visit the quaint **Marsh's Library** ㊵, next door to St. Patrick's. You can then stroll through the old artisan redbrick dwellings in the Liberties, home to the heaviest concentration of the city's antiques stores, to Thomas Street and—just follow your nose— the **Guinness Brewery** ㊶, where you can keep your spirits up in more ways than one. At this point, if you want to see more architecture and modern art, proceed farther west to the Irish Museum of Modern Art in the elegant 18th-century **Royal Hospital Kilmainham** ㊷, and the **Kilmainham Gaol** ㊸. If you don't elect to head this way, turn back down Thomas Street, crossing the Liffey at Bridge Street, which on its north side becomes Church Street. On your left is the **Four Courts** ㊹, just up on the left is **St. Michan's Church** ㊺, and a quick jog over to Bow Street (via Mary's Lane) is the **Old Jameson Distillery** ㊻—here you'll learn all there is to learn about Irish whiskey (including the fact that it is spelled with an "e," to distinguish it from Scotch whisky).

TIMING

Allow yourself a few hours, especially if you want to include the Guinness Brewery and the Irish Museum of Modern Art at the Royal Hospital. Keep in mind that if you want to cover the easternmost sites—Dublin Castle, City Hall, Christ Church Cathedral, and environs—you can easily append them onto a tour of Temple Bar.

Sights to See

★ ㊱ **Christ Church Cathedral.** You'd never know from the outside that the first Christianized Danish king built a wooden church at this site in 1038; thanks to the extensive 19th-century renovation of its stonework and trim, the cathedral looks more Victorian than Anglo-Norman. Construction on the present Christ Church—the flagship of the Church of Ireland and one of two Protestant cathedrals in Dublin (the other is St. Patrick's just to the south)—was begun in 1172 by Strongbow, a Norman baron and conqueror of Dublin for the English crown, and went on for 50 years. By 1875 the cathedral had deteriorated badly, so a major renovation gave it much of the the look it has today, including the addition of one of Dublin's most charming structures: a Bridge of Sighs–like affair that connects the cathedral to the old Synod Hall, which now holds the Viking extravaganza, Dublinia (☞ *below*). Remains from the 12th-century building include the north wall of the nave, the west bay of the choir, and the fine stonework of the transepts, with their pointed arches and supporting columns. Strongbow himself is buried in the cathedral beneath an impressive effigy. The vast, sturdy **crypt**, with its 12th- and 13th-century vaults, is Dublin's oldest surviving structure and the building's most notable feature. ⊠ *Christ Church Pl. and Winetavern St.,* ☎ *01/677–8099.* ▦ *£1* ⊙ *Daily 10–5.*

㉞ **City Hall.** Facing the Liffey from Cork Hill at the top of Parliament Street, this grand Georgian municipal building (1769–79), once the Royal Exchange, was designed by Thomas Cooley and marks the southwestern corner of Temple Bar. Today it's the seat of the Dublin Corporation, the elected body that governs the city. Twelve columns encircle the domed central rotunda, which has a fine mosaic floor and 12 frescoes depicting Dublin legends and ancient Irish historical scenes. Just off the rotunda is a gently curving staircase, a typical feature of most large Dublin town houses. ⊠ *Cork Hill,* ☎ *01/679–6111, ext. 2807.* ▦ *Free.* ⊙ *Weekdays 9–1 and 2:15–5.*

㉟ **Dublin Castle.** Neil Jordan's film *Michael Collins* captured Dublin Castle's near-indomitable status well: Seat and symbol of the British rule of Ireland for 7½ centuries, the castle figured largely in Ireland's turbulent history earlier this century. After extensive renovations, it's now used mostly for Irish and EU governmental purposes. The sprawling **Great Courtyard** is the reputed site of the Black Pool (Dubh Linn, pronounced *dove*-lin) from which Dublin got its name, though today it is lined with stretch limos and security guards. In the Lower Castle Yard, the **Record Tower,** the earliest of several towers on the site, is the largest remaining relic of the original Norman buildings, built by

Dublin West

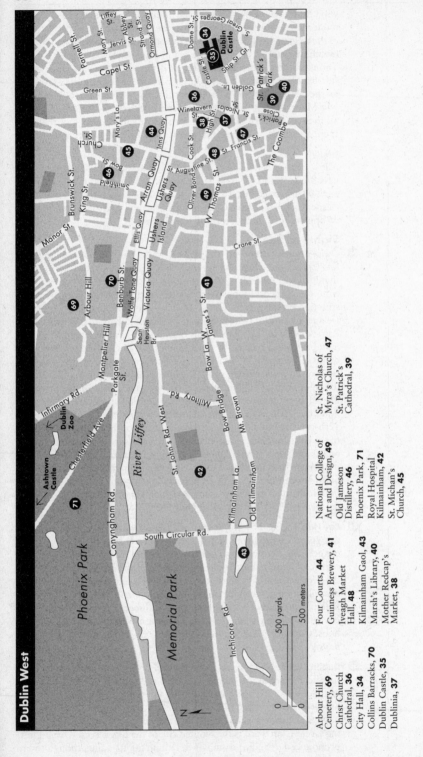

Arbour Hill
Cemetery, **69**
Christ Church
Cathedral, **36**
City Hall, **34**
Collins Barracks, **70**
Dublin Castle, **35**
Dublinia, **37**

Four Courts, **44**
Guinness Brewery, **41**
Iveagh Market
Hall, **48**
Kilmainham Gaol, **43**
Marsh's Library, **40**
Mother Redcap's
Market, **38**

National College of
Art and Design, **49**
Old Jameson
Distillery, **46**
Phoenix Park, **71**
Royal Hospital
Kilmainham, **42**
St. Michan's
Church, **45**

St. Nicholas of
Myra's Church, **47**
St. Patrick's
Cathedral, **39**

King John between 1208 and 1220. Guided tours are available around the principal **State Apartments** (on the southern side of the Upper Castle Yard), formerly the residence of the English viceroys. Now used by the president of Ireland to host visiting heads of state and EU ministers, they are lavishly furnished with rich Donegal carpets and illuminated by Waterford glass chandeliers. The largest and most impressive of these chambers, **St. Patrick's Hall**, with its gilt pillars and painted ceiling, is used for the inauguration of Irish presidents. The **Round Drawing Room**, in Bermingham Tower, dates from 1411 and was rebuilt in 1777; a number of Irish leaders have been imprisoned in the tower, from the 16th century to the early 20th century. The blue oval **Wedgwood Room** contains Chippendale chairs and a marble fireplace. The **Castle Vaults** now holds an elegant little patisserie and bistro.

Also on the grounds of the castle is the **Church of the Holy Trinity** (formerly called Chapel Royal), designed in 1814 by Francis Johnston, who also designed the original General Post Office building on O'Connell Street. Carved oak panels and stained glass depicting viceroys' coats of arms grace the interior. Look up to view the elaborate array of fan vaults that decorates the ceiling. On the outside more than 100 carved heads adorn the walls. St. Peter and Jonathan Swift preside over the north door, St. Patrick and Brian Boru over the east. One-hour guided tours of the castle are available every half hour, but the rooms are closed when in official use, so phone first. The easiest way in to the castle today is via the **Cork Hill Gate**, just west of City Hall. ⊠ *Castle St.,* ☎ *01/ 677–7129.* ▣ *State Apartments £3, including tour.* ⊙ *Weekdays 10– 5, weekends 2–5.*

☾ ❸❼ **Dublinia.** In the old Synod Hall (formerly a meeting place for bishops of the Church of Ireland), attached via a covered stonework Victorian bridge to **Christ Church Cathedral** ·(☞ *above*), Dublin's Medieval Trust has set up an entertaining and informative reconstruction of everyday life in medieval Dublin. The main exhibits use high-tech audiovisual and computer displays; there are also a scale model of what Dublin was like around 1500, a medieval maze, a life-size reconstruction based on the 13th-century dockside at Wood Quay, and a fine view from the tower. For a more modern take on the city, study the noted James Malton series of prints of 18th-century Dublin hanging on the walls of the coffee shop. ⊠ *St. Michael's Hill,* ☎ *01/679–4611.* ▣ *Exhibit £3.95.* ⊙ *Apr.–Sept., daily 10–5; Oct.–Mar., Mon.–Sat. 11– 4, Sun. 10–4:30.*

❹❹ **Four Courts.** Today the seat of the High Court of Justice of Ireland, the Four Courts are James Gandon's second Dublin masterpiece, built between 1786 and 1802, close on the heels of his **Custom House** (☞ *below*), downstream on the same side of the River Liffey. The Four Courts replaced a 13th-century Dominican abbey that stood here earlier. In 1922, during the Irish Civil War, the Four Courts was almost totally destroyed by shelling, and the adjoining Public Records Office was gutted, with many of its priceless legal documents destroyed, including innumerable family records; efforts to restore the building to its original state spanned 10 years. Today the stately Corinthian portico and the circular central hall are well worth viewing. Its distinctive copper-covered dome atop a colonnaded rotunda makes this one of Dublin's most instantly recognizable buildings; the view from the rotunda is terrific. Although there is no tour of the building, you are welcome to sit in while the courts are in session. ⊠ *Inns Quay,* ☎ *01/872–5555.* ⊙ *Daily 10–1 and 2:15–4.*

★ ❹❶ **Guinness Brewery.** Founded by Arthur Guinness in 1759, Ireland's all-dominating brewer—in fact, at one stage the largest stout-producing brewery in the world—is on a 60-acre spread west of Christ Church Cathedral. It happens to be the most popular tourist destination in town—not surprisingly, since the Irish national drink is Guinness stout, a dark brew made with roasted malt. If you're used to lighter, lager-type beers you may find this rich dark concoction, with its thick creamy "head" or "collar," somewhat unusual at first taste. But once the taste is acquired, it soon becomes an addiction, as most any Irishman will tell you! The brewery itself is closed to the public, but the 19th-century **Hop Store,** on Crane Street, part museum and part gift shop, puts on an 18-minute audiovisual presentation. The show ends with the curtain rising on the kind of old-fashioned pub—with mahogany decor, mirrors, and snugs—that is fast becoming hard to find in modern Dublin. You then receive two complimentary glasses (or one pint) of the famous black stout (a smile and a polite request might get you a couple more). The Guinness Zone, a new, interactive exhibit on the second floor, highlights the history of the beer's remarkably successful advertising campaigns, from the famous "Guinness is Good for You" poster ads to the ultrasleek television commercials of the present day. A gift shop sells the best of Guinness memorabilia: posters, bar towels, beer mats, and garments. ⊠ *James' Gate,* ☎ *01/453–3645.* ⌨ *£5.* ⊙ *Apr.—Sept., Mon.–Sat. 9:30–5, Sun. 10:30–4:30; Oct.–Mar., Mon.–Sat. 9:30–4, Sun. noon–4.*

㊸ Kilmainham Gaol. Even farther west than the Royal Hospital, this is a grim, forbidding structure where leaders of the 1916 Easter Uprising, including Pádrig Pearse and James Connolly, were held before being executed in the prison yard. In the 19th century, other inmates here were the revolutionary Robert Emmet and Charles Stewart Parnell, a leading politician (☞ Avondale House *in* Chapter 2). You can visit the cells, a chilling sight, while the guided tour and a 30-minute audiovisual presentation relate a graphic account of Ireland's political history over the past 200 years from a Nationalist viewpoint. You can only visit the prison as part of a guided tour, which leaves every hour on the hour. There is also a small tearoom on the premises. ⊠ *Inchicore Rd.,* ☎ *01/453–5984.* ⌨ *£3.* ⊙ *Apr.–Sept., daily 9:30–5; Oct.–Mar., weekdays 9:30–4, Sun. 10–5.*

㊵ Marsh's Library. A short walk west from St. Stephen's Green and accessed through a tiny but charming cottage garden lies a gem of old Dublin: the city's—and Ireland's—first public library, founded and endowed in 1701 by Narcissus Marsh, the Archbishop of Dublin, then open to "All Graduates and Gentlemen." The two-story, brick, Georgian building has been practically unchanged inside since it was built. It houses a priceless collection of 250 manuscripts and 25,000 16th- to 18th-century books. Many of these rare volumes are locked inside cages, as are the readers who wish to peruse them. The cages were to discourage students who, often impecunious, may have been tempted to make the books their own. The library has recently been restored with great attention to its original architectural details, especially in the book stacks. ⊠ *St. Patrick's Close off Patrick St.,* ☎ *01/454–3511.* ⌨ *£1.* ⊙ *Mon. and Wed.–Fri. 10–12:45 and 2–5, Sat. 10:30–12:45.*

㊳ Mother Redcap's Market. Attached to a pub of the same name (☞ Nightlife and the Arts, *below*), this covered market has everything from linen, old vinyl LPs, antiques, and secondhand books to palm readings and Irish crafts. ⊠ *Back Lane* ⌨ *Free.* ⊙ *Fri.–Sun. 11–6.*

㊻ Old Jameson Distillery. Founded in 1791, this distillery produced one of Ireland's most famous whiskeys for nearly 200 years until 1966, when local distilleries merged to form Irish Distillers and moved to a purpose-built, ultramodern distillery in Middleton, County Cork. Part of the com-

plex was converted into the group's head office, and the distillery itself
was turned into a museum. You can watch a short audiovisual history
of the industry, which actually had its origins 1,500 years ago in Middle Eastern perfume making, and tour the old distillery, where you can
learn about the distilling of whiskey from grain to bottle. You can also
view a reconstruction of a former warehouse, where the colorful nick-
names of former barrel makers are recorded. There's a 20-minute audiovisual show, a 40-minute tour, and a complimentary tasting (remember:
Irish whiskey is best drunk without a mixer—try it straight or with water);
four attendees are invited to taste different brands of Irish whiskey and
compare them against bourbon and Scotch; the staff are confident that
you'll prefer the Irish to anything else, and they have rarely been wrong
in the past! If you have a large group and everyone wants to do this,
phone in advance to arrange it. ⊠ *Bow St.,* ☎ *01/807–2355.* 🖼 *Tour
£3.95.* ☉ *Daily 9:30–5:30; tours every ½ hr.*

★ ㊷ **Royal Hospital Kilmainham.** A short ride by taxi or bus from the city
center, this replica of Les Invalides in Paris is regarded as the most important 17th-century building in Ireland. Commissioned as a hospice for
disabled and veteran soldiers by James Butler, the Duke of Ormonde and
Viceroy to King Charles II, it was completed in 1684, making it the first
classical building in the city and a precursor of Dublin's golden age. It
survived into the 1920s as a hospital, but after the founding of the Irish
Free State in 1922, the building fell into disrepair. Over the last 15 years,
restoration has returned the entire edifice to what it once was.

The structure consists of four galleries around a courtyard and includes
a grand dining hall, 100 ft long by 50 ft wide. The architectural highlight is the hospital's Baroque **chapel,** distinguished by its extraordinary plasterwork ceiling and fine wood carvings. "There is nothing in
Ireland from the 17th century that can come near this masterpiece,"
raves cultural historian John FitzMaurice Mills. Today the Royal Hospital houses the **Irish Museum of Modern Art.** The museum displays
works by non-Irish, 20th-century greats like Picasso and Miró but concentrates on the work of Irish artists. Richard Deacon, Richard Gor-
man, Dorothy Cross, Sean Scully, Matt Mullican, Louis Le Brocquy,
and James Colman are among the contemporary Irish artists represented.
The Café Musée has soups, sandwiches, and other light fare. ⊠ *Kilmainham La.,* ☎ *01/612–9900.* 🖼 *Royal Hospital free, but individual shows may have separate charges; Museum of Modern Art permanent
collection free, small charge for special exhibitions.* ☉ *Royal Hospital Tues.–Sat. 10–5:30, Sun. noon–5:30, tour every ½ hr; Museum of
Modern Art Tues.–Sat. 10–5:30, Sun. noon–5:30; museum tours Wed.
and Fri. 2:30, Sat. 11:30.*

㊸ **St. Michan's Church.** Built in 1685 on the site of an older, 11th-cen-
tury Danish church (Michan is a Danish saint), this Anglican church
is architecturally undistinguished except for its 120-ft-high bell tower.
But its 18th-century organ was supposedly played by Handel for his
first ever performance of the *Messiah,* and its Stool of Repentance is
the only one still in existence in the city; parishioners who were judged
to be "open and notoriously naughty livers" used it to do public
penance. St. Michan's main claim to notoriety, however, is down in
the vaults, where the totally dry atmosphere has preserved a number
of corpses in a remarkable state of mummification. They lie in open
caskets, and if you're strong-hearted, you can shake hands with a former religious crusader or nun! Most of the preserved bodies are thought
to have been Dublin tradespeople. ⊠ *Lower Church St.,* ☎ *01/872–
4154.* 🖼 *£2.50.* ☉ *Apr.–Oct, weekdays 10–12:45 and 2–4:45, Sat. 10–
12:45; Nov.–Mar., weekdays 12:30–3:30, Sat. 10–4:45.*

③⑨ St. Patrick's Cathedral. The largest cathedral in Dublin and also the national cathedral of the Church of Ireland, St. Patrick's is the second of the capital's two Protestant cathedrals (the other is Christ Church (☞ *below*). (The reason that Dublin has two cathedrals is that St. Patrick's originally stood outside the walls of Dublin, while its close neighbor was within the walls and belonged to the see of Dublin.) Legend has it that St. Patrick baptized many converts at a well on the site of the cathedral in the 5th century. The original building, dedicated in 1192 and early English Gothic in style, was an unsuccessful attempt to assert supremacy over Christ Church Cathedral. At 305 ft, it is the longest church in the country, a fact that Oliver Cromwell's troops—no friends to the Irish—found useful, as they made the church's nave into their stable in the 17th century. Their visit left the building in a ruinous state, and its current good repair is largely due to the benevolence of Sir Benjamin Guinness, of the brewing family, who started to finance major restoration work in 1860. Be sure to view the gloriously heraldic **Choir of St. Patrick's,** hung with colorful medieval banners, as well as find the tomb of the most famous of St. Patrick's many illustrious deans, Jonathan Swift, immortal author of *Gulliver's Travels,* who held office from 1713 to 1745. **Swift's tomb** is in the south aisle, not far from that of his beloved "Stella," Mrs. Esther Johnson. Swift's epitaph is inscribed over the robing-room door. Yeats—who translated it thus: "Swift has sailed into his rest; Savage indignation there cannot lacerate his breast"—declared it the greatest epitaph of all time. Other memorials include the 17th-century **Boyle Monument,** with its numerous painted figures of family members, and the **monument to Turlough O'Carolan,** the last of the Irish bards and one of the country's finest harp players. To the immediate north of the cathedral is a small park, with statues of many of Dublin's literary figures and **St. Patrick's Well.** ⊠ *Patrick St.,* ☎ *01/475–4817.* 🎟 *£2.* ☉ *May and Sept.–Oct., weekdays 9–6, Sat. 9–5, Sun. 10–11 and 12:30–3; June–Aug., weekdays 9–6, Sat. 9–4, Sun. 9:30–3 and 4:15–5:15; Nov.–Apr., weekdays 9–6, Sat. 9–4, Sun. 10–11 and 12:30–3.*

The Liberties

A stroll through the Liberties is a walk through working-class Dublin, past and present, good and bad. The name derives from Dublin of the middle ages, when the area south and west of Christ Church Cathedral was outside the city walls and free from the jurisdiction of the city rulers. A certain amount of freedom, or "liberty," was enjoyed by those who settled here, and it often attracted people on the fringes of society, especially the poor.

A Good Walk

Numbers in the text correspond to numbers in the margin and on the Dublin West map.

Start on Patrick Street, in the shadow of St. Patrick's Cathedral (☞ From Dublin Castle to the Four Courts walk, *above*). Look down the street towards the Liffey and a glorious view of Christ Church (☞ *above*). Take a right on Dean Street, where you'll find John Fallons pub (☞ Pubs *in* Nightlife and the Arts, *below*). Take a right off Dean Street onto Francis Street and walk uphill. A number of quality antiques shops (☞ Shopping, *below*) line both sides of the thoroughfare. Halfway up Francis Street, on the right, behind hefty wrought-iron gates, is one of Dublin's most-overlooked treasures, **St. Nicholas of Myra's Church** ④⑦. Continue up Francis Street and take the next right onto Thomas Davis Street (named after a famous patriot and revolutionary—the Liberties has long had a close association with Irish Nationalism). The street is full of classic, two-story redbrick houses. The area, once the heart of "Darlin' Dublin" and the holy source of its distinctive accent, is rapidly becoming yuppified. Back on Francis Street, in an old factory building with its chimney stack intact, is the exciting **Iveagh Market Hall** ㊽. At the top of Francis Street turn left onto Thomas Street. Across the road, on your right side, stands the wonderfully detailed exterior of St. Augustine and St. John, with its grandiose spire dominating the area around. You'll notice churches all over the Liberties; the Bishops thought it wise to build holy palaces in the poorest areas of the city as tall, shining beacons of comfort and hope. Farther up Thomas Street in another converted factory is the **National College of Art and Design** ㊾.

TIMING

Unless you intend on doing some serious antiques shopping, this is a relatively quick stroll—perhaps two hours—as the Liberties is a compact area of small, winding streets.

Sights to See

㊽ **Iveagh Market Hall.** One of the numerous buildings bestowed upon the city of Dublin by Lord Iveagh of the Guinness family, the cavernous, Victorian, redbrick-and-granite Iveagh Market Hall holds a regular, eclectic market from Tuesday to Saturday. ⊠ *Francis St.* ☉ *Tues.–Sat. 9–5.*

㊾ **National College of Art and Design.** The delicate welding of the high-tech, glass, and iron onto the redbrick Victorian facade of this one-time factory makes this school worth a visit. Walk around the cobblestone central courtyard, where there's always the added bonus of viewing some of the students work in mediums such as glass, clay, metal, and stone. ⊠ *Thomas St., Dublin 8,* ☎ *671–1377.*

㊼ **St. Nicholas of Myra's Church.** This church was completed in 1834 in grand neoclassic style. Inside, the highly ornate chapel includes ceiling panels of each of the 12 apostles and a pietà raised 20 ft above the marble altar, which is guarded on each side by angels sculpted by John Hogan while he was in Florence. The tiny nuptial chapel to the right has a small Harry Clarke stained-glass window. ⊠ *St. Nicholas St.*

North of the Liffey

If you stand on O'Connell Bridge or the pedestrian-only Ha'penny span, you'll get excellent views up and down the Liffey, the *abha na life,* which James Joyce transcribed phonetically as Anna Livia in *Finnegan's Wake.* Here, framed with embankments just like those along Paris's Seine, the river is near the end of its 128-km (80-mi) journey from the Wicklow mountains into the Irish sea. And near here, you begin a pilgrimage into James Joyce Country and the fascinating sights of Dublin's northside.

Today the northside—a mix of densely thronged shopping streets and rundown sections (though the property boom is rapidly refurbishing these areas) of once genteel homes—absolutely warrants a walk for three reasons: its major cultural institutions (which include the Gate Theatre, the James Joyce Cultural Centre, the Dublin Writers Museum, and the Hugh Lane Municipal Gallery of Modern Art), the number of sites of significance with ties to Irish Republicanism, and its busy streets. During the 18th century, most of the upper echelons of Dublin society lived in the Georgian houses around Mountjoy Square and shopped along Capel Street, which was lined with stores stocking fine furniture and silver. The construction of Merrion Square on the southside (completed in 1764) and nearby Fitzwilliam Square (completed in 1825), and the decision by Ireland's grandest duke to build Leinster House on the southside, permanently changed the northside's fortunes. The city's fashionable social center crossed the Liffey, and although some of the northside's illustrious inhabitants clung to their houses, this area gradually became more rundown. The northside's fortunes may now be beginning to change, though. Once-derelict swaths of houses, especially on and near the Liffey, are being rehabilitated, and a large new shopping center opened on Mary Street in late 1996. Now a huge shopping mall and entertainment complex are planned for O'Connell Street, right where the defunct Cartlon Cinema stands. Still, the redevelopment that has swept through Temple Bar is only in its early stages here, but precisely because it's a place on the cusp of transition, it's an interesting part of town to visit.

A Good Walk
Numbers in the text correspond to numbers in the margin and on the Dublin City Center map.

Begin at O'Connell Bridge—if you look closely at it you will notice that it is wider than it is long—and head north up **O'Connell Street** ㊿. Stop to admire the monument to Daniel O'Connell, "The Liberator," erected as a tribute to the great orator's achievement in securing Catholic Emancipation in 1829 (note the obvious scars from the fighting of 1916 on the figures). Then continue north to the **General Post Office** ㉑, a major site in the Easter Uprising of 1916. O'Connell leads to the southeastern corner of Parnell Square. Heading counterclockwise around the square, you'll pass in turn the **Gate Theatre** ㉒ and **Abbey Presbyterian Church** ㉓ before coming to the **Dublin Writers Museum** ㉔ and the **Hugh Lane Municipal Gallery of Modern Art** ㉕, both on the north side of the square and both housed in glorious neoclassic mansions; these are the two sites where you should plan to spend most of your time on the northside. Either before you go in or after you come out, you might want to visit the solemn yet serene **Garden of Remembrance** ㉖.

From here, you have two choices: to continue exploring the cultural sights that lie to the northeast of Parnell Square and east of O'Connell Street or to head to Moore, Henry, and Mary streets for a flavor of middle-class Dublin that you won't get on the spiffier southside. If you decide to continue your cultural explorations, jump two blocks northeast of Parnell Square to the **James Joyce Cultural Centre** ㉗, then head farther northeast to the once-glamorous **Mountjoy Square** ㉘. From here, turn south, stopping in at the **St. Francis Xavier Church** ㉙ on Gardiner Street. Head back west to Marlborough Street (parallel to and between Gardiner and O'Connell streets) to visit the **Pro-Cathedral** ㉠. Continue down to the quays and jog a block east to the **Custom House** ㉑. If you decide to shop with the locals, leave Parnell Square via the southwestern corner, stopping first to check out the chapel at the **Rotunda Hospital** ㉒. Moore Street is your first left off Parnell Street and leads directly to Henry Street. Just follow the crowds from there.

TIMING
The northside has fewer major attractions than the southside and, overall, is less picturesque. As a result, you're unlikely to want to stroll as leisurely here. If you zipped right through this walk, you could be done in less than two hours. But the two major cultural institutions covered here—the Dublin Writers Museum and the Hugh Lane Municipal Gallery of Modern Art—each easily deserves several hours, so it's worth doing this walk only if you have the time to devote to them. Also, a number of additional sights connected with James Joyce and *Ulysses*—covered in "ReJoyce! A Walk through *Ulysses* and James Joyce's Dublin"—are in the vicinity, so if you're a devoted Joycean, you should consult the Close-Up box (☞ *below*) before setting out on this walk.

Sights to See

53 **Abbey Presbyterian Church.** A soaring spire marks the exterior of this church, popularly known as Findlater's Church, after Alex Findlater, a noted Dublin grocer who endowed it. Completed in 1864, the church stands on the northeast corner of Parnell Square; the inside has a stark Presbyterian atmosphere, despite stained-glass windows and ornate pews. For a bird's-eye view, take the small staircase that leads to the balcony. ⊠ *Parnell Sq.*

61 **Custom House.** Seen at its best reflected in the waters of the Liffey during the short interval when the high tide is on the turn, the Custom House is the city's most spectacular Georgian building. Extending 375 ft on the north side of the river, this is the work of James Gandon, an English architect who arrived in Ireland in 1781, when construction commenced (it continued for 10 years). Crafted from gleaming Portland stone, the central portico is linked by arcades to the pavilions at either end. Too bad the dome is on the puny size and out of proportion. A statue of Commerce tops the graceful copper dome; statues on the main facade are based on allegorical themes. Note the exquisitely carved lions and unicorns supporting the arms of Ireland at the far ends of the facade. Republicans set the building on fire in 1921, but it was completely restored and now houses government offices. The building opened to the public in mid-1997 after having been closed for many years, and with it came a new exhibition tracing the building's history and significance. ⊠ *Custom House Quay,* ☎ *01/679–3377.* ⊡ *£1:50.* ⊙ *Weekdays 9:30–5, weekends 2–5.*

★ **54** **Dublin Writers Museum.** "If you would know Ireland—body and soul—you must read its poems and stories," wrote Yeats in 1891. Further investigation into the Irish way with words can be found here at this unique museum, set within a magnificently restored 18th-century town house on the north side of Parnell Square. Once the home of John Jameson (of the Irish whiskey family), the mansion is centered on an enormous drawing room, gorgeously decorated with paintings, Adamesque plasterwork, and a deep Edwardian lincrusta frieze. Rare manuscripts, diaries, posters, letters, limited and first editions, photographs, and other mementoes commemorate the life and works of the nation's greatest writers (and there are *many* of them, so leave plenty of time), including Joyce, Shaw, J. M. Synge, Lady Gregory, Yeats, Beckett, and many others. On display are an 1804 edition of Swift's *Gulliver's Travels,* an 1899 first edition of Bram Stoker's *Dracula,* and an 1899 edition of Wilde's *Ballad of Reading Gaol.* There's even a special "Teller of Tales" exhibit showcasing Behan, O'Flaherty, and O'Faolan. Readings are periodically held. The bookshop and café make this an ideal place to spend a rainy afternoon. If you lose track of time and stay until the closing hour, you might want to dine at Chapter One, a highly regarded restaurant in the basement (☞ Dining, *below*), which would have had Joyce ecstasizing about its currant-sprinkled scones. ⊠ *18 Parnell Sq. N,* ☎ *01/872–2077.* ⊡ *£2.95.* ⊙ *June–Aug., Mon.–Sat. 10–6, Sun. 11–5; Sept.–May, Mon.–Sat. 10–5, Sun. 11–5.*

56 **Garden of Remembrance.** Opened in 1966, 50 years after the Easter Uprising of 1916, the garden, within Parnell Square, commemorates all those who died fighting for Irish freedom. A large plaza is at the garden's entrance; steps lead down to the fountain area, graced with a sculpture by contemporary Irish artist Oisín Kelly based on the mythological Children of Lír, who were turned into swans. The garden serves as an oasis of tranquillity in the middle of the busy city. ⊠ *Parnell Sq.* ⊙ *Daily 9–5.*

52 Gate Theatre. The Gate has been one of Dublin's most important theaters since its founding in 1929 by Micháel MacLiammóir and Hilton Edwards, who also founded Galway City's An Taibhdhearc as the national Irish-language theater (☞ Chapter 6). Many innovative productions by Irish playwrights have been staged here, and Dublin audiences have encountered foreign playwrights and actors here for the first time as well, including Orson Welles (his first paid performance) and James Mason, who also performed here early in his career. The show actually begins as soon as you walk into the auditorium—a Georgian masterwork designed by Richard Johnston in 1784 as an assembly room for the Rotunda Hospital complex. Today the theater plays it safe with a major repertory of European and American drama and new plays by established Irish writers. ✉ *Cavendish Row,* ☎ *01/874–4045.*

51 General Post Office. Known as the GPO, it is one of the great civic buildings of Dublin's Georgian era, but its fame derives from the role it played during the Easter Uprising. It has an impressive facade in the neoclassic style and was designed by Francis Johnston and built by the British between 1814 and 1818 as a center of communications. This gave it great strategic importance and was one of the reasons why it was chosen by the insurgent forces in 1916 as a headquarters. Here, on Easter Monday, 1916, the Republican forces, about 2,000 in number, and under the guidance of Pádrig Pearse and James Connolly, stormed the building and issued the Proclamation of the Irish Republic. After a week of shelling, the GPO lay in ruins; 13 rebels were ultimately executed (including Connolly, who was dying of gangrene from a leg shattered in the fighting and had to be propped up in a chair before the firing squad). Most of the original building was destroyed, though the facade survived (you can still see the scars of bullets on the its pillars). Rebuilt and subsequently reopened in 1929, it is still a working post office, with an attractive two-story main concourse. A bronze sculpture depicting the dying Cuchulainn, a leader of the Red Branch Knights in Celtic mythology, sits in the front window. The 1916 Proclamation and the names of its signatories are inscribed on the green marble plinth. ✉ *O'Connell St.,* ☎ *01/872–8888.* ☉ *Mon.–Sat. 8–8, Sun. 10:30–6.*

★ **55 Hugh Lane Municipal Gallery of Modern Art.** Built originally as a town house for the Earl of Charlemont in 1762, this residence was so grand its Parnell Square street was nicknamed "Palace Row" in its honor. Designed by Sir William Chambers (who also built the Marino Casino for Charlemont) in the best Palladian manner, its delicate and rigidly correct facade, extended by two demi-une arcades, was fashioned from the "new" white Ardmulcan stone (now seasoned to gray). Charlemont was one of the cultural locomotives of 18th-century Dublin—his walls were hung with Titians and Hogarths, and he frequently dined with Oliver Goldsmith and Sir Joshua Reynolds—so he would undoubtedly be delighted that his home is now the Hugh Lane Gallery, named after a nephew of Lady Gregory (Yeats's aristocratic patron; ☞ Coole Park *in* Chapter 6) who drowned on the *Lusitania,* which was sunk by the Germans off the coast of County Cork in 1915. Lane collected both Impressionist paintings and 19th-century Irish and Anglo-Irish works. A complicated agreement with the National Gallery in London (reached after heated diplomatic dispute) stipulates that a portion of the 39 French paintings amassed by Lane shuttle back and forth between London and here. From November 1999, you can see Pissarro's *Printemps,* Manet's *Eva Gonzales,* Morisot's *Jour d'Été,* and, the jewel of the collection, Renoir's *Les Parapluies.*

Between the collection of Irish paintings in the **National Gallery of Ireland** (☞ *above*) and the superlative works on view here, you can quickly become familiar with Irish 20th-century art. Irish artists represented here include Roderic O'Conor, well known for his views of the West of Ireland; William Leech, including his *Girl with a Tinsel Scarf* (ca. 1912) and *The Cigarette*; and the most famous of the group, Jack B. Yeats (W. B.'s brother). The museum has a dozen of his paintings, including *Ball Alley* (ca. 1927) and *There Is No Night* (1949). There is also strikingly displayed stained-glass work by early 20th-century Irish master artisans Harry Clarke and Evie Hone. ⊠ *Parnell Sq. N*, ☎ *01/874–1903.* 🎫 *Free.* ☉ *Sept.–Mar.: Tues.–Thurs. 9:30–6, Fri.–Sat. 9:30–5, Sun. 11–5; Apr.–Aug: Tues.–Wed. 9:30–6, Thurs. 9:30–8, Fri.–Sat. 9:30–5, Sun. 11–5.*

❺❼ James Joyce Cultural Centre. Not everyone in Ireland has read James Joyce, but everyone has heard of him—especially since a copy of his censored and suppressed *Ulysses* was one of the top status symbols of the early 20th century. Today, of course, Joyce is acknowledged to be one of the greatest modern authors, and his *Dubliners, Finnegan's Wake,* and *A Portrait of the Artist as a Young Man* can even be read as poetic "travel guides" to Dublin. Now open to the general public, this restored, 18th-century Georgian town house, once the dancing academy of Professor Denis J. Maginni, is a center for Joycean studies and events related to the author. It has an extensive library and archives, exhibition rooms, a bookstore, and a café. Along with housing the **Joyce Museum** (☞ *below*) in Sandycove, the center is the main organizer of "Bloomstime," which marks the week leading up to June 16's Bloomsday celebrations. For a tour of Joyce's Dublin, *see* the Close-Up box "ReJoyce!" A Walk through *Ulysses* and James Joyce's Dublin," *below.* ⊠ *35 N. Great George's St.,* ☎ *01/878–8547.* 🎫 *£2.75.* ☉ *Weekdays 9:30–5, weekends 12:30–5.*

❺❽ Mountjoy Square. Built over the two decades before 1818, this square was once surrounded by elegant, terraced houses, but today only the northern side remains intact. The once-derelict southern side has been restored and converted into apartments. Irishman Brian Boru, who led his soldiers to victory against the Vikings in the Battle of Clontarf in 1014, was said to have pitched camp before the confrontation on the site of Mountjoy Square. Playwright Sean O'Casey once lived here at No. 35 and used the square as a setting for *The Shadow of a Gunman.*

❺⓪ O'Connell Street. Dublin's most famous thoroughfare, 150 ft wide, was previously known as Sackville Street, but its name was changed in 1924, two years after the founding of the Irish Free State. After the devastation of the 1916 Easter Uprising, the street had to be almost entirely reconstructed, a task that took until the end of the 1920s. The main attraction of the street, **Nelson's Pillar,** a Doric column towering over the city center and a marvelous vantage point, was blown up in 1966, the 50th anniversary of the Easter Uprising. After a design competition, plans are afoot to build a spectacular **Millennium Needle** on the sight of the old statue. The new sculpture will be Dublin's tallest structure. The large **monument** at the south end of the street is dedicated to Daniel O'Connell (1775–1847), "The Liberator," and was erected in 1854 as a tribute to the orator's achievement in securing Catholic Emancipation in 1829. Seated winged figures represent the four "Victories,"—courage, eloquence, fidelity, and patriotism—all exemplified by O'Connell. Ireland's four ancient provinces—Munster, Leinster, Ulster, and Connacht—are identified by their respective coats of arms. Look closely and you'll notice that O'Connell is wearing a glove on one hand, as he did for much of his adult life, a self-imposed penance for shooting a man in a duel. Alongside O'Connell is another noted statue, a modern rendition of Joyce's **Anna Livia,** seen as a lady set

REJOYCE! A WALK THROUGH JAMES JOYCE'S DUBLIN AND ULYSSES

JAMES JOYCE'S genius for fashioning high art out of his day-to-day life brought him literary immortality and makes him, even today and possibly for all time, the world's most famous Dubliner. He set all of his major works—*Dubliners, A Portrait of the Artist as a Young Man, Ulysses,* and *Finnegan's Wake*—in the city where he was born and spent the first 22 years of his life, and although he spent the next 36 in self-imposed exile, he never wrote about anywhere else. Joyce knew and remembered Dublin in such detail that he claimed that if the city were destroyed, it could be rebuilt in its entirety from his written works.

Joyceans flock to Dublin annually on June 16 to commemorate **Bloomsday,** the day in 1904 on which Leopold Bloom wanders through the city in *Ulysses.* Why *this* day? It had been an important one for Joyce—when he and his wife-to-be, Nora Barnacle, had their first date. Today Bloomsday has evolved into "Bloomstime," with events taking place in the days leading up to the 16th, then all day and well into the night. Even if you don't make it to Dublin on Bloomsday, you can still roam its streets, sniffing out Bloom's—and Joyce's—haunts.

Begin in the heart of the northside, on **Prince's Street,** next to the **GPO** (☞ Exploring, *above*), where the office of the old and popular *Freeman's Journal* newspaper (published 1763–1924) was located before it was destroyed during the 1916 Easter Uprising. Bloom was a newspaper advertisement canvasser for the *Journal.* Leopold and Molly Bloom's fictional home stood at **7 Eccles Street,** north of Parnell Square. On Great Denmark Street, **Belvedere College** (☎ 01/677–4795)

is housed in a splendid 18th-century mansion. Between 1893 and 1898, Joyce studied here under the Jesuits. A few steps away, the **James Joyce Cultural Centre** (☞ Sights to See *in* Dublin, *above*) is the hub of Bloomsday celebrations. Also on the northside is the site of **Bella Cohen's Brothel** (⊠ 82 Railway St.), in an area that in Joyce's day contained many such houses of ill-repute. Across town on the western edge of the northside, the **New Ormond Hotel** (⊠ Upper Ormond Quay, ☎ 01/872–1811) was an afternoon rendezvous spot for Bloom.

Across the Liffey, walk up Grafton Street to **Davy Byrne's Pub** (☞ Pub Food *in* Dublin, *above*) and then proceed to the **National Library** ((☞ Sights to See *in* Dublin, *above*))—where Bloom has a near meeting with Blazes Boylan, his wife's lover, and looks for a copy of an advertisement—via **Molesworth Street.** No establishment mentioned by Joyce has changed less since his time than **Sweny's Pharmacy** (⊠ Lincoln Pl.), at the back of Trinity College, which still has its black-and-white exterior and an interior crammed with potions and vials.

A NUMBER OF KEY JOYCE SITES lie outside the city center. On February 2, 1882, Joyce was born in the genteel southern suburb of Rathgar, at **41 Brighton Square,** where he spent the first two years of his life. (Bus 15A and Bus 15B make the 5-km/3-mi journey.) Other sites are covered elsewhere in our guide: **Sandymount Strand** and the **James Joyce Martello Tower** (☞ County Dublin—Southside, *below*) and **One Martello Terrace** (☞ Bray *in* Chapter 2).

within a waterfall and now nicknamed by the natives the "floozy in the Jacuzzi." **O'Connell Bridge,** the main bridge spanning the Liffey (wider than it is long), marks the street's southern end.

NEED A
BREAK?
You have a number of good alternatives for a break on the northside. One of Dublin's oldest hotels, the **Gresham** (⊠ Upper O'Connell St., ☎ 01/874–6881), is a pleasant old-fashioned spot for a morning coffee or afternoon tea. **Conway's** (⊠ Parnell St. near Upper O'Connell St., ☎ 01/873–2687), founded in 1745, is reputed to be Dublin's second-oldest pub. For a real Irish pub lunch, stop in at **John M. Keating** (⊠ 14 Mary St. and 23 Jervis St., ☎ 01/873–1567), at the corner of Mary and Jervis streets; head upstairs, where you can sit at a low table and chat with locals.

60 **Pro-Cathedral.** Dublin's principal Catholic cathedral (also known as St. Mary's) was built between 1816 and 1825. Although the severely classical church design is on a suitably epic scale, the building was never granted full cathedral status, nor has the identity of its architect ever been discovered; the only clue is in the church ledger, which lists a "Mr. P." as the builder. The church's facade, with a six-Doric-pillared portico, is based on the Temple of Theseus in Athens; the interior is modeled after the Grecian-Doric style of St-Philippe du Roule in Paris. A Palestrina choir, in which the great Irish tenor John McCormack began his career, sings in Latin here every Sunday at 11. ⊠ *Marlborough St.,* ☎ *01/874–5441.* 🎫 *Free.* ⊘ *Daily 8–6.*

62 **Rotunda Hospital.** Founded in 1745 as the first maternity hospital in Ireland or Britain, the Rotunda was designed on a grand scale by architect Richard Castle (1690–1751), with a three-story tower and a copper cupola. It's now most worth a visit for its **chapel,** with elaborate plasterwork executed by Bartholomew Cramillion between 1757 and 1758, appropriately honoring motherhood. The **Gate Theater** (☞ *above*), in a lavish Georgian assembly room, is also part of the complex. ⊠ *Parnell St.,* ☎ *01/873–0700.*

59 **St. Francis Xavier Church.** One of the city's finest churches in the classical style, the Jesuit St. Francis Xavier's was begun in 1829, the year of Catholic Emancipation, and was completed three years later. The building is designed in the shape of a Latin cross, with a distinctive Ionic portico and an unusual coffered ceiling. The striking, faux-marble high altarpiece, decorated with lapis lazuli, came from Italy. The church appears in James Joyce's story "Grace." ⊠ *Upper Gardiner St.,* ☎ *01/836–3411.* 🎫 *Free.* ⊘ *Daily 7–8:30.*

Along the Grand Canal

At its completion in 1795, the 547-km (342-mi) Grand Canal was celebrated as the longest in Britain and Ireland. It connected Dublin to the River Shannon, and horse-drawn barges carried cargo (mainly turf) and passengers to the capital from all over the country. By the mid-19th century the train had arrived and the great waterway slowly fell into decline, until the last commercial traffic ceased in 1960. But the 6-km (4-mi) loop around the capital is ideal for a leisurely stroll.

A Good Walk

Numbers in the text correspond to numbers in the margin and on the Dublin City Center map.

Begin by walking down the Pearse Street side of Trinity College until you arrive at the Ringsend Road Bridge. Raised on stilts above the canal is the **Waterways Visitors Center** 63. Head west along the bank until you reach the **Mount Street Bridge** ⑭. On the southside is Percy Place, a street with elegant, three-story, terraced houses. On the northside, a small lane leads up to the infamous **Scruffy Murphy's** ⑮ pub. Taking a little detour at the next right, you'll pass a road that leads up to St. Stephen's (☞ *above*). Another right takes you into Powerscourt, a classic, inner-city estate of two-up, two-down terraced houses. Return to the canal and continue your walk along Herbert Place. You can get really close to the dark green water here as it spills white and frothy over one of the many wood-and-iron locks (all still in working order) that service the canal. James Joyce lost his virginity to a prostitute on the next stretch of the Canal, around Lower Baggot Street Bridge, but these banks belong to the lonesome ghost of another writer, Patrick Kavanagh. A life-size **statue of Patrick Kavanagh** ⑯ sits here, contemplative, arms folded, legs crossed on a wooden bench. Less than a mile past Kavanagh's statue the canal narrows as it approaches Richmond Bridge. Just beyond the bridge is the **Irish Jewish Museum** ⑰. To finish your walk in style, take a right onto Richmond Street, past a few antiques stores, until you arrive at **Bambrick's** ⑱, a public house in the best tradition of Dublin.

TIMING

You could walk this section of the canal in half an hour if you hurried, but what's the point? A leisurely pace best suits a waterside walk, so give yourself a couple of hours to visit the Jewish Museum and explore the old streets off the canal.

Sight to See

⑱ **Bambrick's.** This is a pub in the best Irish tradition; long, dark-wood bar, half-empty, frequented mostly by men over 50, with a staff whose sharp, grinning humor borders on being rude.

⑰ **Irish Jewish Museum.** Though Ireland has never had a large Jewish population (it hovers around 1,800 today), in the late 19th century and early 20th century it did become home to roughly 5,000 European Jews fleeing the pogroms of Eastern Europe. Opened in 1985 by Israeli president Chaim Herzog (himself Dublin-educated), the museum has a restored synagogue and a display of photographs, letters, and personal memorabilia culled from Dublin's most prominent Jewish families, though the exhibits trace the Jewish presence in Ireland back to 1067. In homage to Leopold Bloom, the Jewish protagonist of Joyce's *Ulysses*, every Jewish reference in the novel has been identified. The museum is a 20-minute walk or so from St. Stephen's Green. ⊠ *3–4 Walworth Rd.,* ☎ *01/453–1797.* ⊙ *Oct.–Apr., Sun. 10:30–2:30; May–Sept., Tues., Thurs., and Sun. 11–3:30. Also by appointment.*

⑭ **Mount Street Bridge.** This bridge has a wooden lock on either side and is the perfect spot to watch these original gateways to the canal in operation. On the southwest corner of the bridge a small stone monument commemorating the battle of Mount Street Bridge in 1916 and the Irish Volunteers who died on this spot.

⑮ **Scruffy Murphy's.** Many a backroom deal by the country's political power brokers has been made in the backroom of this classy wood-and-brass pub. It's the perfect spot for a pint and a snack.

⑯ **Statue of Patrick Kavanagh.** Patrick Kavanagh, Ireland's great lyric poet, spent the later years of his life sitting on a bench here writing about the canal, which flowed from his birthplace in the Midlands to the city where he would die. In one such poem he tells those who outlive him, "O commemorate me with no hero-courageous tomb, just a canal-bank seat for the passerby." His friends took him at his word and commissioned a life-size bronze of the poet here. ⊠ *Canal bank along Wilton Terrace.*

⑥③ **Waterways Visitors Centre.** At the airy, wood-and-glass visitor center you can learn all about the history of Irish rivers and canals through photos, videos, and models. ⊠ *Grand Canal Quay, Dublin 2* ☎ *677–7501.* ☒ *£2.* ⊙ *June–Sept., daily 9:30–6:30; Oct.–May, Wed.–Sun. 12:30–5.*

Phoenix Park and Environs

Far and away Dublin's largest park, Phoenix Park (the name is an anglicization of the Irish *Fionn Uisce,* meaning clear water) is a vast, green arrowhead-shape oasis north of the Liffey, a 20-or-so-minute walk from the city center. Today—Heaven send what weather it may—Dubliners flock here to "take it aisy." It remains the city's main lung, escape valve, sports center (cricket, soccer, Gaelic games, and polo), and home to the noble creatures of the Dublin Zoo. A handful of other cultural sites near the park are also worth visiting, but to combine a visit to any of them with any of our other walks would be a bit difficult. The Custom House and the Old Jameson Distillery, at the end of the Dublin West walk (☞ *above*), are the sites closest (the Guinness Brewery, (☞ *below*) across the river, is also fairly close). So if you do make it to any of those, be sure to evaluate whether you have enough time to append a visit to one or another of these sites. Otherwise, plan to make a special trip out here, either walking or going by car or cab.

A Good Walk

Numbers in the text correspond to numbers in the margin and on the Dublin West map.

Beginning at the Custom House, walk down the quays on the north side of the Liffey until you come to Blackhall Place. Walk up to Arbour Hill and turn left: The **Arbour Hill Cemetery** ⑥⑨ will be on your left. Directly across Arbour Hill are the **Collins Barracks** ⑦⓪, now a branch of the National Museum (the main entrance is on Benburb Street on the south side). On its east side Benburb becomes Parkgate Street, and it's just a short stroll farther down to the main entrance of **Phoenix Park** ⑦①.

TIMING

Phoenix Park is *big*; exploring it on foot could easily take the better part of a day. If you're looking for a little exercise, head here: Jogging, horseback riding, and bicycling (☞ Outdoor Activities and Sports, *below*) are the ideal ways to explore the park more quickly than you can simply by strolling.

Sights to See

⑥⑨ **Arbour Hill Cemetery.** A total of 14 Irishmen were executed by the British following the 1916 Easter Uprising. They were all buried here, including Pádrig Pearse, who led the rebellion; his younger brother Willie, who played only a minor role in the uprising; and James Connolly, a socialist and labor leader wounded in the battle. Too weak from his wounds to stand, Connolly was tied to a chair and then shot. The burial ground is a simple but formal area, with the names of the dead leaders carved in stone beside an inscription of the proclamation they issued during the uprising. ⊠ *Arbour Hill.* ☒ *Free.* ⊙ *Mon.–Sat. 9–4:30, Sun. 9:30–noon.*

⑦⓪ **Collins Barracks.** Until recently, this was the oldest purpose-built military barracks in the world still in use. Now it's home to the National Museum's collection of glass, silver, costumes, furniture, and other decorative arts. ⊠ *Benburb St.,* ☎ *01/677-7444.* ☒ *Free.* ⊙ *Tues.–Sat. 10–5, Sun. 2–5.*

★ **Phoenix Park.** Europe's largest public park, extending about 5 km (3 mi) along the Liffey's north bank, encompasses 1,752 acres of verdant green lawns, woods, lakes, and playing fields. It's a jogger's paradise, but Sunday is the best time for everyone to visit: Games of cricket, soccer, polo, baseball, hurling—a combination of lacrosse, baseball, and field hockey—and Irish football are likely to be in progress. Old-fashioned gas lamps line both sides of **Chesterfield Avenue,** the main road that bisects the park for 4 km (2½ mi), which was named for Lord Chesterfield, a lord lieutenant of Ireland, who laid out the road in the 1740s. To the right as you enter the park, the **People's Garden** is a colorful flower garden designed in 1864.

Among the park's major monuments are the **Phoenix Column,** erected by Lord Chesterfield in 1747, and the **198-ft obelisk,** built in 1817 to commemorate the Duke of Wellington, the Irish general who defeated Napoleon for the British. (Wellington was born in Dublin but, true to the anti-Irish prejudice so prevalent in 19th-century England, balked at the suggestion that he was Irish: "If a man is born in a stable, it doesn't mean he is a horse," he is reputed to have said.) A tall **white cross** marks the spot from which Pope John Paul II addressed more than a million people during his 1979 visit to Ireland. Often, wild deer can be seen grazing in the many open spaces of the park, especially near here.

You're guaranteed to see wildlife at the **Dublin Zoo,** the third-oldest public zoo in the world, founded in 1830, and just a short walk beyond the People's Garden (☞ *above*). The place looks a little dilapidated, but the government has allocated money for a five-year renovation. Many animals from tropical climes are housed in barless enclosures, while Arctic species swim in the lakes close to the reptile house. The zoo is one of the few places in the world where lions will breed in captivity. Some 700 lions have been bred here since the 1850s, one of whom became familiar to movie fans the world over when MGM used him for their trademark. (As they will tell you at the zoo, he is in fact yawning in that familiar shot: An American lion had to be hired to roar and the "voice" was dubbed.) The children's corner has goats, guinea pigs, and lambs. In summer, the Lakeside Café serves ice cream and drinks. ⊠ *Phoenix Park,* ☎ *01/677–1425.* ▣ *£6.* ⊘ *Apr.–Oct., Mon.–Sat. 9:30–6, Sun. 10:30–6; Nov.–Mar., weekdays 9:30–4, Sun. 10:30–5.*

Both the president of Ireland and the U.S. ambassador have official residences in the park (the president's is known as Aras an Uachtarain), but neither building is open to the public. The Garda Siochana (police) has its headquarters in the park; a small **Garda Museum** contains many relics of Irish police history, including old uniforms. ⊠ *Phoenix Park,* ☎ *01/677–1156, ext. 2250.* ▣ *Free.* ⊘ *Weekdays 9–5; call to confirm.*

Also within the park is a **visitor center,** in the 17th-century fortified **Ashtown Castle;** it has information about the park's history, flora, and fauna. ⊠ *Phoenix Park,* ☎ *01/677–0095.* ▣ *£1.50.* ⊘ *Mar.–May, daily 10–1 and 2–5; June–Sept., daily 9:30–6:30; Oct., daily 2–5; Nov.–Feb., weekends 9:30–4:30.*

. . . .

NEED A
BREAK?

Just before the entrance to Phoenix Park, **Ryan's Pub** (⊠ 28 Parkgate St., ☎ 01/677–6097) is one of Dublin's last remaining genuine, late-Victorian-era pubs.

. . . .

DINING

By Vincent
Jamison

Ireland is going through a culinary renaissance, and Dublin's chefs are leading the charge. They are putting nouvelle spins on traditional Irish favorites such as coddle, stew made with bacon, sausage, and Irish smoked meats. At the heart of the changing food scene are two contrasting—but not opposing—developments: the internationalization of Irish food and the pursuit of authentically Irish food.

Dublin's restaurateurs are one main reason for the move toward a more internationally inflected fare. Many have trained in top restaurants in France, Switzerland, and Germany; others have worked in New York and Chicago; some have been much farther afield—to Thailand, Hong Kong, and Australia. Not surprisingly, they've come back with new ways of thinking about food—from the use of spices to new cooking techniques—and they're not afraid to adapt what they've learned elsewhere to local produce and regional dishes. Some of the chefs get good results by developing a style that reflects a rapprochement between East and West; others succeed through a classical style that could be called Franco-Irish; and still others take their influence from Italy, or the traditions of Anglo-Irish fare, or make an au courant bow to California. European-style cafés (☞ A Thousand Pubs *in* Pleasures and Pastimes, *above*) and brasserie-style restaurants are the latest arrivals—and Dublin can't seem to get enough of either. Of course, sophisticated Dubliners are eager to enjoy the new Continental flavors, but only if the latest fads are taste-tested by sound sense and a sensitive palate. The Irish are not about to let merely newfangled food take over from traditional dishes—and that's good news, because as Ireland rediscovers its authentic food heritage, it is keeping some of its best dishes alive.

Seafood tops that list—not necessarily the traditional cockles and mussels but wild salmon and oysters from the clear Atlantic waters off the west coast; deep-sea fish trawled off the shores of Donegal in the northwest; and lobsters, crabs, and sea urchins gathered in rockier coastal waters. Fresh produce, much of it organically grown, is being treated so imaginatively that even old Irish stalwarts such as potatoes, onions, and carrots have new life. Just look at boxty, or the traditional spud pancakes. At Gallagher's Boxty House, you can now get this centuries-old favorite stuffed with beef marinated in Beamish (Cork's answer to Guinness) or chicken perfumed with Irish Mist. Lamb, beef, and pork and bacon still provide the backbone for many signature dishes, but there is also great interest in venison, quail, and other game—both wild and farmed. There are dozens of excellent cheeses—such as St. Tola goat cheese from County Clare or Carrigburne Brie from Wexford—most produced by small artisan cheese makers. If one of these farmhouse varieties appears on a menu, make a point of trying it.

We have also included some of the city's best addresses for a hearty pub lunch, one of the most popular dining options for Dubliners, especially businesspeople. And if you're expecting soup and sandwiches, think again: Some pubs have excellent carveries where you can get a huge hot lunch for around £5–£6.

Prices

For price ranges *see* Chart 1(A) *in* Smart Travel Tips A to Z. Value-added tax (VAT) will automatically be added to your bill—a 12.5% tax on food, and a government excise tax on drinks. Before paying, check to see whether service has been included. If it has been included, you can pay it with a credit card; but if has not, it's more considerate to the staff to leave the tip (10%–15%) in cash if paying the main bill by credit card.

Many restaurants have recognized that they are priced out of the reach of some diners and offer early bird and/or pre- and post-theater menus with significantly lower set prices at specific times, often from 6:30 to 8 PM.

City Center (Southside)

CHINESE

$$ ✕ **Imperial Chinese Restaurant.** In a city developing a wide choice of ethnic restaurants, this has long been the preferred choice among many of Dublin's Chinese population, especially at lunchtime on Sunday. Behind the elegant facade just off Grafton Street, it has deep-blue carpets, warm-pink walls, a fountain, and an arch. The specialty of the house is dim sum, available at lunchtime only, although there are a number of interesting fixed-price menus as well. ⊠ *12a Wicklow St.,* ☎ *01/677–2580. AE, MC, V.*

CONTEMPORARY

$$$$ ✕ **Peacock Alley.** Conrad Gallagher ran away from school at 12 to be
★   a cook in his native County Donegal. By 18 he was sous-chef at the Plaza in New York, and at 19 *chef de cuisine* at the Waldorf-Astoria's Peacock Alley, whose name he has borrowed. His hotel experience in Manhattan has undoubtedly helped in the elegant new Fitzwilliam Hotel on St. Stephen's Green, where Peacock Alley is ensconced in a stylish 120-seat room with a white-tiled open kitchen at the rear. He is a mercurial and passionate cook, who builds up food on the plate and dabs on multicolored oils and garnishes with painterly precision. His strikingly inventive dishes include smoked salmon with basmati rice, pear, preserved ginger, soy sauce, and quesadilla; deep-fried crab cakes with *katifi* (shredded phyllo pastry); and daube of pot-roasted beef. The strong wine list, excellent service, and lively atmosphere contribute to the whole experience. ⊠ *Fitzwilliam Hotel, 47 S. William St.,* ☎ *01/662–0760. Reservations essential. AE, DC, MC, V.*

$$$ ✕ **Cooke's Café.** Johnny Cooke's Mediterranean-style bistro is a cool spot for visiting movie stars. Cooke is influenced by eclectic Italian-Californian styles, which he serves up with flair on large, white Wedgwood plates in a room that has been sponge-painted in pale gold. Specialties are fresh seafood (except Monday—there is no fishing on Sunday and Cooke insists on absolute freshness): crab salad with spinach, coriander, mango salsa, and lime dressing; and lobster grilled with garlic-herb butter. In season, the roasted game plate with wild mallard and teal, sliced venison and wood pigeon, and a chanterelle-thyme cream sauce is superb. The outdoor seating on nice summer days is a consolation for the slow service during the busiest times. Upstairs is the grill bar Rhino Room, also owned by Cooke. ⊠ *14 S. William St.,* ☎ *01/679–0536. Reservations essential. AE, DC, MC, V.*

$$$ ✕ **La Stampa.** Huge Regency mirrors, little bronze cupids, busts of
★   Roman emperors, candelabra, fake flowers, and large skylights bring neoclassic kitsch to La Stampa's wonderful high-ceiling dining room, between Trinity College and St. Stephen's Green. Menus change frequently to reflect an eclectic, international style. For a main course, you may get a blanquette of monkfish with steamed spring vegetables with coriander cream or roast barbary duck breast with spiced tomato and zucchini tart with a béarnaise sauce. Service is good, and there is an air of fun about the place. ⊠ *35 Dawson St.,* ☎ *01/677–8611. AE, DC, MC, V. No lunch weekends.*

$–$$ ✕ **Side Door.** The Shelbourne Hotel (☞ Lodging, *below*) offers an interesting variation on the usual *très cher* hotel dining room (though it has one of those, too: 27 The Green) and the uninspired coffee shop. This well-designed budget restaurant has oak floors, cream walls, and art deco wood tables and chairs. You can start off with a bowl of Thai soup, a grilled chicken risotto, or Mediterranean vegetable pizza. Main dishes include supreme of chicken marinated in honey and charcoal-grilled rib eye of beef. Designer beers and a good wine list nicely complement the food. ✉ *27 St. Stephen's Green,* ☎ *01/676–6471. AE, DC, MC, V.*

CONTINENTAL

$$$ ✕ **Locks.** Claire Douglas's restaurant on the north shore of the Grand Canal sticks to a fairly straightforward treatment of international food, served up in a relaxed atmosphere. It's popular with business-people and southside locals. Steak and kidney pie as well as *feuillete* (puff pastry) of seafood with a prawn sauce are among the superior main courses. Desserts like pear fool in a tall goblet, or a small chocolate and toffee cake, remind you of classic dishes from another era. ✉ *1 Windsor Terr., Portobello,* ☎ *01/454–3391. AE, DC, MC, V. Closed Sun. No lunch Sat.*

$–$$ ✕ **La Mère Zou.** Eric Tydgadt is Belgian and his wife, Isabel, is from Paris, so it's not surprising that their small basement restaurant is Continental in emphasis. The lunch menu includes six king-size plates; one of them, "La Belge," has a 6-ounce charcoal-grilled rump steak with French fries and a salad with salami, country ham, chicory, and mayonnaise. In the evening, the dishes are more elaborate, with ragout of venison or medallions of monkfish. ✉ *22 St. Stephen's Green,* ☎ *01/661–6669. AE, DC, MC, V. Closed Jan. 1–10. No lunch weekends.*

FRENCH

$$$$ ✕ **Patrick Guilbaud.** Nearly everything is French at this fine restaurant
★ in the Hotel Merrion, including the eponymous owner, his chef, and the maître d'. The setting is modern Dublin design at its very best: a bright and airy room, with a patio leading to the hotel gardens—a fine place to dine on a warm summer evening. Inside, the walls are adorned with paintings that would put many galleries in Ireland to shame. Guillaume Le Brun's cooking is a fluent expression of modern French cuisine—not particularly flamboyant, but coolly professional. Expect superb foie gras, confit of Landaise duck in a delicate phyllo pastry, roe deer with juniper—and also some homage to Irish dishes, from Connemara lobster in season to braised pig's trotters. ✉ *Hotel Merrion, Upper Merrion St.,* ☎ *01/676–4192. AE, DC, MC, V. Closed Sun.– Mon. and late Dec.–mid-Jan.*

$$$$ ✕ **Thornton's.** Chef-owner Kevin Thornton is as restrained and clas-
★ sical in his approach as the Peacock Alley's Conrad Gallagher (☞ *above*)is flamboyant, yet, like Gallagher, he is a naturally gifted chef. In a renovated house with pine floors on the north bank of the Grand Canal, the space is coolly understated; the service is French and quite formal. Thornton's cooking style is light, and his dishes are small masterpieces of structural engineering. In season, he marinates legs of partridge, then debones and reforms the bird, with the breasts presented as a crown. Desserts range from an elegant fig ice cream to chocolate mousse. Although slightly off the beaten path (it's a 20-minute walk or short car ride southwest of St. Stephen's Green) and nowhere near as flashy as some of its competitors, it's worth the trip. ✉ *1 Portobello Rd.,* ☎ *01/454–9067. Reservations essential. AE, DC, MC, V. Closed Sun. No lunch.*

$$$ ✕ **L'Ecrivain.** Chef-owner Derry Clarke's sense of humor is sometimes
★ tested by tipsy patrons who have been known to trip over a life-size sculpture of the writer Brendan Behan on their way out of this elegant French restaurant where paintings of Beckett and other Irish writers adorn the walls. The name means "The Writer," and the food is serious—disciplined and restrained, with the emphasis on fresh Irish produce, especially seasonal ingredients cooked with care and imagination.

78

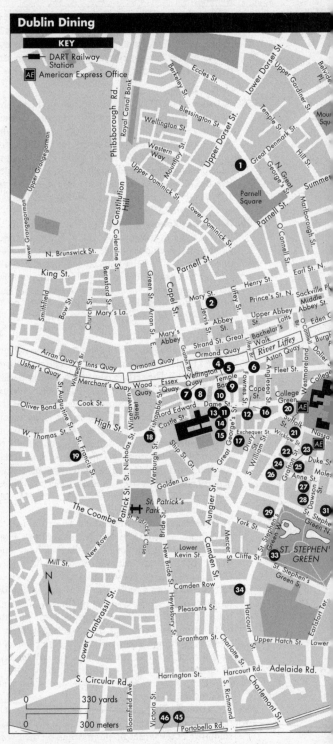
Dublin Dining

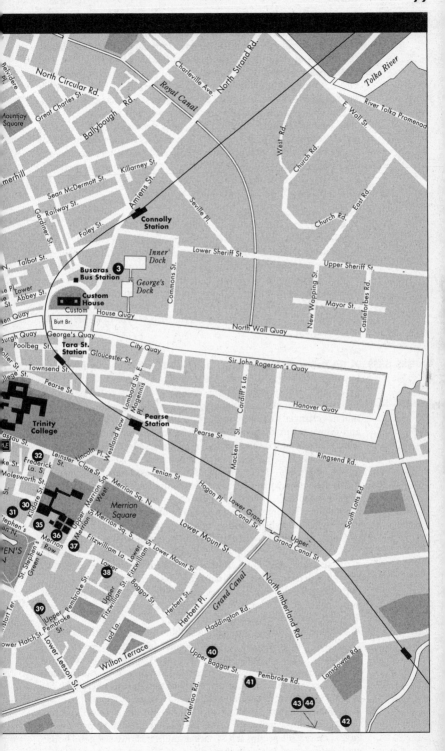

Cured, marinated lamb with prune stuffing is superb. Try one of the unusual first-course salads followed, perhaps, by game in season. Desserts, such as crème brûlée, are given special care. ⊠ *109a Lower Baggot St.,* ☎ *01/661–1919. AE, DC, MC, V. Closed Sun.*

$ ✕ **Mitchell's Cellars.** This popular lunch spot just off St. Stephen's Green is in the vaulted basement of a wine merchant. The quarry-tile floor, whitewashed walls, red-and-white lamp shades hanging over pine tables, and waitresses neatly dressed in navy and white are all basically unchanged since the early '70s, as is the menu. Still, a bustling crowd continues to pack the place, drawn to its country-French home cooking—fare that includes soups and pâtés, quiche lorraine and salads, beef braised in Guinness, and chocolate-and-brandy meringue. ⊠ *21 Kildare St.,* ☎ *01/662–4724. Reservations not accepted. AE, DC, MC, V. Closed Sun., Sat. June–Aug. No dinner.*

INDIAN

$$ ✕ **Rajdoot.** After 32 years in business, this spacious restaurant serves polished Northern Indian, Nepalese, and Rajasthani cuisine. Service is attentive, almost to a fault. You can eat informally at low tables in the reception area or on banquettes in the more formal dining area just behind. Starters include tandoori quail or vegetarian staples such as *pakoras* (chickpea fritters with onions, potato, and cabbage in a spicy deep-fried batter). Duck Jaipur and jumbo prawns with chili garlic are a highlight. ⊠ *26–28 Clarendon St.,* ☎ *01/679–4274. AE, DC, MC, V. Closed Sun.*

IRISH

$$$–$$$$ ✕ **The Commons Restaurant.** This large, elegant dining room is in the basement of historic Newman House (☞ The Center City: Around Trinity College, *in* Exploring Dublin, *above*). The patio doors open onto a paved courtyard for summer aperitifs or alfresco lunches. The restaurant has changed award-winning chefs four times in the last few years, and now a talented young Frenchman, Sebastien Masi, is offering a light treatment of Irish and international themes. Beyond the patio gates lie Iveagh Gardens, a quiet, lovely gem of a park. ⊠ *85–86 St. Stephen's Green,* ☎ *01/478–0530. AE, DC, MC, V. Closed Sun. No lunch Sat.*

$$$ ✕ **The Grey Door.** Just off Fitzwilliam Square and a five-minute walk from St. Stephen's Green, this Irish eatery is in an elegant Georgian town house. The interior is a celebration of Irish craftsmanship, with wooden floors, stylish lighting, handmade tableware; even the logo— of Celtic circles borrowed from Neolithic tombs—is quintessentially Irish. Starters include *brotchan rí* (salmon and leek broth) and Irish nettle and watercress soup. Kildare lamb with boxty potato and fillet of hake with mussel stew continue the Irish spirit into the main courses. In the basement, a less formal restaurant, Pier 32 ($$), has live music most nights. ⊠ *23 Upper Pembroke St.,* ☎ *01/676–3286. AE, DC, MC, V. Closed Sun. No lunch Sat.*

$ ✕ **Burdock's.** In the heart of Viking Dublin, next door to the Lord Edward Pub, Dublin's most famous take-out fish-and-chipper remains steadfastly old-fashioned. Join the inevitable queue and eat on the steps of St. Patrick's Cathedral—the traditional place to consume a Burdock's meal. Be sure to pick up plenty of napkins! ⊠ *Werburgh St.,* ☎ *01/454–0306. No credit cards. Closed Sun.*

$ ✕ **Kilkenny Kitchen.** Housed in the Kilkenny Shop (☞ Shopping, *below*), which specializes in superlative Irish craftsmanship and overlooks Trinity College, this self-service restaurant showcases good homemade buffet food in traditional Irish style. On the menu are a house quiche (with Irish bacon, herbs, and fresh vegetables), good stew, smoked salmon, casseroles, and an imaginative selection of salads. Homemade scones, bread, and cakes, and farmhouse cheeses are also good bets. Lunchtime is busy; expect to share a table. ⊠ *6 Nassau St.,* ☎ *01/677–7066. AE, DC, MC, V. Closed Sun.*

ITALIAN

$ ✕ Gotham Café. This stylish little place just off Grafton Street is very much in tune with the vogue in Dublin for buzzing restaurants with strong Italian–New York leanings. Zipped-up pasta is typically served with a hot chili sauce and Creole sausage; a dozen gourmet pizzas are inventively done with toppings named after hot neighborhoods in other cities: the "Tribeca" has prawns, roasted peppers, zucchini, cilantro, mozzarella, coriander, and hot sauce. ⊠ *8 S. Anne St.,* ☎ *01/ 679–5266. MC, V.*

$ ✕ Il Primo. A few hundred yards from St. Stephen's Green, this lively Italian restaurant has basic decor, with bare tables, old-fashioned and simple but comfortable wood-armed office chairs, stainless-steel cutlery, and paper napkins. But the lovely, large, modern crystal wine glasses give a hint of the good things to come. Generous middle-of-the-road Irish-Italian cuisine changes seasonally. Among the main courses, a delicious creamy risotto with chunky chicken breasts, a scattering of chicken livers, and wild mushrooms is a standout. The wine list, too, is superb. ⊠ *Montague St., off Harcourt St.,* ☎ *01/478–3373. AE, DC, MC, V. Closed Sun.*

$ ✕ Milano. The open, gleaming stainless-steel kitchen off this well-designed room turns out a tempting array of flashy pizzas. On thin pizza crust, choose from such combinations as tomato and mozzarella, ham and eggs, Cajun with prawns and Tabasco, spinach and egg, or ham with anchovies. The wine list, mostly Italian, can make this a surprisingly upscale place for a pizza chain, part of the British-owned Pizza Express group. Last orders are taken at midnight, so keep this in mind if you're looking for a late-night bite. A second branch of the restaurant is in Temple Bar. ⊠ *38 Dawson St.,* ☎ *01/670–7744;* ⊠ *18 Essex St. E., Temple Bar,* ☎ *01/670–3384. AE, MC, V.*

$ ✕ Pasta Fresca. This stylish little Italian restaurant and deli off Grafton Street squeezes a surprising number of people into a fairly small space. Antipasto *misto* (assorted sliced Italian meats) makes a good appetizer— or go for carpaccio *della casa* (wafer-thin slices of beef fillet, with fresh Parmesan, olive oil, lemon juice, and black pepper). The main courses consist of Pasta Fresca's own very good versions of well-known dishes such as spaghetti *alla Bolognese,* cannelloni, and lasagna *al forno.* The pasta is freshly made each day. You'll find lines at lunchtime. ⊠ *3–4 Chatham St.,* ☎ *01/679–2402. AE, DC, MC, V. Closed Sun.*

JAPANESE

$ ✕ Yamamori. Ramen noodle bars offer a staple diet for budget travelers to Japan, but this is the first in Ireland. The meals-in-a-bowl are a splendid slurping experience, and although you will be supplied with a small Chinese-style soup spoon, the best approach is with chopsticks. You can also get an authentic spin on sushi and sashimi dishes as well as delicious chicken teriyaki. ⊠ *71 S. Great George's St.,* ☎ *01/475– 5001. AE, DC, MC, V.*

PAN-ASIAN

$$ ✕ Mao. Everything is Asian fusion at this bustling café, from the little Andy Warhol pastiche of Chairman Mao on the washroom door to the Ho Fun noodles, stir-fried with shaved beef sirloin, pak choy, garlic, and black beans. It pays homage to Thai, Vietnamese, and other Southeast Asian cuisines. Red snapper is served with a tempura batter, chili mussels come in a large bowl with lemongrass, and vegetarian rice-paper rolls arrive stuffed with shiitake mushrooms and bean-thread noodles. Reservations aren't accepted, so go early to be sure of a seat. ✉ *2 Chatham Row,* ☎ *01/670–4899. MC, V.*

RUSSIAN AND SCANDANAVIAN

$$$ ✕ **Old Dublin.** Russian and Scandinavian influences turn up on the menu at this well-established spot, named after an area east of St. Patrick's Cathedral going back a thousand years to Viking times. A series of cozy but elegant low-ceiling rooms are decorated with pristine white linens, well-upholstered chairs, and candlelit tables and further warmed by glowing fires. Specialties include borscht served with mushroom-filled piroshki and blini, and a choice of salted salmons. Familiar dishes such as chicken Kiev and beef Stroganoff are interspersed with surprises such as planked sirloin Hussar, a steak baked between two oak planks, served on an oak platter with salad and sweet pickle. ✉ *90–91 Francis St.,* ☎ *01/454–2028. AE, DC, MC, V. Closed Sun. No lunch Sat.*

VEGETARIAN

$ ✕ **Juice.** This spot serves upscale vegetarian fare (some of it is vegan, or dairy-free, and most of it organic) in a large, airy dining room with brushed stainless steel and dark wine-color lacquer walls. Chef Deb Davis's menu includes a platter of homemade butter-bean and black olive pâté and spinach-and- pistachio pesto, served with bread and crudités, to start. The main course might be a tasty spinach and ricotta cheese cannelloni. ✉ *Castle House, Great George's St.,* ☎ *01/475–7856. MC, V.*

Temple Bar

AMERICAN/CASUAL

$$ ✕ **Elephant & Castle.** One of Temple Bar's most popular and established eateries, Elephant & Castle serves up traditional American food—charcoal-grilled burgers, salads, omelets, sandwiches, and pasta. The brunch on Sunday is always packed. Bare tables fill its two rooms, one of which has a long wooden banquette that runs the length of one wall; the crowds and the absence of soft surfaces mean the noise level can be high. When the service is good, the turnover tends to be quick, although you may be inclined to linger, as its formula—an atmosphere that's both bustling *and* relaxed, generous portions of unfussy *and* well-prepared food—make it a casual Dublin standout. New Yorkers take note: Yes, this is a cousin of the restaurant of the same name in Greenwich Village. ✉ *18 Temple Bar,* ☎ *01/679–3121. Reservations not accepted. AE, DC, MC, V.*

$ ✕ **Bad Ass Café.** Sinéad O'Connor used to wait tables at this lively spot in a converted warehouse between the Central Bank and Ha'penny Bridge (a "Rock 'n Stroll" tour plaque notes O'Connor's past here). Old-fashioned cash shuttles whiz around the ceiling of the barnlike space, which has bare floors and is painted in primary colors inside and out. A wall of glass makes for great people-watching. Although the food—mostly pizzas and burgers—is unexceptional, the Bad Ass can be a lot of fun and is popular with appetites of all ages. ✉ *9–11 Crown Alley,* ☎ *01/671–2596. AE, MC, V.*

CONTEMPORARY

$$$–$$$$ ✕ **The Tea Room.** Simple, sleek, and suave, the highly popular restaurant in the Clarence Hotel (☞ *below*)is one of the least pretentious of Dublin's high-bracket eateries—a pleasant surprise, considering that you may find yourself dining alongside some of the world's most famous stage, catwalk, and screen personalities. Sure, they may be drawn to the place by its equally famous owners, U2, but they keep coming back for the food. Chef Michael Martin is committed to a no-frills-but-plenty-of-fuss cuisine and walks this particularly difficult tightrope with consummate ease. Begin with the carpaccio of wild salmon, with a fried quail egg and a salad of warm potatoes, or the saucisson foie gras and smoked duck. Among the mouthwatering entrées are roast cushion of veal with truffle oil mash and sea bass with a confit of baby fennel and tomato compote. The service is quiet, friendly, and efficient, and manager Alain Kerloc'h is always on hand to suggest an appropriate wine from the extensive list. ⊠ *6–8 Wellington Quay,* ☎ *01/670–7766. Reservations essential. AE, MC, V.*

$$ ✕ **Eden.** The young owners of several of Dublin's new café-style bars,
★ including the Front Lounge and the Globe (☞ *below*), have followed those successes with a popular brasserie-style restaurant with an open kitchen and high wall of glass looking out onto one of Temple Bar's main squares. Patio-style doors lead to an outdoor eating area—a major plus in a city with relatively few alfresco dining spots. Chef Eleanor Walsh creates such dishes as a vegetarian buckwheat pancake filled with garlic, spinach, and cheddar; duck leg confit with lentils; and grilled breast of corn-fed chicken. Desserts include rhubarb crème brûlée and homemade ice creams and sorbets. ⊠ *Meeting House Sq.,* ☎ *01/670–5372. Reservations essential. AE, MC, V.*

$$ ✕ **Mermaid Cafe.** One of the chef-owners dabbles in fine art, and a couple of the large canvases on the walls are carried over into painterly bistro cooking. Lunch, ordered from a blackboard of specials, is an exceptional value—piquant crab cakes, hearty seafood casseroles, venison sausage, or vegetables roasted in a clay dish. Good attention to detail and a thoughtful wine list make this modest restaurant with tall windows looking onto busy Dame Street one of the best eateries in Temple Bar. ⊠ *69 Dame St.,* ☎ *01/670–8236. MC, V. .*

$$ ✕ **Rubicon.** Just down the street from the Shelbourne Hotel (☞ *below*), in a long Georgian room with wooden floors, is this restaurant offering some radical interpretations of international cooking. You might begin with Scandinavian gravlax—salmon cured with sea salt, brandy, lemon juice, mustard, and dill—or a more exotic spicy beef salad with pickled cabbage, papaya, and Thai dressing. Main courses range from piccata of veal with batons of Gruyère coated in marsala cream to duck breast with plum sauce and soy noodles in sesame oil. ⊠ *6 Merrion Row,* ☎ *01/676–5955,* ℻ *01/676–1999. Reservations essential. AE, DC, MC, .V. No lunch Sun.*

FRENCH

$$$–$$$$ ✕ **Les Frères Jacques.** This restaurant in a late-Victorian corner house
★ next to the Olympia Theatre brings a little bit of Paris to Temple Bar. Old prints of Paris and Deauville hang on the green-papered walls, and the French waiters, dressed in white Irish linen and black bow ties, exude a Gallic charm without being excessively formal. Expect traditional French cooking that nods to the seasons. Seafood (depending on fresh fish available at the market) is a major attraction, and lobster, from the tank, is a specialty, typically roasted and flambéed with Irish whiskey. Also recommended is the *magret de canard* (roast breast of duck served with a ginger and grapefruit sauce). A piano player performs Friday and Saturday evenings and the occasional weeknights. ⊠ *74 Dame St.,* ☎ *01/679–4555. AE, DC, MC, V. Closed Sun. No lunch Sat.*

$$ ✕ **Jaskos.** A French restaurant chain of the same name has opened this large, all-day bistro in the space that formerly held the nearby Olympia Theatre's props and where "Amhránn na bhFiann" (pronounced *au*-rawn na veen, "The Soldier's Song"), the Irish national anthem, was composed. If you're looking for comforting food at reasonable prices, this is a good bet. The extensive menu includes *planches* (wooden trays) with things like jumbo shrimps and salad. Among the other standouts are diced foie gras with fresh oysters, a dozen escargots with Pernod and garlic butter, and a rib-eye steak with blue-cheese sauce. ⊠ *64 Dame St.,* ☎ *01/679–7767. AE, DC, MC, V.*

$$ ✗ **La Med.** La Med's Parisian owner-manager has created a clean, two-story dining room overlooking the Liffey on one side and Temple Bar on the other. Its all-day policy means you can get coffee at 11 AM, a well-varied lunch menu at midday, a tapas menu with little pizzas and crostini late in the afternoon, and a full-fledged dinner in the evening. A substantial bouillabaisse, a pastry tart of creamed leek and onion gratin, charcoal-grilled sirloin, and roasted monkfish Basquaise highlight the menu. ⊠ *22 Essex St. E,* ☎ *01/670–7358. AE, MC, V.*

ITALIAN

$ ✗ **Da Pino.** This popular Italian trattoria suffers from a fairly bland combination of salmon and gray decor, but whatever decorative failings it has are more than made up for in simple, affordable cuisine. The delicious *zuppa di pesce e crostacei* (fish and shellfish soup) makes a good starter for the pizzas, among the best in the city center. In keeping with the seafaring theme, try the pizza *al salmone,* a thin-crust pie covered in fresh Irish smoked salmon and capers. ⊠ *38–40 Parliament St.,* ☎ *01/671–9308. Reservations required weekends. AE, DC, MC, V.*

MEDITERRANEAN

$$–$$$ ✗ **Bruno's.** Experienced French-born restaurateur Bruno Berta has a hit on his hands with his Italian-Mediterranean bistro on one of the busiest corners in Temple Bar. Low-slung windows let you watch passersby. Simple but stylish dishes range from starters of fresh crab claws with chilies, lemongrass, and tomato concasse to main dishes of grilled chicken with raisins, dried prunes, Moroccan semolina, and walnut dressing. Friendly service and a relaxed atmosphere make this one of the best bets in the area. ⊠ *30 Essex St E,* ☎ *01/670–6767. AE, DC, MC, V. Closed Sun.*

South City Center: Ballsbridge, Donnybrook, and Stillorgan

CONTEMPORARY

$$$ ✗ **Roly's Bistro.** The crowd, the buzz, the quality of the food, and, above
★ all, the surprisingly reasonable prices have made this big, brasserie-style restaurant one of the capital's most fashionable. It's run by well-known restaurateur Roly Saul and award-winning chef Colin O'Daly. Begin, perhaps, with a wild mushroom soup with sorrel, or crab with pink grapefruit served cold, and continue with roast guinea fowl with grapes and lime sauce, rabbit and pigeon pie with red cabbage, or shellfish bake (an aromatic combination of scallops, prawns, and mussels with tomato and basil). Desserts can be both comforting *and* elegant, like the crème brûlée with homemade praline ice cream. ⊠ *7 Ballsbridge Terr., Ballsbridge,* ☎ *01/668–2611. Reservations essential. AE, DC, MC, V.*

CONTINENTAL

$$$$ ✗ **Le Coq Hardi.** For many years John Howard has been running one
★ of Dublin's best restaurants, in a Georgian house in Ballsbridge. Meeting the challenge posed by newer restaurants and younger chefs, he continues to refine and reinvent his own cooking. One of Howard's signature dishes—a little old-fashioned, perhaps, but still popular—is Coq Hardi, chicken stuffed with potatoes and mushrooms, wrapped in bacon before going into the oven, and finished off with a dash of Irish whiskey. The cheese boards are among the best in the country, and desserts tend to be rich and sumptuously classical French. Service is friendly and relaxed in the plush, comfortable, and quietly elegant dining room. The wine cellar holds many of the world's great wines.

✉ *35 Pembroke Rd., Ballsbridge,* ☎ *01/668–9070. Reservations essential. AE, DC, MC, V. Closed Sun.*

$$$ ✕ **Beaufield Mews.** A 10-minute taxi ride from the city center, this 18th-century coach house with stables still has its original cobbled courtyard and is even said to be haunted by a friendly monk. Inside it's all black beams, old furniture, and bric-a-brac. The most desirable tables overlook the courtyard or the garden or are, less predictably, "under the nun" (the nun in question is a 17th-century portrait). While the main attraction is the atmosphere, the food is based on fresh ingredients, and you'll find old favorites like roast duckling à l'orange as well as wild-salmon steaks simply grilled. ✉ *Woodlands Ave., Stillorgan,* ☎ *01/288–6945. Reservations essential. AE, DC, V. Closed Sun.–Mon. No lunch.*

$$$ ✕ **Patrick Kavanagh Room at the Hibernian Hotel.** Named for the Irish
★ poet, this eatery is one of the most distinguished restaurants affiliated with a hotel in Dublin. Browse through the menu in the cozy, plush sitting room before moving on to the elegant terra-cotta, cream, and green dining room and conservatory beyond. Accomplished chef David Foley turns out sophisticated, complex cuisine. Among the stellar entrées, choose from confit of duck leg served with eggplant, roast peppers, and zucchini with *tapenade* (a caper-anchovy-olive condiment); sole stuffed with crab mousse; or roast fillet of beef with fennel sautéed in olive oil, smoked bacon, and shallot casserole. The desserts are no less elaborate: pears with a champagne sabayon and timbale of winter berries in a Cointreau jelly. ✉ *Hibernian Hotel, Eastmoreland Pl., Ballsbridge,* ☎ *01/668–7666. AE, DC, MC, V. No lunch Sat.*

IRISH

$$$ ✕ **Ernie's Restaurant.** High-quality ingredients, attention to detail, and consistency are the hallmarks of this long-established restaurant only a few minutes by taxi from the city center. Built around a large tree and fountain, the place has a welcoming atmosphere; it's also well known for the late Ernie Evans's large collection of paintings of the West of Ireland. Blue Irish linen and sparkling crystal decorate tables. The seasonal menu always has a variety of catches of the day—grilled sole with spring onion and thyme butter and poached wild salmon on a bed of creamed potato—as well as four or five meat and poultry entrées such as roasted rack of Wicklow lamb with a caramelized onion tart. ✉ *Mulberry Gardens, Donnybrook,* ☎ *01/269–3300. AE, DC, MC, V. Closed Sun.–Mon. and 1 wk at Christmas. No lunch Sat.*

City Center (Northside)

CONTEMPORARY

$$ ✕ **Chapter One.** In the vaulted, stone-walled basement of the Dublin Writers Museum, just down the street from the Hugh Lane Municipal Gallery of Modern Art (☞ North of the Liffey *in* Exploring, *above*), this is one of the most notable restaurants in northside Dublin. Sample dishes such as pressed duck and black pudding terrine with pear chutney as well as roast scallops with smoked bacon and potato-herb salad in a chili dressing. The rich bread-and-butter pudding and the apple and pecan crumble are two stellar desserts. ✉ *18–19 Parnell Sq.,* ☎ *01/873–2266. AE, DC, MC, V. Closed Sun. No lunch Sat., no dinner Mon.*

SEAFOOD

$$ ✕ **Fisherman's Wharf.** This waterfront spot beside the popular Harbourmaster pub, near the northside's Connolly Station, and surrounded by the modernist facades and gray-tinted windows of the International Financial Services Centre is slightly off the beaten path. But when the

sun shines on the lagoon and old docking area just outside, you would-n't want to be anywhere else for an alfresco lunch or dinner. Not surprisingly, the family of fish importers that owns this restaurant concentrates on seafood. Typical fare includes panfried prawns, seafood chowder, and swordfish fillets seared and served on a bed of mixed pepper confit and chili butter. ☒ *International Financial Services Centre, off Amiens St.,* ☎ *01/670–1900. AE, DC, MC, V. Closed Sun.*

Pub Food

Most pubs serve food at lunchtime, some throughout the day. Food ranges from hearty soups and stews to chicken curries, smoked salmon salads, and sandwiches, and much of it is surprisingly good. Expect to pay £4–£5 for a main course. Many pubs do not take credit cards.

✕ **Davy Byrne's.** James Joyce immortalized Davy Byrne's in his sprawling novel *Ulysses.* Nowadays it's more akin to a cocktail bar than a Dublin pub, but it's good for fresh and smoked salmon, salads, and a hot daily special. Food is available at lunchtime and in the early evening. ☒ *21 Duke St.,* ☎ *01/671–1298.*

✕ **John M. Keating.** For a real Irish pub lunch, this old-timer at the corner of Mary and Jervis streets can't be beat. Upstairs you can sit at a low table and chat with locals as you warm up with a bowl of soup and nibble on a sandwich. ☒ *14 Mary St. and 23 Jervis St.,* ☎ *01/873–1567.*

✕ **Old Stand.** Conveniently close to Grafton Street, the Old Stand serves grilled food, including steaks. ☒ *37 Exchequer St.,* ☎ *01/677–0823.*

✕ **O'Neill's.** This fine pub, a stone's throw from Trinity College, has the best carvery (open from 12 to 2:30) of any pub in the city, serving up a hearty lunch for about IR£5–IR£6. ☒ *2 Suffolk St.,* ☎ *01/679–3614.*

✕ **Stag's Head.** Serving the best pub lunch in the city, the Stag's Head is a favorite of both Trinity students and businesspeople. ☒ *1 Dame Ct.,* ☎ *01/679–3701.*

LODGING

"An absolute avalanche of new hotels" is how the *Irish Times* characterized Dublin's hotel boom. It's unlikely that there have ever been more hotels under construction at one time in the capital than there are now, while at the same time, at least one third of the existing hotels are being renovated. New lodgings are opening in all areas of the city, including a couple along the Liffey quays and some in Ballsbridge, an inner "suburb" that's a 20-minute walk from the city center. Demand for rooms means that rates are still high at the best hotels by the standards of any major European or American city (and factoring in the exchange rate means a hotel room can take a substantial bite out of any traveler's budget). Service charges range from 15% in expensive hotels to zero in moderate and inexpensive ones. Be sure to inquire when you make reservations.

Many hotels have a weekend, or "B&B," rate that's often 30%–40% cheaper than the ordinary rate; some hotels also have a midweek special that provides discounts of up to 35%. These rates are available throughout the year but are harder to get in high season. Ask about them when booking a room (they are available only on a prebooked basis), especially if you plan a brief or weekend stay. If you've rented a car and you're not staying at a hotel with secure parking facilities, it's worth considering a location out of the city center, such as Dalkey or Killiney, where the surroundings are more pleasant and you won't have to worry about parking on city streets, which can be difficult.

Dublin has a decent selection of less-expensive accommodations—including many moderately priced hotels with basic but agreeable rooms. As a general rule of thumb, lodgings on the northside of the river tend to be more affordable than those on the south. Many B&Bs, long the mainstay of the economy end of the market, have upgraded their facilities and now provide rooms with private bathrooms or showers, as well as multichannel color televisions and direct-dial telephones, for around £25 a night per person. B&Bs tend to be in suburban areas—generally a 10-minute bus ride from the center of the city. This is not in itself a great drawback, and savings can be significant. For lodging prices, *see* Chart 2(A) *in* Smart Travel Tips A to Z. For additional lodging information, *see* Lodging *in* Smart Travel Tips.

City Center (Southside)

$$$$ ⊞ **Conrad Dublin International.** In a seven-story redbrick and smoked-glass building just off St. Stephen's Green, the Conrad, owned by the Hilton Group, is firmly aimed at international business travelers. Gleaming, light marble graces the large, formal lobby. Rooms are rather cramped and have uninspiring views of the adjacent office buildings, but they are nicely outfitted with natural wood furnishings, painted in sand colors and pastel greens, and graced with Spanish marble in the bathrooms. A note to light sleepers: The air-conditioning/heating system can be noisy. The hotel has two restaurants: the informal Plurabelle and the plusher Alexandra Room. The main bar, Alfie Byrne's, named in honor of Dublin's lord mayor for most of the 1930s (a renowned teetotaller), attempts to re-create a traditional Irish pub atmosphere. ⊠ *Earlsfort Terr., Dublin 2,* ☎ *01/676–5555 or 800/ HILTONS in the U.S.,* 𝔽𝔸𝕏 *01/676–5424. 182 rooms with bath, 9 suites. 2 restaurants, bar, in-room data ports, in-room safes, minibars, no-smoking floor, no-smoking rooms, room service, in-room VCRs, exercise room, concierge, business services, meeting rooms, free parking. AE, DC, MC, V.*

$$$$ ⊞ **Fitzwilliam Hotel.** A relative newcomer to the luxury circuit, the Fitzwilliam has been dubbed a "designer" hotel for its impeccable decor: Everything from light fixtures to luggage racks to staff uniforms is the work of international design leaders. The modern glass building has a large roof garden and overlooks the park. The spacious rooms are furnished in a contemporary, comfortable style. Conrad Gallagher, one of Ireland's young up-and-coming chefs, presides over the rooftop Ireland restaurant. ⊠ *St. Stephen's Green, Dublin 2,* ☎ *01/478–7000,* 𝔽𝔸𝕏 *01/478–7878. 129 rooms, 6 suites. Restaurant, bar, brasserie, in-room data ports, no-smoking rooms, room service, exercise room, laundry service, business services, meeting rooms. AE, DC, MC, V.*

$$$$ ⊞ **Merrion.** The home of Arthur Wellesley, the Duke of Wellington and
★ hero of the Battle of Waterloo, is one of four exactingly restored Georgian town houses that make up part of the capital's newest—and perhaps most luxurious—hotel. The stately rooms are richly appointed in classic Georgian style down to the last detail—from the crisp linen sheets to the Carrara marble bathrooms. Some are vaulted with delicate Adamesque plasterwork ceilings, and others are graced with magnificent, original marble fireplaces. The Garden Wing, at the back of the hotel behind the elegant gardens laid out by Irish landscape designer Jim Reynolds, has smaller rooms than the main house, but they are just as ornate. You know this place has to be one of Dublin's best—

after all, leading Dublin restaurateur Patrick Guilbaud (☞ Dining, *above*) moved his eponymous restaurant here. ⊠ *Upper Merrion St., Dublin 2,* ☎ *01/603–0600,* FAX *01/603–0700. 127 rooms with bath, 18 suites. 2 restaurants, 2 bars, in-room data ports, in-room safes, minibars, no-smoking floor, no-smoking rooms, room service, in-room VCRs, indoor pool, barbershop, beauty salon, massage, steam room, laundry service and dry cleaning, concierge, business services, meeting rooms, free parking. AE, DC, MC, V.*

$$$$ ★ 🏨 **Shelbourne Hotel.** Paris has the Ritz, New York has the Plaza, and Dublin has the Shelbourne. The grand old history (Ireland's constitution was signed in Room 112 in 1921) of this grand old place was written by no less than celebrated novelist and wit Elizabeth Bowen. One step past the ornate, redbrick and white-gingerbread facade and you know you're in in Dublin: Waterford chandeliers, gleaming Old Masters on the wall, and Irish Chippendale chairs invite you to linger in the lobby— as many fabled names have done so since this city showplace opened in 1824 (☞ The Center City: Around Trinity College, *above*). Each guest room is unique; all have fine, carefully selected furniture and luxurious drapes, with splendid antiques in the older rooms. Those in front overlook St. Stephen's Green, but rooms in the back, without a view, are quieter. The impressive suites have separate sitting rooms and dressing areas; the largest, with a mini-network of interconnecting rooms, is named in honor of the late Princess Grace of Monaco, who visited in the 1960s and 1970s. Downstairs the public rooms are awhirl with life: The restaurant, 27 The Green, is one of the most elegant rooms in Dublin; Lord Mayor's Lounge, off the lobby, is a perfect rendezvous spot and offers a lovely afternoon tea—a real Dublin tradition. ⊠ *27 St. Stephen's Green, Dublin 2,* ☎ *01/676–6471 or 800/543–4300 in U.S.,* FAX *01/661–6006. 194 rooms with bath, 9 suites. 2 restaurants, 2 bars, indoor pool, hot tub, sauna, health club, free parking. AE, DC, MC, V.*

$$$$ 🏨 **Westbury.** This comfortable, modern hotel is in the heart of southside Dublin, right off the city's buzzing shopping mecca, Grafton Street. Join elegantly dressed Dubliners for afternoon tea in the spacious mezzanine-level main lobby, furnished with antiques. Alas, the utilitarian rooms—painted in pastels—don't share the lobby's elegance. More inviting are the suites, which combine European decor with tasteful Japanese screens and prints. The flowery Russell Room serves formal lunches and dinners; the downstairs Sandbank, a seafood restaurant and bar, has decor resembling a Joycean-period establishment. ⊠ *Grafton St., Dublin 2,* ☎ *01/679–1122,* FAX *01/679–7078. 203 rooms with bath, 8 suites. 2 restaurants, bar, minibars, no-smoking rooms, room service, laundry service and dry cleaning, free parking. AE, DC, MC, V.*

$$$ 🏨 **Davenport, Mont Clare, and Alexander.** The Davenport's gorgeous, bright-yellow neoclassic facade was built in the 1860s to front a church, but a 1993 conversion remade the building into this hotel, just behind Trinity College, around the corner from Merrion Square, and down the street from the Government Buildings. Beyond the hotel's four-story lobby, few indications of the building's former purpose remain. The reasonably spacious rooms and larger suites are fitted in tasteful, deep colors and functional furnishings. The hotel restaurant, Lanyon's, serves breakfast, lunch, and dinner amid traditional Georgian decor. In the comfortable President's Bar, see how many heads of state you can identify in the photos covering the walls. ⊠ *Merrion Sq., Dublin 2,* ☎ *01/661–6800 or 800/327–0200 in the U.S.,* FAX *01/661–5663. 118 rooms with bath, 2 suites. Restaurant, bar, air-conditioning, minibars, no-smoking rooms, room service, in-room VCRs, laundry service and dry cleaning, concierge, business services, meeting rooms, free parking. AE, DC, MC, V.*

$$ ⊡ **Central Hotel.** Established in 1887, this grand, old-style redbrick hotel is in the heart of the center city, steps from Grafton Street, Temple Bar, and Dublin Castle. Rooms are small but have high ceilings and practical but tasteful furniture; although all have showers, not all have baths, so inquire when booking. Adjacent to the hotel is Molly Malone's Tavern, a lively hotel-bar with plenty of regulars who come for the atmosphere and the live, traditional Irish music on Friday and Saturday nights. The restaurant and Library Bar—one of the best spots in the city for quiet pint—are on the first floor. ⊠ *1–5 Exchequer St., Dublin 2,* ☎ *01/679–7302,* ⨍Ⱥ⨯ *01/679–7303. 67 rooms with bath, 3 suites. Restaurant, 2 bars, room service, laundry service and dry cleaning, concierge, business services, meeting rooms. AE, DC, MC, V.*

$$ ⊡ **Drury Court Hotel.** A two-minute walk from Grafton Street and just around the corner from some of the city's best restaurants, this small hotel opened in March 1996. Rooms are done in subtle greens, golds, and burgundies. The parquet-floored rathskeller dining room serves breakfast and dinner; lunch is served in the casual Digges Lane Bar, frequented by many young Dubliners. ⊠ *28–30 Lower Stephens St., Dublin 2,* ☎ *01/475–1988,* ⨍Ⱥ⨯ *01/478–5730. 30 rooms with bath, 2 suites. Bar, room service, laundry service and dry cleaning, meeting room. AE, DC, MC, V.*

$$ ⊡ **Stephen's Hall All-Suite.** Dublin's only all-suite hotel is in a tastefully modernized Georgian town house just off Stephen's Green. The suites, considerably larger than the average hotel room, include one or two bedrooms, a separate sitting room, a fully equipped kitchen, and bath. They are comfortably equipped with quality modern furniture. Top-floor suites have spectacular city views, and ground-floor suites have private entrances. Morel's Restaurant serves breakfast, lunch, and dinner. ⊠ *14–17 Lower Leeson St., Dublin 2,* ☎ *01/661–0585,* ⨍Ⱥ⨯ *01/661–0606. 37 suites. Restaurant, 2 bars, room-service, no-smoking rooms, meeting rooms, free parking. AE, DC, MC, V.*

$ ⊡ **Avalon House.** Many young, independent travelers rate this cleverly restored, Victorian redbrick building the most appealing of Dublin's hostels. A 2-minute walk from Grafton Street and 5–10 minutes from some of the city's best music venues, the hostel has a mix of dormitories, rooms without bath, and rooms with bath. The dorm rooms and en-suite quads all have loft areas that offer more privacy than you'd typically find in a multibed room. The Avalon Café serves food until 10 PM but is open as a common room after hours. ⊠ *55 Aungier St., Dublin 2,* ☎ *01/475–0001,* ⨍Ⱥ⨯ *01/475–0303. 35 4-bed rooms with bath, 5 4-bed rooms without bath, 4 twin rooms with bath, 4 single rooms without bath, 22 twin rooms without bath, 5 12-bed dorms, 1 10-bed dorm, 1 26-bed dorm. Café. AE, MC, V.*

$ ⊡ **Jurys Christchurch Inn.** Expect few frills at this functional budget hotel, part of a new Jurys minichain that offers a low, fixed room rate for up to three adults or two adults and two children. (The **Jurys Custom House Inn** [⊠ Custom House Quay, Dublin 1, ☎ 01/607–5000, ⨍Ⱥ⨯ 01/829–0400], at the International Financial Services Centre, operates according to the same plan.) The biggest plus is the pleasant location, facing Christ Church Cathedral and within walking distance of most city-center attractions. The rather spartan rooms are decorated in pastel colors and utilitarian furniture. ⊠ *Christ Church Pl., Dublin 8,* ☎ *01/454–0000,* ⨍Ⱥ⨯ *01/454–0012. 182 rooms with bath. Restaurant, bar, no-smoking rooms, parking (fee). AE, DC, MC, V.*

$ ⊡ **Kilronan House.** A five-minute walk from St. Stephen's Green, Deirdre
★ and Noel Comer's guest house is a long-standing favorite—thanks in large measure to the friendly welcome. The large, late-19th-century terraced house, with a white facade, was carefully converted, and the furnishings are updated each year. Richly patterned wallpaper and carpets

grace guest rooms, while orthopedic beds (rather rare in Dublin hotels, let alone guest houses) help to guarantee a restful night's sleep. If you have a dog back home whom you're pining after, you'll appreciate Homer, the Labrador. ⊠ *70 Adelaide Rd., Dublin 2,* ☎ *01/475–5266,* FAX *01/478–2841. 15 rooms with bath. Free parking. MC, V.*

$ ☷ **Number 31.** Two Georgian mews strikingly renovated in the early
★ '60s as the private home of Sam Stephenson, Ireland's leading modern architect, are now connected via a small garden to the grand town house they once served. Together they form a marvelous guest house a short walk from St. Stephen's Green. New owners Deirdre and Noel Comer, who also own Kilronan House (☞ *above*), serve made-to-order breakfasts at refectory tables in the balcony dining room. The white-tiled sunken living room, with its black leather sectional sofa and modern artwork that includes a David Hockney print, will make you think you're in California, not Dublin. ⊠ *31 Leeson Close, Dublin 2,* ☎ *01/676–5011,* FAX *01/676–2929. 19 rooms with bath. No-smoking rooms, laundry service and dry cleaning, free parking. AE, MC, V.*

South City Center—Ballsbridge

$$$$ ☷ **Berkeley Court.** The most quietly elegant of Dublin's large modern hotels, Berkeley Court has a glass-and-concrete exterior designed in a modern, blocklike style set in verdant grounds. Inside, the vast white-tiled and plushly carpeted lobby has roomy sofas and antique planters. The large rooms are decorated in golds, yellows, and greens, with antiques or reproductions of period furniture; bathrooms are tiled in marble. The five luxury suites have a Jacuzzi. The Berkeley Room restaurant has table d'hôte and à la carte menus; the more informal Conservatory Grill, with large windows, serves grilled food and snacks. ⊠ *Lansdowne Rd., Dublin 4,* ☎ *01/660–1711 or 800/550–0000 in the U.S.,* FAX *01/661–7238. 157 rooms with bath, 29 suites. 2 restaurants, bar, room-service, no-smoking rooms, barbershop, beauty salon, exercise room, shops, laundry service and dry cleaning, business service, meeting rooms, free parking. AE, DC, MC, V.*

$$$ ☷ **Doyle Burlington.** Dublin's largest hotel, popular with American tour groups and Irish and European business travelers, is about five minutes by car from the city center. Its impersonal, 1972 glass-and-concrete facade contrasts with the friendly and attentive staff. Public rooms, especially the large bar, have mahogany counters and hanging plants that enhance the conservatory-style setting. The generous-size rooms, in the usual modern plush in neutral tones, have large picture windows. At night, Annabel's nightclub and the seasonal Irish cabaret are both lively spots. Although the Burlington has no sports and health facilities, the Doyle hotel group (☞ *Doyle Tara, below*) has an arrangement that allows you to use the RiverView Sports Club in nearby Clonskeagh for £5 a visit. ⊠ *Upper Leeson St., Dublin 4,* ☎ *01/660–5222,* FAX *01/660–8496. 523 rooms with bath. 2 restaurants, 3 bars, room-service, shops, cabaret (May–Oct.), nightclub, laundry service and dry cleaning, business service, meeting rooms, free parking. AE, DC, MC, V.*

$$$ ☷ **Herbert Park Hotel.** The Herbert Park sits adjacent to a park of the same name and beside the River Dodder. The large lobby has floor-to-ceiling windows and a slanted glass roof. The spacious bar, terrace lounge, and restaurant are Japanese-inspired. Relaxing shades of blue and cream predominate in the nicely sized rooms, which are brightened by green, red, or white bedspreads; all have individually controlled air-conditioning, a large desk, and two telephone lines. Some look onto the park. Two of the suites have large balconies with views of the park or the leafy suburbs. The restaurant has a large terrace where you can

dine in warm weather. ✉ *Ballsbridge, Dublin 4,* ☎ *01/667–2200,* FAX *01/667–2594. 150 rooms with bath, 3 suites. Restaurant, bar, exercise room, business services, free parking. AE, DC, MC, V.*

$$$ 🏨 **Hibernian.** Only a 15-minute walk from the city center, this early
★ 20th-century Edwardian nurses' home designed by Albert E. Murray—one of the architects of the Rotunda Hospital—is now a small luxury hotel. One of the city's most elegant and intimate hostelries, it has retained the distinctive red-and-amber brick facade and has rooms in different shapes. Though they're relatively small, rooms are nicely done in pastels, with deep-pile carpets and comfortable furniture. The public rooms, in cheerful chintz and stripes, include a period-style library and a sun lounge—both comfortable spaces to relax before or after a dinner in the hotel's intimate restaurant, the Patrick Kavanagh Room (☞ *Dining, above*). Amid all this Victorian elegance, the owners haven't forgotten the warming touches. ✉ *Eastmoreland Pl. off Upper Baggot St., Dublin 4,* ☎ *01/668–7666 or 800/414243,* FAX *01/660–2655. 40 rooms with bath. Restaurant, bar, parking (fee). AE, DC, MC, V.*

$$$ 🏨 **Jurys and The Towers.** These adjacent seven-story hotels, a short cab ride from the center of town, are popular with businesspeople and vacationers. They have more atmosphere than most comparable modern hotels, though the Towers has an edge over Jurys, its older (it dates from 1962), larger, less-expensive companion. Jurys has large, plainly decorated rooms with light walls and brown drapes; furnishings are functional but uninspired. The Towers' rooms are a third larger than those of Jurys, decorated in blue and gold with built-in, natural wood furniture; the large beds and armchairs are comfortable. All the suites in both hotels have their own sitting rooms and kitchenettes. The Dubliners Bar, modeled on an old country kitchen, is popular with upwardly mobile locals and guests. ✉ *Ballsbridge, Dublin 4,* ☎ *01/660–5000,* FAX *01/660–5540. Jurys: 300 rooms with bath, 3 suites; the Towers: 100 rooms with bath, 4 suites with kitchenettes. Restaurant, coffee shop, 2 bars, indoor/outdoor pool, hot tub, shop, cabaret (May–Oct.), laundry service and dry cleaning, business services, meeting rooms, free parking. AE, DC, MC, V.*

$$ 🏨 **Lansdowne.** This small Ballsbridge hotel has cozy rooms in Geor-
★ gian style with deep floral-pattern decor. Photos of sports personalities hang on the walls of the Green Blazer bar in the basement, a popular haunt for local businesspeople and fans of the international rugby matches held at nearby Lansdowne Road; you can get a bite to eat here all day. Next to the bar is Parker's Restaurant, which specializes in seafood and grilled steaks. ✉ *27 Pembroke Rd., Dublin 4,* ☎ *01/ 668–2522,* FAX *01/668–5585. 39 rooms with bath, 2 suites. Restaurant, bar, free parking. AE, DC, MC, V.*

$ 🏨 **Ariel Guest House.** This redbrick, 1850 Victorian guest house is one
★ of Dublin's finest, just a few steps from a DART stop and a 15-minute walk from St. Stephen's Green. Rooms in the main house are lovingly decorated with Victorian and Georgian antiques, Victoriana, and period wallpaper and drapes. The 13 rooms at the back of the house are more spartan, but all are immaculate. A Waterford-crystal chandelier hangs over the comfortable leather and mahogany furniture in the gracious, fireplace-warmed drawing room. Owner Michael O'Brien is an extraordinarily helpful and gracious host. ✉ *52 Lansdowne Rd., Dublin 4,* ☎ *01/668–5512,* FAX *01/668–5845. 40 rooms with bath. Breakfast room, free parking. MC, V.*

$ 🏨 **Mount Herbert Guest House.** This sprawling guest house is made up of a number of large Victorian-era houses. It overlooks some of Ballsbridge's fine rear gardens and is right near the main rugby stadium; the nearby DART will have you in the city center in seven minutes. The simple rooms are painted in light shades and contain little besides

92

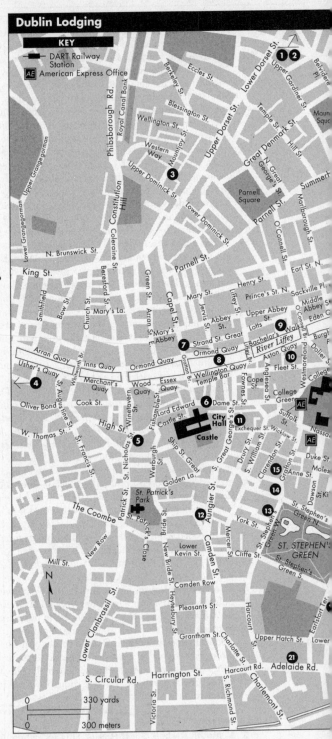

Dublin Lodging

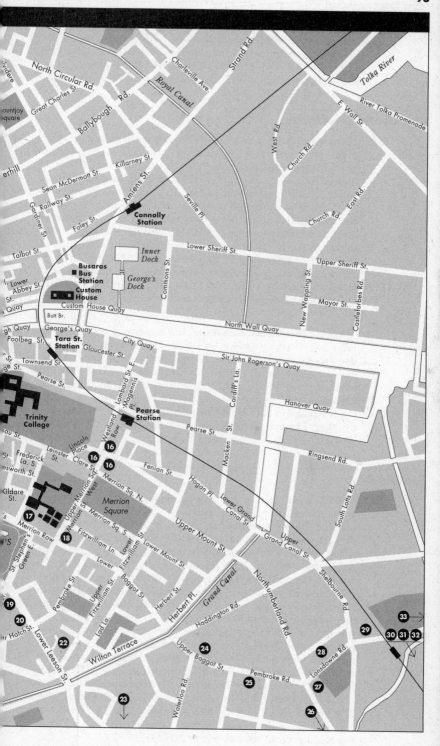

beds, but all have bathrooms and 10-channel TVs. You can relax in the lounge; the large restaurant, overlooking the English-style back garden (floodlit at night) and children's play area, serves three meals a day, with unpretentious dinners of steaks and stews. ⊠ *7 Herbert Rd., Dublin 4,* ☎ *01/668–4321,* FAX *01/660–7077. 200 rooms with bath. Restaurant, bar, gift shop, sauna, business service, meeting rooms, free parking. AE, DC, MC, V.*

City Center (Northside)

$$$$ ⊞ **The Morrison.** Near a number of other new hotels on the quays north of the Liffey, the luxurious Morrison opened in 1998. Halfway between the Ha'penny and Capel Street bridges, it's no more than 10 minutes from Trinity College. The exterior is bland enough, but the highly modern interior was designed by John Rocha, Ireland's most acclaimed fashion designer. He had the last word on everything down to the toiletries and staff uniforms. Rooms are spacious and high-tech, with top-of-the-line entertainment units, satellite TV, and ISDN lines. The Lobo Restaurant has an Asian theme. ⊠ *Ormond Quay, Dublin 1,* ☎ *01/ 879–2999 or 800/447–7462,* FAX *01/878–3185. 88 rooms with bath, 7 suites. 2 restaurants, 2 bars, in-room data ports, minibars, no-smoking rooms, room service, in-room VCRs, laundry service and dry cleaning, concierge, business services, meeting rooms, free parking. AE, DC, MC, V.*

$ ⊞ **Dublin International Youth Hostel.** In a converted convent, Dublin's major hostel has a total of 420 beds divided between private rooms and dorm rooms with 8, 12, 15, or 22 beds. Bathroom facilities are communal, even for private rooms. This is a spartan, low-cost alternative to hotels; if you're not a member of the International Youth Hostel organization, you can stay for a small extra charge. Continental breakfast is included in the rate. The hostel is north of Parnell Square, near the Mater Hospital. ⊠ *51 Mountjoy St., Dublin 1,* ☎ *01/830–1766,* FAX *01/380–1600. 2 twin rooms, 3 3-bed rooms, 2 4-bed rooms, 9 6-bed rooms, and 8-, 12-, 15-, and 22-bed dorms. Restaurant. MC, V.*

Temple Bar

$$$$ ⊞ **The Clarence.** It seems everyone in Ireland knows about the Clarence—an 1852 Temple Bar hotel that used to be a favorite place to stay in the capital with clergy and folks from the provinces. But since the hotel underwent a major renovation in the mid-'90s (ruining much of its elegant charm), you are much more likely to bump into celebrity friends of co-owners Bono and the Edge of U2 than Father O'Casey from Cork. The hotel is understated contemporary to the point of austerity. Stone floors, unadorned oak wainscoting, and a leather-lined elevator set the slightly chaotic tone downstairs, where the Octagon Bar and the Tea Room Restaurant are popular Temple Bar watering holes. Guest rooms are done in a mishmash of earth tones accented with deep purple, gold, cardinal red, and royal blue. With the exception of those in the penthouse suite, rooms are small, but *very* comfortable beds, sparkling bathrooms, and, from the front rooms, views of the Liffey do compensate. The laissez-faire service seems to take its cue from the minimalist decor, so if you like to be pampered, stay elsewhere. ⊠ *6–8 Wellington Quay, Dublin 2,* ☎ *01/670–9000,* FAX *01/670–7800. 46 rooms with bath, 4 suites. Restaurant, bar, no-smoking rooms, minibars, laundry service and dry cleaning, meeting rooms, free parking. AE, DC, MC, V.*

$$ ⊞ **Parliament.** Although the Parliament is in one of Dublin's finest Edwardian buildings, its interior is very much functional, if tidy, and attracts a mostly business clientele. They are drawn by the location, on

Dame Street near the Central Bank and a few blocks down from Trinity College. Rooms are a good size, with a simple, slightly monotonous beige and off-white scheme. The Senate Restaurant and Forum Bar keep up the democratic theme. ☒ *Lord Edward St., Dublin 2,* ☎ *01/670–8777,* 🗚 *01/670–8787. 63 rooms with bath. Restaurant, bar, no-smoking rooms. AE, DC, MC, V.*

$$ 🏨 **Temple Bar.** In a former bank building just around the corner from Trinity College, this hotel has an Art Deco lobby with a large and old-fashioned cast-iron fireplace, natural-wood furniture, and lots of plants. Off the lobby are a small cocktail bar and the bright, open, glass-roofed Terrace Restaurant, which serves sandwiches, pastas, omelets, and fish all day. Mahogany furnishings and autumn green and rust colors adorn guest rooms, nearly all of which have double beds, making them more than a little cramped. The Boomerang nightclub on the premises is open to both guests and the public. ☒ *Fleet St., Dublin 2,* ☎ *01/677–3333,* 🗚 *01/677–3088. 126 rooms with bath, 1 suite. Restaurant, 2 bars, nightclub, parking (fee). AE, DC, MC, V.*

$–$$ 🏨 **Arlington Hotel.** A converted auction house on the quays is the setting for this privately owned boutique hotel. Pass between the gold lions guarding the door and enter a medieval great hall with suits of armor, sumptuous swags, and creaky floors. The theme continues in the bar; boisterous and echo-filled, it's more mead hall than cozy pub. Rich upholstery, romantic lighting, and hearty Irish fare (full breakfast is included in the rates) make the restaurant more intimate. Upstairs the corridors and rooms have a Georgian feel, with soothing pastel yellow or lavender walls; spreads and drapes are awash in golds, rusts, and blues and have patterns and details evocative of tapestries. The hotel also has limited off-street parking, though your way might be blocked by a Guinness truck. ☒ *23–25 Bachelor's Walk, O'Connell Bridge, Dublin 1,* ☎ *01/804–9100,* 🗚 *01/804–9112. 115 rooms. Restaurant, bar, in-room data ports, no-smoking rooms, dance club, baby-sitting, laundry service, meeting rooms, free parking. AE, DC, MC, V.*

South County Dublin Suburbs

$$$ 🏨 **Doyle Tara.** On the main coast road 10–15 minutes from the Dun Laoghaire ferry terminal and 6½ km (4 mi) from the city center, this unpretentious, informal seven-story hotel is also near the Booterstown Marsh Bird Sanctuary (☞ County Dublin—Southside *in* Side Trips, *below*). The best rooms are in the original section and face Dublin Bay; rooms in the addition have slightly more modern decor. The restaurant serves grilled fish, steaks, and omelets. The hotel staff is very personable. ☒ *Merrion Rd., Dublin 4,* ☎ *01/269–4666,* 🗚 *01/269–1027. 113 rooms with bath. Restaurant, bar, no-smoking rooms, laundry service and dry cleaning, free parking. AE, DC, MC, V.*

$$$ 🏨 **Royal Marine.** This 1870 seaside hotel has been completely modernized. The comfortable, capacious rooms have also been refurbished with contemporary decor, though the eight suites with four-poster beds and sitting rooms preserve the lofty ceilings of the original building. Ask for a room at the front of the hotel, facing Dun Laoghaire harbor. ☒ *Marine Rd., Dun Laoghaire, Co. Dublin,* ☎ *01/280–1911,* 🗚 *01/280–1089. 95 rooms with bath, 8 suites. Restaurant, 2 bars, room service, no-smoking rooms, business service, free parking. AE, DC, MC, V.*

$$
★ 🏨 **Fitzpatrick Castle Hill.** With its sweeping views over Dun Laoghaire and Dublin Bay, the Fitzpatrick is worth the 13-km (8-mi) drive from the city center. The original part of the hotel is a 19th-century stone castle, with a substantial modern addition housing rooms; many are furnished with antiques and four-poster beds and have large bathrooms.

The hotel is convenient to golfing, horseback riding, and fishing; the fitness facilities include an 82-ft heated pool. The views from Killiney Hill, behind the hotel, are spectacular; the seaside village of Dalkey and Killiney Beach are both in walking distance. ⊠ *Killiney, Co. Dublin,* ☎ *01/284–0700,* FAX *01/285–0207. 113 rooms with bath. Restaurant, bar, indoor pool, sauna, steam room, health club, meeting rooms, free parking. AE, DC, MC, V.*

$ 🏨 **Bewleys at Newlands Cross.** On the southwest outskirts of the city, this 1998 four-story hotel is a good option if you're planning to head out of the city (especially to points in the Southwest and West) early and don't want to deal with morning traffic. The hotel is emulating the formula recently made popular by Jurys Inns, in which rooms— here each has a double bed, a single bed, and a sofa bed—are a flat rate for up to three adults or two adults and two children. ⊠ *Newlands Cross, Naas Rd., Dublin 22,* ☎ *01/464–0140,* FAX *01/464–0900. 126 rooms with bath. Café, free parking. AE, MC, V.*

Dublin Airport

$$$ 🏨 **Forte Posthouse.** The only hotel at Dublin Airport, this low-rise, red-brick structure with a plain exterior has rooms that are basic but spacious. The Bistro Restaurant serves fish and meat entrées, as well as a selection of vegetarian dishes; Sampans serves Chinese cuisine at dinner only. There's live music in the bar on weekends. You have access to a nearby health club. ⊠ *Dublin Airport,* ☎ *01/844–4211,* FAX *01/ 844–6002. 249 rooms with bath. 2 restaurants, bar, room service, free parking. AE, DC, MC, V.*

$$ 🏨 **Doyle Skylon.** This modern, five-story hotel with a concrete-and-glass facade is on the main road into Dublin city center from the airport. The generous-size rooms are plainly decorated in cool pastels; double beds and a pair of easy chairs are almost the only furniture. A glass-fronted lobby with a large bar and the Rendezvous Room restaurant dominate the public areas. The cooking is adequate but uninspired, with dishes such as grilled steak, poached cod, and omelets. ⊠ *Upper Drumcondra Rd., Dublin 9,* ☎ *01/837–9121,* FAX *01/837–2778. 92 rooms with bath. Restaurant, bar, free parking. AE, DC, MC, V.*

NIGHTLIFE AND THE ARTS

Long before Stephen Daedalus's excursions into nighttown (read Joyce's *A Portrait of the Artist as a Young Man*), Dublin was proud of its lively after-hours scene, particularly its thriving pubs. Lately, however, with the advent of Irish rock superstars (think U2, the Cranberries, Sinéad O'Connor, Bob Geldof) and the resurgence of Celtic music (think *Riverdance*, the soundtrack to *Titanic*), the rest of the world seems to have discovered that Dublin is one of the most happening places in the world. Most nights (including Monday, does anybody have to get up for work? you might wonder), the city's pubs and clubs overflow with young cell phone–toting Dubliners and Europeans who descend on the capital for weekend getaways. The city's 900-plus pubs are its main source of entertainment; many public houses in the city center have live music—from rock to jazz to traditional Irish.

A number of newspapers have informative listings: The *Irish Times* has a daily guide to what's happening in Dublin and in the rest of the country, as well as complete film and theater schedules. The *Evening Herald* lists theaters, cinemas, and pubs with live entertainment. *In Dublin* and the *Big Issue* are weekly guides to all film, theater, and musical events around the city. The *Event Guide,* a weekly free paper that lists music, cinema, theater, art shows, and dance clubs, can be found in pubs and cafés around the city. In peak season, consult the free Bord Fáilte leaflet "Events of the Week."

The Arts

Theater is the dominant performing art in Dublin, but it's by no means the only one. A handful of cinemas, an opera company, classical music, art galleries, and the city's vibrant pub life supplement the wealth of theater you can see. Plans are afoot to build a spectacular new Opera House on the northside of the quays, below O'Connell Bridge.

Art Galleries

Green on Red Galleries. This rather unprepossessing gallery, near the back of Trinity College, is one of Dublin's best, with constantly changing exhibitions featuring the work of some of the country's—and Britain's—most promising up-and-coming artists. ⊠ *Lombard St. E,* ☎ *01/671–3414.* ☼ *Weekdays 11–6, Sat. 11–5.*

Jo Rain Gallery. This small, two-room gallery above a café features a wide range of contemporary art, both national and international. ⊠ *23 Anglesea St., Temple Bar,* ☎ *01/677–9966.* ☼ *Weekdays 11–5:30, Sat. 11–2.*

Kerlin Gallery. Perhaps Dublin's most important commercial gallery, this large space behind Grafton Street exhibits the work of many of Ireland's most important contemporary artists, including such internationally recognized figures as New York–based Sean Scully, Kathy Prendergast (who was awarded a prize at the 1997 Venice Biennale), Paul Seawright (winner of the 1997 Glen-Dimplex Prize, Ireland's equivalent of the Turner Prize), and Stephen McKenna. ⊠ *Anne's La., S. Anne St.,* ☎ *01/670–9093.* ☼ *Weekdays 10–5:45, Sat. 11–4:30.*

Original Print Gallery. An ultramodern building by the same award-winning Dublin architect who designed Temple Bar Gallery (☞ *below*), this place specializes in handmade, limited editions of prints by Irish artists. Also in the building, the **Black Church Print Studio** (☎ 01/677–3629) exhibits prints. ⊠ *4 Temple Bar,* ☎ *01/677–3657.* ☼ *Weekdays 10:30–5:30, Sat. 11–5, Sun. 2–6.*

Rubicon Gallery. This second-floor gallery overlooking St. Stephen's Green holds a number of yearly exhibitions featuring work in all media from sculpture to photography. ⊠ *10 St. Stephen's Green,* ☎ *01/670–8055.* ☼ *Mon.–Sat. 11–5:30.*

Solomon Gallery Not exactly a risk taker, the Solomon has slowly developed a name as one of Dublin's leading fine-art galleries. ⊠ *Powerscourt Townhouse Centre, S. William St.,* ☎ *01/679–4237.* ☼ *Mon.–Sat. 10–5:30.*

Temple Bar Gallery. A flagship of the Temple Bar redevelopment project, this gallery exhibits the work of emerging Irish photographers, painters, sculptors, and other artists in monthly rotating shows. ⊠ *5–9 Temple Bar,* ☎ *01/671–0073.* ☼ *Mon.–Sat. 10–6, Sun. 2–6.*

Classical Music and Opera

National Concert Hall (⊠ Earlsfort Terr., ☎ 01/475–1666), just off St. Stephen's Green, is Dublin's main theater for classical music of all kinds, from symphonies to chamber groups. It's also home to the National Symphony Orchestra of Ireland.

Opera Ireland (⊠ John Player House, 276–288 S. Circular Rd., ☎ 01/453–5519) performs at the Gaiety Theatre (☞ *below*); call to find out what's on and when.

Opera Theatre Company (⊠ 18 St. Andrew St., ☎ 01/679–4962) is Ireland's only touring opera company, performing at venues in Dublin and throughout the country.

St. Stephen's Church (⊠ Merrion Sq., ☎ 01/288–0663) has a regular program of choral and orchestral events in its glorious setting.

Royal Hospital Kilmainham (⊠ Military Rd., ☎ 01/671–8666) presents frequent classical concerts in its magnificent historic interior.

Film

Dublin has two dozen cinema screens in the city center and a number of large, multiscreen cinema complexes in the suburbs, showing current releases made in Ireland and abroad.

Irish Film Centre (⊠ 6 Eustace St., ☎ 01/677–8788; ☞ Temple Bar *in* Exploring, *above*) shows classic and new independent films.

Savoy Cinema (⊠ O'Connell St., ☎ 01874–6000), just across from the General Post Office, is a four-screen theater with the largest screen in the country.

Screen Cinema (⊠ 2 Townsend St., ☎ 01/671–4988), between Trinity College and O'Connell Street Bridge, is a popular three-screen arthouse cinema.

Virgin Multiplex (⊠ Parnell Center, Parnell St., ☎ 01/872–8400), a 12-screen theater just off O'Connell Street, is the city center's only multiplex movie house and shows the latest commercial features.

Jazz

The **Globe** (⊠ 11 S. Great George's St., ☎ 01/671–1220) has live jazz on Sunday afternoons from 5 to 7. The emphasis is on funk fusion and acid jazz, interspersed with classic '50s–'60s sounds. The quality of the music varies, and the audience is often less than attentive.

JJ Smyth's (⊠ 12 Aungier St., ☎ 01/475–2565) is an old-time jazz venue where Louis Stewart, the granddaddy of Irish jazz, has a regular slot.

Pendulum Club (⊠ The Norseman, at Eustace St. and E. Essex St., Temple Bar) is the place to go for good jazz, with some of Ireland's top acts featured as well as guest appearances by internationally recognized musicians. Most gigs start about 9 PM, and there is usually a second set at 10:30 PM; entrance is usually £5–£6.

Rock and Contemporary Music

Mean Fiddler (⊠ Wexford St., ☎ 01/475–8555) is the small Dublin cousin of the famous London venue. There's still plenty of room here for rising Irish and international acts who draw young, lively crowds. After the gig, there's usually a late-night club; your ticket gets you in free.

Olympia Theatre (⊠ 72 Dame St., ☎ 01/677–7744; ☞ Temple Bar *in* Exploring, *above*) puts on its "Midnight from the Olympia" shows every Friday and Saturday from midnight to 2 AM, with everything from rock to country.

The **Point** (⊠ Eastlink Br., ☎ 01/836–3633), a 6,000-capacity arena about 1 km (½ mi) east of the Custom House on the Liffey, is Dublin's premier venue for internationally renowned acts. Call or send a self-addressed envelope to receive a list of upcoming shows; tickets can be difficult to obtain, so book early.

Temple Bar Music Centre (⊠ Curved St., ☎ 01/670–0533)—a music venue, rehearsal space, television studio, and pub rolled into one—buzzes with activity every day of the week. Live acts range from rock bands to ethnic music to singer-songwriters.

Whelan's (✉ 25 Wexford St., ☎ 01/478–0766), just off the southeastern corner of St. Stephen's Green, is one of the city's best—and most popular—music venues, featuring well-known acts performing everything from rock to folk to traditional.

Theater

Abbey Theatre (✉ Lower Abbey St., ☎ 01/878–7222), the home of Ireland's national theater company, stages mainstream, mostly Irish traditional, plays. Its sister theater at the same address, the **Peacock**, offers more experimental drama. W. B. Yeats and his patron, Lady Gregory, opened the theater in 1904, which became a major center for the Irish literary renaissance—the place that first staged works by J. M. Synge and Sean O'Casey, among many others. The original theater burned down in 1951, but it reopened with a modern design in 1966. Seats are usually available for about £12; on Monday all seats are £8.

Andrew's Lane Theatre (✉ 9–11 Andrew's La., ☎ 01/679–5720) presents experimental productions.

Gaiety Theatre (✉ S. King St., ☎ 01/677–1717) is the home of Opera Ireland (☞ *above*) when it's not showing musical comedy, drama, and revues.

Gate Theatre (✉ Cavendish Row, Parnell Sq., ☎ 01/874–4045; ☞ North of the Liffey, *above*), an intimate 371-seat theater in a jewel-like Georgian assembly hall, produces the classics and contemporary plays by leading Irish writers.

Olympia Theatre (✉ 72 Dame St., ☎ 01/677–7744; ☞ Temple Bar *in* Exploring, *above*) is Dublin's oldest and premier multipurpose theatrical venue. In addition to its high-profile musical performances, it has seasons of comedy, vaudeville, and ballet.

Project Arts Centre (✉ 39 E. Essex St., ☎ 01/671–2321) is an established fringe theater.

Tivoli (✉ 135–138 Francis St., ☎ 01/454–4472) brings culture to the heart of old working-class Dublin, the Liberties. Lighter, comedy-based shows and the occasional Shakespeare play are favored.

Samuel Beckett Centre (✉ Trinity College, ☎ 01/608–2266) is home to Trinity's Drama Department as well as visiting groups from around Europe. Dance is often featured.

Nightlife

Dublin has undergone a major nightlife revolution in the last few years and now, for better or worse, bears more than a passing resemblance to Europe's nightclub mecca, London. The old-fashioned discos, once the only alternative for late-night entertainment, have been replaced by a plethora of internationally known dance clubs where style and swagger rule. The streets of the city center, once hushed after the pubs had closed, are the scene of what appears to be a never-ending party; indeed, you're as likely to find crowds at 2 AM on a Wednesday as you are at the same time on a Saturday. Although the majority of clubs cater to an under-30 crowd of trendy students and young professionals eager to sway to the rhythmic throb of electronic dance music, there are plenty of alternatives, including a number of nightclubs where the dominant sounds range from soul to salsa. And if you're looking for something less strenuous, Dublin doesn't disappoint: There are brasseries, bistros, cafés, and all manner of late-night eateries where you can sit, sip, and chat until 2 AM or later.

A relatively new introduction to Dublin's nightclub scene is the professional promoter who organizes theme "parties" and rents space from nightclub owners, paying them a share of the door receipts as rent.

Another trend has been the "reinventing" of some of the old classic pubs—arguably some of the finest watering holes in the world—as popular spots. Despite the changes, the traditional pub has steadfastly clung to its role as the primary center of Dublin's social life. The city has nearly 1,000 pubs ("licensed tabernacles," writer Flann O'Brien calls them). And while the vision of elderly men enjoying a chin wag over a creamy pint of stout has become something of a rarity, there are still plenty of places where you can enjoy a quiet drink and a chat. Last drinks are called at 11:30 PM in spring and summer, and 11 PM in fall and winter; some city-center pubs even have extended opening hours from Thursday through Saturday and don't serve last drinks until 1:45 AM.

A word of warning: Although most pubs and clubs are extremely safe, the lads can get lively—public drunkenness is very much a part of Dublin's nightlife. While this is for the most part seen as the Irish form of unwinding after a long week (or day!), it can sometimes lead to regrettable incidents such as fighting. In an effort to keep potential trouble at bay, bouncers and security men maintain a visible presence in all clubs and many pubs around the city. At the end of the night, the city center is full of young people trying to get home, which makes for extremely long lines at taxi stands and light-night bus stops, especially on weekends. The combination of drunkenness and impatience can sometimes lead to trouble, so act cautiously. If you need late-night transportation, try to arrange it with your hotel before you go out.

Pubs

For the famous "Dublin Literary Pub Crawl" tours, *see* Guided Tours *in* Dublin A to Z at the end of this chapter.

SOUTH CITY CENTER: BALLSBRIDGE, DONNYBROOK, AND STILLORGAN

Byrnes (✉ Galloping Green, Stillorgan, ☎ 01/288–7683) has the airy atmosphere of an old-fashioned country pub, even though it's only 8 km (5 mi) from the city center. It's one of the few pubs that hasn't been renovated.

Dubliner Pub (✉ Jurys Hotel, Ballsbridge, ☎ 01/660–5000) has been remade as an old-fashioned Irish pub; it's a busy meeting place at lunch and after work.

John Fallons (✉ 129 Dean St.), a classy public house in the Liberties, has one of the finest snugs in the city and great photos of old Dublin.

Kiely's (✉ Donnybrook Rd., ☎ 01/283–0208), at first glance, appears to be just another modernized pub, but go up the side lane, and you'll find a second pub, Ciss Madden's, in the same building. Even though it was built in 1992, it's an absolutely authentic and convincing reconstruction of an ancient Irish tavern, right down to the glass globe lights and old advertising signs.

Kitty O'Shea's (✉ Upper Grand Canal St., ☎ 01/660–9965) has Pre-Raphaelite-style stained glass, complementing its lively, sports-oriented atmosphere. Its sister pubs are in Brussels and Paris; this is the original.

O'Brien's (✉ Sussex Terr., ☎ 01/668–2594), beside the Doyle Burlington Hotel, is a little antique gem of a pub, scarcely changed in 50 years, with traditional snugs.

CITY CENTER

Brazen Head (✉ Bridge St., ☎ 01/677–9549), Dublin's oldest pub (the site has been licensed since 1198), has stone walls and open fires that have changed little over the years. It's renowned for traditional-music performances and for lively sing-along sessions on Sunday evenings. A little difficult to find, the Brazen Head is located on the south side of the Liffey quays; turn down Lower Bridge Street, and then make a right into the old laneway.

Café-en-Seine (✉ 40 Dawson St., ☎ 01/677–4369) is a recent conversion to a Parisian-style "locale," with a wrought-iron balcony, art deco furniture, a vaulted ceiling, and a clientele to match: Most are young, cell phone–carrying professionals. Café au lait and alcoholic drinks are served all day until closing.

Cassidy's (✉ 42 Lower Camden St., ☎ 01/475–1429) is a quiet neighborhood pub with a pint of stout so good that President Bill Clinton dropped in for one during a visit to Dublin.

Davy Byrne's (✉ 21 Duke St., ☎ 01/671–1298) is a pilgrimage stop for Joyceans (☞ Close-Up: "ReJoyce! A Walk through *Ulysses* and James Joyce's Dublin," *above*). In *Ulysses,* Leopold Bloom stops in here for a glass of burgundy and a Gorgonzola cheese sandwich. He then leaves the pub and walks to Dawson Street, where he helps a blind man cross the road. Unfortunately, the much-altered pub is unrecognizable from Joyce's day, but it still serves some fine pub grub.

Dockers (✉ 5 Sir John Rogerson's Quay, ☎ 01/677–1692) is a trendy quayside spot east of city center, just around the corner from Windmill Lane Studios, where U2 and other noted bands record; at night the area is a little dicey, so come during the day.

Doheny & Nesbitt (✉ 5 Lower Baggot St., ☎ 01/676–2945), a traditional spot with snugs, dark wooden decor, and smoke-darkened ceilings, has hardly changed over the decades.

Doyle's (✉ 9 College St., ☎ 01/671–0616), a small, cozy pub, is a favorite with journalists from the *Irish Times* just across the street.

The **Globe** (✉ 11 S. Great George's St., ☎ 01/671–1220), one of the hippest café-bars in town, draws arty, trendy Dubliners who sip espresso drinks by day and pack the place at night. There's live jazz on Sunday.

Grogans (✉ 15 S. William St., ☎ 01/677–9320), also known as the Castle Lounge, is a small place packed with creative folk.

Hogan's (✉ 35 Great St. Georges St., ☎ 01/6677–5904), a huge floor space on two levels is jammed on most nights, but the old place maintains its style through it all and the beer is top class.

Horseshoe Bar (✉ Shelbourne Hotel, 27 St. Stephen's Green, ☎ 01/676–6471) is a popular meeting place for Dublin's businesspeople and politicians, though it has comparatively little space for drinkers around the semicircular bar.

Kehoe's (✉ 9 S. Anne St., ☎ 01/677–8312) is popular with Trinity students and academics. The tiny back room is cozy.

McDaid's (✉ 3 Harry St., ☎ 01/679–4395) attracted boisterous Brendan Behan and other leading writers in the 1950s; its wild literary reputation still lingers, although the bar has been discreetly modernized and the atmosphere is altogether quieter.

Dublin Pubs

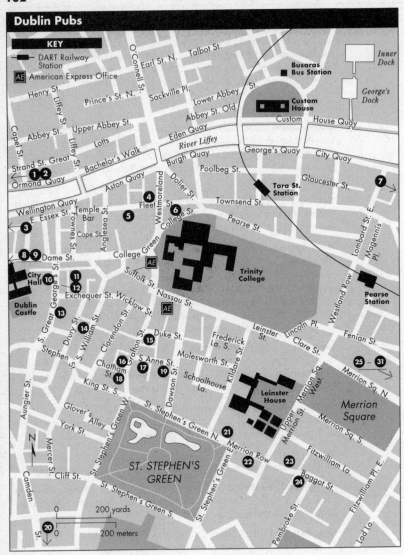

KEY

DART Railway Station

AE American Express Office

Mother Redcap's Tavern (⊠ Back La., ☎ 01/453–8306) is an authentic re-creation of a 17th-century Dublin tavern, with stone walls from an old flour mill, beams, and old prints of the city.

Neary's (⊠ 1 Chatham St., ☎ 01/677–7371), which has an exotic Victorian-style interior, was once the haunt of music-hall artists, as well as of a certain literary set including Brendan Behan. Join the actors from the adjacent Gaiety Theatre for a good pub lunch.

O'Donoghue's (⊠ 15 Merrion Row, ☎ 01/676–2807), a cheerful, smoky hangout, has impromptu musical performances that often spill out onto the street.

Ryan's Pub (⊠ 28 Parkgate St., ☎ 01/677–6097) is one of Dublin's last genuine, late-Victorian-era pubs and has changed little since its last (1896) remodeling.

Stag's Head (⊠ 1 Dame Ct., ☎ 01/679–3701) dates from 1770 and was rebuilt in 1895; theater people from the nearby Olympia, journalists, and Trinity students turn up around the unusual counter, fashioned from Connemara red marble.

Toner's (⊠ 139 Lower Baggot St., ☎ 01/676–3090), though billed as a Victorian bar, actually goes back 200 years, with an original flagstone floor to prove its antiquity, as well as wooden drawers running up to the ceiling, a relic of the days when bars doubled as grocery shops. Oliver St. John Gogarty accompanied W. B. Yeats here, in what was purportedly the latter's only visit to a pub.

COUNTY DUBLIN—SOUTHSIDE

Johnnie Fox's (⊠ Glencullen, Co. Dublin, ☎ 01/295–5647), 12 km (8 mi) from the city center, sits 1,000 ft up in the Dublin Mountains, making it the highest licensed premises in Ireland. It's approached by a winding and steeply climbing road that turns off the main Dublin–Enniskerry road at Stepaside. Steadfastly refusing to bow to the whims of modernization, it has maintained all of its traditional character—oak tables, rough-stone floor flags strewn with sawdust, and ancient bric-a-brac, including copper kettles, crockery, old prints, and guns—appearing very much as it did in the early 19th century, when Daniel O'Connell used it as a safe house for his seditious meetings. Lunch and dinner are served; the specialty is seafood, which is alone worth the journey. In the evenings there is traditional Irish music.

TEMPLE BAR

The Front Lounge (⊠ 33 Parliament St., Temple Bar, ☎ 01/679–3988) is the latest, trendiest offering by the owners of the Globe (☞ *above*). This modern, well-appointed pub caters to a mixed crowd of young professionals, both gay and straight.

Oliver St. John Gogarty (⊠ 57 Fleet St., Temple Bar, ☎ 01/671–1822) is a lively bar that attracts all ages and nationalities and overflows in summer. On most nights there is traditional Irish music upstairs.

Palace Bar (⊠ 21 Fleet St., Temple Bar, ☎ 01/677–9290), scarcely changed over the past 60 years, is tiled and rather barren looking but popular with journalists and writers (the *Irish Times* is nearby). The walls are hung with cartoons drawn by the illustrators who used to spend time here.

Gay and Lesbian Pubs

The **George** (⊠ 89 S. Great George's St., ☎ 01/478–2983), Dublin's two-floor main gay pub, draws an almost entirely male crowd; its nightclub stays open until 2:30 AM nightly except Tuesday.

Out on the Liffey (⊠ 27 Ormond Quay, ☎ 01/872–2480) is Dublin's second gay pub; it draws a mixed crowd of men and women.

Irish Cabaret
BALLSBRIDGE/SOUTH CITY CENTER

Doyle Burlington Hotel (⊠ Upper Leeson St., ☎ 01/660–5222) is a high-class lounge featuring a well-performed Irish cabaret, with dancing, music, and song.

Jurys Hotel (⊠ Ballsbridge, ☎ 01/660–5000) stages a cabaret show similar to that at the Doyle Burlington Hotel (☞ *above*).

NORTH DUBLIN

Abbey Tavern (⊠ Howth, Co. Dublin, ☎ 01/839–0307) has a rip-roaring cabaret with rousing, traditional Irish songs.

CITY CENTER

Castle Inn (⊠ Christ Church Pl., ☎ 01/475–1122) is really just a huge pub that has traditional Irish music and dancing with dinner in a medieval-style banquet hall.

Irish Music and Dancing
SOUTH DUBLIN

Comhaltas Ceoltóiri Éireann (⊠ 35 Belgrave Sq., Monkstown, ☎ 01/280–0295) has boisterous summer evenings of genuine Irish music and dancing.

Harcourt Hotel (⊠ Harcourt St., ☎ 01/478–3677) is where some of the best traditional musicians gather for wild jam sessions.

Nightclubs

The dominant sound in Dublin's nightclubs is electronic dance music, and the crowd that flocks to them every night of the week is of the trendy, under-25 generation. However, there are a couple of clubs where you're more likely to hear tango than techno, such as the weekend nightclub at the Gaiety Theater, Thursday nights at the Pod, and Sunday nights at Lillie's Bordello. **Velure** (☎ 01/670–3750) is one of Dublin's most successful nightclub promoters, organizing live music, DJs, and theme parties throughout the year; call to find out what's going on.

CITY CENTER

The **Da Club** (⊠ 3–5 Clarendon Market, ☎ 01/670–5116), in the refurbished Dublin Arts Club, is one of the most popular spots in town. Despite its small capacity, it has a wide variety of nightly entertainment—from comedy acts to live bands to dance clubs—often running concurrently on its two floors. The venue attracts a young bohemian crowd. It has full bar facilities.

Leeson Street—just off St. Stephen's Green and known as "the strip"—is a main nightclub area from pub closing time to 4 AM, although it has lost its gloss in recent years. Dress at these places is informal, but jeans and sneakers are not welcome. Most of these clubs are licensed only to sell wine, and the prices can be exorbitant (up to £20 for a mediocre bottle); the upside is that most don't charge to get in.

Lillie's Bordello (⊠ Grafton St., ☎ 01/679–9204) is a popular spot for a trendy, professional crowd, as well as for rock and film stars. On Sunday nights, the strict dress code is relaxed for a night of live music and DJs.

The **Pod** (⊠ Harcourt St., ☎ 01/478–0166), also known as the "Place of Dance," is Dublin's most-renowned dance club, especially among the younger set. Entry is judged as much on clothing as on age; it helps to look either stylish or rich, except on Thursday nights, when the club hosts a no-frills, no-nonsense night of dance-floor jazz and funk.

The **Red Box** (⊠ Old Harcourt St. Station, Harcourt St., ☎ 01/478–0166), adjacent to the Pod (☞ *above*) and the Chocolate Bar, can pack in more than 1,000 people and surround them with state-of-the-art sound and light. It regularly hosts Irish and international rock acts as well as celebrity DJs from Europe and the U.S. As do most other Dublin rock venues, the Red Box has full bar facilities.

Rí Ra (⊠ Dame Court, ☎ 01/677–4835) is part of the hugely popular Globe bar (☞ *above*). The name means "uproar" in Irish, and on most nights the place does go a little wild. It's one of the best spots in Dublin for no-frills, fun dancing. Upstairs is more low key.

TEMPLE BAR
The **Kitchen** (⊠ E. Essex St., ☎ 01/677–6359) is in the cavelike basement of the Clarence hotel (☞ Lodging, *above*); its popularity, primarily with an under-30s crowd, owes much to its owners, Bono and the Edge of U2.

OUTDOOR ACTIVITIES AND SPORTS

Health clubs are relatively new to the city, but they are starting to flourish (especially at hotels). Yet there are plenty of other ways to get out and move about. You can explore a beach; cheer on a hometown team; or walk, run, horseback-ride or bike through Phoenix Park.

Beaches

To the north of Dublin city is **North Bull Island,** created over the years by the action of the tides and offering an almost 3-km-long (2-mi-long) stretch of fine sand. Bus 130 from Lower Abbey Street stops by the walkway to the beach (☞ County Dublin—Northside *in* Side Trips, *below*). **Malahide,** a charming village on the northside DART line, has a clean and easily accessible beach, though the current can be strong. The main beach for swimming on the south side of Dublin is at **Killiney** (13 km/8 mi south of the city center), a shingly beach stretching for 3 km (2 mi). The DART train station is right by the beach; the stop is called Killiney. Near Dublin city center, **Sandymount Strand** is a long expanse of fine sand where the tide goes out nearly 3 km (2 mi), but it's not suitable for swimming or bathing because the tide races in so fast. The strand can be reached easily by the DART train.

Participant Sports

If it's essential that you get in a daily workout, you should be able to do so while you're in Dublin, although it will probably take some careful planning. For all its recent changes, the city has only recently embraced health clubs and fitness centers. Check the service information provided for each hotel (☞ Lodging, *above*) for particular fitness amenities; if none are listed, call to inquire, as many of the hotels are adding these amenities.

Bicycling

Bicycling is not recommended in the city center, as traffic is heavy and most roads don't have shoulders, much less bike lanes. Phoenix Park and some suburbs (especially Ballsbridge, Clontarf, and Sandymount), however, are pleasant for biking once you're off the main roads. To the immediate south of Dublin, the Dublin and Wicklow mountains provide plenty of challenging terrain (☞ Chapter 2). Care should always be taken in securing your bicycle when it's left unattended.

Bicycles can be rented for about £35 a week, with an equivalent amount charged for deposit. Nearly 20 companies in the Dublin region rent bicycles; Tourist Information Offices (TIOs) have a full list. Some of the best include the following: **Joe Daly** (⊠ Lower Main St., Dundrum, ☎ 01/298–1485); **McDonald's** (⊠ 38 Wexford St., ☎ 01/475–2586); **Mike's Bike Shop** (⊠ Dun Laoghaire Shopping Center, ☎ 01/280–0417); and **Tracks Cycles** (⊠ 8 Botanic Rd., Glasnevin, ☎ 01/873–2455).

Bowling

Bowling is a popular sport in Dublin; two kinds are played locally. The sedate, outdoor variety is played at **Herbert Park** (⊠ Ballsbridge, ☎ 01/660–1875) and at **Kenilworth Bowling Club** (⊠ Grosvenor Sq., ☎ 01/497–2305). The city has seven indoor 10-pin bowling centers: **Bray Bowl** (⊠ Quinsboro Rd., ☎ 01/286–4455); **Dundrum Bowl** (⊠ Ballinteer Rd., Dundrum, ☎ 01/298–0209); **Leisureplex Coolock** (⊠ Malahide Rd., ☎ 01/848–5722; ⊠ Village Green Center, Tallaght, ☎ 01/459–9411); **Metro Bowl** (⊠ 149 N. Strand Rd., ☎ 01/855–0400); **Stillorgan Bowl** (⊠ Stillorgan, ☎ 01/288–1656); and **Superdome** (⊠ Palmerstown, ☎ 01/626–0700).

Golf

The Dublin region is an idyllic place for golfers, with 30 18-hole courses and 15 9-hole courses, and several more on the way. For detailed information about Dublin's championship courses, including **Portmarnock, St. Margaret's,** and **Royal Dublin,** *see* Chapter 9. Other major 18-hole courses include the following: **Deer Park** (⊠ Howth, ☎ 01/832–6039); **Edmonstown** (⊠ Rathfarnham, ☎ 01/493–2461); **Elm Park** (⊠ Donnybrook, ☎ 01/269–3438); **Foxrock** (⊠ Torquay Rd., ☎ 01/289–3992); **Hermitage** (⊠ Lucan, ☎ 01/626–4781); **Newlands** (⊠ Clondalkin, ☎ 01/459–2903); **Sutton** (⊠ Sutton, ☎ 01/832–3013); and **Woodbrook** (⊠ Bray, ☎ 01/282–4799).

Health Clubs

The health craze has reached laconic Dublin, and health clubs are springing up all over the city. The **Iveagh Fitness Club** (⊠ Christ Church St., Dublin 8, ☎ 01/454–6555) is right next to Christ Church Cathedral and has a pool, sauna, and full weight room. Just off Grafton Street, the **Jackie Skelly Fitness Centre** (41–42 Clarendon St., Dublin 2 ☎ 01/677–0040) is perfect if you're staying in a city-center hotel without a gym.

Horseback Riding

Dublin's environs are excellent for horseback riding. Stables on the city outskirts give immediate access to suitable riding areas. In the city itself, Phoenix Park provides superb, quiet riding conditions away from the busy main road that bisects the park. About 20 riding stables in the greater Dublin area have horses for hire by the hour or the day, for novices and experienced riders; a few also operate as equestrian centers and have lessons. Major stables in the area include the following: **Brittas Lodge Riding Stables** (⊠ Brittas, ☎ 01/458–2726); and **Deerpark Riding Center** (⊠ Castleknock Rd., Castleknock, ☎ 01/820–7141). Outside Dublin, Counties Dublin, Kildare, Louth, Meath, and Wicklow all have unspoiled country territory ideal for horseback riding (☞ Chapter 2).

Jogging

Traffic in Dublin is heavy from early morning until late into the night and it's getting worse, so if you're used to jogging the streets back home be aware that here you'll have to dodge vehicles and stop for lights. (Remember *always* to look to your right *and* your left before crossing a street.) If you're staying in Temple Bar or on the western end of the city and you can run 9 km (5 ½ mi), head to Phoenix Park, easily the nicest place in the city for a jog. If you're on the southside, Merrion Square, St. Stephen's Green, and Trinity College are all good places for short jogs, though be prepared to dodge pedestrians; if you're looking for a longer route, ask your hotel to direct you to the Grand Canal, which has a pleasant path you can run along as far east as the Grand Canal Street Bridge.

Swimming

Dublin has 12 public pools; recommended are: **Townsend Street** (⊠ Townsend St., ☎ 01/677–0503) and **Williams Park** (⊠ Rathmines, ☎ 01/496–1275). Private pools open to the public for a small fee are located at **Dundrum Family Recreation Center** (⊠ Meadowbrook, Dundrum, ☎ 01/298–4654), **Fitzpatrick's Killiney Castle Hotel** (⊠ Killiney, ☎ 01/285–0328), **St. Vincent's** (⊠ Navan Rd., ☎ 01/838–4906), and **Terenure College** (⊠ Templeogue Rd., ☎ 01/490–7071). For a hardier dip, there's year-round sea swimming at the **Forty Foot Bathing Pool** in Sandycove (☞ Side Trips, *below*).

Tennis

Tennis is one of Dublin's most popular participant sports, and some public parks have excellent tennis facilities open to the public. Among the best are **Bushy Park** (⊠ Terenure, ☎ 01/490–0320) ; **Herbert Park** (⊠ Ballsbridge, ☎ 01/668–4364); and **St. Anne's Park** (⊠ Dollymount Strand, ☎ 01/833–8898). Several private tennis clubs are open to the public, including **Kilternan Tennis Centre** (⊠ Kilternan Golf and Country Club Hotel, Kilternan, ☎ 01/295–3729); **Landsdowne Lawn Tennis Club,** (⊠ Londonbridge Rd., Dublin 4, ☎ 01/668–0219); and **West Wood Lawn Tennis Club** (⊠ Leopardstown Racecourse, Foxrock, Dublin 18, ☎ 01/289–2911). For more information, contact **Tennis Ireland** (⊠ 22 Argyle Sq., Donnybrook, Dublin 4, ☎ 01/668–1841).

Spectator Sports

Gaelic Games

The traditional games of Ireland, Gaelic football and hurling, attract a huge following, with roaring crowds cheering on their county teams. Games are held at **Croke Park,** the national stadium for Gaelic games, just north of the city center. For details of matches, contact the **Gaelic Athletic Association** (⊠ Croke Park, ☎ 01/836–3222).

Greyhound Racing

As elsewhere in the world, Greyhound racing is a sport in decline in Ireland. But the track can still be one of the best places to see Dubliners at their most passionate, among friends, and full of wicked humor. **Harolds Cross** (Harolds Cross, Dublin 6, ☎ 01/497–1081) is dilapidated but serves its purpose. **Shelbourne Park** (Shelbourne Park, Dublin 4, ☎ 01/668–3502) is a more stylish place where you can book a table in the restaurant overlooking the track.

Horse Racing

Horse racing—from flat to hurdle to steeplechase—is one of the great sporting loves of the Irish. The sport is closely followed and betting is popular, but the social side of attending racing is also important to Dubliners. The main course in Dublin is **Leopardstown** (☎ 01/289–3607), an ultramodern course on the southside and home of the Hennessey Gold Cup in February, Ireland's most prestigious steeplechase. In the greater Dublin region, other courses include **Fairyhouse** (⊠ Co. Meath, ☎ 01/825–6167), which every Easter Monday hosts the Grand National, the most popular steeplechase of the season; the **Curragh** (☎ 045/441205; ☞ Chapter 2), southwest of Dublin, home of the five Classics, the most important flat races of the season, which are run from May to September; and **Punchestown** (☎ 045/897704) outside Naas, County Kildare, home of the ever-popular Punchestown National Hunt Festival in April.

Rugby
International rugby matches are staged during the winter and spring at the vast **Lansdowne Road Stadium.** Local matches are played every weekend, also in winter and spring. For details, contact the **Irish Rugby Football Union** (⌂ 62 Lansdowne Rd., ☎ 01/668–4601).

Soccer
Although soccer—called football in Europe—is very popular in Ireland (largely due to the euphoria resulting from the national team's successes throughout the late 1980s and early '90s), facilities for watching it are not so ideal; they tend to be small and out of date. **Lansdowne Road,** the vast rugby stadium, is the main center for international matches. For details, contact the **Football Association of Ireland** (⌂ 80 Merrion Sq. S., ☎ 01/676–6864).

SHOPPING

In days gone by, travelers would arrive in Ireland, land of leprechauns, shillelaghs, and shamrocks, and quickly realize that the only known specimens of leprechauns or shillelaghs were those in souvenir-shop windows, while shamrocks only bloomed around the borders of Irish linen handkerchiefs and table cloths. All of this is still true, of course, but today you'll find so much more. The variety and sophistication of stores in Dublin now are quite remarkable, as a walk through Dublin's central shopping area, from O'Connell to Grafton streets, proves. Department stores stocking internationally known fashion-designer goods and housewares stand beside small boutiques that make shopping in the city a personalized and pleasurable experience. Prices can be higher in the smaller shops, but the department stores are less likely to stock specifically Irish crafts. Shopping in central Dublin can mean pushing through crowds, especially in the afternoons and on weekends. Most large shops and department stores are open Monday–Saturday 9–6. Although nearly all department stores are closed on Sunday, some smaller specialty shops stay open. Those with later closing hours are noted below. You're particularly likely to find sales in January, February, July, and August. Don't get confused by the two prices quoted on all goods. As of January 1, 1999, all items had to be listed in Euros as well as Irish pounds.

Shopping Streets

Dublin's dozen or so main shopping streets each have a different character, and it's only by visiting them all that you can really appreciate just how wide a range of items are for sale here. The main commercial streets north of the river have chain stores and lackluster department stores that tend to be less expensive and less design-conscious than their counterparts in the city center on the other side of the Liffey.

City Center (Northside)
Henry Street. Running westward from O'Connell Street, this is the spot where middle-class Dublin shops. Arnotts department store is the anchor; a host of smaller, specialty stores sell CDs, footwear, and fashion. Henry Street's continuation, Mary Street, has a branch of Marks & Spencer and the new Jervis Shopping Centre (☞ *below*).

O'Connell Street. One of Dublin's largest department stores, Clery's, faces the GPO across the city's main thoroughfare—more downscale than southside city streets but still worth a walk. On the same side of the street as the post office is Eason's, a large book, magazine, and stationery store.

City Center (Southside)

Dawson Street. Just east of Grafton Street between Nassau Street to the north and St. Stephen's Green to the south, this is the city's primary bookstore avenue, with Waterstone's and Hodges Figgis facing each other on different sides of the street (☞ Books, *below*).

Grafton Street. Dublin's bustling pedestrian-only main shopping street has two upscale department stores, Marks & Spencer and Brown Thomas. The rest of the street is taken up by smaller shops, many of them branches of international chains such as the Body Shop and Bally, and many British chains. This is also the spot to buy fresh flowers, available at reasonable prices from a number of outdoor stands. Smaller streets off Grafton Street, especially Duke Street, South Anne Street, and Chatham Street, have worthwhile crafts, clothing, and designer housewares shops.

Francis Street. The Liberties, the oldest part of the city, is the hub of Dublin's antiques trade. This street and surrounding areas, such as the Coombe, have plenty of shops where you can browse. If you're looking for something in particular, dealers will gladly recommend the appropriate store to you.

Nassau Street. Dublin's main tourist-oriented thoroughfare has some of the best-known stores selling Irish goods, but you won't find many locals shopping here. Still, if you're looking for classic Irish gifts to take home, you should be sure at least to browse along here.

Temple Bar. Dublin's hippest neighborhood is dotted with small, precious boutiques—mostly intimate, quirky shops that traffic in a small selection of *très* trendy goods, from vintage wear to some of the most avant-garde Irish clothing you'll find anywhere in the city.

Specialty Shopping Centers

City Center (Northside)

Ilac Center (✉ Henry St.) was Dublin's first large, modern, shopping center, with two department stores, hundreds of specialty shops, and several restaurants. The stores are not as exclusive as at some of the other centers, but there's plenty of free parking.

Jervis Shopping Centre (✉ Jervis and Mary Sts.), opened in late 1996, is Dublin's newest city-center shopping mall; it brought with it the major British chain stores.

City Center (Southside)

Powerscourt Townhouse Centre (✉ S. William St.), the former town home of Lord Powerscourt and built in 1771, has an interior courtyard that has been refurbished and roofed over; a pianist often plays on the dais at ground-floor level. Coffee shops and restaurants share space with a mix of antiques and crafts stores, including the **HQ Gallery**, the main showcase of the Irish Craft Council and one of the finest places in Dublin to buy contemporary crafts. You can also buy original Irish fashions here by young designers like Gráinne Walsh.

Royal Hibernian Way (✉ Off Dawson St. between S. Anne and Duke Sts.) is on the former site of the two-centuries-old Royal Hibernian Hotel, a coaching inn that was demolished in 1983. The stylish shops are small in scale and include a branch of Leonidas, the Belgian chocolate firm.

Dublin Shopping

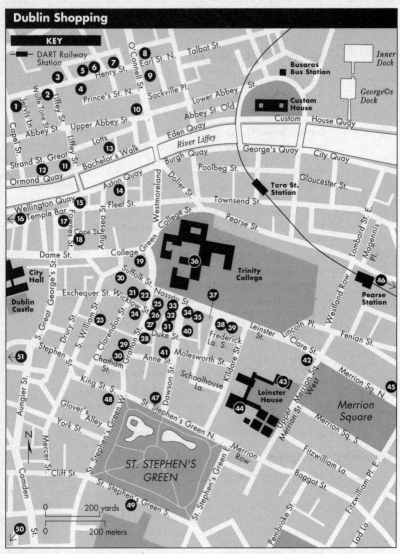

KEY

- DART Railway Station

Inner Dock

George's Dock

Busaras Bus Station

Custom House

Trinity College

Pearse Station

City Hall

Dublin Castle

Leinster House

Merrion Square

Tara St. Station

ST. STEPHEN'S GREEN

St. Stephen's Green Centre (⊠ Northwest corner of St. Stephen's Green), Dublin's largest and most ambitious shopping center, resembles a giant greenhouse, with ironwork in the Victorian style. On three floors overlooked by a vast clock, the 100 mostly small shops sell a variety of crafts, fashions, and household goods.

Tower Design Centre (⊠ Pearse St., ☎ 01/677–5655), east of the heart of the city center (near the Waterways Visitor Centre), has more than 35 separate crafts shops in a converted 1862 sugar-refinery tower. On the ground floor, you can stop at workshops devoted to heraldry and Irish pewter; the other six floors feature hand-painted silks, ceramics, hand-knit items, jewelry, and fine-art cards and prints.

County Dublin Suburbs

Blackrock (⊠ Blackrock, Co. Dublin), to the south, is technically outside of Dublin's city center, but it deserves special mention as one of the most customer-friendly shopping centers around. It's built on two levels, looking onto an inner courtyard, with the giant Superquinn Foodstore, cafés, and restaurants. Blackrock can be reached conveniently on the DART train line; it has its own stop.

Blanchardstown (⊠ Blanchardstown, Dublin 15) is the biggest shopping center in the country. It's a good spot for bargains and a chance to see Dublin families about their everyday lives. The No. 39 bus from Lower Abbey Street goes to Blanchardstown.

Department Stores

Arnotts (⊠ Henry St., ☎ 01/872–1111) has a wide variety of clothing, household, and sporting goods filling three complete floors; the smaller **Grafton Street branch** (⊠ Grafton St., ☎ 01/872–1111) stocks only new fashion and footwear.

A-Wear (⊠ Grafton St., ☎ 01/671–7200; ⊠ Henry St., ☎ 01/872–4644) is a line of shops specializing in fashion for men and women. Many of the items are seasonal and closely follow the ever-changing styles. A steady stream of clothing is supplied by leading Irish designers, including John Rocha.

Brown Thomas (⊠ Grafton St., ☎ 01/679–5666), Dublin's most exclusive department store, stocks the leading designer names in clothing and cosmetics and a wide variety of stylish accessories. It also carries clothing by Irish designers.

Clery's (⊠ O'Connell St., ☎ 01/878–6000) was once the city's most fashionable department store and is still worth a visit, despite its rapidly aging decor. It has four floors of all types of merchandise—from fashion to home appliances—and caters to a distinctly modest, traditional sense of style.

Dunnes Stores (⊠ St. Stephen's Green Center, ☎ 01/478–0188; ⊠ Henry St., ☎ 01/872–6833; ⊠ Ilac Shopping Center, Mary St., ☎ 01/873–0211) is Ireland's largest chain of department stores. All stores stock fashion, household, and grocery items and have a reputation for value and variety.

Eason's (⊠ O'Connell St., ☎ 01/873–3811; ⊠ Ilac Shopping Center, Mary St., ☎ 01/872–1322) is known primarily for its wide variety of books, magazines, and stationery; its larger O'Connell Street branch now sells tapes, CDs, records, videos, and other audiovisual goodies.

Marks & Spencer (⊠ Grafton St., ☎ 01/679–7855; ⊠ Henry St., ☎ 01/872–8833), perennial competitor to Brown Thomas (☞ *above*), stocks everything from fashion (including lingerie) to tasty, unusual groceries. The Grafton Street branch even has its own bureau de change, which doesn't charge commission.

Outdoor Markets

Dublin has a number of open-air markets. **Moore Street,** behind the Ilac center, is open Monday–Saturday 9–6. Stalls lining both sides of the street sell fruits and vegetables; it's also a good spot to come to buy shoes and boots. The traditional Dublin repartée here is renowned in the city. Other open markets are only open on weekends. A variety of bric-a-brac is sold at the **Liberty Market** on the north end of Meath Street, open on Friday and Saturday 10–6, Sunday noon–5:30. The indoor **Mother Redcap's Market** (☞ Dublin West: From Dublin Castle to the Four Courts, *above*), opposite Christ Church, is open Friday–Sunday 10–5; come here for antiques and bric-a-brac. Outside the city center, weekend markets take place in Blackrock and Dun Laoghaire (☞ Side Trips, *below*).

Specialty Shops

Antiques

Dublin is one of Europe's best cities in which to buy antiques, largely due to a long and proud tradition of restoration and high-quality craftmanship. The Liberties, Dublin's oldest district, is fittingly the hub of the antiques trade and is chock-a-block with shops and traders. Bachelor's Walk, along the quays, also has some decent shops. Although the economic boom has created quite a seller's market, bargains are still possible.

Antiques and Collectibles Fairs (☎ 01/670–8295) take place at Newman House (✉ 85–86 St. Stephen's Green) every second Sunday throughout the year.

Conlon Antiques (✉ 21 Clanbrassil St., ☎ 01/453–7323) has a wide selection of antiques, from sideboards to fanlights.

Ha'penny Bridge Galleries (✉ 15 Bachelor's Walk, ☎ 01/872–3950) has four floors of curios, with a particularly large selection of bronzes, silver, and china.

O' Sullivan Antiques (✉ 43–44 Francis St., ☎ 01/454–1143 and 01/453–9659) specializes in 18th- and 19th-century furniture and has a high-profile clientele, including Mia Farrow and Liam Neeson.

Books

You won't have any difficulty weighing down your suitcase with books: Ireland, after all, has produced four Nobel literature laureates in just under 75 years. If you're at all interested in modern and contemporary literature, be sure to leave yourself time to browse through the bookstores, as you're likely to find books available here you can't find back home. Best of all, thanks to an enlightened national social policy, there's no tax on books, so if you only buy books, you don't have to worry about getting VAT slips.

Books Upstairs (✉ 36 College Green, ☎ 01/679–6687) carries an excellent range of special-interest books, including gay and feminist literature, psychology, and self-help books.

Cathach Books (✉ 10 Duke St., ☎ 01/671–8676) sells first editions of Irish literature and many other books of Irish interest, plus old maps of Dublin and Ireland.

Dublin Bookshop (✉ 24 Grafton St., ☎ 01/677–5568) is an award-winning, family-owned bookstore.

Fred Hanna's (⌧ 29 Nassau St., ☎ 01/677–1255) sells old and new books, with a good choice of works on travel and Ireland.

Greene's (⌧ Clare St., ☎ 01/676–2544) carries an extensive range of secondhand volumes.

Hodges Figgis (⌧ 56–58 Dawson St., ☎ 01/677–4754), Dublin's leading independent, stocks 1½ million books on three floors; there's also a pleasant café on the first floor.

Waterstone's (⌧ 7 Dawson St., ☎ 01/679–1415), a large branch of the British chain, has two floors featuring a fine selection of Irish and international books.

Winding Stair (⌧ 40 Ormond Quay, Dublin 1, ☎ 01/873–3292), is a charming new and used bookstore overlooking the Liffey. The little upstairs café is the perfect spot for an afternoon of reading.

China, Crystal, Ceramics, and Jewelry
Ireland is synonymous with Waterford crystal, which is available in a wide range of products, including relatively inexpensive items. But other lines are now gaining recognition, such as Cavan, Galway, and Tipperary crystal. **Brown Thomas** (☞ *above*) is the best department store for crystal; the best specialty outlets are listed below.

Blarney Woollen Mills (⌧ 21–23 Nassau St., ☎ 01/671–0068) is one of the best places for Belleek china, Waterford and Galway crystal, and Irish linen.

Designyard (⌧ East Essex St., ☎ 01/677–8453) carries beautifully designed Irish and international tableware, lighting, small furniture, and jewelry.

House of Ireland (⌧ 37–38 Nassau St., ☎ 01/671–6133) has an extensive selection of crystal, jewelry, tweeds, sweaters, and other upscale goods.

Kilkenny Shop (⌧ 5–6 Nassau St., ☎ 01/677–7066) specializes in contemporary Irish-made ceramics, pottery, and silver jewelry and also holds regular exhibits of exciting new work by Irish craftspeople.

McDowell (⌧ 3 Upper O'Connell St., ☎ 01/874–4961), a jewelry shop popular with Dubliners, has been in business for more than 100 years.

Tierneys (⌧ St. Stephen's Green Centre, ☎ 01/478–2873) carries a good selection of crystal and china. Claddagh rings, pendants, and brooches are popular buys.

Weir & Sons (⌧ 96 Grafton St., ☎ 01/677–9678), Dublin's most prestigious jewelers, sells a wide range of goods in addition to jewelry and watches, including china, glass, lamps, silver, and leather.

Museum Stores
National Gallery of Ireland Shop (⌧ Merrion Sq. W, ☎ 01/678–5450) has a terrific selection of books on Irish art, plus posters, postcards, note cards, and a wide array of lovely bibelots.

National Museum Shop (⌧ Kildare St., ☎ 01/677–7444, ext. 327) carries jewelry based on ancient Celtic artifacts in the museum collection, contemporary Irish pottery, a large selection of books, and other gift items.

Trinity College Library Shop (⌧ Old Library, Trinity College, ☎ 01/608–2308) sells Irish-theme books, Book of Kells souvenirs of all kinds, plus clothing, jewelry, and other lovely Irish-made items.

Music

An increasing amount of Irish-recorded material—including traditional folk music, country-and-western, rock, and even a smattering of classical music—is available.

Celtic Note (⊠ 12 Nassau St., ☎ 01/670–4157), **Claddagh Records** (⊠ 2 Cecilia St., Temple Bar, ☎ 01/679–3664), and **Gael Linn** (⊠ 26 Merrion Sq., ☎ 01/676–7283) specialize in traditional Irish-music and Irish-language recordings.

HMV (⊠ 65 Grafton St., ☎ 01/679–5334; ⊠ 18 Henry St., ☎ 01/872–2095) is one of the larger record shops in town.

McCullogh Piggott (⊠ 25 Suffolk St., ☎ 01/677–3138) is the best place in town for instruments, sheet music, scores, and books about music.

Tower Records (⊠ 6–8 Wicklow St., ☎ 01/671–3250) is the best-stocked international chain.

Virgin Megastore (⊠ 14–18 Aston Quay, ☎ 01/677–7361) is Dublin's biggest music store and holds in-store performances by Irish bands.

Sweaters and Tweeds

If you think Irish woolens are limited to Aran sweaters and tweed jackets, you'll be pleasantly surprised by the range of hats, gloves, scarves, blankets, and other goods you can find. If you're traveling outside of Dublin, you may want to wait to make purchases elsewhere, but if Dublin is it, you still have plenty of good shops to choose from. The tweed on sale in Dublin comes from two main sources, Donegal and Connemara; labels inside the garments guarantee their authenticity. Following are the largest retailers of traditional Irish woolen goods in the city.

An Táin (⊠ 13 Temple Bar Sq. N, ☎ 01/679–0523) carries hyperstylish handmade Irish sweaters, jackets, and accessories

Blarney Woollen Mills (⊠ 21–23 Nassau St., ☎ 01/671–0068) has a good selection of tweed, linen, and woolen sweaters in all price ranges.

Cleo Ltd. (⊠ 18 Kildare St., ☎ 01/676–1421) sells hand-knit sweaters and accessories made only from natural fibers; it also carries its own designs.

Dublin Woollen Mills (⊠ Metal Bridge Corner, ☎ 01/677–5014) at Ha'penny Bridge has a good selection of hand-knit and other woolen sweaters at competitive prices.

Kevin and Howlin (⊠ 31 Nassau St., ☎ 01/677–0257) specializes in hand-woven tweed men's jackets, suits, and hats and also sells tweed fabric.

Monaghan's (⊠ Grafton Arcade, 15–17 Grafton St., ☎ 01/677–0823) specializes in cashmere.

Vintage

Flip (⊠ 4 Upper Fownes St., ☎ 01/671–4299), one of the original stores in Temple Bar, sells vintage and retro clothing from the '50s, '60s, and '70s.

SIDE TRIPS

Dubliners are undeniably lucky. Few populaces enjoy such glorious—and easily accessible—options for day trips. Just outside the city, some of the region's most unique sights—the Joyce Tower, the Marino Casino, Malahide Castle, to name a few—beckon. Once you cross over the Grand Canal, which defines the southern border of the city center, you enter exclusive Ballsbridge and other southern areas of the city and its suburbs. If you do set out for points south and you don't have time to see everything, plan to begin in Ballsbridge. If you have a car, then head to Rathfarnham, directly south of the city. Alternatively, head east and follow the coast road south to Dun Laoghaire (and points even farther south, covered in Chapter 2). Beyond Ballsbridge, these areas are too spread out to cover on foot, and either a car or public transportation (the bus or DART) is the only way to get around. Traveling to and from each of the suburbs will take up most of a day, so you need to pick and choose the excursions you prefer.

County Dublin—Southside

Rathfarnham

Bus 47A from Hawkins St. in the city center goes to both parks in Rathfarnham. Or drive, leaving the city center via Nicholas St. just west of Christ Church Cathedral and following it south through Terenure.

❶ Two parks lie in the suburb of Rathfarnham, due south of the city at the edge of the Dublin Mountains. The 18th-century house in **St. Edna's National Historic Park** has been turned into the **Pearse Museum,** commemorating Pádrig Pearse, leader of Dublin's 1916 Easter Uprising. In the early 20th century, the house was a progressive boys' school, which Pearse and his brother Willie founded. The museum preserves Pearse family memorabilia, documents, and photographs. A lake and nature trails are also on the park's 50-acre grounds, and guides are available for tours of the park or simply for information. ✉ *Grange Rd., Rathfarnham,* ☎ *01/493–4208.* ☞ *Free.* ☉ *Park daily 8:30–dusk; museum May–Aug., daily 10–1 and 2–5:30; Sept.–Apr., daily 10–1 and 2–4.*

☚ ❷ To get to **Marlay Park,** leave St. Enda's Park via Grange Road and walk up the hill for about 1 km (½ mi), turning left at the T junction and continuing another ½ km (¼ mi). The park marks the start of the **Wicklow Way,** a popular walking route that crosses the Wicklow Mountains for 137 km (85 mi), through some of the most rugged landscapes in Ireland (☞ Chapter 2). In addition to its woodlands and nature walks, the 214-acre park has a cobbled courtyard, home to brightly plumaged peacocks. Surrounding the courtyard are crafts workshops, where you are welcome to observe bookbinding and jewelry making and furniture making in process. Every Saturday from 3 to 5, kids can take a free ride on the model steam railway. ✉ *Grange Rd., Rathfarnham,* ☎ *01/493–4059.* ☞ *Free.* ☉ *Nov.–Jan., daily 10–5; Feb.–Mar., daily 10–6; Apr. and Oct., daily 10–7; May and Sept., daily 10–8; June–Aug., daily 10–9.*

Ballsbridge

Take the DART train to Sidney Parade, or Bus 7 or Bus 8 from Burgh Quay (on the south bank of the Liffey, just east of O'Connell Bridge).

Many of Dublin's best hotels and restaurants are in the northern reaches of Ballsbridge, a leafy suburb that is directly across the Grand Canal from the city center. Its major cultural sites, however, are considerably farther south—a bit too far to reach on foot unless you're really an ambitious walker. From the DART station, walk west on Ailesbury Road to Shrewsbury Road, to reach the celebrated (but now temporarily closed) **Chester Beatty Library.** Sir Alfred Chester Beatty (1875–1968), a Canadian mining millionaire, assembled one of the most significant collections of Islamic and Far Eastern art in the Western world, which he then donated to Ireland. Among the library's exhibits are clay tablets from Babylon dating from 2700 BC, Japanese color wood-block prints, Chinese jade books, and Turkish and Persian paintings. The library has been closed since the summer of 1998, but its collections are

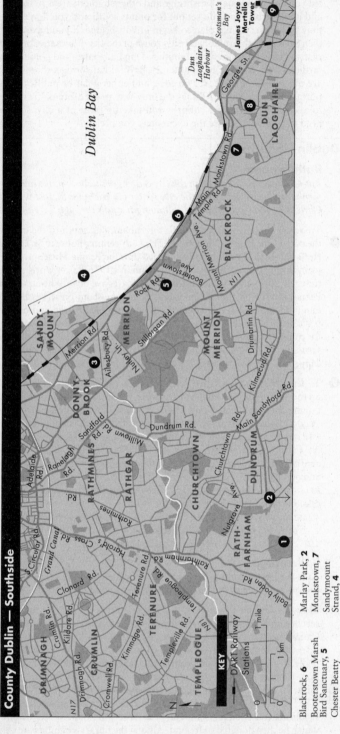

County Dublin — Southside

Dublin Bay

Scotsman's Bay

James Joyce Martello Tower **9**

Dun Laoghaire Harbour

Georges St.

8

DUN LAOGHAIRE

Monkstown Rd. **7**

Main Temple Rd. **6**

BLACKROCK

Mount Merrion Ave.

Booterstown Ave.

N11

Rock Rd. **5**

4

SANDY-MOUNT

Merrion Rd.

Ailesbury Rd.

Nutley Ln. **3**

MERRION

Stillorgan Rd.

MOUNT MERRION

Drumartin Rd.

Kilmacud Rd.

DONNY-BROOK

Sandford

Millltown Rd. Ln.

Dundrum Rd.

Main Sandyford Rd.

Adelaide Rd.

Ranelagh Rd.

RATHMINES

RATHGAR

Rd.

Churchtown Rd.

CHURCHTOWN

DUNDRUM

2

S. Circular Rd.

Grand Canal

Harold's Cross Rd.

Rathmines Rd.

Nutgrove Ave.

RATH-FARNHAM

1

Crumlin Rd.

Kildare Rd.

Drimnagh Rd.

DRIMNAGH

N17

Cromwell Rd.

Kimmage Rd.

CRUMLIN

Clonard Rd.

Terenure Rd.

TERENURE

Templeville Rd.

Templeogue Rd.

TEMPLEOGUE

N81

Rathfarnham Rd.

Ballyboden Rd.

KEY

— DART Railway

■ Stations

N

0 — 1 km
0 — 1 mile

Blackrock, **6**
Booterstown Marsh
Bird Sanctuary, **5**
Chester Beatty
Library, **3**
Dalkey, **9**
Dun Laoghaire and
Sandycove, **8**

Marlay Park, **2**
Monkstown, **7**
Sandymount
Strand, **4**
St. Edna's National
Historic Park, **1**

scheduled to be moved to their new home in Dublin Castle (☞ Dublin West: From Dublin Castle to the Four Courts, *above*), by the year 2000. The number below will provide information in the interim. ⊠ *20 Shrewsbury Rd., Ballsbridge,* ☏ *01/269–2386.* 🎫 *Free.* ☉ *Tues.–Fri. 10–5, Sat. 2–5; tours Wed. and Sat. at 2:30.*

❹ To reach **Sandymount Strand,** double back to the Sydney Parade DART station and keep heading west the few blocks to the beach. Stretching for 5 km (3 mi) from Ringsend to Booterstown, Sandymount was cherished by James Joyce and his beloved from Galway, Nora Barnacle, and it figures as one of the settings in *Ulysses.* (The beach is "at the lacefringe of the tide," as Joyce put it.) When the tide recedes, the beach extends for 1½ km (1 mi) from the foreshore, but the tide sweeps in again very quickly. A sliver of a park lies between the main Strand Road and the beach.

OFF THE BEATEN PATH

SOUTH WALL – East of the city is the South Wall, a long breakwater that stretches 1½ km (1 mi) out into Dublin Bay from the Ringsend power station. The wall is punctuated at its end by **Poolbeg Lighthouse**. On a nice day, it's a wonderful place for a walk and affords stunning views of North Bull Island to the north, Dublin to the west, and the entirety of the bay. It's too far to walk to the wall from the city center, and public transportation runs sporadically, so your best bet is to come out here if you have a car.

Booterstown

Take the DART local train from either Tara St or Pearce St. Or take R118 from the corner of Lower Merrion St. and Merrion Sq.

❺ Booterstown lies along Dublin Bay south of Sandymount. The **Booterstown Marsh Bird Sanctuary** is the largest wildlife preserve in the Dublin area. Curlews, herons, kingfishers, and other fairly rare migratory species come to nest here; information boards along the road describe the birds for visitors. Also on this main road you'll pass **Glena,** the house where Athlone-born John McCormack, one of the best and most popular tenors in the first quarter of the 20th century, died on September 16, 1945. ⊠ *Between the DART line and Rock Rd.,* ☏ *01/454–1786.*

Blackrock

❻ *3 km (2 mi) south of Booterstown. Take the DART line from the city center to Blackrock.*

Fine sea views, swimming, and a major shopping center (☞ Shopping, *above*) draw Dubliners down to Blackrock, a bedroom community where James Joyce's parents lived with their large brood for most of 1892. Above the Blackrock DART station, **Idrone Terrace,** lined with restored, old-fashioned lamps, provides a lovely view across the bay to Howth Peninsula.

Monkstown

❼ *3 km (2 mi) south of Blackrock on R119. Take the DART train from the city center to the Monkstown and Seapoint stations.*

One of Dublin's most exclusive suburbs, Monkstown has two architectural curiosities. John Semple, the architect of Monkstown's **Anglican parish church,** was inspired by two entirely different styles, the Gothic and the Moorish, which he joined into an unlikely hybrid of towers and turrets. Built in 1833 in the town's main square, the church is only open during Sunday services. The well-preserved ruins of **Monkstown Castle** lie about 1 km (½ mi) south of the suburb; it's a 15th-century edifice with a keep, a gatehouse, and a long wall section, all surrounded by greenery. The **Lambert Puppet Theatre** (⊠ Clifton La., ☏ 01/280–0974) stages regular puppet shows and has a puppetry museum.

Dun Laoghaire and Sandycove

8 *2½ km (1½ mi) beyond Monkstown along R119, the Monkstown Crescent.*

After the British monarch King George IV disembarked for a brief visit in 1821, Dun Laoghaire (pronounced dun *lear*-ee) was renamed Kingstown, but it reverted to its original Irish name 99 years later. Its Irish name refers to Laoghaire, the High King of Tara who in the 5th century permitted St. Patrick to begin converting Ireland to Christianity. The town was once a Protestant stronghold of the old ruling elite; in some of the neo-Georgian squares and terraces behind George's Street, the main thoroughfare, a little of the community's former elegance can still be felt.

Dun Laoghaire has long been known for its great harbor, enclosed by two piers, each 2½ km (1½ mi) long. The harbor was constructed between 1817 and 1859, using granite quarried from nearby Dalkey Hill; the west pier has a rougher surface and is less favored for walking than the east pier, which has a bandstand where musicians play in summer. The workaday business here includes passenger-ship and freight-services sailings to Holyhead in north Wales, 3½ hours away (☞ Arriving and Departing by Ferry *in* Dublin A to Z, *below*). Dun Laoghaire is also a yachting center, with the members-only Royal Irish, National, and Royal St. George yacht clubs, all founded in the 19th century, lining the harbor area.

West of the harbor and across from the Royal Marine Hotel and the People's Park, the **National Maritime Museum** is in the former Mariners' church. Its nave makes a strangely ideal setting for exhibits like the French longboat captured during an aborted French invasion at Bantry, County Cork, in 1796. A particularly memorable exhibit is the old optic from the Baily Lighthouse on Howth Head, across Dublin Bay; the herringbone patterns of glass reflected light across the bay until several decades ago. ⊠ *Haigh Terr.,* ☎ *01/280–0969.* 🖂 *£1.50.* ☉ *May–Sept., Tues.–Sun. 1–5.*

From the harbor area Marine Parade leads alongside Scotsmans Bay for 1¼ km (¾ mi), as far as the **Forty Foot Bathing Pool,** a traditional bathing area that attracts mostly nude older men. Women were once banned from here, but now hardy swimmers of both genders are free to brave its cold waters.

A few steps away from the bathing pool stands Sandycove's other claim to fame, the **James Joyce Martello Tower.** Originally built in 1804 when Napoleon's invasion seemed imminent, it was demilitarized in the 1860s along with most of the rest of the 34 Martello towers that ring Ireland's coast. (Martello towers were originally Italian and were constructed to protect the Italian coastline against the possibility of a Napoleonic naval invasion. In Ireland, they were built by the British to protect Irish shores from the same threat and were remarkable for their squat, solid construction, rotating cannon at the top, and—most importantly—their proximity to one another, so that each one is within visible range of the one next to it.) In 1904, this tower was rented to Oliver St. John Gogarty, a medical student who was known for his poetry and ready wit, for £8 a year. He wanted to create a nurturing environment for writers and would-be literati. Joyce spent a week here in September 1904 and described it in the first chapter of *Ulysses,* using his friend as a model for the character Buck Mulligan. The tower now houses the **Joyce Museum,** founded in 1962 thanks to Sylvia Beach, the Paris-based first publisher of *Ulysses.* The exhibition hall contains first editions of most of Joyce's works. Joycean memorabilia include his waistcoat, embroidered by his grandmother, and a tie that he gave to Samuel Beckett (who was Joyce's onetime secretary). The gunpowder magazine stores the Joyce Tower Library, including a death mask of Joyce taken on January 13, 1941. ⊠ *Sandycove,* ☎ *01/280–9265.* ⊡ *£2.* ☉ *Apr.–Oct., Mon.–Sat. 10–1 and 2–5, Sun. 2–6; Nov.–Mar. by appointment.*

DINING

$$$–$$$$ ✕ **Morel's Bistro.** Alan O'Reilly has a stylish, first-floor restaurant over the Eagle House pub on the north side of Dun Laoghaire. The summery Mediterranean colors, striking paintings—large and specially commissioned—and curvaceous (albeit uncomfortable) metal chairs at classically white-clothed tables all create a dashing impression. The seared fillet of salmon with crispy pancetta and savoy cabbage is a terrific entrée. ⊠ *18 Glasthule Rd., Dun Laoghaire, Co. Dublin,* ☎ *01/230–0210. AE, DC, MC, V. No lunch Mon.–Wed. and Sat.*

$$$ ✕ **Brasserie Na Mara.** The first railway in Ireland, opened in 1834, was built from Westland Row (now Pearse Station) in Dublin to Dun Laoghaire. Much of the original station's entrance and ticketing area has been converted into this restaurant, now a brasserie (*na mara* means "of the sea" in Gaelic; the name was kept but the emphasis on seafood jettisoned). Tall Georgian windows overlook the busy Dun Laoghaire ferryport. The menu highlights international dishes with a modern twist, such confit of Barbary duck with pesto potatoes. ⊠ *Dun Laoghaire Harbour, Co. Dublin,* ☎ *01/280–6767. Reservations essential on weekends. AE, DC, MC, V. Closed Sun. and 1 wk at Christmas.*

$ ✕ **Caviston's.** Stephen Caviston and his family have been dispensing fine fare for years from their fish counter and delicatessen in Sandycove. The fish restaurant next door is a lively and intimate place. Typical entrées include panfried scallops served in the shell with a Thermidor sauce and steamed Dover sole with mustard sauce. You can also get a halved lobster with a simple butter sauce for an exceptionally good price. ⊠ *58–59 Glasthule Rd., Dun Laoghaire,* ☎ *01/280–9120. MC, V. Closed Sun.–Mon. and late Dec.–early Jan. No dinner.*

Dalkey

❾ *From the James Joyce Tower in Sandycove, it's an easy walk or quick drive 1 km (½ mi) south to Dalkey. Or take the DART line from the city center to Dalkey.*

Along Castle Street, the town's main thoroughfare, are the substantial stone remains, resembling small, turreted castles, of two 15th- and 16th-century fortified houses. In summer, small boats make the 15-minute crossing from Coliemore Harbour to **Dalkey Island,** covered in long grass, uninhabited except for a herd of goats, and graced with its own Martello tower. From Vico Road, beyond Coliemore Harbour, are astounding bay views as far as Bray in County Wicklow (☞ Chapter 2). On Dalkey Hill is **Torca Cottage,** home of the Nobel Prize–winning writer George Bernard Shaw from 1866 to 1874. You can return to Dalkey Village by Sorrento Road.

County Dublin—Northside

Dublin's northern suburbs remain predominantly working class and largely residential, but there are a few places worth the trip. As with most other suburban areas, walking may not be the best way to get around. A car is recommended but not essential. Buses and trains service most of these areas, the only drawback being that to get from one suburb to another by public transportation means returning back through the city center. Even if you're traveling by car, visiting all these sights will take a full day, so plan your trip carefully before setting off.

Glasnevin

Drive from the north city center by Lower Dorset St., as far as the bridge over the Royal Canal. Turn left, go up Whitworth Rd., by the side of the canal, for 1 km (½ mi); at its end, turn right onto Prospect Rd. and then left onto the Finglas road, N2. You may also take Bus 40 or Bus 40A from Parnell St., next to Parnell Sq., in the north city center.

⑩ Glasnevin Cemetery, on the right-hand side of the Finglas road, is the best-known burial ground in Dublin. Here you'll find the graves of many distinguished Irish leaders, including Eamon De Valera, a founding father of modern Ireland and a former Irish taoiseach and president, and Michael Collins, the celebrated hero of the Irish War of Independence. Other notables interred here include late-19th-century poet Gerard Manley Hopkins and Sir Roger Casement, an Irish rebel hanged for treason by the British in 1916. The large column to the right of the main entrance is the tomb of "The Liberator" Daniel O'Connell, perhaps Ireland's greatest historical figure, renowned for his nonviolent struggle for Catholic rights and emancipation, which he achieved in 1829. The cemetery is freely accessible all day.

⑪ On the northeastern flank of Glasnevin Cemetery, the **National Botanic Gardens** date from 1795 and have more than 20,000 different varieties of plants, a rose garden, and a vegetable garden. The main attraction is the **Curvilinear Range,** 400-ft-long greenhouses designed and built by a Dublin ironmaster, Richard Turner, between 1843 and 1869. The Palm House, with its striking double dome, was built in 1884 and houses orchids, palms, and tropical ferns. ⊠ *Glasnevin Rd.,* ☎ *01/837–4388.* ⊆ *Free.* ☉ *Apr.–Sept., Mon.–Sat. 10–6, Sun. 11–6; Oct.–Mar., Mon.–Sat. 10–4:30, Sun. 11–4:30.*

Marino Casino

⑫ *Take the Malahide road from Dublin's north city center for 4 km (2½ mi). Or take Bus 20A or Bus 24 to the Casino from Cathal Brugha St. in the north city center.*

One of Dublin's most exquisite, yet also most underrated, architectural landmarks, the Marino Casino (the name has nothing to do with gambling—it means "little house by the sea") is a small-scale, Palladian-style Greek temple, built between 1762 and 1771 from a plan by Sir William Chambers. Often compared to the Petit Trianon at Versailles, it was commissioned as a summerhouse overlooking Dublin harbor by that great Irish grandee, Lord Charlemont (☞ Hugh Lane Municipal Gallery of Modern Art *in* North of the Liffey, *above*). While his estate's grand mansion was tragically demolished in 1921, this sublime casino was saved and has now been lovingly restored (thankfully, Sir William's original plans survived). Inside, highlights are the china-closet boudoir, the huge golden sun set in the ceiling of the main drawing room, and the signs of the zodiac in the ceiling of the bijou-size library. When you realize that the structure has, in fact, 16 rooms—there are bedrooms upstairs—Sir William's sleight-of-hand is readily apparent: From its exterior, the structure seems to contain only one room. The tricks don't stop there: The freestanding columns on the facade are hollow so they can drain rainwater, while the elegant marble urns on the roof are chimneys. Last but not least, note the four stone lions on the outside terrace—they were carved by Joseph Wilson, who created the famous British royal coronation coach back in London. All in all, this remains, to quote Desmond Guinness, "one of the most exquisite buildings in Europe." It makes a good stop on the way to

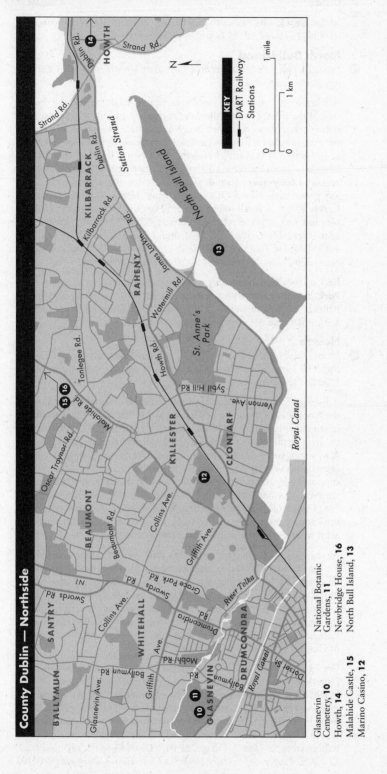

County Dublin — Northside

121

Glasnevin
Cemetery, **10**
Howth, **14**
Malahide Castle, **15**
Marino Casino, **12**

National Botanic
Gardens, **11**
Newbridge House, **16**
North Bull Island, **13**

Malahide, Howth, or North Bull Island. ⊠ *Malahide Rd., Marino,* ☎ *01/833–1618.* ⊡ *£2.* ☼ *June–Sept., daily 9:30–6.*

North Bull Island

⑬ *From Dublin's north city center, take the Clontarf road for 4 km (2½ mi) to the causeway.*

A 5-km-long (3-mi-long) island created in the last century by the action of the tides, North Bull Island is one of Dublin's wilder places, a nature conservancy with vast beach and dunes. The island is linked to the mainland via a wooden causeway that leads to **Bull Wall,** a 1½-km (1-mi) walkway that stretches as far as the **North Bull Lighthouse.** The island is also accessible via a second, northerly causeway, which gives access to **Dollymount Strand.** (The two routes of entry do not meet at any point on the island.) It's reached from the mainland via the James Larkin Road. A small visitor center is largely devoted to the island's bird life. ⊠ *Off the northerly causeway,* ☎ *01/833–8341.* ⊡ *Free.* ☼ *Mar.–Oct., Mon.–Wed. 10:15–1 and 1:30–4, Thurs. 10:15–1 and 1:30–3:45, Fri. 10:15–1 and 1:30–2:30, weekends 10–1 and 1:30–5:30. Nov.–Feb., same hrs except 4:30 closing time weekends.*

Back on the mainland directly across from North Bull Island is **St. Anne's Park,** a public green with extensive rose gardens (including many prize hybrids) and woodland walks; it is freely accessible all day. ⊠ *James Larkin Rd. and Mt. Prospect Ave.*

Howth

★ ⑭ *From Dublin, either take the DART train, which takes about 30 mins; Bus 31B from Lower Abbey St. in the city center; or, by car, take the Howth road from the north city center for 16 km (10 mi).*

A fishing village at the foot of a long peninsula, Howth (derived from the Norse *hoved,* meaning head; it rhymes with "both") was an island inhabited as long ago as 3250 BC. Between 1813 and 1833, Howth was the Irish terminus for the sea crossing to Holyhead in north Wales, but it was then superseded by the newly built harbor at Kingstown (now Dun Laoghaire; ☞ *above*). Today, a marina graces its harbor, which supports a large fishing fleet. Both arms of the harbor pier form extensive walks. Separated from Howth Harbour by a channel nearly 1½ km (1 mi) wide, **Ireland's Eye** has an old stone church on the site of a 6th-century monastery and an early 19th-century Martello tower. In calm weather, local boatmen make the crossing to the island.

At the King Sitric Restaurant on the East Pier (☞ Dining, *below*), a 2½-km (1½-mi) cliff walk begins, leading to the white **Baily Lighthouse,** built in 1814. In some places, the cliff path narrows and drops sheerly to the sea, but the views out over the Irish Sea are terrific. Some of the best views in the whole Dublin area await from the parking lot above the lighthouse, looking out over the entire bay as far south as Dun Laoghaire, Bray, and the north Wicklow coast. You can also see much of Dublin.

Until 1959, a tram service ran from the railway station in Howth, over Howth Summit, and back down to the station. One of the open-topped ☾ Hill of Howth trams that plied this route is now the star at the **National Transport Museum,** a short, 800-yard walk from Howth's DART station. Volunteers have spent several years restoring the tram, which stands alongside other unusual vehicles, including old horse-drawn bakery vans. ⊠ *Howth Village,* ☎ *01/848–0831 or 01/847–5623.* ⊡ *£1.50.* ☼ *Easter–Sept., daily 10–5:30; Oct.–Easter, weekends 2–5:30.*

Next door to the Transport Museum and accessible from the Deer Park Hotel, the **Howth Castle Gardens** were laid out in the early 18th century. The many rare varieties of its fine rhododendron garden are in full flower April–June; there are also high beech hedges. The rambling castle, originally built in 1654 and considerably altered in the intervening centuries, is not open to the public, but you can access the ruins of a tall, square, 16th-century castle and a Neolithic dolmen. ⊠ *Deer Park Hotel, Howth, Co. Dublin,* ☎ *01/832–2624.* ☞ *Free.* ⏲ *Daily 8–dusk.*

DINING

$$$ ✕ **Abbey Tavern.** The original stone walls, flagged floors, blazing turf fires, and old gaslights of the ancient building that houses this old-world tavern all contribute to the historic atmosphere. The upstairs restaurant serves traditional Irish and Continental cuisine and specializes in fish dishes. Sole Abbey (filleted and stuffed with prawns, mushrooms, and herbs) is a house specialty, and fresh Dublin Bay prawns can be cooked to order. Traditional Irish music is performed in a different part of the building. The restaurant is a five-minute walk from the DART station; call for directions. ⊠ *Abbey St., Howth, Co. Dublin,* ☎ *01/839–0307. Reservations essential. AE, DC, MC, V. No dinner Sun.*

$$$ ✕ **King Sitric.** This well-known seafood restaurant is one of Howth's main attractions. It's in a Georgian house on the harbor front, with the yacht marina and port on one side, and with sea views from the upstairs seafood bar, where informal lunches are served in summer. A house specialty is black sole meunière, grilled and finished with a nut-brown butter sauce, but lobster, caught just yards away in Balscadden Bay, is the big treat; it's best at its simplest, in butter sauce. Crab is equally fresh, dressed with mayonnaise or Mornay sauce. ⊠ *East Pier, Howth, Co. Dublin,* ☎ *01/832–5235. AE, DC, MC, V. Closed Sun.*

Malahide

To get here by car, drive from the north city center on R107 for 14½ km (9 mi). Or catch the hourly train from Connolly Station, which takes about 20 mins. Or board Bus 42 to Malahide, which leaves from Beresford Pl. behind the Custom House (service runs every 15 mins; the ride takes about 40 mins).

★ ☪ **⑮** On the coast north of Howth, Malahide is chiefly known for **Malahide Castle,** a picture-book castle occupied by the Anglo-Irish and aristocratic Talbot family from 1185 until 1976, when it was sold to the Dublin County Council. The great expanse of parkland around the castle includes a botanical garden with more than 5,000 species and varieties of plants, all clearly labeled. The castle itself is a combination of styles and periods; the earliest section, the three-story tower house, dates from the 12th century. The medieval great hall is the only one in Ireland that is preserved in its original form, while the National Portrait Gallery features many fine paintings of the Talbot family and 18th- and 19th-century Irish notables. Other rooms are well furnished with authentic 18th-century pieces. Also in the castle is the **Fry Model Railway Museum,** with rare, handmade models of the Irish railway. The castle's self-service restaurant serves good homemade food all day. ⊠ *Co. Dublin,* ☎ *01/846–2184.* ☞ *£3.* ⏲ *Apr.–Sept., weekdays 10–6, Sat. 11–6, Sun. 2–6; Oct.–Mar., weekends 2–5.*

If you're driving, continue from Malahide through Swords on the coastal road (R106) for 8 km (5 mi), turning off N1 as signposted to

☪ **⑯** **Newbridge House** in Donabate. You can also travel from Malahide to Donabate by train, which takes about 10 minutes. From the Donabate train station, the walk to the Newbridge House grounds takes 15 minutes. Built between 1740 and 1760 for Charles Cobbe, Archbishop of Dublin, Newbridge was owned by the Cobee family until 1985, when it, along with most of its furnishings, was purchased by the state. One of the finest Georgian interiors in Ireland, the **Red Drawing Room** is hung with dozens of paintings and decorated with many fine antiques. The **kitchens** of the house still have their original utensils. Crafts workshops and some examples of old-style transportation, such as coaches, are in the courtyard. Beyond the walled garden are 366 acres of parkland and a restored 18th-century animal farm. **Tara's Palace**, a dollhouse that was made to raise funds for children's charities, is also here; it has 25 rooms, all fully furnished in miniature. The exterior of the dollhouse is based on the facades of three great Irish houses—Carton, Castletown, and Leinster. The **coffee shop** is renowned for the quality and selection of its homemade goods. ⊠ *Donabate, Co. Dublin,* ☎ *01/843–6534.* ⌨ *House £2.75, farm £1.* ⊙ *Apr.–Sept., Tues.–Fri. 10–5, Sat. 11–6, Sun. 2–6; Oct.–Mar., weekends 2–5.*

DINING

$$$ ✕ **Bon Appetit.** Owner-chef Patsy McGuirk brought a loyal following from his previous city-center restaurant of the same name when he moved, in 1989, to this substantial Georgian terraced building. The striking floral decor creates a cozy, traditional atmosphere, an impression heightened by the staff of black-jacketed waiters. The traditional Continental menu includes such entrées as warm salad of Dublin Bay king prawns with pine nuts, prawn oil, and shavings of Parmesan, and a generous selection of desserts. Especially recommended are sole McGuirk (filleted, stuffed with prawns and turbot, and baked with white wine and cream); and duckling Grand Marnier (double-roasted duck served on a potato-and-herb stuffing). ⊠ *9 James's Terr., Malahide,* ☎ *01/845–0314. Jacket and tie. AE, DC, MC, V. Closed Sun. No lunch Sat.*

DUBLIN A TO Z

Arriving and Departing

By Bus
Busaras (☎ 01/830–2222) is Dublin's main bus station, just behind the Custom House on the northside.

By Car
Renting a car in Dublin is very expensive, with high rates and a 12½% local tax. Gasoline is also expensive by U.S. standards, at around 60p a liter. Peak-period car-rental rates begin at around £200 a week for the smallest stick models, like a Ford Fiesta. Dublin has many car-rental companies, and it pays to shop around and to avoid "cowboy" outfits (☞ Car Rentals, *below*).

By Ferry
Irish Ferries (⊠ Merrion Row, ☎ 01/661–0511) and **Stena Sealink** (⊠ Ferryport, Dun Laoghaire, ☎ 01/204–7777) have regular car and passenger service between Dublin and Wales (Holyhead). Irish Ferries sails directly into Dublin port. Stena Sealink docks in Dublin port (3½-hour service to Holyhead) and in Dun Laoghaire (**High Speed Service,** known as "HSS," which takes 99 minutes). Prices and departure times vary according to season, so call either company to confirm. In summer reservations are strongly recommended. Dozens of taxis wait to take you into town from both ports, or you can take DART or a bus to the city center.

By Plane
Dublin Airport (☎ 01/844–4900), 10 km (6 mi) north of the city center, serves international and domestic airlines.

AIRPORT SHUTTLE

Dublin Bus (☎ 01/873–4222) operates a shuttle service between Dublin Airport and the city center with departures outside the arrivals gateway; pay the driver inside the coach. The single fare is £3. Service runs from 6:40 AM to 11 PM, at intervals of about 30 minutes (after 8 PM buses run every hour), to as far as **Busaras** (☎ 01/830–2222), Dublin's main bus station, behind the Custom House on the northside. Journey time from the airport to the city center is normally 30 minutes, but it may be longer in heavy traffic.

Buses leave every 20 minutes from outside the arrivals door for the central bus station in downtown Dublin. The ride takes about 30 minutes, depending on the traffic, and the fare is IR£2.50.

A taxi is a quicker alternative than the bus to get from the airport to Dublin center. A line of taxis waits by the arrivals gateway; the fare for the 30-minute journey to any of the main city-center hotels is about £13 plus tip (tips don't have to be large but they are increasingly expected). It's advisable to ask about the fare before leaving the airport.

FROM THE U.K.

Five airlines now serve destinations in Ireland from 19 British airports; major carriers are Aer Lingus, Ryanair, City Jet, British Airways, and British Midland Airways. There are daily services to Dublin from all major London airports; Aer Lingus operates 12 flights from Heathrow Airport, with British Midland operating an additional 10 flights; Ryanair operates several flights from Luton and Stanstead airports, and Virgin Atlantic Cityjet flies from London City Airport. In addition, flights to Dublin leave from Birmingham, Bristol, East Midlands, Liverpool, Luton, Manchester, Leeds/Bradford, Newcastle, Edinburgh, and Glasgow. Prices vary a great deal between companies and at different seasons. Ryanair is known for being the cheapest, but this means cutting back on comfort and services. For reservations and information in Dublin, contact **Aer Lingus** (☎ 01/844–4747), **British Airways** (☎ 800/626747), **British Midland** (☎ 01/283–8833), **City Jet** (☎ 01/844–5566), or **Ryanair** (☎ 01/844–4411).

FROM THE U.S.

The three airlines with regularly scheduled flights from the United States to Dublin are **Aer Lingus** (☎ 01/844–4747), which flies direct from New York, Boston, and Chicago to Dublin; **Continental** (☎ 0800/321324), which flies from New York (Newark Airport) to Dublin daily; and **Delta** (☎ 01/844–4166 or 01/676–8080), which flies direct from Atlanta to Dublin and operates jointly with some of Aer Lingus's flights.

FROM ELSEWHERE IN EUROPE

Major European carriers, such as Air France, Lufthansa, Sabena, SAS, and Alitalia, run direct services to Dublin from most European capital cities and major regional airports, especially those in Germany.

FLYING WITHIN IRELAND

Aer Lingus (☎ 01/844–4747) and **Ryanair** (☎ 01/844–4411) operate flights from Dublin to Cork, Kerry, Shannon, Galway, Knock in County Mayo, and Sligo.

By Train

The main train stations in Dublin are **Connolly Station** (✉ Amiens St.) and **Heuston Station** (✉ End of Victoria Quay). The former provides train services to the north and northwest; the latter to the south and west. Contact the **Irish Rail Travel Centre** (✉ 35 Lower Abbey St., ☎ 01/836–6222) for information.

Getting Around

Traveling around Dublin by public transportation is comparatively easy, although a car is useful for getting to the outlying suburbs. If you're just planning to visit city-center Dublin, definitely plan to do it without a car.

By Bus

Dublin has an extensive network of buses—most of them are green double-deckers. Timetables (£1.50) are available from **Dublin Bus** (⊠ 59 Upper O'Connell St., ☎ 01/873–4222), staffed weekdays 9–5:30, Saturday 9–1. Fares begin at 55p and are paid to the driver, who will accept inexact fares, but you'll have to go to the central office in Dublin to pick up your change as marked on your ticket. Change transactions and the city's heavy traffic can slow service down considerably. Some bus services run on cross-city routes, including the smaller "Imp" buses, but most buses start in the city center. Buses to the north of the city begin in the Lower Abbey Street/Parnell Street area, while those to the west begin in Middle Abbey Street and in the Aston Quay area. Routes to the southern suburbs begin at Eden Quay and in the College Street area. A number of services are links to DART stations, and another regular bus route connects the two main provincial railway stations, Connolly and Heuston. If the destination board indicates AN LÁR, that means that the bus is going to the city center. Late-night buses run weekends, on the hour from midnight to 3 PM; the fare is £3.

By Car

The number of cars in Ireland has grown exponentially in the last few years, and nowhere has their impact been felt more than in Dublin, where the city's complicated one-way streets are congested during the morning and evening rush hours and often during much of the rest of the day. If you can, avoid driving a car except to get you into and out of the city, and be sure to ask your hotel or guest house for clear directions to get you out of the city.

By Taxi

Official licensed taxis, metered and designated by roof signs, do not cruise. Taxi stands are located beside the central bus station, at train stations, O'Connell Bridge, St. Stephen's Green, College Green, and near major hotels; the Dublin telephone directory has a complete list. The initial charge is £1.80 with an additional charge of about £1.60 a kilometer thereafter. The fare is displayed on a meter (make sure it's on). Alternatively, you may phone a taxi company and ask for a cab to meet you at your hotel, but this may cost up to £2 extra. Hackney cabs, which also operate in the city, have neither roof signs nor meters and will sometimes respond to hotels' requests for a cab. Negotiate the fare before your journey begins. Although the taxi fleet in Dublin is large, the cabs are nonstandard and some cars are neither spacious nor in pristine condition. Local taxi companies include **Cab Charge** (☎ 01/677–2222), **Metro** (☎ 01/668–3333), and **VIP Taxis** (☎ 01/478–3333).

By Train

An electric railway system, the **DART** (Dublin Area Rapid Transit; ☎ 01/836–6222) connects Dublin with Howth to the north and Bray to the south on a fast, efficient line. There are 25 stations on the route, which is the best means of getting to seaside destinations such as Howth, Blackrock, Dun Laoghaire, Dalkey, Killiney, and Bray. The service starts at 6:30 AM and runs until 11:30 PM; at peak periods, 8–9:30 AM and 5–7 PM, trains arrive every five minutes. At other times of the day, the intervals between trains are 15 to 25 minutes. Tickets can be bought at stations, but it's also possible to buy weekly rail tickets, as well as weekly or monthly "rail-and-bus" tickets, from the **Irish Rail Travel Centre** (⊠ 35 Lower Abbey St., ☎ 01/836–6222). Individual fares begin at 65p and range up to £1.30. There are heavy penalties for traveling the DART without a ticket. Train services run from **Heuston Station** (⊠ End of Victoria Quay) to Kildare Town west of Dublin via Celbridge, Sallins, and Newbridge, and from **Connolly Station** (⊠ Amiens St.) to more distant locations like Malahide, Maynooth, Skerries, and Drogheda to the north of Dublin and Wicklow and Arklow to the south.

Contacts and Resources

B&B Reservation Agencies

For a small fee, the central reservations system of **Bord Fáilte** (☎ 800/668–668) will book accommodations anywhere in Ireland; have your credit card ready. B&Bs can be booked at local visitor information offices when they are open; however, even these reservations will go through the central reservations system. For more information, *see* Lodging *in* Smart Travel Tips.

Car Rentals

A dozen car-rental companies have desks at Dublin Airport; all the main national and international firms also have branches in the city center. Some reliable agencies include the following: **Avis** (⊠ 1 Hanover St. E, ☎ 01/677–5204; ⊠ Dublin Airport, ☎ 01/844–5204); **Budget** (⊠ 151 Lower Drumcondra Rd., ☎ 01/837–9802; ⊠ Dublin Airport, ☎ 01/844–5919); **Dan Dooley** (⊠ 42–43 Westland Row, ☎ 01/677–2723; ⊠ Dublin Airport, ☎ 01/844–5156); **Hertz** (⊠ Leeson St. Bridge, ☎ 01/660–2255; ⊠ Dublin Airport, ☎ 01/844–5466); **Murray's Rent-a-Car** (⊠ Baggot St. Bridge, ☎ 01/668–1777; ⊠ Dublin Airport, ☎ 01/844–4179).

Embassies

Embassies are open weekdays 9–1 and 2–5. **Australian** (⊠ Fitzwilton House, Wilton Terr., ☎ 01/676–1517). **British** (⊠ 29 Merrion Rd., ☎ 01/205–3700). **Canadian** (⊠ 65 St. Stephen's Green, ☎ 01/478–1988). **U.S.** (⊠ 42 Elgin Rd., ☎ 01/668–8777).

Emergencies

Gardai (police), ambulance, or fire (☎ 999).

DOCTORS AND DENTISTS

Dublin's **Eastern Help Board** (☎ 01/679–0700) can provide the names of doctors. The **Dublin Dental Hospital** (⊠ 20 Lincoln Pl., ☎ 01/662–0766) has emergency facilities and lists of dentists offering emergency care.

HOSPITALS

Beaumont (⊠ Beaumont Rd, ☎ 01/837–7755). **Mater** (⊠ Eccles St., ☎ 01/830–1122). **St. James's** (☎ 01/453–7941). **St. Vincent's** (⊠ Elm Park, ☎ 01/269–4533).

PHARMACIES

Hamilton Long (⊠ 5 Upper O'Connell St., ☎ 01/874–8456) is open Monday–Wednesday and Saturday 8:30–6, Thursday 8:30–8, and Friday 8:30–7.

Temple Bar Pharmacy (⊠ 20 E. Essex St., Temple Bar, ☎ 01/670–9751) is open Monday–Wednesday and Friday–Saturday 9–7, Thursday 9–8.

Guided Tours

BEYOND THE CITY

Bus Éireann (☎ 01/836–6111) organizes day tours out of Busaras, the main bus station, to country destinations such as Glendalough.

ORIENTATION

Dublin Bus (☎ 01/872–0000) has three- and four-hour tours of the city center that include Trinity College, the Royal Hospital Kilmainham, and Phoenix Park. The one-hour City Tour, with hourly departures, allows you to hop on and off at any of the main sites. Tickets are available from the driver or Dublin Bus. From mid-April through September Dublin Bus runs a continuous guided open-top bus tour (£5) that allows you to hop on and off the bus as often as you wish and visit some 15 sights along its route. The company also conducts a north-city coastal tour, going to Howth, and a south-city tour, traveling as far as Enniskerry.

Gray Line Tours (☎ 01/670–8822) runs city-center tours that cover the same sights as the Dublin Bus itineraries (☞ *above*).

TRAIN AND CARRIAGE TOURS

DART Train: Guided tours of Dublin using the DART system are organized by **Views Unlimited** (✉ 8 Prince of Wales Terr., Bray, ☎ 01/286–0164 or 01/285–6121).

Horse-Drawn Carriage: Horse-drawn carriage tours are available around Dublin and in Phoenix Park. For tours of the park, contact the **Department of the Arts, Culture and the Gaeltacht** (☎ 01/661–3111). Carriages can be hired at the Grafton Street corner of St. Stephen's Green, without prior reservation.

WALKING TOURS

Historical and Literary Tours: Historical Walking Tours of Dublin (☎ 01/878–0227), run by Trinity College history graduate students, are excellent two-hour tour introductions to Dublin. The Bord Fáilte–approved tour assembles at the front gate of Trinity College mid-May–mid-October, daily at 11, noon, and 3, with an extra tour on Sunday at 2, and mid-October–mid-May on weekends at noon. The cost is £5. A **Georgian/Literary Walking Tour** leaves from Bewley's Café June–September daily at 11; each tour lasts approximately two hours and costs £5. **Trinity Tours** (☎ 01/608–2320) organizes walks of the Trinity College campus on weekends from March 17 (St. Patrick's Day) through mid-May and from mid-May to September daily; the ½-hour tour costs £3.50 and includes admission to the Book of Kells (☞ Trinity College *in* City Center: Around Trinity College, *above*); tours start at the college's main gate. The **Zozimus Experience** (☎ 01/661–8646) is an enjoyable walking tour of Dublin's medieval past, with a particular focus on the seedy, including great escapes, murders, and mythical happenings. Led by a guide in costume, tours are by arrangement only and run from the main gate of Dublin Castle from 6:45 PM; the cost is £5 per person. Prepare yourself for a surprise!

Musical Tours: Dublin Tourism (☞ Visitor Information, *below*) has a booklet to its self-guided **"Rock 'n Stroll" Trail,** which covers 16 sites with associations to performers such as Bob Geldof, Christy Moore, Sinéad O'Connor, and U2. Most of the sites are in the city center and Temple Bar. The **Musical Pub Crawl** (✉ Discover Dublin, 20 Lower Stephens St., Dublin 2, ☎ 01/478–0191) begins at **Oliver St. John Gogarty's** (✉ Fleet St., Temple Bar) and moves on to three other pubs. Led by two professional musicians who perform songs and tell the story of Irish music, the tour is given May–October, Monday–Thursday and weekends at 7:30 PM; the cost is £6.

Pubs: Colm Quilligan (☎ 01/454–0228) arranges highly enjoyable evening walks of the literary pubs of Dublin, where "brain cells are replaced as quickly as they are drowned." The *Dublin Literary Pub Crawl* is a 122-page guide to those Dublin pubs with the greatest literary associations; it's widely available in Dublin bookstores.

Internet

In the city center are a number of internet cafés that allow you access to the internet and e-mail. All charge between IR£4–IR£6 an hour. **Betacafe** (✉ Arthouse, Curved St., Temple Bar, ☎ 01/671–5717) is a internet café serving coffee and sandwiches. **Cyberia** (✉ The Granary, Temple La. S, Temple Bar, ☎ 01/679–7607) is very popular with students, who tend to spend hours playing computer games. **Planet Cyber Café** (✉ 23 S. Great George's St., ☎ 01/679–0583), in the basement of a video store, is the city's best, with top-of-the-range computers and a good coffee bar.

Lost and Found

Dublin Bus: Contact its headquarters (✉ 59 Upper O'Connell St., ☎ 01/873–4222).

Railways and DART: Contact **Iarnrod Éireann/Irish Rail** (✉ Travel Centre, 35 Lower Abbey St., ☎ 01/836–6222).

Opening and Closing Times

Dublin is gradually becoming a 24-hour city, even though the bus and DART train services close down for the night at 11:30. (A few lines run until dawn on the weekends, and late buses go until 3 AM.) Many taxis run all night, but the demand, especially on weekends, can make for long lines at taxi stands. Many clubs on the Leeson Street strip and elsewhere stay open until 4 AM or later. Sunday, once a day of sabbatical in Dublin, is now often bustling, with some stores open (☞ *below*).

Banks are open weekdays 10–4 and remain open on Thursday until 5. All stay open at lunchtime. Most branches have ATMs that accept bank cards and MasterCard and Visa credit cards (☞ Money *in* Smart Travel Tips). **Museums** are normally open Tuesday–Saturday and Sunday afternoon. **Post offices** are open weekdays 9–1 and 2–5:30, Saturday 9–12:30. Main post offices are open Saturday afternoons, too (look for green signs that say "An Post"). The General Post Office (GPO) on O'Connell Street, which has foreign exchange and general delivery facilities, is open Monday–Saturday 8–8, Sunday 10:30–6:30. To send a postcard to the United States costs 38p, to the United Kingdom 28p.

Pubs open Monday–Saturday at 10:30 AM and 12:30 PM on Sunday. They must stop serving at 11 PM in winter and 11:30 PM in summer, but most pubs take another hour to empty out, as patrons drag out their last drink as long as they can. For a memorable glimpse into a ritual repeated all over Ireland every night, hold out in a pub as long as you can and watch the patrons ignore the bartenders pleading with them to leave. A number of bars in the center of the city have permission to serve until 1 AM on weekend nights.

Stores are open Monday–Saturday 9–5:30 or 9–6, and Thursday until 8. Smaller city-center specialty stores open on Sunday as well, usually 10–6. Most department stores are closed on Sunday.

Safety

What crime there is in Dublin is often drug-related. Sidestreets off O'-Connell Street can be dangerous, especially at night. When you park your car, *do not* leave any valuables inside, even under a raincoat on the back seat or in the trunk; be especially careful parking around the Guinness Brewery and the Old Jameson Distillery (☞ Dublin West: From

Dublin Castle to the Four Courts, *above*), neither of which is in a great neighborhood.

Travel Agencies

American Express (⊠ 116 Grafton St., ☎ 01/677–2874). **Thomas Cook** (⊠ 118 Grafton St., ☎ 01/677–1721).

Visitor Information

The main **Dublin Tourism** (Suffolk St., just off Grafton St., ☎ 01/605–7799, FAX 01/605–7787) is open July–September, Monday–Saturday 8:30–6, Sunday 11–5:30, and October–June, daily 9–6; at **Dublin Airport,** daily 8 AM–10 PM; and at the **Ferryport, Dun Laoghaire,** daily 10–9. **Bord Fáilte,** the Irish Tourist Board, has its own visitor information offices in the entrance hall of its **headquarters** (⊠ Baggot St. Bridge, ☎ 1850/230–330, FAX 01/602–4100), open weekdays 9:15–5:15. A suburban tourist office in **Tallaght** is open March–December, daily 9:30–5.

The **Temple Bar Information Centre** (⊠ 18 Eustace St., ☎ 01/671–5717, FAX 01/677–2525) produces the easy-to-use, annually updated *Temple Bar Guide,* which provides complete listings of the area's hundreds of stores, pubs, restaurants, clubs, galleries, and other cultural venues.

2 DUBLIN ENVIRONS

THE BOYNE VALLEY AND COUNTIES WICKLOW AND KILDARE

Both glory and grandeur are tucked into the folds of the Pale—the counties north, south, and west of Dublin. Here, the scenic-hungry traveler will find some of the richest treasure houses in the land: Castletown, Russborough, and Powerscourt Houses. But there are more than just 18th-century Palladian porticoes here. Celtic crosses, historic churches, the ancient passage graves at Newgrange, and the "monastic city" of Glendalough await—all time-burnished sites that still guard the roots of Irishness.

Updated by
Anto Howard

ONE OF THE LOVELIEST REGIONS in this land of love-
liness, the Pale—the counties immediately north,
south, and west of Dublin—constitutes an area
that seems expressly designed for the sightseer. The entire region is an
open-air museum filled with legendary Celtic sites, grand gardens (little wonder the air is flower-scented), and elegant Palladian country estates. France may have its châteaux of the Loire Valley, England the
treasure houses of Kent and Sussex, Germany its castles of the Rhine,
but today, more and more travelers are discovering that the grand estates of the Pale rank nearly as high in the galaxy of stately style.

Dublin Environs comprise three basic geographical regions: County
Wicklow's coast and mountains, the Boyne Valley, and County Kildare.
Lying tantalizingly close to the south of Dublin is the mountainous county
of Wicklow, which contains some of the most *et-in-arcadia-ego* scenery
in the Emerald Isle. Here, the gently rounded Wicklow Mountains—
to some tastes Ireland's finest—contain the evocative monastic settlement at Glendalough, many later abbeys and churches, and such noted
18th-century estates as Powerscourt and Russborough. Nearby is an
impressive eastern coastline that stretches from Counties Wicklow to
Louth, punctuated by delightful harbor towns and fishing villages. The
coast is virtually unspoiled for its entire length.

North of Dublin lies the Boyne Valley, with its abundant ruins of
Celtic Ireland stretching from Counties Meath to Louth. Some of the
country's most evocative Neolithic ruins—including the famous passage graves at Newgrange—are nestled into this landscape, where
layer upon layer of history penetrates down into earlier, unknowable
ages. It was west of Drogheda—a fascinating town settled by the
Vikings in the early 10th century—that the *Tuatha De Danann,* one-
time residents of Ireland, went underground when defeated by the invading Milesians and became, it is said "the good people" or fairies
of Irish legend. In pagan times this area was the home of Ireland's high
kings and the center of religious life. In those days, all roads led to Tara,
the fabled Hill of Kings. Today, time seems to stand still there—and
you should do so, too, for it is almost sacrilegious to introduce a note
of urgency. At any of the religious sites of the Boyne Valley—Tara, Mellifont Abbey, Monasterboice—be sure to feast your ears on the qui-
etude of centuries gone by. As part of the country's millennium
celebrations, an interpretive center, riverboat trips, and multimedia shows
will commemorate the site of the famous Battle of the Boyne.

Southwest of Dublin are the flat pastoral plains of County Kildare, which
stretch between the western Midlands and the foothills of the Dublin
and Wicklow mountains—both names actually refer to one mountain,
but each marks its county's claim to the land. Kildare has the reputation of being the flattest part of Ireland, a playing field for the breeding, training, and racing of some of the world's premier Thoroughbreds.

Of all the artistic delights that beckon both north and south of Dublin,
few are as enchanting as the imposing country estates of County Wicklow. Here, during the "glorious eighteenth," great Anglo-Irish estates
were built by Irish "princes of Elegance and Prodigality." Only an hour
or two from Dublin, these estates were profoundly influenced by the
country villas of the great Italian architect Andrea Palladio, who
erected the estates of the Venetian aristocracy only a short distance from
the city on the lagoon. As in other parts of Ireland, the ancestral homes
of the dwindling members of the Anglo-Irish ascendancy dot the landscape in the Pale. Today, lords and baronets down on their luck have

turned into hoteliers who welcome guests to castle holidays with adaptable grace.

Pleasures and Pastimes

Dining

Dining out in the area is still essentially a casual affair, but the innovations and experimentation of Dublin's top restaurateurs is influencing the cooking at the finer establishments outside the capital. As in the Southwest (☞ Chapter 5), chefs hereabouts have a deep respect for fresh, locally grown and raised produce. You'll find everything from Continental-style meals to hearty ploughman's lunches. For price ranges ☞ Chart 1(A) *in* Smart Travel Tips A to Z.

Lodging

Counties Wicklow and Kildare offer excellent accommodations, even if the choice may not be vast. If you have only a night or two outside Dublin, try to stay at least one night in one of the area's country-house or manor-house hotels, where some of Ireland's finest hosts welcome you into sometimes glorious, sometimes rustic, but almost invariably comfortable homes. Old-style hotels in Counties Meath and Louth are showing signs of improvement and are becoming ever more popular. Bed-and-breakfasts, as elsewhere in Ireland, are always a delightful option. For price ranges ☞ Chart 2(B) *in* Smart Travel Tips A to Z.

Prehistoric and Monastic Sites

The Boyne Valley, which straddles the county of Louth and runs through the flat heartland of Meath, is home to 10% of all prehistoric monuments in Ireland. Foremost among these is **Neolithic Newgrange,** passage graves built between 2800 and 2400 BC. The **Hill of Tara,** one of the focal points for the ancient high kings of Ireland, was where disputes between clans were settled, new laws were passed, and, eventually, Christianity was proclaimed from the summit by St. Patrick. The advent of Christianity led to the construction of County Wicklow's **Glendalough** monastery, founded by one of St. Patrick's followers, St. Kevin. Later in the 12th century, the first Cistercian house in Ireland, the monastery of **Mellifont,** was founded. North of Mellifont are the ruins of **Monasterboice,** another monastic site where two of the finest high crosses in Ireland stand in the shadow of a 9th-century round tower.

Walking, Hiking, and Biking

Whether you're a novice or veteran hiker, Wicklow's gentle, rolling hills are a terrific place to begin an Irish walking vacation. Devoted hikers come from all over the world to traverse the 137-km (85-mi) **Wicklow Way,** the first long-distance trail to open in Ireland and one of the best. Beginning in Marlay Park (☞ Side Trips *in* Chapter 1), just a few miles south of Dublin, much of the route lies above 1,600 ft and follows rough sheep tracks, forest firebreaks, and old bog roads; rain gear, windproof clothing, and sturdy footwear are essential. Consider participating in one of the walking festivals held at Easter, in May, and in autumn. Biking is also an excellent way to see the area.

Exploring Dublin Environs

All of the towns and sites in the Dublin environs region can be visited on a day trip from the city. This chapter is organized into three different trips, each of which makes a reasonable day trip. Keep in mind that it's easy to lose an hour or so making detours, chatting with locals, and otherwise enjoying the unexpected. The itinerary below covers the area's highlights. If you have fewer than three days, use parts of each day's suggested itinerary to plan your excursion. A car is essential to visit most sights—and don't plan on visiting both the north and south of Dublin in the same day. You can also reach some points of interest by public transport: Bus tours from Dublin cover County Wicklow as far as Glendalough in the southwest and the Boyne Valley to the north; suburban bus services reach into the foothills of the Dublin Mountains; and C.I.E. Expressway services take in the outlying towns. Particularly popular sites have direct connections to Dublin, including Enniskerry and Powerscourt House, Gardens, and Waterfall, which can be reached by taking the No. 44 bus from the Dublin quays area.

Numbers in the text correspond to numbers in the margin and on the Dublin Environs map.

Great Itineraries

IF YOU HAVE 3 DAYS

The four counties surrounding Dublin—Wicklow to the south, Kildare to the west, Meath and Louth to the north—offer memorable historic sites, attractions, and scenery, all of which are best appreciated at a leisurely pace. However, if you have a limited number of days to explore these counties, you can still enjoy the best of Dublin's rich and varied environs. Begin your first day by traveling southward along N11 to **Powerscourt House, Gardens, and Waterfall** ⑲, the opulent Palladian mansion and garden estate, set under the great Sugar Loaf. Keep your spirits up, literally, by taking the road to **Roundwood** ⑳, the highest village in Ireland. Move on to the early Christian monastic settlement of **Glendalough** ㉑, set amid the tranquil Wicklow Mountains forests. Follow R752 south to Rathnew and proceed to **Avoca** ㉕, where you can browse for wool fabric and apparel at Ireland's oldest mill. End your day in ⌖ **Wicklow Town** ㉓, north of Avoca on R754; or, if you want to remain Dublin-based, return to the capital via N11.

Begin your second day with a visit to one of Ireland's grandest mansions, **Castletown House** ㉗ near Celbridge, easily reached via N4, with a left turn at Leixlip, followed by a 8-km (5-mi) drive down R403. Continue south and turn left at Clane until you reach **Naas** ㉙, where you turn left along R410 and go the short distance to Sir Alfred Beit's sumptuous **Russborough House** ㉚—a feast of Old Master paintings, Regency armoires, and Georgian stucco-work. Or, continue west toward **Kildare Town** ㉝, an elegant, prosperous town surrounded by the broad, flat plains of the **Curragh** ㉜. The **National Stud and Japanese Gardens** ㉞ are the real highlight of the area. If you spent your first night in Wicklow, return to Glendalough and proceed onward toward Kildare via the wonderfully scenic Wicklow Gap, a maze of winding roads that take you through the villages of Granabeg, Hollywood (no relation to its American namesake), and Kilcullen. Spend your second night either in nearby ⌖ **Straffan** ㉘ or back in ⌖ **Dublin.**

On your third day, head north of Dublin to Counties Meath and Louth via N3, which will take you to the **Hill of Tara** ②, one of Ireland's most important Celtic sites and home of the Irish kings just after the birth of Christ. Travel back another 2,000 years in time with a visit to **Newgrange** ⑤, home to the most important Neolithic passage tombs in Europe. On your way north to **Monasterboice** ⑩, where one of the finest high crosses in all of Ireland awaits, be sure to visit the small, Georgian village of **Slane** ⑥. Make a stop along N51 at **King William's Glen** ⑦, site of the Battle of the Boyne in 1690 between the Catholic forces of King James II and the Protestant army of King William of Orange—a battle that shaped the course of Irish history. Return to Dublin via N2.

IF YOU HAVE 5 DAYS

Five days should give you ample opportunity to "take it aisy"—or, at least, to take it as easy as you can, considering the array of beautiful sights found in this part of the country. Make a stop in the coastal town of **Bray** ⑱, a Victorian seaside resort founded in the 1850s, before heading south toward **Powerscourt House, Gardens, and Waterfall** ⑲, **Roundwood** ⑳, and on to **Glendalough** ㉑. (If you haven't already explored the towns along Dublin Bay north of Bray but south of Dublin, consult the Side Trips section in Chapter 1 to decide whether or not to visit the County Dublin sights we cover in that section on your way farther south.) For a taste of more recent history, follow N11 a few miles south to Rathnew and drive inland on R752 until you reach **Avondale Forest Park and House** ㉔, the home of the 19th-century Irish leader Charles Stewart Parnell. Overnight in ☷ **Wicklow Town** ㉓, which dates back to Viking days, or near the ☷ **Poulaphouca Reservoir** ㉛, home of the wonderful Rathsallagh House. If you have time, you may want to visit the seaside resort of **Arklow** ㉖ or the **Mount Usher Gardens** ㉒ northwest of Wicklow Town, off N11 beyond Rathnew. Spend your second day visiting the broad flatland of County Kildare, venturing as far south as **Ballytore** ㊱ and **Castledermot** ㊴ before overnighting in ☷ **Straffan** ㉘. On your third day, set off for the Celtic and prehistoric sights of County Meath. Be sure to visit the 12th-century remains of **Mellifont Abbey** ⑨ near **Slane** ⑥, and the town of **Kells** ④, where Ireland's greatest treasure was once unearthed from a bog. Overnight in historic ☷ **Drogheda** ⑧. The following morning, travel north to ☷ **Dundalk** ⑭, the border town of **Omeath** ⑰, and **Inniskeen** ⑬, home of poet Patrick Kavanagh. After lunch, take the **Cooley Peninsula Drive** ⑮ and visit the medieval fishing town of **Carlingford** ⑯, which should take up most of the afternoon. If possible, spend the night in Drogheda, returning to Dublin the next day via the ancient town of **Louth** ⑫ and the market town of **Ardee** ⑪.

When to Tour the Dublin Environs

The wild mountains of Wicklow and the flat pasturelands of Kildare are at their best in spring and summer. However, consider that there is often higher rainfall in March and April. If you're planning to tour the towns and historic sites, winter is a good time to avoid the crush; bring warm clothing and boots, and be prepared for light snow on the hills.

NORTH OF DUBLIN IN THE BOYNE VALLEY

The great prehistoric, pagan, and Celtic monuments of the wide arc of fertile land known as the Boyne Valley excite a grand sense of wonder. As you'll discover, you don't have to be an archaeologist to be awed by Newgrange, Knowth, and Dowth—all set beside the River Boyne—or the sites of the Hill of Tara, Mellifont Abbey, and the high crosses of Monasterboice. Our tour begins at Trim, the locale closest to Dublin, and works its way north. Keep in mind that Omeath and the scenic Cooley Peninsula at the end of this tour are on the border of Northern Ireland. If you make it this far north, consult Chapter 8, particularly our coverage of the Mountains of Mourne, which are just across Carlingford Lough.

Trim

❶ *51 km (32 mi) northwest of Dublin on N3 and R154.*

Resting on the River Boyne, Trim has some of the finest medieval ruins in Ireland. In 1359, on the instructions of King Edward III, the town

Dublin Environs

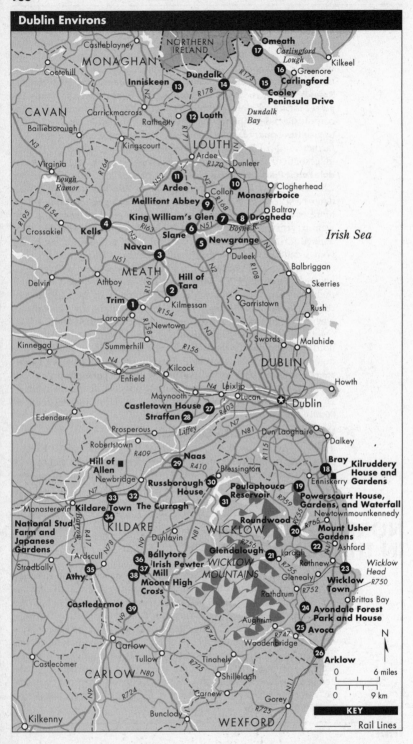

NORTHERN IRELAND

MONAGHAN

Castleblayney

Cootehill

CAVAN

Bailieborough

Virginia

Crossakiel

Kells **4**

Kinnegad

Edenderry

Prosperous

Robertstown

Hill of Allen

Newbridge

National Stud Farm and Japanese Gardens

Monasterevin

Kildare Town **33** **32** **34**

KILDARE

The Curragh

Athy **35**

Stradbally

Ardscull

Castledermot **39**

Castlecomer

Kilkenny

Inniskeen **13**

Carrickmacross

Rathnelly

Kingscourt

Lough Ramor

Delvin

Athboy

Trim **1**

Laracor

Newtown

Summerhill

Enfield

Kilcock

Maynooth

Castletown House **27**
Straffan **28**

Liffey

Naas **29**

Blessington

Russborough House **30**

31

Roundwood **20**

WICKLOW

Dunlavin

Ballytore
Irish Pewter Mill **36** **37**

Moone High Cross **38**

Carlow

Tullow

CARLOW N80

Bunclody

WEXFORD

Dundalk **14**

Omeath **17**

Carlingford Lough

Kilkeel

Carlingford **16** **15** Greenore

Cooley Peninsula Drive

Dundalk Bay

Louth **12**

LOUTH

Ardee

Dunleer

Clogherhead

Ardee **11**

Collon

Monasterboice **10**

Mellifont Abbey **9**

King William's Glen **7** **8** Drogheda

Baltray

Slane **6** **5**

Newgrange

Boyne R.

Duleek

Balbriggan

Skerries

MEATH

Navan **3**

Hill of Tara **2**

Kilmessan

R154

Newtown

Garristown

Rush

Swords

Malahide

DUBLIN

Leixlip

Lucan

☆ Dublin

Dun Laoghaire

Dalkey

Howth

Bray **18** **Kilruddery House and Gardens**

Enniskerry

Powerscourt House, Gardens, and Waterfall **19**

Newtownmountkennedy

Mount Usher Gardens **20**

Ashford

Glendalough **21**

Laragh

22

Rathnew

23 **Wicklow Town**

Wicklow Head

WICKLOW MOUNTAINS

Glenealy

Rathdrum

Avondale Forest Park and House **24**

Avoca **25**

Woodenbridge

Arklow **26**

Aughrim

Tinahely

Shillelagh

Carnew

Gorey

Irish Sea

Poulaphouca Reservoir

N

0   6 miles

0   9 km

KEY

——— Rail Lines

was walled and its fortifications strengthened; in the 15th century several parliaments subsequently were held here. Oliver Cromwell massacred most of its inhabitants when he captured the town in 1649. **Trim Castle,** the largest Anglo-Norman fortress in Ireland, dominates present-day Trim from its 2½-acre site, which slopes down to the river's placid waters. Built by Hugh de Lacy in 1173, the castle was soon destroyed and then rebuilt from 1190 to 1200. The ruins include an enormous keep with 70-ft-high turrets flanked by rectangular towers. The outer castle wall is almost 500 yards long, and five D-shape towers survive. The castle remains are freely accessible at all times. Facing the river is the **Royal Mint,** another ruin that indicates Trim's political importance in the Middle Ages.

The **Yellow Steeple** overlooks Trim from a ridge opposite the castle. The structure was built in 1368 and is a remnant of the 13th-century Augustinian abbey of St. Mary's, which itself was the sight of a great medieval pilgrimage to a statue of the Blessed Virgin. Much of the tower was destroyed in 1649 to prevent its falling into Cromwell's hands, and today only the striking, 125-ft-high east wall remains. The Church of Ireland **St. Patrick's Cathedral** (⊠ Loman St.) dates from the early 19th century, but the square tower belongs to an earlier structure built in 1449. The Trim **visitor center's** "The Power and the Glory" audiovisual display tells the story of the arrival of the Normans and of medieval Trim. ⊠ Mill St., ☎ 046/37227. ⊡ £2.50. ⊙ May–Sept., Wed.– Sun. 9:30–5; Oct.–Apr. by appointment.

If your ancestors are from County Meath, take advantage of the family-history tracing service at the **Meath Heritage and Genealogy Center.** ⊠ Mill St., ☎ 046/36633. ⊡ Free. ⊙ Mon.–Thurs. 9–5, Fri. 9–2.

Several places east and south of Trim are also of interest. At **Newtown,** 1¼ km (¾ mi) east of Trim on the banks of the River Boyne, lie the ruins of what was the largest cathedral in Ireland, built beginning in 1210 by Simon de Rochfort, the first Anglo-Norman bishop of Meath. At **Laracor,** 3 km (2 mi) south of Trim on R158, a wall left of the rectory is where Jonathan Swift (1667–1745), the satirical writer, poet, and author of *Gulliver's Travels,* was rector from 1699 until 1714, when he was made dean of St. Patrick's Cathedral in Dublin. Nearby are the walls of the cottage where Esther Johnson, the "Stella" who inspired much of Swift's writings, once lived. One of the most pleasant villages of south County Meath, **Summerhill,** 8 km (5 mi) southeast of Laracor along R158, has a large square and a village green with a 15th-century cross. South of Summerhill is **Cnoc an Linsigh,** an attractive area of forest walks with picnic sites, ideal for a half day's meandering. Many of the lanes that crisscross this part of County Meath provide delightful driving between high hedgerows and afford occasional views of the lush, pastoral countryside.

Hill of Tara

❷ 14½ km (9 mi) east of Trim on R154, 33 km (21 mi) northwest of Dublin on N3.

Known in popular folklore as the seat of the High Kings of Ireland, the Hill of Tara is one of the country's most important historic sites. The 19th-century ballad by Thomas Moore, "The Harp That Once Through Tara's Halls," was a factor in the over-romanticized view of Tara nearly up to recent times. Systematic excavation by 20th-century archaeologists has led to the less-exciting conclusion that the remains are those of an Iron Age fort that had multiple ring forts, some of which were ruined in the 19th century by religious zealots from England who believed they would find the Ark of the Covenant here. The "Mound of the Hostages," a Neolithic passage grave, most likely gave the place its sacred character. During the hill's reign as a royal seat, which lasted to the 11th century, a great *feis* (national assembly) was held here every three years, when laws were passed and tribal disputes were settled. Tara's decline was predicted one eventful Easter Eve in the 5th century on a night when, according to the Druid religion, no fires could be lit. Suddenly on a hillside some miles away, flames were spotted. "If that fire is not quenched now," said a Druid leader, "it will burn forever and will consume Tara." The fire seen by the court at Tara was lit by St. Patrick at Slane to celebrate the Christian rites of the Paschal. Tara's influence waned with the arrival of Christianity; the last king to live here was Malachy II, who died in 1022.

But like so many of the most prominent sites of the pagan, pre-Christian era, Christianity remade Tara in its own image. Today a modern statue of St. Patrick stands here, as does a pillar stone that may have been the coronation stone (it was reputed to call out in approval when a king was crowned). In the graveyard of the adjacent Anglican church, you'll find a pillar with the worn image of a pagan god and a Bronze Age stone standing on end. However, the main attraction is the Hill of Tara's height: It rises more than 300 ft above sea level, and from its top on a clear day, you can see across the flat central plain of Ireland, with the mountains of east Galway rising nearly 160 km (100 mi) away. In the mid-19th century, the nationalist leader Daniel O'Connell staged a mass rally that is said to have drawn more than a million people— nearly a third of Ireland's population today. In an old Church of Ireland church on the hillside, the **interpretative center** tells the story of Tara and its legends. This can be truly informative, for without expert assistance, it is difficult to identify many of the earthworks at Tara. ⊠ *Hill of Tara,* ☎ *046/25903.* 🎫 *£1.50.* ☉ *May–mid-June and mid-Sept.– Oct., daily 10–5; mid-June–mid-Sept., daily 9:30–6:30.*

Navan

❸ *10 km (6 mi) northwest of the Hill of Tara on N3, 48 km (30 mi) north of Dublin on N3.*

A busy market and mining town with evidence of prehistoric settlements, Navan lies at the crucial juncture of the Rivers Blackwater and Boyne. It took off in the 12th century, when Hugh de Lacy, Lord of Trim, had the place walled and fortified, making it a defensive stronghold of the English Pale in eastern Ireland. The Catholic **St. Mary's Church,** built in 1839, features a late-18th-century wood carving of the Crucifixion, the work of a local artist, Edward Smyth, who at the time was the greatest sculptor Ireland had produced since the Middle Ages. On Friday, the **Fair Green,** beside the church, is the site of a bustling outdoor market. ⊠ *Trimgate St., Navan.* ☉ *Daily 8–8.*

The best views of town and the surrounding area are from the top of the **Motte of Navan,** a grassy mound that tradition—most likely apocryphal—holds to be the tomb of Odhbha, the deserted wife of a Celtic king who died of a broken heart. D'Angulo, the Norman baron, adapted it into a motte-and-baily.

Kells

❹ *16 km (10 mi) northwest of Navan on N3.*

In the 9th century, a group of monks from Iona in Scotland took refuge at Kells (Ceanannus Mór) after being expelled by the Danes. St. Columba had founded a monastery here 300 years earlier, and while some historians think the indigenous monks wrote and illustrated the Book of Kells—the Latin version of the four Gospels and one of Ireland's greatest medieval treasures—most scholars now believe that the Scottish monks brought it with them. Reputed to have been fished out of a watery bog at Kells, the legendary manuscript was removed for safekeeping during the Cromwellian wars to Trinity College, Dublin, where it remains. A large exhibit is now devoted to it in the college's Old Library, where a few of the original pages at a time are on view (☞ Exploring Dublin *in* Chapter 1). A facsimile copy of the Book of Kells is on display in the Church of Ireland **St. Columba's,** in Kells. Four elaborately carved high crosses stand in the church graveyard, while the stump of a fifth is in the marketplace; during the 1798 uprising against British rule, it was used as a gallows.

St. Colmcille's House, a small, two-story, 7th-century church measuring about 24 ft square and nearly 40 ft high, with a steeply pitched stone roof, is similar in appearance to St. Kevin's Church at Glendalough (☞ County Wicklow's Coast and Mountains, *below*) and Cormac's Chapel at Cashel (☞ Chapter 4). Adjacent to St. Colmcille's House, the nearly 100-ft-high **round tower,** which dates prior to 1076, is in almost perfect condition. Its top story has five windows, each facing an ancient entrance to the medieval town.

Dining and Lodging

$ ✕⌂ **Lennoxbrook.** This fine, 200-year-old-plus farmhouse is run by Pauline Mullan, whose children are the fifth generation of the family to occupy the home. A casual, friendly mood prevails throughout the house. Upstairs, the four rooms are decorated with finely patterned wallpaper and period furniture. Lamb and produce are often on the dinner menu (£12 extra). The house, 5 km (3 mi) north of Kells on N3 from Dublin to Cavan, is convenient to Newgrange. The prehistoric forts, passage graves, and other remains dating from 2000 BC on the Loughcrew Hills are a 15-minute drive away. ✉ Co. Meath, ☎ 046/ 45902. 4 rooms with bath. Dining room. MC, V.

Newgrange

★ ❺ 11⅓ km (7 mi) east of Navan on N51.

Newgrange is one of the most spectacular prehistoric tombs in Europe. Built in the 4th millennium BC, which makes it roughly 1,000 years older than Stonehenge, Newgrange was constructed with some 250,000 tons of stones, the nearest source of which was the Wicklow Mountains south of Dublin. How the people who built this tumulus transported the stones here remains a mystery. The mound above the tomb measures more than 330 ft across and is 36 ft high at the front. White quartz stones—somehow hauled the 80 km (50 mi) from the mountains of Wicklow to the south—were used for the retaining wall, while egg-shape gray stones were studded at intervals. The passage grave may have been the world's earliest observatory. It was so carefully constructed that, for five days on and around the winter solstice, the rays of the rising sun still hit a roof box above the lintel at the entrance to the grave. The rays then shine for about 20 minutes down the main interior passageway to illuminate the burial chamber. The site was first restored in 1962 after years of neglect and quarrying. A visit to the passage grave during the winter solstice is considered by many to be the most memorable experience of all, in part due to the luck needed to witness the illumination. There is a nine-year waiting list for one of the 24 places available on each of the five mornings (December 19–23)—and even if you have a place, there is no guarantee that the sun won't be obscured by clouds! However, visitors to the interior of this Bronze Age tomb can also see the effect artificially re-created. The geometric designs on some stones at the center of the burial chamber continue to baffle experts. Access to Newgrange is solely via **Brú na Bóinne** ("palace of the Boyne"), the Boyne Valley visitor center. ☎ 041/24488. ⌨ £3. ⊙ June–mid-Sept., daily 9–7; May and mid-Sept.–Sept. 30, daily 9–6:30; Mar.–Apr. and Oct., daily 9:30–5:30; Nov.–Feb., daily 9:30–5.

The prehistoric sites of **Dowth** and **Knowth** have been under excavation since 1962, and although Dowth is still closed to the public, the partially excavated site at **Knowth** is open between May 1 and October 31. It is far larger and more diversified than the more famous Newgrange tomb (☞ above), with a huge central mound and 17 smaller ones. About one-third of the site has been excavated and can be explored via the visitor center. You can also watch archaeologists at work on the rest of the site. The earliest tombs and carved stones date from the Stone Age (3000 BC), although the site was in use until the early 14th century. In the early Christian era (4th–8th centuries AD) it was the seat of the High Kings of Ireland. ⊠ Knowth, Co. Meath, ☎ 041/24488. ⌨ Newgrange and interpretive center £3; Knowth and interpretive center £2; Newgrange, Knowth, and interpretive center £5. ⊙ June–mid-Sept., daily 9–7; May and mid-Sept.–Sept. 30, daily 9–6:30; Mar., Apr, and Oct., daily 9:30–5:30; Nov.–Feb., daily 9:30–5.

Slane

❻ 2½ km (1½ mi) north of Newgrange, 46 km (29 mi) northwest of Dublin on N2.

The small, Georgian village of Slane was built in the 18th century around a crossroads on the north side of the River Boyne. The **Conyngham Arms Hotel** (☎ 041/24155), at the crossroads in Slane, is an agreeable, family-run establishment that serves a buffet from noon to 3 and a bar menu throughout the day. The 16th-century building known as the **Hermitage** was constructed on the site where St. Erc, a local man who was converted to Christianity by St. Patrick, led a hermit's existence. All that remains of his original monastery is the faint trace of the circular ditch that surrounded it. **Slane Castle,** beautifully situated overlooking a natural amphitheater, was badly damaged in a 1991 fire and is now closed to the public. Back in 1981, Slane's owner, the Anglo-Irish Lord Henry Mountcharles, staged the first of what have been some of Ireland's largest rock concerts; U2, still only one album old, had second billing to Thin Lizzy that year. Most of rock's greatest names have performed here since, including Bob Dylan, Bruce Springsteen, David Bowie, and the Rolling Stones—REM's 1995 show holds the record for attendance, with 70,000. The venue was closed indefinitely following the 1995 show, due in part to protests by locals, who complained that the masses of fans descending upon this quiet town were like marauding armies bent on destruction.

North of Slane town is the 500-ft-high **Slane Hill,** where St. Patrick proclaimed the arrival of Christianity in 433 by lighting the Paschal Fire. From the top, you have sweeping views of the Boyne Valley. On a clear day, the panorama stretches from Trim to Drogheda, a vista extending 40 km (25 mi).

King William's Glen

❼ 7½ km (4½ mi) east of Slane on N51.

On the northern bank of the River Boyne, King William's Glen is where a portion of King William's Protestant army hid before the Battle of the Boyne in 1690. They won by surprising the Catholic troops of James II, who were on the southern side, but many of the Protestant-Catholic conflicts in present-day Northern Ireland can be traced to the immediate aftermath of this battle. The site is marked with an orange and green sign, while part is also incorporated in the nearby, early 19th-century **Townley Hall Estate,** which has forest walks and a nature trail.

Drogheda

❽ *6½ km (4 mi) east of King William's Glen on N51, 45 km (28 mi) north of Dublin on N1.*

One of the most enjoyable historic towns on the east coast of Ireland, Drogheda (pronounced draw-*hee*-da) was colonized in 911 by the Danish Vikings. Two centuries later, the town was taken over by Hugh de Lacy, the Anglo-Norman lord of Trim (☞ *above*) who was responsible for fortifying many locales up and down the River Boyne. At first, two separate towns existed on the northern and southern banks of the river. In 1412, already heavily walled and fortified, Drogheda was unified, making it the largest English town in Ireland. Today, large 18th-century warehouses line the northern bank of the Boyne. Towering over the river is the long **railway viaduct.** Built around 1850 as part of the railway line from Dublin to Belfast, it is still used and is a splendid example of Victorian engineering. Because of its height above the river, the viaduct remains Drogheda's most prominent landmark.

The center of the town, around West Street, is the historic heart of Drogheda. The bank building on the corner of West and Shop streets, called the **Tholsel,** is an 18th-century, square granite edifice with a cupola; it used to house the town hall. **St. Laurence's Gate,** one of the two surviving entrances from Drogheda's original 11 gates in its town walls, has two four-story drum towers and is one of the most perfect examples in Ireland of a medieval town gate.

Butler's Gate, near the Millmount Museum (☞ *below*), predates St. Laurence's Gate by 50 years or more.

The Gothic Revival, Roman Catholic **St. Peter's Church** (⌧ West St.) houses the preserved head of St. Oliver Plunkett. Primate of all Ireland, he was martyred in 1681 at Tyburn in London, where his head was pulled from the execution flames. A severe, 18th-century church within an enclosed courtyard, the Anglican **St. Peter's** (⌧ Fair St.) is rarely open except for Sunday services. If the chapel is closed, it's worth a peek for its setting and the fine views over the town from the churchyard.

Off the Dublin Road south of Drogheda, the **Millmount Museum** shares space in a renovated British Army barracks with crafts workshops, including a pottery and picture gallery and studio. Relics of eight centuries of Drogheda's commercial and industrial past are on display, including painted banners of the old trade guilds; a circular willow and leather coracle (the traditional fishing boat on the River Boyne); and many instruments and utensils from domestic and factory use. Surprisingly, the museum does not have many mementos of the most infamous episode in Drogheda's history, when the English leader Oliver Cromwell sacked the town in 1649, killing 3,000 people. During the attack, Sir Arthur Aston, the town garrison leader and a staunch royalist, was beaten to death with his own wooden leg. ⌧ *Millmount Museum,* ☎ *041/33097.* ⌑ *£2.50.* ⊙ *Tues.–Sat. 10–5:30, Sun. 2:30–5:30.*

En Route   From Drogheda's center, follow R167 north along the northern bank of the River Boyne for 11 km (7 mi) to **Baltray,** which still closely re-

sembles an 18th-century Irish fishing village. From here, continue
north another 8 km (5 mi) to the fishing village of **Clogherhead.** Take
a walk above the local harbor to the heights of Clogher Head for outstanding views north to the Mountains of Mourne (☞ Chapter 8) and
south to Skerries.

Dining and Lodging

$$ ✕ **Buttergate.** Traditional Irish dishes are served at lunch and dinner,
while tasty "light bites" are available throughout the day. If plans to
extend the small conservatory go forward, the splendid view over the
town and the River Boyne will make this one a must-visit while you're
in Drogheda. It's next to the Millmount Museum. ⊠ *Millmount,* ☎
041/34759. MC, V.

$$ ✕▣ **Boyne Valley Hotel and Country Club.** Once owned by a Drogheda
brewing family, this 19th-century mansion sits on 16 acres and is ap-
proached via a 1-km (½-mi) drive. Bedrooms in the main house have
recently been renovated; the newer wing of the hotel has double rooms,
all with contemporary furnishings. A large conservatory houses a bar
and overlooks the grounds, while a large hall is decorated with antiques
and comfy chairs. The Cellar Restaurant specializes in fresh fish. ⊠
Dublin Rd., Drogheda, Co. Louth, ☎ *041/37737,* ℻ *041/39188. 37
rooms with bath. Restaurant, bar, indoor pool, hot tub, sauna, steam
room, 18-hole golf course, 2 tennis courts, health club. AE, DC, MC,
V.*

Mellifont Abbey

❾ *11 km (7 mi) north of Newgrange on N2, 8 km (5 mi) west of Drogheda
on R168.*

On the eastern bank of the River Mattock, which creates a natural border between Counties Meath and Louth here, lie the remains of Mellifont Abbey, the first Cistercian monastery in Ireland. Founded in 1142
by St. Malachy, Archbishop of Armagh, it was inspired by the formal
structure around a central courtyard of St. Bernard of Clairvaux's
monastery, which St. Malachy had visited. Among the substantial
ruins are the two-story chapter house, built in 12th-century English-
Norman style and once a daily meeting place for the monks; it now
houses a collection of medieval glazed tiles. Four walls of the 13th-
century octagonal lavabo, or washing place, still stand, as do some arches
from the Romanesque cloister. At its peak Mellifont presided over almost 40 other Cistercian monasteries throughout Ireland, but all were
suppressed by Henry VIII in 1539 after his break with the Catholic
Church. Adjacent to the car park is a small **architectural museum** depicting the history of the abbey and the craftsmanship that went into
its construction. ⊠ *Mellifont Abbey, Collon,* ☎ *041/26459.* ▣ *£1.50.
☉ May–mid-June and mid-Sept.–Oct., daily 10–5; mid-June–mid-
Sept., daily 9:30–6:30.*

Dining

$$$ ✕ **Forge Gallery Restaurant.** In a converted forge in Collon, north of
Slane on N2, this well-established restaurant is decorated in warm rose
and plum tones and antique furnishings, while an old fireplace throws
comforting warmth and light. The cuisine mixes French Provençale with
a strong hint of traditional Irish cooking. Two popular specialties are
salmon and crab in phyllo pastry and prawns and scallops in a cream
and garlic sauce. Be sure to try one of the seasonal homemade soups.
Paintings in the reception area, done by local artists, are for sale. ⊠
Collon, ☎ *041/26272. Reservations essential on weekends. AE, DC,
MC, V. Closed Sun.–Mon. and mid-Jan.–Jan. 31.*

Monasterboice

⑩ *8 km (5 mi) north of Drogheda on N1, 17 km (11 mi) northeast of Slane on N51.*

Ireland has more carved-stone high crosses than any other European country, and an outstanding collection is in the small, secluded village of Monasterboice. Dated to 923 AD, the **Muireadach Cross** stands nearly 20 ft high and is considered to be the best-preserved example of a high cross anywhere in Ireland. Its elaborate panels depict biblical scenes, including Cain slaying Abel, David and Goliath, and a centerpiece of the Last Judgment. (Figurative scenes are not a characteristic of earlier high crosses, such as those found in Ahenny, County Clare, which are elaborately ornamented but without figures.) From the adjacent, 110-ft-high **round tower,** the extent of the former monastic settlement at Monasterboice is apparent. The key to the tower door is held at the nearby gate lodge.

Ardee

⑪ *14½ km (9 mi) north of Monasterboice on N2.*

The market town of Ardee, formerly at the northern edge of the Pale, has a broad main street and two 13th-century castles. **Ardee Castle** (the one with square corners) was converted into a courthouse in the 19th century. **Hatch's Castle** (with rounded corners) is still a private residence and not open to the public. **St. Mary's Church of Ireland** on Main Street incorporates part of a 13th-century Carmelite church burned by Edward Bruce in early 1316.

All that remains of the **"Jumping Church"** at Kildemock, 3 km (2 mi) southeast of Ardee, are the foundations and one gable wall. Legend has it that this wall, which now sits 2½ ft inside the original foundations, jumped inward to keep out the grave of an excommunicated man who was buried within the walls of the church.

Dining

$$ ✕ **Gables House and Restaurant.** Off the Dublin–Derry road (N2), not far from the Dundalk junction, this family-run spot has traditional decor, with antique mahogany furniture, deep-burgundy velvet curtains, and oil paintings by local artists. Polished tables, silver cutlery, linen napkins, lace coasters, and gleaming leaded-crystal glasses add elegance. Expect generous portions and a French-influenced cooking style. The catch of the day is often monkfish, halibut, or sole. The Gables Medley, made up of cheesecake, profiteroles, and homemade ice cream, is a satisfying way to get a sugar rush. ⊠ *Dundalk Rd., Ardee,* ☏ *041/53789. MC, V.*

Louth

⑫ *11½ km (7 mi) north of Ardee on R171.*

St. Patrick, Ireland's patron saint, was reputed to have built his first church in the hilltop village of Louth in the 5th century and to have made St. Mochta (d. 534) the first bishop of Louth. Still standing at the center of the village is the excellently preserved **St. Mochta's House,** an oratory dating from the 11th century, which has a beautiful, steeply pitched stone roof that can be reached by a stairway. The house is freely accessible, but visitors should watch out for cattle in the surrounding field.

Inniskeen

⑬ *6½ km (4 mi) north of Louth.*

On the road from Dundalk and just over the Louth county boundary in Monaghan, Inniskeen is a small farming town that acts as a social hearth for the area's far-flung community. Patrick Kavanagh (1906–69), the area's most famous poet, is commemorated at the **Inniskeen Folk Museum,** housed in a converted church next to a round tower. Born and raised here, Kavanagh immortalized the town in his early poem "Inniskeen Road"—where as a child he spied on young lovers and their "wink and elbow language of delight"—before becoming one of Ireland's leading poets. He was brought back to the village for burial. ☎ *042/78109. ✉ Donations accepted. ☉ May–Sept., Sun. 3–6, or by appointment.*

Dundalk

⑭ *14½ km (9 mi) east of Inniskeen, 80 km (50 mi) north of Dublin on N1.*

Dundalk, the main town of County Louth (Ireland's smallest county), dates from the early Christian period, around the 7th century. The area near the town is closely connected with Cuchulainn (pronounced coo-cullen)—"a greater hero than Hercules or Achilles," as Frank McCourt, in *Angela's Ashes,* recalls his father claiming (see McCourt's memoir for his father's version of the story). Today, Dundalk is a thriving, if uninspiring, frontier town—only 9½ km (6 mi) from the Northern Ireland border—with a few fine historic buildings. On Mill Street, the **bell tower** of a Franciscan monastery with Gothic windows dates from the 13th century. The Catholic **St. Patrick's Cathedral** stands in Dundalk's town center. It was built between 1835 and 1847, when the Gothic revival was at its height, and is modeled on the 15th-century King's College Chapel (at Cambridge, England), with its buttresses and mosaics lining the chancel and the side chapel walls. The fine exterior was built in Newry granite, and the high altar and pulpit are of carved Caen stone. ✉ Town center, Dundalk. ☉ Daily 8–6.

The **Market House,** the **Town Hall,** and the **Courthouse** are other examples of the town's 19th-century heritage; the last is the most impressive of the three, built in the 1820s in a severe Greek Revival style, with Doric columns supporting the portico. The Courthouse stands north of St. Patrick's Cathedral.

The Church of Ireland's **St. Nicholas** on Market Square incorporates a 15th-century tower. The church was rebuilt in 1707 and has a large, early 19th-century transept. In the graveyard lies the tomb of Agnes Galt, sister of Robert Burns, the 18th-century Scottish poet. ✉ *Market Sq., Dundalk. ☉ During services only.*

The **Dundalk County Museum** is dedicated to preserving the history of the dying local industries, such as beer brewing, cigarette manufacturing, shoe and boot making, and railway engineering. ✉ *Joycelyn St., Dundalk,* ☎ *042/27056. ✉ £2. ☉ May–Sept., Mon.–Sat. 10:30–5:30, Sun. 2–6; Oct.–Apr., Tues.–Sat. 10:30–5:30, Sun. 2–6.*

Dining and Lodging

$$ ✕🏠 **Ballymascanlon Hotel.** On 130 acres just north of Dundalk, this converted Victorian mansion has long had a fine reputation for comfort and good cuisine. Rooms are large and furnished with reproduction period pieces. The restaurant serves Irish and French cuisine and specializes in fresh seafood entrées, such as lobster in season; vegetarian plates are also available. ✉ *Dundalk, Co. Louth,* ☎ *042/71124,*

FAX *042/71598. 75 rooms with bath. Restaurant, 2 bars, indoor pool, hot tub, sauna, steam room, 18-hole golf course, 2 tennis courts, health club. AE, DC, MC, V.*

OFF THE
BEATEN PATH **ARDGILLAN DEMESNE –** Across the Louth border in County Dublin, 18 km (13 mi) south of Dundalk, Ardgillan Demesne is one of the prettiest parks along the coast. Its 194 acres consist of rolling pastures, mixed woodland, and gardens overlooking the Bay of Drogheda, with splendid views of the coastline. The castle was built in 1738 for the Taylor family, one of the principal landowners of the northeast, and consists of two stories over a basement that extends out under the south lawns. The ground-floor rooms are decorated in Georgian and Victorian styles; the first-floor rooms are home to a permanent display of 17th-century maps and host an annual program of exhibitions. ✉ *Balbriggan,* ☎ *01/849-2212.* 🎫 *£2.75.* ☉ *Apr.–June and Sept., Tues.–Sun. 11–6; Oct.–Mar., Tues.–Sun. 11–4:30.*

Cooley Peninsula Drive

⑮ *Beginning in Dundalk, 80 km (50 mi) north of Dublin, 35 km (22 mi) north of Drogheda.*

If you have a car and three or four free hours, the scenic drive around the Cooley Peninsula has some of the finest views of the east coast of Ireland. This is a 64-km (40-mi) round-trip beginning and ending in Dundalk. Beyond the Carlingford Lough on the north side of the peninsula, the Mountains of Mourne rise in the distance. From **Gyles Quay,** a small coastal village with a clean, safe beach, you'll have excellent views southward along the County Louth coast to Clogher Head. A road winds east around the Cooley Peninsula to **Greenore,** a town built in Victorian times as a ferryboat terminal. Today it has become a port for container traffic.

Carlingford

⑯ *6½ km (4 mi) east of Omeath on R173.*

The small, medieval fishing town of Carlingford still has some striking thatched cottages, but what makes it particularly attractive is its natural setting. The mountains of the Cooley Peninsula back right up to the town, the Carlingford Lough lies at its feet, and the Mountains of Mourne rise only 5 km (3 mi) away across the lough.

A massive, 13th-century fortress that rises up over the entrance to Carlingford Lough, **King John's Castle** has an unusual feature: Its west gateway is only wide enough to admit one horseman. At present, of the historic buildings in the town, only the castle is freely accessible to the public. Other remnants from the area's medieval days include a tower from the town wall and one of its gates, which later became the town hall; the 15th-century **Mint Tower House,** with mullioned windows; and **Taaffe's Castle,** a 16th-century fortified town house.

Omeath

⑰ *6½ km (4 mi) northwest of Carlingford on R173.*

The northernmost town on Cooley Peninsula, Omeath was until recently the last main Gaeltacht (Irish-speaking) village in this part of Ireland (most extant Gaeltacht villages are in the Southwest and the West). On the eastern side of the village, you'll find open-air **stations of the cross** at the monastery of the Rosminian Fathers. Jaunting cars (traps pulled by ponies) take visitors to the site from the quayside, which has stalls selling all kinds of shellfish from the nearby lough, including oysters and mussels. A ferry service runs from the quay to Warrenpoint, across the lough in Northern Ireland.

A narrow road climbs the mountains behind Omeath. As you climb higher, the views become ever more spectacular, stretching over the Mountains of Mourne in the north and as far south as Skerries, 32 km (20 mi) north of Dublin. This narrow road leads back to Dundalk.

COUNTY WICKLOW'S COAST AND MOUNTAINS

Make your way to the fourth or fifth story of almost any building in Dublin that faces south and you'll see off in the distance—though amazingly not *that* far off in the distance—the green, smooth hills of the Dublin and Wicklow mountains. On a clear day the mountains are even visible from some streets in and around the city center. If your idea of solace is green hills (and if you're blessed with blue sky), and your visit to Ireland is otherwise limited to Dublin, County Wicklow—or Cill Mhantain, as it is known in Irish—should be on your itinerary.

Not that the secret isn't out: Rugged and mountainous with dark, wooded forests, Central Wicklow is known as the "garden of Ireland" and is a popular picnic area with Dubliners. Set with some of Ireland's grandest 18th-century mansions, it also cradles one of the country's earliest Christian retreats: Glendalough. Nestled in a valley of dense woods and placid lakes, Glendalough and environs can seem (at least during the off-season) practically untouched since their heyday 1,000 years ago. The same granite mountains that have protected Glendalough all these years run into the sea along the east coast, which is home to several popular sandy beaches. Our tour takes you from Dublin down to Arklow, sticking to the east side of the Wicklow Mountains. For the few Wicklow sights on the western side of the mountains, ☞ the County Kildare and West Wicklow tour, *below*. A quick note about getting here: It takes stamina to extract yourself from the unmarked maze of the Dublin exurbs (your best bet is to take N11, which becomes M11, and then again N11), but once you've accomplished that feat, this gorgeous, mysterious terrain awaits.

Bray

⓲ *22 km (14 mi) south of Dublin on N11, 8 km (5 mi) east of Enniskerry on R755.*

One of Ireland's oldest seaside resorts, Bray is a trim village known for its dilapidated summer cottages and sand-and-shingle beach, which stretches 2 km (1 mi). When the trains first arrived from Dublin in 1854, Bray became the number one spot for urban vacationers and subsequently took on the appearance of an English oceanfront town. When the weather is fair, some Dubliners still flock to the faded glory of Bray's boardwalk to push baby carriages and soak up the sun. It's the terminus of the DART train from Dublin, so it's easy to get here without a car. In Bray's old courthouse on Lower Main Street, opposite the Royal Hotel, the **heritage center** in the town hall houses many artifacts from Bray's history, including old photographs and household items. ☒ *Bray,* ☎ *01/286–6796.* 🎟 *Free.* ☉ *May–Sept., weekdays 9–5, Sat. 10–4; Oct.–Apr., weekdays 9:30–1 and 2–4:30, Sat. 10–4.*

Bray Head, a rocky outcrop that juts out over the Irish sea, dominates the town. The steep 9-km (5 ½-mi) cliff trail has great views of the town, sea, and Sugar Loaf mountain to the south. The walk begins at the end of the promenade. The smuggler's cave, Bray Hole, lies at the foot of the Head.

One Martello Terrace (☎ 01/286–8407), at the harbor, is Bray's most famous address. James Joyce (1882–1941) lived here between 1887 and 1891 and used the house as the setting for the Christmas dinner in *A Portrait of the Artist as a Young Man* (☞ Close-Up: ReJoyce! A Walk through James Joyce's Dublin and *Ulysses in* Chapter 1). Today the house is privately owned by an Irish Teachta Dála (member of Parliament, informally known as a "TD"). The phone number we list rings into her constituency office, and someone there should be able to help scholars and devoteés arrange a visit; they recommend calling on Thursday 10 AM–1 PM. Although the residence has been renovated, the dining room portrayed in Joyce's novel still maintains the spirit of his time.

Killruddery House and Gardens are immediately off the Bray–Greystones road just south of Bray. The rare, 17th-century gardens are precisely arranged, with fine beech hedges, Victorian statuary, and a parterre of lavender and roses. The estate, which still belongs to the Earl of Meath, also features a Crystal Palace conservatory. ⊠ *Killruddery,* ☎ *01/286–2777.* ⊡ *£2.* ⊙ *Gardens Apr.–Sept., daily 1–5; house May–June and Sept., daily 1–5; by appointment at other times.*

Dining

$$$ ✕ **Tree of Idleness.** This Greek-Cypriot restaurant, a 10-minute walk
★ from Bray's DART train station, is a pleasant dining spot on the ground floor of a Victorian house along the seafront. It specializes in classic dishes and tasty, hearty portions. The roast suckling pig with caramelized apples is highly recommended. The extensive wine list includes Greek and Cypriot house wines. ⊠ *Seafront,* ☎ *01/286–3498. AE, MC, V. Closed Mon., last wk in Aug., and first wk in Sept. No lunch.*

$ ✕ **Poppies Country Cooking.** Following the success of their remark-
★ able restaurant in Enniskerry (☞ Powerscourt House, Gardens, and Waterfall, *below*), the owners of Poppies decided to open a second restaurant with the same name in Greystones, an old-fashioned seaside resort only a couple of miles south of Bray along the coast. The ceilings are high, the space is airy and bright, and the food is absolutely delicious. If you can, dine here in summer, when you can avail yourself of the sun-drenched garden terrace. ⊠ *1 Trafalgar Sq., Greystones,* ☎ *01/287–4228. No credit cards.*

Outdoor Activities and Sports

The mountains bordering Bray to the south are laced with uncrowded hiking and mountain-bike trails. One of the best is a well-marked path that leads from the beach to the 10-ft-tall cross that crowns the spiny peak of **Bray Head,** which rises 791 ft from the sea. The semidifficult, one-hour climb affords stunning views of Wicklow Town and Dublin Bay.

Powerscourt House, Gardens, and Waterfall

☝ ⑲ *25 km (16 mi) south of Dublin on R117, 32 km (20 mi) north of Glendalough on R755.*

Within the shadow of the famous Sugar Loaf mountain and easily one of the prettiest villages in all of Ireland, **Enniskerry** is built around a sloping central triangular square and surrounded by the wooded Wicklow Mountains. The main reason to visit the area around Enniskerry is the **Powerscourt Estate.** The grounds were originally granted to Sir Richard Wingfield, the first viscount of Powerscourt, by King James I of England in 1609. Richard Castle, the architect of Russborough

House (☞ *below*), designed Powerscourt House in a grand Palladian style, and it was constructed between 1731 and 1743. Alas, the house was gutted in a fire in 1974 immediately following a long period of restoration by the Slazenger family. It's now undergoing an extensive re-restoration; the original ballroom on the first floor— once "the grandest room in any Irish house," according to historian Desmond Guinness—is the only room that gives a sense of the house's former life.

Powerscourt Gardens, considered among the finest in Europe, were first laid out from 1745 to 1767 following the completion of the house and then were radically redesigned in the Victorian style from 1843 to 1875. The redesign was the work of the eccentric, boozy Daniel Robertson, who liked to be tootled around the gardens-in-progress in a wheelbarrow while nipping at his bottle of sherry. He was inspired by the Villa Butera in Sicily, and the gardens thus comprise sweeping terraces, antique sculptures, and a circular pond and fountain flanked by winged horses. There is a celebrated view of the Italianate patterned ramps, lawns, and pond across the beautiful, heavily wooded Dargle Valley, which stairsteps to the horizon and the noble profile of Sugar Loaf mountain. The grounds include many specimen trees (plants grown for exhibition), an avenue of monkey puzzles, a parterre of brightly colored summer flowers, and a Japanese garden. The kitchen gardens, with their modest rows of flowers, are a striking antidote to the classical formality of the main sections. The gardens also offer a self-serve restaurant, crafts center, garden center, and a children's play area. (Enniskerry can also be reached directly from Dublin by taking the No. 44 bus from the Dublin quays area.) ⊠ *Enniskerry,* ☎ *01/286-7676.* 🕮 *Mar.–Oct. £5, Nov.–Feb. £3.50.* ☉ *Mar.–Oct., daily 9:30–5:30; Nov.–Feb., daily 9:30–dusk.*

One of the most inspiring sights to the writers and artists of the Romantic generation, the 400-ft **Powerscourt Waterfall,** 5 km (3 mi) south of the gardens (☞ *above*), is the highest in the British Isles. ⊠ *Enniskerry.* 🕮 *£2.* ☉ *Mar.–Oct., daily 9:30–7; Nov.–Feb., daily 10:30–dusk. Closed 2 wks before Christmas.*

Dining

$ ✕ **Poppies Country Cooking.** Like something out of a fairy tale, this
★ charming café is the perfect spot for breakfast, lunch, or late-afternoon tea (it's open until 7 on weekdays, 8 on weekends). With only a dozen or so tables, it's a cozy place, with a low, pine-paneled ceiling; floral wallpaper and matching cloth lamp shades; and pine farmhouse furniture. Potato cakes, shepherd's pie, lasagna, vegetarian quiche, a variety of house salads (you can order a sampler plate), and the day's soup are the usual fare. The homemade desserts—caramel squares, lemon meringue pie, pavlova—are terrific. You'll be tempted to sit here for hours writing postcards and daydreaming about what it would be like to be a regular. ⊠ *The Square, Enniskerry,* ☎ *01/282–8869. No credit cards.*

Roundwood

② *18 km (13 mi) south of Enniskerry on R755.*

At 800 ft above sea level and set amid spectacular scenery, Roundwood is the highest village in Ireland (not really such a big deal). The Sunday-afternoon market held in the village hall, where cakes, jams, and other homemade goods are sold, livens up what is otherwise a sleepy place. From the broad main street, by the Roundwood Inn (☞ *Dining, below*), a minor road leads west for 8 km (5 mi) to two lakes, **Lough Dan** and **Lough Tay,** lying deep between forested mountains like Norwegian fjords.

Dining

$$$ ✕ **Roundwood Inn.** This 17th-century inn, furnished in a traditional
★ style, with wooden floors, dark furniture, and diamond-shape windows,
is best known for good, reasonably priced bar food ($) eaten at sturdy
tables beside an open fire. The restaurant offers a combination of
Continental and Irish cuisines, reflecting the traditions of the German
proprietor, Jurgen Schwalm, and his Irish wife, Aine. The separate bar
and lounge also serve an excellent menu that includes a succulent
seafood platter of salmon, oysters, lobster, and shrimp. ✉ *Roundwood,*
☎ *01/281–8107. Reservations essential for restaurant. AE, MC, V.*
Restaurant closed Sun. dinner and Mon. except public holidays.

Glendalough

★ ㉑ *54 km (34 mi) south of Dublin on R117 and R755.*

One of Ireland's premier monastic sites, Glendalough is nestled in a
lush, quiet valley deep in the rugged Wicklow Mountains. Set around
two lakes, evergreen and deciduous trees, and acres of windswept
heather, Glendalough flourished as a monastic center from the 6th cen-
tury until 1398, when English soldiers plundered the site, leaving the
ruins that you see today. (The monastery survived earlier 9th- and 10th-
century Viking attacks.) Glendalough's founder was St. Kevin (Co-
emghein, or "fair begotten" in Irish), a descendant of the royal house
of Leinster, who renounced the world and came here to live as a her-
mit before opening the monastery in 550. Note that in high season,
hordes of visitors to Glendalough can make it difficult to appreciate
the quiet solitude that brought Kevin to this valley. The **visitor center**
is a good place to orient yourself and pick up a useful pamphlet. Many
of the ruins are clumped together beyond the visitor center, but some
of the oldest surround the Upper Lake, where signed paths direct you
through spectacular scenery absent of crowds. Most ruins are open all
day and are freely accessible.

Probably the oldest building on the site, presumed to date from St.
Kevin's time, is the **Teampaill na Skellig** (Church of the Oratory), on the
south shore of the **Upper Lake.** A little to the east is **St. Kevin's Bed,** a
tiny cave in the rock face, about 30 ft above the level of the lake, where
St. Kevin lived his hermit's existence. It is not easily accessible; you ap-
proach the cave by boat, but climbing the cliff to the cave can be dan-
gerous and is not recommended. At the southeast corner of the Upper
Lake is **Reefert Church,** also dating from the 11th century, whose ruins
consist of a nave and a chancel. The saint also lived in the adjoining, ru-
ined beehive hut with five crosses, which marked the original boundary
of the monastery. There's a superb view of the valley from here.

The ruins by the edge of the **Lower Lake** are the most important of
those at Glendalough. The **gateway,** beside the Glendalough Hotel, is
the only surviving entrance to an ancient monastic site anywhere in
Ireland. An extensive graveyard lies within, with hundreds of elabo-
rately decorated crosses, as well as a perfectly preserved, six-story
round tower. Built in the 11th or 12th century, it stands 100 ft high,
with an entrance 25 ft above ground level.

The largest building at Glendalough is the substantially intact, 7th- to
9th-century **cathedral,** where you'll find the nave (small for a large church,
only 30 ft wide by 50 ft long), chancel, and ornamental oolite lime-
stone window, which may have been imported from England. South
of the cathedral is the 11-ft-high Celtic **St. Kevin's Cross.** Made of gran-
ite, it is the best-preserved such cross on the site. **St. Kevin's Church**
is an early, barrel-vaulted oratory with a high-pitched stone roof.

A note about getting here directly from Dublin: You can take the **St. Kevin's** bus service (☞ Getting Around *in* Dublin Environs A to Z, *below*). Or, if you're driving from Dublin, head south from Christ Church Cathedral, staying on the main road until you reach Rathfarnham village. From there follow R115, which leads you to Glencree—a beautiful stone village set in a valley—and then on to the Sally Gap. The extra time this takes (versus the main N11/M11/N11) is well worth it, for R115 is one of Ireland's most spectacularly scenic routes; it passes through eye-popping landscape, including awesome, austere mountaintop passes where, as far as the eye can see, you *don't* see anything but mountains. Don't drive this route if you're in a hurry, and don't look for a lot of signage—just concentrate on the glorious views. ⊠ *Glendalough,* ☎ *0404/45325.* 🎫 *£2.* ☉ *Mar.–May and Sept.–Oct., daily 9:30–6; June–Aug., daily 9–6:30; Nov.–Feb., daily 9:30–5; last admission 15 mins before closing.*

Dining and Lodging

$$ ✕🏨 **Glendalough Hotel.** Purists object to how close this old-fashioned, early-19th-century hotel lies to the ruins at Glendalough, but to others it's a convenience. How close is it? Some of the bedrooms, decorated in quiet, pastel colors, overlook the monastery and the wooded mountain scenery; the burble of running water from the Glendassan River audibly enhances the experience. The restaurant also has views of the grounds. The menu is simple but portions are hearty, and the pub is the only one for miles around. ⊠ *Glendalough, Co. Wicklow,* ☎ *0404/45135,* 🖷 *0404/45142. 44 rooms with bath. Restaurant, bar, fishing. AE, DC, MC, V. Closed second wk in Dec. and Jan.*

Mount Usher Gardens

㉒ *14½ km (9 mi) southeast of Roundwood on R764.*

Settled into more than 20 acres on the banks of the River Vartry, Mount Usher Gardens were first laid out in 1868 by Edward Walpole, who owned a Dublin textile firm. Succeeding generations of the Walpole family further planted and maintained the grounds, which today have more than 5,000 species. Eucalypti, azaleas, camellias, and rhododendrons make the most of the riverside locale. Water is visible from nearly every place in the gardens, while bridges span the river. A cluster of crafts shops, including a pottery workshop, and a bookstore and self-service restaurant stand at the entrance. The twin villages of Ashford and Rathnew are to the south and east, and Newtownmountkennedy is to the north. ⊠ *Ashford,* ☎ *0404/40205.* 🎫 *£3.50.* ☉ *Mar. 17–Oct., daily 10:30–6.*

Dining and Lodging

$$$$ ✕🏨 **Tinakilly House.** William and Bee Power have lovingly restored this Victorian-Italianate mansion, built in the 1870s by Captain Robert Halpin (1836–94), who laid the first transatlantic cable lines as captain of *The Great Eastern,* then the biggest ship in the world. (He's honored with a statue in Wicklow Town [☞ *below*].) The lobby has mementos of Captain Halpin and his nautical exploits, including paintings and ship models; impeccable Victorian antiques fill the house. Some bedrooms have four-poster beds, Jacuzzis, sitting areas, and views of the Wicklow landscape, the Irish Sea, or the lovely gardens on the 7-acre grounds. The dining room spotlights French-influenced Irish cuisine, with fresh vegetables from the garden; brown and fruit breads are baked daily. ⊠ *Rathnew, Co. Wicklow,* ☎ *0404/ 69274,* 🖷 *0404/67806. 41 rooms with bath. Restaurant, bar, tennis court. AE, DC, MC, V.*

$$ ✕🏠 **Hunter's Hotel.** One of Ireland's oldest coaching inns, first opened in the early 1700s, sits in a lovely rural setting on the banks of the River Vartry, only 1 km (½ mi) east of Rathnew Village. Period prints, beams, and antiques lend an old-world feel enjoyed by both locals and guests. All bedrooms have delicate flower-print wallpaper and are superbly furnished with Victorian-style pieces. There is a fine restaurant, and in the summer, afternoon tea with homemade scones and jams is served in the magnificent garden that stretches down to the river. ✉ *Rathnew, Co. Wicklow,* ☎ *0404/40106,* 🖷 *0404/40338. 16 rooms with bath. Restaurant, bar. AE, DC, MC, V.*

Wicklow Town

❷❸ *26 km (16 mi) east of Glendalough on R763, 51 km (32 mi) south of Dublin on N11.*

At the entrance to the attractive, tree-lined Main Street of Wicklow Town—its name, from the Danish *wyking alo,* means "Viking meadow"—lie the extensive ruins of a 13th-century Franciscan friary. The **friary** was closed down during the 16th-century dissolution of the monasteries in the area, but its ruins give a sense of Wicklow's stormy past, which began with the unwelcome reception given to St. Patrick on his arrival in 432 AD; inquire at the nearby priest's house (✉ Main St., ☎ 0404/67196) to view the ruins. The old town jail, just above Market Square, is currently being converted into a major **heritage center** (✉ Wicklow Town, ☎ 0404/67324, ext. 126), where visitors can trace their genealogical roots in the area.

The **harbor** is Wicklow Town's most appealing area. Take Harbour Road down to the pier; a bridge across the River Vartry leads to a second, smaller pier, at the northern end of the harbor. From this end, follow the shingle beach, which stretches for 5 km (3 mi); behind the beach is the broad Lough, a lagoon noted for its wildfowl. Immediately south of the harbor, perched on a promontory that has good views of the Wicklow coastline, is the ruin of the **Black Castle.** This structure was built in 1169 by Maurice Fitzgerald, an Anglo-Norman lord who arrived with the English invasion of Ireland. The ruins (freely accessible) extend over a large area; with some difficulty, you can climb down to the water's edge.

Between one bank of the River Vartry and the road to Dublin stands the Protestant **St. Lavinius Church,** which incorporates a variety of earlier elements and unusual details: a Romanesque door, 12th-century stonework, fine pews, and an atmospheric graveyard. The church is topped off by a copper, onion-shape cupola, added as an afterthought in 1771. ✉ *Wicklow Town.* 🎫 *Free.* ☼ *Daily 10–6.*

Dining and Lodging

$ ✕ **Pizza del Forno.** With its red-and-white-check tablecloths, low lighting, and pizza oven blazing away, this is a great vantage point for people-watching on Main Street. Inexpensive pizzas, pasta, steaks, and vegetarian dishes appeal to a wide array of appetites. ✉ *Main St., Wicklow Town, Co. Wicklow,* ☎ *0404/67075. AE, MC, V. Closed Christmas–mid-Feb.*

$$ ✕🏠 **Old Rectory Country House.** Once a 19th-century rectory, this small,
★ charming Greek Revival country house stands on a hillside just off the main road from Dublin on the approach to Wicklow Town. Owners Paul and Linda Saunders have a splendid touch. Black-and-white marble fireplaces, bright colors, original oil paintings, and antique and contemporary furniture decorate the house; the light, spacious guest rooms are done in white and pastel shades with antique Victorian and coun-

try-house furniture. Linda's "Green Cuisine" makes use of fresh ingredients; don't miss her salads and desserts, often made or garnished with edible flowers and herbs. ⊠ *Wicklow Town, Co. Wicklow,* ☎ *0404/67048,* FAX *0404/69181. 8 rooms with bath. Restaurant. AE, MC, V. Closed Jan.–Feb.*

Avondale Forest Park and House

㉔ *17 km (11 mi) southwest of Wicklow Town on R752.*

Outside the quaint village of Rathdrum, on the west bank of the Avondale River, the 523-acre **Avondale Forest Park** was, in 1904, the first forest in Ireland to be taken over by the state. There's a 5½-km (3½-mi) walk along the river, as well as pine and exotic-tree trails. **Avondale House,** on the grounds of the park, resonates with Irish history. The house was the birthplace and lifelong home of Charles Stewart Parnell (1846–91), "The Uncrowned King of Ireland," the country's leading politician of the 19th century and a wildly popular campaigner for democracy and land reform. His career clattered to a halt after he fell in love with a married woman, Kitty O'Shea. When her husband instituted divorce proceedings in 1890, the revelation of Parnell's affair during court hearings ruined his political career, and he died a year later under the strain of the controversy. (In Joyce's *A Portrait of the Artist as a Young Man,* the controversy is dramatized as a keenly contested argument during the Daedalus family dinner.) The house, built in 1779, was acquired by John Parnell, great-grandfather of Charles Stewart, in 1795. It has been flawlessly restored, with the reception and dining rooms on the ground floor filled with Parnell memorabilia, including some of his love letters to Kitty O'Shea and political cartoons portraying his efforts to secure home rule for Ireland. ☎ *0404/46111.* 🎫 *£3, parking £2.* ☉ *May–Sept., daily 10–6; Oct.–Apr., daily 11–5.*

Avoca

㉕ *6½ km (4 mi) south of Avondale Forest Park on R754.*

The small hamlet of Avoca is set amid heavily forested hills at the confluence of the Rivers Avonbeg and Avonmore. Beneath a riverside tree here, the Irish Romantic poet Thomas Moore (1779–1852) composed his 1807 poem "The Meeting of the Waters." There are some pleasant forest walks nearby, with scenic views of the valley. The oldest handweaving mill in Ireland, **Avoca Handweavers,** offers a short tour of the mill, which is still in operation. The store sells a wide selection of its own superb fabrics and woven and knit apparel, some of which is difficult to find elsewhere. ☎ *0402/35105.* 🎫 *Free.* ☉ *Shop daily 9:30–5:30, mill weekdays 8–4:30.*

Arklow

㉖ *11 km (7 mi) south of Avoca on R754*

Arklow's long, bustling main street winds its way down a gently sloping hill. Bread lovers and those with a sweet tooth should stop in at **Stone Oven Bakery** (⊠ 65 Lower Main St., ☎ 0402/39418) at the bottom of the hill. The German-born baker, Egon Friedrich, turns out sourdough breads and delicious sweet treats, including hazelnut-chocolate triangles; the shop can prepare simple cheese and bread sandwiches to go or to eat in the tiny, slightly haphazard café. Down on the waterfront at the **Arklow Pottery Factory** (well signed throughout the town), you can take guided tours and shop for crafts. ☎ *0402/32401.* ☉ *Weekdays 9–5, weekends 10–5.*

The **Maritime Museum,** in the public library building near the railway station, traces Arklow's distinguished seafaring tradition; exhibits include old photographs, some original boats, and the logs of long-dead captains. To get here, take a left at St. Peter's Church as you're heading out of town in the direction of Gorey and Wexford. ⊠ *St. Mary's Rd.,* ☎ *0402/32868.* ⌂ *£2.50.* ⊙ *May–Sept., Mon.–Sat. 10–1 and 2–5; Oct.–Apr., weekdays 10–1 and 2–5.*

Immediately north of Arklow is **Brittas Bay,** an area of white sand, quiet coves, and rolling dunes. It is popular in summer with vacationing Dubliners and is perfect for adventurous kids.

COUNTY KILDARE AND WEST WICKLOW

Horse racing is a passion in Ireland—you'll notice every little town has its betting shop—and County Kildare is the country's horse capital. Nestled between the basins of the River Liffey to the north and the River Barrow to the east, its gently sloping hills and grass-filled plains are perfect for breeding and racing Thoroughbreds. For first-time visitors, the National Stud just outside Naas offers a fascinating glimpse into the world of horse breeding. The Japanese Gardens, adjacent to the National Stud, are among Europe's finest, while Castletown House, in Celbridge to the north, is one of Ireland's foremost Georgian treasures. Our tour makes Dublin your starting point, but you may want to pick up this leg from Glendalough (☞ *above*). The spectacular drive across the Wicklow Gap, from Glendalough to Hollywood, makes for a glorious entrance into Kildare. One last note: Consult Chapter 4 if you make it as far south as Castledermot (the southernmost point in this tour), since Carlow and environs are only 10 km (6 mi) farther south.

OFF THE BEATEN PATH

MAYNOOTH – Before heading to Castletown House, make a quick detour slightly farther west to Maynooth, a tiny Georgian town 24 km (15 mi) west of Dublin. Here you'll find **St. Patrick's College,** once exclusively a center for the training of Catholic priests and now also one of Ireland's most important lay universities. It was established in 1795 on the site of an earlier college founded by the Earl of Kildare in the 16th century, which was suppressed by Henry VIII. The visitor center chronicles the college's history and the history of the Catholic Church in Ireland. The university gardens are worth a stroll; choose between the Path of Saints and the Path of Sinners. ☎ *01/628–5222.* ⊙ *May–Sept., Mon.–Sat. 11–5, Sun. 2–6; guided tours every hr.*

At the entrance to St. Patrick's College lie the ruins of **Maynooth Castle,** the ancient seat of the Fitzgerald family. The Fitzgeralds' fortunes changed for the worse when they led the failed rebellion of 1536, and the castle was finally dismantled in Cromwellian times. The castle keep, the oldest part, dates from the 13th century, and the keep and the great hall are still in reasonable condition. The key can be obtained from Mrs. Saults at 9 Parson Street. ⌂ *Free.*

Castletown House

㉗ *20 km (13 mi) southwest of Dublin on N7, 6½ km (4 mi) south of Maynooth.*

In the early 18th century, a revival of the architectural style of Andrea Palladio (1508–80) swept through England, where architects built dozens of houses reinterpreting a style already 150 years old. The rage swept through Ireland among the Anglo-Irish aristocracy (☞ *also* Russborough House, *below* for another fine example nearby, and for references to others). Arguably the largest and finest example of an Irish Palladian-style house is Castletown, begun in 1722 for William Conolly (1662–1729), the Speaker of the Irish House of Commons and then the country's wealthiest man (he made his fortune in forfeited estates after the Battle of the Boyne). Conolly first hired the Italian architect Alessandro Galilei, who designed the facade of the main block; in 1724, the young Irish architect Sir Edward Lovett Pearce completed the house by adding the colonnades and side pavilions. Conolly's death brought construction to a halt; it wasn't until his great-nephew, Thomas Conolly, and his wife, Lady Louisa (née Lennox), took up residence in 1758 that work on the house picked up again. Throughout the 1760s and '70s, Lady Louisa oversaw the alteration and redecoration of the house. Today Castletown is the largest private house in the country, and it underwent major restorations through 1999. It's also the headquarters of the Irish Georgian Society and contains many examples of its original furniture.

Inside, there are many splendid features, including hall plasterwork by the Lafranchini brothers, Swiss-Italian craftsmen who were active in Dublin in the mid-18th century. The ground-floor **Print Room** is the only 18th-century example in Ireland of this elegant fad. Like oversize postage stamps in a giant album, black-and-white prints were glued to the walls by fashionable young women who unwittingly anticipated the universal impulse among teenagers to cover their bedroom walls with posters. Upstairs at the rear of the house, the **Long Gallery**, almost 80 ft by 23 ft, is the most notable of the public rooms. In the 1770s it was redecorated in Pompeian style and with three Venetian Murano glass chandeliers. The poet Robert Lowell lived here for a time in the 1960s. The house was rescued in 1967 by Desmond Guinness (of the brewing family), then the president of the Irish Georgian Society, and it is now the property of the Irish state. ⊠ *Celbridge, Co. Kildare,* ☎ *01/628–8252.* 🖾 *£2.50.* ⊙ *Apr.–Sept., weekdays 10–6, Sat. 11–6, Sun. 2–6; Oct., Mon.–Sat. 10–5, Sun. 2–5; Nov.–Mar., Sun. 2–5.*

Dining and Lodging

$$$$ ✕🏨 **Moyglare Manor.** Set on 16 pastoral acres dotted with sheep and cows, reached via a ⅘-km (½-mi), tree-lined drive, this majestic Georgian manor house is 29 km (18 mi) west of Dublin. Owner Nora Devlin has exuberantly decorated the house with her renowned antiques collection; fresh flowers further enliven the decor. Velvet chairs, oil paintings, and thickly draped windows are in the drawing room, while the grand bedrooms have four-poster canopy beds, roomy wardrobes, marble fireplaces, and comfortable, chintz-covered armchairs. Lamp-shaded wall sconces add a romantic touch to the formal dining room, where a traditional French menu is served. Rich desserts match the spirit of the house. ⊠ *Maynooth, Co. Kildare,* ☎ *01/628–6351,* 🖾 *01/628–5405. 17 rooms with bath. Restaurant, 2 bars. AE, DC, MC, V.*

Straffan

㉘ *7 km (4½) mi southwest of Celbridge on R403, 25½ km (16 mi) southwest of Dublin on N7.*

Attractively situated on the banks of the River Liffey, Straffan is home to the Kildare Hotel and Country Club (☞ Dining and Lodging, *below*), where Arnold Palmer designed the K Club, one of Ireland's most renowned 18-hole golf courses (☞ Chapter 9). The only one of its kind in Ireland, the **Straffan Butterfly Farm** has a tropical house with exotic plants, butterflies, and moths. Mounted and framed butterflies are available for sale. ⊠ *Co. Kildare,* ☎ *01/627–1109.* 🖾 *£2.50.* ☉ *May–July, daily noon–5:30.*

The **Steam Museum** covers the history of Irish steam engines, handsome machines used in Ireland industrially as well as agriculturally, in such operations as churning butter and threshing corn. There's also a collection of model locomotives. Engineers are present on "live steam days"; phone in advance to confirm. ⊠ *Lodge Park,* ☎ *01/627–3155.* 🖾 *Live steam days £4, other times £3.* ☉ *Easter–May and Sept., Tues.–Sun. 2–6; June–Aug., Mon.–Sat. 2–6, Sun. 2:30–5:30.*

En Route County Kildare has two major canal systems that connect Dublin with the Rivers Shannon and Barrow and the interior Lakelands. Sixteen kilometers (10 mi) west of Straffan, **Robertstown** sits on the **Grand Canal** (the other major canal is the **Royal**, which heads to the northeast from Dublin), where you can take scenic walks and, during the summer, barge trips. Built in the early 19th century to accommodate passengers on the canal, the **Grand Canal Hotel** (☎ 045/870005) offers candlelit dinners and musical entertainment.

Dining and Lodging

$$$$ ✕🏨 **Kildare Hotel and Country Club.** Manicured gardens and the
★   renowned Arnold Palmer–designed K Club golf course (☞ Chapter 9) surround this mansard-roofed former residence built in the 1830s for Hugh Barton, an Irishman who had to flee his extensive vineyards in France after the French Revolution and then decided to create a French country mansion here in Ireland. The spacious, very comfortable guest rooms are each uniquely decorated with antiques and have large windows that overlook either the Liffey or the golf course. The rooms in the old house are highly recommended). The hotel also has a leasing agreement with several privately owned cottages on the property, which guests can rent when they're available—although most look as though they belong on a Florida golf course, not in Ireland. Chef Michel Flamme serves an unashamedly French menu—albeit with the hint of an Irish flavor—at the Byerly Turk Restaurant (named after a famous racehorse). The grounds are spectacular and include a magnificent landscaped garden and the renowned golf course, where membership is de rigueur for Ireland's business elite. ⊠ *Co. Kildare,* ☎ *01/ 627–3333,* 🅵🅰🆇 *01/601–7299. 45 rooms with bath, 20–30 apartments. 2 restaurants, 3 bars, beauty salon, indoor pool, 18-hole golf course, 4 tennis courts, horseback riding, squash, fishing. AE, DC, MC, V.*

$$$ ✕🏨 **Barberstown Castle.** With a 13th-century castle keep at one end, an Elizabethan central section, and a large Georgian country house at the other, Barberstown effortlessly blends 750 years of Irish history. Turf fires blaze in beautifully ornate fireplaces in the three sumptuously decorated lounges. Bedrooms are elegantly furnished with reproduction pieces; some have four-poster beds. The restaurant—half Georgian, half medieval (the latter part is in the ground floor of the castle keep)—serves creatively prepared fare. ⊠ *Straffan, Co. Kildare,* ☎ *01/ 628–8157,* 🅵🅰🆇 *01/627–7027. 22 rooms with bath. Restaurant, bar. AE, DC, MC, V.*

Naas

㉙ *13 km (8 mi) south of Straffan on R407, 30 km (19 mi) southwest of Dublin on N7.*

The seat of County Kildare and a thriving market town in the heartland of Irish Thoroughbred country, Naas (pronounced Nace) is full of pubs with high stools where short men (trainee jockeys) discuss the merits of their various stables. Nass has its own small racecourse, but

Punchestown Racecourse (✉ 3 km/2 mi from Naas) has a wonderful setting amid rolling plains, with the Wicklow Mountains forming a spectacular backdrop. Although horse races are held regularly here, the most popular event is the Punchestown National Hunt Festival.

Russborough House

③⓪ *16 km (10 mi) southeast of Naas on R410.*

One of the highlights of the western part of County Wicklow, Russborough House is among the finest of the Palladian-style villas built throughout Ireland by the Anglo-Irish ascendancy in the first half of the 18th century. (Castletown House [☞ *above*], Emo Court [☞ Chapter 3], and Castle Coole [☞ Chapter 8] are the other bright stars in this constellation.) In 1741, a year after Joseph Leeson inherited a vast fortune from his father, a successful Dublin brewer, he commissioned Richard Castle (architect of Leinster House [☞ Exploring Dublin *in* Chapter 1] and Powerscourt [☞ *above*]) to build this palatial house, and he worked on it until his death (after which Francis Bindon took over). They pulled out all the stops to create a confident, majestic house with a silver-gray Wicklow granite facade that extends for more than 700 ft and encompasses a seven-bay central block, off which radiate two semicircular loggias connecting the flanking wings.

Baroque exuberance reigns in the house's main rooms, especially in the lavishly ornamented plasterwork ceilings executed by the Lafranchini brothers (they also worked at Castletown House). After a long succession of owners, Russborough was bought in 1952 by Sir Alfred Beit, the nephew of the German cofounder (with Cecil Rhodes) of the De Beers diamond operation, and it now belongs to Lady Beit, his widow. In 1988, after two major robberies, the finest works in the Beits' art collection—then considered one of the finest private collections in Europe—were donated to the National Gallery of Ireland (☞ Exploring Dublin *in* Chapter 1). However, works by Gainsborough, Guardi, Reynolds, Rubens, and Murillo remain, as well as bronzes, silver, and porcelain. The views from Russborough's windows take in the foothills of the Wicklow Mountains and a small lake in front of the house; the extensive woodlands on the estate are open to visitors. ✉ *Off N81, Blessington,* ☎ *045/865239.* 🎟 *£3, upstairs bedrooms £1.* ☉ *Apr.–Oct., daily 10:30–5:30.*

Poulaphouca Reservoir

③① *33 km (21 mi) west of Glendalough on R756 and R758.*

Known locally as the **Blessington Lakes,** Poulaphouca (pronounced pool-a-*fook*-a) Reservoir is a large, meandering artificial lake that provides Dublin's water supply minutes from Russborough House. You can drive around the entire perimeter of the reservoir on minor roads; on its southern end lies Hollywood Glen, a particularly beautiful natural spot.

The small market town of **Blessington,** with its wide main street lined on both sides by tall trees and Georgian buildings, lies on the western shore of the lakes and is one of the most charming villages in the area. Founded in the late 17th century, it was once a stop on the Dublin–Waterford mail-coach service in the mid-19th century; until 1932, a quaint steam train ran from here to Dublin, along the side of the main road.

Beyond the southern tip of the Poulaphouca Reservoir, 13 km (8 mi) south of Blessington on N81, you will spot a small sign for the **Piper's**

Stones. A short walk from the road, this Bronze Age stone circle was probably used in a ritual connected with worship of the sun.

Dining and Lodging

$$$$ ✕▣ **Rathsallagh House.** Set amid 530 acres of parkland, these low-
★ slung, ivy-covered, Queen Anne stables converted to a farmhouse in 1798 await at the end of a long drive that winds through a golf course. Kay and Joe O'Flynn oversee a stellar staff and an impeccably run operation. Two drawing rooms are adorned with enveloping couches and chairs, fresh flower arrangements, large windows, and fireplaces, with lots of lamps providing ample light to read or relax by day or night. In the elegant wood-paneled dining room, sconces with silk-covered lamp shades, an open fireplace, and candles softly illuminate the beautifully set tables. Kay's outstanding haute Irish dinner menu changes daily; specialties include paupiette of herb-filled salmon with onion and chive beurre blanc. The route to the house, 49 km (31 mi) southwest of Dublin, is well signposted and is not far from where N756 meets N81, but call ahead for precise directions. ⊠ *Dunlavin, Co. Wicklow,* ☎ *045/403112,* 𝔽𝔸𝕏 *045/403343. 17 rooms with bath. Restaurant, bar, indoor pool, massage, sauna, 18-hole golf course, tennis court, croquet, meeting rooms. AE, DC, MC, V.*

Outdoor Activities and Sports

There are splendid views of the Blessington Lakes from the top of **Church Mountain,** which you reach via a vigorous walk through **Woodenbo-ley Wood,** at the southern tip of Hollywood Glen. Follow the main forest track for about 20 minutes and then take the narrow path that heads up the side of the forest to the mountaintop.

The Curragh

㉜ *8 km (5 mi) southwest of Naas on M7.*

The broad plain of the Curragh, bisected by the main N7 road, is the biggest area of common land in Ireland, encompassing about 31 square km (12 square mi) and devoted mainly to grazing. It's also Ireland's major racing center, home to **Curragh Racecourse** (☎ 045/441205), where the Irish Derby and other international horse races are run.

The **Curragh Main Barracks,** a large camp where the Irish Army trains, has a small museum. One of its prize relics is the armored car once used by Michael Collins, the former head of the Irish Army who, in December 1921, signed the Anglo-Irish Treaty designating a six-county North to remain in British hands, in exchange for complete independence for Ireland's remaining 26 counties. Collins was assassinated in 1922; his life was dramatized in Neil Jordan's 1996 film *Michael Collins.* The car can be seen with permission from the commanding officer. ☎ *045/445000; ask for the command adjutant.*

Kildare Town

㉝ *5 km (3 mi) from the Curragh on M7, 51 km (32 mi) southwest of Dublin on N7 and M7.*

Horse breeding is the basis of Kildare's thriving economy. Right off Kildare's main market square, the **Silken Thomas** (☎ 045/522232) recreates an old-world atmosphere with open fires, dark wood decor, and leaded lights; it's a good place to stop for lunch before exploring the sights here.

St. Brigid's Cathedral (Church of Ireland) is where the eponymous saint founded a religious settlement in the 5th century. The present cathedral, with its stocky tower, is a restored 13th-century structure. It was partially rebuilt about 1686, but restoration work wasn't completed for another 200 years. The stained-glass west window of the cathedral depicts three of Ireland's greatest saints: Brigid, Patrick, and Columba. ⊠ *Off Market Sq.* ☎ *Free.* ☉ *Daily 10–6.*

The 108-ft-high **round tower,** in the graveyard of St. Brigid's Cathedral, is the second highest in Ireland and dates from the 12th century. Extraordinary views across much of the Midlands await those energetic enough to climb the stairs to the top. ☎ *045/521229.* ☎ *60p.* ☉ *May–Sept., daily 10–1 and 2–5.*

❸❹ If you're a longtime horse aficionado, or just curious, the **National Stud Farm,** a main center of Ireland's racing industry, is well worth a visit. Founded in 1900 by Colonel William Hall-Walker (later Lord Wavertree), a brewing heir, and transferred to the Irish state in 1843, the Stud is home to breeding stallions who are groomed, exercised, tested, and bred within the neat white buildings, which are set around immaculately kept green lawns. Spring and early summer, when mares will have new foals, are the best times to visit. Walker believed in astrology; thus, every new foal had its "chart done," and those with unfavorable results were sold right away. He even built the stallion boxes with lantern roofs that allow the moon and stars to work their magic on the occupants. Also on the grounds, the **National Stud Horse Museum** recounts the history of horses in Ireland. Its most outstanding exhibit is the skeleton of Arkle, the Irish racehorse that won major victories in Ireland and England during the late 1960s. The museum also contains medieval evidence of horses, such as bones from 13th-century Dublin, and some early examples of equestrian equipment. ☎ *045/521617.* ☎ *£5, including entry to the Japanese Gardens.* ☉ *Mid-Feb.–mid-Nov., daily 9:30–6.*

★ ❸❹ Adjacent to the National Stud, the **Japanese Gardens** were created between 1906 and 1910 by the Stud's founder, Colonel Hall-Walker, and laid out by a Japanese gardener, Tassa Eida, and his son Minoru. The gardens are recognized as among the finest in Europe, although they're something of an East-West hybrid rather than authentically Japanese. The Scots pine trees, for instance, are an appropriate stand-in for traditional Japanese pines, which signify long life and happiness. The gardens symbolically chart the human progression from birth to death, although the focus is on the male journey, not that of the female. A series of landmarks are situated on a meandering path: The Tunnel of Ignorance (No. 3) represents a child's lack of understanding; the Engagement and Marriage bridges (Nos. 8 and 9) span a small stream; and from the Hill of Ambition (No. 13), you can look back over your past joys and sorrows. It ends with the Gateway to Eternity (No. 20), beyond which lies a Buddhist meditation sand garden. It's a worthwhile destination any time of the year, though it's particularly glorious in spring and fall. ⊠ *South of Kildare Town about 2½ km (1½ mi), clearly signposted to left of market square,* ☎ *045/521617.* ☎ *£5, including entry to the National Stud.* ☉ *Mid-Feb.–mid-Nov., daily 9:30–6.*

Athy

❸❺ *24 km (15 mi) south of Kildare Town on R417, 33½ km (21 mi) south of Naas.*

The River Barrow widens considerably at Athy, an industrial town; though it has seen better days, a recent designation as a heritage town may help spiff things up. Overlooking the river, by the bridge, 16th-century **White's Castle,** now a private house, was built by the earl of

Kildare to defend this strategic crossing. The modern pentagonal **Catholic church** (1963–65) has a striking interior with statues, a crucifix by local artist Brid ni Rinn on the high altar, and stations of the cross by George Campbell. ✉ *Free.* ☉ *Daily 8–6.*

Ballytore

36 *8 km (5 mi) east of Athy, 26 km (16 mi) south of Naas on N9.*

In the 18th and 19th centuries, Ballytore was a Quaker settlement. An old schoolhouse has been converted into a small **Quaker Museum.** Among the pupils at the school was Edmund Burke (1729–97), the orator and political philosopher who was close to Samuel Johnson and Sir Joshua Reynolds. Burke was born in Dublin of a Catholic mother and Protestant father; after studying at Trinity he went to London in 1750. His essay *A Philosophical Inquiry into the Origin of Our Ideas of the Sublime and Beautiful* (1756) was a pioneering psychological study of aesthetic theory that is still read today. ☎ *045/431109.* ✉ *Free.* ☉ *Tues.–Fri. 11–6, Sat. 11–1.*

An old mill was converted into the **Crookstown Heritage Centre,** a museum of the flour-milling and baking industries. Built in 1840, the center helped reduce the effects of the Great Famine in this area. You can get a quick bite in its coffee shop. ☎ *0507/23222.* ✉ *£2.50.* ☉ *Apr.–Sept., daily 10–7; Oct.–Mar., Sun. 2–5:30.*

37 From Ballitore take the main N9 road south for 3 km (2 mi) to Timolin, where the **Irish Pewter Mill** pays splendid tribute to an old Irish craft with its showrooms, factory, and museum. Jugs, plates, and other pewter items are for sale. ☎ *0507/24164.* ☉ *May–Sept., weekdays 9:30–5, weekends 11–4.*

38 South Kildare is home to several well-preserved high crosses, set amid monastic ruins. On N9, 1½ km (1 mi) beyond Timolin, take the signposted right turn at the Moone Post Office and continue for 3 km (2 mi) to the **Moone High Cross,** an ancient Celtic cross that stands 17½ ft high, with 51 sculptured panels showing scriptural scenes.

Dining

$ ✕ **Moone High Cross Inn.** Down the road from the Moone High Cross (☞ *above*), this old pub is packed with a cornucopia of local artifacts, newspaper clippings, and old photographs—all fascinating browsing while you nosh on the eclectic bar food that includes steak, salmon, and bacon and cabbage. Save room for the homemade apple pie. On sunny days, you can sit outside and admire the old signs in the beer garden. ✉ *Bolton Hill, Moone,* ☎ *0507/24112. MC, V. Closed Jan.*

Castledermot

39 *8 km (5 mi) south of Moone on N9.*

On the left side of the village of Castledermot, you'll find an almost perfectly preserved 10th-century **round tower** together with two 10th-century **high crosses,** equally well preserved, on the grounds of the local church. From the church gate, you can walk back to the main road along the footpath that is totally enclosed by trees. On the right side of the road in the village, the substantial ruins of a Franciscan friary, mostly dating from the 14th century, are freely accessible.

Dining and Lodging

$$$ ✕☒ **Kilkea Castle.** Built in 1180 as a defensive Anglo-Norman castle, Kilkea was the longtime home of the FitzGerald family; it was modified in the 17th century and later restored. Eleven rooms are in the castle itself, while the rest are set around an adjacent courtyard; those in the castle are more luxuriously furnished. The restaurant is in what was the great hall of the castle; dishes are based on fresh, seasonal produce, some of it from the old, walled gardens below. The hotel has an extensive sports complex, including an 18-hole golf course and clubhouse. ⌂ *Castledermot, near Athy, Co. Kildare,* ☎ *0503/45156,* ℻ *0503/45187. 36 rooms with bath. Restaurant, 2 bars, indoor pool, hot tub, sauna, steam room, 18-hole golf course, 2 tennis courts, archery, health club, fishing. AE, DC, MC, V.*

DUBLIN ENVIRONS A TO Z

Getting Around

By Bus

Bus services link Dublin with main and smaller towns in the environs. All bus services for the region depart from Busaras, the central bus station, at Store Street. For bus inquiries, contact **Bus Éireann** (☎ 01/836–6111). **St. Kevin's** (☎ 01/281–8119), a private bus service, runs daily from Dublin (outside the Royal College of Surgeons on St. Stephen's Green) to Glendalough, stopping off at Bray, Roundwood, and Laragh en route. Buses leave Dublin daily at 11:30 AM and 6 PM (7 PM on Sunday); buses leave Glendalough weekdays at 7:15 AM and 4:15 PM (9:40 AM and 4:15 PM on Saturday, 9:40 AM and 5:30 PM on Sunday). Oneway fare is £6; round-trip, £10.

By Car

The easiest and best way to tour Dublin's environs is by car, because many sights are not served by public transportation, and what service there is, especially to outlying areas, is infrequent. If you need to rent a car, ☞ Car Rentals *in* Dublin A to Z *in* Chapter 1.

To reach destinations in **County Wicklow,** N11/M11 is the fastest and most clearly marked route. The two more scenic routes to Glendalough are R115 to R759 to R755, or R177 to R755.

To visit destinations in the **Boyne Valley,** follow N3, along the east side of the city and make Trim and Tara your first stops. Alternatively, leave Dublin via N1/M1 to Belfast. Try to avoid the road during weekday rush hours (8 AM–10 AM and 5 PM–7 PM); stay on it as far as Drogheda and start touring from there.

To reach destinations in **County Kildare,** follow the quays along the south side of the Liffey (they are one-way westbound) to St. John's Road West (N7); in a matter of minutes, you're heading for open countryside. Avoid traveling this route during the evening peak rush hours, especially on Friday, when Dubliners are themselves making their weekend getaways.

By Train

Iarnród Éireann trains run the length of the east coast, from Dundalk to the north in County Louth to Arklow along the coast in County Wicklow. Trains make many stops along the way; there are stations in Drogheda, Dublin (the main stations are **Connolly Station** [⌂ Amiens St.], and **Pearse Station** [⌂ Westland Row]), Bray, Greystones, Wicklow, and Rathdrum. From Heuston Station (⌂ Victoria Quay and St. John's Road W), the Arrow, a commuter train service, runs westward to Celbridge, Naas, Newbridge, and Kildare Town. Contact Iarnród Éireann (⌂ Irish Rail, ☎ 01/836–6222) for schedule and fare information.

Contacts and Resources

B&B Reservation Agencies

For a small fee, **Bord Fáilte** will book accommodations anywhere in Ireland through its central reservations system. B&Bs can be booked at local visitor information offices when they are open; however, even these reservations will go through the central reservations system. For more information, ☞ Lodging *in* Smart Travel Tips A to Z.

Car Rentals

☞ Car Rentals *in* Dublin A to Z *in* Chapter 1.

Emergencies

Police, fire, and **ambulance** (☎ 999).

Guided Tours

Bus Éireann (☎ 01/836–6111) runs guided bus tours to many of the historic and scenic locations throughout the Dublin environs daily during the summer. Visits include trips to Glendalough in Wicklow; Boyne Valley and Newgrange in County Louth; and the Hill of Tara, Trim, and Navan in County Meath. All tours depart from Busaras Station, Dublin; information is available by phone Monday–Saturday 8:30–7, Sunday 10–7.

Gray Line (☎ 01/661–9666), a privately owned touring company, also runs many guided bus tours throughout the Dublin environs between May and September.

HORSEBACK RIDING

Wicklow Trail Rides (✉ Grainne Sugars, Calliaghstown Riding Center, Ratcoole, Co. Dublin, ☎ 01/4589236, FAX 01/4588171) takes experienced adult horseback riders on weeklong rides through the Wicklow Mountains (May–September), with overnight stays in country homes and guest houses. Instructional holidays for children and adults at the riding center are also available.

WALKING AND HIKING

The **Wicklow Way** is Ireland's most popular walking route, a 137-km (82-mi) trek through the Dublin and Wicklow mountains. The walk begins in Marlay Park, just south of Dublin city center (☞ Chapter 1), where there are a selection of different trails. For information call ☎ 01/493–4059. County Wicklow also sponsors three annual walking festivals. The two-day **Rathdrum Easter Walking Festival** (☎ 0404/46262) includes hill walks of varying lengths over Easter weekend. The first weekend of May, the **Wicklow Mountains May Walking Festival** (☎ 0404/66058) is centered on Blessington. The **Wicklow Mountains Autumn Walking Festival** (☎ 0404/66058) is based in the Glenmalure area.

Wild Wicklow Tours (☎ 01/280–1899) has a small, 26-seater coach that can take you to the more off-the-beaten-track sites in the mountains and along the coast.

Visitor Information

For information on travel in the Dublin environs and for help in making lodging reservations, contact one of the following Tourist Information Offices (TIOs): **Dublin Tourism** and **Bord Fáilte** (☞ Visitor Information *in* Dublin A to Z, Chapter 1): **Dundalk** (☎ 042/35484, FAX 042/38070); **Mullingar** (☎ 044/48650, FAX 044/40413); or **Trim** (☎ 046/37227, FAX 046/31595).

Mullingar is the head office of tourism for Counties Wicklow, Louth, Meath, and Kildare. During the summer, temporary TIOs are open throughout the environs, in towns such as Arklow and Wicklow Town, in County Wicklow; Drogheda and Dundalk in County Louth; and Kildare Town in County Kildare.

3 THE MIDLANDS

COUNTIES OFFALY, ROSCOMMON, LONGFORD, CAVAN, MONAGHAN, WESTMEATH, THE NORTH TIPPERARY, LAOIS, AND THE SOUTH OF LEITRIM

Unspectacular and unsung, the flat plains of the Midlands form the geographical heart of Ireland. There's water at every turn in this landscape of wide lakes and fast rivers, including the mighty Shannon, Ireland's central artery and the longest river in the British Isles. Among the highlights are Clonmacnoise, Ireland's most important monastic ruins; historic towns with age-old industries such as lace making, and crystal; the gardens of Birr Castle; and some of Ireland's finest Anglo-Irish houses—Strokestown House, Castle Leslie, and Emo Court.

Updated by
Alannah
Hopkin

IRISH SCHOOLCHILDREN WERE ONCE TAUGHT to think of their country as a saucer, with mountains around the edge and a dip in the middle. The dip is the Midlands—or the Lakelands, as it is sometimes also referred to—and this often overlooked region comprises seven counties: Cavan, Laois (pronounced leash), Westmeath, Longford, Offaly, Roscommon, and Monaghan, in addition to North Tipperary and Leitrim.

A fair share of Ireland's 800 bodies of water speckle this lush countryside. Many of the lakes formed by glacial action some 10,000 years ago are quite small, especially in Cavan and Monaghan. Anglers who come to the area have learned to expect to have a lake to themselves, and many return year after year to practice the sport. Because of all the water, much of the landscape lies under blanket bog, a unique ecosystem that's worth exploring. The River Shannon, one of the longest rivers in Europe and the longest in the British Isles, bisects the Midlands from north to south, piercing a series of loughs (lakes): Lough Allen, Lough Ree, and Lough Derg. The Royal Canal and the Grand Canal cross the Midlands from east to west, ending in the Shannon north and south of Lough Ree. Stretches of both canals have been developed for recreational purposes.

The main roads from Dublin to the south and the west cross the area—and these roads ultimately came to eclipse the Shannon and the canals as important transportation arteries—but there is also a network of minor roads linking the more scenic areas. You'll find more conventionally attractive hill and lake scenery in the forest parks of Killykeen and Lough Key. The towns themselves—including Nenagh, Roscommon, Athlone, Boyle, Mullingar, Tullamore, Longford, and Cavan—are not among Ireland's most distinctive, but they are likely to appeal to people hungry for a time when the pace of life was slower and every neighbor's face was familiar. A Midland town's main hotel is usually the social center, a good place from which to experience life as the locals do. You might witness a wedding reception (generally a boisterous occasion for all age groups), a First Communion supper, a meeting of the local Lions Club, or even a gathering of the neighborhood Weight Watchers group. By now you've probably realized: Night owls and thrill seekers should probably head elsewhere.

The Midlands are, last but not least, dotted with some of Ireland's most impressive heritage properties from disparate eras: Strokestown Park House, Birr Castle Gardens, Emo Court and Gardens, Castle Leslie, and the magnificent monastic ruins of Clonmacnoise on the banks of the Shannon.

Pleasures and Pastimes

Dining

Most of the restaurants are simple eateries, ranging in price from inexpensive ($) to moderate ($$), and are often attached to a family hotel. Mullingar, in the center of the Midlands, is the beef capital of Ireland, and the many lakes and rivers of the region provide an abundance of fresh salmon and trout. And since no place in Ireland is more than an hour and a half from the sea, you can also expect to find fresh ocean fish. The approach to cooking may often be conventional, but the ingredients will always be first-rate. For price ranges, ☞ Chart 1(A) *in* Smart Travel Tips A to Z.

Lodging

Although there are some beautifully opulent country-house hotels in the region, accommodations for the most part are often modest affairs. The choice is usually between a small-town hotel offering a reasonable standard of basic comfort or a scenically located, country-house bed-and-breakfast, perhaps overlooking a small lake or river. Either way, informality is the order of the day. For price ranges, ☞ Chart 2(B) *in* Smart Travel Tips A to Z.

Outdoor Activities and Sports

BICYCLING

One of the best ways to immerse yourself in the Midlands is to tour the region on a bicycle. Although the area may not have the spectacular scenery of the more hilly coastal regions, its level terrain means a less-strenuous ride. The twisting roads are generally in good condition, and there are pleasant picnic spots in the many state-owned forests just off the main roads. Bord Fáilte recommends two long tours: one of the Athlone-Mullingar-Roscommon area and another of the Cavan-Monaghan-Mullingar region. Whenever possible, try to avoid the major trunk roads that bisect the region.

BOATING

With 485 km (300 mi) of navigable rivers and numerous island-studded lakes in the region, a boat is the best way to see the Midlands at a leisurely pace and from an unusual and memorable angle. Several companies rent out charter boats of varying sizes for vacations on the water. Most of these vessels hold from six to eight people, and all are operated by the parties who rent them, meaning everyone can be captain for a day.

FISHING

Anglers worldwide are attracted to the region's River Shannon and its system of lakes. Beam, rudd, tench, roach, perch, and hybrids are the main varieties, while pike roam select waters. Monaghan, Cavan, Boyle, and the small lakes to the east and west of Lough Derg are the best coarse fishing areas, while brown-trout lakes and rivers can be found around Birr, Banagher, Mullingar, and Roscommon. For pike, you'll find the most fruitful areas around Cavan, Clones, Cootehill, Castleblaney, Kingscourt, Carrick-on-Shannon, Boyle, Belturbet, and Butlersbridge. The Midlands region hosts several angling festivals, with prize money and fringe events such as sing-alongs, dart games, and card competitions. Castleblaney has a tournament in March; Carrickmacross and Ballinasloe, in May; Athlone, in July and October; and Cootehill, in September.

GOLF

Although the parkland courses of the Midlands may lack the spectacular challenge of Ireland's more famous scenic and coastal greens, they have a quiet charm all their own. On weekdays, at least, you are unlikely to have any trouble booking a tee time. Six 18-hole courses have opened in the Midlands in recent years, considerably reducing the pressure on facilities. Greens fees are generally moderate at around £15.

HIKING AND WALKING

Forest park trails (at Killykeen, Lough Key, and Dun a Ri forest parks) and narrow country roads invite visitors to tour parts of the Midlands on foot. One impressive walking trail to the east of Birr, called the Slieve Bloom Way, runs through the Slieve Bloom Mountains on a 50-km (30-mi) circular route; its attractions include deep glens, rock formations, waterfalls, and views from mountain peaks.

Exploring the Midlands

Our coverage of the Midlands is organized into three different tours: Portarlington–Castlepollard; Longford–Clones; and Boyle–Nenagh. The first two tours can easily be strung together for an extended visit in the Midlands, as they chart a course almost due north from the initial starting point in Portarlington, County Laois. Because our third tour covers sights west of those in the first two tours, keep them in mind if you're flying into Shannon and beginning your explorations of Ireland in the western half of the country. In fact, because the Midlands border virtually every major county of Ireland, there are three places in this chapter where you should be alert to nearby locales we cover in other chapters: The easternmost sites in the Midlands (Emo Court and Coolbanagher) are within a few miles of the westernmost sites in Dublin Environs (☞ Chapter 2); the westernmost sites in the Midlands (Boyle and Lough Key Forest Park) are just across the border from County Sligo (☞ Chapter 7); and the northernmost sites and towns of the Midlands are just across the border from Northern Ireland (☞ Chapter 8).

Numbers in the text correspond to numbers in the margin and on the Midlands map.

Great Itineraries

The Midlands is a relatively small region, but part of its attraction lies in the temptation to follow a loose itinerary and spend time off the beaten path. Ten days would allow for a leisurely exploration of the region by bicycle. Car drivers could cover the same route in five days with plenty of time to improvise. Three days would be enough to sample the central area of the region, which is probably more sensible than driving long distances on small roads in an effort to see everything.

IF YOU HAVE 3 DAYS

Heading east from Shannon Airport, turn off the N7 Limerick–Dublin road for ⊡ **Birr** ㉗, a quiet Georgian town built around its magnificent castle and gardens. Then take the nearby **Bord na Mona Bog Rail Tour** ㉕ near Shannonbridge, a good introduction to the flora and fauna of Ireland's many bogs. While you're in the area, stop at **Clonmacnoise** ㉔, Ireland's most important monastic settlement, which overlooks the River Shannon, and return to Birr for the night. The next day head toward ⊡ **Longford** ⑨ to get another view of bog culture at the **Corlea Trackway Exhibition Centre.** Next, head for **Strokestown** ㉑ and its namesake house, where the award-winning museum documents the causes and effects of the 1845–49 Great Famine. Try to find time to tour the house and gardens as well. Spend the night back in Longford. Book a visit to **Carrigglas Manor** near Longford, a romantic, 1837 Tudor-Gothic house that has Jane Austen associations. If the weather is good, take some fresh air in **Lough Key Forest Park** ⑳ near **Boyle** ⑲, from where you will be well positioned to explore the West or Northwest (☞ Chapters 6 and 7, respectively).

IF YOU HAVE 5 DAYS

Heading from Dublin or from points east in Wicklow and Kildare, start at **Emo Court and Gardens** ①. This is the only large-scale country house designed by James Gandon, the architect responsible for much of Georgian Dublin; the lovingly restored house was recently given to the nation. Move north to the Gothic Revival Charleville Castle outside **Tullamore** ③, then to **Kilbeggan** ④, where you can learn about whiskey making at the Kilbeggan Distillery. If you have time, stop in at the beautiful lakelands setting of the **Belvedere House Gardens** ⑤. Stay in or around ⊡ **Mullingar** ⑥ for the night. In the morning of day

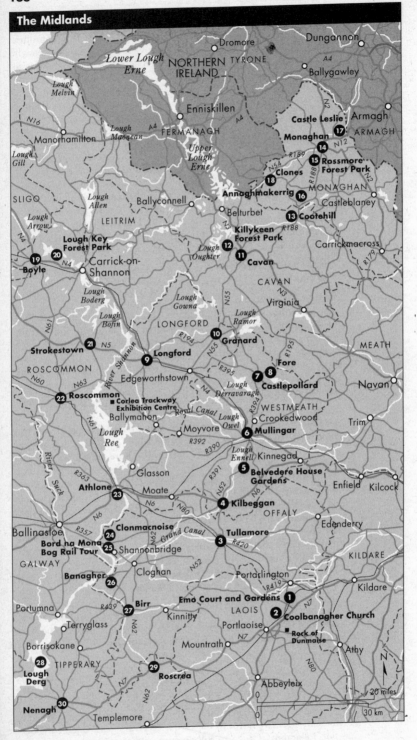

two, briefly explore Mullingar, and then head north on scenic R394 to **Castlepollard** ⑦ and the massive Tullynally Castle and Gardens, the ancestral home of Antonia Fraser, the prolific and highly regarded biographer of the English aristocracy. Crystal aficionados will want to stop in **Cavan** ⑪, while nature buffs can easily spend the afternoon exploring the water-laced **Killykeen Forest Park** ⑫. Spend the night in 🏨 **Cootehill** ⑬, an old-fashioned, friendly County Cavan town popular with the many anglers who frequent this area. Begin your third day visiting 🏨 **Castle Leslie** ⑰, beautifully situated on the shores of Glaslough (the "Green Lake") and home to the talented and mildly eccentric Leslie family. If you're ready for some downtime, you can extend your visit and stay the night. Alternatively, you can either jump across the border to explore the southernmost sights in Northern Ireland (☞ Chapter 8) or head southwest, making a brief stop at **Rossmore Forest Park** ⑮ on your way to the border town of **Clones** ⑱, a lace-making center. On your fourth day, return to Cavan and pick up the road to 🏨 **Longford** ⑨, where the nearby **Carrigglas Manor,** a romantic Tudor-Gothic house, has associations with Jane Austen. To the west lies **Strokestown** ㉑ and its namesake house; its museum devoted to the Great Famine is not to be missed, and the house and newly restored gardens are also worth a look. The **Corlea Trackway Exhibition Centre** merits a quick stop. 🏨 **Athlone** ㉓ is a convenient place to spend the night—from here you're well positioned for an early morning visit to **Clonmacnoise** ㉔, the most important early Christian monastic site in Ireland. Stop at the **Bord na Mona Bog Rail Tour** ㉕ near Shannonbridge on your way to **Banagher** ㉖, where you can either take a 2-hour Shannon cruise (a great trip in good weather) or drive around **Lough Derg** ㉘. Depending on your time, you can choose to end up in either 🏨 **Birr** ㉗, 🏨 **Roscrea** ㉙, or 🏨 **Nenagh** ㉚; from any of these towns you're not far from Shannon Airport and points to the west and southwest.

When to Tour the Midlands

The Midlands are a good year-round choice because, unlike those in the more popular destinations in the West and Southwest, its restaurants, accommodations, and major attractions remain open all year. The area is usually quiet, except at the boating resorts on the Shannon and its loughs, which are heavily booked by Irish vacationers in July and August.

THE EASTERN MIDLANDS

The eastern fringe of the Midlands is about an hour's drive from Dublin, and a visit to the area could easily be grafted onto a tour of Dublin Environs (☞ Chapter 2). Our eastern itinerary begins at Portarlington, the closest village to Dublin in the chapter, and moves northwest to Castlepollard and environs, stopping just short of Longford, the jumping-off point for the Northern Midlands.

Portarlington

72 km (43 mi) southwest of Dublin.

If you enjoy large-scale, domestic architecture, drive to Portarlington, which until recently had a sizable bilingual (English-French) population of Huguenot origin. A quintessential landmark of Irish Palladian ★ ❶ elegance lies just 7 km (4½ mi) south of Portarlington: **Emo Court and Gardens,** one of the finest large-scale country houses near Dublin open to the public. (If you elect to skip over much of the Midlands, at least try to tack on a visit to Emo, especially if you're in County Kildare or Wicklow [☞ Chapter 2].) To come upon the house from the main drive, an avenue lined with magisterial Wellingtonia trees, is to experience one of Ireland's great treasure-house views. Begun in 1790 by James Gandon, architect of the Custom House and the Four Courts in Dublin, Emo (the name derives from the Italian version of the original Irish name Imoe) is thought to be Gandon's only domestic work on as grand a scale as his Dublin civic buildings. Construction continued on and off for 70 years, as family money troubles followed the untimely death of the Emo's first patron and owner, the first Earl of Portarlington.

In 1996, after nearly 30 years of loving restoration, Emo's English-born owner, Mr. Cholmeley Dering Cholmeley-Harrison, donated the house to the Irish nation. The ground-floor rooms have now been beautifully restored and decorated. Among the highlights are the **entrance hall**, with trompe l'oeil in the apses on each side, and the **library**, which has a carved Italian marble mantle with putti frolicking among grapevines. But the showstopper, and one of the finest rooms in Ireland, is the domed **rotunda**—in fact the work of one of Gandon's successors, the Irish architect William Caldbeck—inspired by the Roman Pantheon. The rotunda's blue-and-white coffered dome is supported by marble pilasters with gilded Corinthian capitals. Emo's 55 acres of grounds include a 20-acre lake, lawns planted with yew trees, a small garden (the Clocker) with Japanese maples, and a larger one (the Grapery) with rare trees and shrubs. ⊠ *Emo,* ☎ *0502/26573.* ☏ *Gardens free, house £2.* ☉ *Gardens daily 10:30–5:30; house mid-June–mid-Sept., Tues.–Sun. 10–6, last tour 5:15.*

❷ **Coolbanagher Church,** the familiar name for the exquisite Church of St. John the Evangelist, was, like Emo, designed by James Gandon. On view inside are Gandon's original 1795 plans; there's also an elaborately sculpted 15th-century font from an earlier church that once stood nearby, and adjacent is Gandon's mausoleum for Lord Portarlington, his patron at Emo. The church is open daily in the summer; during other months, ask around in the tiny village for a key, or call the rectory (☎ 0502/24143), which is a 10-minute drive away. ⊠ *1½ km (1 mi) south of Emo Court on R419.* ☉ *May–Oct., daily 9–6.*

Dining and Lodging

$ ✕⛺ **Roundwood House.** Just off N7 at the foot of the Slieve Bloom
★ Mountains, this is a warm, relaxed, classically beautiful 1730s house. Behind the symmetrical Palladian facade lies a simple interior, with family antiques and Persian rugs on well-worn wooden floors in the study, drawing room, and other common rooms. You can stay in one of the large rooms in the main house or in a smaller, cozy room in the original house, which dates from 1650 and is just beyond an herb garden at the back. There are 18 acres of woodland to explore and more-strenuous hill walks in the Slieve Blooms. Hosts Frank and Rosemarie Kennan are likely to share a table with you at dinner. ⊠ *Mountrath, Co. Laois,* ☎ *0502/32120,* 𝔽𝔸𝕏 *0502/32711. 10 rooms with bath. Dining room. AE, DC, MC, V.*

Tullamore

❸ *27 km (17 mi) northwest of Portarlington.*

Tullamore, the county seat of Offaly, is a big country town on the Grand Canal. The main reason to pass through is the **Charleville Forest Castle,** a castellated, Georgian–Gothic Revival manor house set on about 30 acres of woodland walks and gardens, found 1½ km (1 mi) outside Tullamore on N52 to Birr. This magnificent building dates from 1812 and is a fine example of the work of architect Francis Johnston, who was responsible for many of Dublin's stately Georgian buildings. Look for the William Morris–designed dining room with its original wall-paper. Guided tours of the interior are available. ✉ Co. *Offaly*, ☎ 0506/ 21279. 🎫 *£2.50.* ⊙ *May, weekends 2–5; June–Sept., Wed.–Sun. 2–5; Oct.–Apr., groups of 4 or more by appointment.*

Outdoor Activities and Sports

BOATING

A river cruiser for a floating holiday can be rented from **Celtic Canal Cruisers Ltd.** (✉ 24th Lock, ☎ 0506/21861).

GOLF

Tullamore Golf Club (✉ Brookfield, ☎ 0506/21439) is an 18-hole, par-71 parkland course. **Esker Hills Golf &Country Club** (✉ Co. Offaly, ☎ 0506/55999) is a challenging 18-hole, par-71 championship course incorporating natural lakes and woodlands.

Kilbeggan

❹ *11 km (7 mi) north of Tullamore.*

Kilbeggan is known mainly for the **Kilbeggan Distillery,** which was established in 1757 to produce a traditional Irish malt whiskey. It closed down in 1954 and was reopened in 1987 by Cooley Distillery, which now makes its whiskey in County Louth but brings it here to be matured in casks. The distillery has been restored as a museum of industrial archaeology illustrating the process of Irish pot-whiskey distillation and the social history of the workers' lives. ✉ Co. *Westmeath,* ☎ *0506/ 32134.* 🎫 *£3.* ⊙ *Apr.–Oct., daily 9–6; Nov.–Mar., daily 10–4.*

❺ **Belvedere House Gardens,** 19 km (12 mi) north of Kilbeggan, is remarkable for its beautiful setting on the northeast shore of Lough Ennel. Terraced gardens descend in three stages to the waters of the lake and provide a panoramic view of its islands. The estate also contains a walled garden with many varieties of trees, shrubs, and flowers landscaped in the 18th-century style. ✉ Co. *Westmeath,* ☎ *044/40861.* 🎫 *£1.* ⊙ *Apr.–Oct., daily noon–6.*

Mullingar

❻ *24 km (15 mi) northeast of Kilbeggan.*

County Westmeath's major town, Mullingar is a busy commercial and cattle-trading center on the Royal Canal, located midway between two large, attractive lakes, Lough Owel and Lough Ennel. This is an area of rich farmland, and the town is known as Ireland's beef capital; farmers all over Ireland describe a good young cow as "beef to the ankle, like a Mullingar heifer." The buildings in Mullingar date mostly from the 19th century.

The large, Renaissance-style Catholic **Cathedral of Christ the King** was completed in 1939. Finely carved stonework decorates the front of the cathedral, and the spacious interior has mosaics of St. Patrick and St. Anne by the Russian artist Boris Anrep. ✉ *Mary St.,* ☎ *044/48391.* ⊙ *Daily 9–5:30.*

Mullingar's **Military Museum in Columb Barracks** is home to a surprisingly wide array of artifacts that includes weapons from the two world wars; long, canoelike boats of oak from the 1st century AD found in the surrounding lakes; and uniforms and other articles of the old IRA, including a pistol said to have been the property of Michael Collins, who was chief of staff during the War of Independence and the Civil War. ✉ *Columb Barracks,* ☎ *044/48391.* 🎫 *Free.* ⊙ *By appointment only.*

Dining and Lodging

$$$ ✕🏠 **Crookedwood House.** This large, 200-year-old rectory overlook-
★   ing Lough Derravaragh is 13 km (8 mi) north of Mullingar on R394
     Castlepollard road. Proprietors Noel and Julie Kenny added a wing of
     spacious bedrooms and have another nine available nearby in a fine
     period house. The dining room is particularly notable, as Noel is rec-
     ognized as a leading Irish chef. Irresistible delights include a trio of
     salmon, sole, and scallops with lobster sauce, and medallions of beef
     fillet with tomato, cream, and brandy sauce. ⊠ *Mullingar, Co. West-
     meath,* ☎ *044/72165,* FAX *044/72166. 18 rooms with bath. Restaurant.
     AE, DC, MC, V. Closed 2 wks in Nov. No lunch Tues.–Sat., no din-
     ner Sun.*

$ ✕🏠 **Temple.** Almost equidistant from Mullingar, Tullamore, and Athlone
     along N6, Temple is a superb Victorian farmhouse in a parkland set-
     ting. The Fagan family warmly welcomes visitors into large, comfort-
     able rooms furnished with modest antiques. Children have plenty of safe
     areas to roam (this is a working sheep farm), while adults can indulge
     in a relaxation program that includes a choice of yoga, aromatherapy,
     and massage. The house is ideally situated for outdoor activities, such
     as cycling across Clara Bog, walking in the Slieve Bloom Hills, golfing
     at the nearby Delvin Castle, Heath, and Mullingar Golf Clubs, horse-
     back riding, and dinghy sailing. Most guests choose to sample Bernadette
     Fagan's renowned cooking at dinner (book by 10 AM). ⊠ *Horseleap,
     Moate, Co. Westmeath,* ☎ *0506/35118,* FAX *0506/35008. 8 rooms with
     bath. Sauna, steam room, bicycles. MC, V. Closed Nov.–Feb.*

Outdoor Activities and Sports

GOLF

Delvin Castle Golf Club (⊠ Delvin, ☎ 044/64315) is a 9-hole course.
The **Heath Golf Club** (⊠ Portlaoise, ☎ 0502/46533) is a challenging,
18-hole parkland course. **Mullingar Golf Club** (⊠ Belvedere, Mullingar,
☎ 044/48629) is an 18-hole parkland course.

HORSEBACK RIDING

Mullingar Equestrian Centre (⊠ Athlone Rd., ☎ 044/48331) has rid-
ing on the shores of Lough Derravaragh and lessons at all levels. The
center also organizes residential riding holidays.

Castlepollard

❼ *21 km (13 mi) north of Mullingar.*

Castlepollard is an unusually pretty village of multihued, 18th- and 19th-
century houses laid out around a large, triangular green. The biggest
(literally!) nearby attraction is **Tullynally Castle and Gardens,** 1½ km
(1 mi) down the road to Granard, the largest castle in Ireland still lived
in as a family home. How big is it? The total circumference of the build-
ing's masonry adds up to nearly ½ km (¼ mi)—an astonishing ag-
glomeration of towers, turrets, and battlements that date from the first
early fortified building, circa 1655, up through the mid-19th century,
when additions in the Gothic Revival style went up one after another.
Two wings designed by Sir Richard Morrison in 1840 that joined the
main block to the stable court had dramatically different purposes: One
was given over entirely to luxurious quarters for the Dowager Count-
ess; the other housed 40 *indoor* servants. Think of Tullynally the next
time you pay your heating bill: It was one of the first houses in the British
Isles to have central heating.

Tullynally—the name, literally translated, means "Hill of the Swans"—
has been the home of 10 generations of the literary Pakenham family
and the seat of the earls of Longford. Among the living Pakenhams

are the current earl of Longford, Frank Pakenham, the prison reformer and anti-pornography campaigner; wife Elizabeth and daughter Antonia Fraser, both historical biographers; and Antonia's brother Thomas, a historian. In addition to a fine collection of portraits and furniture, the house contains an immense kitchen furnished with many fascinating 19th-century domestic gadgets, including a marmalade cutter and an oversize contraption designed to take the buttermilk out of the freshly churned butter. The grounds also include a landscaped park and formal gardens. ⊠ *Co. Westmeath,* ☎ *044/61159.* ⛫ *Castle and gardens £4, gardens only £2.50.* ☉ *Gardens May–Sept., daily 2–6; castle rooms mid-June–July and mid-Sept.–Sept. 27, guided tours daily 2:30–6.*

Fore

❽ *5 km (3 mi) east of Castlepollard.*

The simple village of Fore is dominated by the remains of **Fore Abbey. St. Fechin's Church,** dating from the 10th century, has a massive, cross-inscribed lintel stone. Nearby are the remains of a 13th-century Benedictine **abbey,** whose imposing square towers and loophole windows resemble a castle rather than an abbey.

THE NORTHERN MIDLANDS

This tour starts in Longford and works its way north, leaving the ancient kingdom of Leinster for Ulster's two most southerly counties, Cavan and Monaghan. (Ulster's four other counties, which now constitute Northern Ireland, are covered in Chapter 8.) The land north of Cavan is characterized by small, round hills called drumlins and is known as "drumlin country."

Longford

❾ *37 km (24 mi) northwest of Castlepollard, 124 km (77 mi) northwest of Dublin.*

Longford, the county seat of County Longford, is a typical little market-town community. Jane Austen fans should consider making a visit to **Carrigglas Manor,** 5 km (3 mi) northeast of Longford on R194 to Granard. The romantic, Tudor-Gothic house, built in 1837 by Thomas Lefroy, offers a glimpse into gracious country living in 18th-century surroundings. His descendants, who still reside here, like to note that as a young man in England Lefroy was romantically involved with the novelist Jane Austen. Why they never married is a mystery, but it is believed that she based the character of Mr. Darcy in *Pride and Prejudice* on Mr. Lefroy. The house still has high-quality plasterwork and many of its original, mid-19th-century furnishings. A magnificent stable yard, part of an earlier house on the site, was designed in 1790 by James Gandon, architect of Dublin's Custom House and Four Courts. Visitors to the stable yard and gardens also have access to a small **costume museum,** which displays mostly 18th-century apparel found in the house. ⊠ *Co. Longford,* ☎ *043/45165.* ⛫ *Stable yard, gallery, and shop free; gardens and museum £2.50.* ☉ *Stable yard, gardens, and museum daily 11–6; house, by appointment only, early June–early Sept., Thurs.–Mon. 2–6.*

Granard

❿ *18 km (11 mi) northeast of Longford.*

The market town and fishing center of Granard stands on high ground near the Longford–Cavan border. The **Motte of Granard** at the southwest end of town was once the site of a fortified Norman castle. In 1932, a statue of St. Patrick was erected here to mark the 15th centenary of his arrival in Ireland. (At least a dozen statues of the patron saint, all virtually identical, were put up that year; see how many others you can spot on your travels.)

Outdoor Activities and Sports

County Longford Golf Club (⊠ Glack, ☎ 043/46310) is an 18-hole parkland course.

Cavan

🕦 *30 km (19 mi) north of Granard, 114 km (71 mi) northwest of Dublin.*

A small, quiet, undistinguished town serving the local farming community, Cavan has two central streets—Main and Farnham—that are parallel to one another. With its pubs and shops, Main Street is like many others in similar Irish towns, while Farnham Street is decorated with Georgian houses, churches, and a courthouse. **Cavan Crystal** is an up-and-coming rival to Waterford in the cut-lead-crystal line; the company offers guided factory tours and access to its factory shop. This is a good opportunity to watch skilled craftspeople at work if you can't make it to Waterford. A major new building housing a visitor center, a glass museum, a restaurant, and a coffee shop opened in 1998. ⊠ *Dublin Rd., Cavan Town, ☎ 049/433–1800. ☜ Free. ◎ Guided tour weekdays at 9:30, 10:30, and 11:30.*

⑫ **Killykeen Forest Park** lies among the beautiful, mazelike network of lakes called Lough Oughter, 11 km (7 mi) north of Cavan. Within the park's 600 acres are a number of signposted walks and nature trails, stables offering horseback riding, and boats and bicycles for rent. Twenty-eight fully outfitted two- and three-bedroom cottages are available for weeklong, weekend, or midweek stays; everything is provided except towels. Rates vary according to season; call for details. ⊠ *Cavan, ☎ 049/433–2541. ☜ Free, parking £1.50. ◎ Feb.–Dec., daily 9–5.*

Dining and Lodging

$$$$ ✕🏨 **Slieve Russell Hotel and Country Club.** This magnificent hotel on
★ 300 acres 26 km (16 mi) west of Cavan makes a convenient break on the Dublin–Sligo journey. Water burbles in the circular fountain before the palatial, neoclassic facade; the spacious lobby gleams with polished marble. The 101 deluxe bedrooms have Jacuzzis, super-king-size beds, and chunky, art deco–style furniture. The sports and spa facilities are outstanding, but for many guests the golfing and excellent freshwater and trout fishing are the main attractions. White linens and wrought-iron chandeliers grace the formal Conall Cearnach restaurant, where the extensive menu includes a variety of traditionally prepared seafood dishes, such as black sole on the bone or salmon hollandaise. The Brackley Buttery restaurant is more informal. ⊠ *Ballyconnell, Co. Cavan, ☎ 049/952–6444, ℻ 049/952–6474. 141 rooms with bath, 10 suites. 2 restaurants, 2 bars, 2 indoor pools, sauna, steam room, 9- and 18-hole golf courses, 4 tennis courts, health club, horseback riding, Ping-Pong, squash, fishing. AE, DC, MC, V.*

$$$ ✕🏨 **Cabra Castle.** This sprawling, gray-stone castle with its crenellated battlements and Gothic windows could have been designed in Hollywood. In fact, it was built in 1699 as the centerpiece of a 1,000-acre estate, most of which now belongs to the Dun a Ri National Park. If you want the full treatment, ask for a "castle room," furnished with more elaborate Victorian antiques than the others. The Victorian-Gothic theme is carried through the bar and the restaurant with varying degrees of success; if you like that sort of thing, be sure to look at

the castle gallery, which has hand-painted ceilings and leaded windows. ⊠ *Kingscourt, Co. Cavan,* ☎ *042/956–7030,* FAX *042/956–7039. 29 rooms with bath. Restaurant, bar, 9-hole golf course, horseback riding, fishing. AE, DC, MC, V.*

$$$ ✕🏠 **MacNean House & Bistro.** Tucked away in the far north on the Cavan-Fermanagh border, this simple guest house and bistro has become a place of pilgrimage for food lovers. The attraction here is the ambitious and inspired cuisine of Neven Maguire, a young Chef of the Year, who cooks alongside his mother while his father oversees the front of the house. Reservations are essential, for although the surroundings are plain and homey, the quality and style of the cooking are first-class. Seafood dishes include steamed fillet of turbot with buttered spinach on a basil-butter sauce, or seasonal game such as saddle of hare stuffed with chicken and pesto mousse on a parsnip puree and rosemary jus. Desserts are Neven's specialty: Try his hazelnut nougat glacé. Given the remoteness of Blacklion, it makes sense to book a room for the night ($) when reserving a table. To reach MacNean House, travel north and west from Cavan on N87, crossing into Northern Ireland, past Florence Court, and out again back into Cavan; the 65-km (40-mi) detour makes sense if you are heading from Dublin to Sligo or Donegal. ⊠ *Blacklion, Co. Cavan,* ☎ *072/53022,* FAX *072/ 53404. 10 rooms with bath. Restaurant (reservations essential). V. Closed Mon.–Tues. June–Sept., Mon.–Wed. Oct.–May. No dinner Sun.*

Outdoor Activities and Sports

There are two golf courses at the **Slieve Russell Hotel** (⊠ Ballyconnell, Co. Cavan, ☎ 049/952–6444); a 9-hole, par-three, parkland course and an 18-hole championship course. Visitors are welcome at the 18-hole **County Cavan Golf Club** (⊠ Arnmore House, Cavan, ☎ 049/433–1283).

Cootehill

⑬ *26 km (16 mi) northeast of Cavan.*

One of the most underestimated small towns in Ireland, Cootehill has a lovely setting on a wooded hillside in the heart of County Cavan. Its wide streets, with their intriguing old shops, are always busy without being congested. Most of its visitors are anglers from Europe, the United Kingdom, and the rest of Ireland.

★ Only pedestrians are allowed through the gates of **Bellamont Forest.** After about a mile of woodlands, the trail leads to the exquisite, hilltop **Bellamont House,** designed in 1728 by Edward Lovett Pearce, architect of the Dublin's Bank of Ireland. Small but perfectly proportioned, it has been virtually unaltered since it was built and is considered one of Ireland's finest Palladian-style houses. It is now a private home but is occasionally opened to the public. If you are interested, inquire locally or at the Tourist Information Office (TIO) in Cavan. Walk up the main street of Cootehill to "the top of the town" (past the White Horse Hotel), and you will see the entrance to the forest.

Dining and Lodging

$ ✕🏠 **Riverside House.** The unpretentious, genuine, old-fashioned Irish hospitality at Joe and Una Smith's farm is appreciated by both serious anglers and nonsporting guests. The substantial Victorian house on 100 acres overlooks the River Annalee. All rooms have peaceful views and are individually decorated with modest antiques and family hand-me-downs. Bring your boots if you want to explore around this working dairy farm. The lodging is signposted 1 km (½ mi) outside town off R188. ⊠ *Co. Cavan,* ☎ *049/555–2150,* FAX *049/555–2150. 6 rooms, 5 with bath. Dining room, boating, fishing. MC, V.*

$ ✕▥ **The White Horse.** This is a typical market-town hotel—it serves as a lively focal point for the community as well as a good grade of budget accommodation. It's particularly popular with visiting anglers. Some rooms in the rambling Victorian building are a bit small; all are plainly decorated, and the quieter ones are at the back. The restaurant, a softly lit, mahogany-furnished room in the interior of the hotel, is popular with town folk, who head here for generous portions and simply cooked dishes. ✉ *Market St., Co. Cavan,* ☎ *049/555–2124,* FAX *049/555–2407. 30 rooms, 24 with bath. Restaurant, 2 bars. AE, MC, V.*

Outdoor Activities and Sports

Rossmore Golf Club (✉ Rossmore Park, near Cootehill, ☎ 047/81316) is an 18-hole parkland course. (*See also* the 18-hole championship golf course at the **Nuremore Hotel**, *below.*)

Monaghan

⓮ *24 km (15 mi) north of Cootehill.*

A former British garrison town, Monaghan is built around a central square known as the Diamond. The town's old **Market House,** elegantly constructed of limestone in 1792, is now the tourist office (☞ Visitor Information *in* Midlands A to Z, *below*). The award-winning **County Museum** traces the history of Monaghan from earliest times to the present through archaeological finds, traditional crafts, artwork, and a variety of other historical artifacts. ✉ *Hill St.,* ☎ *047/82928.* ⌕ *Free.* ◷ *June–Sept., Tues.–Sat. 11–5; Oct.–May, Tues.–Sat. 11–1 and 2–5.*

⓯ Outside town (on R189 Newbliss road), you'll find fresh air in pleasant surroundings at **Rossmore Forest Park,** 691 acres of low hills, small lakes, and pleasant forest walks through rhododendron groves. Signposted nature trails that are freely accessible.

⓰ At **Annaghmakerrig,** 5 km (3 mi) southwest of Newbliss, a small forest park with a lake is the site of **Annaghmakerrig House,** home of the Shakespearian stage director Sir Tyrone Guthrie until his death in 1971. He left it to the nation as a residential center for writers, artists, and musicians. It is not officially open to the public, but anyone with a special interest in the arts or in its previous owner can ask to be shown around, and visitors can wander through and picnic on its grounds. ✉ *Near Newbliss,* ☎ *047/54003.*

Dining and Lodging

$$$ ✕▥ **Nuremore Hotel and Country Club.** This Victorian country house
★ is now a luxury hotel with excellent sporting facilities, including its own trout lake. There are open fires in the large lounge, which is furnished with plump armchairs and Victorian tables. The bedrooms are decorated with mahogany Victorian furniture and coordinated color schemes. The restaurant serves a hybrid French-Irish cuisine in formal surroundings amid a dusky-pink decor. It is 80 km (50 mi) from both Dublin and Belfast, making it a popular weekend retreat for city dwellers. ✉ *Carrickmacross, Co. Monaghan,* ☎ *042/966–1438,* FAX *042/966–1853. 54 rooms with bath, 5 suites. Restaurant, bar, indoor pool, sauna, steam room, 18-hole golf course, 2 tennis courts, health club, horseback riding, squash, fishing. AE, DC, MC, V.*

Castle Leslie

⓱ *11 km (7 mi) northeast of Monaghan.*

Leave Monaghan on N12 and follow it out of town to Castle Leslie, originally a medieval stronghold, which has been the seat of the Leslie family since 1664. The castle sits on the shores of deep, beautiful

Glaslough, which means "green lake," whose waters are mirrorlike on sunny days. The present house was built around 1870 in a mix of Gothic and Italianate styles—Sir John Leslie, who built it, spent years in Italy and picked up many ideas there, including the colonnaded loggia, said to have been copied from Michelangelo's cloister at Santa Maria degli Angeli in Rome. The mildly eccentric Leslie family is known for its literary and artistic leanings—when Jonathan Swift stayed here, he wrote in the guest book: "Glaslough with rows of books upon its shelves/written by the Leslies about themselves." The family has many notable relations by marriage, including the Duke of Wellington and Sir Winston Churchill. Wellington's death mask is preserved at Castle Leslie, as is one of Churchill's baby dresses, along with an impressive collection of Italian works of art, including an Andrea della Robbia chimneypiece. There are 14 acres of gardens with miniature golf and croquet; home-baked teas are served in the tearoom and conservatory. ⊠ *Co. Monaghan,* ☎ *047/88109.* ☞ *£3, including tour.* ☉ *May–Aug., daily 2–6; tour on the hr and other times by appointment.*

Dining and Lodging

\$\$–\$\$\$ ✕▥ **Castle Leslie.** If you want to live like a lord—at least for one night—all the splendor of this famed estate can be yours if the tour isn't enough to satisfy your country-house fantasies. Some of the furniture and paintings predate the existing house, going all the way back to 1660. The large bedrooms have pleasant parkland views and are decked out in Victorian splendor with a wealth of antiques; most beds are either canopied, four-poster, or half-tester. Pre-dinner drinks are served next to a roaring log fire in the drawing room. A four-course menu of Continental cuisine, with five starter and main-course combinations, is served by candlelight; braised partridge in season, coq au vin, or salmon with sesame and ginger vinaigrette typify the entrées. ⊠ *Glaslough, Co. Monaghan,* ☎ *047/88109,* ℻ *047/88256. 14 rooms with bath. Dining room, fishing, boating. MC, V.*

Clones

🔞 *24 km (15 mi) west of Monaghan.*

Clones (pronounced clo-*nez*) was the site, in early Christian times, of a monastery founded by St. Tighearnach, who died here in AD 458. An Augustinian abbey replaced the monastery in the 12th century, and its remains can still be seen near the 75-ft **round tower** on Abbey Street. In the central diamond of the town stands a 10th-century, Celtic high cross, with carved panels depicting scriptural scenes. Nowadays Clones, a small, agricultural market town 1 km (½ mi) from the Northern Ireland border, is one of two lace-making centers in County Monaghan (the other is Carrickmacross). In an attempt to bring in some income, local rectors' wives took up the craft, which was introduced in the 19th century. Crochetwork and small raised dots are two hallmarks of Clones lace. A varied selection is on display around the town and can be purchased at the **Clones Lace Centre** ⊠ *Cara St., Co. Monaghan,* ☎ *047/52125.* ☞ *Free.* ☉ *Mon. and Wed.–Sat. 10–6.*

Dining and Lodging

\$\$\$ ✕▥ **Hilton Park.** To find this large, stately, early Georgian country house,
★ look for a large set of black gates with silver falcons 5 km (3 mi) outside Clones on R183 Ballyhaise road. It has three private lakes on its 500-acre grounds, which include 50 acres of gardens and parkland, a working sheep farm, and an organic market garden. Next door is Clones Golf Club (☞ Outdoor Activities and Sports, *below*). Johnny and Lucy Madden, the friendly hosts, run their house with stylish informality. All rooms are individually decorated with antiques and have

lovely views; some have four-poster beds. Dinner—freshly prepared produce from their market garden, combined with local meat and fish—
is available for guests. ☒ *Clones, Co. Monaghan,* ☎ *047/56007,* 🅵🅰🆇
*047/56033. 6 rooms with bath. Dining room, lake, 9-hole golf course,
croquet, boating, fishing. AE, MC, V. Closed Oct.–Mar.*

Outdoor Activities and Sports

Clones Golf Club (☒ Hilton Park, Clones) is a 9-hole course on limestone that is dry year-round.

NORTH TIPPERARY
AND THE WEST MIDLANDS

Our Midlands tour concludes with the area's western fringe, picking
up in the town of Boyle in County Roscommon. (If you do make it
this far, be sure to consult Chapter 8; locales covered there are close
to Boyle and environs.) The tour skirts the Lough Key, Lough Ree, Lough
Derg, and the River Shannon and, depending how you travel south,
takes you through the hilly landscape of unspoiled County Leitrim—
it, too, dappled with clean, cool lakes, is beloved of anglers for its peaceful, fish-filled waters. Despite a liberal sprinkling of villages, County
Leitrim is almost uninhabited (though it is the home of one of Ireland's
leading writers, John McGahern). Between the area's many bodies of
water, much of the land is bog, a fragile ecosystem that rewards closer
investigation. The towns are small and generally undistinguished, with
the exceptions of Birr and Strokestown, both of which were laid out
by architects and designed to complement the "big houses" that share
their names. The tour then brings you southward, to northern County
Tipperary.

Boyle

⑲ *190 km (118 mi) northwest of Dublin.*

An old-fashioned town on the Boyle River midway between Lough Gara
and Lough Key, Boyle makes a good starting point for visits to the nearby
Curlew Mountains. A massive edifice in the center of town, **King
House** was built about 1730 by the local King family, who moved 50
years later to larger quarters at Rockingham in what is now Lough Key
Forest Park (☞ *below*); that house burned down in 1957. The King
family originally came from Staffordshire, England, and aggressively
worked to establish themselves as local nobility—Edward King, an ancestor of the Kings who settled here, drowned in the Irish Sea in 1636;
he was the subject of Milton's poem *Lycidas*. From 1788 to 1922 the
house was owned by the British Army and used as a barracks for the
Connaught Rangers, known as the fiercest regiment of the British
Army (Wellington called them the "Devil's Own"). After extensive renovations, the house was opened to the public in 1995, with exhibits
on the Connaught Rangers, the Kings of Connaught, and the history
of the house. A coffee shop, popular with locals, serves traditional Irish
breakfasts and hearty lunches, both with plenty of homemade baked
goods on the menu. ☒ *Boyle,* ☎ *079/63242.* 🎫 *£2.50.* ⊙ *May–Sept.,
daily 10–6; Apr. and Oct., weekends 10–6; last tour at 5.*

Another reason to visit Boyle is the ruins of the **Cistercian abbey** (on
N4). The church was founded in the late 12th century when the Romanesque style still prevailed, but as construction went on, the then-
hot Gothic style made it to Ireland, evident in arches on the north side.
A 16th- to 17th-century gatehouse, through which you enter the abbey,
has a small exhibition. The ruins are freely accessible.

⑳ Lough Key Forest Park (☎ 079/62363), part of what was once the massive Rockingham Estate, is 3 km (2 mi) northeast of Boyle. Now a popular base for campers, backpackers, walkers, and anglers, the park consists of 840 acres on the shores of the lake and contains a bog garden, a deer enclosure, and a cypress grove. Ruins from Rockingham days, including the remains of a stable block, church, icehouse, and temple, are also found here. Boats can be hired on the lake, and there is also a restaurant. Parking is £2 (June–September), and the park is freely accessible.

Strokestown

㉑ *28 km (17 mi) south of Boyle.*

★ Strokestown has the widest main street in Ireland—laid out to rival the Ringstrasse in Vienna—which leads to three Gothic arches that mark the entrance to the grounds of **Strokestown Park House.** Home to the Pakenham Mahon family from 1660 to 1979, the house once sat on 27,000 acres and was the second-largest estate in Roscommon, after the King family's Rockingham (☞ *above*). The house has a complicated architectural history, which, to some degree, mirrors the histories of other Anglo-Irish houses. The oldest parts of the house date from 1696, Palladian wings were added in the 1730s to the original block, and the house was extended again in the early 19th century. Its contents are a rich trove specific to the site, as the contents were never liquidated in the auctions experienced by similar houses. The interior is full of curiosities, such as the gallery above the kitchen, which allowed the lady of the house to supervise domestic affairs from a safe distance. Menus were dropped from the balcony on Monday mornings with instructions to the cook for the week's meals. The 4-acre walled pleasure garden is fully restored and boasts the longest herbaceous border in Britain and Ireland. The award-winning **Irish Famine Museum,** housed in the stable yards, documents in detail the disastrous famine (1845–49) and the subsequent mass emigration. ⊠ *Strokestown,* ☎ *078/33013.* ▣ *House £3.25; house, museum, and garden £8.50.* ☉ *Apr.–Oct., daily 11–5:30; by appointment other times for groups.*

Roscommon

㉒ *43 km (27 mi) south of Boyle, 19 km (12 mi) south of Strokestown.*

Roscommon is the capital of County Roscommon, where sheep- and cattle-raising are the main occupations. It's a pleasant little town with many solid stone buildings, including the **Bank of Ireland** in the former courthouse and **county jail.** On the southern slopes of a hill in the lower part of town sit the remains of **Roscommon Abbey.** In the abbey's principal ruin, a church, are eight sculpted figures that represent gallowglasses (medieval Irish professional soldiers) and stand at the base of the choir. The ruins are freely accessible. To the north of Roscommon Town are the weathered remains of **Roscommon Castle,** a large Norman stronghold first built in the 13th century.

Outdoor Activities and Sports

Bikes can be rented from **Brendan Sheerin** (⊠ Main St., Boyle, ☎ 079/62010) .

Athlone

㉓ *29 km (18 mi) southeast of Roscommon, 127 km (79 mi) west of Dublin, 121 km (75 mi) east of Limerick.*

Athlone is the main shopping hub for the surrounding area and an important road and rail junction. The introduction of a bypass has eased traffic congestion, and a local initiative highlighting the attractions of Athlone's recently christened "Left Bank" (behind the castle [☞ *below*]), where many of the buildings date from at least 200 years ago, have combined to make Athlone a more attractive destination.

Athlone Castle is the site most worth visiting in Athlone. Beside the River Shannon, at the southern end of Lough Ree, it was built in the 13th century. After their defeat at the Battle of the Boyne in 1691, the Irish retreated to Athlone and made the river their first line of defense. The castle, which has been substantially altered and repaired, was extensively renovated in 1991 for its 300th anniversary. It remains an interesting example of a Norman stronghold and houses a small museum of artifacts relating to Athlone's eventful past. Admission includes access to an interpretative center depicting the siege of Athlone in 1691, the flora and fauna of the Shannon, and the life of the tenor John McCormack (1884–1945), an Athlone native and probably the finest lyric tenor Ireland has ever produced. ✉ *Town Bridge, Athlone,* ☎ *0902/ 72107.* 🎟 *£2.50.* ⊙ *May–Sept., daily 10–5; Oct.–Apr. by appointment.*

Dining and Lodging

$$$ ✕ **Le Château.** In Athlone's colorful Old Quarter, a Presbyterian church dating from 1860 now houses this unusually romantic restaurant. The furniture may be ecclesiastical, but the decor strikes a nautical note. Candlelit tables are set with large wine glasses, white linen, and fine old bone china. Owner-chef Stephen Linehan relies on fresh local ingredients. Main courses include medallions of veal with smoked bacon, garlic, and herbs, or roast peppered monkfish with fresh herb sauce. For dessert try the lemon tart or, in summer, fresh strawberry vol-au-vents with homemade ice cream. Reflecting the number of visitors to Athlone on Shannon cruisers who stop and eat here, the menu comes in three languages. ✉ *Saint Peter's Port, The Docks,* ☎ *0902/94517. AE, MC, DC, V. No lunch Mon.–Sat.*

$$$ ✕ **Wineport Restaurant.** About 5 km (3 mi) north of town on the shores
★ of Lough Ree, this pleasantly informal restaurant, in a wooden boathouse adorned with memorabilia from the original Lough Ree Yacht Club, has earned several prestigious awards since its debut in 1993. The menu changes every eight weeks, but roast organic venison (from a nearby farm) served in a juniper marinade is a popular year-round main course. New Irish cuisine, for example confit of salmon with a black pudding champ (mashed potato), is a feature of the menu. ✉ *Glasson,* ☎ *0902/85466. AE, DC, MC, V. Closed Mon.– Tues. Nov.–Feb.*

$$$ ✕🏨 **Hodson Bay Hotel.** Instead of staying in Athlone's unremarkable
★ town center, head 4 km (2½ mi) out of town on N63 to this four-story mansion on the shores of Lough Ree. Once an 18th-century family home, the hotel is adjacent to Athlone's golf course (☞ Outdoor Activities and Sports, *below*) and has its own marina. All guest rooms are coordinated in deep pastel shades with well-designed wooden furniture. The bar overlooks the lake, as does L'Escale Restaurant, a romantic, candlelit room with tables set with pink linen. The menu offers imaginative Irish cooking with a French accent. ✉ *Roscommon Rd., Athlone, Co. Westmeath,* ☎ *0902/92444,* 𝖥𝖠𝖷 *0902/92688. 90 rooms with bath, 7 suites. 2 restaurants, bar, indoor pool, sauna, 18-hole golf course, 2 tennis courts, health club, horseback riding, fishing. AE, DC, MC, V.*

Outdoor Activities and Sports

BICYCLING

Rent bikes from **M. R. Hardiman** (✉ Irishtown, Athlone, Co. Westmeath, ☎ 0902/78669).

The Viking is a riverboat that travels up the Shannon to nearby Lough Ree. The ride is 1½ hours, and light refreshments are available. ⊠ *The Strand, Athlone,* ☎ *0902/73383.* 🎫 *£5.* ☉ *Sailings July–Sept., Thurs.–Tues. at 11, 2:30, and 4; Wed. at 4:30.*

A river cruiser for a floating holiday can be rented by the week from **Athlone Cruisers Ltd.** (⊠ Jolly Mariner Marina, Athlone, ☎ 0902/72892) or **S. G. S. Marine** (⊠ Ballykeeran, Athlone, ☎ 0902/85163).

Mount Temple Golf Club (⊠ Campfield Lodge, Moate, ☎ 0902/81545) is a 9-hole parkland course 19 km (12 mi) east of Athlone. **Athlone Golf Club** (⊠ Hodson Bay, Athlone, ☎ 0902/92073 or 0902/92235) is a lakeside, 18-hole parkland course. **Glasson Golf & Country Club** (⊠ Glasson, Athlone, ☎ 0902/85120) is an 18-hole parkland course bordered on three sides by Lough Ree and the River Shannon.

Clonmacnoise

★ ㉔ *20 km (13 mi) south of Athlone, 93 km (58 mi) east of Galway.*

Many ancient sites dot the River Shannon, but the foremost of these is Clonmacnoise, early Christian Ireland's foremost monastic settlement and, like Chartres, a royal site. The monastery was founded by St. Ciaran between 543 and 549 at a location that was not as remote as it now appears to be—near the intersection of two of what were then Ireland's most vital routes: the Shannon River, running north–south, and the Eiscir Riada, running east–west. Like Glendalough, Celtic Ireland's other great monastic site, Clonmacnoise benefitted from isolation; surrounded by bog, it is accessible only via one road or the Shannon.

The monastery was founded on an esker (natural gravel ridge) overlooking the Shannon and a marshy area known as the Callows, which today is protected habitat for the corncrake, a wading bird. Numerous buildings and ruins remain. The small **cathedral** dates as far back as the 10th century but has additions dating from as recently as the 15th century. It was the burial place of kings of Connaught and of Tara, and of Rory O'Conor, the last High King of Ireland, buried here in 1198. The two round towers include **O'Rourke's Tower,** which was struck by lightning and subsequently rebuilt in the 12th century. There are **eight smaller churches.** The smallest is thought to be the burial place of St. Ciaran; the only one not built within the monastery walls is the Nun's Church, about 1 km (½ mi) east. The **high crosses** have now been moved into the visitor center to protect them from the elements (copies stand in their original places); the best preserved of these are the **Cross of the Scriptures,** also known as **Flann's Cross.** Some of the treasures and manuscripts originating from Clonmacnoise are now housed in Dublin; most are at the National Museum, while the 12th-century *Book of the Dun Cow* is at the Royal Irish Academy Library (☞ Chapter 1).

Clonmacnoise survived raids by feuding Irish tribes, Vikings, and Normans for almost 1,000 years, until 1552, when the English garrison from Athlone reduced it to ruin. Since then it has remained a prestigious burial place. Among the ancient stones are many other graves of local people dating from the 17th to the mid-20th century, when a new graveyard was consecrated on adjoining land. ⊠ *Co. Offaly,* ☎ *0905/74195.* 🎫 *£2.50.* ☉ *Mid-June–Sept., daily 9–7; Oct.–May, daily 10–6 or dusk.*

Bord na Mona Bog Rail Tour

★ ㉕ *10 km (6 mi) south of Clonmacnoise.*

As you pass through the small town of Shannonbridge, on either side of the road you'll notice vast stretches of chocolate-brown boglands and isolated industrial plants for processing this area's natural resource. Under the jurisdiction of Bord na Mona, the same government agency that makes commercial use of other boglands, the area is worth exploring. If you would like to have a close look at a bog, take a ride on the **Bord na Mona Bog Rail Tour,** which leaves from Uisce Dubh. A small, green-and-yellow diesel locomotive pulls one coach across the bog at an average of 24 kph (15 mph) while the driver provides commentary on a landscape unchanged for millennia. There are more than 1,200 km (745 mi) of narrow-gauge bog railway, and the section on the tour, known as the Clonmacnoise and South Offaly Railway, is the only partly accessible to the public. ⊠ *Uisce Dubh, near Shannonbridge,* ☎ *0905/74114.* ⊡ *£3.50.* ☉ *Tour Apr.–Oct., daily on the hr 10–5.*

Banagher

㉖ *21 km (13 mi) southeast of Shannonbridge.*

A small but lively village on the shores of the River Shannon, Banagher has a marina that makes the town a popular base for water-sports fans. Anthony Trollope, who came to Ireland as a post office surveyor in 1841, lived and wrote his first book, *The Macdermots of Ballycloran,* here. Charlotte Brontë spent her honeymoon here. **Flynn's** (⊠ Main St., ☎ 0509/51312), a light and spacious Victorian-style bar in the center of town, has a lunch menu of generously filled sandwiches, salad platters, a roast meat of the day, chicken, fish, or burgers and chips. It's a popular spot with the boating crowd and can be busy on weekends.

If you happen to be in Banagher on a Thursday or a Sunday, you can take a 2-hour **Shannon cruise** on *The River Queen,* an enclosed launch that seats 54 passengers and has a full bar on board. ⊠ *Silver Line Cruisers Ltd., The Marina, Banagher,* ☎ *0509/51112.* ⊡ *£4.* ☉ *Cruises June–mid-Sept., Thurs. at 3, Sun. at 2:30 and 4:30, weather permitting.*

Birr

㉗ *12 km (8 mi) southeast of Banagher, 130 km (80 mi) west of Dublin.*

Birr is a quiet, sleepy place with tree-lined malls and modest, Georgian houses. It was recently designated as a heritage town. The settlement's roots go back to the 6th century, but it was much later, in the mid-18th century, that Birr was given its modern-day appearance, as a Georgian building boom took hold.

★ All roads in Birr lead to the gates of **Birr Castle Demesne,** a Gothic Revival castle (built around an earlier 17th-century castle that was damaged by fire in 1823) that is still the home of the earls of Rosse. It is not open to the public, but you can visit the surrounding 150 acres of gardens. The present earl and countess of Rosse continue the family tradition of making botanical expeditions for specimens of rare trees, plants, and shrubs from all over the world. The formal gardens contain the tallest (32 ft) box hedges in the world. In spring, you can see a wonderful display of flowering magnolias, cherries, crab apples, and naturalized narcissi; in autumn, the maples, chestnuts, and weeping beeches blaze red and gold. The grounds are laid out around a lake and along the banks of two adjacent rivers; above one of these stands the castle. The grounds also contain **Ireland's Historic Science Centre,** an exhibition on astronomy, photography, botany, and engineering housed in the stable block. The giant (72-inch) reflecting telescope, built in 1845, remained the largest in the world for the next 75 years and was recently restored. Allow at least 2 hours to see all that's here. ⊠ *Rosse Row, Birr,* ☎ *0509/20336.* 🖭 *£5.* ☉ *Apr.–Oct., daily 9–6.*

Dining and Lodging

$$$ ✕🏨 **Kinnitty Castle.** At the foot of the Slieve Bloom Mountains 16 km (10 mi) east of Birr, Kinnitty is an exuberant, turreted Gothic Revival edifice, rebuilt in 1927 of ashlar granite. Everything is on a large scale: Bedrooms have large four-poster beds and intricately carved chairs, and heavy old beams are incorporated into the bathrooms in the old house. Accommodations in the new wing are smaller. The dining room has enormously tall windows and a dark wood floor. Typical main courses are panfried loin of lamb with its own sweetbreads or ragout of lobster from the tank, finished with Sevruga caviar. ⊠ *Kinnitty, Birr, Co. Offaly,* ☎ *0509/37318,* 🖷 *0509/37284. 37 rooms with bath. Restaurant, bar, tennis court, horseback riding, Ping-Pong, fishing. AE, DC, MC, V.*

$$ ✕🏨 **Tullanisk House.** Set on 700 acres of woodland in its own deer
★ park, this 18th-century dower house for Birr Castle (☞ *above*) has been carefully restored into an elegant accommodation with the atmosphere of a private home. Rooms vary in size, but owner-hosts Susie and George Gossip have decorated each with character. Books and magazines are everywhere, and open fires, board games, and table tennis are available on wet days. Dinner (reservations essential) is served on family china and silverware by candlelight in the classic Georgian dining room. All guests sit at the host's table and share the same menu, which features fresh local produce cooked, usually by George, in classic country-house style, with game as a specialty during winter. ⊠ *Co. Offaly,* ☎ *0509/20572,* 🖷 *0509/21783. 5 rooms with bath. Dining room, hiking, Ping-Pong. AE, MC, V.*

$ ✕🏨 **Dooly's.** This 250-year-old, black-and-white coaching inn is tucked away in a corner of Birr's central square. A log fire burns in the front lobby, which is decorated in the Georgian style. Rooms, which have all been refurbished and modernized, have pastel colors, floral drapes and bedspreads, and plain, dark-pastel walls. The relaxed bar and coffee shop are busy all day; a more formal dining experience is in the Emmet Restaurant. The five-course table-d'hôte dinner menu, an excellent value, may feature medallions of beef flambéd in whiskey and onions or fresh Corrib salmon steak poached in pink peppercorns and white wine. ⊠ *Emmet Sq., Birr, Co. Offaly,* ☎ *0509/20032,* 🖷 *0509/ 21332. 18 rooms with bath. Restaurant, bar, coffee shop, horseback riding, fishing. AE, DC, MC, V.*

$ ✕🏨 **The Maltings.** Set in a picturesque riverside setting near Kinnitty Castle, this beautiful cut-stone and brick malt house has been converted into family-run accommodations. Spacious rooms have small windows, country pine furniture, and simple matching floral drapes and spreads. The cheerful, low-ceiling restaurant overlooks the river and offers good value in plain cooking. ⊠ *Castle St., Co. Offaly,* ☎ 🖷 *0509/21345. 10 rooms with bath. Restaurant, sauna, exercise room. MC, V.*

Lough Derg

㉘ *16 km (10 mi) west of Birr on R489.*

Between Portland and Portumna the River Shannon widens into 32,000 acres of unpolluted water, known as Lough Derg, a popular center for water sports, including waterskiing, yachting, and motor cruising. Fishermen flock here as well for pike- and coarse-angling. There are excellent woodland walks around the shore of the Lough. (Be sure not to confuse this Lough Derg with the lake of the same name in County Donegal, a well-known pilgrimage site, covered in Chapter 7. The well-signposted, scenic **Lough Derg Drive,** approximately 90 km (54 mi), encircles the lake, passing through a number of pretty waterside villages, from Portumna in the north to Killaloe in the south. **Terryglass,** on the eastern shore of Lough Derg and well signposted on R439 from Birr, is popular with water-sports enthusiasts and anglers, as well as regular vacationers seeking an away-from-it-all destination; it is considered one of the prettiest villages in Ireland.

Dining and Lodging

$ ⊡ **Riverrun House.** Typical of the very best of the newer B&Bs around the country, this rambling farmhouse-style building in the middle of the village combines country stylishness with practicality. Clean, clutter-free rooms have duvet-covered king-size beds, framed botanical prints, one or two pieces of antique country pine, and throw rugs on stripped pine floors. Dinner isn't served, but the village has two pub-restaurants. A stream runs through the pretty, south-facing garden, and small children are made especially welcome. ⊠ *Terryglass, Nenagh, Co. Tipperary,* ☎ *067/22125,* FAX *067/22187. 6 rooms with bath. Dining room, tennis court, bicycles. AE, MC, V.*

$ ⊡ **Tír na Fiúise.** Hosts Niall and Inez Heenan and their friendly sheep dog, Ben, offer guests a taste of Irish farm life. Feed the pigs, help make hay, or try your hand at cutting turf. Alternately, if you just want to chill out in the small but comfortable farmhouse, that's okay too. Tir na Fiúise (the name means "Land of Fuchsia") presents genuine peace and quiet on 100 acres next to the pretty lakeside village of Terryglass. Rooms are cozy, bright, simple, and sparklingly clean. Breakfasts of fresh organic produce, homemade yogurts, farmhouse cheeses, and smoked salmon are served until noon. ⊠ *Terryglass, Borrisokane, Co. Tipperary,* ☎ FAX *067/22041. 4 rooms with bath. Boating, fishing, bicycles. MC, V. Closed Nov.–Easter.*

Outdoor Activities and Sports

The 18-hole parkland course at **Birr Golf Club** (⊠ The Glens, Birr, ☎ 0509/20082) is highly recommended by discerning golfers.

Roscrea

㉙ *19 km (12 mi) south of Birr.*

The main Dublin–Limerick road passes through Roscrea, a charming town steeped in religious history, and cuts right through a 7th-century monastery founded by St. Cronan. It also passes the west facade of a 12th-century Romanesque church that now forms an entrance gate to a modern Catholic church. Above the structure's round-headed doorway is a hood molding enclosing the figure of a bishop, probably St. Cronan.

With your back to St. Cronan's, turn left and then right onto Castle Street to visit **Damer House,** a superb example of an early 18th-century town house on the grand scale. It was built in 1725 within the curtain walls of a Norman castle, at a time when homes were often constructed beside or attached to the strongholds they replaced. The house has a plain, symmetrical facade and a magnificent carved-pine staircase inside; on display are exhibits of local historical interest. The 13th-century stone castle is surrounded by a moat and consists of a gate tower, curtain walls, and two corner towers. The house is home to the **Roscrea Heritage Centre.** ⊠ *Castle St., Roscrea,* ☎ *0505/21850.* ⊡ *£2.50.* ☉ *May–Sept., daily 9:30–6; Oct.–Apr., weekends 10–5.*

Outdoor Activities and Sports

Roscrea Golf Club (✉ Demyrale, ☎ 0509/21130) is an 18-hole parkland course with views of the Slieve Bloom Mountains.

Nenagh

③ *35 km (21 mi) west of Roscrea, 35 km (21 mi) west of Limerick.*

Nenagh was originally a Norman settlement; it grew to a market town in the 19th century. Standing right in the center of Nenagh, the **Castle Keep** is all that remains of the original town. Once one of five round towers linked by a curtain wall, and measuring 53 ft across the base, it rises to 100 ft, with 19th-century castellations at the top. The gatehouse and governor's house of Nenagh's old county jail now form the **Nenagh Heritage Centre,** which has permanent displays of rural life in the recent past before mechanization, as well as temporary painting and photography exhibits. ✉ *Kickham St.,* ☎ *067/32633.* 🖭 *£2.* ☉ *Easter–Oct., weekdays 9:30–5, Sun. 2:30–5; Nov.–Easter, weekdays 9:30–5.*

Dining and Lodging

$$ ✕🏨 **Waterman's Lodge.** Perched on a hilltop with bay windows overlooking the Shannon and the hills of County Clare, Brid Ryan's lovely lodge makes an ideal rural retreat. Open fires, piles of books, high ceilings, and timber floors combine to create a relaxing, country-house atmosphere. Rooms have brass or cast-iron beds and modest antiques. Chef Thomas O'Leary's imaginative treatment of seasonal local produce is renowned: Try his roast rack of lamb with a parsley crust, sage-flavored couscous, and lamb au jus. ✉ *Ballina, Killaloe, Co. Clare,* ☎ *061/376333,* ⅢX *061/375445. 10 rooms with bath. Restaurant, horseback riding, fishing. DC, MC, V. No dinner Sun. Closed Dec. 22–mid-Mar.*

$ ✕🏨 **Ashley Park House.** Margaret and P. J. Mounsey invite guests to experience informal country-house living in their 18th-century fishing lodge overlooking Lough Ourna. Formal gardens and 76 acres of beech woodland surround the home, and abundant wildlife can be observed from a rowboat. High ceilings, country views, and an abundance of antiques are features of the large bedrooms. Created from fresh local produce, dinners may even include trout you've caught in the lake. ✉ *Ardcroney, Co. Tipperary,* ☎ ⅢX *067/38223. 5 rooms, 2 with bath. Fishing, boating. No credit cards.*

Outdoor Activities and Sports

BOATING

Shannon Sailing (✉ New Marina Complex, Dromineer, ☎ 067/24499) organizes cruises of scenic Lough Derg by water bus and also hires out cruisers and sailboards.

GOLF

Nenagh Golf Club (✉ Beechwood, ☎ 067/31476) is a typical 18-hole, par-69 Midlands course: green, flat, and not too busy.

THE MIDLANDS A TO Z

Arriving and Departing

By Bus

Bus Éireann (☎ 01/836–6111) runs an express bus from Dublin to Mullingar in 1½ hours, with a round-trip fare of £9. Buses depart three times daily. A regular-speed bus, leaving twice daily, makes the trip in 2 hours.

By Car

Mullingar (the regional capital), Longford, and Boyle are on the main
N4 route between Dublin and Sligo. It takes 1 hour to drive the 55 km
(34 mi) from Dublin to Mullingar, and 2 hours from Mullingar to Sligo.
To get from Mullingar to the southwest, a 150-km (94-mi) trip that
takes about 2 hours, you can take N52 to Nenagh, where it meets N7,
and follow that into Limerick. R390 from Mullingar leads you west
to Athlone, where it connects with N6 to Galway. The 120-km (75-
mi) drive takes about 2½ hours.

By Plane

The principal international airport serving the Midlands is **Dublin Airport** (☎ 01/844–4900). **Sligo Regional Airport** (☎ 071/68280) has daily
flights from Dublin on Aer Lingus. Car-rental facilities are available
at Dublin Airport. For more information on these airports, ☞ Arriving and Departing *in* Chapters 1 and 7.

By Train

A direct-rail service links Mullingar to Dublin (Connolly Station),
with three trains every day making the 1½-hour journey. It costs £7.50
one-way and £12.50 round-trip. Contact **Irish Rail** (☎ 01/836–6222)
for information.

Getting Around

By Bus

The express buses leaving Dublin (☞ Arriving and Departing by Bus,
above) make stops at Mullingar (1½ hrs), Longford (2¼ hrs), Carrick-
on-Shannon (3 hrs), Boyle (3¼ hrs), and Sligo (4¼ hrs). There is also
a daily bus from Mullingar to Athlone and an express service connecting
Galway, Athlone, Longford, Cavan, Clones, Monaghan, and Sligo. Details of all bus services are available from Bus Éireann depots at the
following locations: **Athlone Railway Station** (☎ 0902/72651), **Cavan
Bus Office** (☎ 049/433–1353), **Longford Railway Station** (☎ 043/
45208), **Monaghan Bus Office** (☎ 047/82377), **Sligo Railway Station**
(☎ 071/69888), and **Bus Éireann** (☎ 01/836–6111 in Dublin).

By Car

Most of the winding roads in the Midlands are uncongested, although
you may encounter an occasional animal or agricultural machine crossing the road. In Mullingar, the cattle-trading town, roads can become
badly crowded, however. If you're driving in the north of Counties Cavan
and Monaghan, be sure to avoid "unapproved" roads crossing the border into Northern Ireland. The approved routes into Northern Ireland
connect the towns of Monaghan and Aughnacloy, Castlefinn and Cas-
tlederg, Swalinbar and Enniskillen, Clones and Newtownbutler, and
Monaghan and Rosslea. Those driving a rented car should make sure
it has been cleared for cross-border journeys.

By Train

Trains from Mullingar, departing twice daily every weekday and Sunday, stop at Longford (35 min), Carrick-on-Shannon (1 hr), Boyle (1¼
hrs), and Sligo (2 hrs).

Contacts and Resources

B&B Reservation Agencies

For a small fee—£3, plus a 10% deposit (which is taken off the bal-
ance of your bill when you pay for your accommodations)—**Bord
Fáilte** will book accommodations anywhere in Ireland through its central reservations system. B&Bs can be booked at local visitor information
offices when they are open; however, even these reservations will go

through the central system. For more information, ☞ Lodging *in* Smart Travel Tips A to Z.

Car Rentals

There are a handful of car rental firms in the Midlands: **Hamill's Rent-a-Car** (⊠ Dublin Rd., Mullingar, Co. Westmeath, ☎ 044/48682), **Gerry Mullin** (⊠ North Rd., Monaghan, ☎ 047/81396), **O'Reilly & Sons/Euromobil** (⊠ Dublin Rd., Longford, ☎ 043/46494).

Emergencies

Police, fire, and **ambulance** (☎ 999). For medical and ambulance service, contact Mullingar's **General Hospital** (☎ 044/40221).

PHARMACY

Weir's Chemist (⊠ Market Sq., Mullingar, ☎ 044/48462).

Outdoor Activities and Sports

FISHING

General information about fishing can be obtained in most hotels, B&Bs, and bars. Contact the Irish Tourist Board for more details on angling tournaments (☞ Visitor Information, *below,* for local offices, and Smart Travel Tips A to Z). For information on necessary licenses and permits, contact the **Eastern Regional Fisheries Board** (⊠ Balnagowan Mobhi Boreen, Dublin 9, ☎ 01/837–9209).

Visitor Information

Five Midlands Tourist Information Offices (TIOs) are open all year (not all have fax numbers): **Carrick-on-Shannon** (⊠ The Marina, Co. Leitrim, ☎ 078/20170), **Cavan** (⊠ Farnham St., ☎ 049/31942), **Monaghan** (⊠ Market House, ☎ 047/81122), **Mullingar** (⊠ Dublin Rd., ☎ 044/48650, FAX 044/40413), **Portlaoise** (⊠ James Fintan Lawlor Ave., ☎ 0502/21178).

Another eight Midlands TIOs are open seasonally: **Athlone** (⊠ Church St., ☎ 0902/94630), open April–October; **Birr** (⊠ Rosse Row, ☎ 0509/20110), open May–September; **Boyle** (⊠ Bridge St., ☎ 079/62145), open April–September; **Clonmacnoise** (⊠ Clonmacnoise, ☎ 0905/74134), open April–October; **Longford** (⊠ Main St., ☎ 043/46566), open June–September; **Nenagh** (⊠ Connolly St., ☎ 067/31610), open May–early September; **Roscommon** (⊠ The Square, ☎ 0903/26342), open mid-May–mid-September; **Tipperary** (⊠ James St., ☎ 062/51457), open May–October; **Tullamore** (⊠ Bridge St., ☎ 0506/52617), open mid-June–mid-September. For off-season inquiries about Boyle and Roscommon, consult the Sligo TIO (☞ Visitor Information *in* The Northwest A to Z *in* Chapter 7).

4 THE SOUTHEAST

COUNTIES WEXFORD, CARLOW,
KILKENNY, TIPPERARY, AND WATERFORD

Although the Southeast doesn't have Ireland's wildest scenic landscape, it *does* have plenty to offer—things all Ireland, and the world, enjoy. Time-burnished Kilkenny glows with an old-world atmosphere, while Tipperary's Golden Vale is home to the country's most fertile farmland. Counties Wexford and Waterford are leading holiday destinations for natives in the know, with opera cognoscenti flocking to Wexford's famous festival. And long before Kleenex and Xerox turned their brand names into the thing itself, Waterford set a standard for cut crystal that all the world knows by name.

Updated by Alannah Hopkin

THE IRISH LIKE TO PUT LABELS ON AREAS, and "Ireland's sunny Southeast" is the tag they've taken to calling Counties Wexford, Carlow, Kilkenny, Tipperary, and Waterford. The moniker is by no means merely fanciful: The weather station on the coast at Rosslare reports that this region receives more hours of sunshine than anywhere else in the country. The Southeast, indeed, also has the driest weather in Ireland, with as little as 30 inches of rainfall per year—compared to an average of 80 inches on parts of the west coast. This is saying something in a country where seldom do more than three days pass without a shower of rain, which can vary from the finest light drizzle to a downpour that would convince Olympic swimmers they had never truly come to grips with the element of water. Little wonder the outdoor-loving Irish have made the Southeast's coast a popular vacation area. The whole area is Croesus-rich with natural beauty: not the rugged and wild wonders found to the north and west but an inland landscape of fertile river valleys and lush, undulating pastureland, with a coast that alternates between long, sandy beaches and rocky bays backed by low cliffs. Although the region is blessed with idyllic country sights and small and charming fishing villages, you'll find you never have to travel that far to find the bright lights—the cities of Kilkenny, Waterford, and Wexford.

The Southeast's coastal and inland areas both have a long, interesting history. The kings of Munster had their ceremonial center on the Rock of Cashel, which in the 7th century became an important monastic center and bishopric, and there were other thriving early Christian monasteries at Kilkenny, Ardmore, and Lismore. But the quiet life of early Christian Ireland was disrupted from the 9th century onward by a series of Viking invasions. The Vikings liked what they found here—a pleasant climate; rich, easily cultivated land; and a series of safe, sheltered harbors—so they stayed and founded the towns of Wexford and Waterford. (Waterford's name comes from the Norse Vadrefjord, Wexford's from Waesfjord.) Less than two centuries later, the same cities were conquered by Anglo-Norman barons and turned into walled strongholds. The Anglo-Normans and the Irish chieftains soon started to intermarry, but the process of integration came to a halt in 1366 with the Statute of Kilkenny, based on English fears that if such intermingling continued they would lose whatever control over Ireland they had. The next great crisis was Oliver Cromwell's Irish campaign of 1650, which, in attempting to crush Catholic opposition to the English parliament, brought widespread woe.

Carlow Town, Kilkenny City, Enniscorthy, and Wexford Town together provide an introduction to Irish history. All have remnants of their successive waves of invaders—Celt, Viking, and Norman. The most beautiful is Kilkenny City, an important ecclesiastic and political center up to the 17th century and now a lively market town whose streets still contain many remains from medieval times, most notably St. Canice's Cathedral and a magnificent 12th-century castle that received in turn a sumptuous Victorian makeover. Wexford's narrow streets are built on one side of a wide estuary, and it has a delightful maritime atmosphere. Waterford, although less immediately attractive than Wexford, is also built on the confluence of two of the region's rivers, the Suir and the Barrow. It offers a rich selection of Viking and Norman remains, some attractive Georgian buildings, and also the world-renowned Waterford Glass Factory, open to visitors.

Beyond lies a tranquil countryside with more Edenic pleasures. The road between Rosslare and Ballyhack passes through quiet, atypical, flat countryside dotted with thatched cottages. Beyond Tramore, level, sandy beaches give way to rocky Helvick Head and the foothills of the Knockmealdown Mountains at Dungarvan. Among the inland riverside towns, Carrick-on-Suir and Clonmel each have a special, quiet charm. In the far southwest of County Waterford, near the Cork border, Ardmore presents early Christian remains on an exposed headland, while in the wooded splendor of the Blackwater Valley, the tiny cathedral town of Lismore has a hauntingly beautiful fairy-tale castle.

Anglers will scarcely believe the variety of fishing and scenery along the Rivers Barrow, Nore, and Suir, and especially in the Blackwater Valley area. County Tipperary is the location of the Rock of Cashel, a vast, cathedral-topped rock rising above the plain and one of Ireland's most stunning historic sights. The ancient seat of the kings of Munster, Cashel is also, according to legend, where St. Patrick converted the High King of Ireland to Christianity.

Pleasures and Pastimes

Festivals and the Arts

There are two major arts festivals in the area: Kilkenny Arts Week, held in late August, features classical music, theater, and art exhibits, and the Wexford Opera Festival, where each year in late October and early November three rare operas are given full-scale productions with internationally renowned casts (☞ Nightlife and the Arts *in* Kilkenny City *and* Wexford Town, *below*).

Dining

The restaurants in this region are generally small and informal. Seafood—especially Wexford mussels, crab, and locally caught salmon—appears on most menus, along with local lamb, beef, and game in season. Food is usually prepared in a simple, country-house style, but be ready for some pleasant surprises, as there are a number of ambitious Irish chefs at work in the area in both restaurants and hotels. For price ranges, ☞ Chart 1(A) *in* Smart Travel Tips A to Z.

Lodging

The southeast coast is popular with Irish families during July and August, when it is advisable to book in advance, especially at places right on the coast. For price ranges ☞ Chart 2(B) *in* Smart Travel Tips A to Z.

Outdoor Activities and Sports

BICYCLING

The Southeast is a relatively unchallenging area for cyclists, with the only seriously hilly parts in the Knockmealdown and Comeragh mountains to the south of the region. If you enjoy bird life and sea vistas, try planning a coastal route: Between Arklow and Wexford it is predominantly flat with expanses of sandy beaches. The Hook Peninsula between Wexford and Waterford has a network of small, quiet roads, many of them leading to tranquil fishing villages. Traveling from Waterford to Dungarvan via Dunmore East and Tramore offers a variety of scenery combining cliff-top rides with stretches of beachfront.

GOLF

Some of Ireland's best parkland courses can be found in the Southeast, and there is also a championship links course at Rosslare. Mount Juliet, near Kilkenny, has been publicly acclaimed by Nick Faldo as one of Europe's best. It is one of six 18-hole courses to open in the area in recent years. ☞ Chapter 9 for more details.

HIKING

Two hiking trails cross the region, and the scenery on both is interestingly varied with wooded hills, rich farmland, and several rivers. The South Leinster Way begins in the County Carlow town of Kildavin and makes its way southwest over Mt. Leinster and the River Barrow, terminating in Carrick-on-Suir. A second trail, the Munster Way, picks up where the first ends and leads through the Vee Gap in the Knockmealdown Mountains and on to Clogheen.

HORSEBACK RIDING

If you have any equestrian skills at all, you will probably want to ride some of the fine horses bred in this part of Ireland. Inland, the terrain is mainly arable farmland, while the long, sandy beaches of the coast are regularly used as gallops. Most establishments have riding for about £9 to £12 and hour, and many stables offer hunting packages to the more experienced rider; rates are available on request.

SPECTATOR SPORTS

The people of the Southeast are a sporting lot, and on any given day you're likely to find the stand at the races or the hurling matches overflowing. Greyhound racing is extremely popular here, and Irish dogs are considered to be among the best in the world. Races are held at night, and a bar and restaurant are usually within the stadium. Horse races are also held regularly in the area at small, informal meets. Ask locally about Gaelic football and hurling venues. These skillful and fast-moving games can often be watched for free, or for the nominal entrance price at one of the five Gaelic Athletic Association (GAA) in the area.

Exploring the Southeast

The Southeast is geographically a large region (a car is essential for getting around here), stretching from the town of Carlow near the border of County Wicklow (☞ Chapter 2) in the north to Ardmore near the border of County Cork (☞ Chapter 5) in the south. Outside of the months of July and August, when the Irish themselves head here for their own vacations, the region is relatively free of traffic, making it ideal for leisurely exploration. Wexford, Waterford, and Kilkenny all have compact town centers best explored on foot, and they also make good touring bases.

Numbers in the text correspond to numbers in the margin and on the Southeast, Kilkenny City, Wexford Town, and Waterford City maps.

Great Itineraries

IF YOU HAVE 3 DAYS

Three days is enough time for a greatest-hits itinerary of the Southeast, though it won't leave you much time for meandering along the back roads. Start in the south of the region by taking the main Cork–Wexford road (N25) and heading north to visit the popular seaside resort and cliff-top early Christian monuments at **Ardmore** ㊾. Stop in the famed pubs of **Dungarvan** ㊼ for a *ceili* (Irish dance); then head on to **Lismore** (50), a small, pretty village on the Blackwater River, to tour the gardens of the Duke of Devonshire's spectacular castle. From Lismore drive on along a scenic route known as the Vee Gap to visit another great Irish castle and Lord and Lady Cahir's Swiss Cottage at **Cahir** (51). On the next day, spend the morning visiting that postcard icon, the awe-inspiring **Rock of Cashel** in the market town of **Cashel** (53). Drive via Urlingford on the main N8 to **Kilkenny City** ④–⑪, where you can wander the time-hallowed streets, explore its medieval cathedral, and visit its Victorian baronial castle seat. Head to **Leighlinbridge** ② for a salmon steak at the Lord Bagenal Inn, then on to the unspoiled

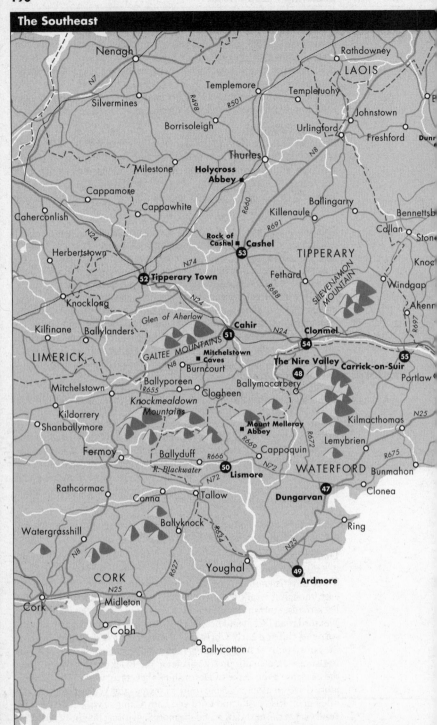

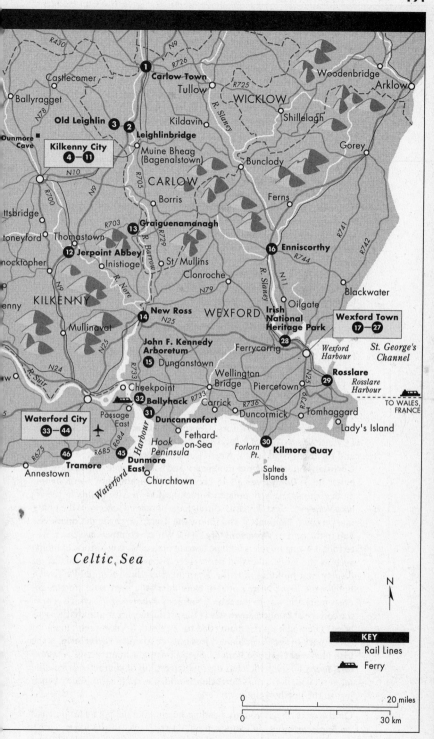

riverside village of **Graiguenamanagh** ⑬ and its Duiske Abbey. On the following morning head for the coast again and have a look at the still vibrant old Viking port of **Wexford** ⑰–㉗. Drive on down this pretty stretch of coast through the picturesque waterside villages of **Kilmore Quay** ㉚ and **Ballyhack** ㉜ and cross by car ferry to **Waterford City** ㉝–㊹, another old Viking settlement on the estuary of the Rivers Suir and Nore-Barrow whose name these days brings to mind the dazzling cut glass that has carried the city's name to the banquet halls of the world. Waterford is on the main Cork–Wexford road.

IF YOU HAVE 5 DAYS

Five days allows for a leisurely sampling of the different regions within the Southeast, with time to get to know its three biggest towns, Kilkenny, Wexford, and Waterford. Start in the north of the region, approaching it through **Carlow Town** ①—a modern center but home to several fascinating historical sights. Cross the River Barrow at **Leighlinbridge** ② and drive down to **Graiguenamanagh** ⑬, an unspoiled and hilly riverside village with a nicely restored Abbey. Continue on through **Jerpoint Abbey** ⑫, a stone-built village on the River Nore with a ruined Cistercian monastery which had been a masterpiece of Irish Romanesque, to **Kilkenny City** ④–⑪, a lovely town that features medieval coaching inns, Tudor almshouses, Georgian streets, and alleyway "slips." Next morning explore the medieval city center with its castle and cathedral on foot. Drive on through Urlingford to the spectacular **Rock of Cashel,** symbol of both Celtic and Christian Ireland, in the market town of **Cashel** (53). Continue to **Cahir** (51) at the foot of the Galtee Mountains where you can visit another kind of castle, this time of Norman vintage, and inspect the town's numerous antiques shops.

Next day drive up through the scenic Vee Gap in the Knockmealdown Mountains past Mount Melleray, home to an order of contemplative monks who welcome visitors. Continue to **Lismore** ㊿, which has the Devonshire seat, one of Ireland's prettiest castles. Then head for the coast and the main road south, which leads to **Ardmore** ㊾, where the early Christians built a cliff-top monastery and round tower. Spend the night either in **Dungarvan** ㊼—a cheerful little fishing town—or inland among the sparsely populated Knockmealdown Mountains in the **Nire Valley** ㊽. Next day drive through the unspoiled scenery of the pretty market town **Clonmel** (54), and follow the River Suir through **Carrick-on-Suir** to the port of **Waterford City** ㉝–㊹. While a commercial center, Waterford is luring travelers with pedestrian malls and new historic exhibits, such as the large collection of recently discovered Viking artifacts on display in a building near the Norman stronghold Reginald's Tower. Follow the River Nore north to **New Ross** ⑭, a busy river port. Signposts mark the way to the **John F. Kennedy Arboretum** ⑮, which is near the cottage at **Dunganstown** where the president's great-grandfather was born. Then pick up the main road to Wexford, a Viking settlement on the estuary of the River Slaney. Just outside town, at **Ferrycarrig,** is the **Irish National Heritage Park** ㉘. Spend the night in attractive **Wexford Town** ⑰–㉗, which has narrow streets full of character. If wildlife interests you, don't miss **Curracloe Strand,** a 9-km (5½-mi) sandy beach just to the north of the town.

On the next day, if you are heading north, take the N11 Dublin road via **Enniscorthy** ⑯, an historic town on the banks of the River Slaney dominated by its Norman castle. If you are heading south with time to spare, take the small coastal road through **Kilmore Quay** ㉚, past thatched cottages and narrow lanes, to **Ballyhack** ㉜, where you can take a car ferry across the harbor to Waterford and the road south.

Finally, a travel companion that doesn't snore on the plane or eat all your peanuts.

When traveling, your MCI WorldCom Card is the best way to keep in touch. Our operators speak your language, so they'll be able to connect you back home—no matter where your travels take you. Plus, your MCI WorldCom Card is easy to use, and even earns you frequent flyer miles every time you use it. When you add in our great rates, you get something even more valuable: peace-of-mind. So go ahead. Travel the world. MCI WorldCom just brought it a whole lot closer.

You can even sign up today at www.mci.com/worldphone or ask your operator to make a collect call to 1-410-314-2938.

EASY TO CALL WORLDWIDE

1 Just dial the WorldPhone access number of the country you're calling from.
2 Dial or give the operator your MCI WorldCom Card number.
3 Dial or give the number you're calling.

France ◆	0-800-99-0019
Germany	0800-888-8000
Ireland	1-800-55-1001
Italy ◆	172-1022
Spain	900-99-0014
Sweden ◆	020-795-922
Switzerland ◆	0800-89-0222
United Kingdom	
To call using BT	0800-89-0222
To call using CWC	0500-89-0222

For your complete WorldPhone calling guide, dial the WorldPhone access number for the country you're in and ask the operator for Customer Service. In the U.S. call 1-800-431-5402.

◆ Public phones may require deposit of coin or phone card for dial tone.

EARN FREQUENT FLYER MILES

American Airlines®
A'Advantage®

Continental Airlines
OnePass

▲ Delta Air Lines
SkyMiles®

■ MILEAGE PLUS®
United Airlines

U·S AIRWAYS
DIVIDEND MILES

MCI WorldCom, its logo and the names of the products referred to herein are proprietary marks of MCI WorldCom, Inc. All airline names and logos are proprietary marks of the respective airlines. All airline program rules and conditions apply.

The first thing you need overseas is the one thing you forget to pack.

FOREIGN CURRENCY DELIVERED OVERNIGHT

Chase Currency To Go® delivers foreign currency to your home by the next business day*

It's easy–before you travel, call 1-888-CHASE84 for delivery of any of 75 currencies

Delivery is free with orders of $500 or more

Competitive rates– without exchange fees

You don't have to be a Chase customer–you can pay by Visa® or MasterCard®

 **CHASE**

THE RIGHT RELATIONSHIP IS EVERYTHING.®

1•888•CHASE84
www.chase.com

When to Tour the Southeast

The Southeast is a good area of Ireland to visit off-season. Restaurants and accommodations are open between November and March, months when many places in the more touristy western regions are closed. And then there's the weather, which serves up significantly less rain than elsewhere, making this a good choice if you're visiting in the spring and autumn. Remember that in July and August, the Irish themselves descend on the coastal resorts, so if you plan to head for the beaches of the Southeast in the summer, be sure to reserve accommodations well in advance.

ON THE ROAD TO KILKENNY CITY AND WEXFORD TOWN

Many sights in this region—notably rich in historical and maritime attractions—make a visit here memorably picturesque. From Carlow Town's small county seat you travel through the farmlands of the Barrow Valley to Kilkenny City—which, from an architectural point of view, is among the most pleasing towns of inland Ireland. The historic city center is endowed with an old-world atmosphere, thanks to the country gentry who made their headquarters here in the 18th century, building themselves fine town houses in the Georgian style. From Thomastown, just outside Kilkenny, another cross-country drive follows the River Nore to New Ross, where it meets the River Barrow, and proceeds to John F. Kennedy's ancestral home and the arboretum planted in his memory. The tour ends in the old Viking port of Wexford Town, now home to a celebrated opera festival, which presents rare works in the restored 18th-century Theatre Royal.

Carlow Town

❶ *83 km (52 mi) south of Dublin.*

Carlow Town was established on the banks of the River Barrow by the Anglo-Normans in the 12th century. Its position on the border of the English Pale—the area around Dublin that was dominated by the English from Elizabethan times on—made it an important strategic center and hence the scene of many bloody battles and sieges. Today Carlow is a lively market town little more than an hour from central Dublin, with a population of about 11,700. The presence of the large Institute of Technology here gives the town a lively buzz.

The Roman Catholic **Cathedral of the Assumption** is one of Carlow Town's most prominent sights. Completed in 1883, the Regency-Gothic-style cathedral is notable for its stained-glass windows and a magnificently sculpted marble monument on the tomb of its builder, Bishop James Doyle (1786–1834), a champion of Catholic emancipation; the monument was carved by the Irish sculptor John Hogan (1800–58). ✉ *Tullow St.,* ☎ *0503/31227.* ☼ *Daily 10–8.*

The ruins of the 13th-century **Carlow Castle** can be found near the bridge on the grounds of Corcoran's Mineral Water Factory. Only the west wall and two towers remain, both offering imposing views of the River Barrow. This castle withstood a siege by Cromwell's troops in 1650, only to be destroyed accidentally in 1814 when a Dr. Philip Middleton attempted to renovate the castle for use as a mental asylum. While setting off explosives to reduce the thickness of the walls, he managed to demolish all but the west wall and its two flanking towers. (Despite what the story might suggest, Middleton was not himself to be a patient.)

The **County Museum** is housed in Carlow's town hall. Exhibits include a reconstructed blacksmith's forge and a preindustrial kitchen. ⊠ *Centaur St.,* ☎ *0503/31759.* 🖃 *£1.* ⊙ *Tues.–Fri. 11–5, weekends 2–5.*

The famous **Browne's Hill Dolmen** is reached by taking a 3-km (2-mi) detour on the road to Tullow (R725) east of Carlow Town. This stone monument dates from 2000 BC and, with a capstone weighing in at 100 tons, is considered the largest in Ireland. Nineteenth-century historians thought that dolmens were Druidic altars, while the peasantry believed them to be giants' graves. They are, in fact, megalithic tombs dating from the Stone Age (circa 3000–2000 BC). The dolmen is accessible through a field gate along the road; there is no entrance fee.

Dining and Lodging

$$$$ ✕ **Danette's Feast.** Tucked into an elegant, antiques-filled rectory outside Carlow on the Hackettstown road, Danette O'Connell's relaxed country house indeed provides the promised feast—but not only one for the tastebuds. Both Danette and partner David Milne are musicians; thus, the background melodies are the perfect accompaniments to the dining experience. Musical evenings—classical soirees followed by an eight-course tasting menu—take place once a month. Danette's love for Mexican food is evident in her main courses: chili rellenos with Parma ham and goat's cheese, or tacos with shredded, twice-cooked beef, perhaps with a margarita sorbet in between. Her other specialty is classic French cuisine; meals might include fresh brill with lemon butter and dill sauce, or fillet of steak in a sauce of smoked bacon, mushrooms, and wine. ⊠ *Urglin Glebe, Co. Carlow,* ☎ *0503/40871. MC, V. Closed Mon.–Tues. No dinner Sun., no lunch Wed.–Sat.*

$ ⌂ **Barrowville Town House.** This elegant 18th-century house, nestled into its own semi-formal gardens, is only minutes away from the town center. The large, bright rooms are in the original house and are decorated with attractive Victorian antiques. Tea and coffee are available all day in a sitting room that overlooks the grounds. Hosts Randal and Marie Dempsey both have previous hotel management experience, so housekeeping standards are impressively high. The breakfast features a buffet including fresh fruit salad, smoked salmon, and an Irish cheeseboard, while the menu lists pancakes, fish platter, kidneys, and liver, as well as the usual fry. ⊠ *Kilkenny Rd., Co. Carlow,* ☎ *0503/43324,* 📠 *0503/41953. 7 rooms with bath. Croquet, fishing. MC, V.*

Outdoor Activities and Sports

GOLF

Carlow Golf Club (⊠ Deerpark, ☎ 0503/31695), 3 km (2 mi) north of the town on the Dublin road, is set in a wild deer park; it remains open all year.

Leighlinbridge

❷ *10 km (6 mi) south of Carlow Town on N9.*

In Leighlinbridge, the first bridge over the River Barrow was built in 1320. On the east bank of Leighlinbridge lie the ruins of **Black Castle,** built in 1181, one of the earliest Norman fortresses constructed in Ireland and the scene of countless battles and sieges over the centuries. A lone, ruined 400-year-old tower stands today.

Dining

$$ ✕ **Lord Bagenal Inn.** This famous old pub beside the River Barrow is today a bar-restaurant with open fires and warm lighting. The bar menu

consists of a basic selection of steaks, poultry, and fresh fish. The restaurant's seasonal menu, which changes weekly, is based on French country cooking and is supplemented by a tempting buffet. Specials might include cod with roasted red peppers and new potatoes or noisettes of local lamb with fresh rosemary. The award-winning wine list holds many finds. ⊠ *Main St.,* ☎ *0503/21668. DC, V. No dinner Sun.–Mon.*

Old Leighlin

❸ *5¾ km (3 mi) west of Leighlinbridge, signposted to the right off N9.*

Worth a quick stop, the tiny village of Old Leighlin is the site of a monastery founded in the 7th century by St. Laserian. It was rebuilt in the 12th century as St. Laserian's Cathedral and enlarged in the 16th century. Guided tours are available. Casey's, the village pub, is renowned for having been in the same family since 1542.

Kilkenny City

❹ *24 km (15 mi) southwest of Leighlinbridge on N10, 121 km (75 mi) southwest of Dublin.*

One of Ireland's most alluring destinations, Kilkenny City cries to be explored by foot or bicycle, thanks to its historic and easily circumnavigable town center. This is a lovely place where the centuries rub elbows, with Georgian streets hard by Tudor stone houses—even the great town castle is a bewitching marriage of Gothic and Victorian styles. From a bird's-eye view, the city (population 10,000) is an impressively preserved, 900-year-old Norman citadel attractively situated on the River Nore, which forms the moat of its magnificently restored castle. In the 6th century, St. Canice (a.k.a. "the builder of churches") established a large monastic school here; the town's name reflects Canice's central role: Kil Cainneach means "Church of Canice." Kilkenny's medieval look wasn't established for another 400 years, when the Anglo-Normans fortified the city with a castle, gates, and a brawny wall.

Kilkenny holds a special place in the history of Anglo-Irish relations. The infamous 1366 Statute of Kilkenny, intended to strengthen English authority in Ireland by keeping the heirs of the Anglo-Norman invaders from becoming absorbed into the Irish way of life, was an attempt at apartheid. Intermarriage became a crime punishable by death. Irish cattle were barred from grazing on English land. Anglo-Norman settlers could lose their estates for speaking Irish, for giving their children Irish names, or for dressing in Irish clothes. The native Irish were forced to live outside town walls in shantytowns. Ironically, the process of Irish and Anglo-Norman assimilation was well under way when the statute went into effect; perhaps if this intermingling had been allowed to evolve, Anglo-Irish relations in this century might have been more harmonious.

By the early 17th century, the Irish Catholics had grown impatient with such repression; they tried to bring about reforms with the Confederation of Kilkenny, which governed Ireland from 1642 to 1648, with Kilkenny as the capital. Pope Innocent X sent money and arms. Cromwell responded in 1650 by overrunning the town and sacking the cathedral, which he then used to stable his horses.

The center city is small and, despite the large number of historic sights and picturesque streets—in particular, Butter Slip and High Street—it can easily be covered in less than 3 hours. One of the most pleasant cities south of Dublin (and one of the most popular in summer, when it can be swamped with visitors), Kilkenny City is a center for well-designed crafts, especially ceramics and sweaters; the premier venue is the Kilkenny Design Centre. The city is also home to more than 50 pubs, many of them on Parliament and High streets, which also support a lively music scene. Many of the town's pubs and shops have old-fashioned, highly individualized, brightly painted facades, created as part of the town's 1980s revival of this Victorian tradition.

⑤ **St. Canice's Cathedral,** on the corner of Dean Street and Parliament Street, is the best place to begin a walking tour of Kilkenny City. In spite of Cromwell's defacements, this is still one of the finest cathedrals in Ireland, and it is the country's second-largest medieval church, after St. Patrick's Cathedral in Dublin. The bulk of the 13th-century structure (restored in 1866) was built in the early English style. Within the massive walls is an exuberant Gothic interior, given a somber grandeur by the extensive use of a locally quarried black marble. Many of the memorials and tombstone effigies represent distinguished descendants of the Normans, some depicted in full suits of armor. Look for a female effigy in the south aisle wearing the old Irish or Kinsale cloak; the 12th-century black marble font at the southwest end of the nave; and St. Ciaran's Chair in the north transept, also made of black marble, with 13th-century sculptures on the arms.

The biggest attraction on the grounds is the 102-ft **round tower,** which was built in 847 and is all that remains of the monastic development reputedly begun in the 6th century, around which the town arose. If you have the energy to climb the tower's 167 steps, the 360-degree view from the top is tremendous. Next door is **St. Canice's Library,** containing some 3,000 16th- and 17th-century volumes. ⊠ *Dean St.,* ☎ *056/64971* ⊠ *£1.* ⊙ *Cathedral Easter–Oct., Mon.–Sat. 9–1 and 2–6, Sun. 2–6; Oct.–Apr., Mon.–Sat. 10–1 and 2–4, Sun. 2–4; tower daily 9–1 and 2–6.*

⑥ The ruins of the **Black Abbey,** south of St. Canice's Cathedral, belong to a 13th-century friary, named after the black capes of the Dominican friars. It has recently been restored as a Dominican church. A museum displaying a number of historical artifacts is next door in the presbytery. ⊠ *Free.* ⊙ *Daily 9–1 and 2–6.*

⑦ Across the street from the courthouse (two blocks east of the Black Abbey ruins), **Rothe House,** dating primarily from 1594, with 1610 additions, is the restored home of a wealthy Tudor merchant. It is now the headquarters of the **Kilkenny Archaeological Society** and houses a motley collection of Bronze Age artifacts, ogham stones, and coal-mining gear. There's also a genealogical research facility that can help you trace your ancestors. ⊠ *Parliament St.,* ☎ *056/22893.* ⊠ *£2.* ⊙ *Apr.–Oct., Mon.–Sat. 10:30–5, Sun. 2–5; Nov.–Feb., Mon.–Sat. 1–5, Sun. 3–5.*

⑧ **Kyteler's Inn** (⊠ *Kieran St.,* ☎ *056/21064*), the oldest in town, is in the cellar of a building notorious as the place where Dame Alice Kyteler, an alleged witch, was accused of poisoning her four husbands. The restaurant retains its medieval aura, thanks to its 14th-century stonework and exposed beams. Its menu features an à la carte dinner, including plainly cooked Irish steak, salmon, and chicken, and, of course, Smithwick's beer, which has been brewed in Kilkenny since the late 18th century. However, the owners can't resist serving witch's broth—really just a homemade vegetable soup.

⑨ The **Tholsel,** or town hall, which was built in 1761 on Parliament Street, stands near the site of the medieval Market Cross.

⑩ The **Tourist Information Office (TIO)** is housed in the **Shee Alms House** (off the east side of High Street). The building was founded in 1582

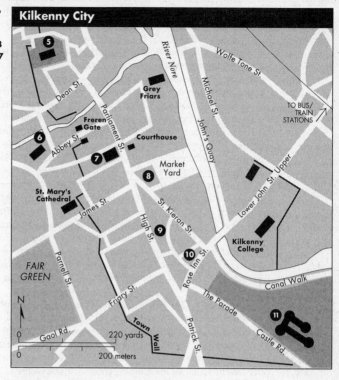

by Sir Richard Shee as a hospital for the poor and served in that capacity until 1895. ⊠ *Rose Inn St.,* ☎ *056/51500.* ⊘ *Apr.–May and Sept., Mon.–Sat. 9–6, Sun. 11–5; July–Aug., Mon.–Sat. 9–8, Sun. 11–5; Oct.–Mar., Mon.–Sat. 9–5.*

★ ⑪ Founded in 1172 and dominating the south end of town, **Kilkenny Castle** served for more than 500 years, beginning in 1391, as the seat of the Butler family—later designated earls and dukes of Ormonde—one of the more powerful clans in Irish history. In 1967 the sixth Marquess of Ormonde handed over the present building, which dates largely from 1820, to the state; since then it's been through a series of restorations. The gray stone building, with two turreted wings and numerous chimneys poking over the battlements, stands amid rolling lawns beside the River Nore in 49 acres of landscaped parkland. Most impressive is the 150-ft-long, aptly named **Long Gallery,** a refined airy hall that contains a collection of family portraits, frayed tapestries, and a skylit, decorated ceiling of carved oak beams adjoined with Celtic lacework and adorned with brilliantly painted animal heads. The **Butler Gallery** houses a collection of modern art and frequently changing exhibitions. ⊠ *The Parade, Kilkenny,* ☎ *056/21450.* ⚐ *Castle tour £3; grounds and Butler Gallery free.* ⊘ *Apr.–May, daily 10:30–5; June–Sept., daily 10–7; Oct.–Mar., Tues.–Sat. 10:30–12:45 and 2–5, Sun. 11–12:45 and 2–5.*

Dining and Lodging

$$$ ✕ **Ristorante Rinuccini.** Kilkenny City's premier Irish-Italian restaurant is in the basement of a Georgian town house opposite Kilkenny Castle. In early evening a harpist sets the mood in the intimate, softly lit dining room, which has red tablecloths and rustic ladder-back chairs. Owner Antonio Cavaliere's menu includes homemade pastas like penne with a smoked salmon, cream, and wine sauce; and spaghetti with fresh

crabmeat, garlic, olive oil, and chili. Humanely raised Irish veal is served in a variety of traditional ways. ⊠ *1 The Parade, Co. Kilkenny,* ☎ *056/61575. AE, DC, MC, V. No dinner Sun.*

$–$$ ✕ **Cafe Sol.** Off the main street near the town hall (Tholsel), this small, cheerful, unpretentious spot is decorated with oilcloth on the tables and Venetian blinds in the windows. Lunches feature excellent baked goods, including scones and date and orange cake produced by owner-chefs Gail Johnson and Eavan Kenny. The mood is more romantic at dinner, with softer lighting and candles on the tables. The à la carte menu is short but enticing: Warm salad of monkfish, salmon, and pine kernels is a popular starter, while main courses include steaks, fresh pasta with homemade pesto, and fish of the day. ⊠ *William St., Co. Kilkenny,* ☎ *056/64987. MC, V. No dinner Sun.–Tues.*

$$ ✕🏠 **Lacken House.** Owner-chef Eugene McSweeney and his wife, Breda, run this Georgian restaurant-with-rooms on the edge of Kilkenny. The nicely outfitted quarters are decorated in pretty Laura Ashley fabrics. Traditional furnishings in the cellar restaurant maintain the period character of the house. Salmon from the nearby Nore is featured as a fillet with a galette of potato and celeriac, served with sage butter sauce. ⊠ *Dublin Rd., Co. Kilkenny,* ☎ *056/61085,* FAX *056/62435. 8 rooms with bath. Restaurant, bar. AE, DC, MC, V. Restaurant closed Sun.–Mon.*

$–$$ ✕🏠 **Langton's.** One of Ireland's most famous "eating pubs," this family-run establishment, a landmark since the 1940s, is a labyrinthine collection of interconnected bars and restaurants. Most of the seating areas have open fires, but different ambiences, ranging from the leather-upholstered gentlemen's club in the Horseshoe Bar to an attempt at art deco in the spacious main dining room. Cuisine is classic "plain Irish," with a big selection of steaks. Roast rack of lamb, grilled black sole on the bone, and vegetarian crepe are all perennially popular. There are eight well-equipped rooms and two penthouse suites overhead. ⊠ *69 John St., Co. Kilkenny,* ☎ *056/65133,* FAX *056/65693. 8 rooms with bath. AE, DC, MC, V.*

$–$$ ✕🏠 **Knocktopher Hall.** This characterful Georgian mansion 17½km (11 mi) south of Kilkenny on N10 makes a memorable touring base. The house was built on the site of an earlier castle in 1740 and added to over the years, ending up with romantic but unclassical gray stone crenellations. A family of peacocks roams the grounds. Bedrooms are large, with 18th-century French beds and relaxing rural views. Golfers and equestrians often stay here and use the sporting facilities at Mount Juliet (☞ Jerpoint Abbey, *below*), only 8 km (5 mi) away. Your well-traveled hosts, English financier John Wilson and his Irish wife, Carmel, treat guests as friends of the family, sharing their drawing room and the large family dining table with them. Both are enthusiastic cooks and produce a five-course dinner of contemporary Irish cuisine (residents only, book by noon) nightly. ⊠ *Knocktopher, Co. Kilkenny,* ☎ *056/68626,* FAX *056/68626. 4 rooms with bath. No credit cards. Closed Dec. 16–Jan. 1.*

$$ 🏠 **Butler House.** This elegant Georgian house, an integral part of the ★ Kilkenny Castle complex, once belonged to the earls of Ormonde. It is now open to guests under the management of the Kilkenny Civic Trust. Ask for a room with a bow window overlooking the garden and castle; those facing Patrick Street are noisier. The restaurant is open for lunch year-round and for dinner June through September. ⊠ *16 Patrick St., Co. Kilkenny,* ☎ *056/65707,* FAX *056/65626. 14 rooms with bath. Restaurant. AE, DC, MC, V.*

$$ 🏠 **Hibernian.** If you've ever wanted to go behind the scenes in a bank, here is your chance. Kilkenny's latest town-center showpiece is this magnificent 1840s bank, which has been converted into a luxurious guest house. A new bedroom wing, restaurant, and bar were recently opened to supplement the nine rooms in the original building. Rooms are enormous, with high ceilings and elegant Georgian-style furniture, each painted in cheerful, solid colors to soften the austere effect of such imposing surroundings. Breakfast is served in the banking hall, which will eventually become a Victorian bar. ⊠ *33 Patrick St., Co. Kilkenny,* ☎ *056/71888,* FAX *05671877. 34 rooms with bath, 4 suites. Restaurant, bar. AE, DC, MC, V.*

Nightlife and the Arts

Kilkenny Arts Week (☎ 056/63663), which runs for nine days around the third week of August, celebrated its 25th anniversary in 1998. Classical music, film, theater, literary events, and visual-arts exhibits take place throughout Kilkenny. The **Cat Laughs** is an early June festival with an international roster of stand-up comedians.

Outdoor Activities and Sports

BICYCLING

Bikes for exploring the quiet countryside around Kilkenny can be rented through **J. J. Wall** (⊠ 88 Mandlin St., Co. Kilkenny, ☎ 056/21236).

GOLF

Kilkenny Golf Club (⊠ Glendine, ☎ 056/65400), 2 km (1 mi) northeast of town, is an 18-hole, par-71, mainly flat course.

SPECTATOR SPORTS

The 1336 Statutes of Kilkenny expressly forbade the ancient Irish game of hurling, today one of this area's most popular sports. Gaelic football and hurling matches are held at **Kilkenny GAA Grounds** (⊠ Nowlan Park, ☎ 056/22481). At **Kilkenny Greyhound Racetrack** (⊠ St. James's Park, ☎ 0504/21013), evening meets are held where betting is the main attraction. **Gowran Park** (⊠ Co. Kilkenny, ☎ 056/26126) holds horse races regularly.

Shopping

Kilkenny is a byword for attractive, original crafts that combine traditional arts with modern elements of design. The town's leading outlet, the **Kilkenny Design Centre** (⊠ Kilkenny Castle, ☎ 056/22118), in the old stable yard opposite the castle, sells ceramics, jewelry, sweaters, and handwoven textiles. The **Sweater Shop** (⊠ High St., ☎ 056/63405) carries a range of knitwear. **P. T. Murphy** (⊠ 85 High St., ☎ 056/21127) specializes in heraldic jewelry. **Nicholas Mosse Pottery** (⊠ Bennettsbridge, ☎ 056/27105) stocks an attractive array of hand-decorated spongeware. **Stoneware Jackson Pottery** (⊠ Bennettsbridge, ☎ 056/27175) makes distinctive, hand-thrown tableware. **Rudolf Heltzel** (⊠ 10 Patrick St., ☎ 056/21497) is known for its striking, modern designs of gold and silver jewelry. You can see glass being blown at the **Jerpoint Glass Studio** (⊠ Stoneyford, ☎ 056/24350)—where the glass is heavy but modern and uncut—and then pick up a bargain in the factory shop.

Jerpoint Abbey

⓬ *14½ km (9 mi) south of Kilkenny on R700.*

Thomastown is a pretty, stone-built village on the River Nore. A short detour 2 km (1 mi) to the south of Thomastown on N9 leads to Jerpoint Abbey, one of the most notable Cistercian ruins in Ireland, dating from about 1180. The church, tombs, and the restored cloisters—decorated with affecting human figures and fantastical mythical creatures—are a must for all lovers of the Irish Romanesque.

Guides are available from mid-June to mid-September. ☎ *056/21755.* ✉ *£2.* ⊙ *Mid-Mar.–May and mid-Sept.–mid-Oct., Wed.–Mon. 10–5; June–mid-Sept., daily 9:30–6:30; otherwise, obtain key from on-site caretaker.*

Dining and Lodging

$$$$ ✕▥ **Mount Juliet.** Within the walls of a 1,400-acre estate on the River
★ Nore, 17 km (11 mi) south of Kilkenny City on N9, lies this imposing, three-story Georgian mansion. Behind its symmetrical, gray
stone facade, many of the house's original features are intact, including
finely stuccoed ceilings and marble mantelpieces. Bedrooms are large
and individually decorated, with mahogany furniture, super-king-size
beds, and original fireplaces. The two major activities here are horseback riding on the extensive trails within the estate and golfing on
the Jack Nicklaus–designed parkland championship course. The
Lady Helen McAlmont Restaurant, a stately room in Wedgwood blue
and white, its tables adorned with crystal, silverware, and fine linen,
serves haute cuisine with Franco-Irish touches from succulent local
produce. ✉ *Co. Kilkenny,* ☎ *056/24455,* ℻ *056/24522. 53 rooms
with bath. 2 restaurants, 2 bars, indoor pool, sauna, 18-hole golf
course, tennis court, archery, croquet, horseback riding, fishing. AE,
DC, MC, V.*

$ ✕▥ **Berryhill.** A charming, creeper-clad 1789 house perched high on
★ a ridge overlooking the River Nore and the picturesque village of Inistioge (southeast of Thomastown), this is a warm, comfortable family home on a working sheep farm. Guests can enjoy the bright, airy
drawing room, with its baby grand piano and a drinks trolley with an
"honesty book." Rooms are decorated in animal themes of an elephant,
a pig, and a frog; the last has a veranda. Breakfast, served at the din-
ing-room table in front of a big open fire, often includes fresh trout.
Dinner, country-house style, can be prebooked. ✉ *Inistioge, Co.
Kilkenny,* ☎ ℻ *056/58434. 3 suites. Croquet, fishing. MC, V. Closed
Nov.–Mar., except when guests rent all 3 rooms.*

Outdoor Activities and Sports

GOLF

For detailed information about **Mount Juliet Golf Club** (✉ Co. Kilkenny,
☎ 056/24455), which frequently hosts the Irish Open, ☞ Chapter 9.

HORSEBACK RIDING

The excellent facilities at **Mount Juliet** (✉ Co. Kilkenny, ☎ 056/24455)
are open to nonresidents.

Graiguenamanagh

⑬ *15 km (9 mi) northeast of Thomastown on R703.*

Graiguenamanagh (pronounced *Grey*-gun-a-manna) is a pretty, unspoiled
village on the banks of the River Barrow at the foot of Brandon Hill.
In the 13th century the early English-style church of **Duiske Abbey** was
the largest Cistercian church in Ireland. The choir, the transept, and
part of the nave of the original abbey church have been incorporated
into the new Catholic church. Purists will be disappointed by the modernization, which was carried out between 1973 and 1983, although
various medieval building techniques were used. This is good walking
country; ask locally for directions to the summit of **Brandon Hill**
(1,694 ft), a 7-km (4½-mi) hike.

Dining and Lodging

$ ✕▥ **Waterside.** All the rooms and the restaurant in this 19th-century
★ stone corn mill on the River Barrow have picturesque views of the water.
The restaurant, which occupies the ground floor of the old mill build-

ing, has exposed pitch-pine beams, decorated windows, and candles and crisp white linens on the tables. Located 27 km (17 mi) southeast of Kilkenny, Waterside is popular with hikers and those who value the nearby riding and golf. ✉ *The Quay, Co. Kilkenny,* ☎ *0503/24246,* FAX *0503/24733. 10 rooms with bath or shower. Restaurant, bar, fishing. MC, V.*

New Ross

🄯 *17 km (11 mi) south of Graiguenamanagh on R705.*

New Ross is a busy inland port on the banks of the River Barrow. Even though it is one of the oldest towns in County Wexford, settled in the 13th century on an ancient monastic site, only the most dedicated history buffs will be tempted to stop and explore the steep, narrow streets above its unattractive docks. The major attraction in New Ross is a cruise up the River Barrow on the **Galley Cruising Restaurant** (☎ 051/421723). You can take in the peaceful farmlands along the riverbank while sampling lunch, afternoon tea, or dinner. The emphasis is on fresh local produce and seafood. The restaurant is open Easter–October only.

Ballylane Farm is a 3-km (2-mi) detour from New Ross on the N25 Wexford road. These 200 acres provide an opportunity to experience a working farm firsthand and to add greatly to your appreciation of the Irish countryside as a working environment. Maps and information sheets are supplied to guide you through fields and woodlands, where you can observe a variety of farm animals and local wildlife. ✉ *New Ross,* ☎ *051/425666.* 🎫 *£3.* ⊘ *Mid-Mar.–Apr., weekends 10–6; May–Oct., daily 10–6; group tour by appointment.*

🄯 The **John F. Kennedy Arboretum** is clearly signposted from New Ross on R733, which follows the banks of the Barrow southward for about 5 km (3 mi). The cottage where the president's great-grandfather was born is in Dunganstown, and Kennedy relatives are still living in the house. About 2 km (1 mi) downroad at Slieve Coillte is the entrance to the arboretum, which has more than 600 acres of forest, nature trails, and gardens, as well as an ornamental lake. The grounds contain some 4,500 species of trees and shrubs and serve as a resource center for botanists and foresters. The top of the park offers fine panoramic views. ✉ *Dunganstown,* ☎ *051/388171.* 🎫 *£2.* ⊘ *Daily 10–dusk.*

Shopping
The **Butlersland Craft Centre** (✉ New Ross, ☎ 051/422612) is on the main N25 2 km (1 mi) east of New Ross and stocks an extensive range of Irish crafts, including clothing, cut glass, wood items, and jewelry. Sample the home baking in the coffee shop.

Enniscorthy

🄯 *19 km (12 mi) northeast of New Ross on N79.*

Enniscorthy, a thriving market town with a rich history, is on the main road between Dublin and Wexford, to the south of the popular resort of Gorey. Built on the steeply sloping banks of the River Slaney, the town is dominated by **Enniscorthy Castle,** constructed by a Norman knight in 1199 and once leased to the English poet Edmund Spenser, author of *The Faerie Queene,* who first came to Ireland in 1580 as secretary to the lord deputy of Ireland (Spenser's prose defense of Lord Grey of Wilton's repressive policies was published posthumously in 1633, 34 years after his death). The castle was the site of fierce battles against Oliver Cromwell in the 17th century and during the Uprising of 1798.

Its square-towered keep now houses the **County Wexford Museum,** which contains thousands of historic items, including a reconstructed dairy and displays of pottery and military memorabilia from the 1798 and 1916 uprisings. The curator is often eager to provide commentary on the exhibits. ⊠ *Castle Hill,* ☎ *054/35926.* ⊡ *£2.* ⊙ *Apr.–mid-Sept., Mon.–Sat. 10–6, Sun. 2–5; mid-Sept.–Mar., daily 2–5.*

The **National 1798 Center** tells the tale of the ill-fated 1798 rebellion. ⊠ *Arnold's Cross,* ☎ *054/37596.* ⊡ *£4.* ⊙ *Mon.–Sat. 9:30–5, Sun. 11–5.*

St. Aidan's Cathedral stands on a commanding site overlooking the Slaney. This Gothic Revival structure was built in the mid-19th century under the direction of Augustus Welby Pugin, the architect of the Houses of Parliament in London.

Outdoor Activities and Sports

GREYHOUND RACING

The **Showgrounds** (⊠ Co. Wexford, ☎ 054/33172) have greyhound racing on Monday and Thursday at 8 PM, with bar and catering facilities available.

HORSEBACK RIDING

Boro Hill House Equestrian Centre (⊠ Clonroche, ☎ 054/44117) organizes residential riding holidays and hunting breaks as well as daily and hourly riding. The center is fully equipped with indoor and outdoor arenas, forest trails, and a cross-country course.

Shopping

Kiltrea Bridge Pottery (⊠ Kiltrea Bridge, Caime, ☎ 054/35107) specializes in large, hand-thrown terra-cotta pots suitable for both indoor and outdoor planting. **Carley's Bridge Pottery** (⊠ Carley's Bridge, ☎ 054/33512) has a selection of handcrafted pottery.

Wexford Town

⑰ *24 km (15 mi) south of Enniscorthy on N11, 142 km (88 mi) south of Dublin.*

From its appearance today, you would barely realize that Wexford is an ancient place—in fact, it was defined on maps by the Greek cartographer Ptolemy as long ago as the 2nd century AD. Its Irish name is Loch Garman, but the Vikings called it Waesfjord—the harbor of the mud flats—which became Wexford in English. Wexford became an English garrison town after it was taken by Oliver Cromwell in 1649. (The Anglo-Norman conquest of Ireland began in County Wexford in 1169, so the British presence has deep roots, and Wexford has been an English-speaking county for centuries.)

The River Slaney empties into the sea at Wexford Town. The harbor has silted up since the days when the Viking longboats docked here; nowadays only a few small trawlers fish out of here. Wexford Town's compact center is set on the south bank of the Slaney, with its main street running parallel to the quays on the riverfront. It can be explored on foot in an hour or two. Allow at least half a day in the area if you also intend to visit the Heritage Park at nearby Ferrycarrig, and a full day if you also want to take in Johnstown Castle Gardens and its agricultural museum, or walk on the nature reserve at Curracloe Beach to the north of the town. The town is at its best in late October, when the Wexford Opera Festival (☞ Nightlife and the Arts, *below*) engenders a carnival atmosphere that affects all walks of life.

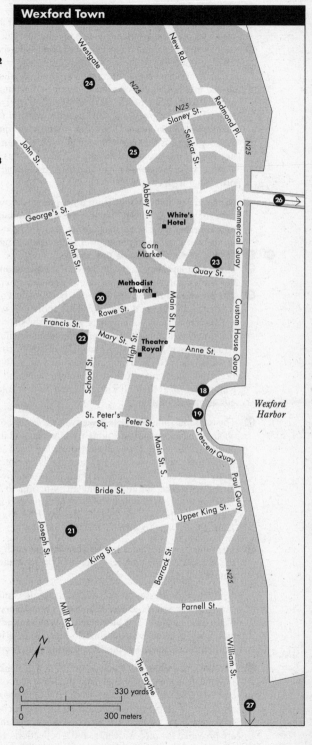

Wexford Town

⑱ The **TIO** on the waterfront at Crescent Quay is a good place to start exploring Wexford Town on foot and to find out about guided walking tours organized by local historians. Standing in the center of Crescent Quay, the large bronze **statue of Commodore John Barry** (1745–1803) commemorates the man who came to be known as the "Father of the American Navy." Born in 1745 in nearby Ballysampson, Barry settled in Philadelphia at age 15, became a brilliant naval fighter during the War of Independence (thus avenging his Irish ancestors), and trained many young naval officers who went on to achieve fame for themselves. **Main Street** (one block inland from the quays), a narrow thoroughfare, is the major shopping street of the town, with a pleasant mix of old-fashioned bakeries, butcher shops, stylish boutiques, and a share of Wexford's more than 90 pubs—friendly places that exude provincial Irish charm.

⑲ Rising above the rooftops from most points in town are the graceful spires of two elegant examples of 19th-century Gothic architecture. These **twin churches** have identical exteriors, their foundation stones were laid on the same day, and their spires both reach a height of 230 ft. The **Church of the Immaculate Conception** is on Rowe Street. The **Church of the Assumption** is on Bride Street. The **Franciscan Church** (⊠ School St.) has a ceiling worth noting for its fine, locally crafted stucco work.

⑳ ㉑

㉒

㉓ The **Wexford Bull Ring** (⊠ Quay St., back toward quays) was once the scene of bullbaiting, a cruel medieval sport that was popular among the Norman nobility. This arena was also the site of another, far more tragic event in 1649, when Cromwell's soldiers massacred 300 panic-stricken townspeople who had gathered here to pray as the army stormed their town. The birthplace of Oscar Wilde's mother, Jane Francis Elgee (who wrote as "Speranza"), was in the old rectory on Main Street near the Bull Ring. Wilde definitely inherited from her his gift as an epigrammatist.

㉔ The red sandstone **Westgate Tower** was the largest of five fortified gateways in the Norman and Viking town walls, and it is the only one remaining. The early 13th-century tower has been sensitively restored. Keep an eye out as you wander around this part of town for other preserved segments of the old town walls. Westgate Tower houses the **Wexford Experience**, an audiovisual introduction to Wexford's history. This presentation lasts for about 30 minutes and is supplemented by seasonal exhibitions. ☎ 053/46506. ⊠ £1. ☉ May–Sept., Mon.–Sat. 10–6, Sun. 2–6; Oct.–Apr., Mon.–Sat. 11–5.

㉕ The ruins of the 12th-century **Selskar Abbey** (south of Westgate Tower) still stand. Here the first treaty between the Irish and the Normans was signed in 1169.

A few more addresses are worth noting as you wander the town's narrow, winding streets. **Oliver Cromwell's temporary residence** is at 29 Main Street South. The **birthplace of William Cody,** father of the famous American showman "Buffalo Bill" Cody, is on King Street. The Cornmarket is the site of the 19th-century poet **Thomas Moore's home.**

㉖ The **Wexford Wildfowl Reserve** on the north bank of the Slaney is a short walk across the bridge from the main part of town. Thirty percent of the world's Greenland white-fronted geese spend their winters on the mud flats, known locally as slobs, which also draw ducks, swans, and other waterfowl. Screened blinds and an observation tower are provided for bird-watchers, and a collection of the various species who live on the slobs has been established at the reception center. The reserve is signposted off R741, 4 km 2½ mi) north of Wexford. ⊠ *North*

Slob, Wexford Harbour, ☎ *053/23129.* ✉ *Free.* ☉ *Apr. 16–Sept., daily 9–6; Oct.–Easter, daily 10–5.*

☚ **Curracloe Strand,** 11 km (7 mi) northeast of Wexford Town, runs for 9 km (5½ mi). Besides being a popular swimming place in summer, it is also home to many migratory birds in the winter.

㉗ The signpost for **Johnstown Castle Gardens** is reached by following N25 for 5 km (3 mi) toward Rosslare. The castle itself, a massive, Victorian-Gothic building in gray stone, is now an agricultural college, but the attractive and well-maintained grounds, with ornamental lakes and more than 200 different trees and shrubs, are open to the public. The main attraction is the **Irish Agricultural Museum,** housed in the quadrangular stable yards. Extensive displays are devoted to rural transportation, farming, and the activities of the farmyard and the farmhouse, with a special exhibit on dairying. The museum also contains an important collection of Irish country furniture. ☎ *053/42888.* ✉ *£2.50.* ☉ *Mon.–Sat. 9–12:30 and 1:30–5, Sun. 2–5.*

★ ☚ ㉘ The **Irish National Heritage Park** at Ferrycarrig, 5 km (3 mi) from Wexford Town on N25, is one of Ireland's most successful and enjoyable family attractions. This 35-acre, open-air theme park beside the River Slaney should not be missed. In about an hour and a half, a guide takes you through 9,000 years of Irish history—from the first evidence of humans on this island, at around 7000 BC, to the Norman settlements of the mid-12th century. Full-scale replicas of typical dwelling places illustrate the changes in beliefs and lifestyles. Highlights of the tour include a prehistoric homestead, a *crannóg* (lake dwelling), an early Christian *rath* (fortified farmstead), a Christian monastery, a horizontal water mill, a Viking longhouse, and a Norman castle. There are also examples of pre-Christian burial sites and a stone circle. Most of the exhibits are "inhabited" by students in appropriate dress who will answer questions. The unspoiled riverside site includes several nature trails. ✉ *Ferrycarrig,* ☎ *053/20733.* ✉ *£3.50.* ☉ *Mid-Mar.–Oct., daily 9:30–6:30; last admission at 5.*

Dining and Lodging

$$ ✕ **La Riva.** This is a characterful and informal first-floor bistro, right in the center of town near the TIO. Informal is the word—tables have plain, unpolished wood tops and the daily specials are chalked up on a board. Charm enters the picture on Thursday, when a guitarist entertains by candlelight. The menu is light and eclectic, with many people opting for two or three starters in order to try as many of owner-chef Frank Chamberlaine's unusual combos as possible. Among the most popular dishes are grilled duck breast with soya and coriander noodles, and local scallops with a rosemary and orange sauce. ✉ *Henrietta St.,* ☎ *053/24330. MC, V. Closed Jan. No lunch.*

$ ✕ **Oak Tavern.** About 2 km (1 mi) from Wexford Town and not far from the gates of the Irish National Heritage Park on the Enniscorthy Road, the pub-restaurant in this old-world inn is a good place to stop on your way back into town. In cold weather, warm yourself beside log fires that blaze in the lounge; in fair weather relax on the riverside terrace. Steaks, local salmon, and plainly cooked seafood are on the menu. ✉ *Enniscorthy Rd.,* ☎ *053/20922. AE, MC, V.*

$$$ 🏨 **White's Hotel.** Housed in an historic 19th-century building fronted by a modern conservatory, this property is a friendly, convivial place conveniently located in the heart of town. Its refurbished old-fashioned passageways, brass trim, and red-velvet decor combine with candlelight and roaring log fires to create a warm ambience. The country-style guest rooms are furnished with Victorian reproductions. Rooms in the new addition to the hotel are more spacious. ⊠ *George's St., Co. Wexford,* ☎ *053/22311,* 🖷 *053/45000. 82 rooms with bath. Restaurant, bar, sauna, steam room, health club. AE, DC, MC, V.*

$ 🖫 **Faythe House.** Quietly situated in the old part of town, this pleasant guest house is only a short walk from the main shopping area. Some rooms have views of the pretty floral and vegetable garden and the harbor beyond, while others look into the street. The decor is muted and homey, but rooms are well equipped for the price range. Breakfast is a highlight here, with an award-winning menu that includes fresh fruit salad, local smoked salmon, and kedgeree or kippers. ⊠ *Swan View,* ☎ *053/22249,* 🖷 *053/21680. 10 rooms with bath. MC, V.*

$ 🖫 **McMenamin's Town House.** Early breakfast by arrangement and an exceptional degree of comfort for its price range make this four-story Victorian villa, a short walk from the railway station in the town center, an ideal stopover en route to or from the Rosslare ferries. Book months rather than weeks in advance if you want a room here during the Opera Festival. The bedrooms are spacious, warm, and immaculately clean, with glorious, large pieces of highly polished Victorian furniture and antique beds, including a mahogany half-tester. There are about eight choices at breakfast, including fresh fish of the day. Don't leave without tasting Kay and Seamus McMenamin's homemade whiskey marmalade. ⊠ *3 Auburn Terr., Co. Wexford,* ☎ 🖷 *053/ 46442. 6 rooms with bath. MC, V. Closed Dec. 18–29.*

$$$ ✕🖫 **Ferrycarrig.** A striking modern hotel with a prime riverside location in the rolling countryside 3 km (2 mi) from Wexford Town on N11, this a favorite of regular visitors to Wexford. The hotel's flamboyant modern architecture and landscaping may not be to all tastes, but the peaceful views over the Slaney estuary make up for this. Choose between dining in the informal 160-seater Bistro or the more formal Tides Restaurant, the latter of which serves modern French cuisine. All the bedrooms have wonderful views of the river and green fields; some also have balconies. ⊠ *Ferrycarrig Bridge, Co. Wexford,* ☎ *053/20999,* 🖷 *053/20982. 90 rooms with bath. 2 restaurants, bar, indoor heated pool, sauna, health club, fishing. AE, DC, MC, V .*

Nightlife and the Arts

Touring companies and local productions can be seen in Wexford at the **Theatre Royal** (⊠ High St., ☎ 053/22400). Hands down, the **Wexford Opera Festival** (☎ 053/22144), held during the last two weeks of October and dribbling into November, is the town's leading cultural event. More than 30 years old, the festival puts on seldom-performed works with top talent from all over the world. As of press time (summer 1999), the operas for the 2000 season had not been announced, but the three operas slated for 1999—Karl Goldmark's *The Queen of Sheba,* Stanislaw Moniuszko's *The Haunted Manor,* and Umberto Giordano's *Siberia*—were representative of the rarity of the operas performed here. Along with an ever-expanding fringe, the festival supplies a variety of musical events from 11 AM to midnight.

Outdoor Activities and Sports

BICYCLING

If you'd like to explore the long, sandy coast of this area at a leisurely pace, bicycles can be rented at the **Bike Shop** (⊠ 9 Selskar St., ☎ 053/ 22514).

HORSEBACK RIDING

Ballingale Farm (⊠ Taghmon, ☎ 053/34387) has facilities for both children and adults, including a cross-country course. **Horetown Equestrian Centre** (⊠ Horetown House, Foulksmills, ☎ 051/565771) specializes in residential riding holidays with cross-country riding and will teach you how to play polo-crosse. **Sheimalier Riding Stables** (⊠ Forth Mountain, Taghmon, ☎ 053/39251) has riding by the hour.

Horse races are held regularly at the **Wexford Racecourse** (⊠ Bettyville, ☎ 053/42307).

Shopping

The **Wool Shop** (⊠ 39 S. Main St., ☎ 053/22247) is the place to go for Aran sweaters. At **Barker's** (⊠ 36–40 S. Main St., ☎ 053/23159) you can find Waterford crystal at factory prices, as well as local pottery and crafts.

ALONG THE COAST TO WATERFORD

This tour follows mainly minor roads along the prettiest parts of the coast in Counties Wexford and Waterford, pausing midway to explore Waterford City on foot.

Rosslare

㉙ *18 km (11 mi) southwest of Wexford Town off N25 on R470.*

Sometimes called Ireland's sunniest spot, the village of Rosslare is a seaside resort with an attractive beach, while Rosslare Harbour, 8 km (5 mi) south of the village, is one of Ireland's busiest ports and the terminus for car ferries from Fishguard, Pembroke, Le Havre, and Cherbourg. Vacationers head here to hike, golf, sun, and bathe for the most part.

Dining and Lodging

$$$ ✕⊡ **Kelly's.** This traditional beachfront weekend retreat has been
★ owned and run by the Kelly family since 1895. Its extensive recreational facilities are a big draw. Guest rooms are done in comfortable, rustic decor, and those facing the front have lovely sea views. Waterford glass chandeliers hang in the Ivy Room, where the menu includes fresh local produce served in classic French style. Casual bistro-style dining in La Marine features Irish produce in a rustic, Mediterranean-style menu. ⊠ *Rosslare, Co. Wexford,* ☎ *053/32114,* ℻ *053/32222. 99 rooms with bath. 2 restaurants, indoor-outdoor pool, sauna, steam room, 18-hole golf course, 4 tennis courts, croquet, health club, horseback riding, jogging, squash, beach, fishing, cabaret. AE, DC, MC, V. Closed Dec.–Feb.*

$ ⊡ **Tuskar House Hotel.** Found in a quiet area near the ferry port, this small, family-run hotel promises simple pleasures. Comfortable rooms, some with balconies, have good views of the sea, especially those in the rear; all are decorated with functional, modern furniture in a bright, cheery palette. Public rooms have lots of polished pine, glass, and greenery. Seafood is a specialty at the restaurant. ⊠ *St. Martin's Rd., Rosslare Harbour, Co. Wexford,* ☎ ℻ *053/33363. 30 rooms with bath. Restaurant, bar. AE, DC, MC, V.*

Nightlife and the Arts

Portholes Bar at the **Hotel Rosslare** (⊠ Rosslare Harbour, ☎ 053/33110) is a popular spot for lively, traditional Irish music most evenings during the summer.

Outdoor Activities and Sports

Rosslare Golf Club (⊠ Rosslare Strand, ☎ 053/32203) is a 27-hole, par-72, championship links. A mixture of links and parkland can be found at the Southeast's newest course, the 18-hole, par-72 **St. Helen's Bay** (⊠ Kilrane, ☎ 053/33669).

Kilmore Quay

③⓪ *22 km (14) mi south of Rosslare on R739.*

A quiet, old-fashioned, seaside village of thatched and whitewashed cottages noted for its fishing industry, Kilmore Quay is also popular with recreational anglers and bird-watchers. From the harbor there is a pleasant view to the east over the flat coast that stretches for miles. **Kehoe's Pub**(☎ 053/29830) is the hub of village activity; its collection of maritime artifacts is as interesting as any museum. During the last two weeks in July, the village hosts a lively **seafood festival** (☎ 053/29922) with a parade, seafood barbecues, and other events.

☙ The **Saltee Islands,** Ireland's largest bird sanctuary, are a popular off-shore day trip from Kilmore Quay. (From mid-May to the end of July, look for boats at the village waterfront or on the marina to take you to the islands.) In late spring and early summer, several million seabirds nest among the dunes and on the rocky scarp on the south of the islands. Even if you are not an ornithologist, it's worth making the trip at these times to observe the sheer numbers of gulls, kittiwakes, puffins, guillemots, cormorants, and petrels.

The **Kilmore Quay Maritime Museum** is onboard the lightship *Guillemot.* The boat, built in 1923, is the last Irish lightship to be preserved complete with cabins and engine room, and it contains models and artifacts relating to the maritime history of the area. ☎ 053/29655. ✉ £2. ☉ May–Sept., daily noon–6; Oct.–Apr. by appointment.

Dining and Lodging

$ ✕ **Silver Fox.** Simplicity and freshness are the keynotes at this busy, family-run seafood restaurant. Chef and co-owner Nicky Cullen offers up to a dozen seafood options, including fresh Kilmore Quay crab or prawn cocktail, Bannow Bay oysters au naturel or hot-buttered on toast, plus a sprinkling of nonseafood options such as stuffed garlic mushrooms or deep-fried St. Killian (local Camembert-like) cheese. This place is popular, so reserve in advance. ✉ *Kilmore Quay,* ☎ 053/29888. *AE, MC, V. Closed Mid-Jan.–mid-Feb.*

$ ▥ **Quay House.** Originally the village post office, this whitewashed guest house is three minutes' walk from the pier. The solid old house has been carefully refurbished with Douglas pine floors throughout and country pine bedroom furniture. Guests, generally outdoor types, are encouraged to socialize in the lounge and the dining room. ✉ *Kilmore Quay, Co. Wexford,* ☎ 053/29988, FAX 053/29808. *6 rooms with bath. Dive shop, fishing. MC, V.*

Shopping

Country Crafts (✉ Kilmore Quay, ☎ 053/29885) overlooks the harbor of Kilmore Quay and has a mixture of Irish-made crafts, antique pine furniture, and paintings by local artists.

En Route On leaving Kilmore Quay, make your way northwest on R736, and then head west through Duncormick and on to Wellington Bridge. Past the bridge, head toward Fethard-on-Sea on the **Ring of Hook** drive. This is a strange and atypical part of Ireland, where the land is exceptionally flat and the narrow roads are straight.

The Ring of Hook leads to **Duncannon,** a small resort with a sandy beach and a delightful nautical atmosphere, on the north side of Waterford Harbour. Its history is marked by the visits of two kings: James II beat a hasty retreat out of Ireland through Duncannon port after his defeat at the Battle of the Boyne in 1690, and his successor, William III, also spent some days here before leaving for England.

③① **Duncannon Fort.** This imposing, 16th-century stone edifice at the water's edge was built on the site of an Iron Age fortification. Restoration work is currently in progress and should be complete by the summer of 2000. ☒ *Co. Wexford,* ☏ *051/389454.* ☑ *£2.* ☉ *May–mid-Sept., daily 10–5:30.*

Ballyhack

★ ③② *34 km (21 mi) west of Kilmore Quay.*

On the upper reaches of Waterford Harbour, the pretty village of Ballyhack, with its square castle keep, wooden buildings, thatched cottages, and green, hilly background, is much admired by painters and photographers. Nowadays a small car ferry makes the five-minute crossing to Passage East and Waterford. The pretty gray stone keep of **Ballyhack Castle** dates from the 16th century. It was once owned by the Knights Templars of St. John of Jerusalem, who held the ferry rights by royal charter; traditionally, they were required to keep a boat at Ballyhack to transport injured knights to the King's Leper Hospital at Waterford. The first two floors have been renovated and house a number of local history exhibits. ☒ *Ballyhack,* ☏ *051/389468.* ☑ *£1.* ☉ *June and Sept., weekdays 10–11 and 2–6, weekends 10–6; July–Aug., daily 10–6.*

Dunbrody Abbey is reached by taking a short detour 5 km (3 mi) north of Ballyhack on the R733 New Ross road. This ruined Cistercian abbey dates from the late 12th century and flourished until about 1539, when Henry VIII instigated the dissolution of the monasteries. Next to the Dunbrody Abbey lies **Dunbrody Castle,** property of the Marquess of Donegall, with a fledgling 1,500-tree yew-hedge maze, tea shop, gift shop, and a small museum. ☒ *Campile,* ☏ *051/425389.* ☑ *£1.50.* ☉ *Apr.–Sept., daily 10–6.*

Dining and Lodging

$$$ ✕ **Neptune Restaurant.** Pierce and Valerie McAuliffe's tiny waterside restaurant—a ferry ride across the River Nore between Counties Waterford and Wexford—has come up with a new concept: cooking school by day, restaurant by night. Mid-June through mid-September, Tuesday through Thursday from noon to 2, it offers "A Taste of Ireland" cooking demonstrations for £20 per person, including lunch and wine. The dinner menu specializes in fresh fish, with such highlights as local salmon and hot crab *Behat* (white crabmeat oven-baked in vegetable sauce with French mustard and cheese). ☒ *Ballyhack Harbour, New Ross,* ☏ *051/389284. AE, DC, MC, V. Closed Dec.–Mar. No lunch Fri.–Mon., no dinner Sun., no dinner Mon. Apr.–May and Sept.–Oct.*

$$$ ✕🏨 **Dunbrody Country House.** This historic country retreat is both stylish and pleasantly informal. Once the home of the seventh Marquess of Donegall, Dermot Chichester, the sprawling, two-story Georgian manor house is now owned and run as a small hotel by Kevin and Catherine Dundon. Kevin is a master-chef with international experience, and Catherine oversees the ongoing restoration program. From the 20 acres of maturely planted, informal parkland, it is an easy stroll to the pretty fishing village of Arthurstown and a short drive to Duncannon Beach. Rooms are spacious with peaceful country views, individually decorated, and furnished with Georgian antiques. The oak-floor dining room overlooks a small sunken garden that is floodlit at night— the walls are a sumptuous dark red, tables are large with Victorian spoonback chairs, and the kitchen is serious and ambitious. ☒ *Arthurstown, New Ross, Co. Wexford,* ☏ *051/389600,* 🆅🆇 *051/389601. 10 rooms with bath, 2 suites. Restaurant, bar, fishing. AE, DC, MC, V. Closed Jan.–Feb. 14.*

Waterford City

❸❸ *5 km (3 mi) west of Ballyhack by ferry and road (R683), 62 km (39 mi) southwest of Wexford Town, 158 km (98 mi) southwest of Dublin.*

The largest town in the Southeast, Waterford, like Wexford Town to the east, was founded by the Vikings in the 9th century and taken over by Strongbow, the Norman invader, in 1170. The city resisted Cromwell's 1649 attacks—his phrase "by Hook or by Crooke" refers to his two siege routes, one via Hook Head, the other via Crooke Village on the estuary—but did not prosper again until 1783, when George and William Penrose set out to create "plain and cut flint glass, useful and ornamental," and thereby set in motion a glass-manufacturing industry without equal. The best Waterford glass was produced from the late 1780s to the early 19th century. This early work, examples of which can be found in museums and public buildings all over the country, is characterized by a unique, slightly opaque cast that is absent from the modern product.

Waterford has better-preserved city walls than anywhere else in Ireland but Derry (☞ Chapter 8). Initially, the slightly run-down commercial center doesn't look too promising. You'll need to park your car and proceed on foot to discover the heritage that the city has made admirable efforts over the past decade to preserve. The compact town center can be visited in a couple of hours. Allow at least another hour if you intend to take the Waterford Crystal factory tour.

The **city quays**—at the corner of Greyfriar's Street and Custom House Parade—are a good place to begin a tour of Waterford City. (The TIO is also down there, at No. 41 The Quay.) The city quays stretch for nearly a mile along the River Suir and were described in the 18th century as the best in Europe.

❸❹ The **Waterford Heritage Centre** on Greyfriar's Street is home to some of the 75,000 historical artifacts excavated from beneath the city in the mid-1980s. Parts of Viking houses are displayed alongside samples of leather work, bone carvings, pottery, and ornate jewelry. ⊠ *Greyfriar's St.,* ☎ *051/871227.* ☜ *£1.50.* ☉ *Apr.–Oct., daily 10–5; Nov.–Mar., weekdays 10–5.*

❸❺ Admission to the Heritage Centre also gives access to the massive, pepper-pot-shape **Reginald's Tower,** a waterside landmark on the east end of Waterford's quays that marks the apex of a triangle containing the old walled city of Waterford. Built by the Vikings for the city's defense in 1003, it has 80-ft-high, 10-ft-thick walls; an interior stairway leads to the top. The tower served in turn as the residence for a succession of Anglo-Norman kings (including Henry II, John, and Richard II), a mint for silver coins, a prison, and an arsenal. It is said that Strongbow's marriage to Eva, the daughter of Dermot MacMurrough, took place here in the late 12th century, thus uniting the Norman invaders with the native Irish. It has recently been restored to its original medieval appearance and furnished with appropriate 11th- to 15th-century artifacts.

❸❻ One of Waterford's finer Georgian buildings, **City Hall,** on the Mall, dates from 1788 and was designed by John Roberts, a native of the city. On the way you'll pass some good examples of domestic Georgian architecture—tall, well-proportioned houses with typically Irish, semicircular fanlights above the doors. The arms of Waterford hang over City Hall's own entrance, which leads into a spacious foyer that originally was a town meeting place and merchants' exchange. The building contains two lovely theaters, an old Waterford dinner service, and

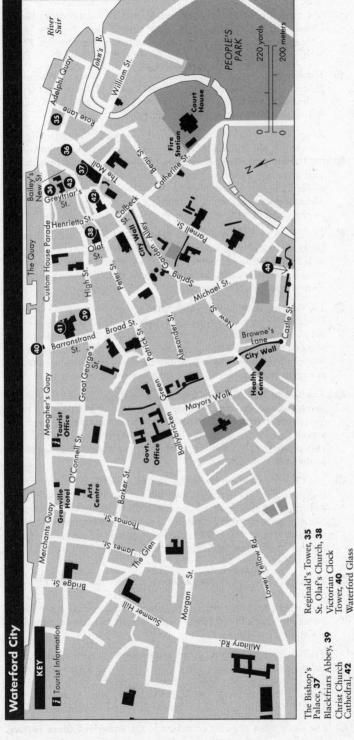

Waterford City

211

KEY

ⓘ Tourist Information

People's Park

220 yards
200 meters

The Bishop's Palace, **37**
Blackfriars Abbey, **39**
Christ Church Cathedral, **42**
City Hall, **36**
French Church, **43**
Holy Trinity Cathedral, **41**

Reginald's Tower, **35**
St. Olaf's Church, **38**
Victorian Clock Tower, **40**
Waterford Glass Factory, **44**
Waterford Heritage Centre, **34**

an enormous 1802 Waterford glass chandelier, which hangs in the Council Chamber (a copy of the chandelier hangs in Independence Hall in Philadelphia). The **Theatre Royal** (☞ Nightlife and the Arts, *below*) is the setting for the annual Festival of Light Opera in October. ⊠ *The Mall,* ☎ *051/873501.* 🎫 *Free.* ☉ *Weekdays 9–1 and 2–5.*

㊲ The **Bishop's Palace** is another building that is among the most imposing of the remaining Georgian town houses. Only the foyer is open to the public. ⊠ *Alongside City Hall on Mall.* 🎫 *Free.* ☉ *Weekdays 9–5.*

As you turn onto Colbeck Street, you'll see one of the remaining portions of the **old city wall**; there are sections all around the town cen-
㊳ ter. The site of **St. Olaf's Church** (⊠ St. Olaf's St.) is reached by taking a left at the top of Colbeck Street and then an immediate right. St. Olaf's was built, as the name implies, by the Vikings in the mid-11th century. All that remains of the old church is its original door, which has been incorporated into the wall of the existing building (a meeting hall).

㊴ The ruined tower of **Blackfriars Abbey** (⊠ High St.), reached via St. Olaf's Street and High Street, belonged to a Dominican abbey founded in 1226 and returned to the crown in 1541 after the dissolution of the monasteries. It was used as a courthouse until Cromwellian forces destroyed it in the 17th century.

㊵ The **Victorian Clock Tower** on Merchant's Quay (visible as you look down Barronstrand Street to the quays) was built in 1864 with public donations. Although it has no great architectural merit, it serves as a reminder of the days when Waterford was a thriving, bustling port. (Now, as elsewhere in Ireland, Waterford's workforce is more likely to be employed in high-tech and service industries than on the waterfront.)

㊶ The Roman Catholic **Holy Trinity Cathedral** (⊠ Barronstrand St. between High St. and the clock tower) has a simple facade and a richly (some would say garishly) decorated interior with high, vaulted ceilings and ornate, Corinthian pillars. Surprisingly, it was built in the late 18th century, when Catholicism was barely tolerated, on land granted by the Protestant city fathers.

㊷ The Church of Ireland **Christ Church Cathedral** (⊠ Henrietta St. near High St.), like Holy Trinity, was designed in neoclassic style by John Roberts (who also designed City Hall). The story of the city from the Norman invasion to the present day is told in an audiovisual presentation. ☎ *051/858958.* 🎫 *£2.* ☉ *Apr.–May and Oct., weekdays 11:30, 2:15, and 3:30; June–Sept., Mon.–Sat. 10:30, 2:15, 3:30, and 4:30, Sun. 2:30 and 4.*

㊸ The roofless ruins of the **French Church** (⊠ Greyfriar's St.), a 13th-century Franciscan abbey, are across Cathedral Square. The church, also known as Greyfriars, was given to a group of Huguenot refugees (hence the "French") in 1695. A splendid east window remains amid the ruins.

If the weather is favorable, consider a **cruise** along Waterford's harbor and the wide, picturesque estuary of the River Suir. A luxury river cruiser departs from the quay beside Reginald's Tower. Tickets can be purchased at the Tourism Information Office. ⊠ *Galley Cruises,* ☎ *051/421723.* ☉ *Tours June–Aug., daily at 3, weather permitting.*

㊹ The city's most popular attraction is the **Waterford Glass Factory,** about 2 km (1 mi) from the TIO. (Take the N25 Waterford–Cork road south from the quay, or ask at the tourist office about the regular bus service.) When the factory opened in 1783, it provided English royalty with a supply of ornate handcrafted flatware, chandeliers, and decorative pieces. Over the years, its clientele and product line diversified, and today the United States is the biggest market. The worthwhile tour of the factory takes you through the specialized crafts of blowing, cutting, and polishing glass—all carried out against a noisy background of glowing furnaces and ceaseless bustle. An extensive selection of crystal is on view (and for sale) in the showroom. To reserve a place in a 60-minute tour, which includes an optional 18-minute audiovisual show, call the factory or the tourist office. ⊠ *Cork Rd., Kilbarry,* ☎ *051/373311.* ⌑ *£3.* ⊙ *Nov.–Mar., weekdays 9–5, tours 9:30–3:15; Apr.–Oct. daily 8:30–6, tours 8:30–4.*

Dining and Lodging

$$$ ✕ **Dwyers of Mary Street.** In an old Royal Irish Constabulary barracks
★ (the original bars are still on the downstairs windows), this French-influenced spot has a menu that changes every two weeks and a lovely pink, green, and cream color scheme. Original paintings grace the walls, and antiques are mixed with modern touches, such as Bauhaus chairs. A typical meal might begin with garlic prawns in a *rösti* nest, followed by boned quail with apples and sultana (raisin) stuffing and seasonal vegetables. ⊠ *8 Mary St.,* ☎ *051/877478. AE, DC, MC, V. Closed Sun. No lunch.*

$$ ✕ **Wine Vault.** Yes, in the cellar of this Elizabeth town house, there really is a wine vault—and what a wine vault: With more than 350 labels, it has won owner David Dennison many awards. The ground floor, which doubled in size in 1999 by taking over the next-door premises, is home to a busy and informal bistro with polished wooden tables where Australian chef Chris Uren puts the emphasis on seafood. Daily specials may include fresh pasta, cumin- and turmeric-spiced risotto, lobster in season, a Butcher's Plate (duck, pork, and beef with mushroom truffle and Madeira jus), or Vegetarian Charlotte of parsnip, roast peppers, and Chinese leaf. ⊠ *High St.,* ☎ *051/853444. AE, MC, V. Closed Sun.*

$ ✕ **Reginald Restaurant and Pub.** Here 20th-century locals—drawn by the snacks and the lunchtime bar food—mix and mingle in a setting that includes a section of the city's 9th-century Viking wall (if only it could speak!). The dinner menu includes fresh monkfish and steamed mussels as well as chicken, veal, and steak dishes. ⊠ *The Mall,* ☎ *051/ 855087. AE, MC, V.*

$$$$ ✕▥ **Waterford Castle.** If coming to the Emerald Isle didn't take you far enough away from your real life, this 17th-century stone castle (with 19th-century additions) on its own 310-acre island in the River Suir may do the trick. The island is 3 km (2 mi) outside Waterford City and can be reached only by car ferry. The Great Hall and the drawing room have fine oak paneling, ornate antique furniture, and tapestries. The luxuriously decorated guest rooms have four-poster beds. Some bathrooms have original tile work and all have reproduction claw-foot tubs. Plush is the word in the Munster Room restaurant, with its detailed plastered ceiling, oak furniture, and deep-burgundy Donegal carpet, where the fare tends to country-style dishes like poached salmon, asparagus served in puff pastry, and bread-and-butter pudding. ⊠ *The Island, Ballinakill, Co. Waterford,* ☎ *051/878203,* ℻ *051/879316. 14 rooms with bath, 5 suites. Restaurant, indoor pool, 18-hole golf course, 2 tennis courts, health club, croquet, fishing. AE, DC, MC, V.*

$$ ▥ **Granville Hotel.** In the heart of Waterford, this floodlit landmark beside the River Suir is one of Ireland's oldest hotels, with many historical connections. The patriot Thomas Francis Meagher was a previous owner, while Charles Stuart Parnell stayed here when campaigning for Home Rule. Recent refurbishment has retained the old-world Georgian character of its public rooms. Bedrooms are decorated in 18th-century style and have good-size bathrooms. Ask for a room at the back if traffic disturbs you. ✉ *Meagher Quay, Co. Waterford,* ☎ *051/305555,* FAX *051/305502. 98 rooms with bath. 2 restaurants, bar. AE, DC, MC, V.*

$ ✕🖾 **Foxmount Farm.** For a pleasant change of pace, you can stay on a working dairy farm in the peaceful countryside. This elegant 17th-century house on its own extensive grounds is about 5 km (3 mi) outside town on the road to the Passage East ferry. The creeper-clad farmhouse has an informal style, with welcoming log fires and intriguing antiques. Your host Margaret Kent is renowned for her evening meals, cooked to order from fresh local produce, as well as fruit and herbs from her own garden—and don't miss her homemade ice cream. ✉ *Passage East Rd., Co. Waterford,* ☎ *051/874308,* FAX *051/854906. 6 rooms, 4 with bath. Dining room, tennis. No credit cards.*

Nightlife and the Arts

Culture buffs won't want to miss the **Garter Lane Arts Centre** (✉ 22a O'Connell St., ☎ 051/855036), the largest such cultural center in Ireland. Call ahead for a schedule of upcoming concerts, exhibits, and theater productions at the center. Interesting work by contemporary artists can be seen at the **Dyehouse Gallery** (✉ Dyehouse La., ☎ 051/878166). The **Waterford Show** tells the story of Waterford's culture and heritage through music, song, and dance. Book at Waterford Crystal or the Tourist Information Office (☎ 051/875788). The show takes place at City Hall, 9 PM Thursday, Saturday, and Sunday, May–September. Cost of £6 includes a glass of wine. **Waterford International Festival of Light Opera** (☎ 051/375437), the only competitive event of its kind, is a great draw for amateur musical societies from throughout Ireland and Great Britain. The festival runs for 17 nights every September at the **Theatre Royal** (✉ City Hall, The Mall, ☎ 051/874402). **T&H Doolan's Bar** (✉ 32 George's St., ☎ 051/872764) hosts traditional Irish music most summer nights and on weekends year-round.

Outdoor Activities and Sports

GOLF

Waterford Castle Golf Club (✉ The Island, Ballinakill, ☎ 051/871633) is an 18-hole, par-72 course that claims to be Ireland's only true island course. **Faithlegg Golf Club** (✉ Faithlegg House, Checkpoint, ☎ 051/382241) is an 18-hole, par-72 course set in mature landscape on the banks of the River Suir.

HORSEBACK RIDING

Horses are available by the hour at **Kilotteran Equitation Centre** (✉ Kilotteran, ☎ 051/384158).

SPECTATOR SPORTS

Gaelic football and hurling can be seen at the **Waterford GAA Grounds** (✉ Walsh Park, ☎ 051/358219).

Shopping

While in Waterford, definitely pay a visit to the world-famous **Waterford Glass Factory** (✉ Cork Rd., Kilbarry, ☎ 051/373311 [☞ *above*]). The showroom displays an extensive selection of Waterford crystal and Wedgwood china. The best selection of crystal in Waterford City itself is on show at **Joseph Knox** (✉ 3 Barronstrand St., ☎ 051/875307). The **Waterford Design Centre** (✉ 44 The Quay, ☎ 051/856666) has three floors devoted to Irish crafts, gifts, and fashion.

Dunmore East

㊺ *16 km (10 mi) east of Waterford via R683 and R684.*

Home to an attractive lighthouse, Dunmore East is a quaint, one-street fishing village of thatched cottages at the head of Waterford Harbour. Plenty of small beaches and cliff walks are nearby, and you get a wonderful view of the estuary from the hill behind the village.

Dining

$$–$$$ ✕ **Ship Restaurant.** Fresh, local seafood is the emphasis at this simply furnished restaurant on the ground floor of a 19th-century house overlooking the bay. The food is an imaginative mixture of French and Irish influences. Start off, perhaps, with deep-fried pastry parcels stuffed with fresh crabmeat, or vichyssoise with smoked mussels. Entrées include grilled or panfried black sole and roulade of Dover sole filled with saffron mousse. ✉ *Co. Waterford,* ☎ *051/383141 or 051/383144. AE, MC, V. Closed Sun.–Mon. Nov.–Mar. No lunch Sept.–May.*

Tramore

㊻ *11 km (7 mi) south of Waterford City on R685.*

Ⓒ Tramore has a 5-km-long (3-mi-long) **beach** that is a popular escape for families from Waterford and other parts of the Southeast, as the many vacation homes and camper parks show. It is Ireland's biggest seaside resort and a dream-come-true for young children, but it is not to everybody's taste. Part of the seafront is overshadowed by a 50-acre amusement park, a miniature railway, and new vacation home developments, although the upper half of town is more quiet and reserved. At the western end of the beach, the sand gives way to rocky cliffs guarded by the Metal Man, a giant cast-iron figure who stands atop a great pillar. It's said that if a young woman hops on one foot around the base of the pillar three times, she will be married within a year. This custom, which is still observed in a lighthearted way, can be traced back to a stone that stood on the spot centuries ago and was used in ancient Celtic fertility rites.

Dining

$ ✕ **Esquire.** Originally built in 1937 as a gentlemen's bar, this quiet retreat retains an air of gentility. Paul Horan, the internationally trained owner-chef, applies his skills to fresh local produce. A full à la carte menu with such dishes as smoked salmon, Irish peppered steak with brandy, and vegetarian specials is served in the restaurant, while a simpler—and faster—bar-food menu is also available. ✉ *Cross Market St.,* ☎ *051/386237. MC, V.*

$$ ✕⊞ **Annestown House.** The stretch of coast between Tramore and Dungarvan is rich in secluded coves, and Annestown House has a private path down to Annestown Cove. The large, white Victorian house is romantically perched above the sea and offers relaxed home comforts. Hosts John and Pippa Galloway provide plenty of room for guests to read or simply lounge about, while the more energetic can tackle the billiards table, tennis, or croquet. Rooms are generally large, with wonderful sea views at the front of the house. Dinner is served at 7:30 PM; book by noon. ✉ *Annestown, Co. Waterford,* ☎ *051/396160,* ℻ *051/396474. 5 rooms with bath. Tennis court, croquet, billiards. AE, MC, V. Closed Dec. 21–30.*

Outdoor Activities and Sports

GOLF

Tramore Golf Club (✉ Newtown Hill, ☎ 051/386170) is an 18-hole championship course overlooked by the Comeragh Mountains.

Horse races are held regularly at **Tramore Racecourse** (✉ Co. Water-ford, ☎ 051/381574).

En Route   You join the coast again 11 km (7 mi) west of Trim on R675 at **Annestown,** a smaller, quieter resort town with a good, sandy beach. The former copper-mining center of **Bunmahon,** now a fishing village popular with vacationers, is 8 km (5 mi) from here. A scenic footpath, signposted from Bunmahon, follows the Mahon River as it tumbles down from the Comeragh Mountains. This pleasant coastal drive highlights views of unusual rock formations in the cliffs interspersed with sand dunes, as well as various rare flowers and birds. Attractive, easily accessible beaches are at **Stradbally** and **Clonea.**

Dungarvan

❹⓽ *42 km (26 mi) southwest of Tramore on R675.*

Gradually the lowlands of Wexford and eastern Waterford, with their covering of soft grasses, give way to heath and moorland; the bog is created and maintained by the wetter climate of the hillier western Waterford countryside. You will see the mountains responsible for this change in climate rising up behind Dungarvan, the largest coastal town in County Waterford. This bustling fishing and resort spot is situated at the mouth of River Colligan, which empties into Dungarvan Bay here. It is a popular base for climbers and hikers.

Dining and Lodging

$$$ ✕ **The Tannery.** Paul Flynn recently returned to Dungarvan after eight years as right-hand man to top chef Nico Ladenis in London, so the menu promises adventurous and extraordinary things. Quiet mainstream jazz provides sophisticated background music in the high-ceiling room with tall windows, which has been created in an old waterside tannery. Classic French cooking is combined with fashionable Thai and Mediterranean influences. Novelties result, including risotto of mussels, vine tomatoes, and chorizo with saffron and arugula, or crab linguine with tomato garlic and ginger. ✉ *Quay St.,* ☎ *058/45420. AE, DC, MC, V. Closed Sun.–Mon. and two wks in Jan.*

$$ ⊞ **Clonea Strand Hotel.** The beachside location and excellent sports facilities are the chief attractions of this family-run hotel. The prevailing modern design is striking and combines a smoked-glass lobby with white-washed and slate-hung bedroom wings. The decor of the rooms is standard hotel-modern, but the views from the windows make up for any plainness, with the Atlantic Ocean on one side and the Comeragh Mountains forming a backdrop on the other. ✉ *Clonea, Co. Waterford,* ☎ *058/42416,* FAX *058/42880. 59 rooms with bath. Restaurant, bar, pool, sauna, 18-hole golf course, 2 tennis courts, exercise room, fishing. AE, DC, MC, V.*

Nightlife and the Arts

The **Seanachie Pub** (✉ Ballymacart, Ring, ☎ 058/46285) is an award-winning place that features traditional music and dancing in the courtyard on Sunday during the summer. A *ceili* (Irish dance) is held nightly during the summer at the Irish-language college **Colaiste na Rinne** (☎ 058/46104) at Ring, an Irish-speaking village 7 km (4½ mi) south of Dungarvan.

Outdoor Activities and Sports

If you are tempted to explore the coast of the Dungarvan area and the nearby Nire Valley on two wheels, bicycles can be rented at **Tony O'Mahony** (✉ 14 Sexton St., Abbeyside, ☎ 058/43346).

FISHING
To rent a skippered boat for deep-sea fishing contact Cormack Walsh at the **Sea Angling Service** (⊠ 42 Lower Main St., ☎ 058/43514).

GOLF
West Waterford Golf Club (⊠ Coolcormack, ☎ 058/43216) is an 18-hole, par-72 parkland course playable year-round.

THE NIRE VALLEY, THE BLACKWATER VALLEY, AND COUNTY TIPPERARY

"It's a long way to Tipperary . . ." so run the words of that famed song sung all over the world since World War I. Actually, Tipperary is *not* so far to go, considering that, as Ireland's biggest inland county, it's within easy striking distance of Waterford and Cork. Moving in from the coastline, this tour takes you through some of Ireland's most lush pasturelands and to some of its most romantic sites, such as Lismore Castle. The Nire Valley, in the mountains between Dungarvan and Clonmel, is a newly popular area for hiking and other outdoor pursuits. The Blackwater Valley is renowned for its beauty, its peacefulness, and its excellent fishing. Some of the finest racehorses in the world are raised in the fields of Tipperary, which is also the county in which you will find the Rock of Cashel—the greatest group of monastic ruins in all Ireland.

The Nire Valley

48 *29 km (18 mi) northwest of Dungarvan on R672, 16 km (10 mi) southeast of Clonmel.*

A visit to the Nire Valley—one of Ireland's lesser-known wilderness walking areas—is an optional detour on the way from Dungarvan to the Blackwater Valley and is worthwhile only if you have time to take a walk in this fairly remote spot. But if you do, this little pocket of land that time forgot will enchant you. The valley of the River Nire starts in the village of **Ballymacarbery** and runs along the base of the Comeragh Mountains. Both forest and mountain walks pass through quiet country where sheep far outnumber people. **Knocknagriffin,** the highest peak in the Comeraghs at 2,476 ft, with views back to Waterford on the coast and inland to Tipperary Town, is easily accessible to a moderately fit walker. Walking instructions and maps are provided locally by **Nire Valley Tourist Information** (☎ 052/36455).

Dining and Lodging

$ X⌗ **Hanora's Cottage.** The cottage, one of Ireland's premier B&Bs,
★ was built in the heart of the Nire Valley by owner Seamus Wall's great-grandparents, John and Hanora, in the late 19th century. The guest rooms, including five new additions, are a generous size by cottage standards and are prettily decorated with chintz curtains and spreads. Nearby golf, riding, and walking are the main activities here (guided walks are offered every Saturday), while the less energetic simply unwind in front of the open fire, which still has the bellows wheel and creel (for hanging pots) from the original cottage kitchen. The evening meal is prepared by the Wall's son Eoin, a promising young chef, and packed lunches are provided using Seamus's famous home-baked brown bread. ⊠ *Ballymacarbery, Co. Waterford,* ☎ *052/36134,* FAX *052/36540. 8 rooms with bath. Dining room. MC, V.*

Outdoor Activities and Sports

Explore the Nire Valley on horseback by joining a guided hack from **Melody's Riding Stables** (⊠ Ballymacarbery, near Clonmel, Co. Tipperary, ☎ 052/36147).

Ardmore

㊽ *24 km (15 mi) south of Dungarvan on N25.*

Ardmore is a delightful village on its own peninsula at the base of a tall cliff, and it's far more restrained in tone than Tramore. Ardmore has ancient roots: In the 5th century, St. Declan is reputed to have disembarked here from Wales, 30 years before St. Patrick arrived in Ireland. Ardmore's monastic remains are found on the top of the cliff. The ruined, 12th-century **Cathedral of St. Declan** has some ogham stones inside and weathered but interesting biblical scenes carved on its west front. The saint is said to be buried in **St. Declan's Oratory,** a small early Christian church that has been partially reconstructed. The 97-ft-high ★**round tower,** one of 70 round towers remaining in Ireland, is in exceptionally good condition and has one of the most spectacular settings. Round towers were built by the early Christian monks as watchtowers and belfries but came to be used as places of refuge for the monks and their valuables during Viking raids. This is the reason the doorway is 15 ft above ground level: Once inside, the monks could pull the ladder into the tower with them.

Lismore

㊿ *40 km (25 mi) northwest of Ardmore on N72.*

The enchanting little town of Lismore is built on the banks of the Blackwater, a river famous for its trout and salmon. Today, with a population of only 920, Lismore is a sleepy village, popular with anglers and romantics. From the 7th to the 12th century, however, it was an important monastic center, founded by St. Carthac (or Carthage), and it had one of the most renowned universities of its time. The only reminders of those days are the village's two cathedrals, a Roman Catholic one from the late 19th century and the Church of Ireland St. Carthage's, which dates from 1633 and incorporates fragments of an earlier church. The latter cathedral also has interesting tombs and effigies.

★ As you cross the bridge entering Lismore, you will be struck by a dramatic view of the magnificent **Lismore Castle,** a vast, turreted gray stone building atop a wooded rock that overhangs the river. There has been a castle here since the 12th century, but the present structure, built by the sixth Duke of Devonshire, dates from the mid-19th century. The castle still remains in the same family and was for many years the Irish home of Fred Astaire's sister, Adele, who married into the family. The house is generally not open to the public, although small groups can rent it out for a premium price during certain times of the year. The upper and lower gardens, open to the public, consist of woodland walks, including an unusual yew walk said to be more than 800 years old, and an impressive display of magnolias, camellias, and shrubs. ☎ *058/54424.* ⌑ *£2.50.* ☼ *May–Sept., daily 1:45–4:45.*

En Route Leave Lismore, heading east on N72 for 6½ km (4 mi) toward Cappoquin, a well-known coarse-angling center, and pick up R669 north into the **Knockmealdown Mountains.** Your route is signposted as the Vee Gap road, the Vee Gap being its summit, from where you'll have superb views of the Tipperary plain, the Galtee Mountains in the northwest, and a peak called Slievenamon in the northeast. If the day is clear, you should be able to see the Rock of Cashel, ancient seat of the kings of Munster, some 32 km (20 mi) away. Just before you enter the Vee Gap, look for a 6-ft-high mound of stones on the left side of the road. It marks the grave of Colonel Grubb, a local landowner who liked the view so much that he arranged to be buried here standing up so that he could look out over the scene for all eternity.

You might like to break your journey and visit the **Mount Melleray Abbey.** The monastery was founded in 1832 by the Cistercian Order in what was then a barren mountainside wilderness. Over the years the order has succeeded in transforming the site into more than 600 acres of fertile farmland. The monks maintain strict vows of silence, but visitors are permitted into most areas of the abbey. It is also possible to stay in the guest lodge by prior arrangement; from Easter on through the summer, book two weeks in advance. ☎ *058/54404,* ℻ *058/52140.* 🎫 *Free.* ⊙ *Daily 9–6.*

Dining and Lodging

$$–$$$ ✕🏨 **Richmond House.** This handsome three-story Georgian country house is set deep in the countryside just outside Cappoquin. The atmosphere is informal, unpretentious, and very relaxing, under the personal supervision of owners Claire and Paul Deevy. The public rooms, with their log fires and traditional rust and cream decor, retain characterful echoes of the old-world country hotel. Paul is a talented chef who uses local produce wherever possible—specially grown salad leaves from one neighbor, Knockanore cheese from another. The menu's selections are usually ravishing. ✉ *Cappoquin, Co. Waterford,* ☎ *058/54278,* ℻ *058/54988. 9 rooms with bath. Restaurant, bar, horseback riding, fishing. MC, V. Sun.–Mon. dinner for residents only. Closed Dec. 23–Feb.*

Cahir

⑤ *37 km (23 mi) north of Lismore on N8.*

Cahir (pronounced care) is a small market town on the River Suir, at the crossroads of the busy N24 and N8 roads. **Cahir Castle,** the town's main attraction, is a massive limestone structure dating from 1164 and built on rock in the middle of the river. There are regular guided tours and an audiovisual display in the lodge. ☎ *052/41011.* 🎫 *£2.* ⊙ *Apr.–June and late-Sept.–mid-Oct., daily 10–6; June–mid-Sept., daily 9–7:30; late Oct.–Mar., daily 10–1 and 2–4:30.*

Dining and Lodging

$ ✕ **Castle Court Hotel.** If you're looking for a quick bite before or after visiting the castle, forego the overpriced eating spots right around the castle and head a block up the hill for the best bar food in town. The square Georgian building has an elegant and comfortable bar with polished mahogany and well-upholstered seats. Choose from the daily hot specials—bacon and cabbage or seafood bake, for example—or order from the extensive sandwich menu. ✉ *Church St.,* ☎ *052/41210. AE, DC, MC, V.*

$ ✕🏨 **Bansha Castle.** In the heart of quiet, wooded country backed by the Glen of Aherlow, about 8 km (5 mi) from Cahir on the N24 Tipperary road, sits this 18th-century stone house, which incorporates a Norman-style round tower. The atmosphere is relaxed and friendly: The family cat occupies the best fireside armchair in the chintz-strewn but unfussy drawing room. Large rooms, all with great views, are simply furnished with plain carpets and mahogany reproduction pieces. Good home cooking using locally grown organic produce is served in the dining room (guests dine at separate tables). A plethora of nearby outdoor activities includes walking, golf, salmon and trout fishing, and horseback riding at a stable across the road. ✉ *Bansha, Co. Tipperary,* ☎ *062/54187,* ℻ *062/54294. 6 rooms, 4 with bath. Dining room. No credit cards.*

$ ✕🏨 **Kilcoran Lodge Hotel.** This handsome, sprawling, 19th-century former hunting lodge sits amid beautiful countryside 6 km (4 mi) outside Cahir beneath the Galtee Mountains. It's conveniently on the main Cork–Dublin (N8) road. Rooms facing the front have the best

views of the heather-covered slopes; all have Victorian-style furnishings and comfortable beds. The furnishings in the public areas
are discreet and stately, and the entire hotel wears the ambience of
a country manor house. ⊠ *Co. Tipperary,* ☎ *052/41288,* ☒ *052/
41994. 23 rooms with bath. Restaurant, bar, indoor pool, health club.
AE, DC, MC, V.*

Outdoor Activities and Sports

Explore the Galtee mountains and the Glen of Aherlow on horseback
with the **Bansha Equestrian Centre** (⊠ Bansha, ☎ 062/54194).

En Route   To your left as you drive from Cahir to Tipperary Town on N24 is the
Glen of Aherlow, a lovely 16-km-long (10-mi-long) wooded stretch skirting the River Aherlow and its tributaries between the Galtee Mountains to the south and the Slievenamuck Hills to the north. The highest
summit in the Galtees is the 3,018-ft Galtymore Mountain.

Tipperary Town

52   *22 km (14 mi) southwest of Cahir on N24.*

Tipperary Town, a dairy-farming center at the head of a fertile plain
known as the Golden Vale, is a good starting point for climbing and
walking in the hills around the Glen of Aherlow. Racehorses are County
Tipperary's most famous export. Try to catch a horse race in the southeast if you can: It makes an enjoyable and inexpensive day out.

Outdoor Activities and Sports

Tipperary Town's racetrack is situated 5 km (3 mi) west of town and
is called, somewhat confusingly, **Limerick Junction Race Course** (⊠ Limerick Junction, ☎ 062/52766).

Cashel

53   *17 km (11 mi) northeast of Tipperary Town on N74.*

Cashel is a market town on the busy Cork–Dublin road, which, in spite
of the incessant heavy traffic running through it, retains some interesting Victorian shopfronts on its Main Street, with four-part windows
divided by timber pilasters. The town has a lengthy history as a center of royal and religious power. From roughly AD 370 until 1101, it
was the seat of the kings of Munster, and it was probably at one time
a center of Druidic worship. Here, according to legend, St. Patrick arrived in about AD 432 and baptized King Aengus, who became Ireland's
first Christian ruler. One of the many legends associated with this
event is that St. Patrick plucked a shamrock to explain the mystery of
the Trinity, thus giving a new emblem to Christian Ireland.

The **Cashel Heritage Tram** provides circular tours of Cashel's historic
sites; you can join and leave at any point. The £3 ticket price includes
two free entries. ☉ Mar.–Oct., Mon.–Sat. 9:30–5:30, Sun. 2:30–5:30;
June–Sept., Tues.–Sat. noon–6.

★   The awe-inspiring, oft-mist-shrouded **Rock of Cashel** is one of Ireland's
most visited sites, but it is no less worthwhile for its popularity. The
rock itself, which is a short walk to the north of the town, rises as a
giant, circular mound 200 ft above the surrounding plain; it is crowned
by a tall cluster of gray monastic remains. Legend has it that the devil,
flying over Ireland in a hurry, took a bite out of the Slieve Bloom Mountains to clear his path (the gap, known as the Devil's Bit, can be seen
to the north of the rock) and spat it out here in the Golden Vale. Take
some time to linger here, sitting on the grass admiring the view of the

plains of Tipperary and absorbing the atmosphere of its pagan and Christian pasts.

The best approach to the rock is along the **Bishop's Walk,** a 10-minute hike that begins outside the drawing room of the Cashel Palace Hotel (☞ Dining and Lodging, *below*) on Main Street. (Ask for directions at the reception desk.) As you enter the monastic site, you'll see ahead a rough stone with an ancient cross; this is where, according to legend, St. Patrick baptized King Aengus. (Patrick was old then and drove his staff into the earth to support himself. After the ceremony, it was discovered that the staff had passed through the king's foot and the grass was soaked with blood. Aengus didn't complain, as he thought that this suffering was part of the initiation rite.) The stone at this site was also the coronation stone of the Munster kings; it dates from as early as the 4th century.

Actually, the stone that you see upon arrival is a replica; the real one is on display in the **museum** across from the entrance. Although the museum with its 15-minute audiovisual display is an innovation that some find inappropriate and unnecessary, it does provide enthusiastic young guides, who will ensure that you do not miss the many interesting features of the buildings atop the Rock of Cashel.

The shell of **St. Patrick's Cathedral** is the largest building on the summit. The 13th-century cathedral was originally built in a flamboyant variation on Romanesque style, but it was destroyed by fire in 1495. The restored building was desecrated during the 16th century in a particularly ugly incident in which hundreds of townspeople who had sought sanctuary in the cathedral were burned to death when Cromwell's forces surrounded the building with turf and set it afire. There is a series of sculptures in the north transept representing the Apostles, other saints, and the Beasts of the Apocalypse. Look for the octagonal staircase turret that ascends beside the **Central Tower** to a series of defensive passages built into the thick walls. From the top of the Central Tower, you'll have a wonderful view of the surrounding plains and mountains. Another passage gives access to the **round tower,** a well-preserved building 92 ft high.

The entrance to **Cormac's Chapel,** the best-preserved building on top of the Rock, is behind the south transept of the cathedral. The chapel was built in 1127 by Cormac Macarthy, king of Desmond and bishop of Cashel (combination bishop-kings were not unusual in the early Irish church). Note the high corbeled roof, modeled on the traditional covering of early saints' cells (as at Glendalough [☞ Chapter 2] and Dingle [☞ Chapter 5]); the typically Romanesque, twisted columns around the altar; and the unique carvings around the south entrance. ⊠ *Rock of Cashel,* ☎ 062/61437. ⊠ *£3.* ☉ *Mid-Mar.–mid-June, daily 9:30–5:30; mid-June–mid-Sept., daily 9–7:30; mid-Sept.–mid-Mar., daily 9:30–4:30.*

The **Bru Boru Heritage Center,** where Irish music, dance, and culture are studied, lies at the base of the rock. Exhibits on aspects of Irish heritage change seasonally, and you can visit the crafts shop, genealogy center, and restaurant (☞ Nightlife and the Arts, *below*). ☎ 062/61122. ⊠ *Heritage Center free, evening song and storytelling £5.* ☉ *Heritage Center June–Oct., daily 9 AM–11 PM; Nov.–May, daily 9–5; evening song and storytelling mid-June–mid-Sept., Tues.–Sun. 9 PM.*

In the same building as the TIO, the **Cashel of the Kings Heritage Center** explains the historic relationship between the town and the rock and includes a scale model of Cashel as it looked during the 1600s.

The center also offers guided tours of the town. ⊠ *City Hall,* ☎ *062/ 62511.* 🎫 *£1.* ☉ *Jan.–May and Sept.–Dec., daily 9:30–5; June–Aug., daily 9:30–7.*

The **G. P. A. Bolton Library,** on the grounds of the St. John the Baptist Church of Ireland Cathedral, has a particularly notable collection of 12,000 rare books and manuscripts on display. ⊠ *John St.,* ☎ *062/61944.* 🎫 *£1.50.* ☉ *Mar.–Oct., Mon.–Sat. 9:30–5:30, Sun. 2:30–5:30.*

Dining and Lodging

$$$$ ✗ **Chez Hans.** This small, converted Victorian church at the foot of
★ the Rock of Cashel oozes old-world charm: Dark wood and tapestries provide an elegant background for tables dressed in beige linen. Traditional French cuisine with a hint of nouvelle takes advantage of fresh Irish ingredients. Specialties include roast rack of spring lamb with a fresh herb crust and tarragon sauce; the steaks are always excellent, as is the fish. ⊠ *Rockside,* ☎ *062/61177. Reservations essential. MC, V. Closed Sun.–Mon. and 1st 3 wks of Jan. No lunch.*

$$ ✗ **Spearman Restaurant.** This small, front-parlor restaurant is hidden away in the center of Cashel, behind the TIO. Stained-glass windows, hunting prints on the walls, art deco–style side lights, and tall-back chairs disguise the fact that this was, until recently, a grocery store. Young local chef John Spearman is gaining a solid reputation for imaginative, affordable food based on the best of fresh local produce. ⊠ *97 Main St.,* ☎ *062/61143. AE, DC, MC, V. Closed Mon. and Nov.–Apr. No dinner Sun.*

$$$$ ✗🏨 **Cashel Palace.** Dramatically set at the foot of the Rock of Cashel,
★ this 1730s redbrick-and-stone bishop's palace is an exquisite accommodation, set back from the street in its own garden. The pine-paneled public rooms are dominated by twin marble fireplaces and carved pillars; a striking, intricately carved, red-pine staircase sweeps upstairs. Four-poster canopy beds, antiques, and spacious bathrooms characterize the luxurious guest rooms; ask for one facing the back so that you can enjoy the breathtaking view of the Rock of Cashel. The menu at the elegant Three Sisters Restaurant relies on game in season, local lamb and beef, and fresh fish imaginatively prepared, while the bistro-style basement Bishop's Buttery serves simple, light meals all day. ⊠ *Main St., Co. Tipperary,* ☎ *062/62707,* 📠 *062/61521. 13 rooms with bath. 2 restaurants, bar, fishing. AE, DC, MC, V.*

$$$ 🏨 **Dundrum House Hotel.** Nestled beside the River Muteen, 12 km (7½ mi) outside busy Cashel, this magnificent, four-story Georgian house is well worth the trek for the quiet of the countryside. Fourteen high-ceiling bedrooms take up the main house; the rest are in a three-story wing built during the house's previous incarnation as a convent. All the rooms have large pieces of early Victorian furniture, lovely views of the surrounding parkland, and relaxing pink-and-green decor. The old convent chapel, stained-glass windows intact, is now a cocktail bar. Elaborate plaster ceilings, attractive period furniture, and open fires make the spacious dining room and lounge inviting. ⊠ *Dundrum, Co. Tipperary,* ☎ *062/71116,* 📠 *062/71366. 60 rooms with bath. 2 restaurants, 2 bars, pool, sauna, steam room, 18-hole golf course, tennis court, fishing. AE, DC, MC, V.*

Nightlife and the Arts

Folksinging, storytelling, and dancing are enjoyed from May through September, Tuesday through Saturday, at the **Bru Boru Heritage Center** (☎ 062/61122) at the foot of the Rock of Cashel.

Outdoor Activities and Sports

The natural features of the mature Georgian estate at Dundrum House Hotel have been incorporated into an 18-hole, par-72 course for the **County Tipperary Golf and Country Club** (⊠ Dundrum House Hotel, Dundrum, ☎ 062/71116). Visitors are welcome every day.

Clonmel

54 *24 km (15 mi) southeast of Cashel on R688.*

As the county seat of Tipperary, Clonmel is set on the prettiest part of the River Suir, with wooded islands and riverside walks. With a population of about 12,500, it is one of Ireland's largest and most prosperous inland towns. There has been a settlement here since Viking days; in the 14th century the town was walled and fortified as a stronghold of the Butler family. The novelist Laurence Sterne (1713–68), author of *Tristram Shandy*, was born here, and the English novelist Anthony Trollope (1815–82) served for a time in the post office. O'Connell Street, the main thoroughfare, runs east–west and close to the river. At one end is the **West Gate**, built in 1831 on the site of the medieval one. Among other notable buildings are the **Court House** (designed by Sir Richard Morrison) and the **Franciscan friary** and **St. Mary's Church of Ireland,** both of which incorporate remains of earlier churches and some interesting tombs and monuments. Clonmel is known in sporting circles as the home of the Tipperary foxhounds and a greyhound-racing center—meets and races are often disrupted by animal lovers.

Dining and Lodging

$ ✕ **Mulcahy's of Clonmel.** This award-winning bar-restaurant serves a selection of salads, snacks, and hot dishes from 10:30 to 7 in the Carvery Food Bar; from 6 PM an extensive à la carte menu is available in the Melleray Restaurant. ⊠ *47 Gladstone St.,* ☎ *052/22825. AE, DC, MC, V.*

$$ ✕▥ **Minella Hotel.** This bowfront, Georgian manor hotel is found in a quiet neighborhood on the bank of the River Suir. The rooms, which are all in wings separate from the main house, afford fine views of the river, particularly those in the front and in the east wing. "Executive" rooms in the new wing are larger, and some have Jacuzzi baths. The Victorian furnishings are comfortable; walls are decorated with hunting prints. The dining room is oak-paneled and has a good reputation for freshly prepared classic cuisine. ⊠ *Coleville Rd., Co. Tipperary,* ☎ *052/22388,* FAX *052/24381. 62 rooms with shower, 8 suites. Restaurant, bar, fishing, bicycles. AE, DC, MC, V.*

Outdoor Activities and Sports

GOLF

Clonmel Golf Club (⊠ Lyreanearla, ☎ 052/24050) is an 18-hole course on the slopes of the Comeragh Mountains that welcomes visitors daily.

SPECTATOR SPORTS

Clonmel is at the very heart of sporting Ireland. Hurling and Gaelic football are played on Sunday at the **Clonmel GAA Grounds** (⊠ Western Rd., ☎ 052/21806). Horse races are held regularly at **Clonmel Racecourse** (⊠ Powerstown Park, ☎ 052/22852). Greyhound races are held at night in a relaxed atmosphere with bar and catering facilities at **Clonmel Greyhound Racetrack** (⊠ Davis Rd., ☎ 052/21118).

Carrick-on-Suir

⑤⑤ *20 km (12 mi) east of Clonmel on N24.*

Uncharacteristically for towns in Ireland, Carrick-on-Suir lies partly in County Tipperary and partly in County Waterford. The beautifully restored **Ormonde Castle** is the town's main attraction. A Tudor manor house, one of the best-preserved Tudor buildings in Ireland, is the most interesting part of the castle. The town is one of several claiming to be the birthplace of Anne Boleyn, and the house is said to have been built in order to entertain her daughter, Queen Elizabeth I, who never visited here. It contains some good, early stucco work, especially in the 100-ft Long Room, and many arms and busts of the English queen. ☎ *051/640787.* ☜ *£2.* ☉ *Mid-June–Sept., daily 9:30–6:30.*

Shopping

The **Tipperary Crystal Factory Shop** (✉ Ballynoran, ☎ 051/641188), a factory outlet that offers free tours of the glass-cutting facility weekdays between 10 and 3:30, also has a showroom in a replica thatched cottage, open daily.

THE SOUTHEAST A TO Z

Arriving and Departing

By Car

Waterford City, the regional capital, is easily accessible from all parts of Ireland. From Dublin, take N7 southwest, change to N9 in Naas, and continue along this highway through Carlow Town and Thomastown until it terminates in Waterford. N25 travels east–west through Waterford City, connecting it with Cork in the west and Wexford Town in the east. From Limerick and Tipperary Town, N24 stretches southeast until it, too, ends in Waterford City.

By Ferry

The region's primary ferry terminal is found just south of Wexford Town at Rosslare. **Stena Sealink** (☎ 053/33115) sails directly between Rosslare Ferryport and Fishguard, Wales. Pembroke, Wales, can be reached on the **B+I Lines** (☎ 053/33311), and there are three sailings weekly to France's Le Havre and Cherbourg on **Irish Ferries** (☎ 053/33158).

By Plane

Waterford Regional Airport (☎ 051/875589) is on the Waterford–Ballymacaw road in Killowen. Waterford City is 9½ km (6 mi) from the airport. A hackney cab from the airport into Waterford City costs approximately £12. **British Airways** (☎ 051/875589 or 800/626747) schedules flights out of this small regional airport daily to Stanstead, England.

Getting Around

By Bus

Bus Éireann (☎ 01/836–6111 in Dublin or 051/873401 in Waterford) makes the Waterford–Dublin journey four times daily for about £6. There are three buses daily between Waterford City and Limerick, and three between Waterford City and Rosslare. The Cork–Waterford journey is made twice daily. In Waterford City, the terminal is Plunkett Station.

By Car

For the most part, the main roads in the Southeast are of good quality and are free of congestion. Side roads are generally narrow and twisting, and drivers should keep an eye out for farm machinery and animals on country roads.

By Train

Waterford City is linked by **Irish Rail** (☎ 01/836–6222 in Dublin or 051/873401 in Waterford) service to Dublin. Trains run from Plunkett Station in Waterford City to Dublin four times daily, making stops at Kilkenny, Thomastown, and Carlow Town. The daily train between Waterford City and Limerick makes stops at Tipperary Town and Clonmel. The train between Rosslare and Waterford City runs twice daily.

Contacts and Resources

B&B Reservation Agencies

For a small fee, **Bord Fáilte** will book accommodations anywhere in Ireland through its central reservations system. B&Bs can be booked at local visitor information offices when they are open; however, even these reservations will go through the central reservations system. For more information, ☞ Lodging *in* Smart Travel Tips A to Z.

Car Rentals

The major car-rental companies have offices at Rosslare Ferryport, and in most large towns rental information can be found through the local tourism office. Typical car-rental prices start at about £40 per day with unlimited mileage, and they usually include insurance and all taxes. **Budget** has offices in Rosslare Harbour (✉ The Ferryport, ☎ 053/33318) and Waterford Airport (☎ 051/421670). **Hertz** has offices in Rosslare Harbour (☎ 053/33238) and Waterford City (☎ 051/878737).

Emergencies

Police, fire, and ambulance (☎ 999). **Waterford Regional Hospital** (✉ Ardkeen, ☎ 051/873321).

Guided Tours

Kilkenny: Walking tours of Kilkenny are arranged by Tynan Tours and operate from Monday through Saturday from the Kilkenny TIO (☎ 056/65929 or 056/51500). Open-Top Coach Tours of Kilkenny depart from the castle gate April–October 10–5 (☎ 01/458–0054).

Waterford City: Burtchaell Tours lead a Waterford walk at noon and 2 PM daily from March through September. It leaves from the Granville Hotel. Call for details and off-season information (☎ 051/873711).

Wexford Town: Walking tours of historic Wexford Town can be pre-booked for groups by contacting Seamus P. Molloy (☎ 053/22663).

Outdoor Activities and Sports

FISHING

For further information on this and other angling activities in the region, contact the **Southern Regional Fisheries Board** (✉ Anglesea St., Clonmel, Co. Tipperary, ☎ 052/23971).

SPECTATOR SPORTS

Tickets to major Gaelic football and hurling matches are available through the **Gaelic Athletic Association** (✉ GAA, Croke Park, Jones's Rd., Dublin 3, ☎ 01/836–3222). For smaller venues, inquire at local TIOs.

Visitor Information

Seven Tourist Information Offices in the Southeast are open all year (not all have fax numbers): **Carlow Town** (✉ Hadden Shopping Center, Tullow St., Co. Carlow, ☎ 0503/31554). **Clonmel** (✉ Community Office, Nelson St., Co. Tipperary, ☎ 052/22960). **Dungarvan** (✉ The

Square, Co. Waterford, ☎ 058/41741). **Kilkenny** (✉ Rose Inn St., ☎ 056/51500, FAX 056/63955). **Rosslare** (✉ Rosslare Ferry Terminal, Kilrane, Rosslare Harbour, Co. Wexford, ☎ 053/33622, FAX 053/33421). **Waterford City** (✉ 41 The Quay, Co. Waterford, ☎ 051/875788, FAX 051/877388). **Wexford Town** (✉ Crescent Quay, Co. Wexford, ☎ 053/23111, FAX 053/41743).

Another five TIOs are open seasonally: **Cahir** (✉ Castle St., Co. Tipperary, ☎ 052/41453), open April–September; **Cashel** (✉ Town Hall, Co. Tipperary, ☎ 062/61333, FAX 062/61789), open April–September; **Lismore** (✉ The Courthouse, Co. Waterford, ☎ 058/54975, FAX 058/53009), open April–October; **New Ross** (✉ Harbour Centre, The Quay, Co. Wexford, ☎ 051/21857), open mid-June–August; **Tipperary Town** (✉ 3 James St., Co. Tipperary, ☎ 062/51457), open May–October; **Tramore** (✉ Railway Sq., Co. Waterford, ☎ 051/81572), open mid-June–August.

5 THE SOUTHWEST

IN AND AROUND CORK AND
KILLARNEY, THE RING OF KERRY,
THE DINGLE PENINSULA, AND
SHANNONSIDE

Spectacular is the word for the Southwest,
where superlatives flow as continuously as
the Rivers Lee and Blackwater. Five-star
scenery is everywhere, from Kinsale along
the coast west to Mizen Head in the far
southwest corner to the glorious mountains
and lakes of Killarney. And the food! Thanks
to its accomplished chefs and the bounty of
farms, fields, lakes, and coast, County Cork
has become to the Irish food world what
California is to America's. You'll also find a
mild climate, the nation's second- and third-
largest cities, and extensive Irish-speaking
areas: What more could you ask for?

CORK, KERRY, LIMERICK, AND CLARE—the sound of these Southwest Ireland county names has an undeniably evocative Irish lilt. A varied coastline, spectacular scenery (especially around the famous lakes of Killarney), and a mild climate have long attracted visitors to this region. Although the Southwest contains Cork and Limerick—Ireland's second- and third-largest cities—its most notable attractions are rural: miles and miles of pretty country lanes meandering through rich but sparsely populated farmland. Even in the two main cities the pace of life is perceptibly slower than in Dublin. To be in a hurry in this region is being ill-mannered. It was probably a Kerryman who first remarked that when God made time, he made plenty of it.

Updated by
Alannah
Hopkin

As you look over thick, fuchsia hedges at thriving dairy farms or stop off at a wayside restaurant to sample the region's seafood or locally raised meat, it is hard to imagine that some 150 years ago this area was decimated by famine. Thousands perished in the fields and the workhouses, and thousands more took "coffin ships" from Cobh in Cork Harbour to the New World. Between 1845 and 1849 the population of Ireland fell by more than a million, or roughly 30% (according to the 1841 census, the Irish population was 8,175,124). Many small villages in the Southwest were wiped out. The region was battered again in the War for Independence and the Civil War that was fought with intensity in and around "Rebel Cork" between 1919 and 1921. Economic recovery only began in the late '60s, which led to a boom in hotel construction and renovation—not always, alas, done in the appropriate style.

Outside of Killarney and Shannon, tourist development remains fairly low-key. The area is trying to absorb more visitors without losing too much of what attracts them in the first place: uncrowded roads, pollution-free beaches and rivers, easy access to golf and fishing, and unspoiled scenery where wildflowers, untamed animals, and rare birds (which have all but disappeared in more industrialized European countries) still thrive.

South of the city of Cork, the main business and shopping town of the region, the resort town of Kinsale is the gateway to a relatively unspoiled coastline containing Roaring Water Bay, with its main islands, and the magnificent, natural harbor, Bantry Bay. The southwest coast of the region is formed by three peninsulas: the Beara, the Iveragh, and the Dingle; the road known as the Ring of Kerry makes a complete circuit of the Iveragh Peninsula. Killarney's sparkling blue lakes and magnificent sandstone mountains, inland from the peninsulas, have a unique and romantic splendor, immortalized in the 19th century by the writings of William Thackeray and Sir Walter Scott. Around the Shannon estuary you enter "castle country," an area littered with ruined castles and abbeys as a result of Elizabeth I's attempt to subdue the old Irish province of Munster in the 16th century. Limerick City, too, bears the scars of history from a different confrontation with the English, the Siege of Limerick, which took place in 1691. Today, it is Limerick's other "scars"—described so memorably in Frank McCourt's noted bestseller, *Angela's Ashes*—that now lure travelers to discover (or rediscover) the city.

Although the Southwest has several sumptuous country-house hotels, it is basically an easygoing, unpretentious region, where informality and simplicity are the keynotes of hospitality. As in the rest of Ireland, social life revolves around the pub, and a visit to your "local" is the best way to find out what's going on. Local residents have not lost their natural curiosity about "strangers," as visitors are called. You will frequently be asked, "Are you enjoying your holiday?" "Yes" is not a good enough answer: What the locals are really after is your life story.

Pleasures and Pastimes

Dining

The Southwest—especially County Cork—rivals Dublin as Ireland's food-culture epicenter. Cork has astonishing resources: sparkling waters full of a wide array of fish, acre after acre of potato fields, cows galore, wild mushrooms and berries, and much more. Cork's dedicated, inventive chefs turn this bounty into a feast—all, it often seems, for your benefit—in food markets (Cork City's English Market, most notably), bakeries, cafés, restaurants, B&Bs, and country houses. In tiny Shanagarry, Darina and Tim Allen train hundreds of chefs every year at their Ballymaloe Cookery School. Outstanding restaurants and the International Gourmet Festival in October draw crowds to Kinsale, the "Gourmet Capital of Ireland." Whether trained at home or abroad, area chefs put a premium on fresh, local (often organically grown) produce. To sample the region's best cuisine, consult our five-day gastronomic tour (☞ Great Itineraries, *below*). For price ranges, *see* Chart 1(A) *in* Smart Travel Tips A to Z.

Lodging

Some of the most sumptuous country-house hotels in Ireland are in the Southwest. You'll also find more modest establishments, many in spectacular seaside locations. Though some country houses appear grand, their main aim is to provide a relaxed stay in beautiful surroundings. A good pair of walking boots and a sensible raincoat are more useful here than a formal wardrobe. If you want to dress for dinner, as some people do, feel free. By and large, however, informality is the order of the day. Keep in mind that facilities may be minimal: Only expensive hotels have fitness centers, for instance. At the least, most hotels can organize golf, deep-sea fishing, freshwater angling, and horseback riding. Most B&Bs have introduced private bathrooms and, in the larger towns, televisions and direct-dial phones in rooms. Accommodations in West Cork, Killarney, and Dingle are seasonal; between November and March, many places close down, but outside these months—especially from July to mid-October—hotels are busy, so book well in advance. If your first choice for a hotel is full, ask for a recommendation to similar lodgings nearby. For price ranges, ☞ Chart 2(B) *in* Smart Travel Tips A to Z.

Nightlife and the Arts

Mid-June through September, you'll find musical entertainment in pubs on most nights; in other seasons, Thursday through Sunday are the busiest times. Dingle is the best place for traditional Irish music; elsewhere, pubs and clubs offer a mix of traditional, country, rock, and jazz. Spontaneous music seisuns are common, especially on the Dingle Peninsula; elsewhere, performances usually begin around 9. Nightclubs are usually attached to hotels or bars; they are open from 10:30 PM until 1 or 2 AM. Expect to pay a £5–£8 cover fee.

Outdoor Activities and Sports

BICYCLING

You'll find some of the most spectacular scenery in the country around **Glengarriff, Killarney,** and **Dingle.** The length of the hills—rather than their steepness—is the challenge here, but without the hills there wouldn't be such great views. A less-strenuous option, equally scenic but on a smaller scale, is the coast of West Cork between **Kinsale** and **Glen-**

garriff. The **Beara Peninsula** proves very popular with cyclists, who enjoy its varied coastal scenery and relative lack of vehicles. Traffic can be a problem in July and August on the **Ring of Kerry,** where there is a lack of alternative routes to the one main circuit. Because of the various mountain ranges in the area, rain is never far off, except on the hottest summer days, so always carry a light, waterproof jacket. The Irish Tourist Board publication "Cycling Ireland" (£2) suggests six bicycling circuits that can be made in the region. For bicycle rentals, expect to pay about £6 per day, or £25 for seven days, with a £40 refundable deposit.

FISHING

Besides having an abundance of facilities for sea angling and a wealth of salmon and trout rivers, the Southwest enjoys the bonus of scenic surroundings—be it the black-slate cliffs of the coast or the lush vegetation of Killarney and the Ring of Kerry. **Shore fishing** is available all along the coast, from Cobh in the east to Foynes in the west. The whole region offers excellent opportunities for **lake and river fishing,** although most anglers head for Waterville or Killarney. Coarse anglers will find pike at Macroom and coarse-angling facilities at Mallow and Fermoy. The **deep-sea fishing** season runs from April to October. Boat rentals cost about £20 per person per day. Boats can be rented at Ballycotton, Cork Harbour in Cobh, Midleton, Passage West, Crosshaven, Kinsale, Courtmacsherry, Clonakilty, Castletownshend, Valentia Island, Fenit, and Dingle.

GOLF

Many of the Southwest's 18-hole courses are world-famous, championship clubs set amid wonderful scenery. The leading courses in the region—**Cork Golf Club, the Old Head Golf Links, Waterville Golf Links, Killarney Golf and Fishing Club,** and **Tralee Golf Club**—are all covered in depth in Chapter 9.

HIKING

The far southwest around Killarney and Dingle is classic hiking country, with spectacular scenery and a feeling of wilderness—even though you're never more than 3 or 4 km (2 or 3 mi) from civilization. On higher ground, fog can come down very quickly, so follow local advice on weather conditions and adjust your schedule accordingly. Two signposted, long-distance walking trails wind through the region: The 214-km (134-mi) **Kerry Way** begins in Killarney and loops around the Ring of Kerry, and the 153-km (95-mi) **Dingle Way** loops from Tralee around the Dingle Peninsula. Both routes consist of paths and "green (unsurfaced) roads," with some stretches linked by surfaced roads. In general, these routes, although rough underfoot, are suitable for families, particularly in summer. The 209-km (130-mi) **Beara Way** mainly is an off-road walk around the rugged Beara Peninsula in West Cork.

The **Blackwater Way** is a 168-km (104-mi) trail that follows the lower slopes of the Knockmealdown Mountains to the rich farms and woodlands of the Blackwater Valley. The **Sheep's Head Way** encircles the Sheep's Head Peninsula and has glorious views of Bantry Bay along its 88-km (55-mi) route. Additional walks can be found in Killarney National Park; Gougane Barra, northeast of Ballylickey off R584 in County Cork; Farran, off N22 about 16 km (10 mi) west of Cork City in County Cork; the Ballyhoura Mountains on the Cork-Limerick border, off N20 at Ballyhea about 16 km (10 mi) north of Buttevant; and Currachase Forest Park, east of Askeaton off N69 in County Limerick.

Exploring the Southwest

Our coverage of the Southwest is organized into seven tours: **Cork City and Environs** (which includes the ever-popular Blarney Castle, home of the Blarney Stone); **East Cork and the Blackwater Valley** (covering Youghal and Ballymaloe); **Kinsale to Glengarriff via Bantry Bay** (Mizen Head, Cape Clear, and other points in the far Southwest); the **Ring of Kerry; In and Around Killarney**; the **Dingle Peninsula**; and **North Kerry and Shannonside.** We begin in Cork (under the assumption that you'll approach from points east) and make a clockwise sweep of the area. We end on the northern fringe, crossing over the border from County Kerry into County Limerick and then briefly dipping into the very southeastern reaches of County Clare in the area immediately around Shannon Airport. If you fly into Shannon, you can easily travel the entire sequence in reverse, or pick and choose from those places that interest you.

Among the most notable attractions in the Southwest are the Lakes of Killarney, which require a day or more; you simply must explore these wonders partly on foot to enjoy them fully. Killarney also makes a good base for discovering the Ring of Kerry and the Dingle Peninsula. The main cities in the area—Cork, Tralee, and Limerick—have quiet charm, but they cannot compete with the magnificent scenery farther west. Kinsale is a favorite starting point for a leisurely drive through the coast west to Bantry, which can take one day or three, depending on your appetite for unscheduled stops and impromptu exploration. Two national parks, Glengarriff near the sea and Gougane Barra in the mountains, are also worth visiting.

Numbers in the text correspond to numbers in the margin and on the Southwest, Cork City, and Killarney Area maps.

Great Itineraries

IF YOU HAVE 3 DAYS

Base yourself in ☒ **Killarney Town** ⑤⓪–⑥⓪ for both nights, and reserve one day for a leisurely exploration of **Killarney**'s famous lakes and mountains. Visit the **Gap of Dunloe** ⑤② on an organized tour and walk or ride horseback through the gap itself, crossing the lake beyond by rowboat. The next day head for the Ring of Kerry via **Killorglin** ④⑨ and enjoy the mix of subtropical vegetation caused by the nearby Gulf Stream and rugged cliffs. You need reasonable visibility for the Ring of Kerry, so if the seaward weather promises mist, head inland instead to **Gougane Barra Forest Park,** where the hermit St. Finbarr had his mountain retreat. Follow the granite-walled **Pass of Keimaneigh** to **Bantry** ㊱. A cliff-top road runs between Bantry and Glengarriff, with wonderful sea views along the 24-km (15-mi) Bantry Bay inlet. The stretch of road between **Glengarriff** ㊲ and Killarney Town, known as the tunnel road, is one of Ireland's most famous scenic routes. It comes into Killarney Town past the **Ladies' View** ⑥⓪, little changed since it impressed Queen Victoria's ladies-in-waiting almost 150 years ago.

IF YOU HAVE 5 DAYS FOR A GASTRONOMIC TOUR

Apart from the innovative chefs working in the kitchens of some of Dublin's finest restaurants, Cork is indisputably Ireland's leading food region (☞ Dining *in* Pleasures and Pastimes, *above*)—with superlative country-house hotels serving food prepared from the freshest local ingredients; the country's leading cooking school; and its self-proclaimed "gourmet capital." If you're a dedicated foodie or you've already done a wider sweep through the country and you want to focus on one region, our five-day itinerary, taking in the Southwest's best food, may be for you. Begin in **Cork City** ①–⑲ and stop in at the not-to-be-missed

ATLANTIC OCEAN

CLARE

Kilkee

Kilrush

Killimer
Tarbert
76 Glin

N67
N68
N69
R523

Mouth of
the Shannon

Ballybunion

Listowel
75

Abbeyfeale

N69
N27
R578

Brandon
Bay

Tralee
Bay

Tralee

73 **74** N21

Castleisland

R577

Kilmakedar Church
Gallarus Oratory

72 Mt. Brandon
Kilcummin
Connor
Pass

DINGLE PENINSULA

Blennerville

Castlemaine

R559
N70
R561

Ballydavid
Dún an Óir
Ballyferriter
Dunquin
Slea Head

70 **71**
68 **69**
67 **63**
65 **64**

62
Dingle
Town

61

R561

Annascaul

Inch

Killorglin

N22

Ventry
Dunbeg

Rossbeigh **48**

49

R562

Killarney
Area

66
Blasket
Islands

Dingle Bay

Glenbeigh **47**
Kerry

Caragh
Lake

50 — 60

N72

Cahirciveen

Ring

N70

IVERAGH PENINSULA

KERRY Upper
Lake

Lake
Leane

Muckross

KILLARNEY
NATIONAL
PARK

N22

Valentia
Island **44**

46

R568

R569

Staigue Fort
41

N70 **39** **Kenmare**

Skellig
Islands **45**

Ballinskelligs
Bay

Waterville

43

N70

Ring

of Kerry

40 **Sneem**

Tahilla

Parknasilla R571

R584

Gougane Barra
Forest Park

Caherdaniel **42**

Kenmare River

N71

37 **Glengarriff**

BEARA PENINSULA

Garnish
Island **38**

Ballylickey

R586

Castletown
Bere

R572

Bantry Bay

36 **Bantry**

Dursey
Island

Bere Island

Durrus

N71

Ballydehob

Schull R592

N71

Skibbereen

32 R596

Liss Ard
Foundation

Castletownsher

Mizen Head
Signal Station

Goleen

Crookhaven

Roaring Water Bay

R595

33 **Baltimore**

34
Sherkin
Island

35

Cape Clear
Island

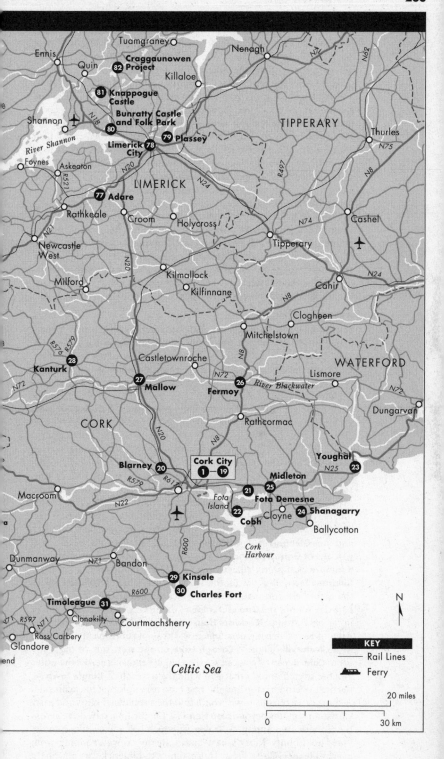

Tuamgraney

Ennis

Quin

Craggaunowen Project 82

Killaloe

Nenagh

Knappogue Castle 81

Bunratty Castle and Folk Park 80

Shannon

River Shannon

Limerick City 78 79 **Plassey**

Foynes

Askeaton

R521

TIPPERARY

Thurles

N75

LIMERICK N24

Adare 77

Rathkeale

Croom

Holycross

N74

Cashel

N21

Newcastle West

N20

Kilmallock

Tipperary

N24

Milford

Kilfinnane

Cahir

R576 R579

Clogheen

Mitchelstown

N8

WATERFORD

Kanturk 28

Castletownroche

N72

Lismore

N72

N72

Mallow 27

26 **Fermoy**

River Blackwater

Dungarvan

CORK

N20

N8

Rathcormac

Youghal 23

N25

Blarney 20

R579

R61

Cork City 1 19

Midleton

25

Macroom

N22

21 **Fota Demesne**

Fota Island

22 **Fota Demesne**

Cloyne

24 **Shanagarry**

Cobh

Ballycotton

R600

Cork Harbour

Dunmanway

N71

Bandon

R600

Kinsale 29

30 **Charles Fort**

Timoleague 31

N71 R597 N71

Clonakilty

Courtmachsherry

Ross Carbery

Glandore

Celtic Sea

N

KEY	
——	Rail Lines
🚢	Ferry

0   20 miles

0   30 km

English Market ⑪. Stay overnight and also dine at the ⛏ **Arbutus Lodge,** where the eight-course "tasting menu" will introduce you to French-Irish haute cuisine complemented by a widely acclaimed wine list. On the next day head out to ⛏ **Ballymaloe House** in **Shanagarry** ㉔, for 50 years the Allen family farm and today run by three generations of the family. The decor is simple but elegant country-style, and the emphasis is on fresh local produce and fish from nearby **Ballycotton.** If you plan carefully, you may be able to fit in a one-day cooking class at the **Ballymaloe Cookery School and Gardens,** 2 km (1 mi) away, also run by the Allen family. At the least, the gardens, with their wide variety of herbs and edible plants, are a pleasant way to see food before it hits the table. Next drive northwest to **Mallow** ㉗ in the Blackwater Valley to ⛏ **Longueville House,** another family-run operation, albeit on a grander scale. Proprietor William O'Callaghan's President's Restaurant earns raves as one of the finest in Ireland; he also runs one of Ireland's only vineyards. From here, head to **Kenmare** ㊴, where the ⛏ **Sheen Falls Lodge** has 300 acres of semitropical gardens beside the fall of the River Sheen; stroll in the gardens before dining in La Cascade restaurant. The following day drive back toward the pretty waterfront village of **Kinsale** ㉙, where spots like the **Oystercatcher** and the ⛏ **Blue Haven Hotel** have helped earn the town the title "Gourmet Capital of Ireland." Return to Cork City the next day.

IF YOU HAVE 7 DAYS

Start at **Bunratty Castle** ⑧⓪, the nearest attraction to Shannon Airport and a must-see for first-time visitors. Continue on to ⛏ **Limerick City** ⑦⑧ and take a look at either the restored **King John's Castle** or the Celtic and medieval treasures at the **Hunt Museum.** Spend the night in Limerick; the following day, head south for **Blarney** ⑳, with its castle, where you can kiss the Blarney Stone and browse through Ireland's largest selection of crafts shops. Then proceed to ⛏ **Cork City** ①–⑲, where you can make an overnight stop. Take a walk around the city center and enjoy the city's lively nightlife, including pubs, restaurants, and theater. The next day head east up to Cork Harbour to visit **Cobh** ㉒, where the Queenstown Heritage Centre documents the history of Irish emigration. Cross the harbor by ferry and visit ⛏ **Kinsale** ㉙, an historic little port built on hilly slopes, with a star-shape fort dating from 1620 on its large, natural harbor. The town is a fashionable resort with gourmet restaurants, crafts shops, and art galleries. The following day, drive through scenic West Cork around Bantry Bay and into **Glengarriff** ㊲, where you can take a boat to the subtropical gardens of **Garnish Island** ㊳, a few minutes offshore. Continue on to **Kenmare** ㊴, a pretty village on a river estuary, and then go on to ⛏ **Killarney Town** ㊵–⑥⓪ via a scenic road known as the Windy Gap. Spend the night here and make an early start the next day, either taking a half-day tour of the **Gap of Dunloe** ㊷ or viewing the splendid scenery in the park around **Muckross House** ㊽. In the afternoon, leave for the Ring of Kerry, driving past **Sneem** ㊵ through subtropical vegetation to ⛏ **Waterville** ㊸ or ⛏ **Caragh Lake** on the west side of the Ring. From **Cahirciveen** ㊻ you can see the Dingle Peninsula across the water and the stretch of road that you will take to reach ⛏ **Dingle Town** ⑥②, the next overnight stop and the best base for exploring the peninsula. A short drive outside town, you'll find the spectacular cliffs and early Christian remains beyond **Slea Head** ⑥⑤. On the final day, drive across the Connor Pass and up to **Tralee** ㊴, which has a lively museum devoted to County Kerry's past and a steam railway running from nearby **Blennerville** ㊳. From Tralee, return to Limerick City and Shannon Airport on the Adare road (N21) or take N69 to Tarbert and the ferry into County Clare to reach Galway and the west of Ireland.

When to Tour the Southwest

The weather is most likely to be warm and sunny in July and August, but there is no guarantee against rain. July and August are the busiest months with Irish, British, and Continental tourists heading for the area in large numbers. Visiting in high season means the bars and restaurants of the area will be lively but also crowded. The best time to visit the Southwest is in the "shoulder seasons"—May through June and September through October, when the weather will still be mild; most if not quite all accommodations and attractions will be open, and crowds can be avoided. Lodging and restaurants outside the main cities are seasonal, and choice will be limited between November and mid-March. However, not everything closes down at this time of year, and the roads and scenic spots will be blissfully uncrowded. It may be wet, but it seldom gets cold in this part of the world.

CORK CITY AND ENVIRONS

The major metropolis of the south, Cork is Ireland's second-largest city (population 175,000), but put this in perspective: Roughly half of Ireland's 3.6 million people live in and around Dublin, a city 10 times the size. Though small relative to the capital, Cork is a spirited, lively place, with a formidable pub scene, some of the country's best traditional music, a respected and progressive university, attractive art galleries, and offbeat cafés.

The city received its first charter in 1185 from Prince John of Norman England, and it takes its name from the Irish word *corcaigh*, meaning "marshy place." The original 6th-century settlement was spread over 13 small islands in the River Lee. Major development occurred during the 17th and 18th centuries with the expansion of the butter trade, and many attractive Georgian-design buildings with wide bowfront windows were constructed during this time. As late as 1770, Cork's present main streets—Grand Parade, Patrick Street, and the South Mall—were submerged under the Lee. Around 1800, when the Lee was partially dammed, the river divided into two streams that now flow through the city, leaving the main business and commercial center on an island, not unlike Paris's Ile de la Cité. As a result, the city features a number of bridges and quays, which, although initially confusing, add greatly to the port's unique character. (A word of warning to drivers: They also can contribute to traffic bottlenecks during rush hours, although the new tunnel under the River Lee should ease the problem.)

"Rebel Cork" emerged as a center of the Nationalist Fenian movement in the 19th century. The city suffered great damage during the War of Independence in 1919–21, when much of its center was burned. Cork is now regaining some of its former glory as a result of sensitive commercial development and an ongoing program of inner-city renewal. The recent opening of the cross-river tunnel—which links the N8 Dublin–Cork road, the N20 Limerick–Cork road, and the N25 Rosslare–Cork road to the roads leading to Cork Airport, Ringaskiddy Ferryport, and the scenic southwest—is expected to drastically reduce the amount of Cork's through-traffic. In late summer and early autumn, the city hosts some of Ireland's premier festivals, including October's huge **Cork Jazz Festival,** which draws about 50,000 visitors from around the world; the **Cork Film Festival,** also in October; and a number of others. ☞ Nightlife and the Arts, *below,* for more information.

Cork City

1 *254 km (158 mi) south of Dublin, 105 km (65 mi) west of Limerick City.*

"Cork is the loveliest city in the world. Anyone who does not agree with me either was not born there or is prejudiced." Whether or not Cork merits this accolade of native poet and writer Robert Gibbings, the city does have plenty to recommend it, including several noteworthy historic sites. These, though spread out, are still best visited on foot; you may want to take a bus to the city's westernmost sights. Patrick Street is the center city's main thoroughfare.

2 **Patrick's Bridge** is a good place to start a walk around the city. From here, you can look across the river to St. Patrick's Hill, where tall Georgian houses have been converted to professional use, mostly as doctors' offices. The hill is so steep that steps are cut into the pavement.

3 The tower of **St. Mary's Pro-Cathedral** dominates in part the slopes of the hilly north city. If you're interested in tracing your Cork ancestors, the presbytery at St. Mary's has records of births and marriages dating from 1784. ⊠ *Cathedral Walk.* ▦ *Free.* ☉ *Daily 9–6.*

4 Also in the north city, **St. Anne's Church** has the pepper-pot Shandon Steeple, which has a four-sided clock and is topped with a golden, salmon-shape weather vane. The Bells of Shandon were immortalized in an atrocious but popular 19th-century ballad of that name. If you climb the 120-ft tower, your reward is being able to ring the bells, with the assistance of sheet tune cards, out over Cork—but be careful to hit the right notes! ⊠ *Church St.,* ▦ *£1; with bell tower £1.50.* ☉ *May–Oct., Mon.–Sat. 9:30–5; Nov.–Apr., Mon.–Sat. 10–3:30.*

Firkin Crane, Cork's former 18th-century butter market, stands beside St. Anne's Church. This round building houses two small performing spaces. Adjacent is the Shandon Craft Market. You can make your way back to the quays along the Lee via the pretty lanes lined with small, tidy houses.

5 **Patrick Street,** which cuts a graceful curve, lies to the south of Patrick Bridge. If you look above some of the standardized plate-glass and plastic shop facades here, you'll see examples of the bowfront Georgian windows that are emblematic of old Cork. The street saw some of the city's worst fighting in the years 1919–21, during the War of Independence. Roches Stores is the largest department store in town; Brown Thomas, next door, is the most upscale. Tall ships that once served the butter trade used to load up at **Merchant's Quay,** right off Patrick Street, before heading downstream to the open sea. The design of the large shopping center on the site today evokes the warehouses of old.

The **bus station** is one block downstream from (west of) Patrick Bridge if you face the river. The Brian Boru Bridge, in front of the bus station, leads to **Kent (Rail) Station,** which is north of the river two blocks to the right. **Winthrop Street** is a pedestrian mall off Patrick Street. Winthrop leads to Oliver Plunkett Street, a busy, narrow road known

6 for its fashion boutiques, jewelry stores, and **General Post Office,** a neoclassic building with an elegant, colonnaded facade. The friendly, old **Long Valley** (⊠ Winthrop St., ☎ 021/427–2144), popular with artists, writers, students, and eccentrics, serves tea, coffee, and pints, as well as oversize sandwiches.

Housed in the 1724 building that was once the city's Custom House,

7 the **Crawford Municipal Art Gallery** is Ireland's most respected provincial art gallery. Its permanent collection includes a number of landscape paintings depicting Cork in the 18th and 19th centuries. Irish painters

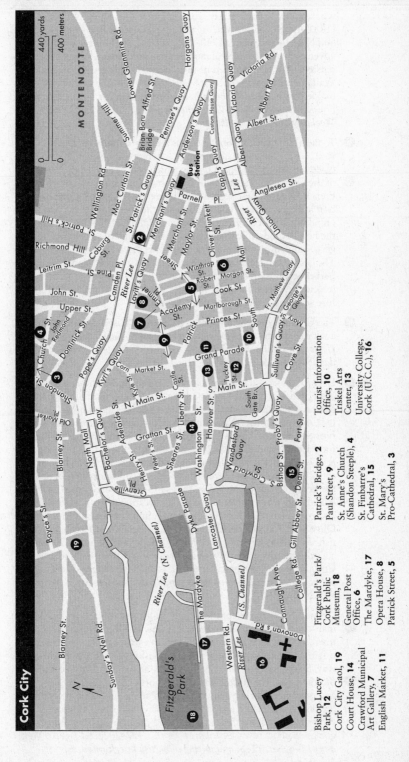

Cork City

Bishop Lucey
Park, **12**
Cork City Gaol, **19**
Court House, **14**
Crawford Municipal
Art Gallery, **7**
English Market, **11**

Fitzgerald's Park/
Cork Public
Museum, **18**
General Post
Office, **6**
The Mardyke, **17**
Opera House, **8**
Patrick Street, **5**

Patrick's Bridge, **2**
Paul Street, **9**
St. Anne's Church
(Shandon Steeple), **4**
St. Finbarre's
Cathedral, **15**
St. Mary's
Pro-Cathedral, **3**

Tourist Information
Office, **10**
Triskel Arts
Center, **13**
University College,
Cork (U.C.C.), **16**

whose work is particularly worth looking for include William Leech (1881–1968), Daniel Maclise (1806–70), James Barry (1741–1806), and Nathanial Grogan (1740–1807). The Crawford regularly mounts adventurous exhibitions of modern Irish and foreign artists. A new extension, due for completion in late 2000, will greatly increase the available exhibition space. Its **café**, run by the Allen family of Ballymaloe (☞ Shanagarry, *below*), is a good place for a light lunch or a homemade sweet treat. ⊠ *Emmet Pl.,* ☎ *021/427–3377.* ⊡ *Free.* ⊙ *Weekdays 9–5, Sat. 9–1.*

8 To the left of the Crawford Gallery is the **Opera House** (⊠ Lavitt's Quay, ☎ 021/427–0022), an unfortunate concrete edifice built in 1965 to replace the ornate old opera house, which was destroyed in a fire. West **9** of the Crawford Gallery, **Paul Street** runs through the heart of the old French Quarter, first settled by Huguenots fleeing religious persecution in France. Pretty lanes radiate off the street, while the piazza is a popular place for street theater and entertainment. The shops here offer the best in modern Irish design—from Donegal tweeds to handblown glass—and, in an alley north of the piazza, a good selection of antiques. The best cakes, fruit tarts, and ice cream in Cork are handmade at **Gingerbread House** (⊠ Paul St. Piazza, ☎ 021/427–6411). Sit at the big refectory tables for a made-to-order sandwich or a roll and coffee before selecting a slice of the day's baking.

10 The Cork City **Tourist Information Office (TIO)** is in the Grand Parade, a wide thoroughfare at the western extreme of Patrick Street. ⊠ *Tourist House, Grand Parade,* ☎ *021/427–3251,* ☎ *021/427–3504.* ⊙ *Weekdays 9–6, Sat. 9–1.*

★ 11 Food lovers should head right for the **English Market,** housed in an elaborate, red-and-brown-brick and cast-iron Victorian building. (Its official name is the Princes Street Market, and it's also known locally as the Covered Market.) A turn-of-the-century predecessor to today's urban farmers' markets, this is a great place to get a sense of Cork's thriving food scene. Among the 140 stalls, keep an eye out for the **Cork Bakery Company,** which produces more than 25 varieties of handmade bread every day. Local coffee lovers claim **Iago,** Sean Calder-Potts's deli, has the best coffee in town; it also sells sandwiches made from its freshly baked *ciabatta* (a slipper-shape Italian bread). Olive oil, olive-oil soap, and olives from Greece, Spain, France, and Italy are all found at the **Olive Stall. Kay O'Connell's Fish Stall,** in the market's legendary fresh-fish alley, sells local smoked salmon. **O'Reilly's Tripe and Drisheen** sells a Cork specialty, tripe (cow's intestines), and *drisheen* (blood sausage). Upstairs is the Farmgate, an excellent café (☞ Dining and Lodging, *below*). ⊠ *Entrances on Grand Parade and Princes St.* ⊙ *Weekdays 9–5:30, Sat. 9–1.*

Opened in 1985 in celebration of the 800th anniversary of Cork's Nor-**12** man charter, **Bishop Lucey Park** is a tiny, green oasis in the center of town. During its excavation, workers unearthed portions of the city's original fortified walls, now preserved just inside the arched entranceway. Sculptures by contemporary Cork artists are scattered through-**13** out the park. The **Triskel Arts Center,** north of the Bishop Lucey Park and reached by an alleyway off Grand Parade, has exhibitions of contemporary arts and crafts, a coffee shop, and a small auditorium that shows films and live theater. It's a good place to get the pulse of artsy goings-on about town. ⊠ *Tobin St.,* ☎ *021/427–2022.* ⊡ *Free.* ⊙ *Weekdays 11–6, Sat. 11–5, and during advertised performances.*

14 The **Court House** (⊠ Washington and S. Main Sts.) with an imposing Corinthian portico, dates from 1835 and is still in use today.

⑮ South of the River Lee's south channel, **St. Finbarre's Cathedral** is reached by taking the footpath across the river in Grand Parade and following the quays westward. (This was once the entrance to medieval Cork.) The three spires of the 19th-century Gothic cathedral are visible up ahead on Bishop Street. St. Finbarre established a monastery on this site around AD 650 and is credited as the founder of Cork. The present cathedral, which was completed in 1879 and underwent major restorations in 1999, belongs to the Church of Ireland and houses a 3,000-pipe organ. ⊠ *Bishop St.,* ☎ *021/496–3387.* ⊠ *Free.* ☉ *Daily 9–6.*

⑯ The main quadrangle of **University College, Cork** (known as U. C. C., with about 10,000 students) is a fine example of 19th-century university architecture in the Tudor-Gothic style, reminiscent of many Oxford and Cambridge colleges. Several ancient ogham stones are on display, as are occasional exhibitions of archival material from the old library. The **Honan Collegiate Chapel**, to the east of the quadrangle, was built in 1916 and modeled on the 12th-century, Hiberno-Romanesque style, which is best exemplified by the remains of **Cormac's Chapel** at Cashel (☞ Chapter 4). Most noteworthy about the chapel are its stained-glass windows (1915), some of the finest of which were created by Harry Clarke, who is widely regarded as Ireland's most distinguished stained-glass craftsman of the period. U. C. C.'s Doric porticoed gates are at the corner of Donovan's and Western roads, about a mile up Washington Street and the Western Road. ☎ *021/427–6871.* ⊠ *Free.* ☉ *Weekdays 9–5.*

⑰ The **Mardyke** is a popular riverside walk where cricket is played on
⑱ summer weekends. Bordered on one side by the Mardyke, **Fitzgerald's Park** contains the **Cork Public Museum**, a Georgian mansion that houses a well-planned exhibit of Cork's history from ancient times to the present, with a strong emphasis on the city's Republican history. ☎ *021/427–0679.* ⊠ *Free.* ☉ *Weekdays 11–1 and 2:15–5, Sun. 3–5.*

From the museum, ask for directions to **Daly Bridge**—or "the shaky bridge," as it is known locally—which will take you across the River Lee
⑲ to Sunday's Well and the **Cork City Gaol.** (If you are driving, continue up Western Road, taking the first right at Victoria Cross for Sunday's Well, and follow the signposts to the Gaol.) This castle-like building, which contains an austere, 19th-century prison, where inmates lived in wretched conditions, has been a surprise success with visitors—perhaps because you feel so good when you leave. Life-size figures occupy the cells, and sound effects help to illustrate the appalling conditions that prevailed in the gaol from the early 19th century through the founding of the state after the 1916 Uprising. A **Radio Museum** in the Governor's House tells the history of broadcasting in Cork. ⊠ *Sunday's Well,* ☎ *021/430–5022.* ⊠ *£3.* ☉ *Oct.–Easter, daily 10–4; Easter–Sept., daily 9:30–5.*

Dining and Lodging

$$$ ✕ **Cafe Paradiso.** This simple, café-style restaurant near the university and across from Jurys Hotel (☞ *below*) serves Mediterranean-style food, which is so tasty that even dedicated meat-eaters forget it's vegetarian. The room is basic, with assorted tables and spindly chairs; the daily special is chalked up on a board, and the food is served on enormous platters. Chef Denis Cotter garners raves for his risottos with seasonal vegetables (such as pumpkin and radicchio), his gougères-choux pastry rings with savory fillings, and his excellent, homemade desserts. ⊠ *16 Lancaster Quay, Western Rd., Co. Cork,* ☎ *021/427–7939. MC, V. Closed Sun.*

$$$ ✕ **Ivory Tower.** Seamus O'Connell is the adventurous, young owner-chef of this small town-center restaurant. Bare wooden floors and stick-back chairs in the first-floor Georgian dining room are warmed by the original artwork on display, but the real star here is the bril-

liantly eclectic menu. O'Connell has cooked in Mexico and Japan and describes his approach as "trans-ethnic fusion." Tagliatelle of flashed squid, wild pheasant tamale, and Cajun blackened swordfish with banana ketchup are just some of the surprising—and very accomplished—combinations offered. ⊠ *35 Princes St.,* ☎ *021/427–4665. MC, V. Closed Sun.–Mon.*

$–$$$ ✕ **Lovett's.** The Lovett family has been setting high standards on the Cork gastronomic scene since 1977. Their Georgian house, surrounded by mature grounds in a prosperous suburb, has a formal dining room lined with portraits of 18th-century Cork society. The establishment is known for its extensive wine list, which focuses on vineyards with Irish origins, making it strong on Bordeaux. As for food, start with hot black-and-white pudding terrine with onion and raisin confit, followed perhaps by black sole on the bone with citrus butter. The brasserie ($) is more informal, with bistro-style wooden tables and rustic stick-back chairs. ⊠ *Churchyard La., off Well Rd., Douglas,* ☎ *021/ 429–4909. AE, DC, MC, V. Closed Sun.–Mon. and 1 wk at Christmas. No lunch Sat.*

$ ✕ **Farmgate Café.** On a terrace above the fountain at the Princes Street
★ entrance to Cork's English Market (☞ *above*), this simple restaurant-café is one of the best lunch spots in town. One side of the terrace is open to the market and operates as self-service; the other side is glassed in and served by waiters (reservations advised). Tripe and drisheen are always on the menu, while daily specials include less challenging but no less traditional dishes such as corned beef with *colcannon* (potatoes and cabbage mashed together with butter and seasonings) and loin of smoked bacon with *champ* (potato mashed with scallions or leeks). The restaurant is open Monday–Saturday 10:30–5; last food orders are taken at 4 PM. A sister restaurant is in Midleton (☞ *below*). ⊠ *English Market, Cork,* ☎ *021/427–8134. MC, V.*

$ ✕ **Isaac's.** This popular brasserie-style restaurant is north of the river (cross at Patrick's Bridge and turn right) in a converted warehouse. High ceilings, well-spaced tables covered in oilcloth, modern art, and jazz music create an eclectic, energetic atmosphere. The East-meets-Mediterranean menu has many tempting options, including warm salads with Clonakilty black pudding and king prawns in spicy tomato sauce. ⊠ *MacCurtain St.,* ☎ *021/450–3805, MC, V. No lunch Sun.*

$ ✕ **Michael's.** This large second-floor room on Cork's main shopping street is the latest venture of talented local chef Michael Clifford, who left the world of haute cuisine to cater, bistro-style, to the diner on a budget—and he does so exceptionally well. The large room has dark walls, cheerful yellow curtains, and well-spaced, oilcloth-covered tables. Start with a warm smoked haddock salad dusted with fines herbes, followed by traditional bacon and cabbage or Irish lamb casserole with roasted peppers and courgettes. Desserts include choux puffs filled with tropical fruits and wild rose syrup, or spicy apple-and-raisin flan. ⊠ *71–72 Patrick St.,* ☎ *021/427–7716. MC, V. Closed Sun.*

$ ✕ **Proby's Bistro.** A striking and stylish modern building with patio tables and sun umbrellas optimistically placed on the terrace, this riverside bistro near St. Finbarre's Cathedral is a short walk from the main shopping area. The spacious ground-floor restaurant has an open fire, oilcloth-covered tables, and a bold Mediterranean decor that suits the light, flavorsome food. The menu is mainly rustic Italian—bruschetta, polenta, risotto, mixed leaf salads with flavored oils—with occasional Eastern influences. ⊠ *Proby's Quay, Crosses Green,* ☎ *021/431–6531. MC, V.*

$$$ ✕🖃 **Arbutus Lodge.** Declan and Patsy Ryan's two-story, hillside villa—
★ only a five-minute drive from the city center, well signposted from St. Luke's Cross—has the ambience of a fancy, private home. Airy guest

rooms are individually decorated with fine antiques and original paintings. The outstanding restaurant, with its large bay window, polished mahogany sideboards, and plush-velvet chairs, is the perfect setting for French-Irish hauté cuisine. For an inexpensive lunch, head to the Gallery Bar, with its panorama of the city. ⊠ *Middle Glanmire Rd., Montenotte, Co. Cork,* ☎ *021/450–1237,* ℻ *021/450–2893. 16 rooms, 4 suites. Restaurant, bar, tennis court. AE, DC, MC, V.*

$$$　✕🏨 **Jurys.** Beside the River Lee, a five-minute walk from the city center, is this modern, two- and three-story structure made of smoked glass and steel. Its large, open lobby-restaurant area features a waterfall and hanging greenery (some of it plastic). Cork's Bar is popular with the locals at lunch and in the early evening. The mezzanine-level Fastnet Restaurant serves an à la carte international menu with an emphasis on fresh local produce. Bedrooms, plain yet spacious, have quilted spreads, small sofas, and floor-to-ceiling picture windows. The most desirable rooms overlook the interior patio garden and pool. ⊠ *Western Rd., Co. Cork,* ☎ *021/427–6622,* ℻ *021/427–4477. 185 rooms with bath. 2 restaurants, 2 bars, pool, sauna, 2 tennis courts, health club, squash court. AE, DC, MC, V.*

$$　✕🏨 **Hotel Isaac's.** This city-center hotel was stylishly renovated from an old warehouse into a busy restaurant and accommodation complex. Rooms are bright and cheerful, with polished wood floors and rustic pine furniture. The restaurant and some of the rooms overlook a tiny courtyard garden with a waterfall cascading down one side. The dining room also operates as Greene's Restaurant, where fresh produce is prepared in a mix of Irish and Mediterranean styles. ⊠ *48 MacCurtain St., Co. Cork,* ☎ *021/500011,* ℻ *021/506355. 36 rooms with bath. Restaurant, cafeteria, Ping-Pong. MC, V.*

$$$$　🏨 **Hayfield Manor.** Built in 1996 in a surprisingly successful pastiche
★　of the country-house style, the manor sits beside the university campus, five minutes' drive from the city center. The marble-floor lobby is dominated by a splendid, carved-wood double staircase, while a wood-paneled library overlooks the walled patio and garden. Rooms are spacious, with unobtrusive decor in a vaguely Louis XV style. The Victorian-style bar serves food until 7 PM. The elegant leisure center is exclusively for the hotel's patrons. ⊠ *College Rd.,* ☎ *021/431–5600,* ℻ *021/431–6839. 53 rooms with bath. Restaurant, bar, indoor pool, sauna, health club. AE, DC, MC, V.*

$$$　🏨 **Quality Hotel & Suites** This luxury hotel on the urban riverside is a two-minute walk from Patrick Street. Spacious, modern one- and two-bedroom suites with kitchen are furnished with handcrafted light-oak furniture. Regular rooms are large, with a similar style of furniture, and half of them have river views. Polished marble floors and warm terra-cotta–color walls enhance the stylish, mezzanine-level bar and restaurant overlooking the river. Four penthouses have terrace views of the city and the river. ⊠ *Morrison's Quay, Co. Cork,* ☎ *021/427–5858,* ℻ *021/427–5833. 28 rooms with bath, 24 suites. Restaurant, bar. AE, DC, MC, V.*

$$　🏨 **Rochestown Park.** Set in 7 acres of mature gardens in the fashionable suburb of Douglas, 5 km (3 mi) south of the city, Rochestown has been built around a Victorian manor house that overlooks its own wooded gardens and the estuary of Cork harbor. However, the new four-lane ring road to the cross-river tunnel runs between the hotel grounds and the estuary, so it is less romantic than it sounds. All the rooms are decorated in a modern style with cotton spreads, wool carpets, and light-oak fixtures. The large health center specializes in thalassotherapy—seaweed wraps and baths. ⊠ *Rochestown Rd., Douglas,* ☎ *021/489–2233,* ℻ *021/489–2178. 115 rooms with bath. Restaurant, bar, pool, sauna, health club. AE, DC, MC, V.*

$ ☷ **Island House.** Young, independent travelers will appreciate the central location and budget rates at this new, five-story riverside hostel. On the ground floor is a café–cum–steak house, while a large self-catering kitchen is available on the fourth floor. Rooms—single, double, triple, or four-bunk—are laid out on corridors accessed by an open terrace. Ask for a river view, as the others overlook neighboring buildings. Pine beds have brightly colored spreads with matching curtains, and all rooms have TV. ⊠ *Morrison's Quay,* ☎ *021/427–1716,* FAX *021/427–1719. 51 rooms, 43 with bath. Restaurant, free parking. MC, V. Closed Dec. 23–28.*

$ ☷ **Jurys Cork Inn.** This modern budget hotel pursues the same policy as its Dublin and Galway counterparts, charging per room, each of which sleeps three adults or two adults and two children. Beside a busy bridge over the River Lee, the inn is a short walk from the city center and bus and rail stations. Rooms are well appointed for the price range: bright and airy with light-wood trim and matching drapes and spreads. ⊠ *Anderson's Quay, Co. Cork,* ☎ *021/427–6444,* FAX *021/427–6144. 133 rooms with bath. Restaurant, bar. AE, DC, MC, V.*

$ ☷ **Victoria Lodge.** This exceptionally well appointed B&B, built in the early 20th century as a Capuchin monastery, is a five-minute drive from the town center; it is also accessible by several bus routes. Breakfast is served in the spacious old refectory with its intact polished benches and paneled walls; the common room is now a television lounge. The simple, comfortable bedrooms feature pastel-color chenille spreads, cotton curtains, and mahogany bureaus. ⊠ *Victoria Cross, Co. Cork,* ☎ *021/454–2233,* FAX *021/454–2572. 30 rooms with bath. AE, MC, V.*

Nightlife and the Arts

FESTIVALS AND SEASONAL EVENTS

Ireland's oldest film festival, the **Cork Film Festival** (☎ 021/427–1711) was established in 1956 and has evolved into one of the country's most important cinema events. New feature-length films and documentaries from Ireland and abroad share the bill with short films, a particular specialty of this festival. It's usually held the second week of October. Near the end of every October, the **Cork Jazz Festival** (☎ 021/427–0463) brings major national and international performers to venues throughout the city.

GALLERIES

The **Lavit Gallery** (⊠ 5 Father Mathew St., off South Mall, ☎ 021/427–7749) has a representative selection of oils and watercolors by members of the Cork Arts Society and other Irish artists, all of which are for sale. Offbeat exhibits can be found at the **Triskel Arts Center** (⊠ Tobin St., off S. Main St., ☎ 021/427–2022). A selection of younger artists' work can be seen at the **Tig Fili** (⊠ Thompson House, MacCurtain St., ☎ 021/455–1989).

MUSIC AND THEATER

Cork Opera House (⊠ Lavitt's Quay, ☎ 021/427–0022) is the city's major hall for touring productions and variety acts. Smaller productions are staged at the **Everyman Palace** (⊠ MacCurtain St., ☎ 021/450–1673), where the ornate Victorian interior has been lovingly restored.

PUBS AND NIGHTCLUBS

La Bodega (⊠ Cornmarket St., ☎ 021/427–2878), a converted wine warehouse, is the hippest—and loudest—spot in town. The bar at the **Metropole Hotel** (⊠ MacCurtain St., ☎ 021/450–8122) is one of the best places for jazz. The **Quality Hotel** (⊠ Morrison's Island, ☎ 021/427–5858) is another good spot for jazz. **Sir Henry's** (⊠ S. Main St., ☎ 021/427–7255) offers dance, indie, and house music Wednesday–Saturday and occasional gigs. Traditional musicians occasionally gather at **An Spailpin Fanach** (⊠ 28 S. Main St., ☎ 021/427–7949). Night owls will appreciate the late-night music club at the Cork Opera House (near stage-door entrance), the **Half Moon** (⊠ Half Moon Street, ☎ 021/427–0022), which features live jazz and blues from up-and-coming local bands most weekends from 11 PM. See *The Examiner* or *The Evening Echo* for details.

Outdoor Activities and Sports

BICYCLES

Rent a bike to explore the city and its environs at **Rothar Cycle Tours** (⊠ 2 Bandon Rd., at Barrack St., ☎ 021/431–3133).

FISHING

Fishing tackle, bait, and licenses, as well as friendly advice on local resources, can be obtained at **T. W. Murray** (⊠ 87 Patrick St., ☎ 021/427–1089).

GOLF

Douglas Golf Club (⊠ Douglas, ☎ 021/489–1086) is a tree-lined, parkland, 18-hole course in the southern suburbs of the city. **Cork Golf Club** (⊠ Little Island, ☎ 021/435–3451 [☞ Chapter 9]). **Lee Valley Golf Club** (⊠ Clashanure, Ovens, ☎ 021/733–1721) is a par-72, 18-hole, championship course 15 minutes west of the city. **Monkstown Golf Club** (⊠ Parkgarriffe, Monkstown, ☎ 021/484–1376) is an 18-hole, par-70, strategically bunkered, parkland course 11 km (7 mi) southeast of the city.

HORSEBACK RIDING

Hitchmough Riding School (⊠ Highland Lodge, Monkstown, ☎ 021/437–1267) has an indoor arena for all-weather riding. **Pinegrove Riding School** (⊠ White's Cross, ☎ 021/430–3857) will provide 1- and 2-hour hacks in the countryside north of the city.

Shopping

ANTIQUES

Irene's (⊠ 22 Marlboro St., ☎ 021/427–0642) sells antique jewelry. **Mills Antiques** (⊠ 3 Paul's La., ☎ 021/427–3528) carries Irish, English, and European paintings, printings, silver, porcelain, and small furniture. For furniture, paintings, and other large decorative objects try **O'Regan's Antiques** (⊠ 3 Paul's La., ☎ 021/427–2902). **Pinnacle** (⊠ 44A MacCurtain St., ☎ 021/427–9788) stocks antique pine, glass, porcelain, paintings, and prints. **Victoria's** (⊠ 2 Oliver Plunkett St., ☎ 021/427–2752) carries interesting jewelry, Victoriana, and period clothes.

BOOKS

Mercier Bookshop (⊠ 18 Academy St., ☎ 021/427–5040), off Patrick Street, sells new books and publishes its own list of Irish and local-interest titles.

CLOTHING

Quills (⊠ 107 Patrick St., ☎ 021/427–1717) has a good selection of Irish-made fashion and casual wear for both women and men. For casual weatherproof clothing, try the **Tack Room** (⊠ Unit 3, Academy St., ☎ 021/427–2704). **Monica John** (⊠ French Church St., ☎ 021/427–1399) sells locally designed high-fashion ladies' wear, as well as some imported lines. Fashion lovers will find a choice of internationally famous designer labels at the tiny but elegant boutique **The Dressing Room** (⊠ 8 Emmet Pl., ☎ 021/4270117), opposite the entrance to the Cork Opera House.

DEPARTMENT STORE

Brown Thomas (⊠ 18 Patrick St., ☎ 021/427–6771) is Cork's leading department store. Previously known as Cash's, the store was renovated in 1998 into an even plusher and more stylish version of its Dublin namesake. The fashion floor is well worth a visit to check out items by Irish and international designers. Refuel at the coffee shop, where healthy open sandwiches and homemade soup are available. The ground floor has an excellent cosmetics hall and a good selection of Irish crystal and designer menswear.

MUSIC

Fans of Irish music should visit the **Living Tradition** (⊠ 40 MacCurtain St., ☎ 021/450–2040).

SHOPPING CENTER

The **Merchant's Quay Shopping Centre** (⊠ Merchant's Quay, ☎ 021/427–5466) is the largest indoor mall in downtown Cork.

SPORTING GOODS

For inexpensive rainwear, go to **Penney's** (⊠ 27 Patrick St., ☎ 021/427–1935). **Matthews** (⊠ Academy St., ☎ 021/427–7633) has a wide selection of sporting gear. **Great Outdoors** (⊠ 23 Paul St., ☎ 021/427–6382) caters to most outdoor sports needs. The **Golf Addict** (⊠ 6 Emmet Pl., ☎ 021/427–3393) stocks everything the serious golfer could need, as well as an amusing range of nonessential golf paraphernalia and gifts.

Blarney

㉕ *10 km (6 mi) northwest of Cork City on R617.*

"On Galway sands they kiss your hands, they kiss your lips at Carney, but by the Lee they drink strong tea, and kiss the stone at Blarney." This famous rhyme celebrates one of Ireland's most noted icons—the Blarney Stone, which is the main reason most people journey to Blarney, a small community built around a village green. (To get here in the peak season of July and August, or if you're en route to Killarney from Cork City, follow the signposts off the main N22 Killarney road at Carrigrohane to avoid Cork's inner-city traffic jams.) North of Blarney is **Blarney Castle,** or what remains of it: The ruined central keep is all that's left of this mid-15th-century stronghold. The castle contains the famed **Blarney Stone,** set in a wall below the castle's battlements; kissing the stone, it is said, endows the kisser with the fabled "gift of gab." It's 127 steep steps to the battlements. To kiss the stone, you must lie down on the battlements, hold on to a guardrail, and lean your head way back. It's good fun and not at all dangerous. Expect a line from mid-June to September 1; while you wait, you can admire the views of the thickly wooded River Lee valley below and chuckle over how the word "blarney" came to mean what it does. As the story goes, Queen Elizabeth I wanted Cormac MacCarthy, Lord of Blarney, to will his castle to the crown, but he consistently refused her request with eloquent excuses and soothing compliments. Exhausted by his comments, the queen reportedly exclaimed, "This is all Blarney. What he says he rarely means."

Visitors can also take pleasant walks around the castle grounds; **Rock Close** contains oddly shaped limestone rocks landscaped in the 18th century and a grove of ancient yew trees that is said to have been the center of Druid worship. ⊠ *Blarney Castle,* ☎ *021/438–5252.* ☞ *£3.50.* ☉ *May and Sept., Mon.–Sat. 9–6:30, Sun. 9–5:30; June–Aug., Mon.–Sat. 9–7, Sun. 9–5:30; Oct.–Apr., Mon.–Sat. 9–sundown, Sun. 9–5:30.*

Two hundred yards from the castle, **Blarney Castle House** was built in 1784 in the style of a Scottish baronial mansion. The three-story, gray stone building has picture-book turrets and fancy, stepped gables. The interior features Elizabethan and Victorian antiques, a fine stairwell, and numerous family portraits. ☎ 021/438–5252. ☜ £3. ☉ June–mid-Sept., Mon.–Sat. noon–5.

Dining and Lodging

$ ✕ **Blair's Inn.** This traditional country pub is just five minutes' drive from Blarney on R578 and is a perfect haven from the tour-bus culture that prevails in the village. The family-run inn has a wooded riverside location and is famed for its exuberant window-box displays. In summer, enjoy the beer garden, while in winter warm wood fires flicker in the cozy interior. Freshly prepared local produce is served in generous portions: favorites include Irish stew with lamb, carrots, and potatoes, as well as corned beef. Live entertainment is booked every Sunday from 9 PM, plus Monday from May to October. ⌧ Cloghroe, ☎ 021/438–1470. MC, V.

Outdoor Activities and Sports

GOLF

Muskerry Golf Club (⌧ Carrigrohane, near Blarney, ☎ 021/438–5297) is an 18-hole, par-71 parkland course.

Shopping

Blarney has more crafts shops than anyplace else in Ireland. Most of these stores are concentrated south and west of the village green, a two-minute walk from the castle. A shopping visit here can be profitably used for price comparison and bargain hunting; in spite of appearances, these shops, in general, will not rip you off. **Blarney Woolen Mills** (☎ 021/438–5280) has the largest stock and the highest turnover. The mills sell everything from Irish-made high fashion to Aran hand-knit items to leprechaun key rings.

Cork Harbour–Fota Island and Cobh

Fota Island, 19 km (12 mi) from Cork City; Cobh, 24 km (15 mi) from Cork City on N25.

To explore Cork Harbour, follow the signposts for Waterford on N25 along the northern banks of the River Lee. Alternatively, a suburban rail service from **Kent Station** (☎ 021/450–6766 for timetable) has stops at Fota Island and Cobh (pronounced cove), and it offers better harbor views than the road.

Outside Cork City on the opposite side of the River Lee, **Blackrock Castle** is a turreted, 16th-century fortification, rebuilt in the 19th century in gray stone with crenellations. A picture-perfect riverside castle, it looks like a visitor attraction but is in fact the corporate headquarters of a local company. Shortly after you get a glimpse of Blackrock, the road leaves the river. The turning for Fota Island and Cobh (R624) is clearly signposted off N25 on the right-hand side about 8 km (5 mi) outside town. Turn right again at the gate lodge of the huge estate on Fota Island.

🖐 ㉑ **Fota Demesne** encompasses a magnificent arboretum (freely accessible) and the 70-acre **Fota Wildlife Park,** an important breeding center for cheetahs and wallabies. It also contains free-ranging monkeys, zebras, giraffes, ostriches, flamingos, emus, and kangaroos. ☎ 021/481–2678. ☜ *Wildlife park £4.40; arboretum and gardens free; parking £1.* ☉ *Mid-Mar.–Sept., Mon.–Sat. 10–6, Sun. 11–6.*

Barryscourt Castle is a 5-km (3-mi) detour (clearly signposted outside the gates of Fota House). The 16th-century structure has a courtyard and flanking towers. The interior is in the process of being furnished with replicas of the appropriate period, including domestic items such as early 20th-century kitchen and laundry equipment. Guided tours are given June–September. The gardens, including a medieval orchard, are also under restoration. The coffee shop is famed for its selection of home-baked cakes. ⊠ *Carrigtwohill,* ☎ *021/488–3864.* ☞ *Free, tour £1.50.* ☉ *Daily 11–6.*

㉒ Many generations who departed the port of Cork on immigrant ships for the New World left from **Cobh,** a pretty fishing port and seaside resort with a considerable 19th-century presence and maritime history.

★ The **Queenstown Project,** in the old Cobh railway station, re-creates the experience of the million emigrants who left the town between 1750 and the mid-20th century. It also tells the stories of the great transatlantic liners, including the *Titanic,* whose last port of call was Cobh, and the *Lusitania,* which was sunk by a German submarine off this coast on May 7, 1915, with the loss of 1,198 lives. Many of the *Lusitania*'s victims are buried in Cobh, which has a memorial to them on the local quay. ⊠ *Old Railway Station,* ☎ *021/481–3591.* ☞ *£3.50.* ☉ *Feb.–Nov., daily 10–6.*

The best view of Cobh is from **St. Colman's Cathedral,** an exuberant neo-Gothic granite church designed by Pugin in 1868. Inside are granite niches that portray scenes of the Roman Catholic Church's history in Ireland, beginning with the arrival of St. Patrick. Cork Harbour opens to the sea some 8 km (5 mi) from Cobh at **Roches Point.** One-hour harbor tours from Marine Transport are a splendid way to take in Cobh's glorious watery environs. ⊠ *Kennedy Pier,* ☎ *021/481–1485.* ☞ *£3.50.* ☉ *Tours May–Sept., daily at 10, 11, noon, 1:30, and 2:30.*

Outdoor Activities and Sports

GOLF

Fota Island Golf Club (⊠ Carrigtwohill, ☎ 021/488–3700) is a par-72, 18-hole course.

WATER SPORTS

Explore Cork Harbour from the water by renting a sailing dinghy from **International Sailing Center** (⊠ 5 E. Beach, Cobh, ☎ 021/481–1237).

En Route The **Cork Harbour Crossing** is a three-minute car ferry that runs from Carrigaloe near Cobh to Glenbrook near Ringaskiddy, cutting out the traveling through Cork City. This is useful if you are heading for Kinsale and West Cork. It operates continuously from 7:15 AM to 12:45 AM daily and costs £3 per car, 60p for pedestrians. Alternately, follow N25 toward Cork to Dunkettle Roundabout and take the cross-river tunnel.

EAST CORK AND THE BLACKWATER VALLEY

Although most visitors to Cork head west out of the city for the scenic coastal areas between Cork and Glengarriff, the east and the north of the county are also worth exploring. East Cork, and Youghal in particular, is popular with Irish tourists for its long, sandy beaches. The main attraction in North Cork is the Blackwater River, which crosses the county from east to west. It is famous for both its trout and salmon fishing and its surrounding scenery. This tour starts in the far corner of the county at Youghal and works its way west toward the Kerry border.

Youghal

㉓ *48 km (30 mi) east of Cork City on N25, 74 km (46 mi) south of Waterford.*

Situated on the mouth of the Blackwater River, on the border between Counties Cork and Waterford, Youghal (pronounced yawl) is an ancient walled seaport with a fine, natural harbor. The town was included in a 40,000-acre land grant given to Sir Walter Raleigh by Elizabeth I in the late·16th century. Local legend states that Sir Walter Raleigh planted the first potatoes in Ireland here, a claim disputed by several other locations (and by all accounts he spent little time here). Its long, sandy beach makes it a popular summer day-trip destination for Corkonians. The town itself is in the throes of some major investment, aimed at updating its appeal.

The **clock tower** (⊠ Main St.), Youghal's main landmark, dates from 1776 and was originally built as a jail. A set of steps beside the clock tower leads up to a well-preserved stretch of the old town walls. From here there is a magnificent panorama of the town and the estuary. The **Youghal Heritage Centre** relates the town's history through an audio-visual presentation. If this whets your appetite, trained guides are available to show you the town; a walking tour takes about an hour and a half. ⊠ *Market Sq.,* ☎ *024/92390.* ⊡ *£1, tour £2.50.* ☉ *June–mid-Sept., daily 9:30–7; mid-Sept.–May, weekdays 9:30–5:30.*

At the Youghal **quays,** you may see today's catch being unloaded from one of the small, brightly painted trawlers that fish these waters. The **Moby Dick Lounge Bar** (⊠ Market Sq., ☎ 024/92756) contains memorabilia of the filming here of John Huston's version of Melville's *Moby-Dick,* in which Youghal masqueraded as New Bedford, Massachusetts. **St. Mary's Collegiate Church** (under the town walls) dates from the 13th century and contains many interesting monuments, including the tomb of Richard Boyle (1566–1643), who succeeded Sir Walter Raleigh as Mayor of Youghal and became the first earl of Cork. The brightly painted monument commemorates his three wives and 16 children and is similar to the monument in St. Patrick's' Cathedral in Dublin, which Sir Richard ordered because he was not sure whether he would die in Dublin or Youghal. ⊠ *Emmet Pl.,* ☎ *024/92350.* ☉ *Key available from adjacent lodge.*

Dining and Lodging

$$$ ✕⊞ **Aherne's.** In the Fitzgibbon family since 1923, Aherne's has a highly
★ regarded seafood restaurant and bar that draw food lovers from Cork City (it's under an hour's drive). Popular main courses include hot buttered lobster, grilled salmon with fresh fennel, and more elaborate creations such as plaice stuffed with oysters in a red-wine sauce. The inexpensive bar food includes seafood pie topped with mashed potatoes. In their own modern wing, the 12 bedrooms are furnished with Victorian and Georgian antiques. ⊠ *163 N. Main St., Youghal, Co. Cork,* ☎ *024/92424,* ℻ *024/93633. 12 rooms with bath. Restaurant, bar, fishing. AE, DC, MC, V.*

$ ✕⊞ **Ballymakeigh House.** Signposted off N25 9½ km (6 mi) west of
★ Youghal, this is the Irish farmhouse of your dreams. From the conservatory behind the creeper-clad house you can breakfast on one of Margaret Browne's fresh strawberry muffins while watching the cows amble home. Reserve by 5 PM for her legendary six-course dinners, which have a set menu of the best local produce available that day; herbs and edible flowers from the Ballymakeigh garden add color to many dishes. The impeccably kept, cozy rooms show the attention to detail. This is the kind of place where most people end up staying much longer than just one night. ⊠ *Killeagh, Co. Cork,* ☎ *024/95184,* ℻ *024/95370. 7 rooms with bath. Dining room, tennis court, Ping-Pong, bicycles. MC, V.*

Outdoor Activities and Sports
Youghal Golf Club (⊠ Knockavery, Youghal, Co. Cork, ☎ 024/92787) is a scenic, 18-hole, par-70 course that overlooks the bay.

Shanagarry

㉔ *27 km (17 mi) west of Youghal via N25 and R632.*

Until recently, Shanagarry was a quiet farming village well off the beaten track, chiefly known for its Quaker connections. The most famous Shanagarry Quaker was William Penn (1644–1718), the founder of the Pennsylvania colony, who grew up in **Shanagarry House,** still a private residence in the center of the village. The entry gates are across from **Shanagarry Castle,** now owned and being restored by the potter and entrepreneur Stephen Pearce (☞ Shopping, *below*). The house's most famous tenant since William Penn was Marlon Brando, who stayed here in the summer of 1995 while filming *Divine Rapture* in nearby Ballycotton.

More recently, **Ballymaloe House** (☞ Dining and Lodging, *below*), one of Ireland's first country-house hotels, on the eastern edge of the village, has brought a stream of visitors to the area. On the other side of Shanagarry, **Ballymaloe Cookery School and Gardens,** run by Darina and Tim Allen (daughter-in-law and son of Ballymaloe House original founders Myrtle and the late Ivan Allen), attracts budding chefs from all over Ireland and, increasingly, from points beyond, to its wealth of cooking classes and programs, which range from one day to 12 weeks. (Its graduates can be found in the kitchens of many Irish restaurants, which often promote the connection.) Darina Allen, one of Ireland's best-known chefs, tends formal herb, fruit, and vegetable gardens, as well as a Celtic maze (not yet knee-high). Though it now stands in the midst of unplanted fields, a folly whose interior is decorated with an astonishing variety of shells is slated to be the centerpiece of additional gardens. ✉ *Kinioth House, Shanagarry, Co. Cork,* ☏ *021/464–6785.* 🎫 *Gardens £3.* ☉ *May–Sept., daily 9–6.*

Five kilometers (3 mi) beyond Shanagarry, the pretty fishing village of **Ballycotton** is built on the top of a cliff overlooking an island where large colonies of seabirds breed. There are pleasant cliff walks and a nearby beach.

Dining and Lodging

$$$ ✕🏨 **Ballymaloe House.** One of Ireland's best-known country houses, Ballymaloe has been the home of Myrtle and the late Ivan Allen (who died in 1998) for nearly 50 years. Gentle hills rise up behind the house, while farmland surrounds it as far as the eye can see. Each color-theme guest room is elegantly, if simply, decorated (rooms do not have TVs). Myrtle, the doyenne of Irish cooking, presides over the dining room, the walls of which are hung with Ivan's notable Irish art collection. Chef Rory O'Connell presents a daily changing, six-course, haute Irish menu that relies on fresh fish from nearby Ballycotton, local lamb and beef, and homegrown herbs and vegetables. The superb, mostly local cheeses served before dessert exemplify Myrtle's long-standing practice of supporting small food purveyors around Cork. Signposted from the main N25 at Midleton, 11 km (7 mi) east of Cobh and 32 km (20 mi) from Cork City), the house can be difficult to find, especially at night, so request exact directions. ✉ *Midleton, Co. Cork,* ☏ *021/465–2531,* 🖷 *021/465–2021. 32 rooms with bath. Restaurant (jacket and tie), bar, pool, tennis court. AE, DC, MC, V.*

Shopping

The ceramicist Stephen Pearce makes tableware and bowls in four signature styles—the newest is a gold porcelain—that are available in many Irish crafts shops. He sells a wide selection at his own **Stephen Pearce Emporium** (✉ Shanagarry, near Cloyne, ☏ 021/464–6262), where he also stocks an interesting range of Irish-made crafts.

Midleton

㉕ *12 km (8 mi) east of Cork City on N25, 15 km (9 mi) northwest of Shanagarry on R629*

Midleton is a pleasant market town at the head of the Owenacurra estuary, near the northeast corner of Cork Harbour. Its gray stone buildings date mainly from the early 19th century. Midleton is famous for its school, Midleton College, founded in 1696, and its distillery, founded in 1825 and modernized in 1975, which manufactures spirits—including Irish whiskey—for distribution worldwide.

The **Jameson Heritage Centre** has tours of the Old Midleton Distillery, to show you how Irish whiskey—*uisce beatha,* "the water of life"—was made in the old days. The old stone buildings are excellent examples of 19th-century industrial architecture, and an impressively large old water wheel is still in operation. The biggest pot-still in the world, a copper dome capable of holding 32,000 imperial gallons of whiskey, is also found here. Early in the tour, requests are made for a volunteer "whiskey taster"—so be alert if this option appeals. The tours ends with a complimentary glass of Jameson's Irish whiskey (or a soft drink). A crafts center and café are also on site. ✉ ☎ *021/461–3594.* 🎫 *£3.95.* ⊙ *Mar.–Oct., daily 9–4:30; Nov.–Feb., tours only, weekdays at 12:30 and 3, weekends at 2 and 4.*

Fermoy

㉖ *35 km (22 mi) north of Cork City on N8, 43 km (27 mi) west of Youghal on R634 (Tallow Rd.), which adjoins N72.*

An army town dating mainly from the mid-19th century, Fermoy is a major crossroads on the Dublin–Cork road; the east–west road that passes through town (N72) is an attractive 98-km (61-mi) alternative route to Killarney. Its bridge spanning the Blackwater is flanked by two weirs dating from 1689. The town is popular with fishers.

Dining and Lodging

$$ ✕🏨 **Ballyvolane House.** An informal country-house atmosphere pervades this imposing 1728 stone mansion surrounded by extensive gardens, beyond which is a 100-acre dairy farm. Dinner is served at a large table in the elegant dining room; family silver is set on white linens. The rooms are exceptionally big, sitting areas are generous, and decor consists of a rich assortment of antiques and family heirlooms. Both dinner and accommodation must be booked at least 24 hours in advance, but the preplanning is well worth it. As you approach from Dublin, the village of Castlelyons is signposted off N8 in Rathcormac, just south of Fermoy. ✉ *Castlelyons, Co. Cork,* ☎ *025/36349,* 𝔽𝔸𝕏 *025/36781. 6 rooms with bath. Dining room, horseback riding, fishing. MC, V.*

Outdoor Activities and Sports

For local information on salmon and trout angling contact the **Salmon Angler's Association** (Liam McGarry, ✉ Moorepark, Fermoy, Co. Cork, ☎ 025/31422).

Mallow

㉗ *30 km (19 mi) east of Fermoy on N72.*

In the 18th century, Mallow was a popular spa, often mentioned in the same breath as Bath. Today it is an angling center and market town. (It's at the intersection of the Cork–Limerick and Waterford–Killarney roads, within an hour's drive of all four towns.) At the bottom of Mallow's Main Street, the **Clock House** is a half-timber building dat-

ing from 1855. It shares the site with the Rakes of Mallow Club, the
headquarters of the notorious 18th-century gamblers, drinkers, and fortune hunters remembered in the song "The Rakes of Mallow." Not
much remains today of Mallow's glory, but the old **Spa Well** can still
be seen in the town center, and there are several interesting facades with
overhanging bay windows on Main Street dating from the 18th and
early 19th centuries. The English novelist Anthony Trollope lived at
No. 139 for a time, and he rode with the Duhallow Hunt, enhancing
the fame of the local pack. The ruins of **Mallow Castle,** which dates
from the late 16th century, are at the bottom of the main street behind
(freely accessible) ornamental gates. The castle was burnt by the Ja-
cobites in 1689, and its stables were later converted into a house,
which is still in use as a private home. From here you can view the white,
fallow deer that are unique to Mallow and were originally presented
by Elizabeth I.

Castletownroche, 12 km (7 mi) east of Mallow, is the site of **Anne's
Grove Gardens,** which were inspired by the ideas of William Robinson, a 19th-century gardener who favored naturalistic planting. Exotic foliage borders paths winding down to the river; magnificent
spring magnolias and primulas summer hydrangeas are among the plants
on view in the rolling countryside. ☎ *022/26145.* ☞ *£3.* ☉ *Mid-
Mar.–Sept., Mon.–Sat. 10–5, Sun. 1–6.*

Dining and Lodging

$$$ ✕🏨 **Longueville House.** The Southwest of Ireland has no shortage of
★   outstanding country-house hotels, but by many accounts Longueville
        wins highest honors. Limestone quoins frame the facade of the large,
        elegant Georgian mansion. The three-story central block, dating from
        1720, is flanked by two somewhat later wings, while a Victorian-era,
        glass-and-iron conservatory punctuates the east end. The stately draw-
        ing rooms, decorated with large, gilt-framed mirrors and oil paint-
        ings, overlook the tranquil lawns and rows of oaks of the 500-acre
        estate, which rolls down to the Blackwater. Bedrooms are comfort-
        able and filled with antiques; the high-ceiling rooms on the first story
        at the front are particularly desirable. At the Presidents' Restaurant
        (named for the portraits of the Republic's presidents on the walls),
        William O'Callaghan, son of founding proprietors Michael and Jane
        O'Callaghan, serves food he describes as "true to its origins," and which
        Vincent Jamison, the Dublin dining critic, calls "some of the finest food
        in Europe." ⊠ *Mallow, Co. Cork,* ☎ *022/47156,* ℻ *022/47459. 20
        rooms with bath. Restaurant, bar, fishing. AE, DC, MC, V. Closed
        Dec. 23–mid-Feb.*

Outdoor Activities and Sports

Mallow Golf Club (⊠ Ballyellis, Co. Cork, ☎ 022/21145) is an 18-hole,
par-72 parkland course with excellent views of the Blackwater Valley.

Kanturk

㉘   *15 km (9 mi) west of Mallow on N72 and R579.*

Kanturk lies at the meeting of two rivers, the Allow and the Dalua.
It is more of a village than a town, but its interesting, Victorian
shopfronts bear witness to its past importance as a market town. **Kan-
turk Castle** (⊠ 2 km outside town on the R579 Banteer Rd., and freely
accessible) was built by a local Macarthy chieftain in 1601, but its
completion was prevented by English neighbors complaining it was
too large for an Irishman. Ornate stone fireplaces and mullioned win-
dows in the five-story shell give some idea of the scope of Macarthy's
ambitions.

OFF THE
BEATEN PATH

MILLSTREET – This town 17 km (10 mi) southwest of Kanturk has come to international attention because of the **Green Glens Arena** (☎ 029/70039), which started life as the home of the Millstreet International Horse Show for show jumpers and now hosts the Eurovision Song Contest, boxing title fights, and concerts by international artists. Millstreet is also 32 km (20 mi) east of Killarney.

Dining and Lodging

$$$$
★

✕⌂ **Assolas Country House.** This ivy-covered 17th-century manor possesses the air of a dignified family home, and hosts Joe and Hazel Bourke have perfected the picture by furnishing the house and its bedrooms with period antiques. Dinner begins in front of the blazing log fire in the drawing room, where guests peruse the night's menu over aperitifs. Old Bourke family silver is on the tables in the red Queen Anne dining room. Hazel's refined culinary skills, as well as the well-manicured gardens, are award-winning. Kanturk is known for its good fishing and hunting, and it is within an hour's drive of Cork, Limerick, and Killarney. ⌧ *Kanturk, Co. Cork,* ☎ *029/50015,* ℻ *029/50795. 9 rooms with bath. Restaurant, tennis court, boating, fishing. AE, MC, V. Closed Nov.–mid-Mar.*

$

✕⌂ **Clonmeen Lodge.** The O'Leary family offers residential riding holidays from its home, a modest, redbrick Georgian lodge on the bank of the scenic Blackwater midway between Kanturk and the Green Glens Arena. Nonriding guests are also welcome to take part in golf, hiking, horseback riding, hunting, fishing, and other outdoor activities. The dinner menu relies on locally produced meat and fish and is served beside an open log fire (reserve by 3 PM); wine is the only alcohol available. ⌧ *Clonmeen, Banteer, Co. Cork,* ☎ *029/56238,* ℻ *029/56294. 6 rooms with bath. Dining room, horseback riding, fishing. MC, V.*

KINSALE TO GLENGARRIFF
VIA BANTRY BAY

This tour takes you on a scenic drive of about 136 km (85 mi) around the unspoiled coast of West County Cork. It starts at the historic old port—and now booming seaside town—of Kinsale and meanders through a variety of seascapes to the lush vegetation of Glengarriff. The drive from Kinsale to Glengarriff can take about 2 hours nonstop, but the whole point of making this journey is to linger anywhere that tickles your fancy. The tour is most enjoyable between May and October, when the weather is still warm enough to explore the area on foot.

Kinsale

★ ㉙ *29 km (18 mi) southwest of Cork City on R600.*

A lovely seaside village, Kinsale is made all the more precious by its relative isolation—though it feels a world apart, in fact it's less than 29 km (18 mi) from Cork. At the tip of the wide, fjordlike harbor opening out from the River Bandon, the town center is nestled around small streets lined by upscale shops and eateries with colorful, pastel facades. Its steep, narrow streets climb up the slopes of Compass Hill. Tall, slate-roof and unusual slate-front houses have an unmistakable Spanish influence, which can be traced back to the Battle of Kinsale in 1601, when the Irish and Spanish joined forces to fight the English—and lost. The loss was a serious one for the Irish aristocracy, and they soon took off for Europe, leaving behind their lands to English settlers. Kinsale went on to become an important fishing port as well as a British army and naval base.

Today Kinsale has a number of fine restaurants—it is often referred to as "the Gourmet Capital of Ireland," a billing it especially lives up to during the first week in October, when it hosts its annual **Gourmet Festival** (☞ Festivals and Seasonal Events). But foodies alone can't claim Kinsale; yacht owners and deep-sea anglers are also a big presence here. A signposted walking tour of the town, with an accompanying booklet (£1 from the Kinsale TIO or Boland's on Pearse Street), will familiarize you with its history.

Cuttings and memorabilia from the wreck of the *Lusitania* (☞ Cobh, *above*) are among the best artifacts in Kinsale's local **museum,** housed in the town's newly renovated 17th-century, Dutch-style courthouse. The 1915 inquest into the *Lusitania*'s sinking took place in the **courtroom,** briefly making it the focus of the world's attention; it has been preserved as a memorial. ⊠ *Old Courthouse, Market Pl.,* ☎ *021/477–2044.* ☞ *£2.* ☉ *Mon.–Sat. 11–5, Sun. 3–5.*

★ ③⓪ On the harbor shore on the east side of the Bandon's estuary, the British built **Charles Fort** in the late 17th century, in the wake of their defeat of the Spanish and Irish forces. One of the best-preserved "star forts" in Europe, it encloses some 12 acres on a cliff top (it's similar to Fort Ticonderoga in New York State). If the sun is shining, take the footpath signposted **Scilly Walk;** it winds along the edge of the harbor under tall, overhanging trees and then through the village of Summer Cove. ⊠ *3 km (2 mi) east of town,* ☎ *021/477–2684.* ☞ *£2.* ☉ *Mid-June–mid-Sept., daily 10–6; mid-Apr.–mid-June and mid-Sept.–Oct., Mon.–Sat. 9–5, Sun. 9:30–5:30; Nov.–mid-Apr., weekdays 8–4:30.*

The **Spaniard Inn** (⊠ Scilly, ☎ 021/477–2436) looks over the town and harbor from a hairpin bend on the road to Charles Fort. Inside, sawdust-covered floors and a big open fire make this onetime fishermen's bar a cozy spot in the winter. In the summer, you can take a pint to the sunny veranda and watch the world go by on land and sea.

Dining and Lodging

$$$$ ✕ **The Vintage.** One of Ireland's original front-parlor, cottage-style restau-
★ rants, the Vintage occupies the ground floor of a 500-year-old town house. Even though this is undeniably a venue for a special occasion, the atmosphere is light, informal, and welcoming. The cozy, low-beamed interior is enhanced by Swiss owner Raoul de Gendre's collection of original art. Tables are beautifully appointed with specially designed glassware, linen cloths, and tall glass candle holders. Seiko de Gendre tends the front of the house, while up to four chefs toil over an ambitious à la carte menu. Classic continental cuisine is supplemented by Irish influences, such as Lobster Dublin Lawyer (whole lobster with mustard-whiskey sauce). Appetizers include caviar and sautéed fresh duck foie gras. The wine list features more than 150 primarily European wines. ⊠ *50 Main St.,* ☎ *021/477–2502. AE, DC, MC, V. Closed Jan.–mid-Mar. No lunch.*

$ ✕ **Crackpots.** The food in Kinsale is great but can be tough on the budget. At Carole Norman's "ceramic café" you can sample the light, eclectic menu without fear of bankruptcy. An old grocery shop has been transformed into a simple but elegant eatery with warm yellow walls and two cozy dining areas, one of which has a small open fire. Behind the restaurant is Carole's pottery workshop; if you like your dinner plate, you can buy it. ⊠ *3 Cork St.,* ☎ *021/477–2847, MC, V. Closed Mon.–Wed. Nov.–Feb.*

$$$ ✕🏨 **Blue Haven.** In the heart of Kinsale, this attractive, yellow- stucco,
★ blue-trim town house combines an acclaimed seafood restaurant with
a small hotel. Rooms are both in the main house and in the house next
door. New rooms have custom-designed dark-oak furniture, canopied
antique beds, and spacious baths; those in the main house, though gen-
erally smaller, are cheerfully decorated with paintings by local artists.
Inexpensive bar food is served until 9:30 PM in the lounge bar, the patio,
and the conservatory, which are all decorated with swagged curtains,
hanging plants, and nautical brass. The quiet, pastel-color restaurant
overlooks a floodlit garden with a fountain adorned by cherubs. ⊠ *3
Pearse St., Co. Cork,* ☎ *021/477–2209,* FAX *021/774–268. 18 rooms
with bath. Restaurant, bar, fishing. AE, DC, MC, V.*

$$$ ✕🏨 **Jim Edwards.** One of the most successful pub-restaurants in Ire-
★ land, this spot is renowned for the quality of its steaks and seafood.
The restaurant is unpretentiously decorated with dark-wood tables, green
place mats, and red carpets and drapes. Portions tend to be exceptionally
generous, and children are welcome. Recommended dishes include
the fricassee of seafood and the succulent char-grilled local steak fillet. The separate bar serves inexpensive fare. Upstairs there are well-
equipped guest bedrooms ($), renovated in 1996. ⊠ *Market Quay, Co.
Cork,* ☎ *021/477–2541. 7 rooms with bath. Restaurant, bar. AE, DC,
MC, V.*

$$ 🏨 **The Moorings.** Only yards from the water's edge in the fishing vil-
lage of Scilly, this hotel has a panoramic view across Kinsale Harbor
and yet is only a few minutes' walk from Kinsale's town center. Hosts
Pat and Irene Jones are full of friendly advice and won't discourage
you if you're tempted to install yourself in the sunny conservatory and
simply watch the boats go by. Nicely sized guest rooms have large tiled
bathrooms, patchwork-quilt spreads, and paintings by local artists. ⊠
Scilly, Co. Cork, ☎ *021/477–2376,* FAX *021/477–2675. 9 rooms with
bath. MC, V.*

$$ 🏨 **Sovereign House.** If you're looking for history in this heritage town,
here is the real thing. Built in 1708 as the home of the Sovereign (Lord
Mayor) of Kinsale, this imposing Queen Anne town house has a symmetrical stone facade and a quiet, central location. The interior is furnished in the baronial style with heavy family heirlooms, exposed
stone work, stone-flagged floors, and original fireplaces. Rooms are
large and luxurious, with many original features, including some massive exposed beams and Victorian-style bathrooms. There is a warm
welcome from your host James McKeown, who will advise on local
golf, fishing, and dining. ⊠ *Newman's Mall Co. Cork,* ☎ *021/477–
2850,* FAX *021/477–4723. 4 rooms with bath. Billiards. MC, V. Closed
Dec. 24–27.*

$ 🏨 **Kilcaw House.** Value for the money, off-road parking, and the per-
sonal attention of Henry and Christina Mitchell, the enthusiastic owners, all make this guest house a good choice. On busy weekends when
the town can be buzzing into the small hours, Kilcaw's location—2 km
(1 mi) outside town on the Cork side of the R600—guarantees peace
and quiet. An open fire in the lobby, polished pine floors, and striking
colors add character to the farmhouse-style building. Rooms are well
equipped, spacious, and uncluttered, with country pine furniture and
throw rugs on the wooden floors. ⊠ *Pewter Hole Cross, Co. Cork,*
☎ *021/477–4155,* FAX *021/477–4755. 7 rooms with bath. AE, MC, V.*

Nightlife and the Arts

Check out the **Spaniard Inn** (⊠ Scilly, ☎ 021/477–2436) for live rock
and folk groups. The **Shanakee** (⊠ Market St., ☎ 021/477–4472) is
renowned for traditional Irish music. The **Bacchus Brasserie** (⊠ Guard-
well, ☎ 021/477–2382) has late-night dancing for the over-25s.

Outdoor Activities and Sports

BICYCLES

Rent a bike from **D &C Cycles** (⊠ 18 Main St., Co. Cork, ☎ 021/477–4884) to explore the picturesque hinterland of Kinsale.

DIVING

Kinsale Dive Centre (⊠ Castlepark Marina Centre, Co. Cork, ☎ 021/477–4959) will take you on a guided wreck dive and rents all necessary equipment.

FISHING

For deep-sea angling contact **Ireland Southwest Angling Ltd.** (⊠ Castlepark Marina Centre, Co. Cork, ☎ 021/477–4959).

HORSEBACK RIDING

Knocknamana Stables (⊠ Minane Bridge, ☎ 021/488–7111) has riding by the hour and cross-country trekking.

WATER SPORTS

The **Oysterhaven Holiday and Activity Center** (⊠ Oysterhaven, ☎ 021/477–0738) offers rental of all sailboarding equipment, including wet suits.

Shopping

Victoria Murphy (⊠ Market Quay, ☎ 021/477–4317) has an interesting selection of small antiques and antique jewelry. **Kinsale Crystal** (⊠ Market St., ☎ 021/477–4463) is a master cutter's studio that sells 100% Irish, hand-blown, hand-cut crystal. **Boland's** (⊠ Pearse St., ☎ 021/477–2161) features some unusual items, including exclusive sweaters, designer rainwear, and linen shirts. The **Keane on Ceramics** (⊠ Pier Rd., ☎ 021/477–2085) gallery represents the best of Ireland's ceramics artists. **Giles Norman Photography Gallery** (⊠ 44 Main St., ☎ 021/477–4373) sells unusual black-and-white photographs of Irish scenes.

En Route Leave Kinsale through its center by following the quays and drive west along the Bandon River toward the bridge on R600. The route takes you through **Garretstown Woods** (signposts for Clonakilty on R600), which are carpeted with wild bluebells in April, then past the edge of Courtmacsherry Bay, running alongside a wide, saltwater inlet that teems with curlew, plover, and other waders. The **Pink Elephant** (⊠ Harbour View, Kilbrittain, ☎ 023/49608) is an irresistible stopping place in good weather—a pink-painted, moderately priced bar and restaurant with sweeping sea views on its own grounds high above Courtmacsherry Bay. The bar serves soup and sandwiches on homemade brown bread; the restaurant features plain home cooking, including local seafood and roasted or grilled meat.

Timoleague

③ *19 km (12 mi) west of Kinsale on R600.*

The small town of Timoleague marks the eastern end of the **Seven Heads Peninsula,** which stretches around to Clonakilty. A mid-13th-century **Franciscan abbey** at the water's edge is Timoleague's most striking monument. (Walk around the back to find the entrance gate.) The abbey was sacked by the English in 1642 but, like many other ruins of its kind, was used as a burial place until recent times. A tower and walls with Gothic-arched windows still stand, and you can trace the ground plan of the old friary—chapel, refectory, cloisters, and wine cellar (at one time the friars were well-known wine importers).

Timoleague Castle Gardens are right in the village. Although the castle is long gone—it has been replaced by a modest early 20th-century house in gray stone—the original gardens have survived. Palm trees and other frost-tender plants flourish in the mature shrubbery; there are two large, old-fashioned walled gardens, one for flowers and one for fruits and vegetables. ☎ 023/46116. ⊠ £2. ⊙ *Easter weekend and June–Aug., daily noon–6.*

Courtmacsherry, the pretty village of multicolor cottages glimpsed across the water, has sandy beaches that make it a popular holiday resort. It can be reached by following the signposts from Timoleague.

Dining and Lodging

$ ✕⌂ **Lettercollum House.** This rambling country-manor house dating from 1861 is 2 km (1 mi) outside the village and looks back across the estuary to Courtmacsherry Bay. Chef-proprietors Con McLoughlin and Karen Austin create an informal but welcoming atmosphere; rooms are large, bright, and airy, with wonderful views. Organic herbs, salads, and soft fruit for the table are grown in a walled garden, and pigs are raised on-site. The restaurant is located in the chapel—Lettercollum was once a convent—which retains its stained-glass windows and confessional. ⊠ *Timoleague, Co. Cork,* ☎ 023/46251, ☒ 023/46270. *9 rooms with bath. Restaurant. MC, V. Closed Nov.–Jan.*

$$$ ✕ **Casino House.** Midway between Kinsale and Timoleague on the coastal R600, this traditional farmhouse was converted to an informal restaurant by owner-chefs Michael and Kerrin Relja. The home is decorated in an uncluttered style, and two small dining rooms—one blue and one green—have private sitting rooms for pre-dinner drinks next to an open fire. Menu highlights include starters of garlic prawn salad and lobster risotto; such mains as roast loin of lamb served with Roman gnocchi; and summer fruits with sabayon as a seasonal dessert. ⊠ *Coolmaine, Kilbrittain,* ☎ 023/49944. *MC, V. Closed Wed. mid-Jan.–mid-Mar.; Easter–Oct.; Mon.–Thurs. Nov., Dec., and early Jan.*

En Route This area is the heart of **West Cork,** where natives have been called "a nation unto themselves" and small, twisted roads are overhung by tall hedges of *Fuchsia magellanica.* Originally imported in the mid-19th century, this garden shrub quickly adapted to the balmy sea air and is widely regarded as a weed—albeit a beautiful one with its delicate, drooping flowers in shades of mauve and red—used here for hedging. In June, the hedges are offset by tall, purple foxgloves and, in August and September, by bright purple heather.

Many of the shops and businesses in the small market town of **Clonakilty,** 9½ km (6 mi) from Timoleague on R600/N71, have abandoned chrome and plastic materials for traditional, hand-painted signs and wooden facades—to very charming effect. The best of the several traditional music pubs in town is **De Barra's** (⊠ 55 Pearse St., ☎ 023/33381). Many fine, sandy beaches are near Clonakilty; the best are at **Inchydoney,** 3 km (2 mi) outside of town.

The **birthplace of Michael Collins** (1890–1922) is signposted about 5 km (3 mi) west of Clonakilty off N71 (just past the tiny village of Lissavaird). The ground plan of the simple homestead where the controversial founder of the modern Irish Army was born has been reinstated by his nephew, and there is a bronze memorial (it's freely accessible). There is another memorial in the nearest village, **Woodfield,** opposite the pub where Collins is said to have had his last drink on the day he was shot in an ambush.

The road briefly joins the sea again at **Rosscarbery,** where you leave the main road by turning left at the signpost for Glandore at the end of the causeway. Glandore and Union Hall are twin fishing villages on either side of the landlocked Glandore Harbour. With its steep hill and pretty church, **Glandore** is a popular spot for visitors from the United Kingdom and Germany. Glandore's influx of affluent visitors and expensive yachts has not been shared in **Union Hall,** where simple fishing trawlers still tie up at the quay. In the area hereabouts, you are truly in the back of beyond, where tiny roads are without route numbers.

Castletownshend (clearly signposted from Union Hall via Rineen) has an unusual number of graciously designed, large stone houses, mostly dating from the mid-18th century, when it was an important trading center. Its main street runs steeply down a hill to the sea. The sleepy town awakens in July and August, when its sheltered harbor bustles. Sparkling views await from the cliff-top perch of St. Barrahane's Church, which has a medieval oak altarpiece and three stained-glass windows by the early 20th-century Irish artist Harry Clarke. The low-beamed interior of **Mary Ann's** (☎ 028/36146), one of the oldest bars in the country, is frequented by a very friendly mix of visitors and locals and is a good place for a pint and a bite of bar food. Writer Edna O'Brien claims that it is her favorite pub in the whole world.

Nightlife and the Arts

Exhibitions by internationally acclaimed artists are held in May and August at the waterside **Warren's Boathouse Gallery** (inquiries to Mary Ann's [☞ *above*]).

Skibbereen

③②   *85 km (53 mi) west of Kinsale.*

Skibbereen is the main market town in this neck of Southwest Cork, and it's a good base for the sights nearby. The weekly cattle market (Wednesday) and country market (Friday)—not to mention the plethora of pubs punctuated by bustling shops and coffeehouses—keep the place jumping year-round.

Garden lovers, take note: Still partially under construction but well worth visiting is the **Liss Ard Foundation.** More than 40 acres are planted with various lakeside gardens designed to highlight the natural beauty of the landscape in an ecologically sound way. Particularly worthwhile is the 10-acre **Sky Garden,** designed by American artist James Turrell to celebrate the beauty of the sky. Allow 2 to 3 hours. An optional guided tour is included in the admission price. ⊠ *On Castletownshend road out of Skibbereen,* ☎ 028/22368. 🎫 £5. ☉ *May–Oct., daily 10–dusk; call for hrs Nov.–Apr.*

Dining and Lodging

$$$$ ✕🏠 **Lissard Lake Lodge.** This renovated, lakeside Victorian lodge offers guests something offbeat: a country house without the usual country-house style. Every room does have a view of beautifully landscaped gardens, but there the resemblance to more traditional houses ends. The minimalist decor relies on black and white and natural woods. In the bedrooms, the huge beds have plump white duvets, while a black pillar contains a TV, VCR, and CD player (CDs and videos can be borrowed from reception). The bathrooms, behind sliding Japanese paper doors, are equipped with stainless-steel sinks and large, white tubs. The one small guest lounge is sparsely furnished even by minimalist standards. Chef and co-owner Claudia Meister oversees a Mediterranean-Asian–flavored menu. ⊠ *Skibbereen, Co. Cork,* ☎ 028/40000, 🗎 028/40001. *26 rooms with bath. Restaurant (reservations essential), bar, tennis court, fishing. AE, DC, MC, V. Closed mid-Jan.–mid-Feb.*

$ ✕🏠 **West Cork Hotel.** This busy, long-established, family-run hotel in a large Victorian building on the River Ilen is decorated with a stylish old colonial ambience. Recently refurbished rooms are comfortable as well as a good value for the price range. The restaurant, famous for its steaks, features such fashionable modern dishes as Louisiana crab-cakes and more traditional favorites. ⊠ *Bridge St., Skibbereen, Co. Cork,* ☎ *028/21277,* FAX *028/22333. 36 rooms with bath. Restaurant, bar, horseback riding, fishing. AE, DC, MC, V.*

$ ✕▥ **Heron's Cove.** You really will see herons outside your window at Sue Hill's idyllic harborside retreat. This modern house, built on the edge of a secluded sea inlet, is only minutes' walk from Goleen's appealing village center. The exceptionally well equipped rooms, furnished in part with antiques, have excellent views from every window. During summer, part of the house and its terrace are turned into an informal restaurant. Fresh local seafood stars on the menu, which also includes lamb, duck, and steak. Fresh herb sauces and homemade mayonnaise make subtle accompaniments, and there's a terrific wine list. Off-season (November–March), evening meals are prepared on request for guests only. ⊠ *The Harbour, Goleen, Co. Cork,* ☎ *028/35225,* FAX *028/ 35422. 5 rooms with bath. Restaurant, fishing. AE, DC, MC V.*

Nightlife and the Arts

The **West Cork Arts Center** has regular exhibits of work by local artists. The on-site crafts shop also sells items made by area artisans. ⊠ *North St., Skibbereen,* ☎ *028/22090.* ☉ *Mon.–Sat. 10–6.*

Outdoor Activities and Sports

Bicycles to explore West Cork's coast and country can be rented from **N. W. Roycroft** (⊠ Ilen St., ☎ 028/21235).

Baltimore

③③ *13 km (8 mi) southwest of Skibbereen on R595.*

The beautiful, crescent-shape fishing village of Baltimore is now a popular sailing center and attracts its share of vacationing families from Ireland and abroad, especially during the peak summer months. The village was sacked in 1631 by a band of Algerian sailors; as a result, watchtowers were installed at the harbor mouth to protect the town.

③④ **Sherkin Island,** one of Baltimore's two famous attractions, is 1 km (½ mi) off the coast, only a 10-minute ferry ride away. Seven ferries are scheduled daily (☎ 028/20125 for times). On the island, you'll find the ruins of **Dún Na Long Castle** and **Sherkin Abbey,** both built around 1470 by the O'Driscolls, a seafaring clan known as the "scourge of the Irish seas." The island's population today is 90, and there are several safe, sandy beaches and abundant wildlife.

③⑤ Even more impressive than Sherkin Island is **Cape Clear Island,** a 2- by 5-km (1- by 3-mi) island that is part of the West Cork Gaeltacht, or Irish-speaking area. The ferry to the island, which is 6 km (4 mi) off-shore, takes about an hour from Baltimore (£9 round-trip; ☎ 028/39119 for sailing times). It's exciting to watch the skipper thread his way through the many rocks and tiny islands of Roaring Water Bay. You have excellent views of the **Fastnet Rock Lighthouse,** focus of a renowned yachting race. Sparsely populated (about 200 residents), the island has one pub and a few simple B&Bs, but it is otherwise rugged and unblemished (electricity from the mainland was not brought over, via an underground cable, until April 1997), and it can be explored on foot in about an hour. Bird-watchers may want to schedule more time: Cape Clear is the southernmost point of Irish territory, and its observatory, the oldest in the Republic, has racked up all kinds of sightings of rare songbird migrants. Whales, dolphins, and large flocks of ocean-going birds can be seen offshore in the summer.

Outdoor Activities and Sports

Sailing dinghies and sailboards can be rented by the hour or the day from **Baltimore Sailing School** (⊠ The Pier, Baltimore, ☎ 028/20141).

Bantry

③⑥   *25 km (16 mi) northwest of Skibbereen on N71.*

Bantry is an unprepossessing town with a large market square at the head of Bantry Bay, where a long plaza attracts artisans, craftspeople, and musicians in summer. As you enter Bantry, on the right-hand side
★   of the road you'll see the porticoed entrance to **Bantry House,** one of Ireland's most magnificent houses, beautifully situated overlooking the sea. First built in the early 1700s, then subsequently altered and expanded later that century, the house as it looks today is largely the vision of Richard White, the second earl of Bantry, who also created the Italianate gardens that surround it. On his European grand tours, Richard gobbled up fine art, furniture, and other antiques, including Aubusson tapestries said to have been ordered by Louis XV for the marriage of Marie Antoinette to the Dauphin. Some of the rooms are now a little shabby, but the beauty of the location compensates for the lack of polish. The long climb to the top of the rear garden pays off with what has been called "one of the great views in Ireland." Next to the house is the **Bantry 1796 French Armada Exhibition Center,** a small but worthwhile museum illustrating the abortive attempt by Irish Nationalist Wolfe Tone and his French ally General Hoche to land 14,000 troops in Bantry Bay to effect an uprising. ⊠ *Bantry House,* ☎ *027/50047.* ◢ *House £5, museum £5.* ⏱ *Mar.–Oct., daily 9–6.*

The glorious sweep of **Bantry Bay** is on your left as you climb out of town past Ballylickey on N71. The balladeers celebrate this bay, which is is a starker, more magnificent prospect than any encountered so far. The sparse, windswept vegetation gives an idea of what the wet and windy winters are like on the more exposed part of this coast.

Dining and Lodging

$$$$ ✕ **Blair's Cove House.** In the converted stables of a Georgian mansion overlooking Dunmanus Bay, gleaming silverware, pink tablecloths, and a large crystal chandelier are set off, jewel-in-the-rough style, against stone walls and exposed beams. A covered, heated terrace overlooks the rose-filled courtyard and fountain and is used in summer. The cuisine is French-Irish (the owners are French) with an emphasis on fresh local produce. ⊠ *Blair's Cove, Durrus, Co. Cork,* ☎ *027/61127. MC, V. Closed Sun.; Mon. Sept.–June; and Nov. 1–Feb. No lunch.*

$$$$ ✕ **Shiro Japanese Dinner House.** One of the biggest surprises of West
★   Cork's culinary world has been the success of this tiny, 20-seat restaurant, which serves authentic Japanese cuisine in an Edwardian house surrounded by palm trees. The room is decorated with watercolors by the talented hostess, Tokyo-born Kei Pilz. ⊠ *Ahakista, Durrus, Co. Cork,* ☎ *027/67030. Reservations essential. AE, DC, MC, V. Closed Jan.–Feb. No lunch.*

$$ ✕🏨 **Sea View House.** Set in its own wooded grounds overlooking Bantry
★   Bay, this large, three-story, 19th-century country-house hotel offers excellent value for the money. Owner-manager Kathleen O'Sullivan keeps an eagle eye on what was, until 1980, her private home. Inlaid antique furniture, polished brass, and ornate curtains set a tone of luxury. Bedrooms with sea views have small sofas in the bay windows; others have views of the wooded gardens. Polished tables in the elegant dining room are set with crocheted mats and linen napkins; service is friendly and informal. ⊠ *Ballylickey, near Bantry, Co. Cork,* ☎ *027/50073,* 𝖥𝖠𝖷 *027/*

51555. 17 rooms with bath. Restaurant, bar, horseback riding, fishing. AE, DC, MC, V. Closed mid-Nov.–mid Mar.

Nightlife and the Arts

During the **West Cork Chamber Music Festival**, roughly 20 concerts are held from the last weekend in June through the first in July in the library at exquisite Bantry House. For information on themes and international guest artists for the 2000 event, or for news of other chamber music concerts held at Bantry House throughout the year, contact organizer Francis Humphrys (⊠ Coomkeen, Durrus, Co. Cork, ☎ 027/61105).

Outdoor Activities and Sports

Bantry Park Golf Club (⊠ Donemark, Co. Cork, ☎ 027/50579) is an 18-hole, par-71 course overlooking Bantry Bay.

Shopping

Manning's Emporium (⊠ Ballylickey, ☎ 027/51049) is a showcase for locally made farmhouse cheeses, pâtés, and salamis—an excellent place to put together a picnic or just to browse. One of the Southwest's larger independents, **Bantry Bookstore** (⊠ New St., ☎ 027/50064) has six rooms full of new, antiquarian, and secondhand books.

Glengarriff

㊲ *14 km (8 mi) northwest of Bantry on N71, 21 km (13 mi) southeast of Kenmare.*

One of the jewels of Bantry Bay is Glengarriff, the "rugged glen" much loved by Thackeray and Sir Walter Scott. The descent into wooded, sheltered Glengarriff reveals yet another kind of landscape: Thanks to the Gulf Stream, it is mild enough down here for subtropical plants to thrive. Trails along the shore are covered with rhododendrons, and they afford beautiful views of the nearby inlets, loughs, and lounging seals. You are also back on the beaten path, with crafts shops, tour buses, and boatmen soliciting your business by the roadside.

㊳ **Garnish Island,** about 10 minutes offshore, features beautiful, formal Italian gardens; shrubberies with rare subtropical plants; and excellent views from the Grecian temple. From the island's Martello tower, built at the end of the 18th century, the British watched for attempted landings by Napoleonic forces, including Hoche's ill-fated one. (The price for the boat ride is fixed at £5 round-trip.) ☎ 027/63040. ☑ £2.50. ☉ July–Aug., Mon.–Sat. 9:30–6:30, Sun. 11–7; Apr.–June and Sept., Mon.–Sat. 10–6:30, Sun. 1–7; Mar. and Oct., Mon.–Sat. 10–4:30, Sun. 1–5; last landing 1 hr before closing.

Glengarriff is the gateway to the **Ring of Beara,** a 137-km (85-mi) scenic drive that encircles the Beara Peninsula on R572. Just beyond the busy fishing port Castletownbere lie the ruins of Dunboy Castle and House (freely accessible). **Dursey Island,** at the tip of the peninsula, is a bird watcher's paradise accessible only by cable car. From Dursey Island, head for tiny **Allihies,** the former site of a huge copper mine, and detour along a precipitous and breathtaking coastal road to Eyeries—a ghost town–like village overlooking Coulagh Bay—and then up the south side of the Kenmare River to Kenmare.

THE RING OF KERRY

Running along the perimeter of the Iveragh Peninsula, the dramatic Ring of Kerry is probably the single most-popular tourist route in Ireland. Stunning mountain and coastal views are around almost every turn of the road. The only drawback: On a sunny day, it seems like half the tourists in Ireland are there, packed into buses, on bikes, or backpacking along the same two-lane road. Because tour buses ply the Ring counterclockwise, we recommend that independent travelers take it clockwise, starting at Kenmare. This is equally convenient whether you're approaching from Glengarriff (on N71) or Killarney (also on N71), which is the traditional starting point. The trip covers 176 km (110 mi) on N70 (and briefly R562) if you start and finish in Killarney; the journey will be 40 km (25 mi) shorter if you only venture between Kenmare and Killorglin. Allow at least one full day to circumnavigate the Ring. And because rain blocks views across the water to the Beara Peninsula in the east and the Dingle Peninsula in the west, pray for sunshine. It makes all the difference.

Kenmare

39 *21 km (13 mi) northwest of Glengarriff, 34 km (21 mi) south of Killarney on N71.*

A small market town at the head of the sheltered Kenmare River estuary, Kenmare was founded in 1670 by Sir William Petty (Cromwell's surveyor general, a multitasking entrepreneur) and today is a popular touring base. Most of its buildings date from the 19th century, when it was part of the enormous Lansdowne Estate, itself assembled by Petty. The **Kenmare Heritage Centre** explains the history of the town and supplies a walking route pointing out places of interest. ☎ *064/41233.* ☑ *£2.* ○ *Easter–Sept., Mon.–Sat. 9:30–5:30.*

Dining and Lodging

$$ ✕ **An Leath Phingin.** The name means "The Half Penny," and this stylish little place with exposed stone walls and modern pine tables specializes in northern Italian cuisine. Never let it be said that Kerry is predictable! The explanation lies in owner-chef Con Guerin's links with Bologna, where he learned the art of making fresh pasta. The combination of Irish and Italian is epitomized by a starter of baked aubergine with olive oil, tomato, local goat's cheese, and basil, or a 12-inch Quattro Formaggi pizza featuring four Irish cheeses—Milleens, Cashel Blue, local goat's, and Gubeen. ☒ *35 Main St.,* ☎ *064/41559. MC, V. Closed Nov.*

$$ ✕ **Cafe Indigo.** Although the theme color of the minimalistic decor is a predictable indigo, the menu features eclectic international combinations. Crispy spring rolls with sweet pepper sauce, seared scallops with celeriac puree and mango vanilla-bean salsa, and bitter chocolate lemon torte with vanilla sauce are recommendations. The Square Pint pub serves tempting bar food downstairs: spiced lentil soup, seafood pie, Irish Stew, and imaginative sandwiches. ☒ *The Square,* ☎ *064/42356. AE, DC, MC, V.*

$–$$ ✕ **Packies.** Owner-chef Maura O'Connell Foley established Kenmare's original first-class restaurant, the Lime Tree, but she has since opted for a quieter life at Packies. The small room has a flagstone floor, an exposed-stone fireplace, and paintings by local artists. The delicious bistro-style menu includes wild smoked salmon with red onion and caper salsa as well as and crab claws with garlic butter or olive oil. ☒ *Henry St., Co. Kerry,* ☎ *064/41508. MC, V. Closed Sun. and Nov.–Easter.*

$$$$ ✕▣ **Park Hotel.** This sprawling, 1897 stone château is one of Ireland's
★ premier country-house hotels. A two-minute walk to town, the 11-acre property has views of the Caha Mountains and terraced lawns that sweep down to the bay. A marble fireplace and a tall grandfather clock preside over the thickly carpeted lobby. Owner-manager Francis Brennan is a stickler for authenticity and has made great efforts to recapture

the hotel's heyday. The bedrooms are individually designed with late-Victorian furniture faithful to the house's original period; walnut or mahogany bedroom suites have matching wardrobes, chests of drawers, and headboards. All bedrooms have finely equipped bathrooms with glossy, Italian-marble tiling. Be sure to sample the modern Irish cuisine of the renowned restaurant, which uses local ingredients in a mélange of Asian and Continental styles. ✉ *Kenmare, Co. Kerry,* ☎ *064/41200,* FAX *064/41402. 50 rooms with bath. Restaurant, bar, 18-hole golf course, tennis court, croquet, Ping-Pong, fishing, bicycles. AE, DC, MC, V. Closed Jan.–Apr. 10.*

$$$$ ✕🖭 **Sheen Falls Lodge.** The magnificent setting—300 secluded acres
★ of lawns, semitropical gardens, and forest between Kenmare Bay and the falls of the River Sheen—is easily matched by this rambling, bright-yellow, slate-roof manor house, built by the descendants of Sir William Petty, and the former seat of the earls of Kerry. The public rooms, decorated in warm orange tones, include a mahogany-paneled library with more than 1,000 books, mainly of Irish interest, and a billiards room adjacent to the bar. The bedrooms have a combination of new and antique furnishings; they all offer stunning bay or river views. The restaurant, La Cascade (it overlooks the falls), serves classic French cuisine. ✉ *Co. Kerry,* ☎ *064/41600,* FAX *064/41386. 45 rooms with bath, 8 suites, 8 superior-deluxe rooms. Restaurant, bar, pool, sauna, steam room, tennis court, croquet, health club, horseback riding, fishing, billiards, library. AE, DC, MC, V.*

$ ✕🖭 **Muxnaw Lodge.** A romantic black-and-white house with steep gables, the lodge was built in 1801 and has a magical view over Kenmare Bay. It is surrounded by mature gardens and trees and is only a short walk from town. Rooms are spacious and cozy, individually decorated with interesting old and antique furniture but also boasting up-to-the-minute conveniences like television and tea- and coffeemaking facilities. The atmosphere in general is genteel, old-world, as if the 20th century had passed the place by. Dinner, featuring local produce and plain home cooking, must be booked by noon. Bring your own wine. ✉ *Castletownbere Rd., Co. Kerry,* ☎ *064/41252. 5 rooms with bath. Tennis court, fishing. No credit cards. Closed Dec. 23–26.*

$ 🖭 **Sallyport House.** Across the bridge on the way into Kenmare, this substantial, 1932 family home has been enlarged to serve as a comfortable B&B. The spotless rooms, all with harbor or mountain views, are furnished with a variety of Victorian and Edwardian antiques. Janey Arthur has placed family heirlooms in all rooms; if you are interested in old Irish furniture, ask for a tour. ✉ *Arthur Family, Co. Kerry,* ☎ *064/42066,* FAX *064/42067. 5 rooms with bath. No credit cards. Closed mid-Nov.–Apr. 1.*

Nightlife

Try **O Donnabhaínós** (✉ Henry St., ☎ 064/41361) for traditional music.

Outdoor Activities and Sports

Seafari (✉ Kenmare Pier, ☎ 064/83171) has 2-hour, eco-nature and seal-watching cruises and also runs the Marine Activities Centre (May–October, weather permitting), which offers sea fishing, sailboat day trips, sailboarding, canoeing, waterskiing, and tube rides.

Shopping

Avoca Handweavers (✉ Moll's Gap, ☎ 064/34720) sells wool clothing and mohair rugs and throws in a wide range of colors and weaves. **Black Abbey Crafts** (✉ 28 Main St., ☎ 064/42115) specializes in fine Irish-made crafts. **Cleo's** (✉ 2 Shelbourne St., ☎ 064/41410) stocks

Irish-made wool and linen, and Irish handknits, which have striking designs, often drawn from Ireland's past.

Sneem

40 *27 km (17 mi) southwest of Kenmare on N70.*

This is one of the prettiest villages in Ireland—and, it can seem, one of the most popular. Sneem (from the Irish for "knot") is settled around an English-style green on the estuary of the Ardsheelaun River, its streets filled with houses washed in different colors. Also, look for "the pyramids" (as they are known locally) beside the parish church. These 12-ft-tall, traditional stone structures with stained-glass insets look as though they have been here forever. In fact, the sculpture park was completed in 1990 to the design of the Kerry-born artist James Scanlon, who has won international awards for his work in stained glass.

41 **Staigue Fort,** signposted 4 km (2½) mi inland at Castlecove, is one of the finest examples of an Iron Age stone fort in Ireland. Approximately 2,500 years old, this structure, made from local stone, is almost circular and about 75 ft in diameter, with only one entrance, on the south side. From the Iron Age (from 500 BC to the 5th century AD) and early Christian times (6th century AD), such "forts" were, in fact, the fortified homesteads for several families of one clan and also where their cattle lived. The walls at Staigue Fort are almost 13 ft wide at the base and 7 ft wide at the top; they still stand at 18 ft on the north and west sides. Within the walls stairs lead to narrow platforms on which the lookouts stood. (Private land must be crossed to reach the fort, and a nominal "compensation for trespass" (50p–£1 is often requested by the landowner.)

Dining and Lodging

$$$$ 🏨 **Parknasilla Great Southern.** A porter in a frock coat and striped gray pants typifies the elegant and slightly stuffy turn-of-the-century atmosphere of this grand old hotel. Previous guests include General de Gaulle, Princess Grace, and George Bernard Shaw, who wrote much of *Saint Joan* while staying here. Although some rooms are a bit plain, they are tastefully decorated in soft pinks and blues. The sheltered coastal location, 3 km (2 mi) south of Sneem, and excellent sporting facilities make it an ideal retreat. ⊠ *Parknasilla, near Sneem, Co. Kerry,* ☎ *064/45122,* 🖷 *064/45323. 85 rooms with bath. Restaurant, bar, pool, sauna, 9-hole golf course, tennis court, horseback riding, windsurfing, boating, waterskiing, fishing, bicycles. AE, DC, MC, V.*

$ ✕🏨 **Tahilla Cove Country House.** The house itself is modern and much-added-to over the years—the attraction is its idyllic location, with its own stone jetty in a sheltered private cove. Guests can enjoy the plump, chintz armchairs and open log fire in the large sitting room or laze on the terrace overlooking 14 acres of subtropical gardens and the cove. Rooms are of varying sizes, comfortably furnished in a homely way, and all but two have sea views. ⊠ *Tahilla Cove, Sneem, Co. Kerry,* ☎ *064/45204,* 🖷 *064/45104. 9 rooms with bath. Restaurant, bar, fishing. AE, DC, MC, V. Closed mid-Oct.–Mar.*

42 **Caherdaniel** is the next village west on N70. Beyond the town is **Derrynane House,** once the home of Daniel O'Connell (1775–1847), "The Liberator," who campaigned for Catholic Emancipation (the granting of full rights of citizenship for Catholics), which became a reality in 1828. The house with its lovely garden and 320-acre estate now forms **Derrynane National Park.** The south and east wings of the house (which O'Connell himself remodeled) are open to visitors and still contain much of the original furniture and other items associated with O'-

Connell. ⊠ *Co. Kerry*, ☎ *066/947–5113.* ⌨ *House £2, parking free.* ⊙ *Jan.–Mar. and Nov.–Dec., weekends 1–5; Apr. and Oct., Tues.–Sun. 1–5; May–Sept., Mon.–Sat. 9–6, Sun. 11–7.*

Waterville, Valentia Island, and the Skelligs

❸ *35 km (22 mi) west of Sneem, 5 km (3 mi) north of Caherdaniel on N70.*

Like many other villages on the Ring, Waterville has a few restaurants and pubs, but little else. It *is* famous for game-fishing opportunities, its 18-hole championship golf course, and for the fact that Charlie Chaplin and Charles de Gaulle once spent their summers here. Salmon and trout fishing are excellent at nearby Lough Currane.

Outside Waterville, a scenic detour is signposted from the main Ring to **Ballinskelligs,** a small, Irish-speaking fishing village with an old monastery, a pub, and a fine sandy beach. In the far northwestern corner of the Ring, **Valentia Island** lies across Portmagee Channel. Some of the romance of visiting an island has been lost since Valentia was connected to the mainland by a road bridge in 1971. The island still gives its name to weather reports, but the station that monitors the Atlantic weather systems has now moved onto the nearby mainland.

★ ❹ The **Skelligs—Little Skellig, Great Skellig,** and the **Washerwoman's Rock**—are distinctive conical-shape rock islands visible from Valentia Island on a clear day. The largest rock, the Great Skellig, or **Skellig Michael,** rises 700 ft out of the Atlantic. It has the remains of a settlement of early Christian monks, reached by climbing 600 increasingly precipitous steps. In spite of 1,000 years' battering by Atlantic storms, the church, oratory, and beehive-shape living cells are surprisingly well preserved.

The **Skellig Experience,** where the road bridge joins Valentia Island, contains exhibits on local bird life, the history of the lighthouse and keepers, and the life and work of the early Christian monks. There is also a 15-minute audiovisual show that allows you to "tour" the monastery without leaving dry land. If, however, you'd like to see the Skelligs up close (landing is prohibited without a special permit), you can take a 1½-hour guided cruise. Little Skellig is the breeding ground of more than 22,000 pairs of gannets, while **Puffin Island** to the north has a large population of shearwaters, storm petrel, and puffins. Photographers will love the boat trip, but sailors are warned that these are choppy waters at the best of times. ⊠ *Valentia,* ☎ *066/947–6306.* ⌨ *Center £3; cruise £15 (includes adm. to center).* ⊙ *Apr.–June and Sept., daily 9:30–5; July–Aug., daily 9:30–7; call to confirm weather-dependent cruise times.*

Dining and Lodging

$$ ✕▥ **Butler Arms.** The white, castellated towers at the corners of this hotel provide a familiar landmark on the Ring. The building has been in the same family for three generations; it has a regular clientele, predominantly male, who come back year after year for the excellent fishing and golf facilities nearby. It was a favorite base for Charlie Chaplin. Although the accommodations are neither smart nor chic, the rambling old lounges with open turf fires are comfortable places to relax and converse. ⊠ *Waterville, Co. Kerry,* ☎ *066/947–4144,* ℻ *066/947–4520. 30 rooms with bath. Restaurant, 2 bars, tennis court, horseback riding, fishing. AE, DC, MC, V. Closed mid-Oct.–Easter.*

$ ✕▥ **Smuggler's Inn.** On a 2-km-long (1-mi-long) sandy beach, Lucille and Harry Hunt's small, family-run guest house has a restaurant with renowned seafood. It's an ideal spot for a leisurely lunch or a quick pint and a sandwich. Bedrooms are individually decorated with chintz spreads and curtains. Seven of them offer great sea views. ⊠ *Cliff Rd., Waterville, Co. Kerry,* ☎ *066/947–4330.* ⅏ *066/947–4422. 10 rooms with bath. AE, DC, MC, V. Closed Dec.–Feb.*

Nightlife
Head for the **Inny Tavern** (Inny Bridge, Waterville, ☎ 066/947–4512) for live Irish music.

Outdoor Activities and Sports
Waterville Golf Links (⊠ Ring of Kerry, Co. Kerry, ☎ 066/947–4102), an 18-hole, par-72 course, is one of the toughest and most scenic in Ireland or Britain (☞ Chapter 9).

Cahirciveen

46 *18 km (11) mi northwest of Waterville on N70, 27½ km (17 mi) southeast of Glenbeigh.*

Cahirciveen (pronounced cah-her-sigh-*veen*) marks the Ring's western fringe, and it is the main market town and shopping center for South Kerry, at the foot of Bentee Mountain. The **O'Connell Memorial Church** (⊠ Main Rd.), a large and elaborate neo-Gothic church that dominates the main street, was built in 1888 of Newry granite and local black limestone to honor the local hero, Daniel O'Connell (☞ Caherdaniel, *in* Sneem *above*); it is the only church in Ireland named for a layman. Following the tradition in this part of the world, the town's modest, terraced houses are painted in different colors—the brighter the better. The **Cahirciveen Heritage Centre** is housed in the converted former barracks of the Royal Irish Constabulary, an imposing, castlelike structure built after the Fenian Rising of 1867 to suppress any further revolts. The community-funded center has well-designed displays depicting scenes from times of famine in the locality, the life of Daniel O'Connell, and the recent restoration of this fine building from a blackened ruin. ⊠ *Barracks, Cahirciveen,* ☎ *066/947–2777.* ▦ *£2.50.* ⊙ *June–Sept., Mon.–Sat. 10–6, Sun. 2–6; Mar.–May and Oct., weekdays 9:30–5:30.*

En Route   The road from Cahirciveen to Glenbeigh is one of the highlights of the Ring. To the north is Dingle Bay and the jagged peaks of the Dingle Peninsula, which will, in all probability, be shrouded in mist. If they are not, the gods have indeed blessed your journey. The road runs close to the water here, and beyond the small village of Kells, it climbs high above the bay, hugging the steep side of Drung Hill before descending to Glenbeigh. Note how different the stark character of this stretch of the Ring is from the gentle, woody Kenmare Bay side.

Glenbeigh

47 *27 km (17 mi) northeast of Cahirciveen on N70, 11½ km (7 mi) west of Killorglin.*

On a boggy plateau by the sea, the block-long town of Glenbeigh is a popular holiday base, offering excellent hiking in the **Glenbeigh Horseshoe**, as the surrounding mountains are known, and exceptionally good trout fishing on Lough Coomasaharn. Worth a quick look, the **Kerry Bog Village Museum** is a cluster of reconstructed, fully furnished cottages, which gives a vivid portrayal of the daily life of the region's working class in the early 1800s. ⊠ *Beside Red Fox Bar,* ☎ *066/976–9184.* ▦ *£2.50.* ⊙ *Mar.–Nov., daily 8:30–7; Jan.–Mar. by request.*

48 **Rossbeigh,** north of Glenbeigh, has about 3 km (2 mi) of soft, sandy coastline backed by high dunes. It faces Inch Strand, a similar formation across the water on the Dingle Peninsula (☞ The Dingle Peninsula, *below*). A signpost to the right outside Glenbeigh points to **Lough**

Caragh, another tempting side excursion to a beautiful expanse of water set among gorse- and heather-covered hills and majestic mountains. The road encircles the lake, hugging the shoreline much of the way.

Dining and Lodging

$$$ ✕🏨 **Caragh Lodge.** Built in the mid-19th century as a fishing lodge, this charming old house by the lake sits in 9 acres of spectacular gardens filled with azaleas, camellias, and magnolias. Two large rooms in the main house are furnished with Victorian and Georgian antiques; rooms in the courtyard and the garden annex are smaller; and a new block has six larger rooms and one suite. Comfortable sitting rooms overlook the lake, as does the dining room. Owner Mary Gaunt supervises the four-course, set dinner menu. ✉ *Caragh Lake, Killorglin, Co. Kerry,* ☎ *066/976–9115,* 𝔽𝔸𝕏 *066/976–9316. 14 rooms with bath, 1 suite. Restaurant, sauna, tennis court, boating, fishing. AE, DC, MC, V. Closed mid-Oct.–mid-Apr. No lunch.*

$$$ 🏨 **Ard na Sidhe.** Sidhe (pronounced sheen) means "Hill of the Fairies,"
★ and this secluded, gabled Edwardian mansion certainly fits a fairy-tale story. The house is built of stone walls, now ivy-covered, and is punctuated by casement windows set in stone mullions. Attractive, large rooms have coordinated carpets and spreads as well as lovely floral drapes on the bay windows; those in the main building are the nicest. Antiques and open fires adorn the traditionally furnished lobby and lounges. The hotel also has delightful, award-winning lakeside gardens. ✉ *Caragh Lake, near Killorglin, Co. Kerry,* ☎ *066/976–9105,* 𝔽𝔸𝕏 *066/976–9282. 20 rooms with bath. Restaurant, bar, boating, fishing. AE, DC, MC, V. Closed Oct.–Apr. 25.*

Outdoor Activities and Sports

Dooks Golf Club (✉ Glenbeigh, ☎ 066/68205) is a challenging traditional links on the shore of Dingle Bay (☞ Chapter 9).

Killorglin

④⑨ *14 km (9 mi) east of Glenbeigh, 22 km (14 mi) west of Killarney.*

The last stop on the Ring before Killarney (or the first, if you're going counterclockwise), the hilltop town of Killorglin is the scene of the **Puck Fair,** three days of merrymaking during the second weekend in August. A large billy goat with beribboned horns, installed on a high pedestal, presides over the fair. The origins of the tradition of King Puck are lost in time. Though some horse, sheep, and cattle dealing still occurs at the fair, the main attractions these days are free outdoor concerts and extended drinking hours. The crowd is predominantly young and invariably noisy, so avoid Killorglin at fair time if you've come for peace and quiet. On the other hand, if you intend joining in the festivities, be sure to book accommodations well in advance.

Dining

$$$ ✕ **Nick's Seafood and Steak.** Owner-chef Nick Foley trained as a veterinary surgeon but prefers life in the kitchen. The old, stone town house has a bar–cum–dining room at street level and a quieter dining room on the floor above. Foley is known for his wide choice of local seafood and his steaks. In winter, sample the haunch of Kerry venison in red-wine and juniper sauce. ✉ *Main St.,* ☎ *066/976–1219. AE, DC, MC, V. Closed Nov. and Mon.–Tues. Dec.–Easter.*

IN AND AROUND KILLARNEY

One of southwest Ireland's most attractive locales, Killarney is also the most heavily visited city in the region (its proximity to the Ring of Kerry and to Shannon Airport help to ensure this). Light rain is typical of the area around Killarney, but because of the region's topography, it seldom lasts long. Indeed, the clouds' approach over the lakes and the subsequent showers can actually add to the spectacle of the ever-changing scenery. The rain is often followed within minutes by brilliant sunshine and, yes, even a rainbow.

Exploring Killarney

87 km (54 mi) west of Cork City on N22, 19 km (12 mi) southeast of Killorglin, 24 km (15 mi) north of Glengarriff.

If writers like Sir Walter Scott and William Thackeray had to struggle finding the superlatives to describe the lakes and mountains of Killarney, it is not surprising that they remain among the most celebrated—and indisputably the most commercialized—attractions in Ireland. Killarney's heather-clad mountains, lush subtropical vegetation, and deep-blue lakes dotted with wooded isles have left a lasting impression on a long stream of visitors, beginning in the 18th century with the English travelers Arthur Young and Bishop Berkeley. Visitors in search of the natural beauty so beloved by the Romantic movement began to flock to the Southwest. By the mid-19th century, Killarney's stunning scenery was considered as exhilarating and awe-inspiring as anything in Switzerland or England's Lake District. The influx of affluent visitors that followed the 1854 arrival of the railway transformed the lives of Kerry's impoverished natives and set in motion a snowball of commercialization that continues today.

But the beauty of the surrounding area—an unbeatable combination of wild mountain scenery and lush foliage—persists. The air smells of damp woods and heather moors. Amazingly, the vegetation is splendid at any time of year. The red fruits of the Mediterranean strawberry tree (*Arbutus unedo*) are at their height in October and November. Also at that time, the bracken turns rust, contrasting with the many evergreens. In late April and early May, the purple flowers of the rhododendron *ponticum* put on a spectacular display. (This Turkish import has adapted so well to the climate that its vigorous growth threatens native oak woods, and many of the purple plants are being dug up by volunteers in an effort to control their spread.)

🐄 You may want to limit time spent in **Killarney Town** itself if discos, Irish cabarets, and singing pubs—the last a local specialty with a strong Irish-American flavor—aren't your thing. Killarney's nightlife is at its liveliest from May to September; Irish and European visitors pack the town in July and August, while peak season for Americans follows in September and October. At other times of the year, particularly from November to mid-March, when many of the hotels are closed, the town is quiet to the point of being eerie. Given the choice, go to Killarney in April, May, or early October.

★ 🐄 On your way to the Gap of Dunloe from Killarney, **Aghadoe,** 5 km (3 mi) outside Killarney on the R562 Beaufort–Killorglin road, is an outstanding place to preview some of the sights to come. Standing beside Aghadoe's 12th-century ruined church and round tower, be sure to remember to breathe as you watch the shadows creep across the Lower Lake, with Innisfallen Island in the distance and the Gap of Dunloe away to the west.

★ 🐄 Massive, glacial rocks form the side of the **Gap of Dunloe,** one of Killarney's primary sights. (The rocks create strange echoes: Give a shout to test it out.) The gap is 7 km (4½ mi) west of Killarney on the R562 Beaufort road and well signposted. The road through the gap stretches

Killarney Area

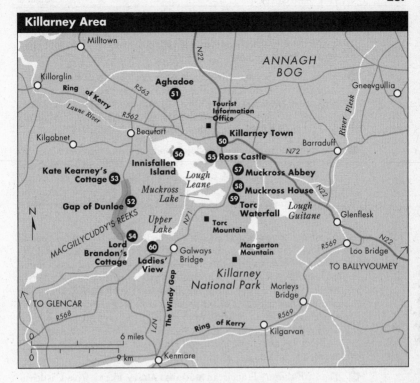

for 6½ km (4 mi)—from ☞ **Kate Kearney's Cottage** to ☞ **Lord Brandon's Cottage**—between MacGillicuddy's Reeks, Ireland's highest mountains to the west, and the Purple Mountains. Five small lakes are strung out beside the road. Cars are banned from the gap, but in summer the first 3 km (2 mi) are busy with horse and foot traffic, much of which turns back at the halfway point.

To see the entire gap and continue on via boat over Upper Lake and Lough Leane, take an organized tour from your hotel or Killarney town center (☞ Guided Tours *in* The Southwest A to Z, *below*). Whether you walk or ride (on horseback or in a jaunting car), you're given 2 hours to get to ☞ **Lord Brandon's Cottage**, at the head of the ☞ **Upper Lake**, where you pick up a boat for the 1¼-hour ride that lands at ☞ **Ross Castle**; from here it's a five-minute walk into town. Most tour companies have a free shuttle service and will pick you up from lodgings within a 5-km (3-mi) radius of Killarney town center. (The value of an organized tour is that you avoid ending up with your car at Dunloe and yourself back in Killarney.)

❸ Kate Kearney's Cottage (✉ Gap of Dunloe, ☎ 064/44116) is a good place to rent a jaunting car (pony and trap) or pony. Kate was a famous beauty who sold illegal *poteen* (moonshine) to visitors from her home, contributing greatly, one suspects, to their enthusiasm for the scenery. Appropriately enough, it's now a pub and a good place to pause for a glass of Irish coffee.

❺ The **Upper Lake** comes into view at the head of the gap, with the lonely Black Valley stretching into the hills at the right. **Lord Brandon's Cottage,** a tea shop serving soup and sandwiches, is open 10 AM to dusk from Easter through September. From here, a path leads to the edge of the lake, and the journey is continued by rowboat. It is an old tradition for the boatman to carry a bugle and illustrate the echoes. Look for caves on the left-hand side when passing through the narrow Middle Lake. The boat passes under Brickeen Bridge and into the **Middle Lake,** where 30 islands are steeped in legends, many of which your boatman is likely to recount.

55 At the end of the journey through the Gap of Dunloe is **Ross Castle,** a fully restored 14th-century stronghold. It was the last place in the province of Munster to fall to Oliver Cromwell's forces in 1652. A later dwelling has 16th- and 17th-century furniture. ☎ *£2.50.* ☉ *May and Sept., daily 9–6; June–Aug., daily 9–6:30; Oct., daily 9–5.*

56 The romantic ruins on **Innisfallen Island** date from the 6th or 7th century. Between 950 and 1350 the *Annals of Innisfallen* were compiled here by monks. (The book survives in the Bodleian Library in Oxford.) You can reach the launch and castle by car. To get to the island, you can rent a rowboat at Ross Castle (£1.50 per hour), or you can join a cruise (£5) in a covered, heated launch.

A half-day trip to Muckross Abbey, Muckross House and Estate, and the Torc Waterfall is another popular excursion from Killarney. Cars are not allowed to drive through the estate grounds, but you'll find a parking lot at the house. Some people choose to make the whole trip by jaunting car, renting one at the stand near the TIO in Killarney. (The cost of a jaunting car is £15–£28, negotiable with the driver, for up to four people. Get an estimate from the TIO.) To save time and money, drive the 4 km (2½ mi) to Muckross Abbey on the N71 Kenmare road, and pick up a jaunting car there. Or, rent a bicycle in town, pack a lunch, and make a day of it.

57 The 15th-century Franciscan **Muckross Abbey,** like ☞ Ross Castle ruined by Cromwell's British troops in 1652, is still amazingly complete, although roofless. An ancient yew tree rises above the cloisters and breaks out over the abbey walls. Three flights of stone steps allow access to the upper floors and living quarters, where you can visit what was once the dormitory, kitchen, and refectory. ⌧ *Muckross Rd.* ☎ *Free.* ☉ *Daily dawn–dusk.*

58 **Muckross House,** a 19th-century, Elizabethan-style manor, now houses the **Kerry Folklife Centre,** where bookbinders, potters, and weavers demonstrate their crafts. The informal grounds here are noted for their rhododendrons and azaleas, the water garden, and the outstanding limestone rock garden. In the park beside the house, the **Kerry Country Life Experience** comprises reconstructed farm buildings and outhouses, a blacksmith's forge, a carpenter's workshop, and a selection of farm animals. It is a reminder of the way things were done on the farm before the advent of electricity and the mechanization of farming. ⌧ *About 1½ km (1 mi) west of the abbey on N71,* ☎ *064/31440.* ☎ *Farms or house £3.80, farms and house £5.50.* ☉ *House Sept.–June, daily 9–5:30; July–Aug., daily 9–7; farms mid-Mar.–Apr., weekends 2–6; May, daily 1–6; June–Sept., daily 10–7; Oct., daily 2–6.*

59 The **Torc Waterfall** is about a 10-minute walk from the parking lot. After your first view of the roaring cascade, it's worth the climb up a long flight of stone steps to the second, less-frequented clearing. If the weather

★ **60** is fine, return to your car and drive on west to **Ladies' View,** a panorama of the three lakes and the surrounding mountains. The name goes back to 1905, when Queen Victoria was a guest at Muckross House. Upon seeing the view of the three lakes, her ladies-in-waiting were said to have been dumbfounded by its beauty. The N71 continues to Kenmare, from where you can complete the circuit by taking the shorter but very narrow Windy Gap route or making a wide sweep via Kilgarvan on R569 and N22, driving back through Killarney to Aghadoe.

Dining and Lodging

$$$$ ✕ **Fredrick's.** Breathtaking views of Killarney's lakes from the rooftop
★ restaurant of the Aghadoe Heights hotel (☞ *below*) make this the ultimate romantic venue. And, as if that weren't enough, the food is outstanding. Silver candelabra, white linen, and fully upholstered chairs
beckon from the tables (ask for one at the front when you book). The
English chef prepares a classic French menu, which varies according
to season. Main courses include classics such as black sole grilled or
meunière or more unusual dishes like medallions of veal with crab souf-
flé. This is one of the most expensive restaurants in Ireland, but it will
provide an unforgettable culinary experience. ⊠ *Aghadoe Heights,* ☎
064/31766. Jacket and tie. AE, DC, MC, V.

$$$ ✕ **Gaby's Seafood.** The best seafood in town packs Gaby's small din-
★ ing room, with its tiled floors, pine booths, and red-gingham cloths
with matching lamp shades. Try the seafood mosaic (seven or eight kinds
of fresh fish in a cream-and-wine sauce) or lobster Gaby (shelled, sim-
mered in a cream-and-cognac sauce, and served back in the shell). ⊠
17 High St., ☎ *064/32519. AE, DC, MC, V. Closed Sun. and mid-
Feb.–mid-Mar. No lunch.*

$$$ ✕ **Strawberry Tree.** There are only eight tables in this tiny, upstairs,
town-center restaurant, but its reputation for imaginative cooking has
spread far and wide. Rustic stone walls, old wooden floors, blue-and-
white linens, and blue-velvet chairs set the stage. Owner-chef Evan Doyle
describes his cooking as very rustic and very Irish, and the fact that all
the food is bought locally from organic growers and free-range pro-
ducers comes out in the tasting. Corned beef is served in cabbage
parcels lined with parsley sauce, salmon is smoked over apple wood,
and pork fillet is stuffed with Clonakilty black pudding. Yer Man's, a
wittily decorated, tiny "olde village pub" underneath, has the same
owner, and it's a good bet for bar food at lunchtime. ⊠ *24 Plunkett
St.,* ☎ *064/32688. AE, DC, MC, V. Closed Dec.–Jan.*

$$ ✕ **Dingles.** If you want to feel more like a local than a visitor, then Gerry
and Marie Cunningham's relaxed town-center restaurant is the place
to go. Open fires, old church pews, and interesting bric-a-brac create
a characterful ambience, while Gerry supplies the warm welcome that
keeps the locals coming back. Marie's cooking uses the best local in-
gredients in simple, unshowy dishes like mussels in cream and herb sauce
as well as baked crab and prawns au gratin. ⊠ *40 New St.,* ☎ *064/
31079. AE, MC, DC, V. Closed Nov.–Mar. No lunch.*

$ ✕ **Sheila's.** Simply furnished with stripped-pine tables and red paper
place mats, Sheila's has fed the people of Killarney and its visitors for
more than 30 years—it was recently handed down from mother to daugh-
ter. The unpretentious menu features such Irish specials as corned beef
with cabbage and Irish stew (Kerry lamb stewed with barley, carrots,
onion, and potatoes). In a town bedeviled by tourist traps, this friendly
spot is an excellent value. The restaurant is licensed to serve wine only.
⊠ *75 High St.,* ☎ *064/31270. AE, DC, MC, V.*

$$$$ ✕🏠 **Aghadoe Heights.** Its location on a bluff 4 km (2½ mi) outside town
(on the Tralee side, signposted off N22) translates into unforgettable
lake views that will long remain with you—especially if enjoyed from
the aerie of the famous hotel restaurant, Fredrick's, one of Ireland's best
(☞ *above*). Eight acres of grounds ensure absolute peace and quiet. The
luxurious interior is a pleasant combination of antique and modern styles.
Most bedrooms have lake views, and all are relatively large, with good-
size bathrooms, matching floral drapes and spreads, lace-covered cush-
ions, and fitted natural wood furniture. Note: The hotel will be closed
until April 2000 for renovations. ⊠ *Aghadoe Heights, Co. Kerry,* ☎
064/31766, 🅵🅰🆇 *064/31345. 60 rooms with bath, 3 suites. Restaurant,
bar, indoor pool, sauna, tennis court, fishing. AE, DC, MC, V.*

$$ ✕🏨 **Beaufort House.** This secluded Georgian house, set in 40 acres of woodland and situated 9 km (5½ mi) outside Killarney on the R562 Killorglin road, is convenient for both Killarney and the Ring of Kerry. An enthusiastic young couple, Donald and Rachel Cameron, renovated the house in 1994. They like to warn their guests that while they offer peace and privacy, two small children and a dog are also in residence. The hall, library, and drawing room all have open fires. The large, uncluttered rooms are furnished with a variety of antiques. The evening meal, often featuring local lamb or home-caught fish, must be booked 24 hours ahead. Three kilometers (2 mi) of private salmon and trout fishing are nearby on the River Laune. ⊠ *Co. Kerry,* ☎ *064/44764,* FAX *064/44764. 4 rooms with bath. Fishing. MC, V. Closed Nov.–Easter, except by arrangement.*

$$ ✕🏨 **Foley's.** Inside this 19th-century former coaching inn in the center of town, chef-owner Carol Hartnett does the cooking and makes use of local ingredients, including superior Irish cream and butter. Roulade of trout stuffed with prawn mousse and grilled T-bone steak with garlic butter are two typical main dishes. The wine list offers more than 200 selections, and a pianist entertains in summer. All rooms in the interconnected town houses above the restaurant are decorated with Victorian antiques and old country furniture, including sofas and chaises lounges; windows are double-glazed, so the rooms are quieter than you would expect. ⊠ *23 High St., Co. Kerry,* ☎ *064/31217,* FAX *064/34683. 32 rooms with bath. AE, DC, MC, V. Closed Nov.–Mar.*

$$ ✕🏨 **The Mills Inn.** If you wince at the idea of Killarney's tour-bus crowds, consider staying 15 minutes' drive from town in this old coaching inn. Ballyvourney is a small, Irish-speaking village on the main Cork–Killarney road, distinguished only by the rapid-flowing River Sullane. But hosts Denis and Mary Scannell rightly claim the inn is "where you meet the real Ireland." It also suits lovers of the outdoor life; special deals are available for golfers and hikers. The inn incorporates an old castle ruin, once a hunting lodge belonging to the Macarthys of Blarney Castle (☞ *above*), as well as a stable yard, pretty gardens, two bars, and a restaurant. Rooms, well insulated from bar and traffic noise, have bright walls and cozy cottage furnishings. The restaurant serves generous portions of local beef and seafood from Kenmare; the main bar, which often hosts live music, has simple, hearty fare such as Irish Stew. ⊠ *Ballyvourney, Macroom, Co. Cork,* ☎ *026/45237,* FAX *026/45454. 12 rooms with bath. Restaurant, 2 bars. MC, V.*

$ ✕🏨 **Climber's Inn.** The name says it all: This place is primarily for walkers and climbers. Its location, 30 km (18 mi) from town in a tiny village at the base of Ireland's highest mountain, Carrantouhill, is an inspiration in itself. Rooms are simple but spotlessly clean and far from spartan, with sturdy pine beds, brightly colored duvet covers and curtains, and power showers. The bar serves award-winning pub grub, including local sea trout from Caragh Lake (a real delicacy, quite unlike commercially reared trout), and the famous Irish stew—Highland lamb casserole. Guided wilderness walks, which could be the most memorable adventure you have in Ireland, can be prebooked. The inn also houses Glencar's post office and shop. ⊠ *Glencar, Co. Kerry,* ☎ *066/976–0101,* FAX *066/976–0104. 10 rooms with bath, 1 dorm with 10 bunks. Bar, fishing. AE, DC, MC, V. Closed Mon.–Thurs. Nov.–mid Mar.*

$$$ 🏨 **Europe.** A secluded lakeside location (a five-minute drive from town) and luxurious but unfussy decor give this modern, five-story hotel the edge over its competitors. Most bedrooms have solid-pine trim, a lake view, and a private balcony. The spacious lounges and lobbies, although a bit impersonal, have picture windows overlooking the lake and mountains, an imaginative display of old carved timber, and antiques. The sports facilities, including an Olympic-size pool, are among

the best and most up-to-date in the area. ✉ *Killorglin Rd., Fossa, Co. Kerry,* ☎ *064/31900,* ⓕⓐⓧ *064/32118. 205 rooms with bath. 2 restaurants, 2 bars, pool, sauna, tennis court, horseback riding, fishing, bicycles. AE, DC, MC, V. Closed Nov.–Mar. 15.*

$$ 🏨 **Glencar House.** Hikers, anglers, and wilderness lovers will be happy out here in the Kerry Highlands, about 20 minutes' drive from Killarney Town and 10 minutes' drive from Killorglin. (From Killarney, turn off the N72 Killorglin road at the sign for Beaufort, and turn right at the first T-junction.) The rambling two-story house was originally built as a hunting lodge in 1670 by the Earl of Lansdowne. Today it is a small, unpretentious country house, with huge elk antlers over the fireplace and stuffed birds and animals at every turn. Rooms are relatively spacious, with country pine furniture and breathtaking views of Killarney's famous mountain range, the MacGillicuddy's Reeks. ✉ *Glencar, Co. Kerry,* ☎ *066/976–0102,* ⓕⓐⓧ *066/976–60167. 18 rooms with bath. Restaurant, bar, fishing. MC, V.*

$ 🏨 **Arbutus.** Run by the friendly Buckley family since it was built more than 60 years ago, this is a good budget hotel in the town center—a short step from the bus and train station and a three-minute walk from the main shopping and dining area. The lobby has an open fire, and the quiet, oak-paneled bar is popular with locals. The rooms in the second-story section are recommended for their roominess and updated furnishings. ✉ *College St., Co. Kerry,* ☎ *064/31037,* ⓕⓐⓧ *064/34033. 44 rooms with bath. Restaurant, bar. AE, DC, MC, V.*

$ 🏨 **Earls Court House.** In a quiet suburb within walking distance of the town center, this comfortable guest house is furnished with interesting antiques collected by Emer Moynihan, who likes to greet her guests with tea or coffee and scones. Bedrooms are spacious, with large bathrooms and an elegant mix of antique and reproduction Victorian furniture. Breakfast is served at mahogany tables in a large, sunny, wooden-floored room; menu choices include pancakes and kippers. ✉ *Woodlawn Junction, Muckross Rd., Co. Kerry,* ☎ *064/34009,* ⓕⓐⓧ *064/ 34366. 11 rooms with bath. MC, V.*

$ 🏨 **Lime Court.** Budget accommodations have been springing up along the Muckross road between Killarney and the national park; this one is only a five-minute walk from the town center. The modern building has two large bay windows at the front, with the rooms in an extension behind it, away from the road. Antiques and large potted plants adorn the reception area, while a baby grand piano anchors the spacious lounge. The relatively large guest rooms overlook green fields and are light, airy, and plainly but comfortably furnished with small sitting areas. ✉ *Muckross Rd., Co. Kerry,* ☎ *064/34547,* ⓕⓐⓧ *064/34121. 16 rooms with bath. Ping-Pong. MC, V.*

Medieval Banquets

The **Killarney Manor Banquet** offers a five-course meal hosted by "Lord and Lady Killarney" in their 1860, castellated manor house. The food, with a choice of poached salmon or roast Kerry lamb for the main course, is served by waitresses in 19th-century costume. The entertainment is excellent by any standards, with a team of professional singers and dancers presenting favorite Irish tunes. ✉ *Loreto Rd.,* ☎ *064/31551.* 🎫 *Entertainment plus 5-course meal and mulled-wine reception £28, entertainment only £10.* ☼ *Apr.–Oct., daily 8 PM: entertainment 8:45–10:45.*

Nightlife and the Arts

Singing bars are popular in Killarney, where a professional leads the songs and encourages audience participation and solos. Try the **Laurels** (✉ Main St., ☎ 064/31149). **Buckley's Bar** (✉ College St., ☎ 064/ 31037) in the Arbutus Hotel has traditional entertainment nightly from June to September. The **Crypt Nightclub** (✉ College Sq., ☎ 064/

31038) is a spook-themed late-night venue for the over-23s. **Gleneagles** (⊠ Muckross Rd., ☎ 064/31870) is the place for big-name cabaret—from Sharon Shannon to the Wolfe Tones—and also has a late-night disco.

Outdoor Activities and Sports

FISHING

Killarney's lakes and rivers have salmon and brown trout. **O'Neill's** (⊠ Plunkett St., ☎ 064/31970) provides fishing tackle, bait, and licenses. To improve your technique contact **Angler's Paradise** (⊠ Loreto Rd., Muckross, ☎ 064/33818), where the Michael O'Brien International Fishing School organizes game, coarse, and deep-sea fishing trips by day or by night.

GOLF

For many people, the two courses at the legendary **Killarney Golf and Fishing Club** (⊠ Mahony's Point, ☎ 064/31034) are the chief reason they're in town; for details *see* Chapter 9. **Beaufort Golf Course** (⊠ Churchtown, Beaufort, ☎ 064/44440) has an 18-hole, par-71 course surrounded by magnificent scenery, and unlike most other Irish golf clubs, it has buggy, trolley, and club-rental facilities.

HIKING AND WALKING

The **Mangerton walking trail** is reached by turning left off N71 midway between Muckross Abbey and Muckross House (following signposts). The summit of **Mangerton Mountain** (2,756 ft) can be reached on foot in about 2 hours—less should you choose to rent a pony (☞ Horseback Riding, *below*). **Torc Mountain** (1,764 ft) can be reached off Route N71; it is a satisfying 1½-hour climb. Do not attempt mountain climbing in the area in misty weather, since visibility can quickly drop to zero. The **Kerry Way,** a long-distance walking route, passes through the **Killarney National Park** on its way to Glenbeigh (detailed leaflet from the TIO). For the less adventurous, four safe and well-signposted nature trails of varying lengths are at hand in the national park. Try the 4-km (2½-mi) Arthur Young's Walk, which passes through old yew and oak woods frequented by Sika deer.

HORSEBACK RIDING

Killarney Riding Stables Ltd. (⊠ Ballydowney, ☎ 064/31686) organizes four- and seven-day treks in Killarney National Park, with accommodation.

Shopping

Shopping in Killarney means crafts and souvenirs, and the most reliable crafts stores are on Main Street and High Street; they all carry a standard range of crystal, handknits, T-shirts, sweatshirts, and tweed hats. **Blarney Woolen Mills** (⊠ 10–11 Main St., ☎ 064/33222) has a large selection of crafts, clothing, and souvenirs. **Bricín Craft Shop** (⊠ 26 High St., ☎ 064/34902) has an interesting collection of handmade crafts including candles, ceramics, and handwoven wool. The **Sweater Company** (⊠ 3 New St., ☎ 064/35406) carries classic, traditional, and designer knitwear. **MacBee's** (⊠ New St., ☎ 064/33622) is a stylish modern boutique stocking the best of Irish high fashion. Visit the **Frank Lewis Gallery** (⊠ 6 Bridewell La., beside General Post Office, ☎ 064/34843) for original paintings and sculptures.

THE DINGLE PENINSULA

The Dingle Peninsula stretches for some 48 km (30 mi) between Tralee (pronounced tra-*lee*) in the east and Slea Head in the west. Small in size yet topographically diverse and brazenly scenic, Dingle's peninsula is composed of rugged mountains and cliffs, interspersed with softly molded glacial valleys and lakes. Along its coast stretch long, sandy beaches and rocky cliffs pounded by the Atlantic Ocean. On the coastal plains, drystone walls enclose small, irregular fields, while exceptional prehistoric and early Christian remains are scattered throughout the peninsula. Dingle is also notorious for its heavy rainfall and an impenetrable sea mist, which can strike at any time of year. (If it does, sit it out in Dingle Town or the village of Dunquin, and enjoy the friendly bars, cafés, and crafts shops.) At its far western end, west of Dingle Town, the peninsula, like parts of County Kerry, is Gaeltacht: Irish is still spoken on a daily basis, although like most other Gaeltacht communities, it is bilingual nowadays, with English as the second language.

The peninsula can be covered in a long day trip of about 160 km (99 mi). (If mist or continuous rain is forecast, postpone your trip until visibility improves.) From Killarney, Killorglin, or Tralee, head for Castlemaine, and take the coast road (R561 and R559) to the town of Dingle. You'll pass through the sheltered seaside resort of Inch, 19 km (12 mi) west of Castlemaine and 45 km (28 mi) northwest of Killarney, where the head of Dingle Bay is cut off by two sand spits that enclose Castlemaine Harbour. Inch has a 6½-km (4-mi) sandy beach backed by dunes that are home to a large colony of natterjack toads.

Annascaul

⑥ *7 km (4½ mi) west of Inch.*

Near the junction of the Castlemaine and Tralee roads, Annascaul was an important livestock center until the 1930s. This explains why such a small village has such a wide road—cattle trading was carried out in the streets—and also why it boasts so many pubs for so few residents. Photographers will be tempted to snap **Dan Foley's** (☎ 066/915–7257) flamboyantly painted pub. Wander in for a pint, and have a chat with Dan, who is also a magician, a farmer, and an expert on local history.

Dingle Town

⑥ *18 km (11 mi) west of Annascaul, 67 km (42 mi) west of Killarney, 45 km (28 mi) west of Killorglin on R561.*

Backed by mountains and facing a sheltered harbor, Dingle, the chief town of its eponymous peninsula, has a year-round population of 1,400 that more than doubles in the summer months. Although many expect Dingle to be a quaint and undeveloped Gaeltacht village, Dingle in fact offers a wide choice of crafts shops, seafood restaurants, and pubs; still, its main streets—the Mall, Main and Strand streets, and The Wood—can be covered in less than an hour. Celebrity hawks, take note: Off-season Dingle is favored as a hideaway by several celebrities, including Julia Roberts, Paul Simon, and Dolly Parton. These and others have their visits commemorated on Green Street's "path of stars."

Dingle's pubs are well known for their music, but among them **O'Flaherty's** (✉ Bridge St., at the entrance to town, ☎ 066/915–1983), a simple, stone-floored bar, is something special and a mecca for traditional musicians. Spontaneous "sessions" occur most nights in July and August, less frequently at other times. Even without music, this pub provides a good spot to compare notes with fellow travelers.

Since 1985 Dingle's central attraction, apart from its music scene, has been a winsome bottle-nosed dolphin who has taken up residence in the harbor. The Dingle dolphin, or **Fungie,** as he has been named, will play for hours with swimmers (a wet suit is essential) and scuba divers, and he follows local boats in and out of the harbor. It is impossible to predict whether he will stay, but boatmen have become so confident of a sighting that they offer trippers their money back if Fungie does not appear. Boat trips (£5) leave the pier hourly in July and August between 11 and 6, weather permitting. At other times, call Jimmy Flannery Sr. (☎ 066/915–1163).

Dining and Lodging

$$ ✕ **Beginish.** Dingle is an oasis in a culinary desert, although this spot
★ is outstanding by any standard. Muted classical music floats through the small rooms, carpeted in pale green, with fresh flowers on the blue-linen tablecloths. The food imaginatively interprets French nouvelle cuisine; specialties include brill fillets on leek fondue with white-wine sauce, and fillet of lamb in phyllo pastry with duxelles. The wine list, with about 100 choices, includes a good selection of half-bottles. ✉ *Green St.,* ☎ *066/915–1588. AE, DC, MC, V. Closed Mon. and mid-Nov.–mid-Mar.*

$ ✕ **Fenton's.** Step beyond the yellow door of this town house to find a cozy, cottage-style restaurant with quarry-tile floors and local art for sale on the walls. The candlelit tables are covered in oilcloth, but the napkins are linen. The bistro-style menu is straightforward and unfussy, allowing for a quick turnover during Dingle's hectic high season. Some dishes, like the cassoulet of mussels in a garlic cream sauce, are available in starter or main-course portions. Sirloin steak is served with caramelized onions and a red-wine sauce. ✉ *Green St.,* ☎ *066/915–1209, AE, DC, MC, V. Closed mid-Nov.–mid-Mar.*

$$$ 🏠 **Dingle Skellig.** A five-minute walk from town center, this is a showcase of Irish craft, art, and design. The light-wood-framed, octagonal reception area has specially commissioned stained-glass doors, and original paintings hang in the corridors. The spacious rooms have modern, pale-wood furniture and drapes and spreads with bold prints; more than half have sea views (if you want one, say so when reserving). Floor-to-ceiling windows in the Coastguard Restaurant look out over Dingle Bay; this is the town's only eatery right at the water's edge, and, as you'd expect, the specialty is seafood. ✉ *Co. Kerry,* ☎ *066/915–1144,* 𝔉𝔄𝔛 *066/915–1501. 110 rooms with bath. Restaurant, bar, pool, steam room, exercise room. AE, DC, MC, V. Closed Dec. 23–27 and Jan.–mid-Mar.*

$ 🏠 **Alpine House.** Dingle is surrounded by a rash of newly built and relatively characterless dormer bungalow-style guest houses. The landmark Alpine is neither spanking new nor old-world. In fact, this plain, family-run, three-story establishment is one of the original guest houses in Dingle, dating from 1963. The location, at the entrance to the town with views over Dingle Bay, is superb. It is quiet, yet Dingle's harbor, pubs, and restaurants are only a two-minute walk away, and private parking is also available. Rooms are bright and cheerful, with pine furnishings, and well equipped for the price range. The value-for-money Alpine has many fans, so book well ahead year-round. ✉ *Mail Rd., Co. Kerry,* ☎ *066/915–1250,* 𝔉𝔄𝔛 *066/915–1966. 10 rooms with bath. MC, V.*

$ 🏠 **Greenmount House.** Wonderful views of the town and harbor await at this modern B&B, a short walk uphill from the town center (turn right at the roundabout at the entrance to Dingle and right again when you come to the first T-junction). A modern bungalow connects to an extension, where six suites each have a sitting room and balcony. Rooms in the original house, though smaller, are impeccable and comfortably decorated with pine beds and floral drapes and spreads. An outstanding breakfast is served in the conservatory, which connects the two buildings. ✉ *Gortanora, Co. Kerry,* ☎ *066/915–1414,* 𝔉𝔄𝔛 *066/915–1974. 12 rooms with bath. Lobby lounge. MC, V.*

$ ⊡ **Pax House.** A kilometer (½ mi) from the town center, this solid modern bungalow has a panorama of Dingle Harbour. Stand on the balcony and watch the fishing boats return with their catch while the sun sets slowly in the west. Rooms are simple but well equipped. Breakfast is a generous affair, with fresh seafood on the menu and a selection of Irish cheeses on the buffet. ⊠ *Upper John St., Co. Kerry,* ☎ *066/915–1650,* ℻ *066/915–1518. 7 rooms with bath. No credit cards.*

Nightlife

Nearly every bar on the Dingle Peninsula, particularly in the town of Dingle, offers music nightly in July and August. **O'Flaherty's** (☞ *above*) is a fine place for traditional music. For sing-along and dance, try **An Reált—The Star Bar** (⊠ The Pier, ☎ no phone).

Outdoor Activities and Sports

BICYCLES

You're likely to remember a bike ride around Slea Head (☞ *below*) for a long time to come. Bicycles may be rented at **Dingle Bicycle Hire** (⊠ The Tracks, ☎ 066/915–2166).

Shopping

Lisbeth Mulcahy at the **Weaver's Shop** (⊠ Green St., ☎ 066/915–1688) sells outstanding handwoven, vegetable-dyed woolen wraps, mufflers, and fabric for making skirts. **Cosai** (⊠ Strand St., ☎ 066/915–2052) sells a variety of Irish-made crafts. Don't miss Dingle's café-bookshop, one of the first in the world. Visit **An Cafe Liteartha** (☎ 066/915–1388), for new and secondhand books of local interest, and friendly conversation.

Ventry

63 *8 km (5 mi) west of Dingle Town on R561.*

The next town after Dingle along the coast, Ventry has a small outcrop of pubs and newsagents and a long, sandy beach with safe bathing and ponies for rent. Between Ventry and Dunquin, you'll find several interesting archaeological sites on the spectacular, cliff-top road along Slea Head.

64 **Dunbeg,** the Iron Age promontory fort, can be seen on the left below the road, after you pass between two tall hedges of fuchsia bushes about 6 km (4 mi) west of Ventry (it's freely accessible; follow the signposts across fields). A fortified stone wall cuts off the promontory, and the landward side is protected by an elaborate system of earthworks and trenches. Within the enclosure is a ruined circular building, with walls up to 22 ft wide. Unlike Staigue Fort on the Ring of Kerry (☞ *above*), this was not a homestead but most probably a refuge in times of danger.

En Route If you continue west along the coast road beyond Dunbeg, you'll see signs indicating "Prehistoric Beehive Huts"—*clocháns* in Irish. Built of unmortared stone on the southern slopes of Mt. Eagle, these cells were used by hermit monks in the early Christian period; some 414 exist between Slea Head and Dunquin. Due to the increase in traffic, some local farmers, on whose land these monuments stand, are charging a "trespass fee" of 50p from visitors.

Slea Head

★ **65** *7 km (5 mi) west of Dingle Town on R561.*

From the top of the towering cliffs of Slea Head, the view of the Blasket Islands and the Atlantic Ocean is unforgettable—guaranteed to stop you in your tracks. Alas, Slea Head has become so popular that tour buses, barely able to negotiate the narrow road, are causing traffic jams, particularly in July and August. **Coumenole,** the long, sandy strand below, looks beautiful and sheltered, but swimming here is dangerous. This treacherous stretch of coast has claimed many lives in shipwrecks—most recently in 1982, when a large cargo boat, the *Ranga,* foundered on the rocks and sank. In 1588, four ships of the Spanish Armada were driven through the Blasket Sound; two made it to shelter, and two sank. One of these, the *Santa Maria de la Rosa,* was found only recently and is currently being excavated by divers during the summer months.

★ **66** The largest of the **Blasket Islands** visible from Slea Head, the **Great Blasket,** was inhabited until 1953. The Blasket islanders were great storytellers and were encouraged by Irish linguists to write their memoirs. *The Islandman,* by Tomás O Crohán, gives a vivid picture of a hard way of life. "Their likes will not be seen again," O Crohán poignantly observed. The **Blasket Centre** explains the heritage of these islanders and celebrates their use of the Irish language with videos and exhibitions. ✉ *Dunquin, Dingle Peninsula,* ☎ *066/915–6371.* 💷 *£2.50.* ☉ *Easter–May and Sept., daily 10–6; July–Aug., 10–7.*

Dunquin

67 *9 km (5½ mi) west of Ventry on R559.*

Once the mainland harbor for the islanders, Dunquin is at the center of the Gaeltacht, and it attracts many students of Irish language and folklore. David Lean shot *Ryan's Daughter* hereabouts in 1969. The movie gave the area its first major boost in tourism, though it was lambasted by critics—"Gush made respectable by millions of dollars tastefully wasted," lamented Pauline Kael—sending Lean into a dry spell he didn't come out of until 1984's *A Passage to India.* **Kruger's Pub** (☎ 066/915–6127), Dunquin's main social center, has long been frequented by artists and writers—including Brendan Behan—and it still is; it's also the only eatery for miles and a good place to stop for a bite.

Dunquin's pier (signposted from the main road) is surrounded by cliffs of colored Silurian rock, more than 400 million years old and rich in fossils. Down at the pier you'll see *curraughs* (open fishing boats traditionally made of animal hide stretched over wooden laths and tarred) stored upside down, usually covered in canvas. Three or four men walk the curraghs out to the sea, holding them aloft over their heads. Similar boats are used in the Aran Islands (☞ Chapter 6), and, when properly handled, they prove extraordinarily seaworthy. If you're interested in going out to the Blaskets, inquire at the pier in June, July, and August for boats heading to Great Blasket during the day, depending on the weather. (There's no scheduled ferry service, nor a phone.)

En Route   Between Dunquin and Ballyferriter, the road skirts **Clogher Strand**—not a safe spot to swim, but a good place to watch the ocean dramatically pounding the rocks when a storm is approaching or a gale is blowing. Overlooking the beach is **Louis Mulcahy's pottery studio.** One of Ireland's leading ceramic artists, Mulcahy produces large pots and urns that are both decorative and functional. He has trained several local people to work in the studio, and visitors are welcome to watch the work in progress and to buy items at workshop prices. ✉ *Clogher Strand,* ☎ *066/915–6229.* ☉ *Daily 9:30–6.*

Ballyferriter

68 *5 km (3 mi) northeast of Dunquin, 14 km (9 mi) west of Dingle on R559.*

Like the other towns at this end of the peninsula, Ballyferriter is a Gaeltacht village, and mainly a holiday spot for vacationers with RVs, many of them German or Dutch. The area around here is great for walking. In 1580, an invasion force of about 600 Spaniards and Italians
69 built a new fortress within **Dún an Óir,** originally an Iron Age promontory fort about 3 km (2 mi) beyond Ballyferriter. They came to support the Catholic-Irish against the Protestant-English. The English successfully bombarded the fort from land and sea, and they then slaughtered all survivors, including many innocent local inhabitants. Dún an Óir—which means "Fort of Gold" in Irish—is now largely obliterated, but folk memory of the massacre is so strong that a memorial was erected on the site in 1980. ▦ *Free.*

One of the best-preserved, early Christian churches in all of Ireland,
70 **Gallarus Oratory** dates from the 7th or 8th century and ingeniously makes use of corbeling—successive levels of stone projecting inward from both side walls until they meet at the top to form an unmortared roof. The structure is still watertight after more than 1,000 years. ▦ *Free.*

71 **Kilmakedar Church** is one of the finest examples of Romanesque (early Irish) architecture surviving. Although the Christian settlement dates from the 7th century, the present structure was built in the 12th century. Native builders integrated foreign influences with their own local traditions, keeping the blank arcades and round-headed windows but using stone roofs, sloping doorway jambs, and weirdly sculpted heads. Ogham stones and other interestingly carved, possibly pre-Christian stones are on display in the churchyard. ▦ *Free.*

72 The summit of **Mt. Brandon** (3,127 ft) is on the left as you cross the **Connor Pass** from south to north (☞ *below*) and is accessible only to hikers. Do not attempt the climb in misty weather. The easiest way to make the climb is to follow the old pilgrims' path, the Saint's Road; it starts at Kilmakedar Church and rises to the summit from Ballybrack, which is the end of the road for cars. At the summit, you'll reach the ruins of an early Christian settlement. The top can also be approached from a path that starts just beyond Cloghane (signposted left on descending the Connor Pass); the latter climb is longer and more strenuous.

En Route From Kilmakedar, return to Dingle on the well-signposted main road (R559); then head north across the **Connor Pass,** a mountain route that passes over the center of the peninsula and offers magnificent views of **Brandon Bay, Tralee Bay,** and the beaches of North Kerry, with **Dingle Bay** in the south. It was from Brandon Bay that Brendan the Navigator (AD 487–577) is believed to have set off on his famous voyages in a specially constructed curragh. On his third trip it is possible that he reached Newfoundland or Labrador, then Florida. Brendan was the inspiration for many voyagers, including Christopher Columbus.

Blennerville

73 *60 km (37 mi) east of Ballyferriter, 5 km (3 mi) west of Tralee on R560.*

Before you reach Tralee, a five-story **windmill** with black and white sails is the main attraction in Blennerville. The surrounding buildings have been turned into a visitor center, with crafts workshops, an audiovisual history of the windmill, hands-on activities like flour grinding, and an exhibition recalling Blennerville's past as County Kerry's main point of emigration during the Great Famine (1845–49). ☎ 066/712–1064. 🖼 £2.50. 🕙 Apr.–Oct., daily 10–5.

A very popular **steam railway** shuttles back and forth between Blennerville and Tralee, with departures from each terminus every half hour April through September. ☎ 066/712–7444. 🖼 £2.50.

Tralee

74 5 km (3 mi) east of Blennerville, 50 km (31 mi) northeast of Dingle on R559.

County Kerry's capital and its largest town, Tralee (population 21,000) has neither ruins nor quaint architecture, yet it makes a go at attracting visitors without them. Tralee has long been associated with the popular Irish song "The Rose of Tralee," the inspiration for the annual **Rose of Tralee International Festival.** The last week of August, Irish communities from around the world send young women to join native Irish competitors; one of them is chosen as the "Rose of Tralee." Visitors, musicians, and entertainers pack the town; a horse race run at the same time contributes to the crowds. Tralee is also the home of **Siamsa Tíre**—the National Folk Theatre of Ireland, which stages dances and plays based on Irish folklore (☞ Nightlife and the Arts, below).

The **Kerry County Museum,** Tralee's major cultural attraction, traces the history of Kerry's people from 5000 BC to the present using dioramas and an entertaining audiovisual show; there's also a streetcar ride through a life-size reconstruction of Tralee in the Middle Ages. ⊠ Ashe Memorial Hall, Denny St., ☎ 066/712–7777. 🖼 £3.50. 🕙 Sept.–July, Mon.–Sat. 10–6; Aug., Mon.–Sat. 10–8.

Ireland's biggest water complex, **AquaDome** has sky-high water slides, a wave pool, raging rapids, water cannons, and other thrills; adults can seek refuge in the Sauna Dome. ⊠ Dingle Rd., ☎ 066/712–8899. 🖼 £4. 🕙 Mid-May–Aug., daily 10–10; Sept.–mid-May, weekdays 2–10, weekends 11–8.

Dining and Lodging

$$$ 🏨 **Ballyseede Castle.** Golfers, take note: The former Fitzgerald Cas-
★ tle is within easy reach of five of the best courses in the region. Victorian additions complement this 15th-century, three-story building. Individually decorated rooms are generously furnished with antiques, and two magnificent drawing rooms with ornamental plasterwork and marble fireplaces complete the picture. Try the Yeats room, which is one of the fanciest. Ballyseede is 3 km (2 mi) east of Tralee on the main Killarney road. ⊠ Co. Kerry, ☎ 066/712–5799, FAX 066/712–5287. 12 rooms with bath. Restaurant, bar, horseback riding, fishing. DC, MC, V.

$$ 🏨 **Abbeygate.** Built in 1995 on the site of Tralee's old marketplace (virtually in the town center, though on a quiet spot behind today's main shopping street), this is an attractive addition to the town's hotels. Nicely sized rooms have country-style wood furniture and large, tiled bathrooms. The Old Market Place Pub, a rambling, imaginatively designed bar, seats 500 people and is built in the traditional style with wood floors, open fires, and a cozy atmosphere. There is bar food at lunchtime and music and dancing nightly from June to September and at least three nights a week at other times. ⊠ Maine St., Co. Kerry, ☎ 066/712–9888, FAX 066/712–9821. 100 rooms with bath. Restaurant, 2 bars. AE, DC, MC, V.

$$ 🏨 **Brandon.** A modern, five-story hotel in the center of town, the Brandon is not especially exciting, but it is the only place in Tralee with a pool and a fitness center. The decent-size rooms are furnished plainly with chunky pine and have uninspiring urban views. The restaurant is reputable. Rates shoot up during the Rose of Tralee Festival (late August) and the Listowel races (third week in September). ⊠ *Princes St., Co. Kerry,* ☎ *066/712–3333,* FAX *066/712–5019. 182 rooms with bath. Restaurant, 2 bars, indoor pool, sauna, steam room, health club, horseback riding, fishing. AE, DC, MC, V.*

Nightlife and the Arts

Try to catch the **National Folk Theater of Ireland** (Siamsa Tíre). Language is no barrier to this colorful entertainment, which re-creates traditional rural life through music, mime, and dance. ⊠ *Godfrey Pl.,* ☎ *066/712–3055.* ✒ *£5.* ☉ *Shows July–Aug., Mon.–Sat. at 8:30; May–June and Sept., Tues. and Thurs. at 8:30.*

Ballad sessions are more popular here than is traditional Irish music. **Horan's Hotel** (⊠ Clash St., ☎ 066/712–1933) has disco music and cabaret acts nightly during July and August and on weekends only during the off-season.

Outdoor Activities and Sports

BICYCLES

Bicycles can be rented from **Tralee Bike Hire** (⊠ Ashe St., ☎ 066/712–7527).

GOLF

You are in the heart of great golfing country in Tralee. For detailed descriptions of **Ballybunion Golf Club** (⊠ Ballybunion, ☎ 068/27146) and **Tralee Golf Club** (⊠ West Barrow, Ardfert, ☎ 066/713–6379), ☞ Chapter 9.

HORSEBACK RIDING

El Rancho Farmhouse and Riding Stables (⊠ Ballyard, ☎ 066/712–1840) specializes in residential trekking holidays on the Dingle trail between Tralee and the Dingle Peninsula.

OFF THE
BEATEN PATH
BALLYBUNION – A detour 41 km (25 mi) northwest of Tralee on N69 and R553 will take you to this seaside resort, famous for its long, sandy beach and championship golf course (☞ Chapter 9). A large bronze statue of President Clinton commemorates a round he played in 1998.

NORTH KERRY AND SHANNONSIDE

Until several decades ago, Shannon meant little more to most people—if it meant anything at all, that is—than the name of the longest river in the British Isles, running for 273 km (170 mi) from County Cavan to Limerick City in County Clare. But mention Shannon nowadays and people think immediately of the major airport, which has become the principal gateway to western Ireland. In turn, what also comes to mind are many of the glorious sights of North Kerry and Shannonside: a slew of historic castles, including Bunratty, Glin, and Knappogue (several feature wonderful medieval banquets); Adare, sometimes called "Ireland's Prettiest Village," and the neighboring Adare Manor, one of Ireland's grandest country-house hotels; and Limerick City, which now attracts visitors tracing the memories so movingly captured in in Frank McCourt's international best-seller, *Angela's Ashes.* Picking up where the Dingle Peninsula route left off, this itinerary begins in Listowel, in the northwest of County Kerry, and then jumps across the Kerry-Limerick border, where the first stop is in Glin, on the south side of the Shannon estuary. Limerick City, the Republic's third largest, and those parts of County Clare on the north side of the Shannon round it out. A hint to travelers arriving at Shannon Airport: If you plan to focus on the Southwest, follow the tours outlined in this chapter from back to front.

Listowel

⑦ *27 km (16 mi) northwest of Tralee on N69.*

A small, sleepy market town, Listowel only really comes alive for its annual horse race during the third week of September. You reach the town from the west by driving along a plain at the base of Stack's Mountain.

Dining

$–$$$ ✕ **Allo's Bar and Bistro.** Just off Listowel's main square, this rustic bar dates from 1859 and serves the best local produce, freshly prepared. Chefs Armel Whyte and Theo Lynch offer local beef and lamb but are best known for their imaginative fish recipes, which often feature oysters and lobster, not otherwise widely available hereabouts. ⊠ *41 Church St.,* ☎ *068/22880. AE, MC, V. No lunch or dinner Sun. No dinner Feb.*

En Route From Listowel, head northeast on N69 18 km (11 mi) to **Tarbert,** the terminus for the **ferry to Killimer** in West Clare, a convenient 20-minute shortcut if you're heading for the west of Ireland. The **Shannon,** with a length of 273 km (170 mi), is the longest river in Ireland or Britain. The magnificent estuary stretches westward for a further 96 km (60 mi) before reaching the sea.

Glin

⑦ *5 km (3 mi) east of Tarbert on N69, 51 km (32 mi) north of Tralee on N69.*

The Fitzgerald family has held the title of Knight of Glin since the 14th century. While the family has built numerous structures in the area, ★ the present **Glin Castle,** situated on the banks of the Shannon, dates only from 1785. Between 1820 and 1836 the 25th knight added crenellations and Gothic details to make the house look more like an ancestral home. A delicate plasterwork ceiling, painted in the original red and green, graces the neoclassic hall, which opens onto a splendid "flying" staircase: two risers that join to a single central tongue. The present Knight of Glin (the 29th), Desmond Fitzgerald, a Harvard-educated art historian, is an expert on Irish decorative arts (and an outspoken arts advocate), so it's fitting that the house has an exceptional collection of Irish 18th-century mahogany and walnut furniture. ⊠ *Co. Limerick,* ☎ *068/34173.* ⊡ *£3.50.* ☉ *May–June, daily 10–noon and 2–4; other times by appointment.*

Dining and Lodging

$$$$ ✕⊡ **Glin Castle.** The Fitzgerald family home offers a genuine experience of Irish castle living in one of the outstanding private houses of the world. The house sits on 500 acres encompassing formal gardens, parkland, and a dairy farm. Ballybunion is the nearest golf course (☞ Chapter 9). The large rooms, though elegantly furnished with the outstanding Irish pieces for which Glin is renowned, are both intimate and comfortable. Country-house cuisine is served in the dining room, where portraits of Fitzgerald ancestors hang on the red walls. The menu makes use of locally produced meat and poultry and freshly caught fish, as well as vegetables and fruit from the walled garden. ⊠ *Co. Limerick,* ☎ *068/34112,* ℻ *068/34364. 6 rooms with bath. Tennis court, croquet, horseback riding, boating, fishing. AE, MC, V.*

En Route Nine kilometers (5½ mi) beyond Glin up N69, **Foynes** was the landing place for transatlantic air traffic in the 1930s and '40s. Flying boats used to land here to refuel before heading on to their European destinations. The **Flying Boat Museum,** in the terminal of the original Shannon Airport, celebrates Foynes's aviation history; it's a must for devoted flying buffs. ☎ *069/65416.* ☒ *£3.* ⊙ *Apr.–Oct., daily 10–5.*

The N69 continues to Limerick through **Askeaton,** where the ruins of a 15th-century Desmond stronghold almost cover a rocky islet on the River Deel. On the bank of the river are the well-preserved ruins of a (freely accessible) 15th-century Franciscan friary.

Castle Matrix, in Rathkeale on R518, dates from 1440, when it was in possession of the earls of Desmond. Confiscated by Elizabeth I, the castle served as a meeting place for the young poets Edmund Spenser and Walter Raleigh in 1589. Raleigh subsequently brought the first potato tubers from North Carolina to Castle Matrix, from where they were distributed throughout south Munster (the old provincial name for the region). In 1962, the late Colonel Sean O'Driscoll, an American architect, bought Castle Matrix and restored it. The library, which serves as the headquarters of the **Irish Heraldry Society,** has an important collection of documents relating to the "Wild Geese," Irish mercenaries who served in European armies in the 17th and 18th centuries. *Rathkeale,* ☎ *069/64284.* ☒ *£3.* ⊙ *May 15–Sept. 15, Sat.–Thurs. 11–5.*

Adare

★ ⑦ *19 km (12 mi) south of Limerick City on N21, 82 km (51 mi) southeast of Tralee on N21.*

A picture-book village with several thatched cottages amid wooded surroundings on the banks of the River Maigue, Adare is rich in ruins; on foot, you can locate the remains of two 13th-century abbeys, a 15th-century friary, and the keep of a 13th-century Desmond castle. Providing that once-upon-a-time allure that has helped make this famous as one of Ireland's prettiest villages, the many stone-built cottages, often adorned with colorful, flower-filled window boxes, have a centuries-old look but were, in fact, built in the mid-19th century by the third Earl of Dunraven, a popular improving landlord, for the tenants on his estate. Nowadays they house various boutiques selling traditional Irish crafts and antiques and also a gourmet restaurant (☞ Wild Geese *in* Dining and Lodging, *below*). Adare Manor, an imposing Tudor–Gothic Revival mansion, which was once the grand house of the Dunraven peerage, is now a celebrated luxury hotel (☞ Adare Manor *in* Dining and Lodging, *below*).

The relationship between the village and its landlord is one of several topics explored in the **Adare Heritage Centre** ☒ ☎ *061/396666.* ☒ *£3.* ⊙ *May–Sept., daily 9–6; Oct.–Apr., daily 10–5.*

Dining and Lodging

$$$ ✕ **Wild Geese.** This low-ceiling thatched cottage opposite the Dunraven Arms (☞ *below*) houses a cozy, characterful series of small dining rooms in which the cooking is seriously good. Co-owner and chef Serge Coustrain trained in classical French cuisine but is not averse to adventurous combinations. Main courses feature light seafood combinations such as panfried fillet of red mullet with vegetable risotto and coriander pesto. Game is a popular option in the winter months. The Wild Geese dessert platter for two features a sample of all desserts, including fantastic homemade ice cream. ☒ *Rose Cottage,* ☎ *061/396451. AE, DC, MC, V. Closed Sun.–Mon. and 3 wks in Jan.*

$$$ ✕⛫ **Dunraven Arms.** This two-story inn in Adare's picturesque village center, established in 1792, oozes old-world charm. Little wonder, then, that it is sometimes the very first port of call with visitors arriving at Shannon Airport, about 40 km (25 mi) northwest; in fact, Charles Lindbergh stayed in the inn's Room 6 while he advised on the design of the airport. The dark walls of the cozy bar and lounges are hung with paintings and prints of horseback riders. The bedrooms are comfortably and tastefully decorated with antiques. Junior suites in the newer wing are furnished with antique four-poster beds. The elegant Maigue Restaurant specializes in modern Irish cuisine, while informal dining is offered in the pretty bar area. ✉ *Main St., Co. Limerick,* ☎ *061/396–633,* 𝔽𝔸𝕏 *061/396–541. 76 rooms with bath, 6 executive suites, 14 junior suites. Restaurant, bar, pool, steam room, health club, horseback riding, fishing. AE, DC, MC, V.*

$$$ ✕⛫ **Mustard Seed at Echo Lodge.** In 1996, after 10 years in the village of Adare, owner-chef Dan Mullane moved his highly regarded restaurant 13 km (8 mi) west to the village of Ballingarry. Its new home, an 1884 former convent on 6 acres, has a series of themed guest rooms— black-and-white, carnival, Chinese, and so on—all of which have views over rolling countryside. Head chef David Norris uses only the best local produce, plus herbs and vegetables from Echo Lodge's own organic garden. Free-range duckling, roast lamb, and seafood such as shark steak show up in imaginative preparations, and there are always good vegetarian options. ✉ *Ballingarry, Co. Limerick 6,* ☎ *09/68508,* 𝔽𝔸𝕏 *069/68508. 12 rooms with bath. Restaurant, bar. AE, MC, V. Closed Sun. to nonguests.*

$$ ✕⛫ **Woodlands House Hotel.** Under the energetic owner-management of the Fitzgerald family, the business has grown from a small B&B to a thriving modern hotel set in 44 acres of grounds on the Limerick side of the village. The friendly welcome is genuine, and independent travelers will be given plenty of touring tips. Rooms are relatively spacious, individually decorated in various modern styles, and well maintained. Ask for one with a view of the pretty gardens. Timmy Mac's bar is a popular meeting place for locals. The Brennan Rooms serves a traditional Irish table d'hôte menu featuring local lamb, pork, and beef and is renowned for its Sunday lunch. More adventurous cooking will be found in the bistro-style coffee shop in Timmy Mac's, which features a range of locally grown organic food. ✉ *Knockanes, Co. Limerick,* ☎ *061/396118,* 𝔽𝔸𝕏 *061/396073. 84 rooms, 8 suites. 2 restaurants, bar, pool, sauna, health club, horseback riding, fishing. AE, DC, MC, V. Closed Dec. 24–26.*

$$$$ ⛫ **Adare Manor.** Until 1988, this Victorian Gothic mansion was the home of the earls of Dunraven. Today it is a grand hotel owned by New Jersey business executive Tom Kane and his wife, Judy. Vast stone arches, heavy Flemish wood carvings, and an elaborately decorated ceiling adorn the lordly central hall, off which are a library and drawing and dining rooms. The glorious 36-ft-high, 100-ft-long gallery, wainscoted in oak, is the architectural highlight, though it is used only for special events. The eight "staterooms" in the original house are the most sumptuous, with huge marble bathrooms, comfortable seating areas, and stone-mullioned windows. Most rooms have super-king-size beds and non-working fireplaces; all have heavy drapes and thick carpets and overlook either the 840 acres of grounds or the River Maigue, which runs right beside the hotel. Adare's golf course, designed by Robert Trent Jones, is considered one of the best courses in Ireland (☞ Chapter 9). ✉ *Adare, Co. Limerick,* ☎ *061/396566,* 𝔽𝔸𝕏 *061/396124. 63 rooms with bath. Restaurant, 2 bars, indoor pool, sauna, 18-hole golf course, horseback riding, fishing. AE, DC, MC, V.*

Outdoor Activities and Sports

GOLF

Adare Manor Golf Club (✉ Adare, ☎ 061/396204) is an 18-hole, par-69 parkland course (☞ Chapter 9).

HORSEBACK RIDING

The **Clonshire Equestrian Center** (✉ Adare, ☎ 061/396770) has all-weather riding facilities and will also organize trail riding and residential holidays.

Shopping

George and Michelina Stacpoole sell an unusual combination of designer knitwear and antiques (✉ Main St., ☎ 061/396409). **Adare Gallery** (✉ Main St., ☎ 061/396898) sells Irish-made jewelry, porcelain, and woodwork, as well as original paintings.

Limerick City

78 *19 km (12 mi) northeast of Adare, 198 km (123 mi) southwest of Dublin.*

At the head of the Shannon estuary and the intersection of a number of major crossroads, Limerick is an industrial port and the fourth-largest city in the Republic (population 60,000). The area around the cathedral and the castle is the old part of the city, dominated by mid-18th-century buildings with fine Georgian proportions. Economic investment is helping to spiff up its former image as an unattractive city marked by high unemployment and a higher crime rate than elsewhere in the Republic. Frank McCourt's 1996 memoir, *Angela's Ashes*—set in Limerick, where McCourt grew up desperately poor—has also helped to pique interest in the city's fortunes today (☞ Close-Up: Rising from the Ashes: Frank McCourt's Limerick, *below*). If you fly into or out of Shannon Airport, you may well pass through here; if you have a few hours to spare, check out the revitalization firsthand. (The answer to the question everyone asks: No, a direct connection is not thought to exist between the city and the facetious five-line verse form known as a limerick—first popularized by the English writer Edward Lear in his 1846 *Book of Nonsense*.)

Like most other Irish coastal towns, Limerick was originally a 9th-century Danish settlement, and in 1197 Richard I granted the city's charter. In 1691, after the Battle of the Boyne, the Irish retreated to the walled city, where they were besieged by William of Orange, who made three unsuccessful attempts to storm the city but then raised the siege and marched away. A year later, another of William's armies overtook the city for two months, and the Irish opened negotiations. The resulting Treaty of Limerick—which guaranteed religious tolerance—was never ratified, and 11,000 men of the Limerick garrison joined the French Army rather than fight in a Protestant "Irish" army.

In the Old Customs House on the banks of the Shannon in the city center, the **Hunt Museum** has the finest collection of Celtic and medieval treasures outside the National Museum in Dublin. Ancient Irish metalwork, European objets d'art, and a selection of 20th-century European and Irish paintings—including works by Jack B. Yeats—are on view. A café overlooks the river. ✉ *Rutland St.,* ☎ *061/312833.* 🎫 *£4.* ☉ *Oct.–Apr., Tues.–Sat. 10–5, Sun. 2–5; May–Sept., Mon.–Sat. 10–5, Sun. 2–5.*

Limerick is a predominantly Catholic city, but the Protestant **St. Mary's Cathedral** is the city's oldest religious building. Once a 12th-century palace—pilasters and a rounded Romanesque entrance were part of the original structure—it dates mostly from the 15th century (the

RISEN FROM THE ASHES: FRANK MCCOURT'S LIMERICK

THE ALCOHOLIC PA. The starving, shivering brood of children. The sheep's head for Christmas. The rags for diapers. The little white coffin. And the long-suffering, abused ma. These are some of the elements that rivet the reader of *Angela's Ashes* (1996, Scribners), Frank McCourt's memoir of his impoverished childhood in Limerick, a rags-to-riches story, with the riches always being more spiritual than material. Called by *Newsweek* "the publishing event of the decade," and compared by some to *The Grapes of Wrath* in its power, pain, and joy, *Angela's Ashes* has sold nearly 2 million hardback copies, won the Pulitzer, and gone Hollywood. The book seems to speak to the Irish in everyone's soul if best-seller lists, from Japan to Germany, are any indication. Not surprisingly, the city of Limerick—the rainsodden setting of this 1930–1940s hard-luck saga—has become a new pilgrimage place for readers eager to partake of the tearfulness of it all. Busloads of McCarthys and O'Dwyers now clamber over the sites described in the book, ending up at South's pub to raise a pint in Frank's honor and to count their blessings.

In the memoir narrated from a child's perspective, Limerick looms as "a gray place with a river that kills." Many children, including McCourt's twin brothers, succumb to tuberculosis, with the rest to run an obstacle course—in shoes with flapping soles—of flea-ridden bedcovers, cane-wielding teachers, doomsday-spouting priests, and fathers who drink their paycheck, beat their wives, and tell their sons to search the skies for the Angel of the Seventh Step, bringer of new babies. Yes, Limerick has its historic sights—King John's Castle, St. Mary's Cathedral, and other landmarks of the town's medieval district—but now the down-and-out addresses of McCourt's childhood draw as much attention from erstwhile visitors.

As it turns out, the slums described so unflinchingly in the book have long been torn down; in fact, Limerick today is flush with new money, renovated 19th-century Georgian row houses, prosperous shopping malls, and restaurants with fancy names like Quenelles. Even the dread River Shannon has undergone a makeover—swans, not refuse, now navigate its flowing stream. Nevertheless, plenty of *Angela's Ashes* sites remain: Leamy's National School on Hartstonge Street, where "Hoppy" O'Halloran and other schoolmasters used to beat any charges who couldn't add 19 to 47; the St. Vincent de Paul Society, where Angela once went begging for furniture and other assistance; People's Park, where Frank once took his younger brothers to make them forget their empty stomachs; plus many other emotional landmarks.

LIKE THE IRISH *SHANACHIE*—storyteller—still spouting tales at many a local pub, Frank McCourt has dug deep into the communal wellspring of Irish memory. The fact that his story has nothing to do with leprechauns and Celtic queens and everything to do with a family history that most families would wish to hide, let alone hang out in the sun to dry, says a good deal about the new Ireland and its people's wish for closure. McCourt's childhood experiences may not have been the happiest, but they are surely worth reading about, remembering, and revisiting, as so many travelers are now making a point of doing.

black-oak carvings on misericords in the choir stalls are from this period), with an extensive 19th-century restoration. A 45-minute son-et-lumière show highlights major episodes from Limerick's history. ⊠ *Bridge St.,* ☎ *061/416238.* ⊠ *Show £2.50.* ⊙ *Mid-June–Sept. 15, daily 7 PM and 9:15 PM.*

First built by the Normans in the early 1200s, **King John's Castle** still bears traces on its north side of the 1691 bombardment. If you climb the drum towers (the oldest section), you'll have a good view of the town and the Shannon. Inside, a 22-minute audiovisual show illustrates the history of Limerick and Ireland; an archaeology center has three excavated, pre-Norman houses; and two exhibition centers display models of Limerick's history from its founding in AD 922. ⊠ *Castle St.,* ☎ *061/411201.* ⊠ *£3.50.* ⊙ *Apr.–Sept., daily 9:30–5; Oct.–Mar., weekends 9:30–5.*

The office of the **Limerick Regional Archives** (⊠ Michael St., ☎ 061/410777) is in the Granary, built in 1774 for grain storage. For a small fee, the archives provides a genealogical research service.

On **O'Connell Street,** you'll find the main shopping area, which consists mostly of modest chain stores. However, the street lies one block inland from (east of) the Arthur's Quay Shopping Centre, a new shopping mall, which, along with the futuristic Tourist Information Center, is one of the first fruits of a civic campaign to develop Limerick's Shannonside quays. **Cruises Street,** a pedestrian thoroughfare, has Limerick's most chic shops (even though they are chiefly high-street multiples) and an inviting atmosphere (with occasional street entertainers); it is on the opposite side of O'Connell Street from the Arthur's Quay Shopping Centre. Off O'Connell Street is the **Dolmen Gallery** (⊠ Honan's Quay, ☎ 061/417929), which specializes in contemporary Irish art exhibits and has a very pleasant restaurant serving healthy, homemade food.

➌ **Plassey,** 5–10 minutes from Limerick on the Ring Road (signposted Dublin N7), is the setting for the University of Limerick, which has a small, nicely landscaped campus.

Dining and Lodging

For lodging convenient to Shannon Airport, ☞ Adare, *above,* and Ennis and Newmarket-on-Fergus *in* Chapter 6.

$$$ ✕ **Quenelle's on the Waterfront.** After five years in the city center, Kieran Pollard and his wife, Sindy Magner, have moved to the stylish new riverfront development near Jurys Inn. Decor is modern and minimalist, with strong colors and polished timber floors. In summer a light Mediterranean-style lunch, available at a lower set price, is served on the terrace. In the evening Kieran's adventurous cooking offers delights: starters like local spiced beef salad with honey and lime vinaigrette, or duck and red onion terrine; and main courses from seafood to locally raised beef, pork, and lamb. From the amuse-bouche presented on arrival to the minted truffles served with the coffee, service is cheerful and the attention to detail is impeccable. ⊠ *Unit Four, Steamboat Quay,* ☎ *061/411111. MC, V. No lunch.*

$$ ✕ **Freddy's Bistro.** Tucked away into a quiet lane between busy O'-Connell and Henry streets, this informal two-story restaurant fills an atmospheric 18th-century coach house. Old brick walls are complemented by the warm color scheme, which glows in candlelight. Pasta with smoked chicken or seafood tagliatelle are popular main courses; for dessert try the hot, sticky toffee pudding. ⊠ *Theatre La., off Lower Glentworth St.,* ☎ *061/316141. MC, V. Closed Sun.–Mon.*

$–$$ ✕ **Jasmine Palace.** Gourmet dining never really caught on in Limerick, but the city abounds in Chinese restaurants. Of several reasonably elegant ones in the town center, this second-floor eatery on the main street (opposite the Royal George Hotel) has been there longest, and many would claim that it's the best. Irish steak is served on a sizzling platter with black bean sauce; the duck and prawn pot is an individual stewpot with pieces of duck and whole king prawns in a rich, spicy sauce. ⊠ *37 O'Connell St., Co. Limerick,* ☎ *061/412484. AE, DC, MC, V.*

$ ✕ **Mortell's.** This simple daytime restaurant decked out in bright pink and mahogany is in the main shopping area. It is both a general café, serving full Irish breakfasts and baked goods, and a seafood restaurant. It has been in the family for more than 40 years, and everything, from the doughnuts to the brown bread to the mayo, is made on the premises. Only the freshest local seafood is served. If you've never tried fish-and-chips, this is the place to start. ⊠ *49 Roches St.,* ☎ *061/415457. AE, DC, MC, V. Closed Sun. No dinner.*

$$$ ✕▣ **Castletroy Park.** Sitting grandly atop a hill on the outskirts of town
★   (follow signs for the N7 Dublin road), with views of the university campus and the surrounding countryside, this large, three-story, red-brick-and-stone hotel is a real gem. The lobby, with its polished wood and Oriental rugs, leads to a large conservatory–cum–coffee shop overlooking an Italian-style courtyard. The guest rooms, scented with potpourri, are decorated with solid wood furniture, muted floral drapes and spreads, and rag-rolled walls. The fitness center, one of the best around, has a large pool. You can mix with the locals in the Merry Pedlar Pub and Bistro or enjoy a formal meal in MacLaughlin's restaurant. ⊠ *Dublin Rd., Co. Limerick,* ☎ *061/335566,* ℻ *061/ 331117. 78 standard rooms with bath, 7 suites, 22 executive rooms. 2 restaurants, bar, in-room data ports, pool, sauna, steam room, health club. AE, DC, MC, V.*

$$ ▣ **Greenhills.** This friendly, family-run hotel is a modern low-rise in a quiet, suburban area where N18 meets the city-center route. Twenty minutes from Shannon and five minutes from the city center, it makes an excellent touring base. The best and newest rooms are in a quiet wing above the fitness center and are big enough to have a small couch, tables, and chairs. All the rooms are color-coordinated in various styles with dark-wood furniture and tiled bathrooms. Children will love the pool, and in high season they can take part in the hotel's children's club. ⊠ *Ennis Rd., Co. Limerick,* ☎ *061/453033,* ℻ *061/ 453307. 55 rooms with bath. Restaurant, bar, coffee shop, pool, sauna, steam room, tennis court, children's programs (ages 4–12). AE, DC, MC, V.*

$ ▣ **Jurys Inn.** Clean, airy, and in good shape, unlike some of Limerick's other budget spots, this is the latest hotel in Ireland's rapidly expanding Jurys chain, which rents per room rather than per person. (The "inn," though, is something of a misnomer, as the hotel is large and relatively anonymous.) Rooms are a good size for the price bracket and have light-wood furnishings. It overlooks an urban stretch of the Shannon now being converted from industrial to leisure use and is a short step from the main shopping and business district. ⊠ *Lower Mallow St., Mount Kennett Pl., Co. Limerick,* ☎ *061/207000,* ℻ *061/400966. 151 rooms with bath. Restaurant, bar. AE, DC, MC, V.*

Nightlife and the Arts

ART GALLERIES

The **Dolmen Gallery** (⊠ Honan's Quay, ☎ 061/417929) shows interesting work by contemporary artists. The **Belltable Arts Center** (⊠ 69 O'Connell St., ☎ 061/319866) has a small auditorium for touring productions and exhibition space. The **Limerick City Gallery** (⊠ Pery Sq.,

☎ 061/310633) has a small, permanent collection of Irish art (most notably Jack B. Yeats's *The Chairplanes*) and mounts interesting shows of contemporary art.

PUBS, CABARET, AND DISCOS

Hogan's (✉ 20-24 Old Clare St., ☎ 061/411279) has a traditional seisun every Tuesday and Friday year-round. Traditional music is featured at **Nancy Blake's Pub** (✉ 19 Denmark St., ☎ 061/416443) year-round Sunday–Wednesday from 9 PM. The **Locke** (✉ 3 George's Quay, ☎ 061/413733), a riverside pub, is one of Limerick's oldest bars, dating from 1724, and has traditional music Sunday, Monday, and Tuesday nights. The Officer's Club upstairs at the **Castle Lane Tavern** (✉ King's Island, ☎ 061/318044) features live dinner entertainment Tuesday through Saturday in the form of an Irish cabaret, culminating in a "hooley" with audience participation. Sessions often take place in the downstairs bar.

Outdoor Activities and Sports

BICYCLES

Bicycles can be rented from **Emerald Cycles** (✉ 1 Patrick St., ☎ 061/416983).

FISHING

Fishing tackle, bait, and licenses can be obtained at **Steve's Fishing Tackle** (✉ 19 Catherine St., ☎ 061/413484).

GOLF

Limerick Golf and Country Club (✉ Ballyneety, ☎ 061/351881) is an 18-hole, par-72 parkland course.

Castletory Golf Club (✉ Golf Links Rd., Castletory, ☎ 061/335753) is a challenging 18-hole, par-71 parkland course in the city suburbs.

HORSEBACK RIDING

Clarina Riding Center (✉ Clarina, near Limerick City, ☎ 061/353087) has riding by the hour.

Shopping

The **Arthur's Quay Shopping Centre** (✉ Arthur's Quay, ☎ 061/419888) near the TIO is the city's biggest indoor mall. **Lane Antiques** (✉ 45 Catherine St., ☎ 061/339307) is an old-world gallery selling antiques, prints, paintings, collectibles, and antiquarian books. **Celtic Bookshop** (✉ 2 Rutland St., ☎ 061/401155) specializes in books of Irish interest.

Bunratty Castle and Folk Park

★ ⑧⓪ *18 km (10 mi) west of Limerick City on N18 (the road to Shannon Airport).*

Likely to be the first Irish castle seen by visitors arriving into Shannon Airport, Bunratty Castle and Folk Park are two of those rare attractions that appeal to all age groups and manage to be both educational and fun. Bunratty Castle, built in 1460, has been fully restored and decorated with 15th- to 17th-century furniture and furnishings. The castle gives a wonderful insight into the life of those times. As you pass under the walls of Bunratty, look for the three "murder holes," which allowed defenders to pour boiling oil on attackers below. On the castle grounds, and every bit as quaint as some first-time visitors expect all of modern Ireland to be, **Bunratty Folk Park** re-creates a 19th-century village street and has examples of the traditional rural housing of the region. Exhibits include a working blacksmith's forge; demonstrations of flour milling, bread making, candle making, thatching, and other traditional skills; and a variety of farm animals in reconstructed small holdings. An adjacent museum of agricultural machinery cannot compete with the furry and feathered live exhibits. Medieval banquets are held at the castle twice nightly (☞ *below*) for those who want to dine on Roast Beast and quaff mead made from fermented honey, apple juice, clover, and heather. ☎ 061/ 361511. ✉ £5.25. ☉ *Sept.–May, daily 9:30–5:30 (last entry 4:15); June–Aug., daily 9:30–7 (last entry 6).*

No visit to Bunratty is complete without a drink in **Durty Nelly's** (☎ 061/364072), an old-world pub with a fanciful decor that has inspired imitations around the world.

Quin

21 km (13 mi) north of Bunratty.

❽ A 15th-century MacNamara stronghold, **Knappogue Castle** has been extensively restored and furnished in 15th-century style. Its name means the "Hill of the Kiss," and, like Bunratty, it's a venue for medieval-style banquets. The castle looks spectacular at night when floodlit. ✉ *Quin,* ☎ 061/368103. ✉ £3. ☉ *May–Sept., daily 9:30–4:30.*

❽ The **Craggaunowen Project,** north of Knappogue Castle, is signposted off the road to Sixmilebridge about 10 km (6 mi) from Quin. **Craggaunowen Castle,** a 16th-century tower house, has been restored with furnishings from the period. Particularly worth seeing are the two replicas of early Celtic-style dwellings that have been constructed on the castle grounds. On an island in the lake, reached by a narrow footbridge, is a clay-and-wattle *crannóg,* a fortified lake dwelling; it resembles what might have been built in the 6th or 7th century when Celtic influence still predominated in Ireland. The reconstruction of a small ring fort shows how an ordinary farmer would have lived in the 5th or 6th century, at the time Christianity was being established. Characters from the past explain their Iron Age (500 BC–AD 450) lifestyle; show you around their small holding, stocked with animals; and demonstrate crafts skills from bygone ages. It is a strange experience to walk across the little wooden bridge above reeds rippling in the lake into Ireland's Celtic past as a jumbo jet passes overhead on its way into Shannon Airport—1,500 years of history compressed into an instant. ✉ *Kilmurry, Sixmilebridge,* ☎ 061/367178. ✉ £4. ☉ *Mid-Mar.–mid-Apr., Fri.–Sun. 10–5; mid-Apr.–mid-May and mid-Sept.–mid-Oct., daily 10–6; mid-May–mid-Sept., daily 9–6.*

Medieval Banquets

If you're a first-time visitor, you may not want to miss the **medieval banquets** held at the Bunratty and Knappogue castles. Do note, though: Both events cater largely to overseas visitors, many of them on organized tours, and they're likely to have little appeal for independent travelers in search of "the real Ireland." But if you're up for it, a warmhearted evening of Irish hospitality should be taken in the lighthearted spirit in which it is offered. Medieval banqueting may not be authentic, but it is fun. At Bunratty, you'll be welcomed by Irish colleens in 15th-century dress, who bear the traditional bread of friendship, then led off to a honey-and-mead reception. Before sitting down at the long tables in the candlelit great hall, you don a bib: You'll need it, because you'll be eating the four-course meal medieval-style—with your fingers! Serving "wenches" take time out to sing a few ballads or pluck the strings of a harp. Because the banquets are so popular, book as far in advance as possible. ☎ *Bunratty and Knappogue: 061/360788.* ✉ *Four-course meal, wine, mead, and entertainment £32.* ☉ *Daily, subject to demand, 5:45 and 8:45.*

In case you want
to see the world.

**At American Express, we're here to make your journey
a smooth one. So we have over 1,700 travel service locations in over 130 countries ready to help. What else
would you expect from the world's largest travel agency?**

do more

In case you want to be welcomed there.

We're here to see that you're always welcomed at establishments everywhere. That's why millions of people carry the American Express® Card – for peace of mind, confidence, and security, around the world or just around the corner.

do more

Cards

To apply, call 1 800 THE-CARD
or visit www.americanexpress.com

In case you're running low.

We're here to help with more than 190,000 Express Cash locations around the world. In order to enroll, just call American Express at 1 800 CASH-NOW before you start your vacation.

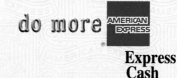

do more

Express Cash

And in case you'd rather be safe than sorry.

We're here with American Express® Travelers Cheques. They're the safe way to carry money on your vacation, because if they're ever lost or stolen you can get a refund, practically anywhere or anytime. To find the nearest place to buy Travelers Cheques, call 1 800 495-1153. Another way we help you do more.

do more   AMERICAN EXPRESS

Travelers Cheques

A *ceili* at Bunratty Folk Park is the next-best thing if you can't get a reservation for a banquet; this program features traditional Irish dance and song and a meal of Irish stew, soda bread, and apple pie. ☎ *061/ 360788. ✆ £27 including wine. ☉ May–Sept., daily 5:45 and 9.*

THE SOUTHWEST A TO Z

Arriving and Departing

By Bus

Bus Éireann operates Expressway services from Dublin to Limerick City, Cork City, and Tralee. Add approximately 1 hour to the journey time by train. Most towns in the region are served by the provincial Bus Éireann network (☎ 01/836–6111 in Dublin, 061/313333 in Limerick, 021/508188 in Cork, or 066/23566 in Tralee).

By Car

The main driving access route from Dublin is N7, which goes 192 km (120 mi) directly to Limerick City; from Dublin, pick up N8 in Portlaoise and drive 257 km (160 mi) to Cork City. The journey time between Dublin and Limerick runs just under 3 hours; between Dublin and Cork it takes about 3½ hours.

By Ferry/Bus

Train connections between Rosslare Harbour and Cork City, Limerick City, and Tralee all involve changing at Limerick Junction, so the journey time is usually longer than by car or bus. It is quicker and cheaper, if less comfortable, to use the long-distance buses that service the ferries. **International Express Supabus** leaves London's Victoria Coach Station daily and travels overnight via Bristol to Fishguard, then on to Cork, Killarney, and Tralee. Timetables can be obtained from any National Express Coach Station or by calling Supabus in Luton, England (☎ 1582/404511). An Irish company, **Slattery's** (☎ 171/482–1604), runs a bus service from London to Cork and Tralee. The journey to Cork via Rosslare is by bus and ferry, and, at about 14 hours, arduous. (A note about both these phone numbers: Since they are U.K. numbers, if you dial from Ireland, first dial 00 [access code] and 44 [the U.K. country code].)

Swansea–Cork Ferries (☎ 1792/456116, which can also be accessed from the U.K.) operates a 10-hour crossing between the two ports on a comfortable, well-equipped boat. Supabus (☞ *above*) will get you to the Swansea ferry from anywhere in the United Kingdom.

By Ferry/Car

From the United Kingdom, the Southwest has two ports of entry: Rosslare (in County Wexford) and Cork City. (☞ The Southeast A to Z *in* Chapter 4, for Rosslare ferry details.) From Rosslare Harbour by car, take N25 208 km (129 mi) to Cork; allow 3½ hours for the journey. You can pick up N24 in Waterford for the 211-km (131-mi) drive to Limerick City, which also takes about 3½ hours.

By Plane

The Southwest has two international airports: Shannon in the West, and Cork on the Southwest coast. **Shannon Airport** (☎ 061/471444), 26 km (16 mi) west of Limerick City, is the point of arrival for all transatlantic flights; it also serves some flights from the United Kingdom and Europe. **Cork Airport** (☎ 021/431–3131), 5 km (3 mi) south of Cork City on the Kinsale road, is used primarily for flights to and from the United Kingdom. Regular 30-minute internal flights are scheduled between Shannon and Dublin, Shannon and Cork, and Cork and Dublin. **Kerry**

County Airport (☎ 066/64644) at Farranfore, 16 km (10 mi) from Killarney, mainly services small planes, but it is gradually increasing its commercial traffic with at least one daily flight from London. ☞ Air Travel *in* Smart Travel Tips A to Z for specific information about airlines.

By Bus from Shannon Airport. Bus Éireann (☎ 061/474311) runs a regular bus service to Limerick City between 8 AM and midnight. The ride takes about 40 minutes and costs £3.50.

By Bus from Cork Airport. Bus service runs between the airport and the Cork City Bus Terminal (✉ Parnell Pl., ☎ 021/450–6066) every 30 minutes, on the hour and the half hour. The ride takes about 10 minutes and costs about £2.

By Taxi. Taxis can be found outside the main terminal building at the Shannon and Cork airports. The ride from Shannon Airport to Limerick City costs about £18; from Cork Airport to Cork City costs about £5.

By Train

From **Dublin Heuston Station** (☎ 01/836–6222), the region is served by three direct rail links to Limerick City, Tralee, and Cork City. Journey time from Dublin to Limerick is 2½ hours; to Cork, 2¾; to Tralee, 3¾. For passenger inquiries: in Limerick, ☎ 061/315555; in Cork, ☎ 021/450–6766; in Tralee, ☎ 066/23522.

Getting Around

By Bus

The provincial bus service, cheaper and more flexible than the train, covers all the region's main centers. Express services are available between Cork City and Limerick City (twice a day); Cork and Tralee (once a day, high season only); and Killarney, Tralee, Limerick, and Shannon (once a day, twice in peak season).

If you plan to travel extensively by bus, a copy of the Bus Éireann timetable (75p from bus terminals) is essential. As a general rule, the smaller the town, and the more remote, the less frequent its bus service. For example, Kinsale, a well-developed resort 29 km (18 mi) from Cork, is served by at least five buses a day, both arriving and departing; Castlegregory, a small village on the remote Dingle Peninsula, has bus service only on Friday.

The main bus terminals are at **Cork** (✉ Parnell Pl., ☎ 021/450–8188); **Limerick** (✉ Colbert Station, ☎ 061/313333); and **Tralee** (✉ Casement Station, ☎ 066/23566).

By Car

A car is the ideal way to explore this region, packed as it is with scenic routes, attractive but remote towns, and a host of out-of-the-way restaurants and hotels that deserve a detour. Roads are generally small, with two lanes (one in each direction). You will find a few miles of two-lane highway on the outskirts of Cork City, Limerick City, and Killarney, but much of your time will be spent on roads so narrow and twisty that it is not advisable to exceed 64 kph (40 mph).

Getting around the Southwest is every bit as enjoyable as arriving, provided you set out in the right frame of mind—a relaxed one. There is no point in imposing a rigid timetable on your journey when you are visiting one of the last places in Western Europe where you are as likely to be held up by a donkey cart, a herd of cows, or a flock of sheep as by road construction or heavy trucks.

By Train

The rail network, which covers only the inner ring of the region, is mainly useful for moving from one touring base to another. Except during the peak season of July and August, only four trains a day run between Cork (or Limerick) and Tralee. More frequent service is offered between Cork City and Limerick City, but the ride involves changing at Limerick Junction—as does the journey from Limerick to Tralee—to wait for a connecting train. Be sure to ascertain the delay involved in the connection. (For passenger inquiries, ☞ Arriving and Departing by Train, *above*.) The journey from Cork to Tralee takes about 2 hours; from Cork to Limerick, about 1¼ hours; from Limerick to Tralee, about 3 hours.

Contacts and Resources

B&B Reservation Agencies

For a small fee, **Bord Fáilte** (the Irish Tourist Board) will book accommodations anywhere in Ireland through its central reservations system. B&Bs can be booked at local visitor information offices when they are open; however, even these reservations will go through the central reservations system. For more information, ☞ Lodging *in* Smart Travel Tips A to Z.

Car Rentals

All the major car-rental companies have desks at Shannon and Cork airports.

Shannon Airport: Avis (☎ 061/471094). **Dan Dooley** (☎ 061/471098). **Euro Dollar** (☎ 061/472633). **Hertz** (☎ 061/471369). **Payless Bunratty** (☎ 061/475549). **Murray's Europcar** (☎ 061/471618).

Cork Airport: Avis (☎ 021/428–1111). **Budget** (☎ 021/431–4000). **Euro Dollar** (☎ 021/434–4884). **Hertz** (☎ 021/496–5849). **Johnson & Perrott** (☎ 021/428–1169). **Murray's Europcar** (☎ 021/496–6736).

Killarney: Avis (☎ 064/36655). **Budget** (☎ 064/34341). **Murray's Europcar** (☎ 064/31237). **Randles** (☎ 064/31237).

Emergencies

Police, fire, and **ambulance** (☎ 999).

DOCTORS AND DENTISTS
Southern Health Board (✉ Dennehy's Cross, Cork, ☎ 021/454–5011).

PHARMACIES
Cork: Phelan's (✉ 9 Patrick St., Co. Cork, ☎ 021/427–2511). **Killarney: P. O'Donoghue** (✉ Main St., Co. Kerry, ☎ 064/31813). **Limerick: Roberts** (✉ 105 O'Connell St., Co. Limerick, ☎ 061/414414).

Guided Tours

Bus Éireann, part of the state-run public-transport network, offers a range of day and half-day guided tours from June to September. They can be booked at the bus stations in Cork or Limerick or at any TIO (☞ Visitor Information, *below*). A full-day tour costs £12; half-day, £7.50, both exclusive of meals and refreshments. Bus Éireann also offers open-top bus tours of Cork City on Tuesday and Saturday in July and August for £4.

Tourist Trails, which allow the visitor to follow a signposted route while reading an accompanying booklet (£1), have been set up in Cork City, Limerick City, Youghal, Kinsale, and Killarney Town. Booklets can be purchased at local TIOs. History buffs should inquire at TIOs for details of guided walking tours, which are organized during the summer by local volunteers.

TOUR OPERATORS

Country House Tours (✉ 71 Waterloo Rd., Dublin 4, ☎ 01/668–6463, FAX 01/668–6578) organizes self-driven or chauffeur-driven group tours with accommodations in private country houses and castles. It also conducts special-interest tours, including gardens, architecture, ghosts, and golf.

Gerry Coughlan of **Arrangements Unlimited** (✉ 1 Woolhara Park, Douglas, Cork City, Co. Cork, ☎ 021/429–3873, FAX 021/429–2488) can prearrange special-interest group tours of the region. Half-day and full-day tours are individually planned for groups of 10 or more to satisfy each visitor's needs.

Into the Wilderness (✉ Climber's Inn, Glencar, Killarney, Co. Kerry, ☎ 066/976–0101) organizes guided walking, climbing, and cycling tours in the Kerry Highlands and Killarney National Park.

Limerick City Tours (✉ Noel Curtin, Rhebogue, Co. Limerick, ☎ 061/311935) offers inexpensive walking tours of Limerick from June to September (and by arrangement other months).

Shannon Castle Tours (✉ Bunratty Folk Park, Bunratty, Co. Clare, ☎ 061/360788) will escort you to an "Irish Night" in Bunratty Folk Park or take you to a medieval banquet at Bunratty or Knappogue Castle (☞ *above*); although the banquets aren't authentic, they are a boisterous occasion and full of goodwill.

KILLARNEY AREA

Destination Killarney (✉ Scott's Gardens, Killarney, Co. Kerry, ☎ FAX 064/32638) is the foremost Killarney tour operator. Besides offering full-day and half-day tours of Killarney and Kerry by coach or taxi, the group will prearrange your visit, lining up accommodations, entertainment, special-interest tours, and sporting activities in one package. A **full-day** (10:30–5) tour costs from £10 to £13 per person, excluding lunch and refreshments. The **Killarney Local Circuit** tour is an excellent **half-day** 10:30–12:30 orientation. The memorable **Gap of Dunloe** tour at £13 includes a coach and boat trip. Add £12 for a horseback ride through the gap. More conventional day trips can also be made to the Ring of Kerry, the Loo Valley, and Glengarriff; the city of Cork and Blarney Castle; Dingle and Slea Head; and Caragh Lake and Rossbeigh.

Gray Line Shannonway Tours (✉ Limerick TIO, Arthur's Quay, Limerick, Co. Limerick, ☎ 061/413088) organizes full-day and half-day coach tours of Killarney and the Shannon region from mid-June through September.

Jaunting cars (pony and trap) that carry up to four people can be rented at a stand outside Killarney TIOs. They can also be found at the entrance to Muckross Estate and at the Gap of Dunloe. A ride costs between £12 and £24, negotiable with the driver, depending on duration (1–2 hours) and route. **Tangney Tours** (✉ Kinvara House, Muckross Rd., Killarney, Co. Kerry, ☎ 064/33358) is the leading jaunting-car company and will also organize tours and entertainment.

The following companies will organize full-day and half-day trips by coach or taxi around Killarney and the Ring of Kerry: **Dero's Tours** (✉ 22 Main St., Killarney, ☎ 064/31251), **Corcoran's Tours** (✉ 10 College ST., Killarney, ☎ 064/36666), **Castlelough Tours** (✉ 7 High St., Killarney, ☎ 064/32496).

Outdoor Activities and Sports

FISHING

Your hotel or the local TIO can suggest places that rent boats. The latter will also recommend locations for coarse and game fishing, or contact the **South Western Regional Fisheries Board** (⊠ 1 Nevilles Terr., Macroom, Co. Cork, ☎ 026/41221).

HIKING

Details about the Southwest's eight long-distance hiking trails, related maps, and guides are contained in the Irish Tourist Board publication *Walking Ireland 2000,* available from Tourist Information Offices (☞ Visitor Information, *below*).

WATER SPORTS

Because of the demands of Irish insurance laws, boat charter is still in its infancy here, with only one company in business for bareboat charter. For the same reasons, dinghy rentals are not widespread, and you will need to demonstrate your competence. Sailboards, on the other hand, are relatively easy to rent. Wet suits (also rentable) are essential for sailboarding except on the hottest days in July and August. Rental of sailboarding equipment, including wet suits, starts at about £10 an hour. Sailing dinghies, as well as sailboards, can be rented by the hour (from about £6) or by the day (from about £20). Dinghy- and sailboard-rental contacts are listed under the towns that provide them.

The average cost of a six-berth yacht between 28 and 35 ft ranges from £120 per person per week (low season) to £200 (high season).

Contact **Sail Ireland Charters** (⊠ Trident Hotel, Kinsale, Co. Cork, ☎ 021/772927, FAX 021/774170) for bareboat charters. For details of residential dinghy sailing courses in the Southwest, contact **Glenans Irish Sailing Club** (⊠ 28 Merrion Sq., Dublin 2, ☎ 01/661–1481).

Visitor Information

Bord Fáilte provides a free information service; its TIOs also sell a selection of tourist literature. For a small fee it will book accommodations anywhere in Ireland.

SEASONAL OFFICES

TIOs in the following towns are open weekdays 9–6, Saturday 9–1: **Bantry** (⊠ Co. Cork, ☎ 027/50229), May–October; **Clonakilty** (⊠ Co. Cork, ☎ 023/33226), June–mid-September; **Dingle** (⊠ Co. Kerry, ☎ 066/915–1188), March–October; **Kenmare** (⊠ Co. Kerry, ☎ 064/41233), April–October; **Kinsale** (⊠ Pier Rd., Co. Cork, ☎ 021/477–2234, 021/477–4417 off-season, FAX 021/774438), March–November; **Youghal** (⊠ Co. Cork, ☎ 024/92390), May–mid-September.

YEAR-ROUND OFFICES

The following TIOs are open weekdays 9–6, Saturday 9–1: **Blarney** (⊠ Co. Cork, ☎ 021/438–1624). **Cork City** (⊠ Grand Parade, Co. Cork, ☎ 021/427–3251, FAX 021/427–3504). **Killarney** (⊠ Aras Fáilte, Beech Rd., Co. Kerry, ☎ 064/31633, FAX 064/34506). **Limerick** (⊠ Arthur's Quay, Co. Limerick, ☎ 061/317522, FAX 061/317939). **Shannon Airport** (⊠ Co. Clare, ☎ 061/471664). **Skibbereen** (⊠ North St., Co. Cork, ☎ 028/21766, FAX 028/21353). **Tralee** (⊠ Ashe Memorial Hall, Denny St., Co. Kerry, ☎ 066/21288).

6 THE WEST

CLIFFS OF MOHER, THE BURREN,
GALWAY CITY, THE ARAN ISLANDS,
CONNEMARA, COUNTY MAYO

With the most westerly seaboard in Europe, the West remains a place apart—the most Irish part of Ireland. Nature's magnificence awaits: the majestic Cliffs of Moher, the eerie expanse of the Burren, the "hidden kingdom" of Connemara, and the Aran Islands, which do constant battle with the stormy Atlantic. But there are also grand baronial houses to visit—Ashford Castle and Kylemore Abbey—and Galway, the city that loves to celebrate. As one of Europe's fastest growing metropolises, it has much to be happy about.

Updated by
Alannah
Hopkin

AS ANY DUBLINER WILL TELL YOU, the West is distinctively different from the rest of Ireland. Within Ireland, the West refers to the region that lies west of the River Shannon; most of this area falls within the old Irish province of Connaught. The coast of this region lies at the far western extremity of Europe, facing its nearest neighbors in North America across 3,200 km (2,000 mi) of Atlantic ocean. While the East, the Southwest, and the North were influenced by either Norman, Scots, or English settlers, the West escaped systematic resettlement and, with the exception of the walled town of Galway, remained purely Irish in language, social organization, and general outlook far longer than the rest of the country. The land in the West, predominantly mountains and bogs, did not immediately tempt the conquering barons. Oliver Cromwell was among those who found the place thoroughly unattractive, and he gave the Irish chieftains who would not conform to English rule the choice of going "to Hell or Connaught."

It wasn't until the late 18th century, when better transport improved communications, that the West started to experience the so-called foreign influences that had already Europeanized the rest of the country. The West was, in effect, propelled from the 16th century into the 19th. Virtually every significant building in the region dates either from before the 17th century or from the late 18th century onward. As in the Southwest, the population of the West was decimated by the Great Famine (1845–49) and by the waves of mass emigration that persisted until the 1950s. Towns were unknown in pre-Christian Irish society, and even today, 150 years after the famine, many residents still live on small farms rather than in towns and villages. Especially during the wet, wintry months, you can still walk out of your country house, hotel, or B&B in the morning and smell the nearby turf fires.

Today, the West is, for many, the most typically Irish part of the country. Particularly in western County Galway, you'll find the highest concentration of Gaeltacht (Irish-speaking communities) in all of Ireland, with roughly 40,000 native Irish speakers making their homes here. When the first entirely Irish-language TV station began broadcasting in late 1996, it was from the tiny village of An Spidéal, on the north shore of Galway Bay in the heart of the Gaeltacht. Throughout this area, you'll see plenty of signs that are in Irish only: Who would suspect that Gaillimh is the Irish for Galway? (☞ Getting Around by Car *in* The West A to Z, *below,* for the Irish names of a few major locales.) But wherever you go in the West, you'll not only see, but more importantly *hear,* the most vital way in which traditional Irish culture survives here: Musicians play in pubs all over the West, and they are recognized as being the best in the Republic (☞ Close Up: A Year-Round Fleadh, *below*).

A major factor in the region's recovery from economic depression has been the lure of its spectacular scenery to visitors. By and large, though, the development that has come with the cultivation of tourism in the West has been mercifully low-key and unobtrusive. Yes, residents of the West have encouraged the revival of such cottage industries as knitting, weaving, and woodworking. But apart from a seaside promenade and fun palace at Salthill, just outside Galway, the area has seen no major investment in public amenities. Alas, this relative unconcern with development cuts both ways: The 5,000-acre Connemara National Park is among the few protected areas in one of Ireland's most important bogland areas. The vast majority of bogland in Connemara and County

Mayo has already been farmed for its peat, leaving bereft swaths of land lamented by environmentalists.

There may be no better sign of the West's aspiration both to move forward *and* still remain tied to its traditions than thatched cottages, which are popular hereabouts as holiday homes. Some of the traditional whitewashed cottages are truly old, while others have been built *to resemble* the old. Of course, there's nothing new about the West's greatest virtue for visitors, apart from its glorious scenery and high-flying capital city: its people. No matter how many times you get out of the car for a photo-op—and we guarantee that you're going to *fly* through rolls of film out here—the stories that you're going to tell when you show your friends and family those pictures are going to be about the *seisun* (informal performance of traditional music) you stumbled upon in a small pub; the tiny, far-from-the-madding-crowds lake near Connemara that you made your own; and the great *craic* ("crack," or good conversation and fun) you're likely to discover wherever you go.

Pleasures and Pastimes

The Arts, Festivals, and Seasonal Events

The Irish in the West love their festivals, and they certainly know how to put on a full celebration. The **Cúirt Literary Festival** and the **Galway Oyster Festival** are but two of many annual events hosted by Galwegians; however, the highlight of the annual festival calendar is the **Galway Arts Festival.** During the second two weeks in July the town—already ordinarily abuzz—hosts theater, film, rock, jazz, traditional music, poetry readings, comedy acts, and visual arts exhibitions, plus a joyous parade by the street theater company Macnas, one of several local troupes to gain international recognition through the festival. Throughout the year, Galway's renovated **Town Hall Theater** lights up its stage for performances by, among many other groups, the 25-year-old Druid Theatre, whose adventurous productions regularly travel to Dublin and London. Not to be outdone by their neighbor to the south, a smaller but very lively festival in Connemara, the **Clifden Community Arts Week,** is held in mid-September, while the **Westport Arts Festival** takes place in the last week of September.

Dining

Because the West has a brief high season—from mid-June to early September—and a quiet off-season, it doesn't have as big a choice of small, owner-operated restaurants as other parts of Ireland. Often the best place to eat is a local hotel—Sheedy's Spa View in Lisdoonvarna, for example, which has one of the few excellent chefs in County Clare, or Rosleague Manor in Letterfrack. The dominant style of cuisine in the West might be called "country-house cooking," with an emphasis on classic, but lovingly prepared, dinner-party fare: homemade pâté, a seafood cocktail, tournedos or salmon hollandaise, and chocolate mousse for dessert. Even at Drimcong House, outside Galway City, Gerry Galvin, arguably Ireland's finest chef, prepares fresh local produce in relatively simple ways, albeit with the kind of subtlety that eludes lesser talents. For price ranges ☞ Chart 1(A) *in* Smart Travel Tips A to Z.

Lodging

Some of Ireland's finest country-house and castle hotels, distinguished old and new hotels, and a good choice of inexpensive B&Bs are all found in the West. Ashford and Dromoland castles are undoubtedly the stars of the region, but less over-the-top places such as Ballynahinch Castle and Cashel House Hotel, both in Connemara, offer similar comfort on a smaller, more intimate scale. The region is short on moderately priced hotels (particularly Galway City), but to compensate, there are wonderful places to stay in the lower price range. One of the great attractions of staying in the West, however much you pay for the night, is the restful atmosphere of so many of the hotels and guest houses, often situated in the middle of a large private estate beside a lake or river, overlooking the sea or distant mountains. Accommodations are busy in July and August, and the best places are also filled in May, June, and September, particularly on weekends, so reserve well in advance. As wonderful as many properties are, facilities like tennis courts and indoor pools are scarce, as are television sets in bedrooms, even in upscale hotels. For price ranges ☞ Chart 2(B) *in* Smart Travel Tips A to Z.

Outdoor Activities and Sports

FISHING

Some of the best angling in Europe is on the West's rivers, lakes, and seas. **Game fishing** for wild Atlantic salmon, wild brown trout, and sea trout is one of the main attractions of the West. The salmon and brown trout season runs from March through September, closing earlier in some waters. Generally, fishing is at its best between mid-May and mid-June. The **sea trout** season starts in late May and runs through September; it has been disappointing in some places in recent years due to the infestation of sea lice. Some improvement was reported in 1999, and strenuous efforts are being made to ensure a good season in 2000. **Shore fishing** is available all along the coast. Boats can be hired from April to October for deep-sea fishing (about £20 per person per day) from the following ports: Doonbeg, Liscannor, and Ballyvaughan in **County Clare**; Roundstone, Spiddle, Clifden, Cleggan, and Inishbofin Island in **County Galway**; and Westport, Ballina, Belmullet, and Killala in **County Mayo**.

HIKING AND WALKING

If you like challenging hills and relatively rough terrain, the West is excellent hiking country. The unusual, almost lunar landscape of the Burren in County Clare is less demanding than the terrain in Connemara. Here, and in the country to the north of Connemara in South County Mayo, the countryside is sparsely populated and subject to sudden changes in weather—usually a portent of rain. There are four signposted trails in the area. The **Burren Way** runs from Lahinch Promenade to Ballyvaughan on the shores of Galway Bay, a distance of 35 km (22 mi). The trail runs through the heart of the Burren's limestone landscape, with ever-changing views of the Aran Islands and Galway Bay. The **Western Way's County Galway section** extends from Oughterard on Lough Corrib through the mountains of Connemara to Leenane on Killary Harbour, a distance of 50 km (30 mi). Its 177-km (110-mi) County Mayo section known as the Western Way (Mayo) continues past Killary Harbour to Westport on Clew Bay, inland to Newport and across the boglands of north County Mayo to the Ox Mountains east of Ballina; this trail includes some of the finest mountain and coastal scenery in Ireland. A new, 387-km (240-mi) hiking route though Irish-speaking Connemara stretches along the shores of Galway Bay from Aiddle to Carraroe, Carna, Letterfrack, and Clonbur.

SPECTATOR SPORTS: SAILING AND HORSE RACING

Galway Hookers, solid, heavy, broad-beamed sailing boats with distinctive, gaff-rigged, brownish-red sails, can still be seen on the waters of Galway Bay. Enthusiasts maintain a small fleet and hold frequent races on the bay in July and August (☞ Kinvara, *below*). Many small **horse races** are held throughout the year in the West, including trotting races, pony races, beach derbies, and the like. Local Tourist Information Offices (TIOs) can provide details. The main event is the **Galway Races,** beginning immediately following the end of the Gal-

way Arts Festival, at the end of July and beginning of August. This boisterous, full-scale festival attracts a massive crowd and all manner of
sideshows, with card sharps, fortune-tellers, rifle ranges, and open-air
concerts.

Pubs and Live Traditional Music

No matter how you choose to spend your time in the West, be sure to
visit at least one pub. For whether or not you drink a pint of Guinness
or any other alcohol, pubs here are more than just bars—they're the
area's vital social centers, places to connect with natives and other travelers, to pick up leads about current and local activities, and, above
all, to hear Irish traditional music played live (☞ Close Up: A Year-
Round Fleadh, *below*).

Shopping

Galway City and Ennis are the West's major shopping areas. Their most
interesting shops carry crafts, Irish-made clothing, jewelry, books, and
antiques. Connemara has a large concentration of crafts shops; it is
the best place in Ireland to buy an Aran sweater—either the traditional,
off-white designs or the plain, linen and cotton Aran-style knits in jewel-
tone red, green, or blue. Galway City is the place to buy a Claddagh
ring. On the Aran Islands, sally rods are woven into attractive baskets
(once used for potatoes or turf), and colorful woven belts, known as
crioses, are hand-plaited from strands of wool. Handwoven woolen
or mohair shawls or rugs provide an affordable touch of luxury. Musical instruments, traditionally made furniture, Connemara marble
jewelry, modern lead crystal, batik, handmade beeswax candles, tweed
place mats, and dried flower arrangements are among the West's many
other goods—in addition to tweeds and sweaters, of course.

Exploring the West

Our coverage of the West is organized into three regional circuits, which
cover this territory from south to north. Our first route, **The Burren and
Beyond—West Clare to South Galway,** picks up minutes from Shannon
Airport and not far from Ennis, the gateway to coastal County Clare.
Our second trip, **Galway and the Aran Islands,** shows you the very best
of buzzing, bustling Galway City and takes you out to the three Aran
Islands, standing guard at the mouth of Galway Bay. Our third journey,
Through Connemara and County Mayo, takes you north of Galway Bay
and west of Galway City into the fabled "hidden kingdom" of Connemara
and beyond to the highlights of County Mayo: monumental Croagh
Patrick, the pretty town of Westport, and the breathtaking Achill Island.
Allow at least four days for exploring the region, seven days if you aim
to visit the Aran Islands and Achill Island. Although distances between
sites are not great, most of the routes in this chapter use the scenic but
slower national secondary routes. Covering 80 km–112 km (50 mi–70
mi) per day on these roads is a comfortable target.

*Numbers in the text correspond to numbers in the margin and on the
West and Galway City maps.*

Great Itineraries

IF YOU HAVE 4 DAYS

Assuming you're arriving in the West via Shannon Airport or by crossing into County Clare via the Killimer–Tarbert ferry, you'll first pass
through either **Ennis** ② or **Kilrush** ③. If the weather's good, head for
the beach town of **Kilkee** ④. If not, head right for the **Cliffs of Moher** ⑥.
Next stop should be the heart of the **Burren** ⑨, though you might want
to stop at the **Burren Display Centre** in Kilfenora first to pick up more
information about Ireland's strangest landscape. Both **Doolin** ⑦ and 🔲

Lisdoonvarna ⑧ are within the Burren and famous for their traditional music. Spend the night in Lisdoonvarna, or in ⛌ **Kinvara** ⑮ or ⛌ **Ballyvaughan** ⑩, both on Galway Bay.

On your second day, head right for ⛌ **Galway City** ⑯–㉚. Spend the morning exploring Galway on foot, poking around its shops, and finding out whether any theater or other performing arts events are on that night. In the afternoon, take a cruise up the River Corrib or drive out along the north shore of Galway Bay to **Salthill** ㉚ and beyond into the Gaeltacht. Eat an early dinner right in Galway before taking in some theater, or drive to one of the restaurants outside town for a leisurely dinner. Whether or not you go to the theater, try to get to a pub in town for some traditional live music and good *craic* before heading off to bed.

On your third day, you can kick around Galway—easily the liveliest city in Ireland after Dublin and the only large city in the West, so be sure you've had your fill of its buzz before you depart. There are plenty of special events to keep you busy, particularly if you're here during a festival. You also might want either to take the ferry out to the **Aran Islands** ㉛ for the day or make the quick trip south to **Coole Park** ⑬ and **Thoor Ballylee** ⑭, the two southernmost sites in the west of Ireland important to W. B. Yeats (most of the rest are in County Sligo [☞ Chapter 7]). Either way, again spend the night in Galway or at one of the country houses outside town (or perhaps even in a B&B on the Aran Islands, if you make it out there). Alternatively, if you're ready for scenery and a smaller town, head out through the moorlands of Connemara through **Oughterard** ㉜ to the Alpine-like coastal village of ⛌ **Clifden** ㊱, where you'll find gorgeous scenery and a surprisingly good selection of pubs and restaurants. Spend the night here or in a country house, hotel, or B&B in or around ⛌ **Cashel** ㉞ or ⛌ **Letterfrack** ㊲.

If you've spent your third night in Galway, follow the alternative day-three itinerary above, but don't linger too long in Clifden. Push on, as should those who stayed the night in or near Clifden, first to **Connemara National Park,** then just beyond to the **Kylemore Valley**'s ㊳ much-photographed **Kylemore Abbey,** which has a breathtaking lakeside location and a better-than-average crafts shop. Continue through **Leenane** ㊴ to ⛌ **Westport** ㊵, the prettiest village in County Mayo and a good place to spend the night. On the way, you won't be able to miss the distinctive conical shape of **Croagh Patrick,** the penitential mountain that was a refuge of St. Patrick during his years spent converting Ireland to Christianity. Try to be in Westport on Thursday, when its old-fashioned farmers' market is held. On your fourth day, make the walk up Croagh Patrick or stroll around Clew Bay seeing how many islands you can count. If the weather cooperates, you might want to venture out to **Achill Island** ㊶. At the end of the day, continue on north to Sligo (☞ Chapter 7) or head for a Midlands destination (☞ Chapter 3).

IF YOU HAVE 7 DAYS

Our four-day itinerary can easily be expanded into a seven-day trip, with the following modifications: Spend a full two days exploring western County Clare, staying one night in the seaside town of **Lahinch** ⑤ (especially if you're a golfer or are traveling with one) and another in any of the towns noted above. Depending on how much time you want to spend in Galway, you might want to make it to **Coole Park** ⑬ and **Thoor Ballylee** ⑭ on one of your first two days in the West, rather than taking a bite out of the time you have for Galway and the Aran Islands. Begin your third (rather than your second) day by heading to ⛌ **Galway City** ⑯–㉚. Plan on spending three full days based either right in or just outside Galway. Spend two of these days in Galway itself and

The West

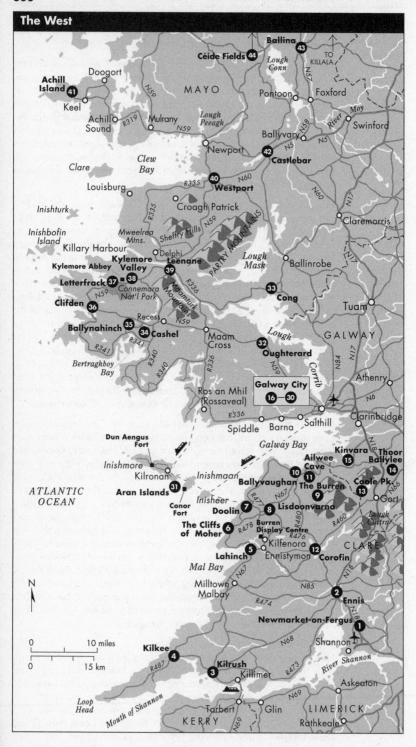

one on a day trip out to the **Aran Islands** ③. On your sixth day, follow our alternative day-three itinerary above, ending up either in ⊡ **Clifden** ③, ⊡ **Cashel** ③, or ⊡ **Letterfrack** ③ for the night. Then follow our day-four itinerary above for your seventh day.

When to Tour the West

"Soft weather," as the Irish call on-again, off-again rainy days, is almost always a possibility in the West, but the months of May and October are likelier to be drier than the rest of the year. The Burren is at its best in May, when the wildflowers are in season. April, May, and October are good times for an off-peak visit. In July and August, expect to rub elbows with Irish families taking their holidays here; these are also the best months to hear traditional music. It doesn't take many visitors to overwhelm Galway City's narrow streets, so if you don't love crowds, steer clear in late July, when the Arts Festival and Galway Race take place back-to-back. Many restaurants and accommodations in Connemara and the Burren are seasonal and close from October to Easter, although thanks to a steady rise in demand, the season is definitely extending slightly each year. If you do choose to visit the West between November and March, your choice of places to stay and to eat will be limited, but you do get to feel as though you have the place to yourself. A word of warning, though: During the winter, the weather in the West can be harsh, with gales and rain sweeping in day after day from the Atlantic.

THE BURREN AND BEYOND— WEST CLARE TO SOUTH GALWAY

County Clare claims two of Ireland's unique natural sites: the awesome Cliffs of Moher and the stark, mournful landscape of the Burren, which hugs the coast from Black Head in the north to Doolin and the Cliffs of Moher in the south. Yet western County Clare is widely beloved among native Irish for a natural phenomenon significantly less unique than these: its beaches. Though just another Irish beach town to some, Kilkee, to name just one, is a favorite summer getaway, the sort of unassuming place that natives beg you not to put into your guidebook. So whether you're looking for inimitable scenery or just a lovely beach to plunk down on for a few hours and relax in the sun (if you're lucky!), this route will introduce you to the natural wonders of the West.

This journey begins at Newmarket-on-Fergus, within minutes of Shannon Airport, and it makes a good jumping-off point for a tour through the West if you've just arrived in Ireland and are planning to head for Galway. It also follows directly from the end of Chapter 5, which concludes 10 km (6 mi) down the road, at Bunratty Castle and Folk Park (and the Knappogue Castle, also nearby), so be sure to take a moment to glance at those sights to decide whether to include them as you get under way. This first tour is also the connecting link between County Limerick (and other points in the Southwest) and Galway City. If you're approaching it from the Southwest and you're not going into Limerick City itself, it's easy to pick up the tour from Killimer, reached via the ferry from Tarbert (☞ Arriving and Departing *in* The West A to Z, *below*).

Newmarket-on-Fergus

❶ *13 km (8 mi) north of Shannon Airport on N18.*

A small town in County Clare, Newmarket-on-Fergus is chiefly remarkable nowadays as the town nearest to Dromoland Castle Hotel, formerly the home of Lord Inchiquin, chief of the O'Brien clan.

Dining and Lodging

$$$$ ✕🍴 **Dromoland Castle.** A popular first stop with affluent American
★   and French visitors arriving at Shannon Airport, Dromoland is the ancestral home of the O'Briens, the descendants of Brian Boru, High King
of Ireland. The massive, turreted, neo-Gothic castle—dating from the
19th century, when it replaced its 16th-century predecessor—looks the
part, standing regally beside a scenic lake, surrounded by tidily landscaped formal gardens and a golf course. Inside, the grand, plushly carpeted rooms are graced with large ancestral portraits, crystal chandeliers,
and oak paneling; hushed, well-dressed guests sit amid all the splendor, sipping tea or drinks. Bedrooms overlook the old Queen Anne sta-
bleyard and feature Regency-style furniture and a pleasant pink or green
color scheme. The vast suites have ruched drapes on the tall windows,
great views over the park, and antiques, many of them Irish-Georgian.
Award-winning cuisine is served in the formal, oak-wainscoted dining
room. ✉ *Co. Clare,* ☎ *061/368144,* 𝔽𝔸𝕏 *061/363355. 74 rooms with
bath. Restaurant, bar, 18-hole golf course, 2 tennis courts, Ping-Pong,
fishing, bicycles. AE, DC, MC, V.*

$ ✕🍴 **Hunter's Lodge.** A comfortable, unpretentious village pub, the lodge
makes an ideal first or last stop for visitors to the West who are traveling via Shannon Airport, 12 km (8 mi) downroad. The pub has an
old-world style, with an open fire and a quiet local trade. Well-equipped
rooms have timber floors with scatter rugs and are attractively decorated with select pieces of old oak furniture. The restaurant, known
for its cheerful service and simply prepared surf and turf, is a good value.
✉ *The Square, Co. Clare,* ☎ *061/368577,* 𝔽𝔸𝕏 *061/368057. 6 rooms
with bath. Restaurant, bar, free parking. AE, DC, MC, V.*

Outdoor Activities and Sports

Dromoland Golf Course (✉ Newmarket-on-Fergus, ☎ 061/368444) is
one of the most scenic in the country, set in a 700-acre estate of rich
woodland on the grounds of the Dromoland Castle Hotel. The 18-hole,
par-71 course has a natural lake that leaves little room for error on a
number of holes.

Ennis

❷ *9½ km (6 mi) east of Newmarket-on-Fergus on N18, 37 km (23 mi)
northwest of Limerick, 138 km (86 mi) north of Tralee.*

A major crossroads and a convenient stop between the West and the
Southwest, Ennis is the county town of County Clare, a pleasant if phys-
ically unremarkable market town that's often bustling. It has always
fostered traditional arts, especially fiddle playing and step-dancing (a
kind of square dance). The **Fleadh Nua** (pronounced fla-*nooa*) festival at the end of May attracts both performers and students of Irish
music. Two statues in Ennis bear witness to the role its citizens have
played in Irish democracy. On a tall limestone column above a massive pediment in the town center stands a **statue of Daniel O'Connell**
(1775–1847), "The Liberator" (☞ Sneem *in* Chapter 5), who was a
member of Parliament for County Clare between 1828 and 1831 and
instrumental in bringing about Catholic Emancipation. Outside the
courthouse (in the town park, beside the River Fergus, on the west side
of Ennis) stands a larger-than-life bronze **statue of Eamon De Valera**
(1882–1975), who successfully contested the election here in 1917, thus
launching a long political career. Although De Valera was born in the
United States, his maternal forebears were from County Clare. He was
the dominant figure in Irish politics during this century, serving as prime
minister for most of the years from 1937 until 1959, when he resigned

as leader of Fianna Fáil, the party he founded, and went on to serve as president until 1973.

Dining and Lodging

$$$$ ✕⊡ **Carnelly House.** This 250-year-old Queen Anne-style, redbrick house is an elegant, convenient base for exploring the West, 5 km (3 mi) south of Ennis and 16 km (10 mi) from Shannon Airport. The perfectly proportioned drawing room has elaborate plasterwork decorations. The large, comfortable bedrooms have canopied or four-poster beds and bucolic views over the 100-acre estate. Dishes such as rack of lamb with garlic and rosemary, pheasant in port, and poached wild salmon are frequent menu items. Hosts Dermot and Rosemarie Gleeson will fill you in on the beguiling house's colorful history. ⊠ *Clarecastle, Co. Clare,* ☎ *065/682–8442,* ℻ *065/682–9222. 5 rooms with bath. Horseback riding, fishing. MC, V.*

Nightlife

Although Ennis is not as fashionable as, say, Galway, it is one of the West's traditional music hot spots. Below are the pubs where you're likeliest to hear sessions, but keep in mind they don't necessarily take place every night and the scene is constantly changing. Phone ahead to check whether a session is happening.

Ciaran's Bar (⊠ 1 Francis St., ☎ 065/684–0180). **Cruise's** (⊠ Abbey St., ☎ 065/684–1800). **Kerins'** (⊠ Lifford, ☎ 065/682–0582). **May Kearney's Bar** (⊠ 1 Newbridge Rd., ☎ 065/682–4888). The **Old Ground** (⊠ O'Connell St., ☎ 065/682–8127). **Paddy Quinn's** (⊠ 7 Market St., ☎ 065/682–8148). The **Temple Gate** (⊠ The Square, ☎ 065/682–3300).

Outdoor Activities and Sports

BICYCLING

Cycle into the Burren on a bike rented from **Michael Tierney** (⊠ 17 Abbey St., ☎ 065/682–9433).

GOLF

Ennis Golf Club (⊠ Drumbiggle Rd., ☎ 065/682–4074) is an 18-hole, par-70 parkland course overlooking the town.

HORSEBACK RIDING

Ballyshannon Riding Establishment (⊠ Ballyshannon House, Quin, ☎ 065/682–5645) has woodland trail riding and beginners' lessons and will provide riding equipment.

Shopping

The **Belleek Shop** (⊠ 36 Abbey St., ☎ 065/682–9607) carries Belleek china, Waterford crystal, and Donegal Parian china, as well as Lladró, Hummel, and other collectible china. **Flax in Bloom** (⊠ 30 Abbey St., ☎ 065/682–0833) has women's and teenagers' fashions with an emphasis on Irish design and classic fabrics. At **Clare Business Center** (⊠ Francis St., ☎ 065/682–0166) you'll find a variety of crafts workshops that sell to the public. **Carraig Donn** (⊠ 29 O'Connell St., ☎ 065/682–8188) stocks Waterford glass and other Irish crystal, Belleek and other fine china, and its own array of knitwear. The **Inis Gallery** (⊠ 11 Chapel Lane, ☎ 065/682–1559) sells Irish fine art prints and maps. Stop off at the **Antique Loft** (⊠ Clarecastle, ☎ 065/684–1969) for collectibles and pine and mahogany antiques.

Kilrush

❸ *43 km (27 mi) southwest of Ennis on N68.*

Like most other mid-19th-century towns in West Clare, Kilrush was laid out with a large central square radiating out into the town's main streets. The widest of these leads to the harbor and the docks. This plan makes the small market town (population 3,000) seem bigger than it actually is. An exhibition entitled **"Kilrush in Landlord Times"** explains the history of the town from its beginnings in the late 18th century; it's also the starting point for a heritage walk through the town's streets that takes you back to the 19th century. ⊠ *Town Sq.,* ☎ *065/ 905–1577.* 🖃 *£1.* ⊙ *May–Sept., Mon.–Sat. 9:30–5:30, Sun. noon–4.*

Outdoor Activities and Sports

Kilrush Golf & Sports Club (⊠ Parknamoney, Ennis Rd., Co. Clare, ☎ 065/905–1138) is an 18-hole, par-70 course that overlooks the Shannon estuary.

Scattery Island Ferries (⊠ Kilrush Marina, Co. Clare, ☎ 065/905–1327) run a 20-minute boat trip to Scattery Island, a picturesque destination that has a ruined 6th-century monastic settlement complete with round tower. From May to early September, two-hour dolphin-watching trips (£10) run out to the Shannon Estuary, where a school of 40 or so bottle-nosed dolphins regularly play. Trips are weather permitting and subject to demand; phone ahead to confirm.

Kilkee

❹ *12 km (8 mi) west of Kilrush on N68.*

Kilkee is one of the most beloved west-coast beach resorts among native Irish people, many of whom have summered here for generations. Its major draw is its safe bathing—both in the waters along its magnificent long, sandy beach and in deep rock pools known as Pollock holes, which remain full at low tide (they attract scuba divers as well as swimmers). From Kilkee, you can take an excursion to **Loop Head Lighthouse** on R487, about a 38-km (24-mi) round-trip. Loop Head is the westernmost point of County Clare, situated at the northern tip of the mouth of the Shannon, the very end of its long estuary.

Outdoor Activities and Sports

Kilkee Golf and Country Club (⊠ East End, ☎ 065/905–6048) overlooks the sea and has spectacular, cliff-edge holes. Founded in 1896, it was expanded in 1994 to an 18-hole, par-72 course.

En Route The main route heads north up the coast on N67. Sandy beaches and more Pollock holes can be found by taking a left off the main road at any sign that indicates STRAND and traveling for about 2½ km (1½ mi).

Lahinch

❺ *47 km (30 mi) north of Kilkee on N67, 30 km (18 mi) west of Ennis on N85.*

A shortcut joins the main tour on N67 at Lahinch, another busy resort village beside a long, sandy beach backed by dunes, best known for its links golf courses and—believe it or not—its surfing. In 1972, the European Surfing Finals were held here, putting Lahinch on the world surfing map. Today Tom and Rosemary Buckley's **Lahinch Surf Shop** (⊠ The Promenade, ☎ 065/708–1543), Ireland's oldest (open since 1990), is ground-zero for County Clare surfers.

Dining and Lodging

$ ✕ **P. J. Egan's.** For all appearances, this is a normal Victorian pub with an open fire and orange lightbulbs casting a romantic glow. The difference is the wine list—good Bordeaux is sold by the case to customers all over Ireland, but Cru Bourgeois and other less-expensive wines are also sold by the bottle at supermarket prices (less than 10% markup compared to the standard 33%) and can be sampled for £2 a glass. ⊠ *Liscannor,* ☎ *065/708–1430, No credit cards.*

$$ ★ ✕⌖ **Aberdeen Arms.** This beautifully refurbished Victorian, seaside hotel is a model of its kind, offering elegance and comfort in a friendly, easy-going setting. Humorous golfing prints hanging on the dark-paneled walls of the bar and grill room appeal to the many golfers who stay here. The newest rooms face the sea and have spectacular skylights and windows. All rooms are large and tastefully decorated with built-in, cream-color melamine closets; plain carpets; and matching cream-floral drapes and spreads. Some rooms have Georgian-style tables and chairs. The main dining room offers an excellent and varied menu of French-Irish cuisine as well as one of the best breakfasts in the county. ⊠ *Lahinch, Co. Clare,* ☎ *065/708–1100,* ẞ̶A̶X̶ *065/708–1228. 55 rooms with bath. 2 restaurants, 2 bars, sauna, 10 tennis courts, health club, fishing, bicycles. AE, DC, MC, V.*

Nightlife
For traditional music try **O'Dwyer's 19th** (☎ 065/708–1440).

Outdoor Activities and Sports
The 6,613-yard, 18-hole, par-72 championship course at **Lahinch Golf Club** (⊠ Co. Clare, ☎ 065/708–1003), which opened in 1892, has challenging links following the natural contours of the dunes. The **Castle Course** (⊠ Co. Clare, ☎ 065/708–1003), the newer 18-hole, par-72 Lahinch course, offers a more carefree round of seaside golf, with shorter holes than the championship course.

Shopping
The **Design Lodge** (☎ 068/708–1744) is a small shop that carries Irish-made goods, including sweaters, linen, tweed, and other fine gift items.

En Route From Lahinch, continue toward the Cliffs of Moher. For the first time on this coast, the road narrows and starts to climb. It twists past small, whitewashed farms and green fields with glimpses of the sea on the horizon.

The Cliffs of Moher

★ ❻ *10 km (6 mi) northwest of Lahinch on R478.*

One of Ireland's most breathtaking natural sites, the majestic Cliffs of Moher rise vertically out of the sea in a wall that stretches over a long, 8-km (5-mi) swath and as high as 710 ft. You can see stratified deposits of five different rock layers in the cliff face. Numerous seabirds, including a large colony of puffins, make their home in the shelves of rock on the cliffs. On a clear day you can see the Aran Islands and the mountains of Connemara to the north, as well as the lighthouse on Loop Head and the mountains of Kerry to the south. **O'Brien's Tower** is a defiant, broody sentinel built at the cliffs' highest point. The parking area is a favorite spot of performers; in the high season, there's likely to be free entertainment—step dancers, fiddle players, or even a one-man band. The **visitor center**, a good refuge from passing rainsqualls, has a gift shop and tearoom. ☎ 065/708–1171. ⌑ *Free.* ⏾ *Cliffs and O'Brien's Tower freely accessible; visitor center mid-Feb.–Apr., daily 10–5; May–June and Sept., daily 10–6; July–Aug., daily 9:30–6:30.*

Doolin

❼ *6 km (4 mi) north of the Cliffs of Moher on R479.*

A tiny village consisting almost entirely of B&Bs, hostels, pubs, and restaurants, Doolin is widely said to have three of the best pubs in Ireland for traditional music (☞ Nightlife *and* Close Up: A Year-Round

Fleadh, *below*). But with the worldwide surge of interest in Irish music during the last decade, the village is more of a magnet for European musicians than it is for young, or even established, Irish artists. On **Doolin Pier,** about 1½ km (1 mi) outside the village, local fishermen sell their catch fresh off the boat—lobster, crayfish, salmon, and mackerel. From spring until early fall (weather permitting), a regular ferry service takes visitors for a 30-minute ride to Inisheer, the smallest of the Aran Islands (☞ *below*). ☎ 065/707–74455. ☎ £15. ☉ *Up to 10 sailings daily mid-Mar.–Oct.; call for schedule.*

Dining and Lodging

$$$ ✕ **Bruach na Haille.** The name means "the bank of the river Aille," and the river can be seen from the side windows of this charming cottage restaurant, owned by John and Helen Browne for 20 years. The low-beamed, cozy rooms have flagstone floors; old dressers laden with colorful delft china; and open turf fires. Lobster from Doolin Pier is usually on the menu, as is a renowned sirloin steak with Irish whiskey sauce. ⊠ *Roadford,* ☎ *065/707–4120. AE, DC, MC, V. Closed Nov.–mid-Mar. No lunch.*

$$ ✕☒ **Aran View House.** On the coast road in the Fanore direction, about 10 minutes' walk from Doolin village, this hotel commands magnificent views of the Aran Islands in the west, Doolin Pier and the Cliffs of Moher in the south, and the gray limestone rocks of the Burren to the north. The 1736 house has been extensively modernized, with lovely antique touches such as four-poster beds and Georgian reproduction furniture. Bay windows in the ambitious restaurant let you savor the views, while the decor impresses with Regency chairs and dusky pink napery. ⊠ *Co. Clare,* ☎ *065/707–4061,* 🖷 *065/707–4540. 19 rooms with bath. Restaurant, bar, fishing. AE, DC, MC, V. Closed Nov.–Mar.*

Nightlife

Doolin's three pubs famous for their traditional music sessions are **Gus O'Connor's** (☎ 065/707–4168), **McDermott's** (☎ no phone), and **McGann's** (☎ 065/707–4133). Gus O'Connor's also serves excellent bar food.

Outdoor Activities and Sports

Cycle along the coast on a bike rented from **Patrick Moloney, Doolin Hostel** (⊠ Co. Clare, ☎ 065/707–4006).

Shopping

Doolin Crafts Gallery (☎ 065/707–4309), beside the cemetery and the church, carries only Irish-made goods, including sweaters, modern lead crystal, linen, lace, and tweed. A jeweler's workshop and a resident batik maker are also on the premises. Don't miss the 1-acre garden, which has more than 600 plants from all over the world. The garden and the Flagship Restaurant are open daily April–October.

Lisdoonvarna

❽ *5 km (3 mi) east of Doolin on R478.*

One of only two spa towns in Ireland (the other is Enniscrone, in western County Sligo), Lisdoonvarna has several sulfurous and iron-bearing springs with radioactive properties, all containing iodine. The town grew up in the late 19th century to accommodate visitors who wished to "take the waters." Its buildings reflect a mishmash of mock-architectural styles: Scottish baronial, Swiss chalet, Spanish hacienda, and American motel. Depending on your taste, it's either lovably kitschy or unappealingly tacky. If you're curious about health cures, the **Lisdoonvarna Spa and Bath House** is worth a visit. Iron and magnesia elements make the drinking water taste terrible (as does most spa water). In comparison, the bathing water is pleasant, if enervating. Electric sulfur baths, massage, wax baths, sauna, and a solarium are available at the spa complex, which sits on the edge of town in an attractive parkland setting. ☎ 065/707–4023. ✉ *Complex free, sulfur baths £5 (book in advance).* ⊙ *Early June–early Oct., daily 10–6.*

In July and August, Lisdoonvarna is a favorite getaway for Irish under-30s. It's also the traditional vacationing spot for the West's bachelor farmers, who used to congregate here at harvest time in late September with the vague intention of finding wives. (Irish farmers are notoriously shy with women and reluctant to marry, often postponing the event until their mid- or late-fifties, if ever.) This tradition is now formalized in the **Matchmaking Festival,** held during late September. Middle-aged singles dance to the strains of country-and-western bands, and a talent contest is held to name the most eligible bachelor.

Dining and Lodging

$ ✕⌂ **Ballinalacken Castle.** On a hill 4 km (2½ mi) outside Lisdoonvarna, this sprawling Victorian lodge is on 100 acres of wildflower meadows beside the 16th-century ruins of an O'Brien stronghold. Its bow windows take advantage of glorious panoramic views of the Atlantic, the Aran Islands, and the Connemara hills. Guest rooms come in all different shapes and sizes; some have marble fireplaces and high ceilings. Six large rooms are in a new wing; all have sea views and dark-wood furniture. The public rooms are a haphazard mix of hand-me-downs, modern items, lovely old Irish oak, and sumptuous, inlaid bureaus. Fresh local seafood and local lamb are served in the modest restaurant. ⊠ *Co. Clare,* ☎ *065/707–4025,* ﬀⱯ *065/707–4025. 12 rooms with bath. Restaurant, bar. MC, V. Closed early Oct.–Mar.*

$ ✕⌂ **Carrigann.** Settled into prettily landscaped gardens and just two minutes' walk from the village center, this small, friendly hotel is popular with hikers, who come for the guided walks and independent exploration. Hosts Mary and Gerard Howard keep a library of special-interest books on the Burren beside the turf fire in the sitting room; their maps and notes are also available. Rooms are modestly furnished but well equipped for the price range. Gerard also runs his own butcher shop, guaranteeing top-quality meat on the hotel's menu. Meals are supplemented by herbs from the garden and fresh local fish. ⊠ *Co. Clare,* ☎ *065/707–4036,* ﬀⱯ *065/707–4567. 20 rooms with bath. Fishing. MC, V. Nov.–Feb.*

$ ✕⌂ **Sheedy's Spa View.** Originally a 17th-century farmhouse, this small,
★ friendly hotel is only a short walk from the town center and the spa wells. It's been in the hands of the Sheedy family since 1855. The rooms are simple, spotlessly clean, and well cared for; most include a Georgian-style coffee table and chairs. Patsy Sheedy and her son, Frankie, who studied abroad, serve French-Irish cuisine at their award-winning, moderately priced Orchid Restaurant. Fresh local lobster with garlic butter and panfried sirloin steak with Cajun root vegetables in a wild mushroom and brandy cream are two of the winners here. ⊠ *Co. Clare,* ☎ *065/707–4026,* ﬀⱯ *065/707–4555. 11 rooms with bath. Restaurant, bar, tennis court. AE, DC, MC, V. Closed Oct.–Mar.*

Nightlife

Country music and ballad singing are popular in the bars of Lisdoonvarna. For traditional music try the **Roadside Tavern** (☎ 065/707–4084).

Shopping

To see an audiovisual presentation on smoking Atlantic salmon, plus live demonstrations of the oak-smoking process, visit the **Burren Smokehouse Ltd.** (☎ 065/707–4432). You can also buy neatly packaged whole sides of salmon to take home.

The Burren

★ ⑨ *Extending throughout western County Clare from the Cliffs of Moher in the south to Black Head in the north, as far southeast as Corofin.*

As you travel north toward Ballyvaughan, the landscape becomes rockier and stranger. Instead of the seemingly ubiquitous Irish green, gray becomes the prevailing color. You're now in the heart of the Burren, a 300-square-km (116-square-mi) expanse that is one of Ireland's fiercest landscapes. The Burren is aptly named: It's an Anglicization of the Irish word *bhoireann* ("a rocky place"). Stretching off in all directions, as far as the eye can see, are vast, irregular slabs of fissured limestone (known as *karst*) with deep cracks between them. From a distance, it looks like a lunar landscape, so dry that nothing could possibly grow on it. In the spring (especially from mid-May to mid-June), the Burren becomes a wild rock garden, as an astonishing variety of wildflowers bloom between the cracks in the rocks, among them at least 23 native species of orchid. The Burren also supports an incredible variety of wildlife, including frogs, newts, lizards, badgers, stoats, sparrow hawks, kestrels, and dozens of other birds and animals. The wildflowers and other plants are given life from the spectacular caves, streams, and potholes that lie beneath the rough, scarred pavements. With the advent of spring, *turloughs* (seasonal lakes that disappear in dry weather) appear on the plateau's surface. Botanists are particularly intrigued by the cohabitation of Arctic and Mediterranean plants, many so tiny (and rare, so please do not pick any) you can't see them from your car window; make a point of exploring some of this rocky terrain on foot. Numerous signposted walks run through both coastal and inland areas. For a private guided tour, contact Mary Angela Keane (☎ 065/707–4003; £25 per hour) or Shane Connolly (☎ 065/707–7168; £10 per person); May and June are peak months for flora, but a tour is worthwhile at any time of year.

In Kilfenora 8 km (5 mi) southeast of Lisdoonvarna on R476, the tiny **Burren Display Centre** has a modest audiovisual display and other exhibits that explain the Burren's geology, flora, and archaeology. ☎ 065/708–8030. ⊠ £2.50. ⊙ June–Aug., daily 9:30–6; Mar.–May and Sept.–Oct., daily 10–5.

Also in Kilfenora, beside the Burren Display Centre, the ruins of a small 12th-century church, once the **Cathedral of St. Fachan,** have been partially restored as a parish church. There are some interesting carvings in the roofless choir, including an unusual, life-size human skeleton. In a field about 165 ft west of the ruins is an elaborately sculpted **high cross** that is worth examining, even though parts of it are badly weathered.

Nightlife

Vaughan's Pub (☎ 065/708–8004) in Kilfenora is known for its traditional music sessions.

Ballyvaughan

⑩ *16 km (10 mi) north of Lisdoonvarna on N67.*

A pretty little waterside village and a good base for exploring the Burren, Ballyvaughan attracts walkers and artists who enjoy the views of Galway Bay and access to the Burren. Outside Ballyvaughan, you'll
⑪ see a signpost to the right for **Ailwee Cave,** the only such chamber in the region accessible to those who aren't spelunkers. This vast, 2-million-year-old cave is illuminated for about 3,300 ft and contains an underground river and waterfall. ☎ 065/707–7036. ⊠ £4.25. ⊙ Early

Mar.–June and Sept.–early Nov., daily 10–6 (last tour at 5:30); July–Aug., daily 10–7 (last tour at 6:30).

Dining and Lodging

$$$ ✕🔟 **Gregan's Castle Hotel.** The Haden family runs this quiet, metic-
★ ulous, large Victorian country house, located at the base of the aptly
named Corkscrew Hill (on N67, midway between Ballyvaughan and
Lisdoonvarna). The house is surrounded by award-winning gardens
and overlooks Galway Bay and the gray mountains of the Burren. All
bedrooms are individually furnished with Georgian and Victorian an-
tiques and William Morris wallpaper; older ones have molded-plaster
ceilings. The spacious rooms on the ground floor have private patio
gardens but lack the splendid views of the rooms upstairs. The restau-
rant, rather formal for this part of the world (jacket and tie are required),
serves updated French cuisine. ✉ *Co. Clare,* ☎ *065/707–7005,* FAX *065/
707–7111. 18 rooms with bath, 4 suites. Restaurant, bar, croquet, fish-
ing, bicycles. AE, MC, V. Closed Nov.–Mar.*

$$ ✕🔟 **Hyland's Hotel.** In the heart of the Burren, this family-run, yel-
low-and-red coaching inn dates back to the early 18th century. A turf
fire greets you in the lobby. Rooms vary in size and shape, but all have
pine furniture and fresh-looking color-coordinated drapes and spreads.
If you like mountain views, ask for a room with a skylight looking out
over the Burren. The restaurant, cheerfully decorated in country pine
with red tablecloths, specializes in simply prepared local produce.
There is live music in the bar most nights from June to mid-September and Irish storytelling once a week. ✉ *Co. Clare,* ☎ *065/707–7037,*
FAX *065/707–7131. 30 rooms with bath. Restaurant, bar. AE, MC, V.
Closed Jan. 6–Feb.*

$ ✕🔟 **Admiral's Rest.** You can guess from the nautical bric-a-brac on
view that this place belongs to a retired naval man—John Macnamara,
who is an expert on the Burren's wildlife. In a modernized cottage on
the coast road between Lisdoonvarna and Ballyvaughan, the restaurant is across the road from the sea, which is visible through the large
windows. Varnished stone floors, stone-topped tables, *sugán* (rope-
seated) chairs, an open wood-and-turf fire, and posies of wildflowers
on the tables make up the rugged decor. Seafood is the mainstay of the
tasty menu. Nine inexpensive B&B rooms with shared baths are available in the bungalow next door. ✉ *Fanore, Co. Clare,* ☎ *065/707–
6105,* FAX *065/707–6161. 9 rooms. AE, MC, V. Closed Nov.–Easter.*

Nightlife

The **Monk's Pub** (☎ 065/707–7059), near the waterfront, has great
music sessions and a friendly ambience.

En Route From Ballyvaughan, it's a 48-km (30-mi) trip circumnavigating Galway Bay to Galway City. If you're eager to get there, skip the next two
towns and head there directly, first passing through Kinvara (☞ *below*).
If you're on a more leisurely pace, head back south through the Burren on R480 and R476 to Corofin.

Corofin

⑫ *23 km (14½ mi) south of Ballyvaughan, 16 km (10 mi) east of Kilfenora
on the R476.*

If you're searching for your Irish roots, Corofin's **Clare Heritage Center** has a genealogical service and advice for do-it-yourselfers. Its displays on the history of the West of Ireland in the 19th century cover
culture, traditions, emigration, and famine, as it exposes some grim statis-
tics. In 1841, for example, the population of County Clare was 286,394.
Fifty years later, famine and emigration had reduced this number to

112,334, and the population continued to decline, reaching an all-time low of 73,597 in 1956. (It is now heading back to the 90,000 mark.) ☎ 065/683–7955. ✉ £2. ⊘ Apr.–Oct., daily 10–6; Nov.–Mar. (genealogy service only), weekdays 9–5; Heritage Center by appointment.

In a 15th-century castle on the edge of Corofin, the **Dysert O'Dea Castle Archaeology Centre** has an exhibition on the antiquities of the Burren. Twenty-five monuments stand within a 1½-km (1-mi) radius of the castle; these date from the Bronze Age to the 19th century, and all are described at the center. ☎ 065/683–7722. ✉ £2. ⊘ May–Sept., daily 10–6.

Coole Park and Thoor Ballylee

24 km (15 mi) northeast of Corofin on N18.

⑬ On the left side north of the little town of Gort is **Coole Park,** once home to Lady Augusta Gregory (1859–1932), W. B. Yeats's patron and his cofounder of Dublin's Abbey Theater (☞ Chapter 8). Yeats visited here often, as did almost all of the other writers who contributed to the Irish literary revival in the first half of the 20th century, including George Bernard Shaw and Sean O'Casey. Douglas Hyde, the first president of Ireland, was also a visitor. The house fell derelict after Lady Gregory's death and was demolished in 1941; the grounds are now a national forest and wildlife park. The only reminder of its literary past is the **Autograph Tree,** a copper beech on which many of Lady Gregory's famous guests carved their initials. Picnic tables make this a lovely alfresco lunch spot. ☎ 091/631804. ✉ Visitor center £2, park free. ⊘ Visitor center mid-Apr.–mid-June and Sept., Tues.–Sat. 10–5, mid-June–Aug., daily 9:30–6:30; park daily 10–dusk.

⑭ **Thoor Ballylee,** signposted 5 km (3 mi) along N66 on the right side of the road north of Coole Park, is a sight Yeats fans won't want to miss. This is one of the only major sites in the west of Ireland associated with the Nobel prize–winning poet that is not in County Sligo (☞ Chapter 7). In his fifties and newly married, Yeats bought this 14th-century Norman tower as a ruin in 1916 for £35. The tower is located beside a whitewashed, thatched-roof cottage, with a tranquil stream running alongside it. Its proximity to Lady Gregory's house at Coole Park made it a desirable location, though it required significant work on Yeats's part to make it livable. He stayed here intermittently until 1929 and penned some of his more mystical works here, including The Tower and The Winding Stair. It's now fully restored with his original decor and furniture. The audiovisual display is a useful introduction to the poet and his times. ☎ 091/631436. ✉ £3. ⊘ Easter–Sept., daily 10–6.

Kinvara

⑮ 13½ km (8½ mi) east of Ballyvaughan, 15 km (9 mi) northwest of Gort on N67, 25 km (15½ mi) south of Galway City.

Whether you're coming from Ballyvaughan or from Gort, Kinvara is worth a visit. The picture-perfect village is a growing holiday base, thanks to its gorgeous bay-side locale, great walking and sea angling, and numerous pubs. Kinvara is best known for its long-standing early August sailing event, **Cruinniú na mBád** (Festival of the Gathering of the Boats), in which traditional brown-sailed Galway hookers laden with turf race across the bay. (Hookers were used until the early part of this century to carry turf, provisions, and cattle across Galway Bay and out to the Aran Islands. A sculpture in Galway's Eyre Square [☞ below] honors their local significance.)

On a rock to the north of Kinvara Bay, the 16th-century **Dunguaire Castle** commands all the approaches from Galway Bay. It is said to be on the site of a 7th-century castle built by the King of Connaught. One of its previous owners, Oliver St. John Gogarty, was a surgeon, man of letters, and model for James Joyce's Buck Mulligan, a character in *Ulysses*. Today Dunguaire is used for a literarily themed medieval banquet that honors local writers and others with ties to the West, including Lady Gregory, W. B. Yeats, Sean O'Casey, and Pádraic Ó'Conaire (☞ Eyre Square *in* Galway, *below*). ⊠ *Kinvara, Co. Galway,* ☎ *091/ 637108.* ⊠ *Castle £2.50; banquets £29.* ☉ *May–Sept., daily 9:30–5; banquets at 5:30 and 8:30.*

Dining and Lodging

$ ✕ **Moran's of the Weir.** Signposted off the main road on the south side of Clarinbridge, this waterside thatched cottage, the home of the Moran family since 1760, houses a simply furnished restaurant at the back that serves only seafood. It's *the* place to stop to sample the local oysters, grown on a bed in front of the restaurant—but only when there is an "r" in the name of the month of your travels! ⊠ *The Weir, Kilcolgan, Co. Galway,* ☎ *091/796113. AE, MC, V.*

$$ ✕☰ **Merriman Inn.** This whitewashed, thatched inn on the shores of Galway Bay may look traditional, but, in fact, it's a midsize hotel. Like its sister property, Brennan's Yard in Galway City, the Merriman is decorated with locally made, well-designed furniture, as well as original crafts, paintings, and sculpture. The bar and lounge both have open fires and a relaxed, friendly atmosphere. Guest rooms are well equipped, but not all have views of Galway Bay, so ask for one when booking. The Quilty Room is a large, airy restaurant adorned with mood-enhancing landscape paintings. Local seafood—such as tournedos of salmon pan-seared with a confit of fennel and a sharp spicy jus—is featured on the French-influenced menu, but you can also try succulent local lamb. ⊠ *Kinvara, Co. Galway,* ☎ *091/638222,* FAX *091/637686. 32 rooms with bath. Restaurant, bar, meeting room. AE, DC, MC, V.*

$ ✕☰ **Burren View Farm.** On the edge of Galway Bay, 5 km (3 mi) west of Kinvara, this simple B&B is relatively isolated on a working sheep and cattle farm and has a million-dollar view. Stone-walled fields dotted with sheep surround the yellow, two-story house. The breakfast room, sun lounge, and front bedrooms look out across a wide sea inlet to the gray expanse of the Burren. Rooms are plain and homey but clean and well maintained. Wholesome evening meals, Irish or Continental style, are cooked on request. ⊠ *Doorus, Kinvara, Co. Galway,* ☎ *091/637142,* FAX *091/638131. 5 rooms, 2 with bath. Dining room, tennis court, fishing. AE, DC, MC, V.*

Nightlife and the Arts

The first weekend in May, Kinvara hosts the annual **Cuckoo Fleadh** (☎ 091/637145). You can hear traditional music most nights at the **Winkles Hotel** (⊠ The Square, ☎ 91/637137).

GALWAY CITY AND THE ARAN ISLANDS

Galway is often said to be a state of mind as much as it is a specific place. The largest city in the West today (population 60,000) and the ancient capital of the province of Connaught, Galway is "the place where the clocks seem to run without the urgencies of elsewhere," as the writer Cormac MacConnell put it. In addition, Galway has always been the chief trading post for the Aran Islands, those "fragments of Connemara flung offshore," again to quote MacConnell. Although Inishmore, Inishmaan, and Inisheer—islands whose very names have the ring of poetry—receive upwards of 100,000 visitors per year (most of them between June and August), a voyage out to these Aran isles is still, for many visitors to Ireland, among their most unforgettable experiences. Few other places enhance their understanding of Irish folkways and Gaelic culture as these legendary locales.

Galway City

⑯ *27 km (12½ mi) north of Kinvara, 219 km (136 mi) west of Dublin, 105 km (65 mi) north of Limerick.*

As almost any Galwegian will tell you, theirs is the fastest-growing city in all of Ireland. And if that doesn't impress you, how about this: It's the fastest-growing city *in all of Europe*. It's an astonishing fact, and once you arrive, you have to wonder where this city can possibly grow. For even though Galway is the largest city in the West, its heart is *tiny*—a warren of streets so compact that if you spend more than a few hours here, you'll soon be strolling along with the sort of easy familiarity you'd feel in your hometown.

For many Irish people, Galway is a favorite weekend getaway, the liveliest place in the Republic, and the city of festivals. Good roads and rail links with the capital make it the number one destination within Ireland for jaded Dubliners. It's also a university town: University College Galway (or UCG as it's locally known) is a center for Gaelic culture (Galway marks the eastern gateway to the West's large Gaeltacht). A fair share of UCG's 9,000 students study the Irish language, while hundreds of European and American university and college enrollees take a semester abroad here; hence, Galway is a sort of Irish frontier town of youth culture. On weekends, and especially festival weekends, you'll see as many pierced and tattooed teenagers and twentysomethings here as you'd find at a Cranberries concert.

But its students aren't its only avant-garde, as Galway has long attracted writers, artists, and musicians. The last keep the traditional music pubs lively year-round—the de facto centers of culture in a town that has no major cultural sites and institutions apart from UCG. Its two small but internationally acclaimed theater companies draw a steady stream of theater people. This cosmopolitan, bohemian populace and its left-coast geography make Galway something like the San Francisco of Ireland.

And although you're not conscious of it when you're in the center of town, Galway is—like its California counterpart—spectacularly situated, on the north shore of Galway Bay, where the River Corrib flows from Lough Corrib out into the sea. If you're lucky, you may get a Galwegian to sing you his or her rendition of the song "Galway Bay," once memorably crooned by Bing Crosby. Barely a 10-minute walk or 5-minute drive out of town, Grattan Road, which runs along the bay's northern shore out to the nearby seaside village of Salthill, has spectacular vistas across the vividly blue bay to the south shore's Black Head and beyond to the three Aran Islands (☞ *below*).

By what magic does Galway look the way it does? Its founders were Anglo-Normans who arrived in the mid-13th century and fortified their settlement against "the native Irish," as local chieftains were called. Galway became known as "the City of the Tribes" because of the dominant role in public and commercial life of the 14 families who founded it. Their names, still common in Galway and elsewhere in Ireland, recur regularly in any account of Irish history and culture: Athy, Blake, Bodkin, Browne, D'Arcy, Dean, Font, French, Kirwan, Joyce, Lynch, Morris, Martin, and Skerret. Particularly in and around its main pedestrian-oriented street—the name of which changes from Williamsgate to William to Shop to High to Quay—the city's medieval heritage is apparent everywhere: in the intimate two- and three-story stucco buildings, the windy streets, the narrow passageways, and the cobblestones underfoot. In the early 1980s, Galway was the first city in Ireland to revive the old Irish tradition of hand-painted wooden shop signs with Gaelic lettering. Modern sculptures, floral hanging baskets, and window boxes are further signs of Galway's deep-seated civic pride.

The question facing Galway today is: What price success? Galway's growth and popularity mean that at its busiest moments, pedestrians jam-pack its narrow, one-way streets, teetering off its even narrower sidewalks. If there's a city that doesn't sleep in Ireland, this is it. In fact, if you want to be guaranteed a quiet night's sleep, either ask for a room in the back of your center-city hotel or simply stay outside of town. First-time visitors here during late July's annual Galway Races week may be surprised to find that helicopters are a common form of transportation to shuttle revelers between the races and parties. There's something emblematic about whirring helicopters and galloping horses, bound together in the same fate, the modern machines and the ancient prancers moving the crowds to great heights, both figuratively and literally. Galwegians and their guests cheer on these emblems of present and past and in this probably guarantee their own future.

A Good Walk

Orient yourself at **Eyre Square** ⑰, part of which is occupied by **Kennedy Park.** Before you really get going, you may want to stop in at the **Tourist Information Office** ⑱ off the southeast corner of the square. At the top (north side) of Eyre Square, turn left down Williamsgate Street. This is the spine of old Galway. Its name changes four times before it reaches the River Corrib, successively called **William Street, Shop Street, High Street,** and **Quay Street.** If you have any postcards to mail, you may want to stop at the General Post Office, on the left side of Eglinton Street, the first right off Williamsgate Street. At the corner of William and Shop streets, **Lynch's Castle** ⑲ is one of Galway's oldest buildings. Continue down Shop Street to the pedestrian way just beyond Abbeygate Street; here **Lynch Memorial Window** ⑳ and **Collegiate Church of St. Nicholas** ㉑ are adjacent to one another. James Joyce fans might want to make the 30-second detour across Lombard and Market streets to Bowling Green, site of the **Nora Barnacle House** ㉒.

It's a minute's walk from the church to **Tíg Neachtain** ㉓ (Naughton's in English, pronounced *knock*-tons), a pub (popular with locals) at the corner of Cross Street and Quay/High Street. This corner is the very heart of old Galway's main historic and commercial district: Nearly all the city's best restaurants, bars, boutiques, art galleries, and crafts, antiques, and bookstores line the narrow, winding streets and alleys in this vicinity. Nothing is more than a five-minute walk from anything else. If this area is bursting at the seams, one block to the east of Shop Street/High Street, between Abbeygate and Cross streets, Middle Street is a significantly less trafficked, up-and-coming, and still somewhat undiscovered thoroughfare that has a number of worthwhile stores and restaurants, as well as the national Irish-language theater.

The **Spanish Arch** ㉔ and the **Galway City Museum** ㉕ are adjacent, right on the river's east bank, across from the Jurys Galway Inn parking lot. Just beyond Jurys (☞ *below*) but before crossing the Wolfe Tone Bridge, turn right onto the pedestrian path that parallels the river. Follow it past the William O'Brien Bridge to the **Salmon Weir Bridge** ㉖ (you'll need to jog off the path onto Abbeygate Street just short of the bridge to gain access to it). As you cross the bridge, look ahead to the **Cathedral of Our Lady Assumed into Heaven and St. Nicholas** ㉗ (known locally simply as "the cathedral"). A five-minute walk down University Road brings you to **University College Galway** ㉘. For a pretty stroll back to the center of town, turn right onto Canal Road and follow it back to the intersection of Dominick Street, Fairhill, and Raven Terrace. From here it's a brief jog to Claddagh Quay, which will take you out to the **Claddagh** ㉙. If you're out this far, you may want to continue on to **Salthill** ㉚; otherwise, head back to the center of town.

TIMING

You could easily take this walk in a morning or afternoon (less the walk out to Salthill), although if you browse in stores, chat with locals, or stop off for a pint or a cup of tea, you could stretch it out into a *very* leisurely all-day excursion. You may want to plan your day so you hit only what most interests you, leaving time to explore along the bay, get out to Salthill, or take a bay cruise.

Sights to See

㉗ **Cathedral of Our Lady Assumed into Heaven and St. Nicholas.** On an island forming the west bank of the River Corrib beside the Salmon Weir Bridge, Galway's largest Catholic church was dedicated by Cardinal Cushing of Boston in 1965. The cathedral was built on the site of the old Galway jail; a white cross embedded into the pavement of the adjacent parking lot marks the site of the cemetery that stood beside the prison.

㉙ **Claddagh.** On the west bank of the Corrib estuary, this district was once an Irish-speaking fishing village outside the walls of the old town. The name is an Anglicization of the Irish *cladach,* which means "marshy ground." It retained its own strong, separate identity until the 1930s, when its traditional thatched cottages were replaced by a conventional housing plan and its unique character and traditions were largely lost. One thing has survived: the Claddagh ring, composed of two hands clasped around a heart with a crown above it (symbolizing love, friendship, and loyalty), is still used by many Irish people as a wedding ring. Traditionally, the ring is worn with the heart facing into you if you're married or otherwise unavailable and with the heart facing outward (indicating your heart is open) if you're still looking for Mr. or Ms. Right. Reproductions in gold or silver are favorite souvenirs of Galway.

㉑ **Collegiate Church of St. Nicholas.** Built by the Anglo-Normans in 1320 and enlarged in 1486 and again in the 16th century, the church contains many fine carvings and gargoyles dating from the late Middle Ages, and it is one of the best-preserved medieval churches in Ireland. Legend has it that Columbus prayed here on his last stop before setting off on his voyage to the New World. On Saturday mornings, a **street market,** held in the pedestrian way beside the church, attracts two dozen or so vendors and hundreds of shoppers. ⊠ *Lombard St.* ☜ *Free.* ☉ *Daily 8–dusk.*

⑰ **Eyre Square.** The largest open space in central Galway on the east side of the Corrib, Eyre Square encompasses a hodgepodge of monuments and concrete and grassy areas. In the center is **Kennedy Park,** a patch of lawn named in honor of John F. Kennedy, who spoke from here when he visited the city in June 1963. At the north end of the park, a 20-ft-high steel **sculpture** standing in the pool of a fountain represents the brown sails seen on Galway hookers, the area's traditional sailing boats (☞ *Kinvara, above*). Seated beside this sculpture is the genial stone **figure of Pádraic Ó'Conaire,** a pioneer of the Irish-language revival at the turn of the century who was born in Galway (his birthplace fronting on the docks is marked with a plaque). When he died in a Dublin hospital in 1928, his only possessions were his pipe (a replica of which he

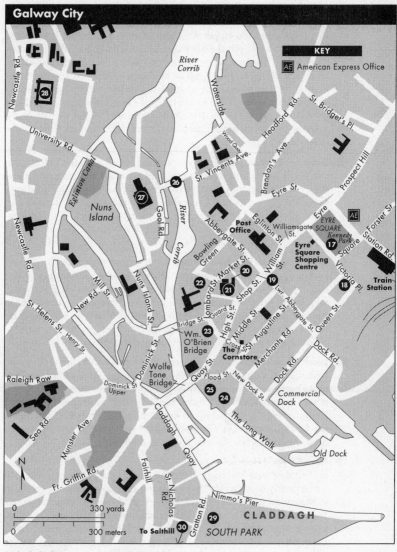

Galway City

KEY

AE American Express Office

River Corrib

Waterside

Newcastle Rd.

University Rd.

28

Eglinton Canal

Nuns Island

27

Gaol Rd.

River Corrib

26

St. Vincents Ave.

Wood Quay

Headford Rd.

St. Bridget's Pl.

Brendan's Ave.

Eyre St.

Prospect Hill

Abbeygate St.

Bowling Green

Post Office

Eglinton St.

Williamsgate St.

EYRE SQUARE

Kennedy Park

17

AE

Station Rd.

Forster St.

Market St.

20

Shop St.

William St.

Eyre Square Shopping Centre

Victoria Pl.

18

Train Station

Newcastle Rd.

Mill St.

Nuns Island St.

22

21

19

Lwr. Abbeygate St.

St. Helens St.

Henry St.

New Rd.

Guard St.

High St.

Middle St.

St. Augustine St.

Merchants Rd.

Queen St.

Dock Rd.

Bridge St.

23

Wm. O'Brien Bridge

Cross St.

The Cornstore

Dominick St.

Wolfe Tone Bridge

Quay St.

Flood St.

New Dock St.

Dock Rd.

Commercial Dock

Raleigh Row

Sea Rd.

Dominick St. Upper

25

24

The Long Walk

Old Dock

Munster Ave.

N

Fr. Griffin Rd.

Claddagh Quay

Fairhill

St. Nicholas Rd.

Grattan Rd.

Nimmo's Pier

CLADDAGH

0   330 yards

0   300 meters   To Salthill 30   29   SOUTH PARK

holds here), his tobacco, and an apple. Now the entrance to Kennedy Park, the **Browne Doorway** was taken in 1905 from the Browne family's town house on Upper Abbeygate Street; it has the 17th-century coats of arms of both the Browne and Lynch families, called a "marriage stone," because when the families were joined in marriage their coats of arms were, too. Keep an eye out for similar if less elaborate versions of the entranceway as you walk around the old part of town. The **bronze cannons** were presented at the end of the Crimean War to the Connaught Rangers, a legendary regiment of the British Army made up of Irish men recruited from the west of Ireland (☞ King House *in* Boyle *in* Chapter 3).

㉕ **Galway City Museum.** Next door to the Spanish Arch (☞ *below*), the city's civic museum contains an array of materials relating to local history: old photographs, antiquities (the oldest is a stone axe head carbon-dated to 3500 BC), and other historical gewgaws. Behind the existing museum, a new museum is scheduled to open in 2000. ⊠ *Spanish Arch,* ☎ *091/567641.* 🎫 *£1.* ⊙ *Mid-Mar.–Sept., daily 10–1 and 2:15–5:15; Oct.–mid-Mar., Tues.–Thurs. 10–1 and 2:15–5:15.*

⑳ **Lynch Memorial Window.** Embedded in a stone wall above a built-up Gothic doorway, the window marks the spot where, according to legend, James Lynch FitzStephen, mayor of Galway in the early 16th century, condemned his son to death after he confessed to murdering a Spanish sailor who had stolen his girlfriend. When no one could be found to carry out the execution, Judge Lynch hanged his son himself, ensuring that justice prevailed, before retiring into seclusion.

⑲ **Lynch's Castle.** Now a branch of the Allied Irish Banks, this is the finest remaining example in Galway of a 16th-century fortified house—fortified because neighboring Irish tribes persistently raided the village, whose commercial life excluded them. Decorative details on its stone lintels are usually found only in southern Spain. Like the Spanish Arch (☞ *below*), it serves as a reminder of the close trading links that once existed between Galway and Spain. ⊠ *Shop St.*

㉒ **Nora Barnacle House.** On June 16, 1904, James Joyce (1882–1941) had his first date with Nora Barnacle, who would later become his wife. He subsequently chose to set *Ulysses* on this day, now known universally as Bloomsday (☞ Close Up: ReJoyce! A Walk through *Ulysses* and James Joyce's Dublin *in* Chapter 1)—"a recognition of the determining effect upon his life of his attachment to her," as Joyce's biographer Richard Ellman has said. Nora was born here, the daughter of a poor baker; today it has a modest collection of photographs, letters, and memorabilia, and a small gift shop. ⊠ *4 Bowling Green,* ☎ *091/564743.* 🎫 *£1.* ⊙ *Mid-May–mid-Sept., Mon.–Sat. 2–5; off-season by appointment.*

★ ㉖ **Salmon Weir Bridge.** The bridge itself is nothing special, but in season—from mid-April to early July—shoals of salmon are visible from its deck as they lie in the clear river water before making their way upstream to the spawning grounds of Lough Corrib. It is a memorable sight.

㉚ **Salthill.** Three kilometers (2 mi) west of Galway, Salthill is a lively, hugely popular seaside resort with its own fun palace. Its promenade is the traditional place "to sit and watch the moon rise over Claddagh, and see the sun go down on Galway Bay"—in the words of the city's most famous song.

㉔ **Spanish Arch.** Built in 1584 to protect the quays where Spanish ships unloaded cargoes of wines and brandies, the arch now stands in the parking lot opposite Jurys Galway Inn. It's easily (and often) mistaken for a pile of weathered stones, yet it's another reminder of Galway's—and Ireland's—past links with Spain (☞ Kinsale *in* Chapter 5).

㉓ **Tig Neachtain.** You can hear traditional music every night at this popular pub, which stands at a busy little crossroads in the heart of the old town. Grab a spot at one of its old-fashioned partitioned snugs at lunchtime for an inexpensive selection of imaginative bar food. It's a good place to mingle with local actors, writers, artists, musicians, and students, although it can get sardine-can crowded. ✉ *17 Cross St.,* ☎ *091/566172.*

⑱ **Tourist Information Office.** Just off Eyre Square, around the corner from the bus and train station and the Great Southern Hotel, this is the place to make reservations and find out about the latest happenings in and around town. ✉ *1 Victoria Pl.,* ☎ *091/563081.* ☉ *Weekdays 9–6, Sat. 9–1.*

㉘ **University College Galway (UCG).** Across the River Corrib, in the northwestern corner of the city, UCG was opened in 1846 to promote the development of local industry and agriculture, but today it's a center for Irish-language and Celtic studies. The Tudor-Gothic-style quadrangle, completed in 1848, is worth a visit, though much of the rest of the campus is architecturally undistinguished. Its library boasts an important archive of Celtic-language materials, and in July and August, it also hosts courses in Irish studies for overseas students.

Dining and Lodging

$$$ ✕ **Drimcong House.** A 300-year-old lakeside house north of Galway
★ City is the home of one of Ireland's most highly regarded restaurants. Its chef-owner, Gerry Galvin, is widely known for his extraordinarily inventive cooking. Galvin's wife, Marie, supplies the kitchen with herbs and vegetables organically grown on their own land. The evening begins around the fireplace in the parlor, where after ordering a cocktail you pore over the week's handwritten menu. The entrées, unfussy and simple, are exactingly executed. Panfried loin of lamb is served in consommé with herb dumplings, and grilled salmon is served with a watercress and radish salad with an anchovy dressing. Desserts, such as a hot apple croûte with praline ice cream and custard sauce, sparkle. The elegant, understated dining room is decorated with prints and original paintings by contemporary Irish artists, and the service is exceptional. You're virtually guaranteed an unforgettable experience. To get here, take N59 (the Oughterard–Clifden road) 13 km (8 mi) north from Galway to the village of Moycullen; the driveway is on the right. ✉ *Moycullen,* ☎ *091/555115. Reservations essential. AE, DC, MC, V. Closed Sun.–Mon. and late Dec.–mid-Mar. No lunch.*

$$$ ✕ **Kirwan's Lane Creative Cuisine.** A newly revamped alley at the river end of Quay Street is home to Mike O'Grady's stylish modern restaurant. Blue-stained wooden tables, narrow floor-to-ceiling windows, and a quarry-tile floor set the stage for a sophisticated, fashionable menu. Fresh prawn cocktail is served with sauce Marie-Rose and a passionfruit mayo, while confit of duck leg comes with braised red cabbage, star anise, and balsamic oil. Main courses have similarly unpredictable twists—rack of lamb is served with sweet potato mash, basil oil, and apricots, while fresh fillet of cod is accompanied by spring onion risotto. ✉ *Kirwan's La.,* ☎ *091/568266. AE, DC, MC, V. Closed Sun.*

$$$ ✕ **Nimmo's.** Swiss chef Stephan Zeltner, who established himself on the Galway scene with a small restaurant above Naughton's pub (☞ *above*), has now moved to a riverside location in an old stone building with a separately run wine bar downstairs. The long, spacious second-floor room has original paintings on the walls and well-spaced tables set with white linen. He prepares robust food, exemplified by panfried chicken breast with duck foie gras or noisettes of venison with apple and Calvados. ⊠ *Spanish Arch,* ☎ *091/563565. AE, DC, MC, V. Closed Sun. No lunch.*

$$ ✕ **Malt House.** Hidden away in an alley off High Street in the center of old Galway, Barry and Therese Cunningham's bustling pub-restaurant has long been popular with both locals and visitors for good food served in informal surroundings. You can either eat in the bar itself or in the fancier main room (beamed ceilings, white, rough-cast walls, and chintz curtains) just off the bar. Fresh prawns panfried in garlic butter is a popular seafood option, while the sirloin steak with green peppercorn sauce and the rack of lamb with a parsley crust should please landlubbers. ⊠ *Old Malte Arcade, High St.,* ☎ *091/563993. AE, DC, MC, V. Closed Sun. Oct.–Apr.*

$$ ✕ **K.C. Blakes.** K.C. stands for Casey, as in owner-chef John Casey, who turned a medieval stone town house once associated with city founders the Blake family into a dark, ultramodern eatery. Dishes range from traditional Irish beef-and-Guinness stew to international cuisine; everything is prepared with fresh ingredients. ⊠ *10 Quay St.,* ☎ *091/ 561826. AE, MC, V. No lunch.*

$–$$ ✕ **McDonagh's Seafood Bar.** The McDonaghs are one of Galway's most entrepreneurial families, in charge of several hotels and this spot, a longtime town landmark. After a major mid-1997 renovation, it's now partly a fish-and-chips bar and partly a "real" fish restaurant. If you've yet to try fish-and-chips, this is the place to start: cod, whiting, mackerel, haddock, or hake is deep-fried in a light batter and served with a heap of freshly cooked chips (French fries). Or try Galway oysters au naturel, or a bowl of mussels steamed in wine and garlic. ⊠ *22 Quay St.,* ☎ *091/565001. AE, MC, V. No lunch Sun. Oct.–Apr.*

$ ✕ **Bridge Mills.** Renovations have altered this 400-year-old former grain mill beside the River Corrib into a restaurant and minimall. You can even sit outdoors beside a bubbling stream and watch local fishermen pulling salmon out of the river. Lunch fare includes fresh salads, sandwiches, and hot specials. The dinner menu is more substantial, with large steaks and vegetarian choices, such as spinach and ricotta cannelloni. ⊠ *O'Brien's Bridge,* ☎ *091/566231. AE, MC, V. No dinner Oct.–mid-May.*

$ ✕ **Hooker Jimmy's Steak and Seafood Bar.** The Glanville family has its own trawler operating out of nearby Spiddal, thus ensuring that the seafood from Galway Bay is as fresh as possible. Dark green paintwork and soft-toned upholstery give a mellow feeling to their new premises near Jurys Inn. In summer, take a seat on the terrace overlooking the River Corrib. Lobster is a favorite of the loyal, youngish clientele who appreciate the no-frills, value-for-money policy. ⊠ *The Fishmarket, Spanish Arch,* ☎ *091/568351. AE, DC, MC, V.*

$$$$ ✕🏨 **Glenlo Abbey.** Five minutes outside the city on N59 Clifden road, Glenlo Abbey is surrounded by its own golf course and has views over Lough Corrib. Built in 1740, it was previously a private home (not a monastery, as the name implies). The lobby resembles a gentlemen's club, with its solid parquet floors, leather Chesterfield sofas, and old, leather-bound books. The spacious bedrooms are in a newer wing and have Georgian-style furniture and super-king-size beds. The bathrooms have marble walls and some, whirlpool baths. The Pullman Restaurant, two Orient Express carriages installed in the grounds, offer a novelty dining experience; informal bar food is served in the Oak Cellar Bar. In the oddly spelled Ffrench Room, Irish and international cuisine is served in formal, Regency-style surroundings. ⊠ *Bushy Park, Co. Galway,* ☎ *091/526666,* 🅵🅰🅾 *091/527800. 38 rooms with bath, 6 suites. 2 restaurants, bar, sauna, 9-hole golf course, tennis court, fishing. AE, DC, MC, V.*

$ ✕🏨 **Cregg Castle.** On a 165-acre wildlife preserve about 15 km (9 mi) north of Galway on N17 (turn left for Corrandulla just beyond Claregalway), this 17th-century castle is pleasantly informal. The Brodericks, the owners, all play instruments, and traditional sessions often take place around the huge, log-and-turf fire in the Great Hall. Bedrooms vary in shape and size and are decorated mainly with sturdy Victorian bygones. Breakfast is served until noon around an antique dining table that seats 18 people. The restaurant is licensed to serve wine only; reservations for dinner should be made by 3 PM. ⊠ *Corrandulla, Co. Galway,* ☎ FAX *091/791434. 10 rooms, 5 with bath. No credit cards. Closed Nov.–Feb.*

$$$ 🏨 **Ardilaun House.** This lovely, 19th-century house lies at the end of
★ a tree-lined avenue in a quiet suburb, midway between the city center and the Salthill promenade—about five minutes' drive from both. Open fires, fresh flower arrangements, and Regency-style furniture characterize the quiet public rooms overlooking the gardens. The individually designed bedrooms are decorated with a pink, gray, or green color scheme and Irish-made mahogany furniture with brass trim. For views of the bay, book an even-numbered room on the top floor. Other rooms, which are just as pleasant, overlook the flower garden, shrubberies, and a fountain. ⊠ *Taylor's Hill, Co. Galway,* ☎ *091/521433,* FAX *091/521546. 81 rooms with bath, 7 suites. Restaurant, 2 bars, indoor pool, sauna, health club. AE, DC, MC, V.*

$$$ 🏨 **Galway Great Southern.** Built in 1845 to coincide with the arrival of the railway, and grandly situated on the southeastern side of Eyre Square, this is still the best address in town. A pianist tickles the ivories in the large lobby, which, like the two bars, is a popular gathering spot. All the guest rooms are decorated in tastefully muted, color-coordinated schemes, with Georgian-style tables and chairs. The large, deluxe rooms in the original building have tall ceilings and windows and are particularly elegant, though those at the front directly above the bar can be noisy late into the night. Rooms at the back are newer; those in the back on the fifth floor have views of Galway Bay, as does the swimming pool. French-Irish cuisine is served at the formal Oyster Room. ⊠ *Eyre Sq., Co. Galway,* ☎ *091/564041,* FAX *091/566704. 112 rooms with bath, 3 suites. Restaurant, 2 bars, indoor pool, sauna. AE, DC, MC, V.*

$$ 🏨 **Brennan's Yard.** Beside the historic Spanish Arch and an easy walk from Galway's shops and restaurants, this tall, four-story stone building in the dockland area has been strikingly converted into a pleasant modern hotel. The large windows in the bar look across the sea to the Claddagh (☞ *above*), as do some of the bedrooms—ask for a sea view when booking. The cozy rooms have small windows because of the age of the building, but they are very well designed, color-coordinated in deep pastels, and individually furnished with antique pine pieces and paintings by local artists. ⊠ *Lower Merchant's Rd., Co. Galway,* ☎ *091/568166,* FAX *091/568262. 24 rooms with bath. Restaurant, bar. AE, DC, MC, V.*

$ 🏨 **Jurys Galway Inn.** At the foot of Galway's busy main Quay Street, right on the banks of the Corrib, this newly built, four-story hotel offers good-quality budget accommodation. Each room is big enough for three adults, or two adults and two children, and the Jurys fixed-price policy applies to all of them. The light, airy rooms have modern pine fittings, plain carpets and walls, double-glazed windows, and fully equipped bathrooms. Those overlooking the river are quieter than those in front. The atmosphere unavoidably tends toward anonymous-international, but it's centrally located and the level of comfort is high for the price range. ⊠ *Quay St., Co. Galway,* ☎ *091/566444,* FAX *091/568415. 128 rooms with bath. Restaurant, bar, parking (fee). AE, DC, MC, V.*

$
★   ⊞ **Norman Villa.** Dee and Mark Keogh's Victorian town house, midway between the city center and the seaside promenade of Salthill, is
ideally located, away from the bustle but within easy walking distance
of both places. Brightly painted walls, Victorian brass beds with Irish
linen sheets, varnished floorboards, wooden shutters, and fun, offbeat
paintings and artifacts make for a lively, pleasant decor. ⊠ *86 Lower
Salthill, Co. Galway,* ☎ FAX *091/521131. 5 rooms with bath. Free
parking. No credit cards. Closed Jan. 10–31.*

Nightlife and the Arts

Because of its small size and concentration of pubs and restaurants,
Galway can seem even livelier at 11 PM than it is at 11 AM. On week-
ends, when there are a lot of students and other revelers in town, Eyre
Square and environs can be rowdy late at night after pub-closing time.
On the plus side, if you've been staying out in the countryside and you're
ready for a little nightlife, you're certain to find plenty of it here.

FESTIVALS AND SEASONAL EVENTS

The **Galway Arts Festival** (☎ 091/583800), the city's premier annual
event, spans the last two weeks in July and includes drama, film,
music, children's events, and a huge parade. The **Galway Races** at
Ballybrit Race Course (to the north of town off N17) start the day after
the arts festival ends for a week of mad revelry. At the end of September, the **Galway International Oyster Festival** (☎ 091/527282) in-
dulges visitors with the "food of the gods." Mid-April's **Cuirt Literary
Festival** (☎ 091/565886) brings in leading Irish and international writers for a week of readings and other events.

PUBS AND OTHER NIGHT SPOTS

The best area for traditional music is the Quay Street–Shop Street area
between Eyre Square and the Spanish Arch. You will usually find a session after about 9 PM at the **Quays** (⊠ Quay St., ☎ 091/561777), **Neách-
tain's** (⊠ 17 Cross St., ☎ 091/561720), **Taaffe's** (⊠ 19 Shop St., ☎
091/564066), **Crane's** (⊠ 2 Sea Rd., ☎ 091/587419), and the **Cottage
Bar** (⊠ Lower Salthill, ☎ 091/526754). **Cuba** (⊠ Eyre Sq., ☎ 091/
565991), on three floors, draws diners and salsa lovers for Cuban cock-
tails and cigars to the beat of Latin music from DJs and live bands.
Le Graal (⊠ 38 Lower Dominick St., ☎ 091/567614), licensed to sell
wine only, is a bar-brasserie that metamorphoses into a lively, late-night
spot. **Aras na Gael** (⊠ 45 Lower Dominick St., ☎ 091/526509) is one
of the few Irish-speaking pubs in the city center.

THEATER

The **Town Hall Theatre** (⊠ Courthouse Sq., Woodquay, ☎ 091/569777),
opened in 1995 in the city's former town hall, is lit virtually every night.

The **Druid Theatre** company (⊠ Chapel La., ☎ 091/568617) is respected
for its adventurous and accomplished productions, mainly of 20th-cen-
tury Irish and European plays. The players perform at the Royal
Court's small stage in London; when they're home, they usually appear at the Town Hall—which is where they eventually brought their
1997–98 success, Martin McDonagh's *Leenane Trilogy,* which opened
in London and later traveled to Sydney, Australia, and off-Broadway.

An Taibhdhearc (⊠ Middle St., ☎ 091/562024), pronounced awn *tie*-
vark, was founded in 1928 by Hilton Edwards and Micháel
Macliammóir as the national Irish-language theater. It continues to produce first-class shows, mainly of Irish works in both the English and
the Irish languages.

Macnas (⊠ Fisheries Field, Salmon Weir Bridge, ☎ 091/561462) is an
internationally renowned, Galway-based troupe of performance artists

A YEAR-ROUND FLEADH

DUBLIN MAY BE THE POLITICAL capital of Ireland, but Galway is the center of its traditional-music universe, a place where you can hear this music all through the year, whether or not there's a *fleadh*, or traditional music festival, going on. ☞ **Galway City** and its environs have given birth to some of the most durable names in Irish music: De Danann, Arcady, singers Dolores and Seán Keane, and the mercurial accordion genius Mairtín O'Connor. Seán Ryan, acknowledged master of the tin whistle, has been playing every Sunday at ☞ **Crane's** for nearly 20 years. The hottest sessions these days take place at the ☞ **Cottage Bar** in Lower Salthill, where up-and-coming young musicians are drawn by the cozy atmosphere and the fine acoustics. In the city itself, there's still plenty of music to be found at old reliables such as ☞ **Neaćhtain's,** ☞ **Taaffe's,** and ☞ **Aras na Gael.**

South of Galway the fishing village of ☞ **Kinvara** hosts the annual **Cuckoo Fleadh,** a small but growing festival that will turn 10 years old in 2003. Resident musicians like De Danann alumni Jackie Daly and Charlie Piggott play regularly at **Winkles Hotel,** where, in 1989, a very young and relatively unknown accordion player got together with a few friends for a casual recording session. The resulting album, *Sharon Shannon,* went platinum virtually overnight, becoming the most successful traditional-music recording ever

released. Today, Shannon, who grew up on a farm outside Corofin, County Clare, and played her first accordion when she was 11, is one of Ireland's leading traditional Irish musicians.

Down the road, the lively market town of ☞ **Ennis**—where Shannon took lessons from local maestro Frank Custy—has lately come into its own, attracting a growing cadre of musicians—the Custys, Siobhán and Tommy Peoples, Josephine Marsh, P. J. King, flute player Kevin Crawford, and, most recently, accordion whiz kid Murt Ryan, newly arrived from Tipperary. Sessions take place at an ever-changing roster of pubs; ☞ **May Kearney's,** ☞ **Ciaran's,** and, most notably, ☞ **Cruise's** are all hot venues. This last pub boasts an adjacent concert venue where a few years ago a group of local musicians recorded a lovely live album, *The Sanctuary Sessions.* Still available through stores specializing in traditional music, the album is an excellent introduction to Irish music, with the featured artists including most of the above-mentioned musicians as well as banjo player Mary Shannon and the wonderful Galway singer Seán Tyrrell. In May, Ennis is home to the ☞ **Fleadh Nua** festival—which celebrated its 25th year in 1998—with concerts, competitions, workshops, and *ceilís* (Irish dancing and song).

— By Sarah McQuaid

who have raised street theater to new levels. Their participation in the Galway Arts Festival's annual parade is always much anticipated.

High-quality work by local artists can be found at **Kenny's Bookshop & Art Galleries** (☞ Shopping, *below*). The art gallery at **University College Galway** (☎ 091/524411) has a number of exhibits each year.

Outdoor Activities and Sports

BICYCLING
Set off to explore the Galway area, especially its coast, by renting a bike from **Celtic Cycles** (⊠ Queen St., ☎ 091/566606).

FISHING
You can get fishing licenses, tackle, and bait at **Freeny's** (⊠ High St., ☎ 091/562609). **Murt's** (⊠ 7 Daly's Pl., Woodquay, ☎ 091/561018) can also handle your fishing needs.

GOLF
The **Galway Golf Club** (⊠ Blackrock, Salthill, ☎ 091/522033) is an 18-hole, par-71 course with excellent views of Galway Bay, the Burren, and the Aran Islands. Some of the fairways run close to the ocean. **Galway Bay Golf and Country Club** (⊠ Renville, Oranmore, ☎ 091/790500) is an 18-hole, par-72, parkland course designed by Christy O'Connor Jr. on the shores of Galway Bay.

RIVER CRUISING
A **Corrib Cruise** from Wood Quay (behind the Town Hall Theatre at the Rowing Club) is a lovely way to spend a fine afternoon; it lasts 1½ hours and travels 8 km (5 mi) up the River Corrib and about 6 km (4 mi) around Lough Corrib. You can also rent the boat for an evening. ☎ 091/568903. ☜ £5. ☼ *May–Sept., daily at 2:30 and 4:30.*

TENNIS
There are nine courts at the **Galway Lawn Tennis Club** (⊠ Threadneedle St., Salthill, ☎ 091/522353) available to nonmembers at £4 per hour.

WATER SPORTS
Galway Sailing Center (⊠ Renville, Oranmore, ☎ 091/794527) offers dinghy sailing and board sailing on Lough Corrib or on coastal waters. Instruction is also available. **Bow Waves** (⊠ 11 Ashleigh Grove, Knockacarra, ☎ 091/591481) schedules individually tailored trips around Galway Bay on high-performance inflatables. Life jackets and wet gear are included in the price. Ride the waves for thrills, or take it easy on a seal and dolphin watch.

Shopping

For a brief overview of Galway's shopping scene, ☞ A Good Walk, *above*.

BOOKSTORES
Kenny's Bookshop & Art Galleries (⊠ High St., ☎ 091/562739) has five floors of books of Irish topics, mainly secondhand and antiquarian, as well as prints, maps, and a small art gallery. **Charlie Byrne's Bookshop** (⊠ The Cornstore, Middle St., ☎ 091/561766) sells a large, varied selection of used books and remainders.

CLOTHING, CRAFTS, AND GIFTS
Don't miss **Design Concourse Ireland** (⊠ Kirwan's La., ☎ 091/566016), a spectacular one-stop shop for the best in Irish handcrafted design. **Design Ireland Plus** (⊠ The Cornstore, Middle St., ☎ 091/567716; ⊠ The Grainstore, Lower Abbeygate St., ☎ 091/566620) has an excellent range of contemporary Irish-made crafts and clothing. **Faller's Sweater Shop** (⊠ 25 High St., ☎ 091/564833; ⊠ 35 Eyre Sq., ☎ 091/

561255) has the choicest selection of Irish-made sweaters, competitively priced. **Meadows & Byrne** (⊠ Castle St., ☎ 091/567776) sells the best in modern household items. **O'Máille's** (⊠ 16 High St., ☎ 091/562696) carries Aran sweaters, handwoven tweeds, and classically tailored clothing. Browse in **Treasure Chest** (⊠ William St., ☎ 091/567237) for china, crystal, gifts, and classic clothing.

JEWELRY
The **Claddagh Jewellers** (⊠ Eyre Sq., ☎ 091/562310) has a wide selection of traditional Claddagh rings and other jewelry.

MALLS
Slightly off the beaten path, the **Cornstore** (⊠ Middle St.) has some stylish shops that tend to be less crowded than their competitors on the main street. On the southwest side of Eyre Square and imaginatively designed to incorporate parts of the old town walls, the **Eyre Square Shopping Centre** (⊠ Eyre Sq.) offers a wide range of moderately priced clothing and household goods.

MUSIC
Specializing in Irish traditional music, **Mulligan** (⊠ 5 Middle St. Court, ☎ 091/564961) carries more than 6,000 CDs, records, and cassettes.

VINTAGE GOODS
Twice as Nice (⊠ 5 Quay St., ☎ 091/566332) sells a mix of new and vintage men's and women's clothing, linens, lace, and jewelry at reasonable prices.

The Aran Islands

③ *48 km (30) mi by boat from Galway City, about 24 km (15 mi) by boat from Ros an Mhil (Rossaveal); flights from Connemara Airport.*

Jutting from a belligerent ocean, the Aran Islands—Inishmore, Inishmaan, and Inisheer—are remote western outposts of the ancient province of Connaught (though they are not the country's westernmost points; that honor belongs to the Blasket Islands [☞ Chapter 5]). These three natural wonders were once as barren and austere as the limestone pavements of the Burren, of which they are essentially a continuation. Today, the land is parceled into small fields surrounded by stone walls, the limestone having been lifted in great ramparts against the pounding ocean. The views from here are spectacular: Witness the uninterrupted expanse of the Atlantic on the western horizon; to the northeast, the Connemara coast and its Twelve Bens; and to the southeast, County Clare's Burren and the Cliffs of Moher.

The islands have been populated for thousands of years, and the Irish-speaking inhabitants have adhered to the traditions of their ancestors—hardy, plain-living fisherfolk and farmers—while adapting to the changes brought by tourism: daily air service to Galway (subsidized by the government), motorized curraghs, multichannel TVs, and all the usual modern home conveniences. Yet islanders retain a distinctness from mainlanders, preferring simple home decor, very plain food, and tightly knit communities. Crime is virtually unknown in these parts; at your B&B, you'll find no locks on the guest-room doors, and the front-door latch will be left open.

Many islanders have sampled life in Dublin or cities abroad but have returned to raise families, keeping the population stable at around 1,500. Through the years, the islands have also attracted writers and artists, including J. M. Synge (1871–1909), who learned Irish on Inishmaan and wrote about its people in his play *Riders to the Sea*. The film *Man of Aran,* made on Inishmore in 1932 by the American director Robert

Flaherty, is a classic documentary recording the islanders' dramatic battles with sea and storm. (The film is shown in the Community Hall in Kilronan, Inishmore, every afternoon during July, August, and early September).

The best time to visit the islands is May and early June while the unusual, Burren-like flora is at its best and before the bulk of the approximately 200,000 annual visitors arrive. (For details on getting to the Aran Islands, ☞ Getting Around *in* The West A to Z, *below*.)

Inis Mór (Inishmore)

With a population of 900, Inishmore is the largest of the islands and the closest to the Connemara coast. It's also the most commercialized, its appeal slightly diminished by road traffic. In the summer, ferries arriving at **Kilronan,** Inishmore's main village and port, are met by minibuses and pony and cart drivers, all eager to show visitors "the sights." More than 8 km (5 mi) long and about 3 km (2 mi) wide at most points, with an area of 7,640 acres, the island is just a little too large to explore comfortably on foot in a day. The best way to see it is really by bicycle; bring your own or hire one from one of the three vendors right near the quay: **Aran Bicycle Hire** (☎ 099/61132), **Costello's** (☎ 099/61241), and **Burke and Mullin** (☎ 099/61402). All operate May through October. The **Aran Heritage Centre** explains the history and culture of the islanders who for many years lived in virtual isolation from the mainland. ☎ *099/61355.* ☒ *£2.* ☉ *Apr.–Oct., daily 10–7.*

★ The main attraction on Inishmore is **Dún Aengus,** one of the finest prehistoric monuments in Europe, dating from about 2000 BC. Spectacularly set on the edge of a 300-ft cliff overlooking a sheer drop, the fort has defenses consisting of three rows of concentric circles. Who the builders were defending themselves against is a matter of conjecture. From the innermost rampart there's a great view of the island and the Connemara coast.

LODGING

The only hotel on the islands is on Inis Oirr, but there's no shortage of B&Bs, mostly in simple family homes. The best way to book is through the **Galway City TIO** (☞ Galway, *above*). Each island has at least one wine-licensed restaurant serving plain home cooking. Most B&Bs will provide a packed lunch and an evening meal (called high tea) on request.

$ ☷ **Kilmurvey House.** At the foot of Dún Aengus fort, about 6½ km (4 mi) from the quay and the airport (accessible by minibus), this rambling 200-year-old stone farmhouse is the first choice of many visitors to the island—about 60% of them American. Proprietor Teresa Joyce recently added five rooms to the four large rooms in the old house and three previously added ones; she also added private baths to all the rooms previously lacking them. ☒ *Kilmurvey, Aran Islands, Co. Galway,* ☎ *099/61218,* ☎ *099/61397. 12 rooms with bath. Dining room. MC, V. Closed Nov.–Apr.*

NIGHTLIFE

The place to go for traditional music is the **American Bar** (☒ Kilronan, ☎ 099/61130).

Inis Meáin (Inishmaan)

The middle island in both size and location, Inishmaan has a population of about 300 and can be comfortably explored on foot. In fact, you have no alternative if you want to reach the island's major antiquities: Conor Fort, a smaller version of Dun Aengus; the ruins of two early Christian churches; and a chamber tomb known as the Bed of

Diarmuid and Grainne, dating from about 2000 BC. You can also take wonderful cliff walks above secluded coves. It's on Inishmaan that the traditional Aran lifestyle is most evident. Until the mid-1930s or so, Aran women dressed in thick, red-woolen skirts to keep out the Atlantic gales, while the men wore collarless jackets, baggy trousers made of homespun tweed with *pampooties* (hide shoes without heels, suitable for walking on rocks), and a wide, hand-plaited belt called a *crios* (pronounced krish). Most islanders still don hand-knitted Aran sweaters, though nowadays they accompany them with jeans and sneakers.

Inis Oirr (Inisheer)

The smallest and flattest of the islands, Inisheer can be explored on foot in an afternoon, though if the weather is fine, you may be tempted to linger on the long, sandy beach between the quay and the airfield. In the summer, Inisheer's population of 300 is augmented by high school students from all over Ireland attending the Gaeltacht, or Irish-language school. Only one stretch of road, about 500 yards long, links the airfield and the village. The **Church of Kevin,** signposted to the southeast of the quay, is a small, early Christian church that gets buried in sand by storms every winter. Every year the islanders dig it out of the sand for the celebration of St. Kevin's Day on June 14. A pleasant walk through the village takes you up to **O'Brien's Castle,** a ruined, 15th-century tower that sits on top of a rocky hill—the only hill on the island.

It's worth making a circuit of the island to get a sense of its utter tranquillity. A maze of footpaths runs between the high stone walls that divide the fields, which are so small that they can support only one cow each, or two to three sheep. Those that are not cultivated or grazed turn into natural wildflower meadows between June and August, overrun with harebells, scabious, red clover, oxeye daisies, saxifrage, and tall grasses. It seems almost a crime to walk here—but how can you resist taking a rest in the corner of a sweet-smelling meadow on a sunny afternoon, sheltered by high stone walls with no sound but the larks above and the wind as it sifts through the stones? "The back of the island," as Inisheer's uninhabited side facing the Atlantic is called, has no beaches, but people still swim off the rocks.

LODGING

$ ☎ **Hotel Inisheer.** A pleasant, modern low-rise in the middle of the island's only village, a few minutes' walk from the quay and the airstrip, this simple, whitewashed building with a slate roof and half-slated walls has bright, plainly furnished rooms. The five newer rooms are slightly larger than the other 10. The restaurant (open to nonguests) is the best bet on the island, although much of the food is imported frozen. ⊠ *Lurgan Village, Aran Islands, Co. Galway,* ☎ *099/75020,* FAX *099/75099. 15 rooms, 12 with bath. Restaurant, bar, bicycles. AE, DC, MC, V. Closed Oct.–Apr. 1.*

THROUGH CONNEMARA AND COUNTY MAYO

Bordered by the long expanse of Lough Corrib on the east and the deeply indented, jagged coast of the Atlantic on the west, rugged, desolate western County Galway is known as Connemara. Like the American West, it's an area of spectacular, almost myth-making geography—of glacial lakes; gorgeous, silent mountains; lonely roads; and hushed, uninhabited boglands. The Twelve Bens, "the central glory of Connemara," as author Brendan Lehane has called them, together with the Maamturk Mountains to their north, lord proudly over the area's sepia boglands. More surprisingly, stands of Scotch pine, Norwegian spruce, Douglas fir, and Japanese Sitka grow in Connemara's valleys and up hillsides—the result of a concerted national project that has so far reforested 9% of Ireland. In the midst of this wilderness, you'll find few people, for Connemara's population is sparse even by Irish standards. Especially in the off-season, you're far more likely to come across sheep strolling its roads than another car.

Two main routes—one inland, the other coastal—lead through Connemara. To take the inland route described below, leave Galway City on the well-signposted outer-ring road and follow signs for N59—Moycullen, Oughterard, and Clifden. If you choose to go the coastal route, you'll travel due west from Galway City to Rossaveal on R336 through Salthill, Barna, and Spiddle—all in the heart of the West's strong Gaeltacht, home to roughly 40,000 Irish speakers. Although this is one of the most impressive and unspoiled coastal roads in Ireland, it has been scarred by modern one-story concrete homes—a sort of faux-Spanish hacienda style favored by locals. (Most of the traditional thatched houses in the West are now used as vacation homes.) You can continue north on R336 from Rossaveal to Maam Cross and then head for coastal points west, or pick up R340 and putter along the coast.

Oughterard

③② *27 km (17 mi) west of Galway City on N59.*

Small and pretty Oughterard (pronounced *ook*-ter-ard) is the main village on the western shores of **Lough Corrib** and one of Ireland's leading angling resorts. The lough is signposted to the right in the village center, less than 1½ km (1 mi) up the road. From mid-June to early September, local boatmen offer trips on the lough, which has several islands. It is also possible to take a boat trip to Cong (☞ *below*), at the north shore of the lough. Midway between Oughterard and Cong, **Inchagoill Island** (the Island of the Stranger), a popular destination for a half-day trip, has several early Christian church remains. The cost of boat rides is negotiable; expect to pay about £6 per person.

Lodging

$$ ✕🔛 **Ross Lake House.** Five kilometers (3 mi) from Oughterard and well off the beaten track, this Georgian house is a low-key country hideaway. Managed by an enthusiastic couple, Henry and Elaine Reid, the house is set near a stream and within 5 acres of colorful gardens (in spite of the name, there is no lake in the grounds, but plenty of them nearby.) The interior is comfortable rather than stylish, with modest Victorian antiques and welcoming open fires. Guest rooms in the converted stables are simpler and a little smaller than those in the house, but all have peaceful garden views. A table d'hôte dinner menu offers good-quality, plain country-house cooking. ✉ *Roscahill, Co. Galway,* ☎ *091/550189,* 🖷 *091/550184. 13 rooms with bath. Restaurant, bar, tennis, horseback riding, fishing. AE, DC, MC, V. Closed Nov.–mid-Mar.*

$$$ 🔛 **Connemara Gateway.** This adventurously designed, modern low-rise with traditional, gray-slate roofs above whitewashed walls combines the best of the old and the new. With a nod to the classic Irish cottage, the lobby and bar are decorated with wooden and cast-iron artifacts and chintz sofas. Guest rooms have modern furniture, floral wall panels with matching drapes, and fluffy mohair coverlets. All have sitting areas beside the large teak-framed windows, which overlook the gardens and the distant hills. There's a strong tour-bus trade, but it doesn't spoil the charming atmosphere. The hotel is about 1 km (½ mi) outside the village on the Galway side of the N59. ✉ *Co. Galway,* ☎

091/552328, FAX *091/552332. 62 rooms with bath. Restaurant, bar, indoor pool, sauna, tennis court, fishing. AE, DC, MC, V. Closed Dec.–mid Feb.*

Nightlife

For good music try **Faherty's** (☎ 091/552194).

Outdoor Activities and Sports

Oughterard Golf Club (✉ Co. Galway, ☎ 091/552131) has an 18-hole, par-70 parkland course suitable for novices and those who wish to improve their games.

En Route   As you continue northwest from Oughterard on N59, you'll soon pass a string of small lakes on your left; their shining blue waters reflecting the blue sky is a typical Connemara sight on a sunny day. Sixteen kilometers (10 mi) northwest of Oughterard, the continuation of the coast road (R336) meets N59 at **Maam Cross** in the shadow of Leckavrea Mountain. Once an important meeting place for the people of north and south Connemara, it's still the location of a large monthly cattle fair. Walkers will find wonderful views of Connemara by heading for any of the local peaks visible from the road. Beyond Maam Cross, some of the best scenery in Connemara awaits on the road to **Recess,** 16 km (10 mi) west of Maam Cross on N59. At many points on this drive, a short walk away from either side of the main road will lead you to the shores of one of the area's many small loughs. Stop and linger if the sun is out—even intermittently—for the light filtering through the clouds gives splendor to the distant, dark-gray mountains and creates patterns on the brown-green moorland below. In June and July, it stays light until 11 PM or so, and it is worth taking a late-evening stroll to see the sun's reluctance to set. In Recess, **Joyce's** (☎ 095/34604) carries a good selection of contemporary ceramics, handwoven shawls, books of Irish interest, original paintings, and small sculptures.

Cong

③③ *23 km (14 mi) northeast of Maam Cross on R336.*

Resting on a narrow isthmus between Lough Corrib and Lough Mask on the County Mayo border, the pretty, old-world village of Cong—an optional detour from Maam Cross—is dotted with ivy-covered thatched cottages and dilapidated farmhouses. It was here that the film *The Quiet Man* was made, exploiting the scenic beauty of the area in full Technicolor effectiveness. Cong is surrounded by many stone circles and burial mounds, but its most notable ruins are those of the **Augustine Abbey** (✉ Abbey St., ☎ no phone), dating from the early 13th century and still exhibiting some finely carved details. It can be seen overlooking a river near fabulous Ashford Castle (☞ Lodging, *below*). Cong's 15 minutes of fame came in 1952, when John Ford filmed *The Quiet Man,* one of his most popular films, here; John Wayne plays a prizefighter who goes home to Ireland to court the fiery Maureen O'Hara. (Pauline Kael called the film "fearfully Irish and green and hearty.") The **Quiet Man Heritage Cottage** is an exact replica of the cottage used in the film, with reproductions of the furniture and costumes, a few original artifacts, and pictures of Barry Fitzgerald and Maureen O'Hara on location. ✉ *Cong, Co. Mayo,* ☎ *092/46089.* ☞ *£2.50.* ☉ *Mar.–Nov, daily 10–6.*

Lodging

$$$$ 🏰 **Ashford Castle.** Perched at the head of Lough Corrib, surrounded
★   by neatly manicured lawns and gardens, this massive, flamboyantly turreted and crenellated castle was built in 1870 for the Guinness fam-

ily in a mock-Gothic baronial style, incorporating an earlier 1228 structure built by the De Burgos family. Now American-owned, Ashford is one of Ireland's most luxurious castle-hotels. Large oil paintings in gilt frames hang from the castle's carved stone walls above polished-wood paneling, illuminated by crystal chandeliers. Deluxe rooms have generous sitting areas, heavily carved antique furniture, and extra-large bathrooms. The suites are vast and faultless, furnished with Georgian antiques and blissfully comfortable. The bedrooms in the discreetly added new wing were recently refurbished; all are individually designed and furnished with selected Victorian antiques. ⊠ Co. Mayo, ☎ 092/46003, ℻ 092/46260. 72 rooms with bath, 11 suites. 2 restaurants, 2 bars, sauna, steam room, 9-hole golf course, 2 tennis courts, health club, horseback riding, boating, fishing, bicycles. AE, DC, MC, V.

Cashel

③④ 8 km (5 mi) south of Recess on R340.

Cashel is a quiet, extremely sheltered angling center at the head of Bertraghboy Bay. General de Gaulle is among the many people who have sought seclusion here. A word of caution in this area: Stray sheep, bolting Connemara ponies, cyclists, and reckless local drivers are all regular hazards on the narrow mountain roads hereabouts.

Dining and Lodging

$$$ ✕🏠 **Cashel House.** Quietly secluded on 40 acres of woodlands at the
★ head of Cashel Bay—with exotic shrubs flowering and Connemara ponies grazing out back—Kay and Dermot McEvilly's luxurious country house has possibly more antiques and curios per square foot than any other hotel in Ireland. Intricately carved oak tables, Biedermeier bureaus, gilt mirrors, Georgian bookcases, ormolu clocks, and other knickknacks are liberally scattered around the lobby, lounge, library, and downstairs corridors. More antiques and curios turn up in the bedrooms, which have king-size beds (canopied in the 13 minisuites), pink-and-green drapes and spreads, and brass bedside lamps. For a view of the sea rather than the garden, ask for a front room. In the dining room, the table d'hôte menu, with more choices than at many other country houses, is particularly strong on fresh local seafood. ⊠ Co. Galway, ☎ 095/31001, ℻ 095/31077. 19 rooms with bath, 13 suites. Restaurant, tennis court, horseback riding, beach, boating, fishing, bicycles. AE, DC, MC, V. Closed Jan. 10–31.

$$$ 🏠 **Zetland Country House.** Built for the Earl of Zetland on a hill overlooking secluded Cashel Bay, John and Mona Prendergast's mid-Victorian hunting lodge is an unforgettable experience within the wilderness beauty of Connemara. Mature grounds and flowering shrubs are surrounded by views of the rocky, heather-covered shores and the jewel-like waters of Cashel Bay. A dining room with massive antique sideboards adorned with family silver overlooks the bay, as does the large and blissfully quiet sitting room. Bedrooms are large and many have sea-views, but those with garden views are also attractive. The comfortable quarters are elegantly furnished with Georgian and Victorian antiques of polished mahogany. ⊠ Co. Galway, ☎ 095/31111, ℻ 095/31117. 19 rooms with bath. Restaurant, bar, tennis court. AE, DC, MC, V. Closed Nov.–Mar.

Outdoor Activities and Sports

Cashel Equestrian Center (⊠ Cashel House, ☎ 095/31001) offers scenic treks and the chance to ride a Connemara pony on its home ground.

Ballynahinch

35 *10 km (6 mi) west of Cashel on R341.*

Along the shores of Ballynahinch Lake you'll enter more forested country. Woodland in this part of Ireland indicates the proximity of a "big house" whose owner can afford to plant trees for pleasure and prevent their being cut down for fuel.

Lodging

$$$ 🏰 **Ballynahinch Castle.** Built in the late 18th century on the Owenmore
★   River, Ballynahinch was once the home of Richard Martin (1754–1834), who was known as "Humanity Dick," the founder of the Royal Society for the Prevention of Cruelty to Animals. Therefore, it may come as a shock—especially to animal lovers—that fishing and hunting are now permitted on the 40 walkable wooded acres that surround the castle. This noted, comfort without ostentation is the hallmark here. The tiled lobby with Persian rugs has two inviting leather chesterfields in front of an open fire. The biggest bedrooms, in the discreetly added ground-floor wing, have four-poster beds, Georgian-style mahogany furniture, and floor-to-ceiling windows overlooking the river. Rooms in the old house are equally comfortable and quiet. The castle is signposted off N59 between Recess and Clifden. ⊠ *Recess, Co. Galway,* ☎ *095/31006,* 𝙵𝙰𝚇 *095/31085. 18 rooms with bath, 10 suites. Restaurant, bar, tennis court, croquet, fishing, horseback riding, bicycles. AE, DC, MC, V. Closed Dec. 20–26.*

Clifden

★ 36 *23 km (14 mi) west of Recess, 79 km (49 mi) northwest of Galway City on N59.*

With roughly 1,100 residents, Clifden would be called a village by most, but in these parts it is looked on as something of a metropolis. It is far and away the prettiest town in Connemara, as well as its unrivaled "capital." Clifden's first attraction is its location—perched high above Clifden Bay on a forested plateau, its back to the spectacular Twelve Ben Mountains. The tapering spires of the town's two churches add to its Alpine feel. A selection of small restaurants, lively bars with music most nights in the summer, pleasant accommodations, and excellent walks make the town a popular base. It's quiet out of season, but in July and August crowds flock here, especially for August's world-famous **Connemara Pony Show.** Horse breeders come from around the world to check out Ireland's finest yearlings and stallions. Clifden's popularity, which has led to a chaotic one-way traffic system and loud techno music blasting out of certain bars, means that if you're over 25 and value your peace and quiet, you'd best choose a base outside town.

A 2-km (1-mi) walk along the beach road through the grounds of the ruined **Clifden Castle** is the best way to explore the seashore. It was built in 1815 by John D'Arcy, the town's founder, who laid out the town's wide main street on a long ridge with a parallel street below it. D'Arcy was High Sheriff of Galway, and his greatest wish was to establish a center of law and order in what he saw as the lawless wilderness of Connemara. Before the founding of Clifden, the interior of Connemara was largely uninhabited, with most of its population clinging to the seashore. Take the aptly named **Sky Road** to really appreciate Clifden's breathtakingly scenic setting. Signposted at the west end of town, this high, narrow circuit of about 5 km (3 mi) heads west to Kingstown, skirting Clifden Bay's precipitous shores.

Dining and Lodging

$$ ✕ **Destry's.** Owned by Paddy and Julia Foyle of Quay House (☞ *below*), this upbeat, extrovert town-center eatery on two floors is named for the Marlene Dietrich film *Destry Rides Again*. The decor combines film memorabilia with local bric-a-brac—look for the skull that sits on top of a Georgian fanlight. The menu is similarly unpredictable, eclectic with a strong Mediterranean influence, making use of good-quality olive oil and fresh herbs. The signature dessert is Lethal Chocolate Pud, made with a carefully guarded secret recipe. ⊠ *The Square, Co. Galway*, ☎ *095/21722. MC, V. Closed Nov.–mid-Mar. and Mon.*

$$ ✕ **O'Grady's Seafood.** A Clifden institution, this intimate, town-center restaurant serves fresh local produce, primarily seafood, more modishly than you might expect in the wilds of Connemara. Once a shop, the small main room is decorated in dark pinks and reds with wrought-iron dividers between the tables. Typical main courses might include a duo of monkfish and blackened scallops on a cilantro duxelles with two sauces, or crisp breast of duckling in its own juice with sweet caramelized onions. ⊠ *Market St., Co. Galway*, ☎ *095/21450. AE, MC, V. Closed Sun.*

$$$ ✕🛏 **Rock Glen Manor House.** Cross the bridge at the west end of town
★ and walk ⅘ km (½ mi) down the R341 Roundstone road to find John and Evangeline Roche's beautifully converted shooting lodge, built in 1815. On windy days, a tiny Connemara pony, Gregory, stands sentinel at the entrance gates and enjoys the breeze. Riding boots and tennis rackets in the hall make this feel more like a private home than a top-class hotel. A turf fire warms the large, sunny drawing room, with plump white armchairs, magazines, books, and board games. Guest rooms are nicely furnished with Georgian pieces, with fluffy mohair or chintz bedspreads and fully tiled bathrooms. In the Victorian-style restaurant, you might enjoy such dishes as roasted rack of lamb with an herb crust and mushroom duxelles. ⊠ *Co. Galway*, ☎ *095/21035,* 𝕗𝕒𝕩 *095/21737. 29 rooms with bath. Restaurant, bar, tennis court, horseback riding, fishing. AE, DC, MC, V. Closed Nov.–mid-Mar. No lunch.*

$$ ✕🛏 **Erriseask House.** The rambling, two-story modern house is on its
★ own private beach along the rocky shore of Mannin Bay. Warm wooden floors, well-crafted furniture, and an admirable lack of clutter combine to create a restful and very comfortable interior. Chef Stefan Matz has won many awards for his fine cooking, which is planned daily. Freshly turf-smoked fillet of beef is a house specialty. ⊠ *Ballyconneely, Co. Galway*, ☎ *095/23553,* 𝕗𝕒𝕩 *095/23639. 8 rooms with bath, 5 suites. Restaurant. AE, DC, MC, V. Closed Nov.–Mar.*

$$ 🛏 **Quay House.** A roaring turf fire in the sitting room greets visitors to this three-story Georgian house, Clifden's oldest building (1820). It's a short walk from the busy town center, and an oasis of calm beside the harbor quay. Rooms are unusually spacious, and those in the main house are imaginatively decorated with deep-colored walls and witty bygones; all but one have sea views. Seven studio rooms with tiny kitchens and balconies overlooking the harbor were added in 1998. Proprietors Julia and Patrick Foyle also tucked in homey touches such as books and model boats. The award-winning restaurant, Destry's (☞ *above*), has moved to the town center. ⊠ *Connemara, Co. Galway*, ☎ *095/21369,* 𝕗𝕒𝕩 *095/21608. 14 rooms with bath. Fishing. MC, V. Closed Nov.–mid-Mar. except by arrangement.*

Nightlife

The best place in town for music is the **Abbeyglen Castle** (⊠ Sky Rd., ☎ 095/21201), which has sessions in the bar most nights from June to September and occasional visits by big-name acts.

Outdoor Activities and Sports

BICYCLING

Explore Connemara by renting a bike from **John Mannion** (⊠ Railway View, ☎ 095/21160).

GOLF

On a dramatic stretch of Atlantic coastline, the 18-hole, par-72 course at the **Connemara Golf Club** (⊠ Ballyconneely, south of Clifden, ☎ 095/23502) measures 7,174 yards.

HORSEBACK RIDING

Errislannan Manor Connemara Pony Stud and Riding Center (⊠ Connemara, ☎ 095/21134) provides mountain treks, instruction, and courses for children.

Shopping

Millar's Connemara Tweeds (⊠ Main St., ☎ 095/21038) is a general art-and-crafts gallery with a good selection of traditional tweeds and hand knits. The **Celtic Shop** (⊠ Main St., ☎ 095/21064) carries high-quality crafts. **Linda's Spinning Studio** (⊠ Derrylea, ☎ 095/21888) sells handwoven wool products and offers demonstrations of the craft.

En Route   Continue toward Letterfrack through the **Inagh Valley,** which is flanked by two impressive mountain ranges with distinctive, conical-shape peaks, rising almost directly—without any foothills—to over 1,968 ft.

Letterfrack

❸⑦   *14 km (9 mi) north of Clifden on the N59.*

The 5,000-acre **Connemara National Park** lies southeast of the village of Letterfrack. Its **visitor center** covers the area's history and ecology, particularly the origins and growth of peat—and presents the depressing statistic that more than 80% of Ireland's peat, 5,000 years in the making, has been destroyed in the last 90 years. You can also get details on the many excellent walks and beaches in the area. ☎ *095/41054.* ⌑ *Park free; visitor center £2.* ☉ *Park freely accessible; visitor center Apr.–May and Sept., daily 10–5:30; June, daily 10–6:30; July–Aug., daily 9:30–6:30.*

Dining and Lodging

$$$ ✕▥ **Renvyle House.** A lake at its front door, the Atlantic Ocean at its back door, and the mountains of Connemara as a backdrop make for an enthralling setting for this hotel 8 km (5 mi) north of Letterfrack. Once the retreat of the man of letters Oliver St. John Gogarty, Renvyle's has a rustic, informal ambience, with exposed beams and brickwork and numerous open turf fires. All the comfortable guest rooms, elegantly decorated in a floral country-house style, have breathtaking views. The softly lit restaurant's table d'hôte menu is based on the traditional country-house style. The hotel is a great place to pursue outdoor activities: Golf, fishing, and horseback riding are all at hand. ⊠ *Renvyle, Co. Galway,* ☎ *095/43511,* ℻ *095/43515. 65 rooms with bath. Restaurant, bar, pool, 9-hole golf course, 2 tennis courts, horseback riding, fishing. AE, DC, MC, V. Closed Jan.–Feb.*

$$$ ✕▥ **Rosleague Manor.** Anne and Patrick Foyle's pink, creeper-clad, ★ two-story Georgian house sits on 30 lovely acres of wooded grounds overlooking Ballinakill Bay and the mountains of County Mayo and Connemara. Inside, the clutter of walking and shooting sticks beneath the grandfather clock in the hall sets the tone, which is fairly informal. The solidly comfortable bedrooms are furnished with well-used Victorian and Georgian antiques, four-poster or large brass bedsteads, and drapes that match the William Morris wallpaper. The best rooms are at the front on the first floor, overlooking the bay. At dinner in the award-winning restaurant, baked monktail with crispy capers and balsamic vinegar is a typical entrée. ✉ Co. *Galway,* ☎ *095/41101,* ℻ *095/41168. 19 rooms with bath. Restaurant, bar, sauna, tennis court, horseback riding. AE, MC, V.*

Nightlife

For traditional music, try the **Bards' Den** (☎ 095/41042).

Outdoor Activities and Sports

Little Killary Adventure Center (✉ Salruck, Renvyle, near Letterfrack, Co. Galway, ☎ 095/43411) provides sailing and windsurfing instruction on sheltered, coastal waters.

Shopping

Connemara Handcrafts (☎ 095/41058) carries an extensive selection of crafts and women's fashions made by the stellar Avoca Handweavers (☞ Chapter 2); there's also an above-average coffee shop.

Kylemore Valley

③⑧ *6½ km (4 mi) between Letterfrack and the intersection of N59 and R344.*

One of the more conventionally beautiful stretches of road in Connemara passes through Kylemore Valley, which lies between the Twelve Bens to the south and the naturally forested Dorruagh Mountains to the north. Kylemore (the name is derived from Coill Mór, Irish for "big wood") looks "as though some colossal giant had slashed it out with a couple of strokes from his mammoth sword," as John FitzMaurice Mills has

★ written. **Kylemore Abbey,** one of the most photographed castles in all of Ireland, lies about ¾ km (½ mi) back from the Kylemore Valley road, visible across a reedy lake (one of three that lie along the road) with a backdrop of wooded hillside. The vast Gothic Revival, turreted, gray stone castle was built as a private home between 1861 and 1868 by Mitchell Henry, a member of Parliament for County Galway, and his wife, Margaret, who had fallen in love with the spot during a carriage ride while on their honeymoon. The Henrys spared no expense—the final bill for their house is said to have come to £1.5 million—and employed mostly local laborers, thereby abetting the famine relief effort (this area was among the worst hit in all of Ireland). In 1920, nuns from the Irish Abbey of the Nuns of St. Benedict, fleeing their abbey in Belgium during World War I, eventually sought refuge in Kylemore, which had been through a number of owners and decades of decline after the Henrys. Still in residence today, the Benedictine nuns now run a girls' boarding school here. Three reception rooms and the main hall are open to the public, as are a crafts center and simple cafeteria. An exhibition and video explaining the history of the house can be viewed year-round at the abbey, and the grounds are freely accessible most of the year. A newly restored 6-acre walled Victorian garden opened in 1999. Ask at the crafts shop for directions to the **Gothic Chapel** (a five-minute walk from the abbey), a tiny replica of Norwich Cathedral built by the Henrys. (Norwich was built by the English Benedictines, in a felicitous anticipation of Kylemore's fate.) ☎ 095/41146. ☜ *Chapel free, exhibition £3, garden £3.* ☯ *Crafts shop Mar. 17–Nov. daily 10–6; cafeteria Easter–Nov., daily 9:30–6; grounds Easter–Nov., daily 9–dusk; exhibition and garden Easter–Nov., daily 9–5:30.*

Beyond Kylemore, the road travels for some miles alongside **Killary Harbour,** a narrow fjord (the only one in Ireland) that runs for 16 km (10 mi) between County Mayo's Mweelrea Mountains to the north and County Galway's Dorruagh Mountains to the south. The harbor has an extremely safe anchorage, 13 fathoms (78 ft) deep for almost its entire length and sheltered from storms by mountain walls. The rafts floating in Killary Harbour belong to fish-farming consortia who artificially raise salmon and trout in cages beneath the water. This is a matter of some controversy all over the West, with some residents fearing the long-term effect of pollution from certain fish-farming practices on wild salmon and trout. Although some people indeed welcome the employment opportunities, others bemoan the visual blight of the rafts on the otherwise unspoiled scenery.

Leenane

㊣ *18 km (12 mi) northeast of Letterfrack on N59.*

Nestled idyllically at the foot of the Maamturk Mountains and overlooking the tranquil waters of Killary Harbour, Leenane is a tiny village noted for its role as the setting for the 1990 film *The Field*, which starred Richard Harris. Its name features in Martin McDonagh's *Leenane Trilogy,* an unflattering view of rural Irish life featuring a cast of tragi-comic grotesques. However, although it was an international hit for Galway's Druid Theatre Company in 1997, it brought a renown that the people of Leenane presumably could have done without. Leenane's **Sheep and Wool Center** illustrates the traditional industry of North Connemara and West Mayo. More than 20 breeds of sheep graze around the house, and there are live demonstrations of carding, spinning, weaving, and the dyeing of wool with natural plant dyes. ☎ 095/42231. ☞ £2. ☉ *Apr.–June and Oct., daily 9:30–7; July–Aug., daily 9 AM–7 PM.*

Dining and Lodging

$$ ✕🏨 **Delphi Lodge.** In the heart of what is arguably Mayo's most spec-
★ tacular mountain and lake scenery, 6 km (4 mi) northwest of Leenane, this attractive Georgian sporting lodge with a lovely lakeside setting is heavily stocked with fishing paraphernalia. Owners Peter and Jane Mantle are gracious hosts and valuable storehouses of information and stories. The bright, spacious bedrooms, some of which have lake views, feature pine furniture, floral curtains, and wonderfully comfortable beds. Guests dine together; there is an excellent wine list and a self-service bar. ☒ *Leenane, Co. Mayo,* ☎ 095/42211, ℻ 095/42296. *12 rooms with bath. AE, MC, V. Closed Mid-Dec.–mid-Jan.*

En Route Westport is the next stop on our route, and you have two options for getting there. The first is to take the direct route on N59. The second is to detour through the **Doolough Valley** between the Mweelrea Mountains (to the west) and the Sheeffry Hills (to the east) and on to Westport via Louisburgh (on the southern shore of Clew Bay). This latter route adds about 24 km (15 mi) to the trip to Westport, but devotees of this part of the West claim that it'll take you through the region's most impressive, unspoiled stretch of scenery. If you opt for the longer route, turn left onto R335 1½ km (1 mi) beyond Leenane. Just after this turn, you'll hear the powerful rush of the Aasleagh Falls. You can park over the bridge, stroll along the river's shore, and soak in the splendor of the surrounding mountains.

Either way you go, look out as you travel north for the great bulk of 2,500-ft **Croagh Patrick**; its size and conical shape make it one of the West's most distinctive landmarks. On clear days a small, white building is visible at its summit (it stands on a half-acre plateau), as is the wide path that ascends to it. The latter is the **Pilgrim's Path,** which about 25,000 people, many of them barefoot, follow each year to pray to St. Patrick in the oratory on its peak. St. Patrick spent the 40 days and nights of Lent here during the period he was converting Ireland to Christianity. The traditional date for the pilgrimage is the last Sunday in July;

in the past, the walk was made at night, with pilgrims carrying burning torches, but that practice has been discontinued. The climb can be made in about 3 hours (round-trip) on any fine day and is well worth it for the magnificent views of the islands of Clew Bay, the Sheeffry Hills to the south (with the Bens visible behind them), and the peaks of Mayo to the north. The climb starts at Murrisk, a village about 8 km (5 mi) outside Westport on the R335 Louisburgh road.

Westport

★ ④ *32 km (20 mi) north of Leenane on R335.*

By far the most attractive town in County Mayo, Westport is on an inlet of Clew Bay, a wide expanse of sea dotted with islands and framed by mountain ranges. The architect James Wyatt planned the town in the late 18th century when he was employed to finish nearby Westport House (☞ *below*). Westport's streets radiate from its central **Octagon,** where an old-fashioned farmers' market is held on Thursday mornings; look for work clothes, harnesses, tools, and children's toys for sale. Traditional shops—ironmongers, drapers, and the like—dot the streets that lead to the Octagon, while a riverside mall is lined with tall lime trees. The town is a popular fishing center and has several good beaches close by.

About 2 km (1 mi) outside town (and clearly signposted from the Octagon) is Westport's **Quay.** (If you're driving north on N59, you'll come to a left turn-off for the Quay before you arrive in Westport proper.) A large warehouse has been attractively restored as holiday apartments, and the Quay has some good bars and decent restaurants, but its central attraction is **Westport House,** a stately home built on the site of an earlier castle. The house was originally begun in 1730 to the designs of Richard Castle (☞ Leinster House *in* Chapter 1 and Powerscourt and Russborough Houses *in* Chapter 2), added to in 1778, and completed in 1788 by architect James Wyatt for the marquess of Sligo. The rectangular, three-story house is furnished with late-Georgian and Victorian pieces. Family portraits by Opie and Reynolds, old Irish silver, and a collection of old Waterford glass are all on display. The home is superbly situated beside a lake with a small formal garden; additional gardens are undergoing restoration. A word of caution: Westport isn't your usual staid country house. The old dungeons, which belonged to the earlier castle (believed to have been the home of the 16th-century warrior queen, Grace O'Malley) now house video games, and the grounds have given way to a small amusement park for children and a children's zoo. If these elements don't sound like a draw, arrive early when it's less likely to be busy. ☎ *098/25430.* ☞ *House £6; family day ticket for all attractions £29.* ☉ *House May and Sept., weekends 2–5; grounds and house June, daily 2–6; July–Aug. 21, Mon.–Sat. 11:30–6, Sun. 2–6; Aug. 22–31, daily 2–6.*

Twelve kilometers (7 mi) north of Westport on N59 on the Beltra River, the pleasant village of **Newport** is popular from March to September with salmon fishermen.

Dining and Lodging

$$ ✕ **Quay Cottage.** Fishing nets, glass floats, lobster pots, and greenery hang from the high-pitched, exposed-beam roof of this tiny, waterside cottage located at the entrance to Westport House. Both an informal wine bar and a shellfish restaurant, it attracts a youngish crowd in search of a good time and good food. Rush-seated chairs, polished-oak tables, and an open fire in the evenings add to the comfortable, none-too-formal atmosphere. Try the chowder special (a thick vegetable and

mussel soup), garlic-butter crab claws, or a half-pound steak fillet, and be sure to sample the homemade brown bread. The restaurant is licensed to serve wine only. ⊠ *The Quay, Co. Mayo,* ☎ *098/26412. AE, MC, V. Closed Jan.*

$$$ ✕⊞ **Newport House.** This handsome, creeper-covered Georgian house beside the Newport River dominates the little town of Newport, 12 km (7 mi) north of Westport on N59. Kieran and Thelma Thompson's grand and elegant private home has spacious public rooms furnished with gilt-framed family portraits, Regency mirrors and chairs, handwoven Donegal carpeting, and crystal chandeliers hanging from ornate stucco ceilings. In the dining room, oysters, smoked salmon, roast breast of duck, charcoal-grilled veal steak, and similar hearty country-house fare are served, along with homemade ice creams and sorbets for dessert. The sweeping staircase, lighted by a lantern and a glass dome, leads to an airy gallery and the bedrooms. Bright and less elaborate than the public rooms, these are decorated with pretty chintz drapes and a mix of Victorian antiques and old furniture. Most bedrooms have sitting areas and good views of the river and gardens; others have such compensations as the enormous Jacobean four-poster in Room 10. ⊠ *Co. Mayo,* ☎ *098/41222,* FAX *098/41613. 19 rooms with bath. Restaurant, bar, fishing. AE, DC, MC, V. Closed Oct.–mid-Mar.*

$$ ✕⊞ **Olde Railway Hotel.** By far the best bet in Westport's town center, this Victorian railway hotel offers both character and comfort. Fishing trophies, Victorian plates, framed prints, and watercolors brighten up the lobby and lounge. A mix of Victorian and older pieces decorate the sunny bedrooms, which have double-glazed, Georgian sash windows. Two top picks: Room 209 has a heavy, Victorian bed and a river view; and Room 114, which has a Victorian chaise lounge and a large Georgian wardrobe. Overlooking the landscaped gardens, the Conservatory Restaurant serves fresh local produce and game specialties. ⊠ *The Mall, Co. Mayo,* ☎ *098/25605,* FAX *098/25090. 24 rooms with bath. Restaurant, 2 bars, fishing. AE, MC, V. Closed mid-Jan.–mid-Feb.*

Nightlife

A good spot to try for traditional music is the **Ardmore Pub** (⊠ The Quay, ☎ 09825994). In Westport's town center try **Matt Molloy's** (⊠ Bridge St., ☎ 098/26655), owned by a member of the Chieftains, where traditional music is of course the main attraction.

Outdoor Activities and Sports

BICYCLING

Enjoy the spectacular scenery of Clew Bay at a leisurely pace on a rented bike from **J. P. Breheny & Sons** (⊠ Castlebar St., ☎ 098/25020).

FISHING

Fishing tackle, bait, and licenses can be obtained at **Patrick Kelly** (⊠ Bridge St., ☎ 098/25982).

GOLF

Westport Golf Club (⊠ Carrowholly, ☎ 098/25113), beneath Croagh Patrick, overlooks Clew Bay. Designed by Fred Hawtree in the early 1970s, the 18-hole, par-73 course has twice been the venue for the Irish Amateur Championship.

HORSEBACK RIDING

Drummindoo Stud and Equitation Center (⊠ Castlebar Rd., ☎ 098/25616) will take you on the Clew Bay Trail, a three-day trek riding on the superb beaches around Clew Bay staying in farmhouses along the route. Alternatively, you can rent a horse by the hour.

Shopping

McCormack's (⊠ Bridge St., ☎ 098/25619) has a traditional butcher shop downstairs, but upstairs it's an attractive gallery and café with work by local artists for sale. **Carraig Donn** (⊠ Bridge St., ☎ 098/26287) has its own range of knitwear and a good selection of crystal, jewelry, and ceramics. **Satch Kiely** (⊠ Westport Quay, ☎ 098/25775) carries fine antique furniture and decorative pieces.

En Route If you're heading out to Achill Island, N59 follows the shores of **Newport Bay** (the northern shore of Clew Bay) for 19 km (12 mi) west from Newport to Mulrany, where R319 branches off to the left for Achill.

Achill Island

★ ㊶ *16 km (10 mi) west of Mulrany, 58 km (36 mi) northwest of Westport.*

Heaven on earth in good weather, when its splendid scenery can be fully appreciated, Achill Island is a destination you'll probably want to head for—but only if you'll be able to *see* its cliff walks and sandy beaches. At 147 square km (57 square mi) and only 20 ft away from the mainland, this mass of bogs and wild heather is the largest island off Ireland's coast. A short causeway leads from the mainland to **Achill Sound,** the first village on the island. The main road runs through rhododendron plantations to **Keel,** which has a 3-km (2-mi) beach with spectacular cathedral-like rock formations in the cliffs at its east end. There's a longer scenic route signposted ATLANTIC DRIVE. **Dugoort,** on the north shore of the island, is a small village with a beautiful golden strand. Nearby is the cottage used by Heinrich Böll, German writer and Nobel prizewinner, whose *Irish Diary,* written in the 1950s, has introduced many visitors to this part of Ireland. The cottage today is part of a center for German-Irish cultural exchanges. On Achill's north coast above Dugoort, 2,204-ft **Slievemore** is the island's highest summit. Until just a few years ago, the people of Achill made a very poor living. Tourism has improved things, as has the establishment of cottage industries (mainly knitting) and shark fishing, which is popular from April to July. Alas, Achill's popularity has led to a rash of new, not always appropriate development, most noticeably clusters (or "villages") of bleak concrete vacation cottages that stand empty for 10 months out of 12.

Lodging

$ ▥ **Ostan Gob A'Choire.** In the first village you approach arriving from the mainland, this small, waterside, two-story town house (its name means "Achill Sound Hotel") has a brick-and-plate-glass bedroom extension. All bedrooms have sea views, but the nicer ones, with tweed curtains and reproductions of Georgian furniture, are in the old building. The smaller rooms are already a little worn, but they are spotlessly clean and have pleasant views of the sound. *Ceilís* (Irish dancing and song) are staged in the Alice's Harbour Inn, as the bar is called, most weekends. ⊠ *Achill Sound, Co. Mayo,* ☎ *098/45245,* ℻ *098/45621. 36 rooms with bath. Restaurant, bar, bicycles. MC, V. Closed Oct.–Mar.*

Outdoor Activities and Sports

Tour the cliffs of Achill on a bike from the **Achill Sound Hotel** (⊠ Co. Mayo, ☎ 098/45245). Bikes can also be rented from **O'Malley's Island Sports** (⊠ Keel P.O., Achill, ☎ 098/43125).

En Route The shortest route to Ballina (N59 via Bangor and Crossmolina) runs for about 24 km (15 mi) across desolate, almost uninhabited bog, some of which has had its turf cut down to rock level by successive generations searching for fuel. Once the novelty has worn off, it's a bleak, boring drive. Unless time is short, we suggest you take the longer but more interesting route by backtracking to Newport and continuing through Castlebar, Pontoon, and Foxford.

Castlebar

㊷ *40 km (26 mi) east of the Achill Islands, 18 km (11 mi) east of Westport, 17½ km (11 mi) east of Newport on R311.*

The administrative capital of Mayo, Castlebar is a tidy little town with an attractive, tree-bordered green. In 1879 Michael Davitt founded the Land League here, in the Imperial Hotel. Hatred of landlords ran high in the area, due to the ruthless, battering-ram evictions ordered by the Earl of Lucan. The disappearance in the 1960s of his high-living successor, the seventh earl, after the violent death in London of his children's nanny, is said to have given today's tenants a perfect pretext for withholding their rents. The same **Imperial Hotel** (⊠ The Green, ☎ 094/21961) is worth a visit to check out its Gothic-style dining room, where the simply prepared country food is probably unchanged since Michael Davitt's day. Although coffeemaking isn't a strong point around here, either, the **Linen Hall Arts Centre** (⊠ Linenhall St., ☎ 094/ 23733) serves espresso and cappuccino in its café; grab a cup after viewing the art exhibitions and performances often scheduled here.

If you're driving the 50 km (31 mi) from Westport northeast to Ballina, there is a choice of two routes. The longer and more scenic is via the tiny, wooded village of Pontoon, skirting the western shore of Lough Conn and passing through the rough bogland of the Glen of Nephin, beneath the dramatic heather-clad slopes of Nephin Mountain 2653 ft). The shorter route follows N5 and N58 to Foxford, a pretty village with several crafts and antiques shops. A good place for a break is at the **Foxford Woollen Mills Visitor Center,** where you can explore the crafts shop and grab a bit at the restaurant. The "Foxford Experience" tells the story of the woollen mill (famous for its tweeds and blankets) from the time of the famine—when it was founded by the Sisters of Charity to combat poverty—to the present day. ⊠ Foxford, ☎ 094/56756. ⊡ £3. ☉ Sept.–June, Mon.–Sat. 10–6, Sun. 2–6; July–Aug., Sun. noon–6; tour every 20 mins.

Ballina

㊸ *40 km (25 mi) northeast of Castlebar on N9.*

Ballina's chief attraction is fishing for salmon and trout in the River Moy and nearby Lough Conn. Although it is the largest town in County Mayo (population 7,500), to some eyes, Ballina's town center may appear run-down; however, its unspoiled, old-fashioned shops and pubs contain many treasures. Try the bar food at **Gaughan's** (⊠ O'Rahilly St., ☎ 096/21151), where the classic wooden interior dates back to the mid-19th century. On the same street, **McGrath's Foodland Delicatessen** (☎ 096/21198) is an old-fashioned grocery handy for picnic materials.

Dining and Lodging

$$ ✕🏨 **Enniscoe House.** A pink Georgian mansion on the shores of Lough Conn, 4½ km (3 mi) south of Crossmolina and 20 km (13 mi) west of Ballina, Enniscoe sits on 150 acres crisscrossed with pleasant walks and 3¼ km (2 mi) of peaceful lakeshore. Owner Susan Kellett inherited the house, and she has been busy preserving and enhancing the property. She's converted many of the farm buildings into offices, which now house a number of independent organizations, including a Mayo genealogy center and the Cloonamoyne Fishery. The formal ornamental garden is also undergoing renovations. Colorful corridors, fishing motifs, and quirky, slightly crooked stairways combine to make this a wonderfully appealing spot. Meals include fruits grown in the organic garden. ✉ *Castlehill, Ballina, Co. Mayo,* ☎ *096/31112,* FAX *096/31773. 6 rooms with bath. Restaurant, fishing. AE, MC, V. Closed mid-Oct.–Mar.*

$$$ 🏨 **Downhill Hotel.** Delightfully situated on 40 wooded acres beside a gushing tributary of the River Moy (just off the N59 Sligo road), this hotel is a popular spot with anglers and outdoor types. The late-Victorian main house feels a little gloomy downstairs, but it is comfortable. Rooms in the new wing tend to be smaller than those in the main house, but the former have good views of the river across the garden. Rooms in the main house are decorated with Georgian-style furniture and tastefully coordinated quilts and drapes. There's music in the bar on weekends and midweek in July and August. ✉ *Co. Mayo,* ☎ *096/21033,* FAX *096/21338. 50 rooms with bath. Restaurant, 2 bars, indoor pool, hot tub, sauna, steam room, 3 tennis courts, exercise room, squash, fishing. AE, DC, MC, V.*

$$ 🏨 **Mount Falcon Castle.** Owner-manager Constance Aldridge's rambling Victorian-Gothic country house 5 km (3 mi) outside Ballina is within easy reach of several beautiful, small beaches. Aldridge is renowned for putting guests at ease and encouraging them to mingle, and she makes children especially welcome. You can salmon fish on the River Moy right on the hotel's extensive grounds; horseback riding, sea fishing, and golf are nearby. Rooms are furnished comfortably with a mix of antiques and heirlooms, and they overlook the wooded grounds. In the dining room, the country-style home cooking, which takes advantage of local produce, has a fine reputation. ✉ *Co. Mayo,* ☎ *096/70811,* FAX *096/71517. 10 rooms with bath. Restaurant, tennis court, fishing. AE, DC, MC, V. Closed Feb.–mid-Apr.*

Outdoor Activities and Sports

BICYCLING

Head for the coast north of Ballina on a bike from **Gerry's Cycle Center** (✉ 6 Lord Edward St., ☎ 096/70455).

FISHING

Fishing bait, tackle, and licenses can be obtained from **John Walkin** (✉ Tone St., ☎ 096/22442).

GOLF

Enniscrone Golf Club (✉ Enniscrone, ☎ 096/36297), 13 km (8 mi) north of Ballina, is an 18-hole, par-72 course. The **Carne Golf Course** at Belmullet Golf Club (✉ Belmullet, ☎ 097/82292), 72 km (45 mi) west of Ballina, is a recent addition to the list of Ireland's renowned links courses (☞ Chapter 9).

THE NORTH MAYO COAST

Killala, 12 km (7½) mi north of Ballina, is a pleasant little seaside town overlooking Killala Bay. This was the scene of the unsuccessful French invasion of Ireland, led by Wolfe Tone in 1798. The history of this tiny bishopric goes back much further, though, as evidenced by its round, 12th-century tower.

Killala is the gateway to the north Mayo coast, a dramatic, windswept stretch of cliffs continuing to Erris Head on the Mullet peninsula in the far west of the county. The sparsely inhabited landscape beneath an ever-changing sky consists of small farms and open moorland. The small roads and stunning views are attractive to cyclists, but be warned: The wind howls in across the Atlantic directly from Iceland, the nearest land mass. Although there are no signposted trails on this coast, there are plenty of cliff footpaths and small roads for walkers to explore. Don't miss the blow-holes on **Downpatrick Head,** great gaps in the rocks through which plumes of water spew in rough weather.

44 Nowadays, the chief reason for visiting this coast is the **Céide Fields.** Widely recognized as one of Europe's most significant megalithic sites, the fields consist of rows and patterns of stones that have been preserved under a 5,000-year-old bog. These stones are the remnants of dwelling places and stone-walled fields built by a peaceful, well-organized farming community. A striking glass-and-steel pyramid houses the visitor center, where displays and an audiovisual show bring this strange landscape to life. Admission includes an optional guided walk through an excavated section of the stones; wet-weather gear is provided when necessary. The Ceide Fields is on R314, 5 km (3 mi) west of Ballycastle. ⊠ *Ballycastle, Co. Mayo,* ☎ *096/43325.* ✆ *£2.50.* ⊙ *Mid-Mar.–May and Oct., daily 10–5; June–Sept., daily 9:30–6:30; Nov., daily 10–4:30.*

Shopping

Hackett &Turpin (⊠ Carrowteige, Ballina, ☎ 097/88925) is a factory outlet for Irish sweaters. From R314 beyond the Céide Fields, follow signs for Benwee Head.

THE WEST A TO Z

Arriving and Departing

By Bus

Bus Éireann (☎ 01/836–6111 in Dublin, 021/508188 in Cork, 061/313333 in Limerick) operates a variety of expressway services into the region from Dublin, Cork City, and Limerick City to Ennis, Galway City, Westport, and Ballina, the principal depots in the region. Expect bus rides to last about one hour longer than the time by car.

By Car

The 219-km (136-mi) Dublin–Galway trip takes about 3 hours. From Cork City take N20 through Mallow and N21 to Limerick City, picking up the N18 Ennis–Galway road in Limerick. The 209-km (130-mi) drive from Cork to Galway takes about 3 hours. From Killarney the shortest and most pleasant route to cover the 193 km (120 mi) to Galway (3 hrs) is N22 to Tralee, then N69 through Listowel to Tarbert and the ferry across the Shannon Estuary to Killimer in County Clare, joining N68 in Kilrush, and then picking up N18 in Ennis. The ferry leaves Tarbert every hour on the half hour and takes 20 minutes, avoiding a 104-km (65-mi) detour through Limerick City. It costs £7 one-way, £10 round-trip. (Ferries return from Killimer every hour on the hour.)

By Plane

The West's most convenient international airport is **Shannon** (☎ 061/471444), 25 km (16 mi) east of Ennis in the Southwest (☞ The Southwest A to Z *in* Chapter 5). **Galway Airport** (☎ 091/752874), near Galway City, is used mainly for internal flights, with steadily increasing U.K. traffic. **Horan International Airport** (☎ 094/67222), at Knock in County Mayo, is also used mainly for internal flights. A small airport for internal traffic only is also located at **Knockrowen,** Castlebar, in County Mayo (☎ 094/22853). Flying time from Dublin is 25–30 minutes to all airports. No scheduled flights run from the United States to Galway or Knock; use Shannon Airport (☞ The Southwest A to Z *in* Chapter 5).

Aer Lingus has daily flights from London's Heathrow Airport to Galway and Knock via Dublin; the trip takes about 2 hours. **Ryanair** flies to Knock daily from London's Luton Airport; flying time is 80 minutes. **Loganair** flies to Knock from Birmingham, Manchester, and Glasgow.

BETWEEN THE AIRPORT AND THE CITIES

Galway: Galway Airport is 6½ km (4 mi) from Galway City. No regular bus service is available from the airport to Galway, but most flight arrivals are taken to Galway Rail Station in the city center by an airline courtesy coach. Inquire when you book. A taxi from the airport to the city center costs about £7.

Knock: If you're flying from Dublin to Horan International Airport in Knock, you can pick up your rental car at the airport. Otherwise, inquire at the time of booking about transport to your final destination: No regular bus service is available from Horan International Airport.

By Train

Galway City, Westport, and Ballina are the main rail stations in the region. For County Clare, travel from Cork City, Killarney Town, or Dublin's Heuston Station to **Limerick City** (☎ 061/315555) and continue the journey by bus. Trains for Galway, Westport, and Ballina leave from Dublin's **Heuston Station** (☎ 01/836–6222). The journey time to Galway is 3 hours; to Ballina 3¾ hours; and to Westport 3½ hours. Train passengers can call for information in Galway (☎ 091/564222), Ballina (☎ 096/71818), and Westport (☎ 098/25253).

Getting Around

By Bus

In July and August, the provincial bus service is augmented by daily services to most resort towns. Outside these months, many coastal towns receive only one or two buses per week. Bus routes are often slow and circuitous, and service can be erratic. A copy of the Bus Éireann timetable (50p from any station) is essential. The main bus stations are located at **Ennis** (☎ 065/682–4177), **Galway City** (✉ Ceannt Station, ☎ 091/562000), **Westport** (✉ Railway station, ☎ 098/25711), and **Ballina** (☎ 096/71800).

By Car

A car is essential in the West, especially from September through June. Although the main cities of the area are easily reached from the rest of Ireland by rail or bus, transport within the region is sparse and badly coordinated. If a rental car is out of the question, your best option is to make Galway your base and take day tours (available mid-June through September) west to Connemara and south to the Burren, and a day or overnight trip to the Aran Islands. It *is* possible to explore the region by local and intercity bus services, but you will need plenty of time.

The West has good, wide main roads (National Primary Routes) and better-than-average local roads (National Secondary Routes), both known as "N" routes. If you stray off the beaten track on the smaller Regional ("R") or unnumbered routes, particularly in Connemara and County Mayo, you may encounter some hazardous mountain roads. Narrow, steep, and twisty, they are also frequented by untended sheep, cows, and ponies grazing "the long acre" (as the strip of grass beside the road is called) or simply straying in search of greener pastures. If you find a sheep in your path, just sound the horn, and it should scramble away. A good maxim for these roads is "You never know what's around the next corner." Bear this in mind, and adjust your speed accordingly. Hikers and cyclists constitute an additional hazard on narrow roads in the summer.

Within the Connemara Irish-speaking area, signs are in Irish only. The main signs to recognize are Gaillimh (Galway), Rós an Mhil (Rossaveal), An Teach Doite (Maam Cross), and Sraith Salach (Recess). A good map, available through newsagents and TIOs, gives Irish and English names where needed.

By Ferry to the Aran Islands

Between June and September, **Aran Ferries** (✉ TIO, Victoria Pl., Eyre Sq., ☎ 091/568903 or 091/592447) has daily sailings from Galway Docks, a five-minute walk from Eyre Square, at 10:30 AM in June, July, and September, 9:30 and 1:30 in August. The crossing takes 90 minutes and costs £18 round-trip. The same company runs a boat from Rossaveal, 32 km (20 mi) west of Galway City, which makes the crossing in 20 minutes and costs £12–£15 round-trip. The shuttle bus from Galway costs £3. For £20 round-trip on the same route you can have one night at a B&B on the islands.

Island Ferries (☎ 091/565767), which has a booking office on Victoria Place opposite the TIO in Galway City, has a one-hour crossing from Rossaveal for £12 round-trip, with up to five sailings a day in summer, weather permitting. Bicycles are transported free, and discounts are available for families, students, and groups of four or more. If you stay a night or two on the islands, ask about accommodations when booking your ferry, as there are some very competitive deals, including free nights in a hostel for backpackers.

If you are heading for **Inisheer,** the smallest island, the shortest crossing is from Doolin in County Clare (☞ The Burren and Beyond—West Clare to South Galway, *above*).

BY FERRY BETWEEN THE ISLANDS

Frequent **interisland ferries** are available in summer months, but tickets are nontransferable, so ask the captain of your ferry about his interisland schedule if you plan to visit more than one island; otherwise, your trip can become expensive.

By Plane to the Aran Islands

Aer Arann (☎ 091/593034) has four flights daily on weekdays, and two flights on weekends. During July and August planes leave every half hour. The flights call at all three of the Aran Islands and leave from Connemara Airport (☎ 091/593034) near Galway. The journey takes about six minutes and costs £35 round-trip, or £44 including one night's bed-and-breakfast. For £25 you can fly one-way and travel one-way by boat from Rossaveal. Ask about other special offers at the time of booking.

By Train

Rail transportation is not good within the West. The major destinations of Galway City and Westport/Ballina are on different branch lines. Connections can only be made between Galway and the other two cities by traveling inland for about an hour to Athlone (☞ Arriving and Departing by Train, *above,* and Chapter 3).

Contacts and Resources

B&B Reservation Agencies

For a small fee, **Bord Fáilte** will book accommodations anywhere in Ireland through its central reservations system. B&Bs can be booked at local TIOs (☞ Visitor Information, *below*) when they are open; however, even these reservations will go through the central reservations system. For more information, ☞ Lodging *in* Smart Travel Tips A to Z.

Car Rentals

If you haven't already picked up a rental car at Shannon Airport (☞ The Southwest A to Z *in* Chapter 5), try the following:

Galway City and Vicinity: Avis (☎ 091/568886). **Budget** (☎ 091/566376). **Eurodollar** (☎ 091/771929). **Euro Mobil** (☎ 091/753037). **Hertz Rent A Car** (☎ 091/752502). **Murray's** (☎ 091/562222). **O'Mara's Rent-a-Car** (☎ 091/564663).

Horan International Airport, Knock: Diplomat Rent A Car (☎ 094/67252). **Murray's** (☎ 094/67221).

Emergencies

Police, fire, and **ambulance** (☎ 999).

DOCTORS AND DENTISTS

County Clare: Mid-Western Health Board (⊠ Catherine St., Limerick, Co. Limerick, ☎ 061/316655). **Counties Galway and Mayo: Western Health Board** (⊠ Merlin Pk., Galway City, Co. Galway, ☎ 091/751131).

PHARMACIES

Galway: Matt O'Flaherty (⊠ 39 Eyre Sq., Co. Galway, ☎ 091/562927). **Westport: O'Donnell's** (⊠ Bridge St., Co. Mayo, ☎ 098/25163).

Guided Tours

The only full- and half-day guided tours in the region start from Galway. Galway City's **TIO** (☞ Visitor Information, *below*) has details of walking tours of Galway, which are organized by request.

Coras Iompar Eireann (CIE), the Irish National Bus Company, coordinates two full-day tours, one covering Connemara and the other the Burren (each £9). Tours run from early June to late September only, with the widest choice available between mid-July and mid-August. Book in advance at Galway City's **Ceannt Railway Station** (☎ 091/562000) or the **Salthill TIO** (☎ 091/520500), which also serve as departure points.

Galway Tours runs a day tour through Connemara and County Mayo and another to the Burren in July and August and on certain bank holiday weekends. Tickets can be booked at the TIO in Galway City (☞ Visitor Information, *below*).

Outdoor Activities and Sports

BICYCLING

All TIOs (☞ Visitor Information, *below*) in the West provide lists of suggested cycle tours.

BOARD AND DINGHY SAILING

One- and two-week courses in sailing and board sailing are available at the **Glénans Center,** based on an otherwise uninhabited island in Clew Bay near Westport. Contact the center's head office (⊠ 28 Merrion Sq., Dublin, ☎ 01/661–1481).

FISHING

Details of the numerous fisheries in the area are available from the local TIOs (☞ Visitor Information, *below*), or consult the Irish Tourist Board leaflet "Angling Ireland" (£2). Similar leaflets are available on coarse-angling (angling for freshwater fish) and sea-angling.

HIKING

For backcountry walking, consult "Irish Walk Guides—The West," a pamphlet available at local TIOs (☞ Visitor Information, *below*), and take local advice on weather conditions.

Visitor Information

Bord Fáilte provides free information service, tourist literature, and an accommodations booking service at its TIOs.

MAIN OFFICES

The following offices are open all year, weekdays 9–6 and Saturday 9–1: **Ennis** (⊠ Clare Rd., Co. Clare, ☎ 065/682–8366). **Galway City** (⊠ 1 Victoria Pl., Eyre Sq., Co. Galway, ☎ 091/563081, FAX 091/565201). **Oughterard** (⊠ Main St., Co. Galway, ☎ 091/552808, FAX 091/552811). **Westport** (⊠ The Mall, Co. Mayo, ☎ 098/25711, FAX 098/26709).

SEASONAL OFFICES

These offices are open as indicated, weekdays 9–6 and Saturday 9–1: **Achill** (⊠ Co. Mayo, ☎ 098/45384), June–August. **Aran Islands (Inishmore)** (⊠ Co. Galway, ☎ 099/61263, FAX 099/61420), mid-March–October 5. **Ballina** (⊠ Co. Mayo, ☎ 096/70848), late March–September. **Castlebar** (⊠ Co. Mayo, ☎ 094/21207), May–mid-September. **Clifden** (⊠ Co. Galway, ☎ 095/21163), April–September. **Cliffs of Moher** (⊠ Co. Clare, ☎ 065/708–1171), Easter–October. **Kilkee** (⊠ Co. Clare, ☎ 065/905–6112), June–August. **Kilrush** (⊠ Co. Clare, ☎ 065/905–1047), June–August. **Salthill** (⊠ Salthill, Co. Galway, ☎ 091/520500), May–September. **Thoor Ballylee** (⊠ Near Gort, Co. Clare, ☎ 091/31436), mid-March–September.

7 THE NORTHWEST

YEATS COUNTRY, DONEGAL BAY, THE NORTHERN PENINSULAS

On an island where there's no shortage of majestic scenery, the Northwest claims its fair share: Cool, clean waters from the roaring Atlantic Ocean shape the landscape into long peninsulas—a raw, sensual landscape that looks like Earth is still under construction, above which soar breezy, rocky crests. Clouds and rain linger over proud mountains, soft glens, raw cliffs, sandy beaches, and heathered bogs, to be chased within minutes by sunshine and rainbows. Two brothers, the writer William Butler Yeats and the painter Jack, immortalized this land in their work. Walk in their footsteps, and you'll be struck anew at the dance of nature and art.

Updated by
Geoff Hill

GLANCE AT A MAP OF IRELAND THAT HAS scenic roads marked in green, and chances are your eye will quickly be drawn to the far-flung peninsulas of the Northwest. At virtually every bend in the roads of counties Donegal, Leitrim, and Sligo there's something to justify all those green ribbons. But what that something is *now* may not be what it is an hour from now. As they say, if you don't like the weather, just wait five minutes. The air, the light, and the colors of the countryside change as though with a turn of a kaleidoscope. Look once, and see scattered, snow-white clouds flying above tawny slopes. Look up, and suddenly the sun has brilliantly illuminated magnificent reds and purples in the undergrowth. The fickle skies brighten and darken at will, tempting a spectrum of subtle shades from the unkempt gorse and heather, then washing the grassy meadows greener than any green you've ever seen.

The Northwest covers the most northerly part of Ireland's Atlantic coastline, running from Sligo in the south along Donegal's remote, windswept peninsulas to Malin Head in the far north. These maritime landscapes are said to have given their colors to the most famous local product, handwoven tweed, which reflects the browns of the peaty heathland and the purples of the heather. Donegal, a sparsely populated rural county of small farms and fishing boats, shares its inland border with Northern Ireland; the border is partly formed by the River Foyle. Inland from Sligo is Leitrim, a county best known for its numerous lakes and loughs, some of which join up with the River Shannon, on the easterly border of this region (and which is covered with greater depth in Chapter 3).

County Donegal was part of the near-indomitable ancient kingdom of Ulster, which was not conquered by the English until the 17th century. By the time the English were driven out in the 1920s, they had still not eradicated rural Donegal's Celtic inheritance. It thus shouldn't come as a surprise that County Donegal contains Ireland's largest Gaeltacht (Irish-speaking area). Driving in this part of the country, you'll either be frustrated or amused whenever you come to a crossroads: Signposts show only the Irish place-names, often so unlike the English versions as to be completely unrecognizable. All is not lost, however: Maps generally give both the Irish and the English names, and locals are usually more than happy to help out with directions (in English)—usually with a yarn thrown in.

Tucked into the folds of the Northwest's hills, modest little market towns and unpretentious villages with muddy streets go about their business quietly. In the squelchy peat bogs, cutters working with long shovels pause to watch and wave as you drive past. Remember to drive slowly along the country lanes, for around any corner you may find a whitewashed thatched cottage with children playing outside its scarlet door, a shepherd leading his flock, a wayward sheep or two looking philosophical about having strayed from their field, or a farmer wobbling along in the middle of the road on his old faithful sit-up-and-beg bicycle.

A raw and sensual landscape—it almost seems as if the earth were still under construction here—the Northwest is overwhelmingly rural and underpopulated. That's not to say there isn't a bit of hurly-burly here. The Northwest's boomtown, Sligo Town, is in the throes of a major renaissance—on a typical weekday, its little winding streets are as busy as those of Galway and it seems to be giving Dublin's Temple Bar a run for its money when it comes to stylish restaurants and trendy people—an amazing feat for a town of only 23,000 souls. Sligo Town pulses not only in the present but with the charge of history, for it was the childhood home of W. B. and Jack Yeats, the place that, more than any other, gave rise to their particular geniuses—or, as Jack put it: "Sligo was my school and the sky above it." More bright lights are found in Letterkenny, which boasts the longest main street of any town in Ireland. Glenveagh National Park exemplifies the surprising alliance between nature and culture you'll find in the Northwest: Here, perched on the edge of a glorious lake in the midst of 24,000 acres of some of Ireland's most thrilling wilderness, sits a fairy-tale castle that reflects the life and times of the man who owned it for 50 years: Henry McIlhenny, the millionaire American philanthropist and art collector whose Impressionist paintings now hang in one of the finest art museums in America.

Keep in mind, though, that the whole region—and County Donegal in particular—attracts plenty of visitors during July and August; this is a favorite vacation area for people who live in neighboring Northern Ireland. To be frank, a few places are quite spoiled by popularity with tourists and careless development. The Rosses Peninsula on Donegal's west coast, still sometimes described as beautiful, is marred by too much building. Bundoran, on the coast between Sligo Town and Donegal Town, a cheap and cheerful family beach resort full of so-called "Irish gift shops" and "amusement arcades," is another place to pass through rather than visit. On the whole, though, the Northwest is big enough, untamed enough, and grand enough to be able to absorb all of its summer (and weekend) tourists without too much harm.

Pleasures and Pastimes

The Brothers Yeats

Just mention Sligo to a Yeats lover and you'll get an immediate sign of recognition. Just as Dublin is, literarily, the city of James Joyce, Sligo and environs are bound to the life and work of W. B. Yeats (1865–1939)—and, no less, his brother, Jack B. (1871–1957), one of Ireland's most important 20th-century painters, whose expressionistic landscapes and portraits are as emotionally fraught as his brother's poems are lyrical and plangent. Before you go, grab a volume of W. B.'s poems—as you gaze over Lough Gill, you really should have in hand "The Lake Isle of Innisfree"—or read Ray Foster's magisterial first volume of Yeats's life, which appeared in mid-1997 and in which Foster, professor of Irish history at Oxford, assessing W. B.'s accomplishments, notes that he was "both serially and simultaneously, a playwright, journalist, occultist, apprentice politician, revolutionary, stage-manager, diner-out, dedicated friend, confidant, and lover of some of the most interesting people of his day." Walking Sligo's streets today, or exploring the surrounding countryside, it's not hard to imagine yourself following in their steps—a feat made all the more interesting by how precisely, and with what feeling, the brothers Yeats captured the landscape in their poems and paintings. In 1923, W. B. was the first of four Irish writers to receive the Nobel Prize for Literature (George Bernard Shaw in 1925 and Seamus Heaney in 1995 followed him to Stockholm; Samuel Beckett was in Tunisia when his Nobel Prize was awarded in 1970).

Dining

Although the Northwest has not been considered a great gastronomic center, in the last few years Sligo Town has established itself as a sort of last stop for food lovers, with a number of food-related shops worth visiting. On the dining front, here and there, newcomers are serving up well-above-average food in memorable settings, though overall, the majority of restaurants offer plain and simple fare such as traditional Irish lamb stew or bacon and cabbage served with generous helpings of potatoes (often prepared in at least two ways on the same plate), washed down with creamy, lip-smacking pints of Guinness. You're likely to find the finest food at the higher-quality country houses, where chefs elegantly prepare local meat, fish, and produce in a hybrid Irish-French haute cuisine. Another new trend: Several of the area's more successful restaurants have recently added accommodations, making them good overnight destinations. For price ranges ☞ Chart 1(A) *in* Smart Travel Tips A to Z.

Lodging

True, it's the farthest-flung corner of Ireland, but the Northwest has a steady stream of arrivals—especially in July and August, when visitors seek out its joys. Residents of Northern Ireland are particularly apt to use the Northwest as a nearby weekend getaway. As a result, good bed-and-breakfasts and small hotels can be found throughout the region. In the Northwest's two major towns—Sligo Town and Donegal Town—as well as the small coastal resorts in between, traditional provincial hotels have been modernized (albeit not always elegantly), yet they retain some of the charm that comes with older buildings and personalized service. Away from these areas, your options are more restricted, and your best overnight choice, with some exceptions, is usually a modest guest house offering bed, breakfast, and an evening meal. Because of its large Gaeltacht population, you should consider staying in an Irish-speaking home; the local Tourist Information Office (TIO) can be helpful in making a booking with an Irish-speaking family. The Northwest is also home to a number of first-class country-house hotels where you can expect the gracious professionalism you'll find in comparable properties elsewhere in Ireland. For price ranges, ☞ Chart 1(B) *in* Smart Travel Tips A to Z.

Nightlife

As in other regions in Ireland where there are few large towns, the pub in the Northwest is the center of nightlife. Always ask locally or at your hotel if there is a nearby pub with a weekly *seisun,* or an informal performance of traditional folk music. Many hotels or large pubs, particularly at resort towns in season, put on some form of entertainment—a disco or live music—most nights of the week. Discos (often called "dances") are usually full of local and visiting teenagers and twentysomethings. These discos are far from sophisticated but are often a lot of fun (and great for meeting people). When there isn't a disco, you will find some kind of live music, usually a local traveling band that plays rock-and-roll standards and country-and-western music. These appeal to an older crowd, often the parents of the kids who danced the night away in the same place the night before.

Outdoor Activities and Sports

BICYCLING

Steep hills, winding and poorly kept roads, occasionally strong winds, and the frequent possibility of cold weather and rain make the Northwest one of Ireland's most challenging areas for cyclists. Now the good news: Plenty of low-cost accommodations, astonishing scenery, empty roads, and a chance to stop and chat with the locals can make either serious touring throughout all of the region or gentle meandering around a small area an immensely rewarding experience.

FISHING

The angling in Ireland's Northwest is of the highest class, attracting enthusiasts and connoisseurs from the world over. Yet there's so much space and so much water that it can feel as if you have the whole place to yourself. There are a dozen sea-fishing festivals during the season, open to visiting anglers. Anglers will find that the best area for brown trout is around Bundoran, including Lough Melvin. In western County Donegal, you'll have good opportunities for catching sea trout. Plenty of salmon and brown trout live in the rivers of southern County Donegal and northern County Sligo. More brown trout can be found in the loughs near Dunfanaghy in northern County Donegal, near Bundoran on the border of Donegal and Sligo counties, and in the border area of Sligo and Leitrim counties. Pike anglers and coarse anglers can cast their lines in the abundant County Leitrim lakes.

GOLF

The Northwest has a large number of 9- and 18-hole courses, most in seaside locations, and several of them are world-class. The Northwest's best 18-hole courses all welcome visitors; ☞ Chapter 9 for the four best courses in the region. Expect to pay greens fees of around £15–£30 a day.

HIKING AND WALKING

Trails in the Northwest provide the experienced walker with challenging opportunities. It helps to be able to read a map, and on high ground you're wise not to take any chances with the weather, which can suddenly turn wet and misty. The mountain districts (such as the Blue Stacks, near Donegal Town) offer rough walks with dramatic views. Long-distance footpaths may be found across County Donegal, in County Leitrim, and around Lough Gill in County Sligo. Good shorter trails are also accessible within Glenveagh National Park.

SURFING

There's great surfing along the Atlantic shores of Counties Donegal and Sligo. Head to Strandhill, Rossnowlagh, and Bundoran on the Sligo and south County Donegal coasts (if you need to rent equipment) or to Marble Strand and Rosapenna in north County Donegal (if you have your own gear). These areas have excellent conditions for world-class surfing.

Sweaters, Tweeds, and China

Most of the Aran sweaters you'll see throughout Ireland are made in County Donegal, the area most associated today with high-quality, handwoven tweeds and hand-knit items. Made of plain, undyed wool and knit with distinctive crisscross patterns, Aran sweaters are durable, soft, often weatherproof, and can be astonishingly warm. Not so long ago, these pullovers were worn by every County Donegal fisherman, usually made to a design belonging exclusively to his own family. Today there's a greater variety in patterns, but most of the sweaters still have that unmistakable Aran look. High-quality machine-made tweeds, especially tweed jackets, also have a long history in the area and are widely available. Locally made parian china is a thin, fine, and pale product of very high quality and workmanship. Elaborate flower motifs and a basket-weave design are two distinctive features of this china, which has been a specialty of Belleek, on the Donegal-Fermanagh border, for more than 100 years. In recent years, it has also developed in and around Ballyshannon.

Exploring the Northwest

Our coverage of the Northwest is organized into three autonomous routes, although they can easily be linked if you want to poke around the area over five or so days. The first journey begins in Sligo Town and covers its immediate environs—all the major sights within a roughly 24-km (15-mi) radius, many of which have strong associations with Yeats. The second trip skirts the entirety of Donegal Bay, from Mullaghmore in the south to Glencolumbkille to the far north and west, before heading inland as far as Ardara. The last route begins at the other end of Donegal, in Letterkenny, and covers the far northwest corner of County Donegal before swinging you back around to the Inishowen Peninsula, the tip-top of Ireland, delicately balanced between the Republic and Northern Ireland. If you decide to explore this chapter from back to front (this makes sense if you're arriving in the Northwest from Northern Ireland), begin with the last itinerary, in Letterkenny; skip the trip to the Inishowen peninsula; and pick up the middle tour from either Glebe House or Burtonport.

Numbers in the text correspond to numbers in the margin and on the Yeats Country and Around Donegal Bay, Sligo Town, and the Northern Peninsulas maps.

Great Itineraries

IF YOU HAVE 2 DAYS

Start your tour in **Sligo Town** ①–⑧, the cozy heart of County Sligo. The settlement is dominated by the stark outline of the hill that rears up to the north of the town: This is Yeats's "bare Ben Bulben," in whose shadow he asked to be buried. To whet your appetite for the works of Sligo's most famous poet, have a look at the memorabilia in the **Niland Gallery** ③, where there are also some of the starkly atmospheric oils painted by his brother, Jack. Take along a volume of Yeats's poetry (or at the least his poem "The Lake Isle of Innisfree") as you follow the signposted Yeats Trail around woody, gorgeously scenic **Lough Gill** ⑫, where you'll begin to understand why this land inspired some of Yeats's finest poems. After the road north passes Yeats's simple grave in **Drumcliff** ⑱ churchyard, make a detour to **Lissadell House** ⑲, the home of the beautiful, aristocratic Gore-Booth sisters to whom Yeats was a frequent visitor, and then head on to **Creevykeel** ㉑, a fine important court tomb dating from 3000 BC. Drive through **Ballyshannon** ㉓, where the River Erne empties into Donegal Bay, and continue on to the large village of ☒ **Donegal Town** ㉔, a good place to stay the night, for this is where the roads of the area meet and then go their own ways to the north and west.

On the next day take the road to the thriving fishing port of **Killybegs** ㉖, beyond which point the views of Donegal Bay improve as the road twists and turns before descending into Kilcar, a village (like others hereabouts) known for its tweed making. The road then crosses a stretch of barren moorland and reaches **Glencolumbkille** ㉗, a scenic hamlet spread out around the rocky harbor of Glen Bay; it has associations with the reclusive and controversial early Christian missionary St. Columba. On the far side of the Glengesh Pass, the small village of **Ardara** ㉘ is the center of the region's tweed heritage and also a good spot to hear traditional music. Return from here southward to Donegal Town and either to Dublin (☞ Chapter 1) via Ballyshannon or to Galway (☞ Chapter 6) via Sligo.

IF YOU HAVE 5 DAYS

For your first two days, follow the first day of the two-day itinerary above, but take *two* whole days to do it. You may want to push on at the end of your second day to ☒ **Ardara** ㉘ and visit the tweed heritage center there rather than stop at ☒ **Donegal Town** ㉔, though both have a range of accommodations and some nightlife. On your third day, follow the coast road from Ardara up to Dungloe. Your rate of progress from here on will depend much on the weather and your pace, as the heathery headlands offer innumerable side excursions. North

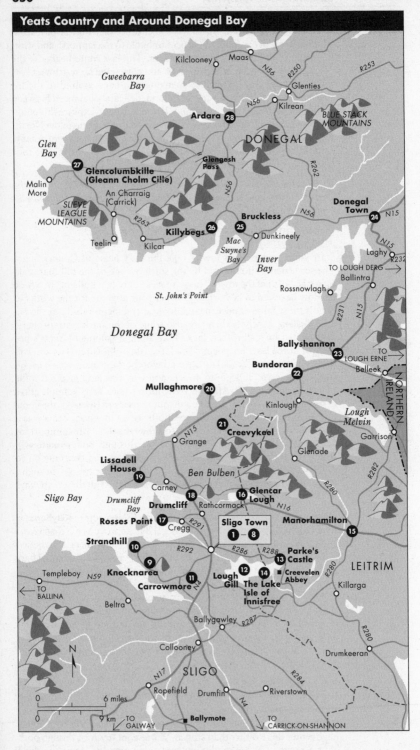

Gweebarra Bay

Kilclooney

Maas

R250

R253

Glenties

N56

Kilrean

Ardara 28

DONEGAL

BLUE STACK MOUNTAINS

Glen Bay

27 **Glencolumbkille (Gleann Cholm Cille)**

Glengesh Pass

R262

Malin More

An Charraig (Carrick)

N56

Donegal Town 24 N15

SLIEVE LEAGUE MOUNTAINS

R263

Killybegs 26 25 **Bruckless**

Dunkineely

N56

N15

Teelin

Kilcar

Mac Swyne's Bay

Laghy

R232

Inver Bay

TO LOUGH DERG

Ballintra

St. John's Point

Rossnowlagh

R231

N15

Donegal Bay

Ballyshannon 23

TO LOUGH ERNE

Belleek

Bundoran 22

NORTHERN IRELAND

Mullaghmore 20

Kinlough

Lough Melvin

Garrison

21 **Creevykeel**

N15

Grange

Glenade

R282

Lissadell House 19

Ben Bulben

R280

Carney

18

16 **Glencar Lough**

N16

Sligo Bay

Drumcliff Bay

Drumcliff

Rathcormack

Manorhamilton

Rosses Point 17

Cregg

R291

Sligo Town

1 — 8

R286 R288

Parke's Castle 13

15

Strandhill 10

R292

Creevelen Abbey

LEITRIM

Templeboy

N59

9

12 14

Killarga

TO BALLINA

Knocknarea

Carrowmore

11

N4

Lough Gill

The Lake Isle of Innisfree

Beltra

Ballygawley

R287

Drumkeeran

R280

Collooney

R284

N

SLIGO

N17

Ropefield

Drumfin

N4

Riverstown

0   6 miles

0   9 km

TO GALWAY

Ballymote

TO CARRICK-ON-SHANNON

of Dungloe is a large Irish-speaking parish known as the **Rosses** ㊶, which has a wild Atlantic coast off which is the island of **Aranmore** ㊸, accessible form Burtonport. Working northward around this peninsula brings you to **Gweedore Headland** ㊵ and Bun Beag (Benbeg). From here another optional circuit can be made of the Gweedore Headland, with its bleak dramatic terrain (somewhat marred by modern bungalow development), which will bring you to Bloody Foreland Head, named for the vivid reds that appear on the rock face during the long western sunsets. Meenlaragh, east along the same headland, is the departure point for **Tory Island** ㊴, a rocky, inaccessible place that has nevertheless been inhabited since prehistoric times. Some of the Tory Island fishermen have developed a sideline producing naive art.

🎦 **Dun Fionnachaid** ㊲ is a pleasant village built in the Plantation era on the shores of Sheephaven Bay, within easy reach of **Ards Forest Park** ㊱, which has trails leading to prehistoric sites. **Doe Castle** ㉟, romantic and dramatically perched on the water's edge, occupies the southern end of Sheephaven Bay and stands at the foot of Muckish Mountain. **Carraig Airt** ㉝, a small village with some enjoyable old-fashioned pubs, gives access to a signposted Atlantic Drive around the **Rosguill Peninsula** ㉞. From here either head south through attractively sleepy Milford to **Ramelton** ㉚, a hilly little town on the edge of **Lough Swilly** ㉛, one of the loveliest of Donegal's big fjordlike inlets, to 🎦 **Letterkenny** ㉙, a convenient base for exploring the rest of the county; or head north to 🎦 **Rathmullan** ㉜, where a number of hotels are right on the shores of Swilly. If you enjoy modern and contemporary art, on your next day head for the **Glebe House and Gallery** ㊻, which exhibits works by major Impressionists, Picasso, Jack Yeats, and the art of the Tory Islanders. If the outdoors beckons, head west for **Glenveagh National Park** ㊹, which also boasts a delightful Victorian-castle country house; if archaeology is your passion, then head east to the dramatic fort of **Grianan Ailigh** ㊼, which provides a spectacular panorama of Donegal, Derry, and the Inishowen Peninsula. From Letterkenny head northeast across the border into Northern Ireland and the city of Derry (☞ Chapter 8) or south for Sligo Town and Galway (☞ Chapter 6).

When to Tour the Northwest

In July and August, the Northwest gets busy with families from Northern Ireland, Dublin, and Great Britain. Musicians play most nights at village pubs, and the weather may be warm enough for hardy folk to swim in the sea, but accommodations may be hard to come by. Between November and February, in contrast, the area is empty of tourists, and with good reason: Gales bring cold, lashing rain in from the Atlantic, shrouding the wild, lonely scenery that is the Northwest's greatest asset. What's more, because so many of the area's hotels are seasonal, you'll have a limited choice. The best months to visit here are easily April, May, June, September, and October.

YEATS COUNTRY—SLIGO TOWN AND ENVIRONS

Just as James Joyce made Dublin his own through his novels and stories, Sligo is indelibly associated with the lyrical poems of William Butler Yeats (1865–1939), Ireland's first of four Nobel laureates. The poet intimately knew and eloquently celebrated in verse not only Sligo Town itself but the surrounding countryside with its lakes, farms, woodland, and dramatic mountains that rise up not far from the center of town. Often on this route, you'll have glimpses of "bare Ben Bulben's head," as Yeats called flat-topped Ben Bulben Mountain, which looms over the

western end of the Dartry range. The areas covered here are the most
accessible parts of the Northwest, easily reached from Galway.

Sligo Town

★ ❶   *60 km (37 mi) northeast of Ballina, 138 km (86 mi) northeast of Gal-*
way, 217 km (135 mi) northwest of Dublin.

The only sizable town in the whole of the Northwest, Sligo (population 23,000) is the best place to begin a tour of Yeats Country. Currently in the throes of an economic boom—Europe's largest videotape
factory is just outside of town, it's the center of Ireland's plastics industry, and the streets ring with the bite of buzz saws and the tang of
resin as new apartments, shopping malls, and cinema complexes are
tastefully erected behind traditional facades—Sligo retains all the
charm of smaller, sleepier villages, yet by day it's as lively and crowded
as Galway, its considerably larger neighbor to the southwest. Locals,
students from the town's college, and visitors bustle past its historic
buildings and along its narrow sidewalks and winding streets and
crowd its one-of-a-kind shops, eateries, and traditional pubs. More than
any other town in the Northwest, Sligo has a buzz and energy that come
as a surprise to anyone who hasn't visited recently.

Squeezed onto a patch of land between Sligo Bay and Lough Gill, Sligo
is clustered on the south shore between two bridges that span the
River Garavogue just east of where it opens into the bay. The new pedestrian zone along the south shore of the river between the two bridges
means that you can now enjoy vistas of the river right in the center of
town.

Sligo was often a battleground in its earlier days: It was attacked by
Viking invaders in 807 and, later, by a succession of rival Irish and Anglo-
Norman conquerors. In 1642, the British soldiers of Sir Frederick
Hamilton fell upon Sligo, killing every visible inhabitant, burning the
town, and destroying the interior of the beautiful medieval abbey.
Then, between 1845 and 1849, more than a million inhabitants died
in the potato famine or fled to escape it—an event poignantly captured
in the words of a letter from local father Owen Larkin to his son in
America in 1850, inscribed on a brass plaque down by the river: "I
am now I may say alone in the world all my brothers and sisters are
dead and children but yourself. We are all ejected out of Lord Ardi-
laun's ground, the times was so bad and all Ireland in such a state of
poverty that no person could pay rent. My only hope now rests with
you, as I am without one shilling and I must either beg or go to the
poorhouse." Stand there a moment by the river, then turn again to the
bustling heart of Sligo today, and marvel at humanity's capacity to reinvent itself.

❷   At the **Yeats Memorial Building** the annual Yeats Summer School is con-
ducted every August (☞ Seasonal Events *in* Nightlife and Arts, *below*).
The **Sligo Art Gallery** shows rotating exhibits of contemporary art. Across
the street is Rohan Gillespie's innovative **sculpture of the poet,** draped
in a flowing coat overlaid with excerpts from his work. It was unveiled
in 1989 by Michael Yeats, W. B.'s son, in commemoration of the 50th
anniversary of his father's death. ✉ *Hyde Bridge,* ☎ *071/45847.* ✉
Free. ☉ *Mon.–Sat., 10–5:30.*

❸   The **Niland Gallery** houses one of Ireland's largest collections of works
by Jack B. Yeats, who once said, "I never did a painting without
putting a thought of Sligo in it (Beckett once wrote that Yeats painted
"desperately immediate images"). Among his works here are *The Is-*
land Funeral (1923), *Sailor Home from the Sea* (1912), and *Leaving*

WITHOUT KODAK MAX
photos taken on 100 speed film

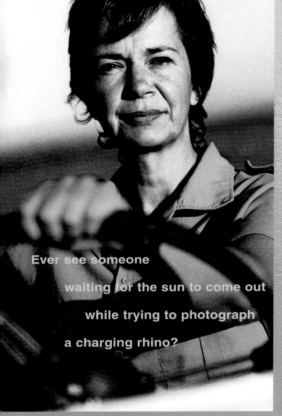

Ever see someone

waiting for the sun to come out

while trying to photograph

a charging rhino?

New!
Kodak Max film:

*Now with better color,
Kodak's maximum
versatility film gives
you great pictures in
sunlight, low light,
action or still.*

WITH KODAK MAX
photos taken on Kodak Max 400 film

It's all you need
to know about film.

www.kodak.com

Distinctive guides packed with up-to-date expert advice and smart choices for every type of traveler.

Fodor's. For the world of ways you travel.

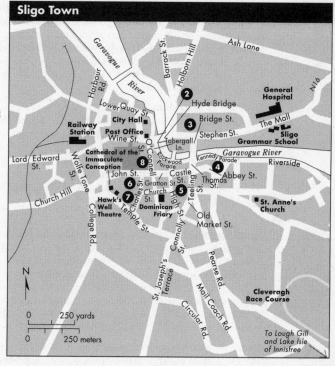

Sligo Town

the Far Point (1946). The collection also includes paintings by John Yeats (father of Jack and W. B.), who had a considerable reputation as a portraitist. Other items at the **museum** that you may see on request are a collection of W. B.'s first editions and such intriguing memorabilia as the author's personal letters and the Irish tricolor flag that draped his coffin when he was buried at nearby **Drumcliff** (☞ *below*). A major new gallery extension planned to open in May 2000 will allow the Niland to show much more work by Yeats, Sean Keating, Paul Henry, and other leading Irish artists of the 20th century. ⊠ *Stephen St.,* ☎ *071/42212.* ☞ *Free.* ☉ *Library Tues.–Fri. 10–5, Sat. 10–1 and 2–5; museum June–Sept., Tues.–Sat. 10–noon and 2–4:50, Oct.–mid-Dec. and mid-Mar.–May, Tues.–Sat. 2–4:50.*

❹ The **Sligo Abbey,** the town's only existing relic of the Middle Ages, was built for the Dominicans by Maurice FitzGerald in 1253. After a fire in 1414, it was extensively rebuilt, only to be destroyed again by Cromwell's Puritans under the command of Sir Frederick Hamilton in 1642. Today the abbey consists of a ruined nave, aisle, transept, and tower. Some fine stonework remains, especially in the 15th-century cloisters. ⊠ *Abbey St.* ☞ *Free.* ☉ *Usually open—if not, key with caretaker (name and address pinned to door).*

❺ The **Courthouse** (⊠ Teeling St.), built in 1878 in the Victorian Gothic style, has a flamboyant, turreted sandstone exterior; it is not open to casual visitors. After it was built, the structure became a symbol for English power. The Courthouse takes its inspiration from the much larger Law Courts in London. Just north of the Courthouse on the east side of Teeling Street, look for the window designating the law firm of **Argue and Phibbs,** one of Sligo's most popular photo-ops.

The **Dominican Friary,** still a functioning church, is west of the Courthouse on High Street; from High Street, take a left onto Church Street.

At the end of Church Street, turn right onto Charles Street. You will notice along these streets that Sligo has numerous churches of all denominations. Presbyterians, Methodists, and even Plymouth Brethren are represented here, as well as Anglicans (Church of Ireland) and, of course, Roman Catholics. According to the Irish writer Sean O'Faolain, "The best Protestant stock in all Ireland is in Sligo." The Yeats family was part of that stock.

6 Designed in 1730 by Richard Castle, who designed Powerscourt and Russborough Houses in County Wicklow (☞ Chapter 2), little **St. John's Cathedral** (Church of Ireland) has a handsome square tower and fortifications. In the north transept you'll find a memorial to Susan Mary Yeats, mother of W. B. and Jack. Next door is the larger and newer Roman Catholic **Cathedral of the Immaculate Conception** (with an entrance on Temple Street), consecrated in 1874. ⊠ *John St.* ☎ *Free.* ☉ *No set hrs.*

7 County Sligo's **TIO** (Tourist Information Office) is useful for the whole of the Northwest. It's around the corner from St. John's Cathedral, in the same building as the **Hawk's Well Theatre.** The TIO sells an excellent "Tourist Trail" walking map of Sligo, designed by no less than the resident Bishop of Killala. It will also give you details of boat tours of Lough Gill, complete with recitals of Yeats's poetry—an excellent way to see the lough. ⊠ *Temple and Charles Sts.,* ☎ *071/61201.* ☎ *Free.* ☉ *Sept.–mid-Mar., weekdays 9–1 and 2–5; mid-Mar.–mid-June, weekdays 9–6, Sat. 10–2; mid-June–Aug., Mon.–Sat. 9–8, Sun. 10–6.*

8 Sligo's most famous pub is **Hargadon's** (⊠ 4 O'Connell St., ☎ 071/70933), a dark, old-style public house with cozy, private, wood-paneled snugs (cubicles); stone or wood floors; rust-red interior walls; and a handsome golden-oak and green-painted facade. It's a good place for a bowl of stew and a creamy pint of Guinness. Around the corner on Wine Street are the offices of the local weekly newspaper, the *Sligo Champion,* whose editor grandly declared in its first issue in 1836: "Let no one think the *Champion* will be a vehicle of slander—we are determined never to sully our pages with personalities."

Dining and Lodging

$ ✕ **Bistro Bianconi.** The all-white decor—blond wood and white-tile floors—lives up to the name. But the minimalism ends there: The menu is a virtual display of fireworks, with a page-long selection of gourmet pizzas baked in the wood-burning oven, with toppings both traditional and innovative. Baked cannelloni and ravioli are other Italian favorites. ⊠ *44 O'Connell St., Sligo,* ☎ *071/41744. AE, MC, V. No lunch.*

$$$$ ✕▥ **Cromleach Lodge.** Christy and Moira Tighe run this highly regarded,
★ small country hotel on a hillside overlooking Lough Arrow. The modern building has a pleasant, country-style interior; bedrooms are spacious, decorated in relaxing pastel shades, and have views out over the lough. Under Moira's direction, the restaurant (reservations required) is particularly notable; all the tables in the three small dining rooms offer panoramic views. Fillet of turbot with chablis and chive sauce and loin of lamb with rosemary juice are two typical and delicious entrées. The hotel is off N4 at Castlebaldwin, 27 km (17 mi) east of Sligo and 8 km (5 mi) east of Ballymote. ⊠ *Lough Arrow, Castlebaldwin, Co. Sligo,* ☎ *071/65155,* ℻ *071/65455. 10 rooms with bath. Restaurant, bar, fishing. AE, DC, MC, V. Closed Nov.–Jan.*

$$$$ ✕▥ **Markree Castle.** From the front, this fortresslike 1640 castle looks slightly forbidding and cold, but seen from the garden in the back, it is spare and elegant. The ancestral home of Charles Cooper, who now owns and manages it with his wife, Mary, Markree is Sligo's old-

est inhabited castle. It sits on a 1,000-acre estate 11 km (7 mi) south of Sligo Town just off the N4 Dublin road. The public rooms include the oak-paneled entry hall, with a large stained-glass window at the top of the grand staircase; a skylit gallery that doubles as the bar; and a formal dining room with ornate, Louis XIV plasterwork. Upstairs the layout is a bit warrenlike: Bedrooms (somewhat haphazardly furnished) are spread over a number of floors and wings, though bathrooms have been modernized. The kitchen offers up an excellent table d'hôte menu, and on Sunday a traditional lunch attracts a sizable, family-oriented crowd. ⊠ *Collooney, Co. Sligo,* ☎ *071/67800,* ℻ *071/67840. 30 rooms with bath. Restaurant, bar, horseback riding. AE, DC, MC, V.*

$$$ ✕⊞ **Coopershill.** Seven generations of the O'Hara family have lived ★ in this three-story Georgian farmhouse since it was built in 1774. Beyond the elegant, symmetrical stone facade, with its central Palladian window, the large public rooms are furnished with appealing period antiques and overstuffed furniture; deer heads hang in the vast hallways. The spacious, beautifully furnished bedrooms have pretty floral wallpaper, and most have four-poster or canopy beds; there are no TVs. In the tranquil dining room overlooking the woods, Irish-style meals and a wide choice of wines are served by candlelight from a grand sideboard set with family silver and crystal. After dining, guests can walk the 500 acres of grounds amid undisturbed wildlife. Coopershill is signposted from Drumfin crossroads, 17 km (11 mi) southeast of Sligo on the N4 Dublin road. ⊠ *Riverstown, Co. Sligo,* ☎ *071/65108,* ℻ *071/65466. 6 rooms with bath. Dining room, tennis court, boating, fishing. AE, DC, MC, V. Closed Nov.–mid-Mar.*

$$$ ✕⊞ **Silver Swan Hotel.** Standing in the center of town on the Hyde Bridge, this comfortable, mid-range hotel and restaurant has a wonderful view of the Garavogue River rushing beneath the bridge. Although the '60s-style exterior will disturb style purists, the interior has been redecorated and the bedrooms refurbished with dark-wood, modern decor. Wednesday nights feature live traditional Irish music. Noise can be a problem, so ask for a room away from the louder public rooms below. ⊠ *Hyde Bridge, Sligo, Co. Sligo,* ☎ *071/43231,* ℻ *071/42232. 29 rooms with bath or shower. Restaurant, bar. AE, DC, MC, V.*

$$$ ✕⊞ **Sligo Park Hotel.** A mile out of town on N4 (the main Dublin road), this is a modern, well-designed, and extremely comfortable establishment with a friendly staff, an excellent restaurant with a well-chosen wine list, and a first-rate fitness center. Dancing and piano entertainment take place on some evenings. Although its predictable, reliable comforts appeal to business travelers, it makes a reasonable base for visitors to Yeats Country. ⊠ *Pearse Rd., Sligo, Co. Sligo,* ☎ *071/60291,* ℻ *071/69556. 110 rooms with bath or shower. Restaurant, bar, indoor pool, 2 tennis courts, health club. AE, DC, MC, V.*

$$ ✕⊞ **Temple House.** Off the beaten track on more than 1,000 acres, this vast Georgian mansion and working organic farm has been in owners Sandy and Deb Perceval's family since 1665. Rooms are furnished with Georgian and Victorian furniture, with highly polished mahogany tables and sideboards and the original rugs. Guests can visit formal terraced gardens and a private lake with waterside footpaths. The huge bedrooms have authentic Victorian curtains, marble-top washstands, polished floorboards, dressing tables, and huge shuttered windows. Deb prepares the evening meal (book by 3 PM), using farm-fresh produce accompanied by fine wines. The traditional Irish breakfasts are generous. There are no TVs. Because of Sandy's allergies, guests are asked to avoid using perfumes, deodorants, and aerosols. ⊠ *Ballymote, Co. Sligo,* ☎ *071/83329,* ℻ *071/*

83808. 5 rooms with bath or shower. Dining room, boating, fishing. AE, MC, V. Closed Dec.–Mar.

Nightlife and the Arts

PUBS AND CLUBS

Open later than most other pubs, **Toffs** (✉ Kennedy Parade, ☎ 071/46731) has a sizable dance floor that teems with Sligo's younger set bopping to a mix of contemporary dance music and older favorites. A few miles south of town, a popular spot with the locals, the **Thatch** pub (✉ Thatch, Ballisodare, ☎ 071/67288) has traditional music "sessions" on Thursday and Sunday.

SEASONAL EVENTS

Established in 1959, the **Yeats International Summer School** takes place during the first two weeks of August. Scholarly lectures, poetry readings, and various side events are open to the public. For details contact the Yeats Society (✉ Yeats Memorial Building, Hyde Bridge, ☎ 071/42693).

Dozens of high-profile and local performers take part in the **Sligo Arts Festival** (☎ 071/69802), held during late May and early June.

THEATER

Sligo Town's **Hawk's Well Theatre** hosts amateur and professional companies from all over Ireland (and occasionally from Britain) in a variety of shows. Most of the summer season is devoted to the works of popular Irish playwrights. ✉ *Temple St.,* ☎ *071/61526.* ✆ *£5–£10.* ☉ *Box office Mon.–Sat. 10–6; call for show times.*

Outdoor Activities and Sports

BICYCLING

Explore Lough Gill, Rosses Point, and other areas of scenic beauty by renting a bicycle from **Gary's Cycles** (£7 per day, £30 per week). (✉ Quay St., ☎ 071/45418).

GOLF

County Sligo Golf Club (✉ Rosses Point, ☎ 071/77186), also known as Rosses Point, is one of Ireland's great championship links (☞ Chapter 9).

HORSEBACK RIDING

For riding in the countryside around Sligo contact the **Sligo Equitation Centre** (✉ Carramore, ☎ 071/61353).

Shopping

Sligo Town has the Northwest's most thriving shopping scene, with a nice variety of food-related, crafts, and hand-knits shops, many with colorful storefronts. The **Cat & the Moon** (✉ 4 Castle St., ☎ 071/43686) specializes in an eclectic and stylish mix of Irish-made crafts, jewelry, pottery, ironwork, and scarves. The gourmet deli **Cosgrove and Son** (✉ 32 Market St., ☎ 071/42809), selling everything from Parma ham to Carageen moss, boiled in milk as a local cure for stomach upsets, is a good place to stock up for a picnic or food for the road. **Cross Sections** (✉ 2 Grattan St., ☎ 071/42265) sells lovely tableware, glassware, and kitchenware. **Tír na nÓg** (✉ Grattan St., ☎ 071/62752), Irish for "Land of the Young," sells essential oils, organic foods, and other health-oriented items; a sister store across the street sells cards and posters. In addition to stylish sweaters, **Carraig Donn** (✉ 41 O'Connell St., ☎ 071/44158) carries a selection of pottery, glassware, linens, and children's kilts. The **Gourmet Parlour** (✉ Bridge St., ☎ 071/44617), across the Garavogue on the north side of town, sells breads, sweets, and home-made jams and chutneys.

Knocknarea

9 *8 km (5 mi) southwest of Sligo Town on R292 Strandhill Rd.*

Knocknarea is the "cairn-heaped grassy hill," as Yeats called it, rising 1,083 ft to the southwest of Sligo Town on a promontory that juts into Sligo Bay. The mountain is also memorably depicted in W. B.'s brother Jack's painting *Knocknarea and the Flowing Tide*. A car park on R292 gives pedestrian access (a 45-minute walk) to the summit, where there's a tremendous view of the mountains of Counties Donegal and Sligo. At its summit, and visible from a huge distance, sits a huge cairn—a heaped-stone monument made with 40,000 tons of rock. The cairn is traditionally associated with "passionate Maeve," as Yeats called her, the 1st-century AD Celtic queen of Connaught who went to war with the men of Ulster in a bid to win the mighty Bull of Cuailgne and was subsequently killed while bathing in a lake. The story is told in the *Táin*, the greatest of all the Irish heroic legends. Romantics like to think that Maeve is buried in this massive cairn, although archaeologists suspect that it more likely covers a 3,000-year-old passage grave—and who's to say both aren't right? Either way, it's a pleasant climb on a summer day. There are tremendous views from the cairn, and nature has installed a handy stream for washing your boots as you take the laneway back down.

10 Continuing west from Knocknarea on R292, you'll come to **Strandhill**, a seaside resort with a touch of charm. It has a good, sandy beach, stretches of which are favored by surfers. Aficionados can rent a suit and board for £5 an hour from **Strandhill Surf Club** (☎ 071/68332) beside the beach.

11 A short drive southeast of Knocknarea (on the minor road back to Sligo Town), **Carrowmore** is the largest group of megalithic tombs in all of the British Isles. The oldest of the 60 tombs, dolmens, and other ruins here predate those at Newgrange (☞ Chapter 2) by roughly 700 years; most are communal tombs dating from 4800 BC, though, unfortunately, more than 100 have been badly damaged, leaving around 40. A restored cottage houses a small exhibition about the tombs. ⊠ *Carrowmore, Co. Sligo*, ☎ *071/61534.* 🖾 *£1.50.* ☉ *May–Sept., daily 9:30–6:30.*

Dining

$–$$ ✕ **Strand Restaurant.** This casual spot serves appealing bar food from noon to 5; dinner service begins at 6. Among the items on the restaurant's à la carte menu are avocado pear with goat's cheese and monkfish with Pernod sauce, followed by hazelnut meringue with brown bread ice cream and Irish cheeses. It's popular for its traditional Irish Sunday lunch, which might include a light grilled rainbow trout with parsley butter or a more substantial roast rib of beef with horseradish sauce. Light paneling, cozy booths, and a peat fire make the Strand's pub a comfortable place to relax on a breezy Sligo evening. ⊠ *Shore Rd., Strandhill, Co. Sligo*, ☎ *071/68641. MC, V. Closed Mon.*

Lough Gill

★ **12** *1½ km (1 mi) east of Sligo Town on R286.*

Beautiful, gentle Lough Gill lies to the east of Sligo Town, and if you're pressed for time, it's a pleasurably quick trip. (Take Pearse Road south out of town, and go through one set of traffic lights, soon after which you'll see a green sign for Lough Gill and Innisfree pointing to the left. Take this turn; you'll shortly see the Cleveragh Race Course on your left. Pass through a modern housing development before arriving at the crest of a hill, where you'll find a gorgeous vista of the lough and the Lake Isle of Innisfree [☞ *below*]. At the bottom of the hill, turn left, and you'll wind your way back to town.) Or you can take a more leisurely trip, making a 37 km- (24-mi) circuit of the lough; the itinerary that follows takes you on this longer drive. Leave Sligo Town via Stephen Street, which turns into N16 (signposted to Manorhamilton and Enniskillen). Turn right almost at once onto R286. Within minutes you will find gorgeous views of the lake so adored by the young Yeats. In fact, Lough Gill in Irish means simply "Lake Beauty." When the soldiers of Sir Frederick Hamilton sacked Sligo in 1642, legend has it that they flung the silver bell of the abbey into the depths of Lough Gill, where today it is said that only the pure can hear it ring. In fine weather the lough is serenity itself: sunlight on the meadows all around, a gossamer of telegraph wire draped over the woods down to a loughside cottage, the lap of water, a salmon leaping, a yacht sailing by.

⑬ On R288 on the eastern shore of Lough Gill, **Parke's Castle** is a sturdy, fortified house built in the 17th century by an English planter (a colonist settling on Irish lands confiscated from Catholic owners) who needed the strong fortifications to defend himself against a hostile populace. What made relations worse is that he obtained his building materials mainly by dismantling a historic fortress on the site, which had belonged to the clan leaders of the O'Rourkes of Breffni (once the name of the district). The entrance fee includes a short video show on the castle and local history. There's also a snack bar. In the summer, boat trips of the lough leave from here. Times vary, but the Sligo TIO will have up-to-date information. ⊠ *Fivemile Bourne, Co. Leitrim,* ☎ *071/64149.* ⊡ *£2.* ☉ *June–Sept., daily 9:30–6:30; Apr.–May and Oct., daily 10–5.*

A short distance south of Parke's Castle, the handsome remains of **Creevelea Abbey** stand on the other side of the River Bonet and can be reached by a few minutes' walk along a footpath. In fact not an abbey but a friary, Creevelea was founded for the Franciscans in 1508 by a later generation of O'Rourkes. It was the last Franciscan community to be founded before the suppression of the monasteries by England's King Henry VIII. Like many other such ruined abbeys, the place still has religious meaning for the local people, who treat it with reverence. One curiosity of this abbey is the especially large south transept; notice, too, its endearing little cloisters, with well-executed carvings on the pillars of St. Francis of Assisi. The abbey is signposted at Dromahair. ⊠ ⊡ *Free.* ☉ *Freely accessible.*

Lake Isle of Innisfree

⑭ *15 km (9 mi) south of Sligo Town via Dromahair on N4 and R287.*

In 1890 William Butler Yeats was walking through the West End of London when, seeing in a shop window a ball dancing on a jet of water, he was suddenly overcome with nostalgia for the lakes of his Sligo home. It was the moment, and the feeling, that shaped itself into his most famous poem, "The Lake Isle of Innisfree":

> I will arise and go now, and go to Innisfree,
> And a small cabin build there, of clay and wattles made:
> Nine bean-rows will I have there, a hive for the honey-bee,
> And live alone in the bee-loud glade. . .
> I hear lake water lapping with low sounds by the shore;
> While I stand on the roadway, or on the pavements grey,
> I hear it in the deep heart's core.

Though there is nothing particularly visually exceptional about Innisfree (pronounced *innish*-free), the "Lake Isle" is a must-see if you're a Yeats fan. To reach Innisfree, drive through the little village of Dromahair to take R287, the minor road that heads back along the south side of Lough Gill toward Sligo Town. Turn right at a small crossroads, after 4 or 5 km (2 or 3 mi), where signposts point to Innisfree. A little road leads another couple of miles down to the lakeside, where you can see the island just offshore.

Across the water on the southwestern end of Lough Gill, a little beyond the Innisfree turnoff, is a tranquil nature walk with particularly picturesque panorama of the lake and of Cottage Island from the top of **Dooney Rock**; this is where the poet daydreamed, contemplated the lake's islands, and imagined a fiddler on the rock who made "folk dance like a wave of the sea." A brochure from the wooden box in the parking lot details the particulars of the area's diverse flora, as well as a few interesting historical tidbits.

Manorhamilton

⑮ *25 km (15 mi) west of Sligo Town.*

The small rural town of Manorhamilton was built in the 17th century for the Scottish planter Sir Frederick Hamilton, who had been given the local manor house by Charles I of England (hence the town's name). The manor itself is now an ivy-covered ruin, and there's not much to see here. The surrounding scenery, however, is spectacular. To reach the town, come back along R287 toward Dromahair, but instead of turning into that village, continue driving—the road number changes to R280—toward Manorhamilton.

Take N16, signposted to Sligo Town, for about 10 km (6 mi) until you **⑯** reach the little turning that heads right to **Glencar Lough.** The turn is signposted "waterfall," and you'll discover several waterfalls here, with a parking lot and footpath leading to one of the highest. The lake is fed by the River Drumcliff and other streams at the foot of the Dartry Mountains: "Where the wandering water gushes/From the hills above Glencar/In pools among the rushes/That scarce could bathe a star," as Yeats put it in his poem "The Stolen Child."

Stay on Lough Glencar's right bank, and you'll reach a fork in the road: A left heads back to N16 and Sligo Town, a right weaves across the country toward N15 and the villages of Drumcliff and Carney. You should take the right, but don't worry if you miss it: Almost any other right turn off N16 will lead you in the same direction. And sure there's no hurry—you're in Ireland now.

Rosses Point

⑰ *8 km (5 mi) northwest of Sligo Town on the R 281.*

Yeats and his brother, Jack, often stayed at Rosses Point during their summer vacations, and it is obvious why they returned. Glorious pink and gold summer sunsets wash over the seemingly endless stretch of sandy beach. **Coney Island** lies just off Rosses Point. Local lore has it that the captain of the ship *Arathusa* christened Brooklyn's Coney Island after this island, but there's probably more legend than truth to this, as it is widely agreed that New York's Coney Island was named after the *konijn,* Dutch for wild rabbits, that abounded there during the 17th century. Two popular sportsmen's havens, the County Sligo Golf Club, which has magnificent views of the sea and Ben Bulben, and the Sligo Yacht Club, are also here.

Drumcliff

⑱ *7 km (4½ mi) north of Sligo Town on N15.*

W. B. Yeats lies buried with his wife, Georgie, in an unpretentious grave in the cemetery of Drumcliff's simple Protestant church, where his grandfather was rector for many years. Yeats actually died on the French Riviera in 1939, but it took almost a full decade for his body to be brought back here—to the place that more than any other might be called his soul-land. In the poem "Under Ben Bulben," he spelled out not only where he was to be buried but also what should be written on the tombstone: "Cast a cold eye/On life, on death./Horseman, pass by!" It is easy to see why the majestic Ben Bulben (1,730 ft), with its sawn-off peak (not unlike Yosemite's Half-Dome), made such an impression on the poet: The mountain gazes calmly down upon the small church, as it does on all of the surrounding landscape—and at the same time stands as a sentinel facing the mighty Atlantic.

In addition to its significance as a Yeats site, Drumcliff is where St. Columba, a recluse and missionary who established Christian churches and religious communities in Northwest Ireland, is thought to have founded a monastic settlement around AD 575. The monastery that he founded before sailing off to the Scottish isle of Iona flourished for many centuries, but all that is left of it now is the base of a **round tower** and a carved **high cross** (both across N15 from the church) dating from around AD 1000, with scenes from the Old and New Testaments, including Adam and Eve with the serpent and Cain slaying Abel.

Right next to the church, the **Old Stables Tea House and Craft Shop** (☎ 071/44956) is a good place to stop for a snack and to pick up some Yeats poetry and books about him; it's open March through October.

Lissadell House

⑲ *14½ km (9 mi) northwest of Sligo Town, 3½ km (2 mi) west of Drumcliff, signposted from N15.*

Beside the Atlantic waters of Drumcliff Bay, on the peninsula that juts out between Donegal and Sligo bays, Lissadell is an austere but classic Georgian residence built in 1834 by Sir Robert Gore-Booth. An enlightened landlord, he mortgaged the house to help his poverty-stricken tenants during the famine years. His descendants still own Lissadell, which is filled with all manner of artifacts brought back from every corner of the globe by the family, who were great travelers. Aficionados of all things Yeatsian will appreciate the house, for the family became good friends of William Butler Yeats, who recalled seeing the house often as a child from his grandmother's carriage. On a visit to the house in 1894, he met the two Gore-Booth daughters, Eva and Constance, and subsequently recalled their meeting in verse: "The light of evening, Lissadell,/Great windows open to the south,/Two girls in silk kimonos." Eva became a poet, while sister Constance Markievicz led a dramatic political life as a fiery Irish nationalist, taking a leading role in the 1916 Easter Uprising against the British. She survived the uprising, going on to become the first woman member of the Dáil (Irish Parliament).

"That old Georgian mansion," as Yeats called it, was designed by the London architect Francis Goodwin. Its two most notable features are a dramatic 33-ft-high gallery, with 24-ft-tall Doric columns, clerestory windows, and skylights; and the dining room, where Constance's husband, Count Markievicz, painted portraits of members of the family and household employees on the pilasters. A copy of Yeats's poem "In

Memory of Eva Gore-Booth and Con Markievicz" is displayed beside the main gate at the entrance. The woods of the Lissadell estate have become a forestry and wildlife reserve—it serves as a home to Ireland's largest colony of the barnacle goose, along with several other species of wildfowl, and is a fine place for bird-watchers. ☎ 071/63150. ▨ £2.50. ⊙ June–mid-Sept., Mon.–Sat. 10:30–12:30 and 2–4:30.

AROUND DONEGAL BAY

As you drive north from Sligo Town to Donegal Town, the glens of the Dartry Mountains (home of Ben Bulben) gloriously roll by to the east, while coastal fields break open here and there to give startling views across the waters of Donegal Bay to the west. In the distance, the Donegal hills beckon on the far horizon. This stretch is dotted with numerous prehistoric sites, and it has become the Northwest's most popular vacation area, though it is, alas, no French Riviera. You'll pass a few small and unremarkable seashore resorts, and, in some places, you may find that haphazard and fairly tasteless construction detracts from the scenery. In between these minor resort developments, you'll find wide-open spaces free of traffic and full of fresh air. The most interesting part of this tour lies on the north side of the bay—all that rocky indented coastline due west of Donegal Town. Here you enter the heart of away-from-it-all County Donegal.

Mullaghmore

⑳ *20 km (13 mi) northeast of Lissadell House, 37 km (24 mi) north of Sligo Town.*

In the high season, the picturesque, usually sleepy fishing village of Mullaghmore becomes congested with tourists. Its main attractions: a 3¼-km-long (2-mi-long) sandy beach; the turreted, fairy-tale Classie Bawn, the late Lord Louis Mountbatten's home (he, his grandson, and a local boy were killed when the IRA blew up his boat in the bay in 1979); and Ben Bulben, rising up off in the distance. A short drive along the headland intersects unobstructed views beyond the rocky coastline out over Donegal Bay. When the weather is fair, you can see all the way across to St. John's Point and Drumanoo Head in Donegal.

Dining and Lodging

$ ✕🖫 **Beach Hotel.** If there's a chill in the air, you can warm up at the roaring fires in the restaurant and residents' lounge of this large harborside Victorian hotel. The pale peach building is decorated in a nautical theme to commemorate the loss of three galleons of the Spanish Armada in the bay in September 1588. Enjoy wonderful views of the pier and the bay from the hotel bars, or tuck into the de'Cuellar Restaurant's acclaimed seafood menu (**$**). Top starters include hot crab claws with garlic, while favorite main courses are dressed lobster and the house seafood platter. Just save room for the homemade brown bread ice cream. ⊠ *Mullaghmore, Co. Sligo,* ☎ *071/66103,* ℻ *071/66448. 28 rooms with bath. Restaurant, 2 bars, indoor pool, hot tub, sauna, steam room, exercise room, hot tub, horseback riding. AE, MC, V.*

Creevykeel

㉑ *3 km (2 mi) southeast of Mullaghmore, 16 km (10 mi) north of Drumcliff on N15.*

Creevykeel is one of Ireland's best megalithic court-tombs. The site (signposted) lies off the road, just beyond the edge of the village of Cliffony. You'll see a burial area and an enclosed open-air "court" where rituals were performed around 3000 BC. Bronze artifacts found here are now in the National Museum in Dublin (☞ Exploring Dublin *in* Chapter 1).

Bundoran

㉒ *12 km (8 mi) north of Creevykeel on N15.*

Across the County Donegal line, Bundoran is one of Ireland's most popular seaside resorts, a favorite haunt of the Irish from both the North and the South. If souvenir shops and amusement arcades aren't your thing, north of the town center is a handsome beach at **Tullan Strand,** washed by good surfing waves. Between the main beach and Tullan, the Atlantic has sculpted cliff-side rock formations that the locals have christened with whimsical names such as the Fairy Bridges, the Wishing Chair, and the Puffing Hole (this last one blows wind and water from the waves pounding below).

Outdoor Activities and Sports

FISHING

Good fishing is 6½ km (4 mi) away from Bundoran at **Lough Melvin.** Ask locally for **Pat Barrett's Tackle Shop** (⊠ Co. Donegal, ☎ no phone) for bait, tackle, and local information.

GOLF

Bundoran Golf Club (⊠ Bundoran, Co. Donegal, ☎ 072/41302) is an 18-hole, par-69 course on the cliffs above Bundoran beach.

Ballyshannon

㉓ *6½ km (4 mi) north of Bundoran on N15.*

The former garrison town of Ballyshannon rises gently from the banks of the River Erne and has good views of Donegal Bay and the surrounding mountains. The town is a typical hodgepodge of shops, arcades, and hotels, but its triangular central area has several bars and places to grab a snack. The biggest and most popular pub is the green-shuttered **Seán Óg's** (⊠ Market St., ☎ 072/51585), which serves light Irish meals all day and features traditional music in the evenings. The town was also the birthplace of the prolific Irish poet William Allingham. Each year in early August, the normally quiet village springs to life with a grand festival of folk and traditional music (☞ Nightlife and the Arts, *below*).

Exquisite chinaware and porcelain is made at the **Donegal Irish Parian China Factory** (☞ Shopping, *below*), the Republic's largest manufacturer of parian china (so named because it resembles the clear, white marble from the Greek island of Paros). Both Donegal Parian and the older, more well-known Belleek Pottery (6½ km (4 mi) away, on the border between the Republic and the North[☞ Chapter 8]), make delicate, cream-color pottery by traditional methods, to a large degree by hand. There's a free 15-minute tour, a 10-minute video, and a showroom, shop, and tearoom. ⊠ On N15 just south of Ballyshannon, ☎ 072/51826. ☼ May–Sept., daily 9–5:30.

To the southeast of Ballyshannon, **Lough Erne** marks an ancient frontier, as the River Erne crossing here was for centuries the gateway into the Ulster region. Through the medieval period Ballyshannon was the southern stronghold of the O'Donnell clan, whose lands eventually became County Donegal. Today Lough Erne and its nearby sites are within the borders of the North[☞ Around Counties Tyrone, Fermanagh, Armagh, and Down *in* Chapter 8].

Dining and Lodging

$$$ ✕⍒ **Sand House Hotel.** Behind the mock manor-house exterior of this 19th-century former fishing lodge lies a large, modern hotel. Right on Donegal Bay, about 8 km (5 mi) northwest of Ballyshannon and 16 km (10 mi) south of Donegal Town, this makes a peaceful, well-positioned base for sightseeing along the coastline; the hotel has access to 3 km (2 mi) of beach. Renovated, well-kept bedrooms are beautifully decorated with antiques and overlook either the sea or the Donegal hills. The restaurant caters to the plain, hearty appetites of Irish vacationers looking for something a bit special. Fresh seafood, including Donegal Bay oysters and mussels, is the daily specialty. ✉ *Rossnowlagh, Co. Donegal,* ☎ *072/51777,* ℻ *072/52100. 45 rooms with bath. Restaurant, bar, tennis court, horseback riding, Ping-Pong, surfing, fishing. AE, DC, MC, V. Closed Nov.–Easter.*

Nightlife and the Arts

In early June, during the **Ballyshannon Drama Festival,** the town hosts different drama companies for a program of mainly Irish plays. Held on the bank holiday weekend at the beginning of August, the **Ballyshannon Music Festival** (☎ 072/51088) is one of Ireland's largest and best folk-music events. Visitors can hear both well-known and unknown folk and traditional musicians, while impromptu "sessions" pop up at pubs. A party atmosphere prevails, attracting up to 12,000 visitors annually.

Shopping

Donegal Irish Parian China Factory (☞ *above*) sells its wares at lower prices than you'll see in retail stores. The least-expensive items (spoons or thimbles) cost around £5. A full tea set starts at about £250.

From Ballyshannon, R230 runs along the south bank of the River Erne toward Belleek. You'll find **Celtic Weave China** (Cloghore, Ballyshannon, Co. Donegal, ☎ 072/51844) right beside the Garda (Irish police) checkpoint, 1½ km (1 mi) before the border to Northern Ireland. This small, family business specializes in the basket-weave design and in elaborate floral decoration, and they can make a single piece of china to your specifications. Extremely delicate-looking, hand-painted china "flower baskets" are also available (though in fact this type of chinaware is not as fragile as it appears). Prices range from £6 to £1,500, but most pieces cost less than £100.

The goods of the best-known producer of Belleek chinaware, **Belleek Pottery** (☎ 013656/58501 in Northern Ireland), can be found in the shops of Donegal and Sligo. For more information on the factory, ☞ Chapter 8.

OFF THE BEATEN PATH

LOUGH DERG – From Whitsunday to the Feast of the Assumption (that is, from June to mid-August), tens of thousands determinedly beat a path to this lonely, out-of-the-way lake, ringed by heather-clad slopes. In the center of the lough, Station Island—known as St. Patrick's Purgatory—is one of Ireland's most popular pilgrimage sites, even though it is also the most rigorous and austere of such sites in the country. Pilgrims stay on the island for three days, taking no sleep and no food except black tea and dry toast. They walk barefoot around the island, on its flinty stones, to pray at a succession of shrines. The pilgrimage has been followed since time immemorial; during the Middle Ages, it attracted large numbers of devotees from foreign lands. To reach the shores of Lough Derg, turn off the main N15 Sligo–Donegal road in the village of Laghy onto the minor R232 Pettigo road, which hauls itself over the Black Gap and descends sharply into the border village of Pettigo, about 21 km (13 mi) from N15. From here, take the Lough Derg access road for 8 km (5 mi).

Note: Nonpilgrims may not visit the island from June to mid-August. If you would like to know more about St. Patrick's Purgatory in order to become a pilgrim, write to Reverend Prior. ✉ *Lough Derg, Pettigo, Co. Donegal.*

En Route   About a mile before you arrive at the next stop on the tour, Donegal Town, a sign on the right points to **Donegal Craft Village** (☞ Shopping *in* Donegal, *below*).

Donegal Town

 21 km (13 mi) north of Ballyshannon on R232, 66 km (41 mi) northeast of Sligo Town.

With a population of about 3,000, Donegal is Northwest Ireland's largest small village—marking the entry into the back-of-the-beyond of the wilds of County Donegal. The town is centered on the triangular Diamond, where three roads converge (N56 to the west, and N15 to the south and the northeast) and the mouth of the River Eske pours gently into Donegal Bay. You should have your bearings in five minutes, and seeing the historical sights takes less than an hour; if you stick around any longer, it'll probably be to do some shopping—arguably Donegal's top attraction.

Donegal was previously known in Irish as Dun na nGall, "Fort of the Foreigners": The foreigners in question were Vikings, who set up camp here in the 9th century to facilitate their pillaging and looting. They were driven out by the powerful O'Donnell clan (originally Cinel Conail), who made it the capital of Tyrconail, their extensive Ulster territories. Donegal was rebuilt in the early 17th century, during the Plantation period, when Protestant colonists were planted on Irish property confiscated from their Catholic owners.

The triangular **Diamond,** like that of many other Irish villages, dates from this period. Once a marketplace, it has a 20-ft obelisk monument to the Four Masters (☞ *below*). On the north side of the Diamond, **McGroarty's Bar** (☎ 073/21049) is a good place to stop for a casual bite; lunch is served from noon to 3 October–April and noon to 5 May–September, but snacks are served all day, including smoked salmon or dressed crab, and a variety of sandwiches. **Magee's** (☞ Shopping, *below*), also on the north side of the Diamond, is a general clothing store, founded in 1866. Much of the stock that carries Magee's label is made in the store's own factory beside the River Eske, a short walk from the shop. Magee's tweed jackets, said to be among the best in the world, are reasonably priced here. ✉ *The Diamond,* ☎ *073/21100.*

Near the north corner of the Diamond, **Donegal Castle** was built by clan leader Hugh O'Donnell in the 1470s. More than a century later, this structure was the home of his descendant Hugh Roe O'Donnell, who faced the might of the invading English and was the last clan chief of Tyrconail. In 1602 he died on a trip to Spain while trying to rally reinforcements from his allies. In 1610, its new English owner, Sir Basil Brooke, reconstructed the little castle, adding the fine Jacobean fortified mansion with towers and turrets that can still be seen today (he was responsible for the Diamond, as well). The small enclosed grounds are pleasant; inside, there are only a few rooms to see, including the garderobe (the rest room) and a great hall with an exceptional vaulted wood-beam roof. ✉ *Tirchonaill St.,* ☎ *073/22405.* ⬚ *£2.* ☉ *Easter–Oct., daily 9:30–5:45. Closed Nov.–Easter.*

The ruins of the **Franciscan abbey,** founded in 1474 by Hugh O'Donnell, are a five-minute walk south of town at a spectacular site perched above the Eske, where it begins to open up into Donegal Bay (take N15, cutting off almost immediately for the parking area and pier behind the Hyland Central Hotel). The complex was burned to the ground in 1593, razed by the English in 1601, and ransacked again in 1607; the ruins include the choir, south transept, and two sides of the cloisters, between which lie hundreds of graves dating back to the 18th century. The abbey was probably where the *Annals of the Four Masters* was written from 1632 to 1636. The *Annals* chronicles the whole of Celtic history and mythology of Ireland from earliest times up to the year 1618. The **Four Masters** were four monks who believed (correctly, as it turned out) that Celtic culture was doomed after the English conquest, and they wanted to preserve as much of it as they could. At the National Library in Dublin, you can see facsimile pages of the monks' work (☞ Exploring Dublin *in* Chapter 1); the original is kept under lock and key. ▣ *Free.* ☉ *Freely accessible.*

Dining and Lodging

$ ✗ **Blueberry Tea Room.** This pleasant, ground-floor restaurant and café is across the street from Donegal Castle. Proprietors Brian and Ruperta Gallagher serve breakfast, lunch, afternoon tea, and a light evening meal. Daily specials—such as Irish lamb stew, a variety of pasta dishes, and vegetarian quiche—are served from noon to 6. Soups, sandwiches, salads, and fruit are on the regular menu, and and brown scones are baked daily. ▣ *Castle St.,* ☎ *073/22933. V. Closed Sun. mid-Sept.–May.*

$$$$ ✗▦ **St. Ernan's House.** On its own wooded tidal island in Donegal Bay,
★ a five-minute drive from town, St. Ernan's is one of the most spectacularly situated country houses in Ireland. The two-story house was built by a nephew of the Duke of Wellington in 1826. Today Brian and Carmel O'Dowd, the meticulous owner-managers, foster a relaxed, serene atmosphere. Guest rooms are simple but elegant, with antiques and views of the bay. Dinner (open to nonguests), in the intimate and elegant dining room, is based on fresh local produce, prepared in the Irish country-house style; the five-course meal changes nightly. Pigeon and quail with oyster mushrooms is a typical starter; lamb in a rich red wine sauce or wild salmon with a green herb sauce might follow. A stroll around the island is a perfect way to finish off the evening. ▣ *St. Ernan's Island, Co. Donegal,* ☎ *073/21065,* FAX *073/22098. 12 rooms with bath. Dining room. MC, V. Closed Nov.–Easter.*

$$$ ✗▦ **Harvey's Point.** At the foot of the Blue Stack Mountains, nestled beside Lough Eske, this Swiss-owned hotel has spacious, well-equipped bedrooms, all overlooking the lake. The split-level, wood-panel dining room, which also has lake views, has warm peach decor, Tiffany lamps, and locally made granite-top tables. The French cuisine leans toward a nouvelle presentation, with several lobster entrées on the menu; it might be served whole with a choice of two sauces, alongside rice and mussels, or garnished with tomatoes and red cabbage. Fisherman's Platter, a selection of five kinds of fish, is also served with two sauces, and sirloin steak is served with a demi-glaze sauce, topped with garlic butter. Homemade ice cream with profiteroles and chocolate sauce is a special dessert. ▣ *Lough Eske, Co. Donegal,* ☎ *073/22208,* FAX *073/22352. 20 rooms with bath. Restaurant, bar, tennis court, boating, bicycles. AE, DC, MC, V.*

$$$ ▦ **Hyland Central.** Right on Donegal's central square, this family-run hotel is affiliated with Best Western. The slightly shop-worn public areas have a touch of old-world style. Although some of the bedrooms are spacious, their decor—simple built-ins and imitation black-leather and teak furniture—is nothing to write home about. On the plus side: Rooms in the back have huge picture windows with lovely views of Donegal Bay. The efficient staff serves good, filling food in the large

dining room. ⊠ *The Diamond, Co. Donegal,* ☎ *073/21027,* FAX *073/ 22295. 90 rooms with bath. Dining room, indoor pool, steam room, health club. AE, DC, MC, V.*

Nightlife and the Arts

During the summer, people pack **McGroarty's Bar** (☞ *above*) for traditional music each Thursday night. The **Abbey Hotel** (⊠ The Diamond, ☎ 073/21014) has music every night in July and August and a disco every Sunday night throughout the year.

Outdoor Activities and Sports

Rent a bike from **C. J. Doherty** (⊠ Main St., Co. Donegal, ☎ 073/21119).

Shopping

Long the principal marketplace for the region's wool products, Donegal Town has several smaller shops with local handweaving, knits, and crafts. The main store in town, **Magee's** (⊠ The Diamond, ☎ 073/ 21100), carries renowned private-label tweeds for both men and women (jackets, hats, scarves, suits, and more), as well as pottery, linen, and crystal. **Simple Simon's** (⊠ The Diamond, ☎ 073/22687), the local health-food store, has crafts, cards, essential oils, and other whole-earth items. About 1½ km (1 mi) south of town, beside the main N15, the **Donegal Craft Village** is a complex of workshops where you can buy pottery, handwoven goods, and ceramics from local young craftspeople and watch the items being made. A coffee shop sells snacks; shops are usually open 9 to 5.

En Route   The main road west is N56, which runs slightly inland from a magnificent shoreline of rocky inlets with great sea views; it's worthwhile turning off the road from time to time to catch a better sight of the coast. About 6½ km (4 mi) out of Donegal Town, N56 skirts **Mountcharles,** a bleak hillside village that looks back across the bay.

Bruckless

㉕   *19 km (12 mi) west of Donegal Town on N56.*

Don't be fooled by the round tower in the churchyard at Bruckless: It's a 19th-century belfry, not an authentic medieval structure. Soon after Bruckless, N56 turns inland across the bogs toward Ardara, but this tour stays by the shore. The road now becomes R263, which runs through attractive heathland and wooded hills down to Killybegs.

Dining and Lodging

$ ✕🏠 **Bruckless House.** A two-story, 18th-century farmhouse on the north side of Donegal Bay, 8 km (5 mi) outside Killybegs and within an easy drive of Glencolumbkille, Ardara, and Donegal Town, this unusual bed-and-breakfast stands on 19 acres of woods, gardens, and a meadow where Irish draft horses and Connemara ponies roam. Public rooms in the main building have a fine view of Bruckless Bay; their Asian decor reflects years spent in Hong Kong by the owners, Clive and Joan Evans. The more conventional but comfortable bedrooms share a large bathroom upstairs. A separate two-bedroom, self-catering gatelodge, the former servants' quarters, is at the entrance to the estate. Wholesome breakfasts are prepared with fruit from the Evanses' prize-winning garden, freshly laid eggs from their hens, and milk and cream from the resident cow. ⊠ *Co. Donegal,* ☎ *073/37071,* FAX *073/37070. 4 rooms, 2 with bath; one 2-bedroom gatelodge. Dining room. AE, MC, V. Closed Oct.–Mar.*

$ ✕🏠 **Castle Murray House Hotel.** Panoramas of distant mountains, the sapphire-blue waters of MacSwyne's Bay, and the long, narrow unspoiled peninsula, punctuated at its tip by a lighthouse, await visitors to this hotel 1½ km (1 mi) out on the 9½-km-long (6-mi-long) St. John's Point Peninsula. The original house has been extended and modernized; rooms are basic but comfortable. Natives trek here for the restaurant ($$), where Thierry Delcros, the French-born owner-chef, prepares superb French cuisine. Selections might include phyllo-wrapped parcel of duck or the specialty of the house, prawns and monkfish in garlic butter. The hotel is 21 km (13 mi) west of Donegal Town. ✉ *St. John's Point, Dunkineely, Co. Donegal,* ☎ *073/37022,* ℻ *073/37330. 10 rooms with bath. Restaurant, bar. MC, V. Closed mid-Jan.–mid-Feb. and Mon.–Tues. mid-Feb.–Easter and Oct.–mid-Jan.*

Killybegs

㉖ *6½ km (4 mi) west of Bruckless, 28 km (17 mi) west of Donegal Town on R293.*

Trawlers from Spain and France are moored in the harbor at Killybegs, one of Ireland's busiest fishing ports. Though it's one of the most industrialized places along this coast, it's not without some charm, thanks to its waterfront location. Killybegs once served as a center for the manufacture of Donegal hand-tufted carpets, which can be found in the White House and the Vatican. The **Harbour Store** (✉ Main St., ☎ 073/32122), right on the wharf, has plenty to make both fishermen and landlubbers happy, including boots and rain gear, competitively priced sweaters, and unusual bright yellow or orange fiberglass-covered gloves (made in Taiwan!).

Dining and Lodging

$$ ✕▥ **Bay View Hotel.** Directly across from Killybegs's harbor, the Bay View is the town's most bustling spot. The recently redecorated hotel is spare and modish, nicely paneled in light wood. The modern, functional bedrooms are pleasantly decorated in pale colors. The Irish table d'hôte menu changes daily in the comfortable, efficient dining room. Bruckless mussels in a white wine and garlic sauce and braised young duckling served with market vegetables and an orange and cherry coulis typify the fare. The hotel has extensive leisure facilities and is well placed for seeing the glorious north shore of Donegal Bay. Special rates include greens fees for Portnoo (outside Ardara) and Murvagh (outside Donegal) for golfers. ✉ *Main St., Co. Donegal,* ☎ *073/31950,* ℻ *073/31856. 40 rooms with bath. Restaurant, bar, indoor pool, sauna, health club. AE, MC, V.*

En Route After Killybegs, R263 narrows, climbs, and twists, giving even better views of Donegal Bay before descending again into pretty **Kilcar,** a traditional center of tweed making. The next village, signposted by its Irish name, An Charraig (Carrick), clings to the foot of the **Slieve League Mountains,** whose dramatic, color-streaked ocean cliffs are, at 2,000 ft, the highest in Ireland and among the most spectacular. To see them, take the little road to the Irish-speaking village of Teelin, 1½ km (1 mi) south from Carrick. Then take the narrow lane (signposted to Bunglass) that climbs steeply to the top of the cliffs. For an even more thrilling perspective, some hardy folk walk on the difficult coastal path from Teelin.

Glencolumbkille (Gleann Cholm Cille)

㉗ *8 km (5 mi) west of Carrick, 27 km (17 mi) west of Killybegs on R263.*

At the far end of a stretch of barren moorland, the tiny hamlet of Glencolumbkille (pronounced glen-colm-*kill*) clings dramatically to the rockbound harbor of Glen Bay. Because it is at the heart of County Donegal's shrinking Gaeltacht, or Irish-speaking region, it has a strong, rural Irish flavor, as do its pubs and brightly painted row houses. Its name means St. Columba's Glen (or, alternatively, Columba's Glen Church); the legend goes that St. Columba, the Christian missionary (☞ Drumcliff *in* Yeats Country, *above*), lived here during the 6th century with a group of followers. Some 40 prehistoric cairns, scattered around the village, have become connected locally with the St. Columba myths. The **House of St. Columba,** on the cliff top rising north of the village, is a small oratory said to have been used by the saint himself. Inside, stone constructions are thought to have been his bed and chair. Every year on June 9, starting at midnight, local people make a 3-km (2-mi) barefoot procession called "An Turas" (the journey) around 15 medieval crosses and ancient cairns, collectively called the stations of the cross. Near the beach in Glencolumbkille is the **Folk Village,** an imaginative museum of rural life. Three small cottages, with bare-earth floors, represent the very basic living conditions of the 1720s, 1820s, and 1920s. The complex, built after local priest Father McDyer imaginatively started a cooperative to help combat rural depopulation, includes an interpretative center, 1881 schoolhouse, nature walk, tea shop, and crafts shop selling local handmade products, including, intriguingly, wines made from fuchsias and bluebells. ☎ 073/30017. FAX 073/30248. ✍ £2. ☉ *Easter–Sept., Mon.–Sat. 10–6, Sun. noon–6; Oct., weekdays 11–3.*

Ardara

★ ㉘ *28 km (17 mi) northeast of Glencolumbkille. 40 km (25 mi) northwest of Donegal Town.*

Fortuitously situated at the head of a lovely ocean inlet, the unpretentious, old-fashioned hamlet of Ardara (pronounced ar-dar-*ah*) is built around the L-shape intersection of its two main streets. (If you come from Glencolumbkille, expect a scenic drive full of hairpin curves and steep hills as you cross over Glengesh Pass.) Ardara has been an important wool-trading center for centuries. Great cloth fairs were once held on the first of every month, and cottage workers in the surrounding countryside still provide Ardara (and County Donegal) with high-quality, handwoven cloths and, especially, hand knits. If you're looking for a chunky Aran sweater, "Ireland's capital of handwoven tweeds and knitwear," as Ardara bills itself, has no fewer than nine stores to choose from (☞ Shopping, *below*). The **Ardara Heritage Centre** celebrates Donegal's history of producing tweed and knitwear. A weaver works at a traditional loom, while photographs and displays provide a historical overview; there's also an audiovisual show. *Main St.,* ☎ *075/41704.* ✍ *£2.* ☉ *Daily 9:30–6.*

There are a number of pubs where you can hear traditional music year-round (☞ Nightlife and the Arts, *below*). The long-established **Nesbitt Arms** (Main St., ☎ 075/41103) is a good place for a reasonably priced drink and snack. If you're traveling in the high season, a word of caution: During the summer, it doesn't take a lot of visitors to overcrowd this small spot.

Dining and Lodging

$$ ✕☑ **Woodhill House.** John and Nancy Yates's spacious home stands
★ on 4 acres of wooded grounds only ½ km (¼ mi) from Ardara. The cream-color exterior is Victorian, but parts of the interior and the coach house date from the 17th century. High ceilings and marble fireplaces are in the fine public rooms; the hall has a lovely round table and stained-glass window. Bedrooms are less grand but large, with superb views of the Donegal highlands. Visitors and locals alike enjoy frequent Irish folk music sessions presented in the bar. The 40-seat restaurant uses

fresh, local ingredients on its Cordon Bleu à la carte menu, with meals prepared in a French-Irish style. Entrées might include duck in port wine sauce, salmon with garlic and spinach sauce, accompanied by seasonal vegetables, or rack of lamb with herbs picked from the family garden. The elaborate desserts are all homemade. ⊠ *Donegal Rd., Co. Donegal,* ☎ *075/41112,* FAX *075/41516. 9 rooms with bath. Restaurant, bar, horseback riding, fishing. AE, DC, MC, V.*

$ ⊞ **Green Gate.** If you're looking for an alternative to country houses and village hotels, Frenchman Paul Chatenoud's remote cottage overlooking Ardara, the Atlantic, and spectacular Donegal scenery is one of the most beautiful little guest houses in Ireland. The four spare rooms, in a converted stone outbuilding with a thatched roof, have new baths; only one has a view. Chatenoud, even more charming than his hideaway, is eager to point guests toward Donegal's best-kept secrets. It's worth visiting here for a peek at the glowing compliments in the guest book. To reach the hotel, follow the sign for Donegal and turn right after 200 yards. ⊠ *Ardvally, Co. Donegal,* ☎ *075/41546. 4 rooms with bath. No credit cards.*

$ ⊞ **Greenhaven House.** Only a few minutes from the village, Eileen and Ray Molloy's modern, one-story home has its own gardens and marvelous views of the nearby mountains and bay. You'll be warmed by a peat fire in the lounge and wake up to a hearty breakfast (included). The Molloys can advise you on shopping for hand knits and other items. ⊠ *Portnoo Rd., Co. Donegal,* ☎ *075/41129,* FAX *075/41129. 6 rooms with shower. Dining room, lounge. V. Closed Dec.*

Nightlife and the Arts

For a small, old-fashioned village, Ardara has a surprising number of pubs, many of them offering evenings of traditional music. The **Central Bar** (⊠ Main St., ☎ 075/41311) has music almost every night during the summer and on weekends the rest of the year. One of the smallest bars in the Republic, **Nancy's Pub** (⊠ Front St., ☎ 075/41187) has some corners that make you wonder if you've wandered into the owners' sitting room; it finds space for a folk group several nights a week in the high season.

The **Weavers' Fair and Vintage Weekend,** planned for June 2000, has as much to do with music, dance, and revelry as it does with the sale of homespun items; for further details, call Bosco McGill (☎ 075/41262).

Outdoor Activities and Sports

Rent a bike (£7 per day, £30 per week) from **Donal Byrne** (⊠ West End, Ardara, ☎ 075/41156).

Shopping

Many handwoven and locally made knitwear items are on sale here; some stores commission goods directly from knitters, and prices are about as low as you'll find anywhere. Handsome, chunky Aran handknit sweaters (£60–£100), cardigans (similar prices), and scarves (£16) are all widely available. Stores also carry ready-to-wear tweeds—sports jackets for women run up to about £120; for men, up to about £150. Shops also stock a selection of traditional Irish products, such as glassware and linen, from other parts of the country. **Campbells Tweed Shop** (⊠ Front St., ☎ 075/41128), **E. Doherty (Ardara) Ltd.** (⊠ Front St., ☎ 075/41304), and **C. Bonner & Son** (⊠ Front St., ☎ 075/41303) are all recommended.

NORTHERN DONEGAL

Traveling on northern County Donegal's country roads, you'll feel that you have escaped at last from the world's hurry and hassle. There's almost nothing up here but scenery, and plenty of it: broad, island-studded loughs of deep, dark tranquillity; unkempt, windswept, sheep-grazed grasses on mountain slopes; ribbons of luminous greenery following sparkling streams; and the mellow hues of wide bog lands, all under shifting and changing cloudscapes. This itinerary—apart from Inishowen Peninsula, which is included as a separate excursion at the end—could take anywhere from one day to a week, depending on how low a gear you slip into after a few breaths of Donegal air. It begins in Letterkenny, the largest town in the county (population 6,500), but if you want to pick up the journey from Ardara, then follow the itinerary in reverse. If you choose to abbreviate the trip, try at least to catch the rewarding Fanad and Rosguill peninsulas and the drive around Sheephaven Bay. Just one word of warning: Don't be a bit surprised if you find a sheep standing in the middle of a mountain road looking as though you, rather than it, are in the wrong place.

Letterkenny

㉙ *55 km (34 mi) northeast of Ardara, 51 km (32 mi) northeast of Donegal Town, 35 km (21 mi) west of Derry.*

Now one of the fastest-growing towns in all of Ireland, Letterkenny, like Donegal to the south, is at the gateway to the far Northwest; you're likely to come through here if you're driving west out of Northern Ireland. Letterkenny's claim to fame has been that it has the longest main street in the whole country, though none of its shops or pubs are particularly special, but lots of locals bustling around make it an interesting place to get a feel for what it's like to live in a modest-size Irish town today. If you're here in the middle of August you could catch the **Letterkenny Folk Festival,** which attracts musicians from all over Europe. The large, neo-Gothic Victorian St. Eunan's Cathedral towers over Letterkenny. The main County Donegal **TIO,** loaded with maps, literature, and advice, is 1½ km (1 mi) south on the Derry road, N13. ☎ *074/21160.* ☉ *Sept.–May, weekdays 9–5; June, Mon.–Sat. 9–6; July–Aug., Mon.–Sat. 9–8, Sun. 10–2.*

Dining and Lodging

$$ ✕▥ **Mount Errigal Hotel.** One of County Donegal's smartest and most modern hotels, although not at all posh, this property appeals to both business and family-vacation visitors. Service is friendly and professional. The clean and comfortable bedrooms are efficiently arranged, with characterless, pale-color furnishings. The Glengesh, the hotel's softly lit restaurant, decorated in the Roman style, serves popular Irish cooking. The bar buzzes with locals seeking a relaxed night out, and folk music, jazz, or dancing is frequently scheduled on weekends. ⊠ *Ballyraine, Co. Donegal,* ☎ *074/22700,* ℻ *074/25085. 105 rooms with bath or shower, 2 suites. Restaurant, 2 bars, indoor pool, sauna, health club, nightclub. AE, DC, MC, V.*

Ramelton

㉚ *13 km (8 mi) north of Letterkenny on R245.*

A small, handsome, former Plantation town built by the prosperous Stewart family, Ramelton (or Rathmelton, though the pronunciation is the same) climbs uphill from a river harbor close to Lough Swilly. The village was the birthplace of Francis Makemie (1658–1708), who preached here before emigrating and founding the American Presbyterian church. In the 18th century it was an important port that exported salmon, butter, grain, linen, and iodine (made from the local seaweed). Houses of wealthy merchants of the time lined the Mall, but

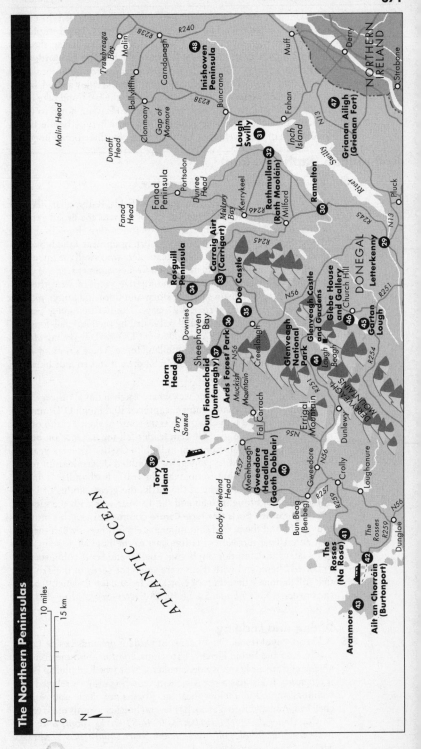

The Northern Peninsulas

10 miles
15 km

N

ATLANTIC OCEAN

Malin Head
Trawbreaga Bay
Malin
Ballyliffin
Carndonagh
R238
R240
Inishowen Peninsula
48
Clonmany
Gap of Mamore
Buncrana
Muff
Derry
NORTHERN IRELAND
Strabone
Dunaff Head
Fahan
Inch Island
N13
47
Grianan Ailigh (Grianan Fort)
Portsalon
Dunree Head
Fanad Peninsula
Lough Swilly
31
32
Rathmullan (Rath Maoláin)
Ramelton
30
Letterkenny
29
Pluck
N13
Fanad Head
Kerrykeel
Milford
R246
Mulroy Bay
River Swilly
DONEGAL
R245
R251
Carraig Airt (Carrigart)
33
Doe Castle
R245
N56
Church Hill
Glebe House and Gallery
46
45
Gartan Lough
R254
Rosguill Peninsula
34
35
36
Creeslough
Glenveagh Castle and Gardens
44
Lough Beagh
Glenveagh National Park
Sheephaven Bay
Downies
Ards Forest Park
37
38
Horn Head
Dun Fionnachaidh (Dunfanaghy)
Muckish Mountain
DERRYVEAGH MOUNTAINS
Fal Carrach
Errigal Mountain
R251
R254
Tory Sound
Dunlewy
N56
39
Tory Island
Bloody Foreland Head
Meenlaragh
R257
Gweedore Headland (Gaoth Dobhair)
40
Gweedore
N56
Crolly
Loughanure
R257
Bun Beag (Benbeg)
41
The Rosses (Na Rosa)
R259
The Rosses
Dungloe
N56
R259
42
Ailt an Chorráin (Burtonport)
43
Aranmore

the coming of the railway to nearby Letterkenny heralded the end of Ramelton's prosperity. However, Lough Swilly continued to play its part in history, sheltering vast fleets of British ships during the First World War, when Ireland was still part of the Empire. The **Bridge Bar** (✉ Bridge End, ☎ 074/51119) has long been a favorite of locals and summertime visitors as a place to meet for a drink; enjoy a good, hearty meal (dinners are served upstairs, away from the bar); and take in the bands that regularly pack the place at night. Heading north to Rathmullan, take the waterside road (R247), which runs beside **Lough Swilly,** one of the loveliest of Donegal's big, fjordlike ocean inlets.

Rathmullan (Rath Maoláin)

③ *11 km (7 mi) north of Ramelton on R247.*

An ancient harbor village set among green fields, Rathmullan (its Irish name means "ring fort of Maoláin") looks across the broad expanse of Lough Swilly to the Inishowen hills on the eastern shore. In the last five years or so, holiday homes have sprung up near Lough Swilly's sandy shores, bringing with them vacationers who swell the town's ordinarily tiny population and make for a livelier summer scene. If you'd like to take an hour or two and familiarize yourself with this unspoiled little town's main sights, history, and flora and fauna, pick up *Rathmullan: A Walking Tour,* a 28-page, handwritten guide penned by resident Margaret Carton and published by the National Trust for Ireland. It's available at the County Donegal TIO (☞ Letterkenny, *above*), Letterkenny bookshops, or Rathmullan House. There's nothing quite comparable for any other town in Ireland, so if this sounds like your cup of tea, don't pass it up.

Rathmullan's modest harbor was where English naval officers, posing as ordinary merchant seamen, captured Red Hugh O'Donnell in 1587. They invited him aboard to taste some of their "cargo of foreign wines," and the sociable clan leader fell for it. Once on board, he was shipped to imprisonment in Dublin Castle. After six years he escaped and returned to Donegal with added determination to defend his homeland—but to no avail. In 1607, Rathmullan's harbor was the scene of the Flight of the Earls, the great exodus of Ulster nobility which brought to an end the 13-year war with the English. The **Flight of the Earls Heritage Centre** commemorates this momentous event and the period that immediately followed, when the million-acre Ulster territories became part of the English domain. Two years later the Plantation era began: English and Scots colonists were "planted" here, and with them were sown the seeds of the Troubles that still dominate the affairs of Northern Ireland (☞ Chapter 9) across the border. ☎ *No phone.* 🎫 *£1.50.* ⊙ *Easter–Sept., Mon.–Sat. 10–6, Sun. noon–6:30.*

Dining and Lodging

$$$ ✕🏨 **Fort Royal Hotel.** On 18 acres of verdant grounds beside Lough Swilly, Ann and Robin Fletcher's spacious, comfortable hotel, once an aristocratic private home, is a decent alternative to the Rathmullan House (☞ *below*). It attracts a regular clientele, who enjoy its relaxed professionalism and marvelous location. Rooms are clean, and resident chef Tim, Ann and Robin's son, has several hotelier awards to his credit. ✉ *Co. Donegal,* ☎ *074/58100,* 🖷 *074/58103. 15 rooms with bath or shower. Bar, 9-hole golf course, tennis court, squash, beach. AE, DC, MC, V. Closed Nov.–Mar.*

$$$ ✕🏨 **Rathmullan House.** Behind the signature facade of this two-story,
★ cream-color mansion awaits one of Ireland's most appealing country houses—a rambling place that is elegant *and* relaxed, and well situ-

ated for visiting all of Donegal. Robin and Bob Wheeler are the friendly, gracious owner-managers. The public rooms, which include the bright-yellow drawing room, library, and a coffee room, are decorated with fine antiques and oil paintings; all are elegant without being stuffy. Bedrooms vary from old-fashioned basic to grand, but all have antiques, well-appointed bathrooms, elegant wallpaper and fine fabrics; five are suitable for disabled guests. Rooms in the front overlook Lough Swilly, whose long, sandy, deserted beach lies steps from Rathmullan's front door, separated only by a ribbon of trees and the award-winning gardens. In a pavilion with a tented ceiling and floor-to-ceiling windows, the dining room has views of the gardens and the lake, as well as a delicious menu, which changes nightly. Breakfast (included) is a feast. ✉ *Co. Donegal,* ☎ *074/58188,* ℻ *074/58200. 26 rooms with bath or shower. Dining room, bar, indoor pool, steam room, tennis court, croquet, beach. AE, DC, MC, V. Closed Jan.*

$$–$$$ ✕🏨 **Water's Edge.** Dawn and Kevin Cairns recently added 11 bedrooms, 9 with sea views, to their popular restaurant, set in a converted row of old cottages on the western shore of Lough Swilly. The cozy, romantic dining room has wooden beams, oak tables, deep-burgundy decor, and linen tablecloths and napkins. Influenced by the owners' travels, the menu is based primarily on fresh, local, seasonally available ingredients. Fish is the main event in summer (although it is available fresh every day of the year); steaks, chicken, duckling, and scallops predominate in the winter. Queen Sofia's Delight, a rich, meringue-based dessert made with seasonal fruit and fresh cream, is a specialty. ✉ *Ballyboe, Co. Donegal,* ☎ *074/58182,* ℻ *074/58007. 11 rooms with bath. MC, V. Closed Nov.–mid-Mar.*

Outdoor Activities and Sports

Horses are available for excursions to the nearby Fanad Peninsula at **Rockhill Trekking Center** (✉ Kerrykeel, ☎ 074/50012).

En Route   Extending north from here is the barren and rock-strewn **Fanad Peninsula.** The signposted Fanad Scenic Drive takes you 27 km (17 mi) up along the west shore of Lough Swilly to low-lying Fanad Head at its northern tip, then down again through the tiny resort village of Kerrykeel, with views of long, narrow Mulroy Bay twisting and turning to your right. If you want to cut the journey short, you can take the back road directly from Rathmullan to Kerrykeel for 9½ km (6 mi).

Carraig Airt (Carrigart)

㉝   *14 km (9 mi) north of Ramelton on R245.*

A small village with a lot of charm and many old-fashioned pubs, Carraig Airt (Carrigart) is at the base of a slender isthmus. This is the neck **㉞** of the extremely beautiful **Rosguill Peninsula,** which has a rocky heart and a fringe of sand dunes and beaches and is encircled by the signposted 15 km (9 mi) **Atlantic Drive.** It's not as far off the beaten track as you might think; you'll see several caravan sites and housekeeping cottages, popular with visitors from Northern Ireland. At the little resort of **Downings** (Na Dúnaibh), there's a long, sandy beach; good fishing; and a chance to buy linen directly from **McNutts of Donegal Ltd.** (☎ 074/55643) and tweeds from **John McNutt Homespun Tweeds Factory** (☎ 074/55158).

★   To the west of the Rosguill Peninsula, **Sheephaven Bay** has shallow, meandering inlets and sandy shores. At the foot of Muckish Mountain and the southern end of Sheephaven Bay, protected on three sides **㉟** by the sea and by a moat on its fourth side, stands **Doe Castle,** a tall, weather-beaten tower at the center of a complex structure enclosed within sturdy defenses. Described by attacking English forces in 1587 as "the strongest fortress in all the province," the impressive edifice dates from at least 1440, when it became the home of MacSweeney Doe, one of the "gallowglasses" (from the Irish *gall o glach*)—foreign mercenaries employed by the O'Donnell clan. Despite the castle's present poor condition, it was still occupied by his descendants until 1890. MacSweeney Doe's curiously carved tombstone is fixed to the southwest tower of the outer wall. ⊠ *Near Creeslough.* ☎ *Free.* ☉ *Usually open; if locked, inquire at caretaker's cottage on approach path.*

Outdoor Activities and Sports

Horses for hacking or trekking on the Rosguill Peninsula can be rented at **Carrigart Riding School** (⊠ Co. Donegal, ☎ 074/53717).

Ards Forest Park

36 *13 km (8 mi) west of Carrigart on N56.*

Clinging to Sheephaven Bay's southwest shore, the 1,188-acre Ards Forest Park (reached by passing through adjacent Creeslough [pronounced *creesh*-la]) is the former wooded estate of a Capuchin friary; the friary itself is still occupied by the Capuchins. Four prehistoric, fortified sites and one dolmen lie within the grounds, which offer some of the most varied landscape of any of Ireland's national forest parks, including rivers, loughs, salt marshes, valleys, and, of course, the bay. If the weather is fine, the park's forest trails and picnic sites are great places to enjoy the scrubbed sea air. ☎ 074/53271. ☎ *Free; £2 parking per car weekends Easter–June and July–Sept.* ☉ *Daily 8 AM–9 PM.*

Dun Fionnachaid (Dunfanaghy)

37 *8 km (5 mi) northwest of Ards Forest Park.*

On the very edge of Sheephaven Bay, Dun Fionnachaid (Dunfanaghy) is a tidy, former Plantation village. If you're ready for a short break, both hotels noted below serve decent, unpretentious, local fare for about £8 for lunch. When the tide goes out, the vast sand flats of **Killyhoey Beach** are uncovered and the sea recedes into the far distance, but as it rises again, the sands are submerged in double-quick time. On the west side of Dunfanaghy, the signpost to **McSwyne's Gun** (McSwyne is the old spelling of MacSweeney) leads to a huge, natural blowhole that gives out a deafening bang when the tide rushes in during rough weather.

★ **38** A little back road runs from Dunfanaghy up to **Horn Head,** the most spectacular of County Donegal's Atlantic headlands. From its sheer 600-ft cliffs, the views along the coast to the other headlands ranged one behind the other are spectacular. Bird-watchers, take note: The cliffs are home to hundreds of seabirds, including puffin and guillemot.

Dining and Lodging

$$ ✕🏨 **Arnold's Hotel.** Right at the entrance to the village, this friendly hotel has been run by three generations of the Arnold family and is a favorite with Irish vacationers. Rooms are unassuming and relaxed; the best overlook the landscaped garden. Guests have the option of eating the generous, traditional Irish meals in the dining room or in the more casual Garden Bistro. Special-interest classes, such as photography, writing, bridge, wine-tasting, and bird-watching, are available for guests on the weekends. ⊠ *Main St., Co. Donegal,* ☎ *074/36208,* FAX *074/36352. 30 rooms with bath and shower. Dining room, bar, tennis court, horseback riding, baby-sitting. AE, DC, MC, V. Closed Dec.–mid-March and weekdays Nov.*

En Route West of Dunfanaghy the terrain is rougher, wilder, and rockier; you're also likely to hear the Irish language being spoken. The N56 reaches round 11 km (7 mi) to Fal Carrach (Falcarragh), the site of an Irish-language college. Another 13 km (8 mi) around the rugged seashore, in good weather, you can catch a ferry from Meenlaragh (near Gortahork) to Tory Island.

Tory Island

39 *14½ km (9 mi) offshore.*

Harsh weather and difficult currents make Tory Island fairly inaccessible. (The boat trip lasts more than an hour on seas that are rough even on the best days; be prepared to get soaked, too.) Despite being rocky, ocean-battered, and barren (not even a single tree), the island has been inhabited since prehistoric times. Islanders speak their own dialect and refer to the mainland as "Ireland." Prehistoric and medieval relics are scattered about the landscape. Poised on the cliffs is the partly ruined, pink-granite **round tower** with its conical cap still intact. At Tory Island's eastern end, the prehistoric **Balor's Fort** was purportedly the residence of Balor, the terrifying, one-eyed Celtic god of night and darkness. At the northeastern tip, the **Wishing Stone** has the power, it is said, to destroy enemies. Still talked about is the time (1884) when the stone's powers were invoked against the British gunboat *Wasp*, whose passengers (mainly policemen) had come to collect taxes—something the islanders were unaccustomed to paying. The ship sank, and all but six of the crew were lost.

Most of the islanders live the simple life of fisherfolk, though quite a few have unexpected sidelines as artists. In 1968, the well-known Irish painter Derek Hill met islander James Dixon, who felt that he could do a better job of painting than Hill. Many other Tory Island residents thought they could, too, and today the Tory Island artists, depicting their own life and landscape in a naive style using nothing more than standard house paints, are widely acclaimed and have exhibited elsewhere in Ireland (☞ Glebe House and Gallery *in* Gartan Lough, *below*) and abroad. **Dixon's Gallery** (☞ Tory Island Hotel, *below*) sells the work of the Tory islanders; prices range from £50 to £200.

Dining and Lodging

$ ✕🏠 **Tory (Ostan Thoraig).** After living and working in England for 10 years, native islander Pat Doohan returned with his wife, Berney, to build and run Tory Island's only accommodation. (He also watches over Dixon's Gallery [☞ *above*].) The comfortable guest rooms are large, sunny, and nicely decorated in a peach, blue, and green palette, with matching curtains and bedspreads; all have TVs and phones. A fireplace warms the bar, which is a popular local hangout and is the only place on the island that sells draft beer. Traditional music sessions and *ceili* dancing regularly liven things up. The restaurant overlooks the sea. ✉ *Tory Island, Letterkenny, Co. Donegal,* ☎ *074/35920,* FAX *074/35613. 14 rooms with bath. Restaurant, bar. MC, V. Closed Dec.–Mar.*

Gweedore Headland (Gaoth Dobhair)

40 *27 km (17 mi) south of Meenlaragh on R257.*

When you return from Tory Island to Meenlaragh, you're on the edge of the Gweedore Headland, which can be circumnavigated on the coast road (R257). Gweedore is rocky, sparsely covered with heather and gorse, and low-lying until you reach its farthest point, **Bloody Foreland Head.** This dramatic name for once does not recall the slaughter of some historic battle but describes instead the vivid red hues of the gaunt rock face when illuminated at sunset.

The Rosses (Na Rosa)

④ *13 km (8 mi) south of Bloody Foreland Head on R259.*

The next distinctive headland south of Gweedore (on the road south after you pass through Bun Beag [Benbeg] and Croithli [Crolly]) is the Rosses (Na Rosa in Irish, meaning "the headlands")—even more beautiful than Gweedore. The bleak but dramatic terrain here, as at Gweedore, has not benefited from a liberal sprinkling of modern bungalows. The coast road (R259) struggles over the inhospitable, stony landscape, crisscrossed with water channels and strewn with more than 100 lakes. Yet quite a number of people manage to survive here, many of them Irish speakers (this is the heart of the Donegal Gaeltacht). The decline of population and living standards was reversed by Patrick Gallagher (1873–1964), who became known as Paddy the Cope. Son of a poor local family, he left school at 10, went to Scotland as a farmhand, and saved enough money to return home in the 1950s and buy a small holding of his own. Gallagher, affectionately remembered throughout the area, persuaded the citizens around the Rosses to set up cooperatives to bring in new farming methods and machinery, as well as cooperatively owned stores to keep prices down.

Ailt an Chorráin (Burtonport)

④ *16 km (10 mi) southwest of Crolly on R259.*

This village of Ailt an Chorráin (Burtonport), which claims to land more salmon and lobster than any other fishing port in Ireland, is the departure point for a trip over to **Aranmore,** 6½ km (4 mi) offshore. Aranmore means "big island," and it is indeed the largest and most populous of County Donegal's rocky offshore fragments. The ride out takes 25 minutes, but although it's fairly accessible, the island still feels remote and ungoverned. It has been inhabited for thousands of years (about 1,000 people live on it today), and it offers good fishing as well as striking cliff scenery and views back onto the Rosses; there's a prehistoric fort on its south side. ⌨ *Ferry £2.* ☉ *7 crossings daily.*

Back on the mainland, if you follow the coast another 6½ km (4 mi) southeast, R259 rejoins N56 at **An Clochan Liath** (Dungloe), a pleasant little fishing town regarded as the capital of the Rosses, though there's little to do or see here.

En Route   From Dungloe, start the journey back to Letterkenny. The N56 takes you 13 km (8 mi) direct to Croithli (Crolly), a quicker journey than going back along the coast road. Stay on N56 north until you're a couple of miles beyond Gaoth Dobhair (Gweedore) village, on the little River Clady, and take R251 to skirt the south side of **Errigal Mountain** to the village of Dunlewy, 26 km (16 mi) east of Dungloe. This whole drive passes through some of the best scenery in all of County Donegal. Serene Errigal looks especially grand from Dunlewy. On the edge of Dunlewy Lough, the **Lakeside Centre,** or Ionad Cois Locha, is an interesting spot to pause for a look at a reconstructed, 19th-century weaver's home where you can watch a demonstration of old-style weaving and audiovisual show, then have a guided tour of traditional cottages. Half-hour boat trips on the lake include storytelling and a history of the area. There's also a café and crafts shop. ☎ *075/31699.* ⌨ *Weaving demonstration, show, and tour £3, boat trip £3.* ☉ *Apr.– May, Sat. 11–6, Sun. noon–7; June–Sept., Mon.–Sat. 11:30–6, Sun. 12:30–7.*

Glenveagh National Park

★ ㊹ *16 km (10 mi) east of Dunlewy on R251, 27 km (17 mi) northwest of Letterkenny.*

Bordered by the Derryveagh Mountains (Derryveagh means "forest of oak and birch"), Glenveagh National Park encompasses 24,000 acres of wilderness—mountain, moorland, lakes, and woods—that has been called "the largest and most dramatic tract in the wildest part of Donegal." Within its borders, a thick carpet of russet-color heath and dense woodland rolls down the Derryveagh slopes into the broad, open valley of the River Veagh (or Owenbeagh), which opens out into Glenveagh's spine: long and narrow, dark and clear **Lough Beagh.** (The park, in profile, looks like a backpacker marching off to the northwest.)

The Glenveagh lands have long been recognized as a remote and beautiful region. Between 1857 and 1859, John George Adair, a ruthless gentleman farmer, assembled the estate that now makes up the park. In 1861, he evicted the estate's hundreds of poor tenants without compensation and destroyed their cottages. Nine years later, Adair began to build **Glenveagh Castle** on the eastern shore of Lough Veagh, but he soon departed for Texas. He died in 1885 without returning to Ireland, but his widow, Cornelia, moved back to make Glenveagh her home. She created the four different **gardens** covering 27 acres, planted the luxuriant rhododendrons here, and began the job of making this flamboyantly turreted and battlemented 19th-century folly livable.

The gardens and castle as they appear today are almost entirely an American invention—the product of the loving attentions of Glenveagh's last owner. U.S. millionaire Henry P. McIlhenny bought the estate in 1937 and, beginning in 1947, lived here for part of every year for almost 40 years; his other homes included a mansion on Philadelphia's Rittenhouse Square. McIlhenny's grandfather invented the gas meter, and he was a distant cousin of the creators of Tabasco sauce. An avid art collector and philanthropist (he was president of the Philadelphia Museum of Art, to which he bequeathed his outstanding 19th-century European art collection), McIlhenny decorated every inch of the house himself and entertained lavishly. (Greta Garbo slept in the Pink Bedroom on a visit.) McIlhenny was something of an eccentric: His staff of more than 40 were required to wear Austrian-inspired clothes—the women wore dirndls—he chose himself, inspired by his annual trips to Salzburg and other Austrian music festivals. The house has been maintained just as it was on his last occupancy in 1983; later that year, he made a gift of the house to the nation. He had sold the government the surrounding land in 1975, which it opened to the public in 1984 as Ireland's third national park.

Beyond the castle, footpaths lead into more remote sections of the park, including the **Derrylahan Nature Trail,** a 1½-km (1-mi) signposted trail where you may suddenly catch sight of a soaring falcon or chance upon a shy red deer. The park is home to one of Ireland's two largest herds; the other is at Killarney (☞ Chapter 5). Guided walks are held May through October. The visitor center at the park's entrance has a permanent exhibition on the local way of life and on the influence of climate on the park's flora and fauna. Skip the sleep-inducing audiovisual and instead have a bite to eat in the cafeteria. ⊠ *Glenveagh National Park, Church Hill, Letterkenny,* ☎ *074/37088 or 074/37090.* 🖃 *£2, guided tour of castle £2.* ☉ *Easter–May and Sept.–Oct., daily 10:30–6:30; June–Aug., daily 10:30–7:30. Closed Fri. in Oct.*

Gartan Lough

④⑤ *13 km (8 mi) southeast of Glenveagh on R251, 17 km (11 mi) north-west of Letterkenny.*

Close to Church Hill village, Gartan Lough is technically within the national park and is administered partly by the park authorities. The lake and the surrounding mountainous country are astonishingly beautiful. St. Columba was supposedly born here in AD 521, and the legendary event is marked by a huge cross at the beginning of a foot-path into the national park. Nearby are other dubious "relics" of the saint, which are popularly believed to possess magical powers, such as the Natal Stone, where he is thought to have first opened his eyes, and the Stone of Loneliness, where he is said to have slept. However, the superstitions do rub off: The soil of Gartan was carried by sol-diers from the area to the trenches of the First World War as a pro-tective relic.

④⑥ On the northwest shore of Gartan Lough, just off R251, sits **Glebe House and Gallery,** a fine Regency manor with 25 acres of gardens. For 30 years, Glebe House was the home of the distinguished landscape and portrait artist Derek Hill, who furnished the house in a mix of styles with art from around the world; in 1981 he gave the house and its con-tents, including his outstanding art collection, to the nation. Highlights include paintings by Renoir and Bonnard, lithographs by Kokoschka, ceramics and etchings by Picasso, and the paintings *Whippet Racing* and *The Ferry, Early Morning* by Jack B. Yeats, as well as Donegal folk art produced by the Tory islanders (☞ *above*). The decoration and fur-nishings of the house, including original William Morris wallpaper, are worth a look as well. ⊠ *Church Hill,* ☎ *074/37071.* ☞ *£2.* ⊗ *Easter and mid-May–Sept., Sat.–Thurs. 11–6:30.*

At the **Colmcille Heritage Centre** you can learn more about St. Columba and his times. Return to R251 and turn right almost at once onto R254 in Church Hill; straightaway you'll arrive at the exhibition and inter-pretation center, which features medieval manuscripts, stained glass, and displays tracing the decline of the Celtic religion and the rise of Irish Christianity. From Church Hill, if you stay on R251, you'll be back in Letterkenny after 16 km (10 mi). ⊠ *Gartan, Church Hill,* ☎ *074/37306.* ☞ *£2.* ⊗ *May and Sept.–Oct., Mon.–Sat. 10:30–6:30, Sun. 1–6:30; June–Aug., Mon.–Sat. 10–6:30, Sun. noon–6:30.*

Grianan Ailigh (Grianan Fort)

★ **④⑦** *29 km (18 mi) northeast of Letterkenny on N13.*

A circular stone Celtic fort, the Grianan Ailigh (Grianan Fort), defi-nitely merits a visit, although it is, like the Inishowen Peninsula (☞ *below*), northeast of Letterkenny and thus closer to Northern Ireland (☞ Chapter 8) than the majority of Donegal sites covered here. The fortress sits on top of an 810-ft hill; on a fine day, the panorama of the rolling Donegal and Derry landscape is breathtaking. To the north lies the Swilly estuary, flowing around Inch Island into Lough Swilly. On either side rise the hills of the Fanad and Inishowen peninsulas, though they're often partly veiled by mists. As for the fort, what you'll see is a circular stone enclosure with a diameter of about 76 ft, which you can enter through a gate (it's open most of the year). Inside, earth ramparts and concentric defenses punctured by passages surround a sturdy central structure. No one knows when Grianan Fort was built, but it was probably an Iron Age fortress: Its position was accurately recorded in the 2nd century AD by the geographer Ptolemy of Alexan-dria. In the 5th century it became the seat of Ulster's O'Neill chieftains and remained so until the 12th century, despite serious attempts by their enemies to destroy it, especially in the year 674 and again in 1101. The present-day fortress, however, owes a good deal to overzealous "restoration" in the 1870s by Dr. Walter Bernard, a Derry historian; before that, it was in ruins. To get here, take the main Derry road (N13) from Letterkenny. Keep a lookout for signs to Buncrana, because the easy-to-miss sign for the fort is opposite. Instead of turning to Buncrana, take the narrow lane that climbs and turns for more than a mile to the top of the hill.

Inishowen Peninsula

48 *Peninsula circuit from Fahan to Muff via Malin Head and Inishowen Head: 161 km (100 mi).*

The most northerly point in all of Ireland, the huge Inishowen Peninsula is a grandly green, wild piece of land with a solid, mountainous interior. It is enclosed by Lough Swilly on one side, Lough Foyle on another, and the battering Atlantic to the north. Despite a string of small and untempting coastal resorts, it remains unspoiled and less traveled than most other parts of the country. If you decide to make the 160-km (100-mi) Inishowen circuit (known as the "Inishowen 100," for its length in miles) plus the 64-km (40-mi) round-trip to reach it from Letterkenny, you'll need to allow at least one whole day, though it is possible to make an abbreviated visit in less time.

From Grianan Ailigh, go back to N13 and cross straight over to take the Buncrana turning. You'll shortly meet R238, the main route from Derry to Buncrana. Turn left here; the first town you'll come to is **Fahan** (pronounced fawn), which has monastic ruins that include the early Christian **St. Mura cross slab.** After the village, opposite the North West Golf Club, signs on the right show the entrance to the IDA (Irish Industrial Authority) industrial estate. Turn in here, and you'll find the **National Knitting Centre** (Lisfannon, ☎ 077/62355), which offers residential courses in traditional Irish hand knitting; the center also sells fine knit goods.

A popular, downscale beach resort favored by Derry denizens, **Buncrana** has a 14th-century O'Doherty tower that gradually became part of an 18th-century mansion. Shortly after you pass Buncrana, turn left at the fork in the road away from R238 onto the coast road, which will take you past the 19th-century fort on Dunree Head, up and over the spectacular viewpoint of the **Gap of Mamore,** where the 1,250-ft **Croagh-carragh** rises up on one side and the 1,361-ft **Mamor Hill** echoes it on the other. The road heads north toward **Dunaff Head,** where Lough Swilly opens into the ocean. Rejoin R238 at Clonmany and take it through **Ballyliffin,** another small resort town with an O'Doherty tower on the beach, and a convenient place for a snack or meal. Ballyliffin's **Strand Hotel** (☎ 077/76107) is a family-run establishment that serves pub lunches as well as an eclectic menu in the restaurant. Rooms ($) are also available.

By the junction of R238 and R240, you'll see a church with a curious remnant of early Christianity against one wall—the decorated, 7th-century **Donagh Cross,** accompanied by a couple of pillar stones. The strange carvings on the stones clearly date from a pre-Christian period. Around the corner from the Donagh Cross, **Carndonagh,** the area's main market town, has several more medieval monastic remains; **Slieve Snaght,** Inishowen's highest peak, at 2,019 ft, lies just southwest of town. As it runs up beside Trawbreaga Bay, R238 turns into R242 shortly before the picturesque village of Malin; it's another 16 km (10 mi) up to **Malin Head,** the most northerly point in all of Ireland and an important spot for birds migrating south in autumn. Although it has good views, Malin Head is not as dramatic a spot as some of the other headlands.

From Malin Head, take the signposted route across the peninsula to **Moville,** a sleepy waterside resort on the Lough Foyle side. From here, it's 8 km (5 mi) to **Inishowen Head,** the peninsula's rocky eastern tip. On the way to the head, at **Greencastle,** you'll see the fortifications of foreigners who tried to control the nine counties of Ulster: a 14th-century, Anglo-Norman fortress and an English fort built five centuries later to defend against French support for the Irish. The drive along the lough shore toward Derry (☞ Chapter 8), though attractive, is punctuated by small, uninteresting villages whose modernized pubs cater to visitors from Derry. If you want to turn away from Derry toward Letterkenny before reaching the border, take R239 from Muff to **Bridge End,** home to one of the most attractive of Ireland's many new Catholic churches.

Dining and Lodging

$$–$$$ ✕🍴 **Restaurant St. John's.** A cozy, old-fashioned atmosphere prevails
★   at this restored lakeside Georgian house, which has been known for 20 years for its restaurant. Pictures of old Derry hang in the turquoise-and-pink dining room, and white Donegal linen is used for tablecloths and napkins. Phil McAfee, who does the cooking, is scrupulous about using only organic vegetables and local produce in the peak of its season. Homemade bread is baked daily to serve with the fresh garden soups and pâtés. The six-course table d'hôte menu changes monthly and offers appetizers such as seafood chowder or a terrine of salmon and monkfish wrapped in spinach. Fillets of brill with herbs and fennel sauce, and Donegal rack of lamb, served with mascarpone risotto and rosemary, are typical main courses. Desserts include homemade ice creams and Carrageen moss with fruit coulis. ✉ *Fahan, Co. Donegal,* ☎ *077/60289,* 🖷 *077/60612. 5 rooms with bath. MC, V. Closed mid-Feb.–mid-Mar.*

Outdoor Activities and Sports

For hacking and trekking on the Inishowen Peninsula contact **Lenamore Stables** (✉ Muff, ☎ 077/84022), which also has four self-catering rooms ($) above the stables.

THE NORTHWEST A TO Z

Arriving and Departing

By Bus

Bus Éireann (☎ 071/60066 locally or 01/836–6111 in Dublin) can get you from Dublin to Sligo Town in 4 hours for £8 one-way, £11 round-trip. Three buses a day from Dublin are available. Another bus route, four times a day from Dublin (five on Friday), goes to Letterkenny, in the heart of County Donegal, in 4¼ hours, via a short trip across the Northern Ireland border; it's £10 one-way, £13 round-trip. Other Bus Éireann services connect Sligo Town to other towns all over Ireland.

By Car

Sligo, the largest town in the Northwest, is relatively accessible on the main routes. The N4 travels the 224 km (140 mi) directly from Dublin to Sligo, but you need to allow at least 4 hours for this journey. The N15 continues from Sligo Town to Donegal Town and proceeds from Donegal Town to Derry City, just over the border in the province of Northern Ireland. The fastest approach for anyone driving up from the

West and the Southwest is on N17, connecting Sligo to Galway, though the landscape is undistinguished.

By Plane

The principal international air-arrival point to the Northwest is the tiny airport at Charlestown, near Knock, whose official name is **Horan International Airport** (☎ 094/67247), 54½ km (34 mi) south of Sligo Town. Locally it is known simply as Knock Airport. **City of Derry Airport** (☎ 01504/810784), a few miles over the border, receives flights from Manchester and Glasgow. City of Derry is a particularly convenient airport for reaching northern County Donegal. A small airfield is at **Carrickfinn** (☎ 075/48232) near Dungloe. **Sligo Airport** (☎ 071/68280 or 071/68318) at Strandhill, 8 km (5 mi) west of Sligo Town, is the other area airport.

Ryanair has flights to Knock Airport from London Stansted daily. **Aer Lingus** has direct flights from Birmingham to Sligo Airport on Friday. **Macair** provides direct flights to Carrickfinn Airport near Dungloe from Birmingham and Edinburgh. **British Airways Express** flies to Carrickfinn from Glasgow and also flies to Eglinton Airport from Manchester and Glasgow.

BETWEEN THE AIRPORTS AND YOUR DESTINATION

By Bus. If you aren't driving, Knock Airport becomes less attractive, as you'll have no easy public transportation link to your destination, except the once-a-day (in season) local bus to Charlestown, 11 km (7 mi) away. Nor can you rely on catching a bus at the smaller airports, except at Sligo Airport, where buses run from Sligo Town to meet all flights.

By Car. Knock Airport has a convenient car-rental desk. You can also pick up rental cars at Sligo and Eglinton (Derry) airports.

By Taxi. Cabs sometimes wait outside Knock Airport to meet incoming flights, but passengers arriving at the other airports may have to phone a local taxi company. Phone numbers of taxi companies are available from airport information desks and are also displayed beside pay phones inside the airport terminals.

By Train

Sligo Town is the northernmost direct rail link to Dublin. From Dublin three trains a day are available, and the journey takes 3 hours and 20 minutes. The fare is £13.50 one-way or day-return, £18 round-trip. The train stops at Ballymote (20 mins from Sligo), Boyle (40 mins), and Carrick-on-Shannon (50 mins). However, if you want to get to Sligo Town by rail from other provincial towns, you'll be forced to make some inconvenient connections and take roundabout routes. The rest of the region has no railway services. Contact **Irish Rail** (☎ 01/836–6222).

Getting Around

By Bus

Bus Éireann services operate out of Sligo Town (☎ 071/60066) and Letterkenny (☎ 074/21309) to destinations all over the region, as well as to other parts of Ireland. From Sligo Town, you can reach almost any point in the region for less than £10. **McGeehans** (☎ 075/46150) is one of several local bus companies linking towns and villages in the Northwest.

By Car

Roads are uncongested, but in some places they are in a poor state of repair (French bus drivers refused to take their buses into County

Donegal a few summers back, as a gesture of protest about the state of the roads). In the Irish-speaking areas, signposts are written only in the Irish (Gaelic) language, which can be confusing. You need to prepare beforehand for this by checking the Irish names of places on your route.

Contacts and Resources

B&B Reservation Agencies

For a small fee, **Bord Fáilte** will book accommodations anywhere in Ireland through its central reservations system. B&Bs can be booked at local visitor information offices when they are open; however, even these reservations will go through the central reservations system. For more information, ☞ Lodging *in* Smart Travel Tips A to Z.

Car Rentals

You can rent a car in Sligo Town from **Euro Mobil** (☎ 071/67291). **Murray's Europcar** (☎ 071/68400) rents cars from Sligo Airport. **Murray's Europcar** (☎ 078/33013) also has a branch at Knock Airport. A medium-size four-door costs around £50 per day with unlimited mileage (inclusive of insurance and taxes), or around £220 per week. If you're planning to tour mostly northern County Donegal, you may find it more convenient to rent a car in Derry from **Ford** (☎ 01504/360420). Conversely, if you're planning to drive a rental car across the border to Northern Ireland, inform the company in advance and check the insurance policy.

Emergencies

Police, fire, and **ambulance** (☎ 999).

HOSPITALS

Letterkenny General Hospital (✉ High Rd., Letterkenny, Co. Donegal, ☎ 074/22022). **Sligo General Hospital** (✉ Dromahair Rd., Sligo Town, Co. Sligo, ☎ 071/42161).

Guided Tours

Walking tours of Sligo Town usually depart twice daily in July and August from the TIO. They are free and last about 1 to 1½ hours. However, the guides are generally students, so a tip of £1 or £2 is welcome. Check details with the TIO (☎ 071/61201). For a friendly, relaxed, minibus tour of the area in July and August, call **John Houze** (☎ 071/42747 or 086/833–9084, FAX 071/54321). He is a knowledgeable guide who leads popular tours to Lough Gill (£6.50 morning tour, £7.50 afternoon) and north of Sligo Town to Drumcliff, Lissadell House, and Creevykeel (£6.50). **Bus Éireann** (☎ 071/60066 or 074/21309) has budget-priced, guided, one-day bus tours of the Donegal Highlands and to Glenveagh National Park which start from Bundoran, Sligo Town, Ballyshannon, and Donegal Town.

Nightlife and the Arts

Outside Sligo Town, the Northwest features few serious arts activities and events, though there are a number of festivals and seasonal events. The local press, including the *Donegal Democrat,* the *Leitrim Observer,* and *Sligo Champion,* has useful events listings.

Outdoor Activities and Sports

BIRD-WATCHING

For more information, contact the **Irish Wild Bird Conservancy** (✉ 8 Longford Pl., Monkstown, Co. Dublin, ☎ 01/280–4322).

FISHING

A **fishing license** is not needed for sea fishing or for coarse and pike angling. For game fishing (salmon and sea trout), the license costs £3 for one day, £10 for 21 days, or £25 for a full season. The full-season license is valid throughout the whole country; there's also a local annual license, valid only in the Northwest, for £12. Senior citizens are exempt from these costs. You can obtain licenses for County Donegal from the **Northern Regional Fisheries Board** (⊠ Ballyshannon, Co. Donegal, ☎ 072/51435). For licenses in Counties Sligo and Leitrim, contact the **North-Western Regional Fisheries Board** (⊠ Ballina, Co. Mayo, ☎ 096/22623). Some tackle shops are also permitted to sell licenses.

If you want full **information** on fishing in the Northwest waters, suitable accommodations, details of boat rentals, and so on, ask the Irish Tourist Board (☞ Visitor Information *in* Smart Travel Tips A to Z) for the annual *Anglers' Guide*.

Bait, tackle, and local information can be found at the following places:

County Donegal: John McGill (⊠ Main St., Ardara, ☎ no phone); O'-Doherty's (⊠ Main St., Donegal Town, ☎ no phone); and Pat Barrett (⊠ Finner Rd., Bundoran, ☎ 072/41504).

County Leitrim: The Creel or Geraghty's (⊠ Main St., Carrick-on-Shannon, ☎ The Creel: 078/20166; Geraghty's: 078/21316) and Aodh Flynn (⊠ Deerpark, Manorhamilton, ☎ no phone).

County Sligo: Barton Smith (⊠ Hyde Bridge, Sligo Town, ☎ 071/42356).

GOLF

For a full list of golf courses in the region, contact the Irish Tourist Board (☞ Visitor Information *in* Smart Travel Tips A to Z) or local TIOs (☞ Visitor Information, *below*). For detailed information about the Northwest's championship courses, including Carn Golf Course, Donegal Golf Club, County Sligo Golf Club, and Enniscrone Golf Club, ☞ Chapter 9.

HIKING

For information about Northwest walking routes, contact **Field Officer, Long Distance Walking Routes Committee** (⊠ Cospoir, 11th floor, Hawkins House, Dublin 9, ☎ 01/873–4700).

HORSEBACK RIDING

For information on recognized establishments that offer full riding vacations including lodging, contact the **Association of Irish Riding Establishments** (⊠ Mespil Hall, Kill, Co. Kildare, ☎ 045/877208 or 045/877299).

SURFING

Ask the **Irish Surfing Association** (⊠ Tigh-na-Mara, Rossnowlagh, Co. Donegal, ☎ 073/21053) for specific information on surfing in the region.

Visitor Information

The TIO in **Sligo Town** (in the extreme south of the region) is the main visitor information center for the whole Northwest. ⊠ *Áras Reddan, Temple St.,* ☎ *071/61201,* ℻ *071/60360.* ☉ *Sept.–May, weekdays 9–1 and 2–5; June, Mon.–Sat. 9–1 and 2–6; July–Aug., Mon.–Sat. 9–8, Sun. 10–2.*

If you are traveling in County Donegal in the North, try the TIO at **Letterkenny,** about 1½ km (1 mi) out of town. ⊠ *Derry Rd.,* ☎ *074/*

21160, FAX *074/25180.* ⊘ *Sept.–May, weekdays 9–1 and 2–5; June, Mon.–Sat. 9–1 and 2–6; July–Aug., Mon.–Sat. 9–8, Sun. 10–2.*

SEASONAL OFFICES

These offices are open only during the summer months (usually the first week in June to the second week in September):

Bundoran (⊠ Main St., Co. Donegal, ☎ 072/41350). **Donegal Town** (⊠ Quay St., Co. Donegal, ☎ 073/21148, FAX 073/22762). **Dungloe** (⊠ Village Center, Co. Donegal, ☎ 075/21297).

8 NORTHERN IRELAND

BELFAST, THE ANTRIM COAST, DERRY,
LOUGH ERNE, AND THE MOUNTAINS
OF MOURNE

With peace—precious peace—abiding, it's
a fine time to discover this overlooked corner
of Europe. Northern Ireland offers a great
bounty of treasures, including Palladian
stately houses, the Giant's Causeway, and
two rapidly changing cities—Derry and
Belfast, both noted for Victorian architecture
and other irresistible pleasures. Now that
significant progress has been made toward
an end to the longstanding, headline-making
conflict known as the Troubles, why not
discover this heritage-rich array of delights?

Updated by
Geoff Hill

LEGEND HAS IT THAT WELL OVER A MILLENNIUM ago a marauding chieftain caught sight of the shores of Northern Ireland from the deck of his boat and offered this green fertile land to whichever of his two sons could first lay hand on it. As the two rival sons rowed for the shore in their separate boats, one began to draw ahead—whereupon the other drew his sword, cut off his own hand, and threw it onto the beach—and so, by blood and sacrifice, won this new province. To this day the arms of Northern Ireland feature this same severed limb: the celebrated "Red Hand of Ulster."

From this bardic tale to the "Troubles" of today, Northern Ireland has had a long and often ferocious history. But come here and you'll find any thoughts of violence vanishing in the face of the country's outstanding natural beauty; its magnificent, stately houses; and the genuine, open hospitality of its inhabitants. The Six Counties, or Ulster (as Northern Ireland is often called), cover less than 14,245 square km (5,500 square mi) in all, but within their boundaries they contain some of the most unspoiled scenery you could hope to find—the granite Mountains of Mourne; the Giant's Causeway, made of extraordinary volcanic rock; more than 320 km (200 mi) of coastline with long, unspoiled beaches and hidden coves; and rivers and island-strewn lakes that provide fabled fishing grounds, among them the largest freshwater lake in Europe, Lough Neagh. Ancient castles and Palladian-perfect 18th-century treasure houses are as numerous on the ground here as almost anywhere else in Europe, and each has its own tale of heroic deeds, dastardly treachery, or lovelorn ghosts. Northern Ireland not only shelters this great heritage in stone, but it also holds an even greater legacy in its celebrated descendants. Nearly one in six of the more than 4½ million Irish who made the fateful journey across the Atlantic to seek their fortune in the New World was from Ulster, and of this group (and from their family stock), more than a few left their mark in America: Davy Crockett, President Andrew Jackson, General Ulysses S. Grant, President Woodrow Wilson, General Stonewall Jackson, financier Thomas Mellon, merchant Paul Getty, and writer Edgar Allen Poe.

Present-day Northern Ireland, a province under the rule of the United Kingdom, includes six of the old Ulster's nine counties and retains its sense of separation, both in the vernacular of the landscape and (some say) in the character of the people. The hardheaded and industrious Scots-Presbyterians, imported to make Ulster a bulwark against Ireland's Catholicism, have had a profound and ineradicable effect on the place. The North appears to boast more factories, neater-looking farms, better roads, and—in its cities—more of the two-story, redbrick houses typical of Great Britain than does the Republic. For all that, the border between north and south is of little consequence to visitors.

Ireland's ancient history truly began in the North when settlers came to the banks of the River Bann 9,000 years ago. Five thousand years later Bronze Age settlers built the great stone circles idiomatic to Counties Down and Tyrone, and later the Iron Age brought the Celts. St. Patrick, son of a Roman official and once a slave in County Antrim, returned to spread Christianity in the 5th century. But from the first Norman incursions in the 12th century onward, the English made greater and greater inroads into Ireland, endeavoring to subdue what they believed was a potential enemy. Ulster proved the hardest part to conquer, but in 1607 Ulster's beaten Irish nobility fled their homeland forever, many of them going to France and Spain, in the great exodus known as the Flight of the Earls. Their abandoned lands were distributed by the English to "the Planters"—staunch Protestants from England and Scotland.

After three centuries of smoldering tensions and religious strife, 1916 saw the Easter Uprising and then, in the parliamentary elections of 1918, an overwhelming Nationalist vote across Ireland for Sinn Féin ("We Ourselves"), the party that believed in independence for all of Ireland. In the five northeastern counties of Ulster, however, only 7 seats went to the Nationalists, and 22 to the Unionists, who wanted to remain an integral part of the United Kingdom. At 2:10 AM on December 6, 1921, in the British prime minister's residence at 10 Downing Street, Michael Collins signed the Anglo-Irish Treaty, designating a six-county North to remain in British hands, in exchange for complete independence for Ireland's 26 counties as the Irish Free State.

Fast-forward to 1968, when, in the spirit of the student protesters in Paris and Washington, and after 40 years of living with an apparently permanent and sectarian Unionist majority, students in Belfast's Queen's University launched a civil rights movement, claiming equal rights in jobs, housing, and opportunity. The brutality with which these marches were suppressed in front of the world's press led to worldwide revulsion, riots, and counter-riots. The Irish Republican Army (IRA), which had lain dormant for decades, hijacked what was left of the shattered civil rights movement, which once had a smattering of Protestant students among its ranks. Armed British troops who had been first welcomed by many in the Catholic ghettos as protectors from Protestant paramilitaries now found themselves welcomed by neither side. Britain imposed Direct Rule. No one was happy, and the decades of guerrilla conflict that ensued between the IRA, the UDA/UVF (Protestant/Loyalist paramilitaries), and the British government continued in a mix of lulls and terrors—apart from the IRA's annual Christmas "truce"—until the summer of 1994, when the "Provos," as they are colloquially known, called an ongoing cease-fire, confirmed in July 1997.

Belfast reveled in its new peace: New hotels, shopping malls, and restaurants came off dusty drawing boards. People who had not seen the city's center for a quarter of a century gazed at its bright lights. Today, the IRA and Loyalist cease-fires are still in place, but major divisions remain: The various shades of Unionism are closely identified with the "planted" Protestant population, while Nationalists and Republicans are inextricably associated with the "native" Irish community, which traces its genetic inheritance back to the Iron Age Celtic invaders and which is almost entirely Catholic. Today, in blue-collar Protestant areas you'll see curbstones and lampposts painted in the British colors of red, white, and blue; entwined British and Red Hand Ulster flags fluttering from tall poles raised in pocket-handkerchief front yards; and countless signs and crests declaring proud devotion to Ulster and the Queen. By contrast, in Irish Republican and Nationalist Catholic districts, you'll note the green, white, and gold of the Irish Republic's Tricolor flickering in the breeze. Still, the province's new regional parliament, or Assembly, was up and running in 1999, and both sides were at last talking rather than fighting.

Don't worry if this all seems impossibly complex: Even locals say wryly, "If you understand Northern Ireland politics, you're missing the point." In any case, the province's turbulent history cannot mask the fact that it is a region incredibly rich in natural beauty and artistic treasures, such as the great Georgian estates and Belfast's Victorian architecture. For overseas travelers, Northern Ireland remains one of the increasingly rare forgotten spots of Europe.

Pleasures and Pastimes

Dining

While it has nowhere near the number of innovative restaurants as Dublin (which is five times more populous), Belfast has witnessed an influx of international influences with new restaurants, bistros, wine bars, and—as in Dublin—European-style café-bars where you can get good food *and* linger over a drink.

By and large, though, hearty, unpretentious cooking predominates, with good-quality, fresh local fish and meat simply prepared. You're virtually guaranteed to find certain traditional dishes on menus here, such as Guinness and beef pie; champ (creamy, buttery mashed potatoes with scallions); oysters from Strangford Lough; Ardglass herring; mussels from Dundrum; and smoked salmon from Glenarm. A widespread favorite is the Ulster fry, an inexpensive pub plate of bacon, black pudding, mushrooms, sausages, tomatoes, and eggs, served with potato or soda bread—one of the reasons Northern Ireland has one of the highest rates of heart disease in the world. The delights of ethnic restaurants, including Chinese, Japanese, Indian, Persian, and Thai, are now found in Belfast, and even beyond.

Casual dress is quite acceptable at most establishments, though jeans are usually discouraged. As for the cost of a meal here, by the standards of the Republic or the United States, or even the rest of the United Kingdom, restaurant prices are surprisingly moderate. A service charge of 10% may be indicated on the bill; it is customary to pay this, unless the service was bad. For price ranges, ☞ Chart 1(B) *in* Smart Travel Tips A to Z.

Festivals

Festivals, marches, and other excuses to gather fill the calendar in Ulster—certainly as much as in the South, and possibly more so than. Every village in Nationalist areas has its own annual celebration; such *fleadhs* (festivals, pronounced flahs) are especially common in June and July. If you're interested in the Troubles, you may want to see the often-controversial Orangemen's (Unionist) March on July 12 and the Ancient Order of Hibernians (Nationalist) marches of August 15, but be aware that in recent years some Orange marches have led to ugly confrontations as they've traversed Nationalist/Republican areas. The **Belfast Folk Festival** in September is a weekend of traditional Irish music and dance at downtown locations. The **Belfast Festival at Queen's University,** which lasts three weeks each November, is the North's cultural high point of the year. Its heady mix of drama, music, dance, and film is centered on the Queen's University campus—the most pleasant area of town. ☞ The Arts, *below,* for more detailed information about these and other festivals.

Lodging

Since the advent of the 1994 cease-fire, major hotel chains both in the Republic and abroad have been investing in the North. Low-cost guest houses (often family-run), offering bed and breakfast, are probably the best way to meet locals; most B&Bs provide an evening meal as well, if needed. In Belfast's environs visitors can choose from the humblest terraced town houses or farm cottages to the grandest country houses. Dining rooms of country-house lodgings frequently reach the standard of top-quality restaurants. All accommodations in the province are inspected and categorized by the Northern Ireland Tourist Board, which publishes all names, addresses, and ratings in the handbook *Where to Stay* (£4.99). For price ranges, see Chart 1(B) *in* Smart Travel Tips A to Z.

Outdoor Activities and Sports

BICYCLING

Roads are good and fairly traffic-free, so cycling is popular. Once in the countryside you will often have the run of long, winding roads. There's no need to have a bike of your own—many towns offer places to rent them.

BIRD-WATCHING

The province has an unexpectedly wide range of habitats and bird species for such a tiny area. The best time to come is winter, but even in summer visitors can participate in first-class bird-watching, especially on the Antrim uplands, all down the Antrim coast, and on the nearby islands.

FISHING

With a 606-km (466-mi) coastline, part on the Atlantic and part on the Irish Sea, as well as major lakes and an abundance of unpolluted rivers, the North is a great place for anglers. Set your rod for salmon on the Bann, Bush, and Foyle rivers and for brown trout in their tributaries. There are bigger lake trout in Loughs Neagh, Melvin, and Erne, while pike and other coarse (white) fish abound in the Erne. Turbot and plaice are taken off the north coast, where sea bass may be caught from the shore. For specific information on fishing, ☞ Fishing *in* Contacts and Resources *in* Northern Ireland A to Z, *below.*

HIKING AND WALKING

Northern Ireland is magnificent walking country. Ask at tourist offices for details of their local walking and cycling trails, 14 of which spring off the **Ulster Way,** an 896-km (560-mi) trek for serious hikers that runs around the six counties and links up with marked trails on the other side of the border. The terrain never demands more than a pair of sturdy walking shoes, and you don't have to walk the whole trail. Many cities and towns have their own historic trails; for further information, ☞ Hiking and Walking *in* Contacts and Resources *in* Northern Ireland A to Z, *below.*

HORSEBACK RIDING/PONY TREKKING

Sitting on the back of a horse or pony is a great way to travel into places that are out of bounds to motorists. Woodland, beaches, and rough country become accessible on guided rides, some suitable for complete beginners. There are some 35 riding and trekking centers around the province, and several of them offer accommodations (☞ Contacts and Resources *in* Northern Ireland A to Z, *below*).

SPECTATOR SPORTS

As on the rest of the island, people in Ulster take their sport seriously, particularly Saturday's **soccer** and **rugby** and Sunday's **hurling** and **Gaelic football** events. Dates of local matches are listed in local newspapers. **Greyhound racing** has roots deep in the Celtic psyche. During the summer, you'll come across the very English sport of **cricket** being played throughout the province. There are two **horse racing** tracks—the one at Downpatrick is particularly atmospheric. One oddity is the ancient precursor of bowls, called **bullets,** which is still played in County Armagh. It involves throwing bowls (originally they were cannonballs, hence the name) along a narrow, winding country lane; the first to cover 3 km (2 mi) is the winner. The All-Ireland Championship for this sport is held in early August in Armagh. Tourist offices carry details of local and province-wide events.

Shopping

The best of the North's traditional products, many made according to time-honored methods, include the exquisite linen and superior handmade woolen garments that you might associate only with the Republic of Ireland. Handmade lacework also remains a handicraft from the countrywomen of some Northern Ireland districts. Visitors should keep an eye out for hand-cut crystal from County Tyrone and for the mellow, cream-color parian china of Belleek. Traditional music CDs and the unadorned blackthorn walking stick are two good choices at the other end of the price scale.

Exploring Northern Ireland

With as fine a setting as you'll find anywhere in Britain, the city of Belfast is Northern Ireland's main gateway. A naturally lively, friendly city, Belfast has plenty of distinguished hotels and restaurants, fascinating museums, Victorian architecture and—proof of the city's strong maritime connections—the shipyards that once built the ill-fated *Titanic,* which still contain the world's largest dry dock. It is testimony to the spirit of Belfast that the long years of sectarian violence have not dimmed its vivacity. Northern Ireland's second city, Derry, is also looking to the future and has an appealing personality all its own—beautiful rows of Georgian houses are being restored, and new museums, tourist attractions, and craft shops are opening apace in the small city center, which is still enclosed by its medieval walls and one of Europe's best-preserved examples of a fortified town.

Along the shores of the North's coasts and lakes, green, gentle slopes descend majestically into hazy, dark-blue water against a background of more slopes, more water, and huge, cloud-scattered skies. The Antrim Coast is among the most scenic in all of Ireland, while Dunluce Castle, the Giant's Causeway, and the small towns along the east coast give the traveler a choice of sites along the excellent roads. Enniskillen, in County Fermanagh, is bright and bustling, and the surrounding Lough Erne has magnificent lake views, as well as one of Ireland's most impressive round towers, on Devenish Island. On the other side of Enniskillen stand Castle Coole and Florence Court, two of the most graceful mansions of the 18th-century Anglo-Irish nobility.

Numbers in the text correspond to numbers in the margin and on the Northern Ireland and Belfast maps.

Great Itineraries

IF YOU HAVE 2 DAYS

The first day leave the bustling Victorian industrial metropolis of **Belfast** ①–⑪, the starting and ending point of your itinerary, and head north to the remarkable natural formations of the **Giant's Causeway** ⑰ and the teetering cliff-top remains of **Dunluce Castle** ⑱ via the breathtaking **Glens of Antrim** ⑮, ending the day in the dramatically rejuvenated city of 🖼 **Derry** ㉒–㉚. The next day head south to the tranquil beauty of **Lough Erne** with visits to the ancient monastic site of **Devenish Island** ㉞, the historic town of **Enniskillen** ㉟, and the exquisite neoclassic beauty of **Castle Coole** ㊱. Finish your second day back in 🖼 **Belfast.**

IF YOU HAVE 4 DAYS

Leave **Belfast** ①–⑪ and head north to the **Glens of Antrim** ⑮ with a look at the characteristic twin towns of rugged **Cushendall** and pretty **Cushendun** before heading for the **Giant's Causeway** ⑰ and **Dunluce Castle** ⑱. Then follow the coast road via Downhill as far as 🖼 **Derry** ㉒–㉚, where you'll spend the night. The following day head south for **Belleek** ㉜, home of the famous pottery, via the emotive **Ulster-American Folk Park** and the reconstructed dwellings of the **Ulster History Park** ㉛; don't miss the holy islands of **White** ㉝ and **Devenish** ㉞. Spend the night in or around the historic town of 🖼 **Enniskillen** ㉟. The next day follow the road to leafy **Armagh** ㊲, Ireland's ecclesiastical capital, and **Navan Centre,** on the site of the legendary fort of the Red Branch Knights. Continue to the magnificent **Mountains of Mourne** ㊳ via Bessbrook, a pretty Quaker model village that also happens to be home to the busiest military helicopter base in Europe. Pass through Newry and Kilkeel, finishing the day in 🏨 **Portaferry.** The last day make your way to Belfast along the shores of Strangford Lough to the fairy-tale gardens of **Mount Stewart** ㊵ and the brilliantly designed **Ulster Folk and Transport Museum** ⑬. Return to Belfast.

When to Tour Northern Ireland

The best time to visit the area is from May to September, when the weather is a little friendlier to travelers, especially in coastal and lake areas. Apart from holiday weekends there should be no trouble getting accommodation anywhere outside Belfast. If heading for Belfast, book in advance. Most of the city's cultural events—except early August's lively West Belfast Festival—take place in the autumn.

BELFAST

➊ *167 km (104) mi north of Dublin.*

Belfast was a great Victorian success story, an industrial boomtown whose prosperity was built on trade—especially linen and shipbuilding (the *Titanic* was built here). The key word here, of course, is *was*—linen is no longer a major industry, and shipbuilding has severely suffered. For the last two decades, news about Belfast was news about the Troubles—until the 1994 cease-fire. Since then, the North's capital city has benefited from major hotel investment, gentrified quaysides, a heralded performing arts center, and heartfelt efforts on the part of the tourist board to claim for the North its share of the visitors pouring into the Euro-buzzing Emerald Isle. On July 20, 1997, the cease-fire was officially reestablished, and this embattled city began its quest for a newfound identity. This is a fascinating place in the throes of a major historical transition, a city with some of the warmest, wryest people in all of Ireland; a fair amount of new construction; and, most of all, a palpable will to move forward.

Before English and Scottish settlers arrived in the 1600s, Belfast was a tiny village called Béal Feirste (Sandbank Ford) belonging to Ulster's ancient O'Neill clan. With the advent of the Plantation period, Sir Arthur Chichester, from Devon in southwest England, received the city, and his son was made Earl of Donegall. Protestant French Huguenots fleeing persecution settled near here, bringing their valuable linen work skills. In the 18th century, Belfast saw a phenomenal expansion: Its population doubled in size every 10 years, despite an ever-present sectarian divide. Although the Anglican gentry despised the Presbyterian artisans—who, in turn, distrusted native Catholics—Belfast's growth continued at a dizzying speed. In 1849, Queen Victoria paid a visit (she is recalled in the names of buildings, streets, bars, monuments, and other places around the city), and in the same year, the university opened and took the name Queen's College. Nearly 40 years later, in 1888, Victoria granted Belfast its city charter. Today its population is 300,000—one-quarter of all Northern Ireland's citizens.

Exploring Belfast

Belfast is a fairly compact city, its center made up of roughly three contiguous areas that are easy to navigate on foot, though from the south end to the north it's about an hour's leisurely walk. At Belfast's southern end, the **Queen's University area** is easily the most appealing part

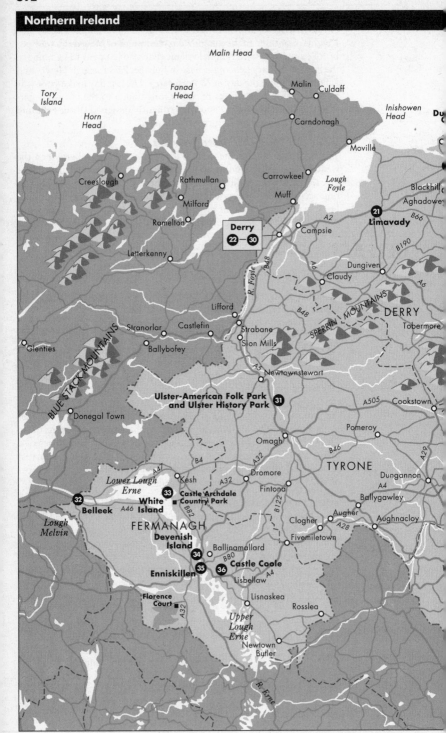

Tory Island

Horn Head

Fanad Head

Malin Head

Malin

Culdaff

Carndonagh

Inishowen Head

Du

Moville

Creeslough

Rathmullan

Milford

Carrowkeel

Lough Foyle

Blackhill

Aghadowe

Ramelton

Muff

Derry

22 — 30

Campsie

A2

Limavady

21

B66

Letterkenny

B48

R. Foyle

A6

Dungiven

B190

Claudy

Lifford

B48

Castlefin

Strabane

Sion Mills

SPERRIN MOUNTAINS

DERRY

Tobermore

Stranorlar

Glenties

BLUE STACK MOUNTAINS

Ballybofey

A5

Newtownstewart

Ulster-American Folk Park and Ulster History Park

31

A505

Cookstown

Donegal Town

Omagh

Pomeroy

B46

TYRONE

A29

Dungannon

A4

Ballygawley

Aughnacloy

A47

Lower Lough Erne

Kesh

B4

A32

Dromore

Fintona

B122

Clogher

Augher

A28

Fivemiletown

32

Belleek

A46

White Island

33

Castle Archdale Country Park

B82

FERMANAGH

Lough Melvin

Devenish Island

34

Ballinamallard

B80

Castle Coole

35

36

Enniskillen

Lisbellaw

A4

Florence Court

A32

Lisnaskea

Rosslea

Upper Lough Erne

Newtown Butler

R. Erne

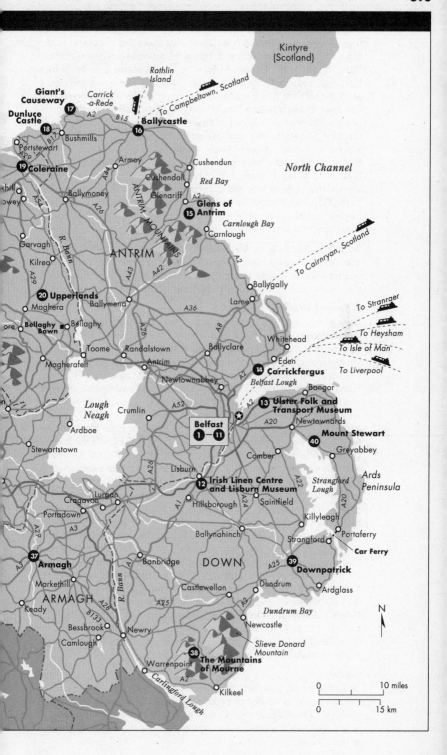

of the city. Within are the university, Botanic Gardens, charming B&Bs, and entire streets of fine, intact 19th-century, two- and three-story buildings. The many pubs and restaurants also make this the center of the city's nightlife. At the north end, between University Street and Shaftesbury Square, is the **Golden Mile,** with hotels, major civic and office buildings, and some restaurants, cafés, and stores. The area doesn't quite glow the way the name suggests, but even if you don't end up staying here, you're likely to pass through it often. City Hall marks the northern boundary of the Golden Mile and the southern end of the (theoretically) pedestrian-only **central district,** which extends from Donegall Square north almost to St. Anne's Cathedral. This is the old heart of Belfast, and it's still a bustling, frenetic place—the equivalent of Dublin's Grafton and Henry streets in one—where both locals *and* visitors shop. Cafés, pubs, offices, and stores of all kinds, from department stores to the Gap and Waterstone's (there's even a Disney store), occupy the historic redbrick and white-Portland-stone buildings and modern architecture that line its narrow streets.

Behind St. Anne's is the **Cathedral Quarter,** a maze of cobbled streets that the city fathers plan to transform over the next few years into a combination of Temple Bar in Dublin and the Left Bank in Paris. Walk there now, and see for yourself the transformation taking place.

A Good Walk

Begin your stroll at the centrally located **Europa Hotel** ② and the **Grand Opera House** ③ next door. Even if you're just starting out, at least poke your head in the glorious **Crown Liquor Saloon** ④, a restored Victorian gin palace across the street from the Europa. Turn right from the Crown along Great Victoria Street and then right again onto Howard Street to reach Belfast's Donegall Square, dominated by its columned and domed **City Hall** ⑤. The gray building on Donegall Square's northwest corner is the **Linenhall Library.** To the right of the library, on the corner of Wellington Place and Queen Street, is the main **Northern Ireland Tourist Board Information Centre** ⑦, and to the left is the start of Donegall Place, Belfast's main shopping street. Stroll up to Royal Avenue; then turn right onto Donegall Street to see **St. Anne's Cathedral** ⑥. Walk east down **High Street** to busy Victoria Street. From here, as you walk toward the leaning **Albert Memorial Clock Tower** ⑧, you'll see parts of Belfast's historic shipyards and two of the world's largest cranes in the Harland and Wolff shipyard, which built the *Titanic.* Return west to the city center by busy Chichester Street; the new Waterfront Hall [☞ Nightlife and the Arts, *below*] is on the river at the end of this street, one block east of Victoria Street. If you're ready for more walking, head south one block to May Street; you'll pass behind City Hall just before coming to Bedford Street, which turns into Dublin Road—together they constitute the eastern flank of the **Golden Mile.** Continue on to **Queen's University** ⑨, the **Botanic Gardens** ⑩, and the **Ulster Museum** ⑪, these last three in the **Stranmillis** area of the city. If you don't want to walk, head to Donegall Square East, where you can catch a black taxi or the Stranmillis or Malone bus.

TIMING

Belfast, a small, compact city, is suitable for walking tours. Much of the city center is limited to pedestrians, and, therefore, traffic isn't a problem. The walking tour above could be completed in a couple of hours, but you'll want to leave yourself a little more time to browse at your leisure.

Sights to See

❽ **Albert Memorial Clock Tower.** Tilting a little to one side, not unlike Pisa's more notorious leaning landmark, the clock tower was named for

Queen Victoria's husband, Prince Albert. The shipyard cranes beyond—Samson and Goliath—are two of the world's largest. The tower is not open to the public. ⊠ *Victoria Sq.*

★ ⑩ **Botanic Gardens.** Laid out in 1827 on land that slopes down to the River Lagan, tucked between **Queen's University** (☞ *below*) and the **Ulster Museum** (☞ *below*), these gardens are a glorious haven of grass, trees, flowers, curving walks, and wrought-iron benches where it was not unusual, in their Victorian heyday, to find 10,000 of Belfast's citizens strolling on a Saturday afternoon. Begun in 1839 and completed in 1852, the **Palm House,** constructed of curved iron and glass, is the oldest curvilinear greenhouse in the world—a technical marvel designed by Charles Lanyon in 1839. The **Tropical Ravine House,** though not architecturally distinguished, has an outstanding collection of tropical flora. If you stay in the university area, this is easily the nicest place in Belfast for an early morning stroll or jog—and if it's cold and rainy you can always take shelter in the steamy jungles of the Tropical Ravine. A wander around the free museum takes in such exhibits as the Egyptian mummy Takabuti and the magnificent Girona collection of gold jewelry from three Spanish galleons that sank off the County Antrim coast in 1588. ⊠ *Stranmillis Rd.,* ☎ *028/9032–4902.* ☞ *Free except during concerts.* ⊙ *Gardens daily dawn–dusk; Palm House and Tropical Ravine House weekdays 10–5, weekends 1–5.*

★ ⑤ **City Hall.** Built between 1898 and 1906, the massive, exuberant Renaissance Revival City Hall dominates Donegall Square. Modeled on St. Paul's Cathedral in London, it was designed by Brumwell Thomas, who was knighted but had to sue to get his fee. Before you enter, take a stroll around Donegall Square, where you'll find statues of Queen Victoria; a monument commemorating the *Titanic* (built in Belfast); and a column honoring the U.S. Expeditionary Force, which landed in the city on January 26, 1942—the first contingent of the U.S. Army to land in Europe. When U.S. president Bill Clinton visited in November 1995, a huge reception was held on the green front lawn; it included a performance by hometown boy Van Morrison, whose "Days Like This" had become an unofficial anthem of the 1994 cease-fire. Head inside under the porte cochere at the front of the building. From the entrance hall (the base of which is a **whispering gallery**), the view up to the heights of the 173-ft **Great Dome** is a feast for the eyes. With its complicated series of arches and openings, stained-glass windows, Italian marble inlays, decorative plasterwork, and paintings, this is Belfast's most ornate public space—homage to the might of the British empire. The guided tour gives access to the Council Chamber, Great Hall, and Reception Room, all upstairs. ⊠ *Donegall Sq.,* ☎ *028/ 9032–0202.* ☞ *Free.* ⊙ *Mon.–Sat. 9–5; guided tours June–Sept., weekdays at 10:30, 11:30, and 2:30; Oct.–May, weekdays at 2:30.*

★ ④ **Crown Liquor Saloon.** Opposite the Europa Hotel on Great Victoria Street and now owned by the National Trust (the U.K.'s official conservation organization), the Crown is one of Belfast's glories: a late-19th-century pub with richly carved woodwork around cozy snugs (cubicles), leather seats, colored tile work, and abundant mirrors. It's all been kept immaculate, is still lit by gas, and is the perfect setting for a pint of Guinness and a plate of oysters. When you settle in your snug, note the little gunmetal plates used by the Victorians for lighting their matches. ⊠ *46 Great Victoria St.,* ☎ *028/9024–9476.* ⊙ *Daily 11:30 AM–midnight.*

② **Europa Hotel.** A landmark in Belfast, the Europa (☞ Lodging, *below*) is a monument to the resilience of the city in the face of the Troubles. The most bombed hotel in western Europe, it has been targeted 11 times

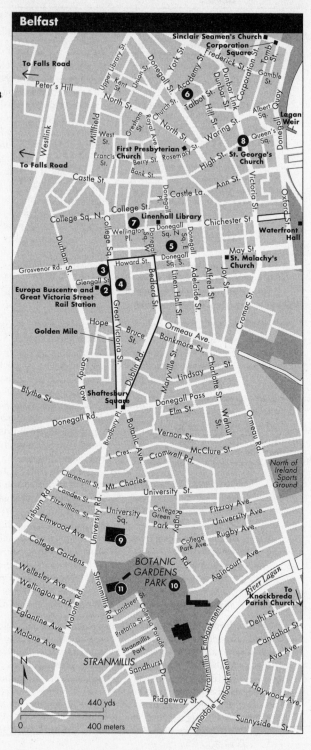

by the IRA since the early '70s and refurbished every time. Today, owned by affable Ulster millionaire hotel magnate Billy Hastings, it shows no signs of its explosive history. ⊠ *Great Victoria St. at Glengall St.*

Golden Mile. The **Europa** (☞ *above*) and the **Crown** (☞ *above*) mark the northern end of this arrowhead-shape area extending from Howard Street on the north to Shaftesbury Square at the southern tip, bordered on the west by Great Victoria Street and on the east by Bedford Street and Dublin Road. The Crown is far from being the only impressive old pub on this stretch—most of Belfast's evening life takes place in bars and restaurants here. Alternatives include a number of nearby replicated Victorian bars with more locals and fewer visitors, such as **Robinson's,** two doors from the Crown; the **Beaten Docket** on the other side of the Crown; the **Spinner's,** behind the Crown; and **Morrison's,** a haunt of media types on nearby Bedford Street.

★ ❸ **Grand Opera House.** Designed in 1894 by the famous theater architect Frank Matcham, this reveals the Victorian age's fascination with the East. Beautifully restored in the '70s, the Grand Opera House (☞ Nightlife and the Arts, *below*). is worth a visit, even if you don't go to a show, for a chance to admire the opulence of the gilt moldings, ornamental plasterwork, and exquisite ceiling fresco by contemporary Irish artist Cherith McKinstry. It was the site of Van Morrison's 1984 album *Live at the Grand Opera House, Belfast.* By far the best way to see and enjoy the place is to attend a show; musicals, operas, and conventional theater all share billing. ⊠ *Great Victoria St.,* ☎ *028/9024–1919.*

★ **High Street.** Off High Street, especially down to Ann Street (parallel to the south), run narrow lanes and alleyways called entries. Though mostly cleaned up and turned into chic shopping lanes, they still hang on to something of their former raffish character, including distinctive pubs with little-altered Victorian interiors. Among the most notable are the following: the **Morning Star** (⊠ Pottinger's Entry off High St.), with its large windows and fine curving bar; **White's Tavern** (⊠ Winecellar Entry off High St.), Belfast's oldest pub, founded in 1630, which, although considerably updated, still has a warm and comfortable ambience, with plush seats and a big, open fire; **Magennis's Whiskey Café** (⊠ 84 May St.), in splendid counterpoint to the Waterfront Hall's space-age ambience; and **McHugh's** (⊠ Queen's Sq.), in what is reckoned to be the city's oldest extant building, dating from 1710.

Linenhall Library. This gray building on Donegall Square's northwest corner is in fact a comfortable private library, founded in 1788 and designed by Charles Lanyon. The library, significantly expanded in 1998, has an unparalleled collection of 80,000 documents relating to the Troubles; it is also a perfect hideaway for relaxing with a newspaper. An early librarian, Thomas Russell, was hanged in 1803 for supporting an Irish uprising. On the walls are paintings and prints that show Belfast views and landmarks—much of this artwork is for sale and makes excellent and original souvenirs or gifts. ⊠ *17 Donegall Sq. N,* ☎ *028/9032–1707.* ▦ *Free.* ⊙ *Weekdays 9:30–5.30, Sat. 9:30–4.*

❼ **Northern Ireland Tourist Board Information Centre.** Recently relocated into new quarters, this is the main point for picking up maps and details for travel in Northern Ireland. The new office, in Donegall Square beside City Hall, incorporates the plush, comprehensive Belfast Welcome Centre. ⊠ *Wellington Place/Queen St.,* ☎ *028/9024–6609,* 𝗙𝗔𝗫 *028/9031–2424.* ⊙ *Sept.–June, Mon. 9:30–5:15, Tues.–Sat. 9–5:15; July–Aug., Mon. 9:30–7, Tues.–Sat. 9–7, Sun. noon–4.*

NEED A
BREAK?
At the start of Royal Avenue, turn left into Bank Street to find **Kelly's Cellars** (✉ 30 Bank St., ☎ 028/9032–4835), a traditional bar with character. Specialties include Ulster fry as well as champ (potatoes mashed with butter and spring onions) and sausages. Two centuries ago, Kelly's Cellars was the regular meeting place of a militant Nationalist group, the Society of United Irishmen, whose leader, Wolfe Tone (who was a Protestant), is remembered as the founder of Irish Republicanism.

⑨ Queen's University. Dominating University Road is Queen's University itself. The main university buildings, modeled on Oxford's Magdalen College and designed by the ubiquitous Charles Lanyon, were constructed in 1849 in a Tudor Revival style. The long, handsome red-brick-and-sandstone facade of the main building has large leaded windows, with three square towers and crenellations galore. **University Square,** really a terrace, is another treasure from the same era. There is a new Seamus Heaney library, named after the Ulster-born 1997 Nobel prize-winning poet. ✉ *University Rd.,* ☎ *028/9033–5252.* ☉ *May–Sept., Mon.–Sat. 10–4; Oct.–Apr., weekdays 10–4.*

⑥ St. Anne's Cathedral. A somber heaviness and deep, rounded arches are the hallmarks of the Irish neo-Romanesque style, and both elements dominate this large edifice, which is basilican in plan and was built at the turn of the 20th century. Lord Carson (1854–1935), who was largely responsible for keeping the six counties inside the United Kingdom, is buried here beneath a suitably austere gray slab. New landscaping around the cathedral is one indication of the improving fortunes of this area. ✉ *Donegall St.,* ☎ *028/9032–8332.* 🎫 *Free.* ☉ *Weekdays 9:15–4:45, Sat. 9:15–4*

Stranmillis. Once its own village, now the off-campus quarter, Stranmillis is one of Belfast's more appealing neighborhoods, filled with tree-lined residential streets on which you'll see scurrying academics and find a wide choice of ethnic eateries. Reached via Stranmillis Road (near the **Ulster Museum** [☞ *below*]), the neighborhood is home to "Little Paris," a stretch of shops and cafés. The community reaches down to the riverside towpath along the Lagan. **Malone Road** joins the river farther south, close to the out-of-town **Giant's Ring** (off Ballyleeson Road), a large, neolithic earthworks focused on an impressive dolmen. To get this far, unless you're a vigorous walker (it's possible to come all the way on the Lagan towpath), you'll be happier driving in a car or taking a bus: Ulsterbus 13 passes close to the site, and on the return journey it will take you back to Donegall Square.

★ **⑪ Ulster Museum.** In the southwest corner of the **Botanic Gardens** (☞ *above*), the museum has three floors devoted to the history and prehistory of Ireland and, in particular, Northern Ireland, together with a considerable collection of 19th- and 20th-century fine art. A skeleton of the now-extinct Irish giant deer is a highlight of the natural history section. Other major holdings are the trove of jewelry and gold ornaments—as well as a cannon and other armaments—recovered from the Spanish Armada vessel *Girona* and two sister galleons sunk off the Antrim coast in 1588. Perhaps the most imaginative, user-friendly sections are on the first floor; one colorfully traces the rise of Belfast's crafts, trade, and industry; the other tells the story of the Nationalist movement and explains the separation of the North from the rest of the country. A small café is on level three, and a free guidebook is available at the reception desk. ✉ *Stranmillis Rd.,* ☎ *028/9038–3000.* 🎫 *Free.* ☉ *Weekdays 10–5, Sat. 1–5, Sun. 2–5.*

OFF THE
BEATEN PATH

CHURCHES AROUND THE CITY – Belfast has so many churches you could visit a different one nearly every day of the year and still not make it to all of them. The oldest house of worship is the Church of Ireland **Knockbreda Parish Church** (⊠ Church Rd. off A24 on the south side of city). This dark, sturdy, and atmospheric structure was built in 1737 by Richard Cassels, who designed many of Ireland's finest mansions. It quickly became *the* place to be buried—witness the vast, 18th-century tombs in the churchyard. Closer to the city center, the **First Presbyterian Church** (⊠ Rosemary St.) dates from 1783 and has an interesting elliptical interior. It also hosts lunchtime concerts. The Church of Ireland's **St. George's** (⊠ High St.), built in 1816, has a tremendous Georgian portico and pretty box pews. Roman Catholic **St. Malachy's** (⊠ Alfred St.), built in 1844, features fine stonework, including an astonishing fan-vaulted ceiling. By the riverfront is one of the most appealing churches, Presbyterian **Sinclair Seamen's Church** (⊠ Corporation Sq. off Donegall Quay). It was designed by—guess who—Charles Lanyon, the architect of Queen's University (☞ *above*), and has served the seafaring community since 1857. A maritime theme pervades the building: The pulpit is shaped like a ship's prow; the bell is from HMS *Hood,* sunk in 1916; and even the collection plates are shaped like lifeboats!

Dining

Cooking in Belfast is going through as profound a revolution as in Dublin. The choice of restaurants is more limited, but two or three of the best kitchens are a match for anything else in Ireland. The best chefs—Michael Deane, the Rankins, and Robbie Miller—have worked abroad and have brought back a sophisticated awareness of international cooking styles. Beyond the top-tier places, there are many other spots where you'll find good-quality, fresh local fish or meat prepared in a simple style but without much polish.

$$$–$$$$
★

✕ **Roscoff.** Celebrity TV chefs Paul and Jeanne Rankin, innovative cooks who travel widely, run this Golden Mile spot—consistently acclaimed as one of the best in the six counties and talked about a good deal throughout Ireland. The long, stylish room has a modern, minimalist decor, a bit like the cuisine featured by the Rankins (Paul is from Belfast, Jeanne from the Canadian Prairies). Dishes can be Asian-influenced, such as pork with ginger, spicy fried cod with chili jam and a sesame vinaigrette, char-grilled Moroccan lamb with couscous, or roast monkfish with grilled tomatoes and black beans. The stellar desserts might include crème brûlée with fresh mango puree or snap cigars filled with honey and pine-nut ice cream served with sharp marinated plums. When the Rankins travel, though, the overall standards tend to suffer in their absence. ⊠ *Shaftesbury Sq. at end of Great Victoria St.,* ☎ *028/9033–1532. AE, DC, MC, V. Closed Sun. No lunch Fri.*

$$$

✕ **Deane's.** Chef Michael Deane became celebrated for his accomplished food in a tiny open kitchen in an equally tiny Victorian railroad station a few miles outside Belfast. Early in 1997, he sold out to move to a much larger two-story room—a brasserie downstairs and formal restaurant upstairs—in the center of Belfast, close to City Hall. Deane's tastes are eclectic, though he has worked in Bangkok, and Thai influences particularly shine in his subtle way with spices. Squab is a Deane specialty. He turns locally shot wild squab into a starter served in a light lasagna with celeriac leaves, spinach and foie gras, while for a main dish he dry-marinates a squab with cinnamon sticks for two days, then serves it in an olive oil curried stock, with coriander seed and leaves, apple, ginger, and soy sauce, all on a bed of risotto. The ravioli of lobster is a standout. Deane took a gamble moving to these much bigger premises, and it seems to have worked, if the lunchtime crowds at his tables are anything to go by. ⊠ *38–40 Howard St.,* ☎ *028/9033–1134. AE, MC, V. Closed Sun. and 2 wks in July.*

$$$　✕ **Shanks.** Golf clubhouses don't usually spell welcome to peripatetic
★　　gourmands, but Shanks is decidedly different. Robbie and Shirley Miller's cool temple to the contemporary, designed by London design guru Terence Conran, sits on a vast 3,000-acre estate. The bar is wood and zinc; David Hockney pieces hang on the walls. Like many of Ireland's other best young chefs, Robbie Miller studied under Roscoff's Paul Rankin, and he spares nothing to produce wonderful fish and game dishes. How demanding is he? A scuba diver handpicks large, fresh scallops from the Copeland Islands in the Irish Sea, as they are more tender than scallops dredged by a trawler off the sea bottom. Shanks is about 19 km (12 mi) from Belfast, signposted off the Crawfordsburn Road (turn *right* off the Belfast–Bangor Road, or you can take a train from Belfast to Bangor and then a taxi). ⊠ *Blackwood Golf Centre, Crawfordsburn Rd., Bangor, Co. Down,* ☎ *028/ 9185–3313. Reservations essential. AE, MC, V. Closed 2 wks in July. No lunch Sat.–Mon.*

$–$$$　✕ **Chez Delbart.** Better known among locals by an alternative name— Frogities—this is the third and smallest of the trio of eateries founded by French ex-submariner M. Delbart, who promotes his heritage with the Eiffel Tower motif that adorns the exterior. Open in the evenings only, Frogities packs in a student clientele, particularly on weekends, who come back again and again for staples like the crepes and brochettes. ⊠ *10 Bradbury Pl.,* ☎ *028/9023–8020. AE, DC, MC, V. Closed Sun.–Mon. No lunch.*

$–$$$　✕ **La Belle Époque.** Relaxed and intimate, this well-established restaurant is charmingly French, with art nouveau decor reminiscent of Paris. The menu features smoked salmon stuffed with fish mousse in a horseradish sauce as an appetizer and a main course of fillet of beef with whole grain mustard cream sauce. For dessert you can't go wrong with the freshly made fruit sorbets. The set-price lunch menu is an excellent value. ⊠ *61 Dublin Rd.,* ☎ *028/9032–3244. Reservations essential. AE, DC, MC, V. Closed Sun.*

$$　✕ **Antica Roma.** Cecil B. DeMille's Rome rubs shoulders with Little Italy in this restaurant's astonishing trompe l'oeil murals of the interior of a Roman villa, which justify anyone's first visit. The menu has a surprisingly appealing Celtic interpretation of Italian cuisine. Seafood—especially clams, mussels, and squid— is particularly good. ⊠ *67 Botanic Ave.,* ☎ *028/9031–1121. AE, MC, V. Closed Sun. No lunch Sat.*

$$　✕ **Benedict's** The newest addition to Bradbury Place in the heart of Belfast's Golden Mile (below), this neo-Gothic entertainment complex and hotel includes an upstairs restaurant where chef Jim McLaughlin specializes in seafood and venison with strong Asian and French influences. Dine early if you want to avoid the noise from the crowded bar and disco downstairs—then go down and dance off dessert. ⊠ *7– 21 Bradbury Place,* ☎ *028/9059–1999. AE, MC, V.*

$$　✕ **Café Society.** Though the little tables outside on the sidewalk in the summer may not give Café Society a Parisian air, the second-floor window tables have the best view of bustling Belfast. The food is splendid, too. Seared scallops with fennel and olives as well as grilled buffalo mozzarella are among the distinctive starters. The mixed fish grill of grouper, red snapper, and salmon served with polenta is the delight among the entrées. ⊠ *3 Donegall Sq. W,* ☎ *028/9043–9525. MC, V. Closed Sun. No lunch.*

$–$$　✕ **Nick's Warehouse.** On a narrow, cobbled street near the increasingly fashionable Laganside area, Nick Price's cool, cozy wine bar and adjacent restaurant are among Belfast's most relaxing watering holes.

The busy bar serves warm salads in a range of nut oils, as well as tiny, tasty casseroles. In the slightly more formal restaurant, favorites are duck with red cabbage and apple compote, and halibut with langoustine and sweet peppers. The wine and imported beer lists are impressive. ⊠ *35 Hill St.,* ☎ *028/9043–9690. Reservations essential for restaurant. AE, MC, V. Closed Sun. No dinner Mon.*

$–$$ ✕ **The Strand.** In the University area, this dark and intimate bistro with candlelit tables attracts students and professors with its adventurous, unusual menu. Recommended dishes include Irish lamb noisettes and baked eggplant. For dessert try the cream-laden gâteaux. Vegetarian entrées are available, such as a flan of broccoli and cashews. ⊠ *12 Stranmillis Rd.,* ☎ *028/9068–2266. AE, DC, MC, V.*

$–$$ ✕ **Sun Kee.** This unpretentious little spot has the mark of all truly good Chinese restaurants—the Chinese people who live in the area eat here, tucking into huge portions while watching the large TV in the corner, then rushing upstairs for a quick game of mah-jong. The decor is simple, but the food is terrific. While you can't go wrong with beef in green pepper sauce and *char sui* (marinated and barbecued) pork, this is also a good place to take a risk with dishes such as duck's web or fish-head soup, eel, and roasted pork belly. The helpful staff will even choose for you if you tell them your tastes. ⊠ *38 Donegall Pass,* ☎ *028/ 9031–2016. MC, V. No lunch.*

$ ✕ **Kitchen Bar.** A great spot to mingle with city-center office workers, this place is known for its lunches—Irish stew, the Ulster fry, and host Pat Catney's famous Paddy's Pizza, made on a base of traditional Irish soda bread. Wash everything down with the selection of draft beers (real ale aficionados flock here for its annual beer festival during the first week of October). There's traditional music on Friday nights. ⊠ *16 Victoria Sq.,* ☎ *028/9032–4901. MC, V.*

$ ✕ **Roscoff Café.** If you're looking for the Roscoff (☞ *above*) experience without breaking the bank, this city-center bakery-café has a Parisian feel to it, especially if the weather is fine and you can sit at the tables outside. Try the walnut bread, sun-dried tomato bread, focaccia (for which Roscoff is renowned), and the delicious soups and desserts. ⊠ *21 Fountain St.,* ☎ *028/9031–5090. AE, DC, MC, V. Closed Sun. No dinner Mon.–Wed. and Sat., no lunch Thurs.–Fri.*

Lodging

Airport and Environs

$$$$ 🏨 **Stakis Park Templepatrick.** On 220 acres of wooded parkland with its own 18-hole championship golf course, this modern hotel is 10 minutes from Belfast International Airport and 20 minutes from Belfast city center. Rooms are generously equipped, with satellite TV and full bathroom. The location is particularly good if you're planning a brief visit to the province and don't want to stay in the city. ⊠ *Castle Upton Estate, Templepatrick Co. Antrim BT39 0DD,* ☎ *028/9443–5500,* FAX *028/9443–5511. 129 rooms with bath, 1 suite. Restaurant, bar, indoor pool, sauna, 18-hole golf course, exercise room, meeting rooms. AE, DC, MC, V.*

$$$ 🏨 **Dunadry Inn and Country Club.** Ten minutes from Belfast International Airport, this spacious, whitewashed former mill on 10 acres of land is a hotel of considerable charm. Renovations made use of large wooden components from the old mill's massive linen beetling (polishing) engines in the stairwell and a gallery over the bar. Its bedrooms are large; the best open onto the inner courtyard. The restaurant is a popular spot for local weddings, so you may find yourself in the midst of a real Irish celebration. ⊠ *2 Islandreagh Dr., Dunadry, Co. Antrim BT41 2HA,* ☎ *028/9438–5050,* FAX *028/9438–5055. 83 rooms with* *bath. Restaurant, bar, indoor pool, croquet, exercise room, meeting rooms. AE, MC, V.*

Golden Mile

$$ 🖼 **Jurys Belfast Inn.** The first Jurys north of the border brings the chain's flat-rate pricing formula—one price for up to three adults or two adults and two children—to the Golden Mile. Once you get past the forbidding warehouse-like exterior, a spacious, marble-tiled foyer with warm green and salmon hues awaits. Some rooms overlook College Square, the cricket lawn of the elegant dusky brick Royal Belfast Academical Institution, built in 1814 by Joan Soane. The Arches Restaurant offers well-prepared hotel fare. Tartan fabrics and dark wood decorate the Inn Pub, which serves a lunch-only hot buffet. ⊠ *Fisherwick Pl. BT2 7AP,* ☎ *028/9053–3500,* ℻ *028/9053–3511. 190 rooms with bath. Restaurant, bar, meeting rooms. AE, DC, MC, V.*

Outside the City Center

$$$$ 🖼 **Culloden Hotel.** Eight kilometers (5 mi) from the city center on A2, this 19th-century, former Scottish baronial mansion stands amid 12 acres of parkland. One of only two five-star hotels in Northern Ireland—the other is the Belfast Hilton—it's the flagship in a fleet of hotels run by local hotelier Billy Hastings. Public areas have ornate woodwork, Louis XV chandeliers, decorative plasterwork, and stained glass. Guest rooms, both in the original section and in a newer wing, are decorated with silk-and-velvet fabrics and have fine views. The dining areas include the French Mitre Restaurant, with mahogany tables and a garden view, and the Grill Bar, which serves both snacks and full meals. The hotel is close to the Ulster Folk and Transport Museum (☞ Side Trips, *below*). No-smoking rooms are available. ⊠ *142 Bangor Rd., Holywood, Co. Down BT18 0EX,* ☎ *028/9042–5223,* ℻ *028/9042–6777. 77 rooms with bath, 10 suites. Restaurant, grill, indoor heated pool, sauna, tennis court, croquet, squash, nightclub, laundry services. AE, DC, MC, V.*

$$$$ 🖼 **The McCausland Hotel.** Clean and simple lines, a feeling of space and light, and an aura of sumptuous minimalism are the hallmarks of this pair of 1867 grain warehouses, which have become Belfast's newest luxury hotel, with the original cast-iron pillars and beams retained throughout. Bedrooms are more traditional country-cottage style but entirely comfortable and well equipped. Dining, under the capably inspired hands of chef Eamonn O'Cathain, is in the Marco Polo bar-bistro or the more formal Merchants Restaurant. On the edge of the blossoming Laganside area (*above*), the hotel is a 5-minute walk from the city center and 20 minutes from the start of the Golden Mile (*above*). ⊠ *34-38 Victoria St., Co. Antrim BT1 3GH,* ☎ *028/9022–0200,* ℻ *01232/220220. 60 rooms with bath, 4 suites. Restaurant, brasserie, bar, exercise room, meeting rooms. AE, DC, MC, V. Closed Dec. 25–27.*

$$$ 🖼 **Rayanne House.** This country house and restaurant in leafy Holywood, 10 km (6 mi) from Belfast city center, has won numerous national prizes for its food and hospitality. Rooms are airy, with traditional decor and nice views of the gardens. The menu is Irish with European influences—and the food so delicious that you may have trouble rising from the table to go exploring ⊠ *60 Demesne Rd., Holywood, Co. Down BT18 9EX,* ☎ *028/9042–5859,* ℻ *028/9042–3364. 6 rooms with bath. Dining room. AE, MC, V.*

$ 🖼 **The Cottage.** Aptly named, this lovely little B&B in Mrs. Elizabeth Muldoon's immaculate white home, 8 km (5 mi) east of Belfast, has a charming, flower-filled garden in the back. It's as rural a setting as you're likely to find so close to the city center. The traditional country-house decor combines beautiful antiques and modern comforts in the bedrooms. ✉ *377 Comber Rd., Dundonald BT16 0XB,* ☎ *028/9187–8189. 2 rooms with bath. No credit cards.*

University Area

$$$ 🏨 **Dukes Hotel.** Although this distinguished redbrick Victorian building has only 21 rooms, it has such big-hotel amenities as a spacious lobby, extensive exercise facilities, and a restaurant that leans toward healthful, local cuisine. The color scheme is smart gray, enlivened with plenty of greenery, and a waterfall splashes down parallel to the stairs. The comfortable rooms are well equipped; many have views of the hills beyond the city. ✉ *65–67 University St. BT7 1HL,* ☎ *028/9023–6666,* 🖷 *028/9023–7177. 21 rooms with bath. Restaurant, bar, sauna, exercise room, meeting rooms. AE, DC, MC, V.*

$$$ 🏨 **Wellington Park Hotel.** Formerly a private residence and currently run by the Mooney family, this modernized establishment is among the best in this area of town. The quiet bedrooms are well designed, with built-in wooden furniture; some feature sleeping lofts. Live music and good food are featured at the bar and restaurant. ✉ *21 Malone Rd. BT9 6RU,* ☎ *028/9038–5050,* 🖷 *028/9038–5055. 75 rooms with bath or shower. Restaurant, bar, laundry service, meeting rooms. AE, DC, MC, V.*

$$–$$$ 🏨 **Ash-Rowan Guest House.** Multiple award-winning former restau-
★ rateurs Sam and Evelyn Hazlett own and run this outstanding B&B in a spacious Victorian home on a tranquil residential avenue. Every bedroom has been decorated in a tasteful, individual style, and each has a private bath and TV. Guests have access to a library. Breakfasts and dinners, prepared by the owners, are first-rate; the house is no-smoking. ✉ *12 Windsor Ave. BT9 6EE,* ☎ *028/9066–1758,* 🖷 *028/9066–3227. 5 rooms with bath. Dining room, library. MC, V. Closed Dec.*

$$–$$$ 🏨 **Madison's.** This is one of Belfast's liveliest spots, with a terrific location on tree-, café-, and shop-lined Botanic Avenue, a few minutes' walk from the university. The hotel is run with gracious aplomb by the Mooney family (proprietors of the Dunadry Inn and Wellington Park Hotel [both ☞ *above*]). Its facade and public areas are decorated in a modish Barcelona-inspired take on art nouveau. The bedrooms, in cool yellows and rich blues, are sparely furnished but comfortable. Guests have access to the extensive fitness facilities of Queen's University, including a terrific pool. ✉ *59 Botanic Ave. BT7 1JL,* ☎ *028/ 9033–0040,* 🖷 *028/9032–8007. 35 rooms with bath. Restaurant, bar, business services. AE, MC, V.*

$$ 🏨 **Old Rectory.** Mary and Jerry Callan's well-appointed house, built in 1896 as a rectory, is decorated in pastels and has good views of the countryside. Complimentary whiskey is served by the fire each evening. Rare in Ulster B&Bs, a healthy alternative to the hearty Ulster fry is served at breakfast. ✉ *148 Malone Rd. BT9 5LH,* ☎ *028/9066–7882,* 🖷 *028/9068–3759. 4 rooms with bath. No credit cards.*

Nightlife and the Arts

Nightlife

Belfast has dozens of pubs packed with relics of the Victorian and Edwardian periods. Although pubs typically close around 11:30 PM, many city-center/Golden Mile nightclubs often stay open till 1 AM.

CITY CENTER/DOCKS

Pat's Bar (✉ 19–22 Prince's Dock St., ☎ 028/9074–4524) has regular first-rate sessions of traditional music. **Madden's Bar** (✉ 74 Smithfield St., ☎ 028/9024–4114) is another popular pub with traditional tunes. The **Kitchen Bar** (✉ 16 Victoria Sq., ☎ 028/9032–4901) is a real ale bar with traditional music on Friday nights. Near the Kitchen Bar, **Bittles Bar** (⊠ 70 Upper Church La., ☎ 028/9031–1088), on Victoria Square, has informal music sessions on weekends. The **Rotterdam** (⊠ 54 Pilot St., ☎ 028/9074–6021) features folk, jazz, and blues performers. **McHugh's** (⊠ 29–30 Queen's Sq., ☎ 028/9024–7830), in Belfast's oldest building, dating from 1711, is three floors of bars, restaurants, and live music at weekends. **Kelly's Cellars** (⊠ 30-32 Bank St., ☎ 028/9032–4835), open since 1720, offers blues on Saturday nights.

GOLDEN MILE AREA

Robinsons Bars (⊠ 38 Great Victoria St., ☎ 028/9024–7447), next to Crown Liquor Saloon, is a popular pub that appeals to a young crowd; it has folk music in its Fibber Magee's bar Saturday and rock in its Rock Bottom basement on Wednesday. The **Beaten Docket** (⊠ 48 Great Victoria St., ☎ 028/9024–2986) is a noisier, modern pub that attracts a young crowd; it features up-to-the-minute music. **Limelight** (⊠ 17 Ormeau Ave., ☎ 028/9032–5968) is a disco-nightclub with cabaret on Tuesday, Friday, and Saturday, and music on other nights. **Morrisons** (⊠ 21 Bedford St., ☎ 028/9024–8458) has a music lounge upstairs, where there's a mix of jazz, rock, and discussions for film buffs arranged by local directors in conjunction with the Northern Ireland Film Council; Saturday, it's rock; Sunday, Irish music. At press time, the **Manhattan** (⊠ 23 Bradbury Pl., ☎ 028/9023–3131), a.k.a. the M-Club, was Belfast's hottest place for dedicated clubbers, with TV soap-opera celebrities flown in weekly to mix with the local nighthawks. Next door, **Benedict's** (⊠ 7–21 Bradbury Pl., ☎ 028/9059–1999) is a bar, music venue, disco, 150-seat restaurant and hotel. The **Crescent Town House** (⊠ 13 Lower Crescent, ☎ 028/9032–3349) is a cool, postmodern version of Benedict's (*above*).

UNIVERSITY AREA

The **Empire Music Hall** (⊠ 42 Botanic Ave., ☎ 028/9032–8110), a deconsecrated church, is the city's leading music venue. Stand-up comedy nights are usually on Tuesday. The **Botanic Inn** (⊠ 23–27 Malone Rd., ☎ 028/9066–0460), known as "the Bot" to its student clientele, is a big, popular disco-pub. The **Eglantine Inn** (⊠ 32–40 Malone Rd., ☎ 028/9038–1994), known as "the Egg," faces the Bot across Malone Road. **Lavery's Gin Palace** (⊠ 12 Bradbury Pl., ☎ 028/9032–7159) mixes old-fashioned beer drinking downstairs with dancing upstairs. **Cutter's Wharf** (⊠ 4 Lockview St., ☎ 028/9066–2501), down by the river south of the university, is at its best on summer evenings and at the Sunday jazz brunch.

The Arts

The **Northern Ireland Arts Council** (☎ 028/9038–5200) produces the monthly *Artslink* poster-brochure, which lists what's happening throughout Belfast and the North; it's widely available throughout the city. The **Belfast Festival at Queen's University,** which lasts three weeks each November, is the city's major arts festival. For information, contact the Festival Office (25 College Gardens, BT9, ☎ 028/9066–6321). At press time, the future of the **Belfast Folk Festival,** usually held in September, was uncertain; there is no festival office. For updates, contact the Northern Ireland Arts Council.

ART GALLERIES

Ormeau Baths Gallery. The white, airy spaces of this former municipal bathhouse 1now display the work of major contemporary international and Irish artists. ⊠ *18a Ormeau Ave.,* ☎ *028/9032–1402.* ☺ *Tues.–Sat. 10–6.*

Fenderesky Gallery. Iranian philosopher Jamshid Mirfenderesky's gallery is one of the few in Ireland with a stable of modern Irish artists known throughout Europe. ✉ *Crescent Arts Centre, 2 University Rd.,* ☎ *028/9023–5245.* ⊙ *Tues.–Sat. 11:30–5:30.*

Bell Gallery. Nelson Bell's Victorian home in the leafy university suburbs is a mecca for many of Ireland's more traditional painters. ✉ *13 Adelaide Park, Malone Rd.,* ☎ *028/9066–2998.* ⊙ *Weekdays 9–5 and by appointment.*

FILM

Belfast has several city-center movie theaters that show the major new British and American box-office favorites. **Virgin Cinemas** (✉ Dublin Rd., ☎ 028/9024–3200 for information and 028/9055–5176 for credit-card booking [both 24 hrs]) has 10 screens. **Curzon Cinema** (✉ Ormeau Rd., ☎ 028/9064–1373) has three screens. **Queen's Film Theatre** (✉ University Sq. Mews, off Botanic Ave., ☎ 028/9024–4857), Belfast's main art cinema, shows domestic and foreign movies on its two screens.

MAJOR MULTIPURPOSE VENUES

Grand Opera House. This beautifully restored Victorian playhouse has no company of its own but books shows from all over the British Isles and sometimes farther afield. It puts on a constant stream of West End musicals and plays of widely differing kinds, plus occasional operas and ballets. ✉ *Great Victoria St.,* ☎ *028/9024–9129.* ▣ *U.K.£6–U.K.£30.*

Waterfront Hall. Everyone in Belfast is still singing the praises of this civic structure, which opened in January 1997. From the looks of it, the hall is an odd marriage of *Close Encounters*–modern and Castel Sant'Angelo–antique. It houses both a major 2,235-seat concert hall (used for ballet, symphony, rock, and Irish music) and a 500-seat studio space (for modern dance, jazz, and experimental theater). The river-view Terrace Café restaurant and two bars make it convenient to eat or have a pint before or after your culture fix. ✉ *Lanyon Pl.,* ☎ *028/9033–4400.*

MUSIC

King's Hall. This is the major venue for pop and rock concerts. ✉ *484 Lisburn Rd.,* ☎ *028/9066–5225.*

Ulster Hall. Home to the Ulster Orchestra, the hall has a splendid Victorian organ. Rock concerts are occasionally scheduled here. Led Zeppelin fans, take note: The world stage debut of "Stairway to Heaven" took place here in March 1971. ✉ *Linenhall St.,* ☎ *028/9032–3900.*

OPERA AND THEATER

Belfast Civic Arts Theatre. Near the university area, this venue specializes in comedies and other lightweight productions. ✉ *41 Botanic Ave.,* ☎ *028/9031–6900.*

Crescent Arts Centre. "The Crescent" to its habitués, this huge, rambling black stone building off the campus end of Bradbury Place is a focus for experimental theater and dance, provocative art in its Fenderesky Gallery (☞ *above*), and experimental jazz. ✉ *2–4 University Rd.,* ☎ *028/9024–2338.*

Lyric Theatre. In the south of Belfast, the Lyric stages thoughtful drama inspired by traditional and contemporary Irish culture. ✉ *Ridgeway St.,* ☎ *028/9038–1081.* ▣ *U.K.£5.50–U.K.£11; call to confirm prices.*

Old Museum Arts Centre (OMAC). A powerhouse of challenging, avant-garde theater and modern dance, OMAC also has a risk-taking art gallery. ✉ *7 College Sq. N,* ☎ *028/9023–5053.*

Opera Northern Ireland. Humperdinck's *Hansel and Gretel,* Britten's *A Midsummer Night's Dream,* Leoncavallo's *Pagliacci,* and Puccini's *Gianni Schicchi* were scheduled in past years; performances are at the Grand Opera House (☞ *above*). ☎ *028/9032–2338.*

Shopping

Belfast's main shopping streets include **Donegall Place, High Street, Royal Avenue,** and several of the smaller streets connecting them. The whole area is mostly traffic-free (except for buses and delivery vehicles), so you'll find it pleasant to wander and window-shop. **Hoggs** (✉ 10 Donegall Sq. W, ☎ 028/9024–2232) stocks a good selection of linen, Tyrone crystal, Belleek china, and miniatures. **Castle Court** (✉ 10 Royal Ave., ☎ 028/9023–4591) is the city's largest, most varied upscale shopping mall. Opposite Castle Court, **Smyth's Irish Linens** (✉ 65 Royal Ave., ☎ 028/9024–2232) carries a large selection of handkerchiefs, tablecloths, napkins, and other linen goods, which make excellent souvenirs or presents. **Craftworks** (✉ Bedford House, 16–22 Bedford St., ☎ 028/9024–4465) stocks inexpensive crafts by local designers. The **Steensons** (✉ Bedford House, Bedford St., ☎ 028/9024–8268) sell superb, locally designed jewelry. **Smyth and Gibson** (✉ Bedford House, Bedford St., ☎ 028/9023–0388) makes and sells beautiful, luxurious linen and cotton shirts and accessories. If you've an interest in bric-a-brac, visit the renovated **St. George's Market,** a flea market on May Street, every Tuesday and Friday morning. The long thoroughfare of **Donegall Pass,** running from Shaftesbury Square at the point of the Golden Mile east to Ormeau Road, is a unique mix of biker shops and antiques arcades, and a good place to stroll.

Side Trips

The two sights below are closer to Belfast than others covered in this chapter. However, none of the sites along the Ards Peninsula and the north coast are more than a few hours' drive from Belfast—perfect for day trips.

Irish Linen Centre and Lisburn Museum

In the 18th, 19th, and early 20th centuries, linen, a natural fabric woven from the fibers of the flax plant, was the basis of Ulster's most important industry—and thus of much of its folk history and song. A century ago, 240,000 acres were given over to flax, whose pretty blue flowers sparkle for just a week in early July, and 400 acres were designated as "bleach greens," where the woven fabric whitened in the summer sun. Eventually, American cotton and Egyptian flax killed off the mass-production linen trade, which had been centered on Lisburn, in mills powered by the River Lagan. What now survives of the linen industry does so by producing high-quality designer fabrics, plus traditional expensive damask.

⓬ Today at the **Irish Linen Centre and Lisburn Museum** (✉ 12 km/8 mi southwest of Belfast), a series of rooms traces this history. Weaving is demonstrated on a turn-of-the-century hand loom (although the attached shop has a disappointing choice of linen goods). If you're looking for a more intensive investigation of the linen industry, tours of the **Linen Homelands** are offered. The six-hour bus tour (with a break for lunch) visits three different sites: the Irish Linen Centre; a modern, operational linen spinning and weaving factory; and the last working water-powered scutching mill (where flax fibers are broken down) in Ireland. In July you may catch the splendid sight of just a few fields of lilac-blue flax flowers bending in the light summer breeze. Tours are given May–September, Wednesday 10–4 (the cost is U.K.£9, lunch extra; no tours July 5, 12, 19), and begin at the Banbridge Gateway Tourist Information Centre (✉ 200 Newry Rd., Banbridge, ☎ 028/4062–3322). Reservations are essential for this more intensive tour. ✉ *Market Sq., Lisburn,* ☎ *028/9266–3377.* ◪ *Free.* ⊙ *Mon.–Sat. 9:30–5.*

Ulster Folk and Transport Museum

⑬ Devoted to the province's social history, the excellent Ulster Folk and Transport Museum is 16 km (10 mi) northeast of Belfast, set in some 70 acres around Cultra Manor, encircled by a larger park and recreation area. It vividly brings the North's past to life with a score of reconstructed buildings transported here from around the region; these structures represent different facets of northern life—a traditional weaver's dwelling, terraces of Victorian town houses, an 18th-century country church, a village flax mill, a farmhouse, and a rural school. Inside you'll usually find a cheery fire and an appropriately dressed attendant who will explain what it was like actually to live in them. You start your visit with the **Folk Gallery,** which explains the background of each building. Across the main road (by footbridge) is the beautifully designed **Transport Museum,** where exhibits include locally built airplanes and motorcycles; the iconoclastic car produced by former General Motors whiz kid John De Lorean in his Belfast factory in 1982; and a moving section on the *Titanic,* the Belfast-built luxury liner that sank on her first voyage, in 1912, killing 1,500 of the passengers and crew. A miniature railway runs on Saturday in summer. ⊠ *Cultra, near Holywood,* ☎ *028/9042–8428.* ⌑ *U.K.£4.* ☉ *Apr.–June and Sept., weekdays 9:30–5, Sat. 10:30–6, Sun. noon–6; July–Aug., Mon.–Sat. 10:30–6, Sun. noon–6; Oct.–Mar., weekdays 9:30–4, weekends 12:30–4:30.*

AROUND COUNTIES ANTRIM AND DERRY

Starting and finishing in Belfast, you can take a circular route through a portion of the North that allows you to pass through some fair-size towns, as well as drive in open country through splendid natural scenery. From medieval towns such as Carrickfergus, you'll travel past the natural wonder of the Giant's Causeway and the man-made brilliance of the castle at Dunluce before arriving in the old walled city of Derry.

Carrickfergus

⑭ *16 km (10 mi) northeast of Belfast, 24 km (15 mi) south of Larne.*

Carrickfergus, on the shore of Belfast Lough, grew up around its ancient castle. When the town was enclosed by ramparts at the start of the 17th century, it was the only English-speaking town in Northern Ireland. Not surprisingly, this was the loyal port where William of Orange chose to land on his way to fight the Catholic forces at the Battle of the Boyne in 1690. However, the English did have one or two small setbacks, including the improbable victory in 1778 of John Paul Jones, the American naval hero, over the British warship HMS *Drake.* (This, by the way, was America's first naval victory during the Revolutionary War.) After the sea battle, the inhabitants of Carrickfergus stood on the waterfront and cheered Jones because they supported the American Revolution.

Carrickfergus Castle, one of the first and one of the largest of Irish castles, is still in good shape. An impressive sight, perched on a rock ledge, it was built in 1180 by John de Courcy, provincial Ulster's first Anglo-Norman invader. Apart from being captured briefly by the French in 1760, the castle stood as a bastion of British rule right up until 1928, at which time it still functioned as an English garrison.

Walk through the castle's 13th-century gatehouse into the Outer Ward. Continue into the Inner Ward, the heart of the fortress, where the five-story keep stands, a massive, sturdy building with walls almost 8 ft thick. Inside the keep, you'll find the **Cavalry Regimental Museum** with historic weapons and an impressive, vaulted Great Hall. These days Carrickfergus Castle hosts entertaining medieval banquets (inquire at Carrickfergus tourist information office, ☎ 028/9336–6455, or the Northern Ireland Tourist Board, ☎ 028/9024–6609); if you're here at the beginning of August, you can enjoy the annual Lughnasa festival, a lively medieval costume entertainment. ☎ 028/9335–1273. ◻ U.K.£3. ☉ Apr.–Sept., Mon.–Sat. 10–6; Oct.–Mar., Mon.–Sat. 10–4.

The **Andrew Jackson Centre,** in a thatched cottage 2 km (1 mi) northeast of Carrickfergus, tells the tale of U.S. president Andrew Jackson, whose parents emigrated from here in 1765. This cottage was not their actual home but a reconstruction of an 18th-century thatched cottage thought to resemble it. ◻ Boneybefore, Larne Rd., ☎ 028/9336–6455. ◻ U.K.£1.20. ☉ Apr.–May, weekdays 10–4, weekends 2–4; June–Sept., weekdays 10–6, weekends 2–6.

Structures that remain from Carrickfergus's past are **St. Nicholas's Church,** built by John de Courcy in 1205 and remodeled in 1614, and the handsomely restored North Gate in the town's medieval walls. Dobbins Inn on High Street has been a popular hotel for more than three centuries.

Dining and Lodging

$$$ ✕▥ **Galgorm Manor.** The Gillies bar is decidedly Irish, the dining room cosmopolitan, the manor house itself photogenic, and the estate grounds—where guests may go riding and practice archery—cinematic. Full privileges to Galgorm Castle, an 18-hole, par-72 golf course five minutes from the hotel, are an added treat. The River Maine, a good brown-trout river, flows within sight of many of the large rooms. Galgorm is off A42 3 km (2 mi) west of Ballymena, 32 km (20 mi) inland of Larne, 40 km (25 mi) north of Belfast. ◻ 136 Fenaghy Rd., Ballymena BT42 1EA, ☎ 028/2588–1001, ℻ 028/2588–0080. 23 rooms with bath. Restaurant, bar, horseback riding, fishing, meeting rooms. AE, MC, V.

En Route   As you head away from Carrickfergus on A2, you'll pass through the village of Eden, where **Castle Dobbs** was the home of Arthur Dobbs, the 18th-century British governor of North Carolina. Signposted on the left, 2½ km (1½ mi) off the road, **Dalway's Bawn,** built in 1609, is the best surviving example of an early *bawn,* or fortified farmhouse occupied by a Protestant Planter.

Glens of Antrim

★ ⓯   *Nine glens in the 86 km (54 mi) between Larne and Ballycastle.*

Soon after Larne, the coast of County Antrim becomes spectacular—wave upon wave of high, green hills curve down to the hazy sea, dotted with lush and gently curved glens, or valleys, first carved out by glaciers at the end of the last Ice Age. A narrow, winding, two-lane road (A2, known locally as the Antrim Coast Road) hugs the slim strip of land between the hills and the sea, bringing you to the magnificent Glens of Antrim, nine wooded river valleys running down from the escarpment of the Antrim Plateau to the eastern shore. Until the building of this road in 1834, the glens were home to isolated farming communities—people who adhered to the romantic, mystical Celtic legends and the everyday use of the Irish language. The Glens are worth several days of serious exploration. Even narrower B-roads curl west off A2, up each of the beautiful glens where trails await hikers.

Carnlough

24 km (15 mi) north of Larne, 22½ km (14 mi) east of Ballymena, 43 km (27 mi) from Ballycastle.

A little resort made of white limestone, Carnlough overlooks an endearing harbor within stone walls. The sandy beaches can be reached by crossing over the limestone bridge on Main Street, built especially for the Marquis of Londonderry. The small harbor, once a port of call for fishermen, now shelters pleasure yachts. Carnlough is surrounded by a group of hills that rise 1,000 ft from the sea. There is a small tourist office inside the post office.

Dining and Lodging

$$$ ✕⊞ **Londonderry Arms Hotel.** This ivy-covered, traditional inn right on Carnlough Harbour was built as a coaching inn in 1848. What awaits are lovely seaside gardens, gorgeous antique furnishings, regional paintings and maps, lots of fresh flowers, and Georgian-period decor. In 1921 Sir Winston Churchill inherited it; since 1947 it has been owned and run by the hospitable O'Neill family. Both the original and the newer rooms have lovely Georgian antiques and luxurious fabrics, and they are immaculately kept. The restaurant serves substantial, traditional Irish meals that rely on fresh, local seafood, simply prepared. ⊠ *20 Harbour Rd. Co. Antrim BT44 0EU,* ☎ *028/2888–5255,* ⅻ *028/ 2888–5263. 35 rooms with bath. Restaurant, bar. AE, DC, MC, V.*

$$$ ⊞ **Ballygally Castle.** At the Larne end of the North Antrim coast drive, 40 km (25 mi) from Belfast, stands an impressive, turreted castle that faces Ballygally Bay. Built by a Scottish lord in 1625, the castle cheerfully invites visitors to enjoy a good night's sleep, a hearty breakfast, and its Dungeon Bar, whose substantial stone walls justify the name. Modern facilities integrate with old Scots baronial design, though a recent extension jars with the original style. Bedrooms, some in the castle turrets—one complete with milady's ghost—are individually decorated with comfortable furnishings. In the dining room a decent table d'hôte evening meal is served to music, on Saturday, and a Sunday high tea is also available. ⊠ *274 Coast Rd., Ballygally, Co. Antrim BT40 2RA,* ☎ *028/2858–3212,* ⅻ *028/2858–3681. 31 rooms with bath. Dining room, bar, fishing, baby-sitting. MC, V.*

En Route   Between Carnlough and Ballycastle the scenery becomes even more stunning. Glenariff, opening onto Red Bay at the village of Glenariff (also known as Waterfoot), is considered the loveliest of the glens. A good day trip is **Glenariff Forest Park,** the largest and most accessible of Antrim's valleys. Inside are picnic facilities and dozens of good hikes, notably the 5½-km (3½-mi) **Waterfall Trail** (follow the blue arrows), which offers outstanding views of Glenariff River and its waterfalls and passes by small but swimmable loughs. Detailed maps are available at the visitor center, which has a small self-serve cafeteria. ⊠ *98 Glenariff Rd.,* ☎ *028/2175–8232.* ⅻ *U.K.£1.* ☉ *Nov.–May, daily 8 AM–8 PM; June–Oct., daily 8 AM–10 PM.*

At Cushendall, you'll see Turnley's Tower—a curious, fortified square tower of red stone, built in 1820 as a curfew tower and jail for "idlers and rioters"—standing at a crossroads in the middle of the village. If you would like a break from the Antrim coast, stay on A2 direct to Ballycastle. But if you would prefer to stay by the sea, turn left at the tower in the direction of **Cushendun,** a tiny jewel of a village designed by Clough Williams-Ellis, who also designed the famous Italianate village of Portmeirion in Wales. From this part of the coast you can see the Mull of Kintyre on the Scottish mainland. If you have firm nerves, take the narrow and precipitous coastal road north past dramatically beautiful **Murlough Bay** to **Fair Head**; others will prefer to rejoin A2 via B92, left, after a few miles and descend—passing on the left the ruins of the Franciscans' 16th-century **Bonamargy Friary**—into Ballycastle.

Ballycastle

⑯ *20 km (13 mi) east of Bushmills, 16 km (10 mi) east of Giant's Causeway.*

Ballycastle is the main resort town in the glens, at the northern end of the Glens of Antrim drive. People from the province flock here in the summer. The town is shaped like an hourglass—with its strand and dock on one end, its pubs and chippers on the other, and the 1 km (½ mi) Quay Road in between. Beautifully aged shops and pubs line its Castle, Diamond, and Main streets.

From Ballycastle town you have a view of L-shape **Rathlin Island,** where in 1306 the Scottish king Robert the Bruce took shelter in a cave (under the east lighthouse) and, according to the popular legend, was inspired to continue his armed struggle against the English by watching a spider patiently spinning its web. It was on Rathlin in 1898 that Guglielmo Marconi set up the world's first cross-water radio link, from the island's lighthouse to Ballycastle. Bird-watching and hiking are the island's main activities. Unless the sea is extremely rough, a ferryboat makes regular journeys (twice daily in winter, more frequently in summer). Although the island is only 9½ km (6 mi) away from shore, the trip can take 45 minutes; make sure that you'll be able to return the same day.

Every year since 1606, on the last Monday and Tuesday in August, Ballycastle has hosted the **Oul' Lammas Fair,** a modern version of the ancient Celtic harvest festival of Lughnasa (Irish for "August"). Ireland's oldest fair, this is a very popular two-day event at which sheep and wool are still sold alongside the wares of more modern shopping stalls. Treat yourself to the fair's traditional snacks, "dulse" (sun-dried seaweed) and "yellow man" (rock-hard yellow toffee).

Off the coast, 8 km (5 mi) west of Ballycastle, you can see the **Carrick-a-Rede** rope bridge, which spans a 60-ft gap between the mainland and Carrick-a-Rede Island. The island's name means "rock in the road" and refers to how it stands in the path of the salmon who follow the coast as they migrate to their home rivers to spawn. For the past 150 years salmon fishermen have set up the rope bridge in late April, taking it down again after the salmon season ends. The bridge is open to the public and offers some heart-stopping views of the crashing waves below. If you summon up the nerve to cross it once, of course you then have to do it again to get back to the mainland. ⊠ *Signposted on B15.* ☞ *Free.* ☉ *Apr.–Sept., daily.*

Giant's Causeway

★ **⑰** *19⅓ km (12 mi) west of Ballycastle, 86 km (54 mi) north of Belfast.*

The Giant's Causeway is Northern Ireland's premier tourist attraction—a singularly strange natural phenomenon consisting of a mass of 37,000 mostly hexagonal pillars of volcanic basalt, clustered like a giant honeycomb and extending hundreds of yards into the sea. Legend has it that the causeway was created 60 million years ago when boiling lava, erupting from an underground fissure that stretched from Northern Ireland to the Scottish coast, crystallized as it burst into the sea, and formed according to the same natural principle that structures a honeycomb. As all Ulster folk know, though, the scientific truth is that the columns were created as stepping stones by the giant Finn McCool in a bid to reach a giantess he'd fallen in love with on the Scottish island of Staffa (where the causeway resurfaces). Unfortunately, the giantess's boyfriend found out, and in the ensuing battle Finn pulled out a huge chunk of earth and flung it toward Scotland. The ensuing hole became Lough Neagh, and the sod landed to create the Isle of Man. Boiling lava, indeed.

To reach the causeway, you can either walk 1½ km (1 mi) down a long, scenic hill or take a minibus from the visitor center. West of the causeway, **Port-na-Spania** is the spot where the 16th-century Spanish Armada galleon *Girona* went down on the rocks. The ship was carrying an astonishing cargo of gold and jewelry, some of which was recovered in 1967 and is now on display in the Ulster Museum in Belfast (☞ Belfast, *above*). Beyond this, **Chimney Point** is the name given to one of the causeway structures on which the Spanish fired, thinking that it was Dunluce Castle, which is 8 km (5 mi) west.

Arriving by car at the Giant's Causeway, at first you'll reach a cliff-top parking lot beside the **visitor center,** which houses displays about the area and an audiovisual exhibition explaining the formation of the causeway coast. ⊠ *Causeway Head, near Bushmills,* ☎ *028/2073–1855.* ▣ *Visitor center: audiovisual exhibition U.K.£1, static exhibition U.K.50p, parking U.K.£2.* ☉ *Causeway freely accessible; visitor center May–June and Sept.–Oct. daily 10–6; July–Aug., daily 10–7; Nov.– Apr., daily 10–5 (closes earlier according to demand).*

Bushmills

10 km (6 mi) northeast of Coleraine, 14 km (8½ mi) east of Portstewart.

The oldest licensed distillery in the world, Bushmills was first granted a charter by King James I in 1608, though historical records refer to a distillery here as early as 1276. Bushmills produces the most famous of Irish whiskeys—its namesake, Bushmills—and what is widely regarded as the best, the rarer black-label version known to aficionados as Black Bush. One-hour tours begin in the mashing and fermentation room, proceed to the maturing and bottling warehouse, and end with a complimentary shot of *uisce beatha,* the "water of life," in the visitor center–cum–gift-shop. ⊠ *Bushmills Distillery, Bushmills,* ☎ *028/2073–1521.* ▣ *U.K.£3.* ☉ *Apr.–Oct., Mon.–Sat. 10–4; Nov.–Mar., weekdays 10–4.*

Lodging

$$–$$$ 🏨 **Bushmills Inn.** Roy Bolton and Richard Wilson have overseen the transformation of this cozy old coaching inn, found just off the diamond—or main square, as they're referred to in Ulster. Stripped pine, peat fires, and gas lights warm the public rooms. The livery stables now house the informal restaurant, serving fresh and hearty food, and the bar, always full of good spirits; out front are three tables so that you can dine and drink alfresco. Some of the bedrooms are quite small, so ask to see before you decide. The distillery is a stroll away, as is the salmon-filled River Bush. ⊠ *25 Main St., Bushmills BT57 8QA,* ☎ *028/2073–2339,* ₣₳ₓ *012657/32048. 32 rooms with bath/shower. Restaurant, bar, meeting rooms. MC, V.*

Dunluce Castle

★ ⑱ *8 km (5 mi) west of Giant's Causeway.*

Halfway between Portrush and the Giant's Causeway, dramatically perched on a cliff at land's end, Dunluce Castle is one of the North's most evocative ruins. Originally a 13th-century Norman fortress, it was captured in the 16th century by the local MacDonnell clan chiefs—the so-called "Lords of the Isles." They enlarged the castle, paying for some of the work with their profits from salvaging the Spanish galleon *Girona* (☞ Ulster Museum *in* Belfast, *above*) and made it an important base for ruling northeastern Ulster. Perhaps they expanded the castle a little too much, for in 1639 faulty construction caused the kitchens (with its cooks) to plummet into the sea during a storm. Nearby is the **Dunluce Centre,** an entertainment complex with rides, a live show about myths and legends, a viewing tower, shops, and a restaurant. ⊠ *Port Ballintree,* ☎ *028/7082–4444.* 🎟 *U.K.£4.* ☉ *Mar.–June and Sept., weekdays noon–5, weekends 10–9; July–Aug., daily 10–9.*

Portrush and Portstewart are the two subsequent seaside towns. Portrush's main attraction is the **Royal Portrush Golf Club** (☞ Chapter 9), one of Ireland's premier, championship courses. **Portstewart Strand,** to the west of town, has some of Ireland's best surfing.

Dining

$$$ ✕ **Ramore Restaurant and Wine Bar.** On Portrush's picturesque har-
★ bor, where a haven of boats are tucked away from the resort's brasher amusements, this spot does double duty. The daily offerings at the wine bar ($) are posted on a blackboard. Upstairs, the draws are panoramic views and chef George McAlpin's Pacific Rim–inflected way with local Atlantic fish and shellfish, which together make up one of Northern Ireland's top dining experiences. Menus change every three months, but Grand Marnier soufflé, a regular dessert, is always an indulgent way to finish. ⊠ *The Harbor,* ☎ *028/7082–4313 restaurant; 028/7082–3444 wine bar;* ℻ *028/7082–3194. MC, V in restaurant only. Restaurant closed Sun.–Mon. Wine bar closed Sun. No lunch in restaurant.*

Coleraine

➒ *10 km (6 mi) south of Portrush, 13 km (8 mi) southwest of Dunluce Castle, 48 km (30 mi) east of Derry.*

Dating from the 5th century BC, Coleraine became the seat of the University of Ulster in 1968. The River Bann, flowing through the town, divides the county of Antrim from that of Derry. As well as being a fishing town, Coleraine boasts an important linen industry.

Some of Ireland's oldest remaining relics, dating from the very first inhabitants of this island (about 7000 BC), were found on Mountsandel just to the south of Coleraine. One of the many dolmens in this region is called Slaghtaverty after an evil dwarf who mesmerized women using his magical harp. He was buried alive and upside down by the great Finn McCool (maker of the Giant's Causeway), so that the sounds of his harp would not escape from the ground.

Lodging

$$ 🏠 **Greenhill House.** This charming, Georgian country house, about 13 km (8 mi) south of Coleraine, is a peaceful retreat run by Elizabeth and James Hegarty. Guests enjoy the pleasantly decorated bedrooms, substantial breakfasts, and excellent dinners of locally caught fish, Ulster beef, and homemade bread and cakes. Dinner should be booked by noon. ⊠ *24 Greenhill Rd., Aghadowey, Co. Londonderry BT51 4EU,* ☎ *028/7086–8241,* ℻ *028/7086–8365. 6 rooms with bath. Dining room. MC, V. Closed Nov.–Feb.*

$ 🏠 **Camus House.** Follow the road along the Bann Valley south from Coleraine 6½ km (4 mi) out of town, and you'll arrive at this appealing farmhouse, parts of which date from 1685. Today it's a relaxed and gracious guest house, elegantly furnished, with a snug sitting room with a stone fireplace. Proprietor and salmon fisher Josephine King provides a friendly atmosphere and a hearty breakfast. The pleasant bedrooms, decorated in pastel colors, have tasteful, modern furnishings, reading lamps, and large closets. ⊠ *27 Curragh Rd., Castle Row, Coleraine, Co. Londonderry BT51 3RY,* ☎ *028/7034–2982. 3 rooms share 1 bath and shower room. Breakfast room. No credit cards.*

Upperlands

20 *32 km (20 mi) southwest of Coleraine, 56 km (35 mi) northwest of Belfast.*

Upstream from Coleraine, the River Bann—rich in eels for roasting and smoking and in salmon for poaching—flows out of Lough Neagh. On its left bank are the towns and fortifications of the 17th-century Planters, built by London's Livery Companies, whose descendants developed the linen industry. In the tiny town of Upperlands, visitors can tour **William Clark and Sons,** a working linen mill where age-old wooden machinery beetles (polishes) threads for the linen linings of suits for England's Royals. There is also a small linen museum. ⊠ *Upperlands, Maghera,* ☎ *028/7964–2214.* ▩ *U.K.£1.* ☉ *Mon.–Thurs. 9–5, Fri. 9–noon.*

Dining and Lodging

$$$ ✕▦ **Ardtara House.** A 19th-century Victorian home built by a de-
★ scendant of the founder of the town's first linen mill, Ardtara is the North's finest country-house hotel. In the mid-'90s, Maebeth Fenton—a New York–based public relations executive (her clients include the Northern Ireland Tourist Board) who grew up nearby—oversaw a luxurious renovation. The gorgeously furnished terra-cotta and pink drawing room, with original plaster moldings and a marble fireplace, looks out on the wide front lawn and tennis court. The eight large bedrooms are furnished with antiques; each has a fireplace, as do some of the elegantly appointed marble bathrooms. The hotel's restaurant is in the former snooker room, with dark paneled walls, a wallpapered hunting scene, and a huge skylight. Peat-smoked rack of lamb with champ and rosemary gravy, or salmon with champagne sauce, is a stellar entrée. You'll feel the calm and relaxed atmosphere Fenton and the rest of the staff strive for the moment you walk in, and you won't want to leave it behind. ⊠ *8 Gorteade Rd., Upperlands, Co. Londonderry BT46 5SA,* ☎ *028/7964–4490,* ▥ *028/7964–5080. 8 rooms with bath. Restaurant, tennis court, meeting room. AE, MC, V.*

Limavady

21 *21 km (13 mi) west of Coleraine, 34 km (21 mi) northwest of Upperlands, 27 km (17 mi) east of Derry.*

In 1851, at No. 51 on Limavady's Georgian main street, Jane Ross wrote down the tune played by a traveling fiddler and called it "Londonderry Air," better known now as "Danny Boy." While staying at an inn on Ballyclose Street, William Thackeray (1811–63) wrote his rather lustful poem "Peg of Limavaddy" about a barmaid. Among the many Americans descended from Ulster emigrants was President James Monroe, whose relatives came from the Limavady area.

Dining and Lodging

$$$$ ✕▦ **Radisson Roe Park Hotel & Golf Resort.** One of the North's most deluxe resorts, the Radisson rests amid 155 acres of countryside on the banks of the River Roe. Bedrooms are decorated in cream and blue, with satellite TV and other amenities. Guests have a variety of dining options: The Courtyard Restaurant is formal and international; the

Coach House, an American brasserie, is a relaxed place where golfers congregate; and O'Cahan's Bar takes its name from a local chieftain besieged on a riverside promontory, whose Irish wolfhound leapt an impossible chasm to bring relief—doubtless an inspiration to golfers flagging at the ninth. ⊠ *Roe Park, Limavady, Co. Londonderry BT49 9LB,* ☎ *028/7772–2222,* FAX *028/7772–2313. 64 rooms with bath. 2 restaurants, 2 bars, indoor pool, beauty salon, sauna, steam room, 18-hole golf course, exercise room, horseback riding, fishing, baby-sitting, meeting rooms. AE, DC, MC, V.*

Derry

㉒ *109 km (68 mi) north of Belfast, 53 km (33 mi) north of Omagh.*

Derry's name is a shadow of its history. Those in favor of British rule call the city Londonderry, its old Plantation-period name; the "London" part was tacked on in 1613 after the Flight of the Earls (☞ Rathmullan *in* Chapter 7), and the city and county were handed over to the Corporation of London, which represented London's merchants. They brought in a large population of English and Scottish Protestant settlers, built new towns for them, and reconstructed Derry within the city walls, which survive almost unchanged to this day. Both before then and after, Derry's sturdy ramparts have withstood many fierce attacks and have never been breached, which explains the city's coy sobriquet, "The Maiden City." The most famous attack was the historic siege of 1688–89, after 13 apprentice boys slammed the city gates in the face of the Catholic king James II. The inhabitants, who held out for 105 days and were reduced to eating dogs, cats, and laundry starch, nevertheless helped to secure the British throne for the Protestant king William III.

Whatever you choose to call it, Derry is one of Northern Ireland's most underrated towns. If Belfast was the Beethoven of Northern Ireland, Derry would be the Mozart—fey, witty, and a touch surreal. Despite the derelict factories along the banks of the River Foyle and a reputation marred by Troubles-related violence, the city has worked hard to move forward. Such efforts show in the quaint, bustling town center, encircled by 20-ft-tall, 17th-century walls. The city's winding streets slope down to the Foyle, radiating from the Diamond—Derry's historic center where St. Columba founded his first monastery in 546. Fine Georgian and Victorian buildings sit side by side with gaily painted Victorian-fronted shops, cafés, and pubs.

Derry, incidentally, has links to Boston that date as far back as the 17th and 18th centuries, when many Derry residents escaped their hardships at home by emigrating to that U.S. city and beyond. Aviation fans, take note: Derry was where Amelia Earhart touched down, on May 21, 1932, after her historic solo flight across the Atlantic. Local lore has it that the first man to reach her airplane greeted her in typically unfazed Derry fashion: "Aye, and what do you want, then?"

㉓ **City walls.** To really experience Derry's history, stroll along the parapet walkway atop the ramparts of these walls, built between 1614 and 1618 and one of the few intact sets of city walls in Europe. Pierced by eight gates (originally four) and as much as 30 ft thick, the gray stone ramparts are only 1½ km (1 mi) all around; today most of the life of the town actually takes place outside of them. You can walk the walls on your own, following the sites below in an counterclockwise direction; or, from June through September, you join one of the guided walks from the city's new tourist Information Centre (*below*). ▣ *Free.*

㉔ **Tourist Information Centre.** This is the most strategic place to start your tour of the city, whether by yourself or on one of the guided walks.

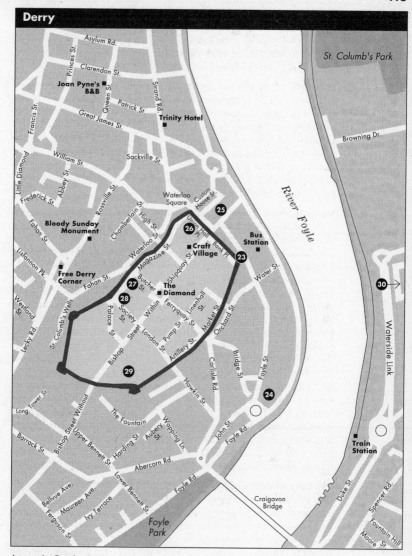

Derry

Apprentice Boys'
Memorial Hall, **28**

Calgach Centre, **27**

City walls, **23**

Guildhall, **25**

St. Columb's
Cathedral, **29**

Tourist Information
Centre, **24**

Tower Museum, **26**

Workhouse
Museum, **30**

Tours are currently run by the erudite Tommy Carlin and last just under 2 hours. ⊠ *44 Foyle St.,* ☎ *028/7126–7284 or 028/7137–7577,* 𝖥𝖠𝖷 *028/7137–7992.* 🎫 *Free; tours £3.20.* ☉ *July–Sept., weekdays 9–7, Sat. 10–6, Sun. 10–5; Easter–June, Mon.–Thurs. 9–5:15, Fri. 9–5, Sat. 10–5; Oct.–Easter, Mon.–Thurs. 9–5:15, Fri. 9–5.*

㉕ **Guildhall.** At the entrance to the old city, this ornate Victorian stone and sandstone building dates from 1890 and has impressive stained-glass windows. These were actually shattered by two IRA bombs in June 1977 and rebuilt by the Campbell's firm in Belfast, who had installed the original windows in 1890 and still had the original plans—-now that's a filing system! The Guildhall, where Derry city council meets monthly, is the site of musical recitals and heated political rallies. ⊠ *Guildhall Sq.,* ☎ *028/7137–7335.* 🎫 *Free.* ☉ *Weekdays 9–5; guided tours July–Aug. and by appointment.*

㉖ **Tower Museum.** This multiple award-winning museum, which chronicles the history of Derry, is inside the reconstructed O'Doherty's Tower, which was originally built in 1615 by the O'Dohertys for their overlords, the O'Donnells, in lieu of tax payments. Highlights include a small section on the eccentric Bishop Frederick Augustus Hervey (1763–1803), who livened up Sunday by making his curates sprint naked along nearby Magilligan Strand while he whipped them. The vivid "Story of Derry" exhibition covers the city's history, from its origins as a monastic settlement in an oak grove and including the beginnings of the Troubles in 1969, after years of institutionalized discrimination in jobs and public housing (a well-known Derry innuendo is that the skeleton in the city's coat of arms was actually a Catholic waiting for a house). It is, in fact, Walter de Burgo, a forebear of singer Chris de Burgh, who was starved to death in the dungeons of Greencastle after a dispute with his cousin William. A small but poignant exhibition details the history of the Troubles in the city, while a large new exhibition on the Spanish Armada is scheduled to open in the autumn of 2000. There's also an excellent virtual museum on-site celebrating the life and legacy of St. Columb. ⊠ *Union Hall Pl.,* ☎ *028/7737–2411.* 🎫 *U.K.£3.50.* ☉ *Sept.–June, Tues.–Sat. 10–5; July–Aug., Mon.–Sat. 10–5, Sun. 2–5.*

㉗ The **Calgach Centre** is the home of the **Fifth Province**, an inspired high-tech celebration of the city's history from its earliest days, as well as its importance in creating the Irish diaspora of 17 million people. You begin by sitting on a neolithic mound while the voice of veteran British actor Richard Harris intones in a ghostly voice the history of Derry, from the sylvan oak grove beloved by the chieftain Calgach, right up to the city's finest hour, when local boy Bernardo O'Higgins was made president of Chile. From there it's into a comfortable armchair for a virtual-reality time trip through the coming of the Vikings and the Normans, the flight of the Irish nobility from English persecution in 1601, and the famine of 1845–49, when 1½ million emigrated to the United States and a million more died of starvation. It's moving stuff, grippingly presented. The center is also the home for touring exhibitions. Call for details. ⊠ *4–22 Butcher St.,* ☎ *028/7737–3177.* 🎫 *U.K.£3.* ☉ *Mon.–Thurs. 9–5:30, Fri. 9–5; shows weekdays at 11:30 and 2:30.*

㉘ **Apprentice Boys' Memorial Hall.** This Scottish baronial edifice, built in 1867 and extended in 1933 to house the exclusively Protestant organization (which was set up in 1715 to honor the memory of the 13 apprentices who slammed the gate in the face of the Catholic king James in December 1688 and began the famous siege), is only now being made open to the public. Inside you will find the initiation room, in which 20,000 men have sworn allegiance to the code of the organization formed to uphold the defiant spirit of those original 13. An upstairs bar and dance hall, both spurned by the more temperate members the room for the more severe sister organization the Royal Black Preceptory, has walls lined with 12 banners representing the lost tribes of Israel. In the ladies' room, one of the more curious sights is a photograph of a splendid Italian matriarch wearing the sash of fellow Protestant organization the Orange Order. She is, in fact, *Signora* E. B. Cabenna, the descendant of one of the Italian workmen brought over by the magnificently eccentric Bishop Frederick Augustus Hervey (*above*) to work on his churches. Naturally, the bishop couldn't have Catholics rebuilding Protestant churches, so the workmen were forced to convert before taking up their tools. A magnificently chaotic museum has shelves and glass cases filled to the brim with furniture and firearms, books and bombs, and swords and sculpture. It's a wonderful glimpse into a hitherto closed world. ⊠ *Society St.,* ☎ *no phone.* 🎫 *Donations accepted by arrangement.* ☉ *Tours by arrangement only. Call Derry TIC 028/7126–7284 or 028/7137–7577.*

As you stand on the walls at this point, you are face-to-face with two symbols of Derry's divided nature. The truncated column to your left is all that is left of the **Walker Memorial,** a statue of the governor of Derry during the siege. It was blown up by the IRA in 1973, and the story goes that the statue's head rolled down the hill into the Catholic Bogside, where it was captured by a local youth. He ransomed it back to the Protestants for a small fortune, and today it sits on the shoulders of a replica of the original statue beside the Apprentice Boys' Memorial Hall. With an irony that would have delighted both Bishop Hervey and Signora Cabenna, the replica had to be made where the plans of the original statue were kept: in Dublin, that city that is all things alien to northern Protestants.

From here, you can see the valley where the Troubles began with the original civil rights marches in 1969. At **Free Derry Corner** is the white gable wall where Catholics defiantly painted the slogan "You are now entering Free Derry" as a declaration of a zone from which police and the British Army were banned until 1972, when the army broke down the barricades. That same year, 13 civil rights marchers were shot by British soldiers in an event that rankles Catholics to this day. "Bloody Sunday," as it became known, is commemorated by the mural of a civil rights march. Farther along the wall is the Church of Ireland **St. Augustine's Church,** where the original 6th-century city monastery stood.

Roaring Meg, one of the original cannons from the 1688–89 siege, still looks out from Double Bastion, the next corner on the ramparts. The building behind you is the old **First Presbyterian Primary School,** now the **Verbal Arts Centre** (*below*), which hosts fine art exhibitions and storytelling events.

㉙ **St. Columb's Cathedral,** built in 1633 in simple Planter's Gothic style, was the first Protestant cathedral built in the United Kingdom after the reformation. In the vestibule is the 270-pound mortar ball, which during the siege was fired over the wall with an invitation to surrender sent by King James. Legend has it that when they read it, every man, woman, and child in the city rushed to the walls and shouted, "No surrender!"—a Protestant battle cry to this day. In addition to its intricate, corbeled roof and austere spire, the church contains the oldest and largest bells in Ireland (dating from the 1620s), and it is a treasure house of Derry Protestant emblems, memorials, and relics from the 1688–89 siege. The **Chapter House Museum** has the oldest surviving map of Derry (from 1600) and the Bible owned by Governor George Walker (*above*) during the siege. Nearby is the spot where in

1870 Cecilia Alexander wrote the hymn "There Is a Green Hill Far Away." ✉ *Museum: Off Bishop St.,* ☎ *028/7126–7313,* 🖃 *Free; minimum donation of U.K.£1 recommended.* ☉ *Mar.–Oct. daily 9–1 and 2–5; Nov.–Feb., daily 9–1 and 2–4.*

㉚ Workhouse Museum. Across the River Foyle from the city walls, this 1832 structure was built to alleviate poverty but was the end of the road for people who had tried to make their lives better but had failed. During the famine years, the city was the main emigration port for Northern Ireland, and many families came here hoping to get on a boat, failed, and ended up in the workhouse in utter despair. Inside, families were separated, and this was often the last time children saw their parents alive. During the famine years of 1845–49, 1½ million people left Ireland and one million died, and the museum captures the despair of those dark days.

Many of the descendants of those who left, of course, came back during the Second World War, when thousands of U.S. servicemen arrived in the city in 1942 to turn it into a base for the Battle of the Atlantic. Today a small museum in the workhouse chronicles the story of that battle, from the Yanks' arrival in the January rain (which prompted one of them to ask if the city's barrage balloons were actually there to stop the place from sinking) through the end of the war when 64 U-boats lined up in the harbor to surrender, like a convention of retired sharks, to 1946, when the city's biggest export was G.I. brides. ✉ *23 Glendermott Rd.,* ☎ *028/7131–8328.* 🖃 *Free.* ☉ *Mon–Sat. 10–4:30.*

The **Boston Tea Party** (✉ 10 and 13–15 Craft Village, ☎ 028/7126–9667), a small tea shop down an alley nearly opposite the Richmond Shopping Centre on Shipquay Street, is a nice spot for a snack or lunch break. **McGilloway's** (✉ 165 Strand Rd., ☎ 028/7126–2050) is an unpretentious but excellent seafood restaurant. Derry is packed with agreeable pubs, but **Badgers** (✉ 16 Orchard St., ☎ 028/7136–0763) has the best range of simple wholesome food. Plus it's the watering hole for local media types, artists, writers, and musicians. If you're feeling homesick for an American accent, head for the **Gravy Bistro** (✉ 32 Carlisle Rd., ☎ 028/7136–0300), where home-cooked lunches and dinners have French and Italian leanings; there's no license, so bring your own bottle.

Dining and Lodging

$-$$ ✕ **Oyster's.** All aboard for this cozy hillside restaurant with a nautical theme. Starters include chorizo sausage and linguini or seafood chowder with smoked bacon. Standout mains are Thai seared salmon with egg noodles, sea bass with smoked salmon, vanilla and leek mash, and peppered lamb with rosemary and cherry tomatoes. Upstairs, there's a more informal bistro, which does great fish-and-chips. ✉ *Spencer Rd.,* ☎ *028/7134–4875. MC, V.*

$$$ ✕🖃 **Beech Hill.** Past a fairy-tale gatehouse and set among clumps of beech trees, streams, and a duck pond, Beech Hill is a grand 1792 country home very much attuned to the present. Chef Ward Birkhill, who has been cooking since he was 13 and trained with the tempestuous Marco Pierre White in London, draws many Northwest politicos from both sides of the border (with Eurocrats in tow) who appreciate his sophisticated menu. The vast honeymoon suite, with a four-poster bed, overlooks the gardens. The house is 3 km (2 mi) south of the city, left off A6. ✉ *32 Ardmore Rd., Derry BT47 3QP,* ☎ *028/7134–9279,* FAX *028/7134–5366. 27 rooms with bath. Restaurant, bar, sauna, hot tub, exercise room, meeting rooms. AE, MC, V.*

$$$ ✕⌂ **The Trinity.** On the banks of the River Foyle, past the Guildhall and not far outside the city walls, the cool, stylish, and friendly Trinity is Derry's only city-center hotel. The spacious bedrooms are decorated with rosewood and several hues of green; amenities include coffeemakers and satellite TV. The hotel is home to a number of watering holes: Nolan's Snug, the European-style café-bar, and the hotel's bistro restaurant, which offers such specialties as scallop of pork stuffed with wild mushrooms and Parmesan. The roof garden makes a pleasant sanctuary. ✉ *22–24 Strand Rd., Derry BT48 7 AB,* ☎ *028/ 7127–1271,* FAX *028/7127–1277. 40 rooms with bath, 3 suites. Restaurant, 3 bars, meeting rooms. AE, DC, MC, V.*

$ ✕⌂ **Joan Pyne's.** All architectural life is in the little enclave outside Joan Pyne's, from art deco to neo-Gothic. No. 16 was originally a Victorian merchant's family home built to Georgian proportions, then a rectory and bank before Joan began the process of turning it into the city's grandest guest house. Previous guests include the late Hurd Hatfield, star of the movie *The Picture of Dorian Gray.* Joan also owns a similar but smaller house three minutes' walk away, which serves as an annex. ✉ *16 Queen St., Derry BT48 7EQ,* ☎ *028/7126–4223,* FAX *028/7126–6913. 12 rooms, 4 with bath. MC, V.*

Nightlife and the Arts

It may be only the North's *second*-largest city, but to its residents, Derry is thought to be first in spirit.

ART GALLERIES

The **Orchard Gallery** (✉ Orchard St., ☎ 028/7126–9675) has gained a Europe-wide reputation in the fields of political and conceptual art. The **Context Gallery** (✉ 5–7 Artillery St., ☎ 028/7137–3538) is a close competitor. The **McGilloway Gallery**(✉ Shipquay St., ☎ 028/7136–6011) stocks a broad selection of representational modern Irish art. Owner Ken McGilloway offers wine on Friday evenings until 9 PM.

The **Verbal Arts Centre** (✉ Mall Wall, ☎ 028/7126–6946) hosts regular exhibitions and storytelling events, re-creating the great old Irish tradition of fireside tales.

PUBS AND CLUBS

Traditional Irish music can be found at **Peadar O'Donnell's** (✉ 63 Waterloo St., ☎ 028/7137–2318). The **Gweedore Bar** (✉ 16 Waterloo St., ☎ 028/7126–3513) is a favorite for hip-hop and house music. **Squire's Nightclub** (✉ 33 Shipquay St., ☎ 028/7126–6017) is the place for disco.

THEATER AND OPERA

Brian Friel, of *Philadelphia Here I Come* fame, premiered much of his work in the **Guildhall** (☞ *above*) through the **Field Day Theatre Company** (✉ Foyle Arts Centre, Lawrence Hill, ☎ 028/7136–0196). Other theater productions take place at the **Rialto Entertainment Center** (✉ 5 Market St., ☎ 028/7126–0516), the **Foyle Arts Centre** (✉ Lawrence Hill, ☎ 028/7126–6657), and the **Playhouse** (✉ 5–7 Artillery St., ☎ 028/7126–8027).

Shopping

Shopping in town is generally low-key and unpretentious, but some gems of Irish craftsmanship can be found here. Stroll up Shipquay Street to find small stores and an indoor shopping center. Stop at the **Donegal Shop** (✉ 8 Shipquay St., ☎ 028/7126–6928) for Irish linen, tweeds, and woolens. Off Shipquay Street, the **Derry Craft Village** has a romantic maze of shops, residential apartments, and workshops in an an 18th-century setting, complete with crafts demonstrations, costumes, and, of course, souvenirs galore. Where Shipquay reaches the Diamond, you'll find **Austin's** (✉ 2 the Diamond, ☎ 028/7126–1817), a large store stocking Tyrone crystal, Belleek china, and other quality Northern Irish goods. **Bookworm** (✉ 16 Bishop St., ☎ 028/7128–2727) is "the best bookshop in Ireland," according to writer Nuala O Failain, while **Thomas the Goldsmith** (✉ 7 Pump St., ☎ 028/7137–4549) stocks exquisite work by international jewelry designers. The Donegal designer fashions of **Edel MacBride** (✉ 2 Castle Gate, ☎ 028/7126–6166) are worn by Jane Seymour, Olivia Newton-John, and Hillary Rodham Clinton.

En Route   From Derry, head across County Tyrone toward Enniskillen. Take A5 south via Strabane to Omagh. **Strabane,** birthplace of the surreal novelist Brian O'Nolan, alias Flann O'Brien, does not offer much interest apart from the well-preserved, 18th-century **Gray's Print Shop** (✉ 49 Main St., ☎ 028/7188–4094). John Dunlap (1746–1812), who apprenticed here as a printer before emigrating to Philadelphia, founded America's first daily newspaper, the *Philadelphia Packet,* in 1771, and was also the man who printed and distributed the American Declaration of Independence. James Wilson, grandfather of President Woodrow Wilson, also emigrated from here. The original **Wilson family home** (✉ Ligford Rd., ☎ 028/8224–3292), a simple thatched cottage, still with much of the original 18th-century furniture, survives at Dergalt, 3 km (2 mi) along the Plumbridge road. It can be visited by knocking at the farmhouse next door, still owned and worked by the Wilson family. For a delightfully rustic alternative route, drive along the minor road B48, which skirts the foot of the **Sperrin Mountains** and reaches all the way to Omagh.

Alternatively, you may want to head north from Derry to the **Inishowen Peninsula,** the northernmost point of Ireland (☞ Chapter 7).

AROUND COUNTIES TYRONE, FERMANAGH, ARMAGH, AND DOWN

During the worst of the Troubles, parts of these four counties that border the Republic were known as bandit country. But now visitors can enjoy a worry-free drive through the calm countryside and stop in at some very "Ulster" towns, distinct from the rest of Ireland. The area includes the great houses of Castle Coole and Florence Court; the ancient, ecclesiastical city of Armagh; and the wild Sperrin Mountains.

Ulster-American Folk Park and Ulster History Park

③①   *27 km (17 mi) south of Strabane, 5 km (3 mi) north of Omagh.*

The Ulster-American Folk Park has been designed to re-create a Tyrone village of two centuries ago, a log-built American settlement of the same period, and the docks and ships that the emigrants to America would have used. The centerpiece of the park is an old whitewashed cottage, now a museum, which is the ancestral home of Andrew Mellon (1855–1937), the U.S. millionaire banker and philanthropist. Another thatched cottage is a reconstruction of the boyhood home of Archbishop John Hughes, founder of New York's St. Patrick's Cathedral. Exhibitions trace the contribution of the Northern Irish people to American history. The park also features a crafts shop and café. ✉ *Camphill, Co. Tyrone, on A5 between Strabane and Omagh,* ☎ *028/8224–3292.* 🖭 *U.K.£3.50.* ⊙ *Easter–Sept., Mon.–Sat. 11–6:30, Sun. 11:30–7; Oct.–Good Fri., weekdays 10:30–5; last admission 1½ hrs before closing.*

On B48, another 6 km (4 mi) northeast of the Ulster-American Folk Park, the **Ulster History Park** documents Irish history from the first known settlers to the 12th-century arrival of the Normans. The open-air displays include lath and rawhide huts, primitive farms and stockades, a round tower, and an oratory. Hours are identical to those at the Ulster-American Folk Park (☞ *above*). ⊠ *Cullion, Lislap, Gortin,* ☎ *028/8264–8188.* ☞ *U.K.£3.*

Omagh

43 km (27 mi) northeast of Enniskillen.

Omagh, the county town of Tyrone, lies close to the Sperrin Mountains, with the River Strule to the north. Playwright Brian Friel was born here. Sadly, it is more recently known as the scene of the worst atrocity of the Troubles, when an IRA bomb killed 29 people in August 1998. The town has two places of worship—a Church of Ireland church and a Catholic double-spire church.

Belleek

❷ *41½ km (26 mi) southwest of Omagh.*

The old town of Belleek sits on the northwestern edge of Lower Lough Erne and is home to the world-famous Belleek Pottery. On the riverbank stands the visitor center of **Belleek Pottery Ltd.,** producers of Belleek chinaware and porcelain. Here a factory, a showroom, a permanent exhibition, a Belleek pottery museum, and a café are all under one roof. On weekdays, a tour of the factory starts every half hour. You'll find hardly any noise coming from machinery in the workshops, however—everything at Belleek is handmade, using the exact process that was invented in 1857. The showroom is filled with beautiful gifts, but prices are high: A cup and saucer set costs about U.K.£25–U.K.£30, and a bowl in a basket-weave style (very typical of Belleek) could cost you several hundred pounds. ⊠ *Belleek, Co. Fermanagh,* ☎ *028/ 6865–8501.* ☞ *U.K.£2.* ☉ *Shop and showroom Sept.–May, weekdays 9–6, Sat. 10–6; June–Aug., daily 9–8. Tours Mon.–Thurs. 9:15–12:15 and 2:15–4:15, Fri. 9:15–3:15.*

En Route   North of Omagh the country is pretty and rustic, with small farm villages within sight of the bare Sperrin Mountains. Heading east from the town on A505, you'll discover a pensive landscape of moist heath and bog. Left of the road, **Beaghmore** is a strange Bronze Age ceremonial site preserved for millennia beneath a blanket of peat: It has seven stone circles and 12 cairns. Farther along, A505 reaches **Wellbrook Beetling Mill,** where locally made linen was first "beetled," that is, pounded with noisy, water-driven hammers to give it a smooth finish. The mill is kept in working order by the National Trust. ⊠ *Corkhill,* ☎ *028/8675–1735.* ☞ *U.K.£1.60.* ☉ *Apr.–May and Sept., weekends 2–6; Easter and June–Aug., Wed.–Mon. 2–6.*

About 6½ km (4 mi) beyond Wellbrook is **Cookstown,** an odd Plantation village with a single, broad main street more than 1½ km (1 mi) long. From here, head down on the back lanes to **Lough Neagh,** at 396 square km (153 square mi) the largest lake in the British Isles, noted for an abundance of eels. On its shore at **Ardboe** stands a remarkable 10th-century high cross more than 18 ft tall and richly carved with biblical scenes.

Lough Erne

131 km (82 mi) west of Belfast, 100 km (62 mi) south of Derry.

On the journey beside Lough Erne, pause to catch your breath while eating up the lovely view of green hills extending down to the still lake water.

Castle Archdale Country Park, signposted down a narrow road about 6½ km (4 mi) from the Kesh, has a lakeside marina, an open-air country museum, and a World War II exhibition featuring the Battle of the Atlantic. ☎ *028/6862–1588.* 🎟 *Free.* ☉ *Call for hrs.*

Lake and River Cruising

Inland cruising on the Erne waterway—777 square km (300 square mi) of lakes and rivers—is one of the North's major treats. Upper and Lower Lough Erne are enclosed by some of Ireland's finest scenery and are studded with more than 100 little islands. Out on the lakes and the River Erne, which links them, you'll have all the solitude you want, but you'll find company at lough-side hostelries. To hire a boat, contact **Erne Charter Boat Association** (✉ Belleek Charter Cruising, Erne Gateway Centre, Corry, Belleek, ☎ 028/6865–8027). Expect to pay at least U.K.£300 to hire a four-berth cruiser for two or three nights.

White Island and Devenish Island

4 km (2 ½ mi) and 16 km (10 mi) north of Enniskillen.

From Castle Archdale, a ferry (☎ 028/6862–1731) runs from June through September, Tuesday through Sunday (U.K.£2.25), taking passengers to see the carved Celtic figures on **White Island.** After you drive 13 km (8 mi) farther from Castle Archdale Park, where B82 joins A32, a small sign shows the way to catch the little boat (☎ 028/6632–3110) that runs from April through September, Tuesday through Sunday (U.K.£2.25) over to **Devenish Island.** The extensive but ruined 12th-century monastery on Devenish features Ireland's best example of a round tower—it is 82 ft tall—and a richly carved high cross.

Enniskillen

43 km (27 mi) southwest of Omagh, 77 km (48 mi) west of Armagh.

Enniskillen is the pleasant, smart-looking capital of County Fermanagh and the only place of any size in the county. Its town center is strikingly situated on an island in the River Erne between Upper and Lower Lough Erne. The principal thoroughfares, Townhall and High streets, are crowded with old-style pubs and rows of redbrick Georgian flats, and the waterfront **Enniskillen Castle** is one of the best-preserved monuments in the North. Built by the Maguire clan in 1670, this stronghold houses the local history collection of the **Fermanagh County Museum** and the polished paraphernalia of the **Royal Inniskilling Fusiliers Regimental Museum.** A Heritage Centre also stands within the curtilage of the castle. ✉ *Wellington Rd.,* ☎ *028/6632–5000.* 🎟 *U.K.£1.50.* ☉ *May–Sept., Tues–Fri. 10–5, Sat. and Mon. 2–5; July–Aug also Sun. 2–5; Oct.–Apr., Mon. 2–5, Tues.–Fri. 10–5.*

The spires of the daunting 19th-century St. Michael's and St. MacArtin's cathedrals, both on Church Street, preside over the town. Farther west down Church Street are High Street's pubs and restaurants.

At the riverside in Enniskillen, the 16th-century **Water Gate** is handsomely turreted, a protection against enemies of the town.

Beyond the West Bridge in Enniskillen lies **Portora Royal School,** established in 1608 by King James I. Its grounds contain the ruins of Portora Castle. Among the writers educated here were Samuel Beckett and Oscar Wilde, the pride of the school until his trial for homosexuality.

Among the several relaxed and welcoming old pubs in Enniskillen's town center, the one with the most appeal is **Blake's of the Hollow** (✉

6 Church St., ☎ 028/6632–2143) on the main street, a place hardly altered since it opened in 1887. Its name derives from the facts that the heart of the town lies in a slight hollow and the pub's landlord is named William Blake. Don't ask if he's related to the great poet of the same name—everybody does, and he isn't!

Castle Coole

★ ㊱ *3 km (2 mi) southeast of Enniskillen.*

In the 18th century and through most of the 19th, the Loughs of Erne and their environs were remote places—far from Ireland's bustling cities. But it was just this isolated green and watery countryside that attracted the Anglo-Irish gentry. They built grand houses—among them, one widely considered to be the finest: Castle Coole. This "uncommonly perfect" mansion (to quote the eminent architectural historian Desmond Guinesss) stands in its own landscaped oak woods and parkland at the end of a long, tree-lined driveway. Although the Irish architect Richard Johnston made the original drawings in the 1790s and was responsible for the foundation, the castle was, for all intents and purposes, the work of James Wyatt, commissioned by the first Earl of Belmore. One of the best-known architects of his time, Wyatt, who was based in London, did much work in Ireland, but he only visited the country once, and he never came here. Alexander Stewart was the resident builder-architect who oversaw much of the building's construction. The architect wasn't the only imported element; in fact, much of Castle Coole was transported over from England, including the main facade, which is clad in Portland stone shipped from Dorset to Ballyshannon and then hauled over land by horse and cart. And what a facade it is: In perfect symmetry, white colonnaded wings extend from either side of the mansion's three-story, nine-bay center block, with a pedimented central portico. It is perhaps the apotheosis in Ireland of the 18th-century's reverence for the Greeks, and it bears a touch of Palladian sensibility.

Inside, the house is remarkably well preserved; most of the lavish plasterwork and original furnishings are still in place. On its completion in September 1798, the construction had cost U.K.£70,000 and the furnishings another U.K.£22,000, compared to the U.K.£6 million cost of a restoration in 1995–96, during which anything not in keeping with the original design was removed. The saloon is one of the finest rooms in the house, with a vast expanse of oak flooring, gilded Regency furniture, and gray scagliola pilasters with Corinthian capitals. The present earl of Belmore still lives on the estate and uses one wing of the house. ⊠ Co. Fermanagh, ☎ 028/6632–2690. 🎟 U.K.£2.80. ☉ Easter, Sept., and weekends 1–6; May–Aug., Fri.–Wed. 1–6; last tour 5:15 PM; Oct.–Apr., house closed.

Horseback Riding/Pony Trekking

If you're over in the Enniskillen/Lough Erne area, the **Ulster Lakeland Equestrian Park** (⊠ Necarne Castle, Irvinestown, ☎ 028/6862–1919) can teach you to ride or take you on a pony trek through the 200 rolling acres of this Gothic-looking castle's rolling parkland. Rates begin at U.K.£8 for 30 minutes. There are rooms to stay in, a bar, and a restaurant.

Lodging

$$$ 🏠 **Blessingbourne.** This faux Elizabethan, Victorian-era house, with mullioned windows, stables, and carriage museum, sits on a pretty circular lake. Meals can be eaten with the Lowry family, the proprietors. One of the bedrooms has a four-poster bed. A visit makes the diversion to Fivemiletown—so named as it is five Irish miles from anywhere—

worthwhile. ⊠ *Fivemiletown, Co. Tyrone BT75 0QS,* ☎ *028/ 8952–1221. 4 rooms. Dining room. No credit cards.*

En Route   Set within an enchanted park—it is reputed that you can hear the "song of the little people" here—**Florence Court** is one of the most impressive of the North's grand Anglo-Irish mansions. Built around 1730 for John Cole, father of the first earl of Enniskillen, the three-story Palladian mansion was struck by fire in the 1950s; however, a loving restoration has replicated much of the abundant rococo plasterwork in the dining room, Venetian room, and, particularly, the famous staircase, all ascribed to Robert West, one of Dublin's most famous stuccadores (plaster workers). The house is 11 km (7 mi) south from Enniskillen on A4 and A32. ☎ *028/6634–8249.* ▱ *U.K.£2.80.* ◷ *Mansion Easter, Apr., and Sept., weekends 1–6; May–Aug., Wed.–Mon. 1–6. Grounds year-round, 10 AM–1 hr before dusk.*

Armagh

③⑦ *64 km (40 mi) west of Belfast, 77 km (48 mi) east of Enniskillen.*

The small but ancient ecclesiastical city of Armagh, despite the pleasing Georgian terraces around the elegant Mall east of the town center, can seem drab. Having suffered as a trouble spot in the sectarian conflict, though, it is now the scene of some spirited and sympathetic renovation. Here St. Patrick founded a church, and the town has remained a religious center to the present day; in fact, *two* Armagh cathedrals are dedicated to Ireland's patron saint. Despite the 1921 partition of Ireland into two parts, the seat of the Catholic Archbishop of All Ireland remains here, as does the seat of the Archbishop of the Anglican Church of Ireland.

Armagh's main attraction is the **Astronomy Centre and Planetarium and Observatory.** The observatory here has been in continuous use since 1791. The planetarium contains models of spacecraft, video shows of the sky, and hands-on computer displays. The **Earthorium exhibition** explores the world from three levels—its interior, surface, and atmosphere. The outdoor, 30-acre **AstroPark** features a model solar system. A **16-inch telescope** is open two nights per month, September through April (call for specific dates). The planetarium's **Robinson Dome,** also known as "the 10-inch dome" for the 1875 Grub telescope it houses, is open in summer months. ⊠ *College Hill,* ☎ *028/3752–3689 planetarium; 028/3752–4725 observatory.* ▱ *AstroPark and Robinson Dome free; hall of astronomy and Earthorium U.K.£1; special shows and other exhibitions U.K.£3.50.* ◷ *Planetarium weekdays 10–4:45, weekends 1:15–4:45; show weekdays at 3, weekends at 2 and 3; Robinson Dome Apr.–Sept., weekdays 9:30–4:30.*

Dedicated to St. Patrick, the pale limestone, Victorian-Gothic **Catholic Cathedral,** whose two spires rise above a hill at the north end of Armagh Town, is best seen from a short distance, allowing the viewer to take in the full majesty of it.

Near the town center in Armagh, a squat, battlemented tower identifies the **Protestant cathedral,** in simple, early 19th-century Perpendicular-Gothic style. It stands on the site of much older churches and contains several relics of Armagh's long history, including sculpted, pre-Christian idols. This cathedral claims to be the burial place of Brian Boru, the great High King—that is, king of all Ireland—who visited Armagh in 1004 and was received with great ceremony. Ten years later, at the Battle of Clontarf, he drove the Vikings out of Ireland but was killed after the battle was won.

Past the 13th-century Franciscan friary ruins, in the stables of the former archbishop's demesne, the **Palace Stables Heritage Centre** presents a diorama of everyday life—upstairs and downstairs—in the 18th-century days of the extremely wealthy Baron Rokeby, Church of Ireland Archbishop Richard Robinson. He commissioned local architect Francis Johnston, who had designed much of Georgian Dublin, to create a new Armagh out of the slums into which it had degenerated. The archbishop gave the city a clean water supply and a sewer system, then turned the city's racecourse into an elegant mall. He paved and lit the streets; financed improvements to the Bishop's Palace and the Protestant cathedral; and endowed the public library, the observatory, the Royal School, and the county infirmary. ⊠ *Palace Demesne, Friary Rd.,* ☎ *028/3752–9629.* 🖼 *U.K.£3.* ⊙ *Apr.–Sept., Mon.–Sat., 10–6, Sun. 1–6; Oct.–Mar., Mon.–Sat. 10–5, Sun. 2–5.*

Just outside Armagh, **Navan Fort** is Ulster's Camelot—the region's ancient capital. Excavations date evidence of activity going back to 700 BC. The fort has strong associations with figures of Irish history and legend. Thousands of years ago it is said to have been the site of the palace of Queen Macha; subsequent legends call it the barracks of the legendary Ulster warrior Cuchulain and his Red Branch Knights. Remains dating from 94 BC are particularly intriguing: A great conical structure, 120 ft in diameter, was formed from five concentric circles made of 275 wooden posts, with a 276th, about 12 yards high, situated in the center. In a ritual whose meaning is not known, it was filled with brushwood and set on fire. The Navan Centre rehearses the knight's tales—Ireland's *Iliad* and Ulster's *Camelot* combined. ⊠ *3 km (2 mi) west of Armagh on A28,* ☎ *028/3752–5550.* 🖼 *Centre U.K.£3.95; fort free.* ⊙ *Fort freely accessible; Centre Apr.–June and Sept., weekdays 10–6, Sat. 11–6, Sun. noon–6; July–Aug., Mon.–Sat. 10–7, Sun. 11–7; Oct.–Mar., weekdays 10–5, Sat. 11–5, Sun. noon–5.*

En Route Leave Armagh to the southeast on A28, driving toward Newry. Instead of going the entire way on the main road, after about 9½ km (6 mi), you'll have a more enjoyable drive if you take B133, on the right. This will lead you through a rustic, drumlin landscape of vivid green pastures. The appearance of villages changes as you return toward the River Bann; houses and farms begin to resemble those of Britain rather than those in the Republic.

Lodging

$$$ 🏨 **Drumsill Hotel.** On 15 acres of mature wooded grounds, this modern hotel is 1½ km (1 mi) northwest of Armagh on A29 road, signposted the Moy. Bedrooms are clean and functional. The formal Gallery Restaurant has an adventurous menu, with such starters as peppered chicken salad and main courses of duck breast with balsamic pear and scallion salad. Lemon lush pie is a standout dessert. Bond's Wine Bar features live music weekends. ⊠ *35 Moy Rd., Armagh BT61 8DL,* ☎ *028/3752–2009,* 🖷 *028/3752–5624. 10 rooms with bath. Restaurant, wine bar, meeting rooms. AE, MC, V.*

$$ 🏨 **Dean's Hill.** Jill Armstrong's elegant guest house was built, as the name suggests, for the cathedral's dean in 1760, and it has been in the Armstrong family for more than 100 years. Each of the three bedrooms, their period architectural features largely intact, has its own bath. One has a four-poster bed, another a fireplace. A self-catering apartment in the courtyard sleeps four. Despite the rural setting, Armagh's historic center is only a 10-minute walk away. ⊠ *College Hill, Armagh BT61 9DF,* ☎ *028/3752–4923. 3 rooms with bath, 1 apartment. Tennis court, croquet. No credit cards.*

The Mountains of Mourne

38 *16 km (10 mi) south of Downpatrick, 51 km (32 mi) south of Belfast.*

In the words of the popular song by Percy French, the Mountains of Mourne "sweep down to the sea"—from 2,000-ft summits. East of the unprepossessing though historically important border town of Newry, this area was long considered ungovernable, its hardy inhabitants living from smuggling contraband into the numerous rocky coves on the seashore. Much of the Mourne range is still inaccessible except on foot. The countryside is gorgeous: high, windswept pasture and moorland threaded with bright streams, bound by a tracery of drystone walls, and dotted with sheep and whitewashed farmhouses snuggled in stands of sycamore. It's the perfect landscape for away-from-it-all walkers, cyclists, and serious climbers. Climbers should inform their hotel or the **Northern Ireland Centre for Outdoor Activities** (⊠ Bryansford, Newcastle, ☎ 028/4372–2158) when and where they're heading before setting off.

Newcastle, a bracing Victorian cold-water bathing station, is the main center for visitors to the hills. Looming above Newcastle is **Slieve Donard,** its panoramic, 2,805-ft summit grandly claiming views into England, Wales, and Scotland "when it's clear enough"—in other words, rarely, say the pessimists. **Castlewellan Forest Park** comprises 1,150 acres of forested hills running between the Mourne Mountains and Slieve Croob. With its lake, secluded arbors, and **arboretum,** the park makes an excellent introduction to the area. ⊠ *Main St., Castlewellan,* ☎ *028/4377–8664.* ⊠ *Car U.K.£3; pedestrians U.K.£1.50.* ☉ *Daily dawn–dusk.*

Covering 1,200 acres and entered through picturesque Gothic gateways, **Tollymore Forest Park** extends up the valley of the River Shimna. There are many pretty stone bridges over the sparkling waters. ⊠ *Tully-brannigan Rd., Newcastle,* ☎ *028/4372–2428.* ⊠ *Car: U.K.£3; pedestrians: U.K.£1.50.* ☉ *Daily dawn–dusk.*

Farther into the mountains, the road to the **Silent Valley** reservoir parklands leads to further mountain views and excellent photo ops. Take B27 from Kilkeel; after 6 km (4 mi), turn right. ☎ *028/9074–6581.* ⊠ *Car U.K.£3; pedestrians U.K.£1.50.* ☉ *Apr.–Sept. daily 10–6:30; Oct.–Mar. 10–4.*

Outdoor Activities and Sports

The **Royal County Down** (⊠ Newcastle, ☎ 028/4372–3314) is considered by many golfers to be one of the finest courses in the world (☞ Chapter 9).

Lodging

$$$ 🏨 **Burrendale Hotel & Country Club.** Owner Sean Small's personality has made this low-slung, modern building, shaded by clumps of beech, into one of the most relaxing establishments on the North's east coast. Staff members are cheery; bedrooms are decorated in quiet tones. The Cottage Kitchen and Vine restaurants are competent (the former casual, the latter more formal) and particularly aim to please the many local customers, who like their plates overflowing. ⊠ *51 Castlewellan Rd., Newcastle, Co. Down BT33 0JY,* ☎ *028/4372–2599,* FAX *013967/22328. 68 rooms with bath. 2 restaurants, 2 bars, indoor pool, hot tub, sauna, steam rooms, exercise rooms, meeting rooms. AE, MC, V.*

$$$ 🏨 **Glassdrumman Lodge.** For those who wish to be pampered as well as immersed in the ancient Kingdom of Mourne, Graeme and Joan Hall's eclectically simple and stylish lodge is the place. The outside of the house

is less than spectacular, but those at the impressively busy estate grow their own crops, raise their own farm animals, churn their own butter, and bake their own bread. Rooms are decorated in bright colors and have large windows, which take advantage of the glorious views. The Halls think of everything, including overnight laundry service and complimentary car washing. Horseback riding and trekking can also be arranged. ⊠ *Mill Rd., Annalong, Co. Down BT34 4RH,* ☎ *028/ 4376–8451,* ☎ *028/4376–7041. 10 rooms with bath, 2 suites. Restaurant, horseback riding, laundry service, business services, meeting rooms. AE, MC, V.*

$$$ 🏨 **Slieve Donard Hotel.** A lavish, redbrick monument to Victoriana, this turreted, Victorian hotel stands like a palace on spacious green lawns at one end of Newcastle's 6½-km (4-mi) sandy beach. Guests will feel as if they are stepping back to the town's turn-of-the-century heyday as an elegant seaside resort, even though the rooms now have every modern comfort. Ask for a room overlooking the water. At the entrance to the grounds, the relaxed Percy French gatehouse pub serves adequate seafood dishes; music is presented every Saturday night. The Royal County Down Golf Club is next door. ⊠ *Downs Rd., Newcastle, Co. Down BT33 0AH,* ☎ *028/4372–3681,* ☎ *028/4372–4830. 130 rooms with bath. Dining room, bar, indoor pool, beauty salon, hot tub, steam room, 2 tennis courts, 2 exercise rooms. AE, DC, MC, V.*

Downpatrick

㊵ *35 km (22 mi) south of Belfast, 50 km (31 mi) east of Newry.*

Downpatrick used to be called "Plain and Simple Down" but had its name changed by the Norman knight John de Courcy, who moved to the town in 1176 and set about promoting St. Patrick (the 5th-century Briton who, captured by the Irish, became a slave in the Down area and later escaped to France, where he learned about Christianity, and bravely returned to try to convert the local chiefs). Although it is not true that Patrick brought a new faith to Ireland—there was already a bishop of Ireland before Patrick got here—he must have been a better missionary than most because he did indeed win influential converts. The clan chief of the Down area gave him land at the village of Saul, near Downpatrick, to build a monastery.

Downpatrick's hilltop **cathedral,** which lay ruined from 1538 to 1790 and was reopened in 1818, preserves parts of some of the earlier churches and monasteries that have stood on the site since the 6th century. Even before that time, the cathedral site had long been an important fortified settlement, and Down takes its name from the Celtic word "dun," or fort. In the churchyard, a somber slab inscribed "Patric" supposedly the saint's tomb, which is a bit of a fraud, since no one knows where Patrick is buried. It might be here, at Saul, or, some scholars argue, more likely at Armagh.

For some hard facts concerning the patron saint of Ireland, visit the **St. Patrick Heritage Centre** next to the cathedral; it's housed, together with the **Down Museum,** inside a former 18th-century jail. ⊠ *The Mall,* ☎ *028/4461–5218.* 🎫 *Free.* ☉ *Mid-June–mid-Sept., weekdays 11–5, weekends 2–5; mid-Sept.–mid-June, Tues.–Fri. 11–5, weekends 2–5.*

Portaferry

30 km (18½ mi) south of Newtownards, 13 km (8 mi) east of Downpatrick.

You'll have to cross Strangford Lough on the 24-vehicle car ferry from Strangford to reach Portaferry (U.K.£4 per car and driver, 80p per additional passenger), another quiet fishing village with old fortifications to guard this once-strategic channel, which joins the lough to the sea. The ferry crossing takes 10 minutes or less, and boats leave every half hour throughout the day. Departures from Strangford are on the half hour and hour, and from Portaferry on the three-quarter hour and the quarter hour: weekdays 7:30 AM–10:30 PM, Saturday 8 AM–11 PM, and Sunday 9:30 AM–10:30 PM.

Exploris, Portaferry's unusual aquarium, has models of the underwater environment in Strangford Lough and examples of 70 species that call the lough their home. Some of these creatures may not be what you expect: seals, which the aquarium staff regularly find and rescue from death on nearby shores (and, in one mysterious episode, the middle of an inland field), as well as several large, long-lived species of fish which still live in the lake. ⊠ *The Rope Walk,* ☎ *028/4272–8062.* ⊠ *U.K.£3.50.* ☉ *Apr.–Aug., Mon.–Sat. 10–6, Sun. 1–6; Sept.–Mar., Mon.–Sat. 10–5, Sun. 1–6.*

Dining and Lodging

$$$ ✕⌗ **Portaferry Hotel.** Standing on the quayside (or "strand") over-
★ looking the narrow channel that connects Strangford Lough to the sea, this centuries-old, comfortable, whitewashed inn offers well-kept, simply furnished double rooms. The main action takes place in the popular bar and restaurant, home to huge breakfasts, country lunches, and old-fashioned—and reasonably priced—evening meals. Live Strangford oysters, stuffed mussels, Dublin Bay prawns, scallops with bacon and garlic, and grilled turbot are briskly served to the Belfast and Dublin regulars who appreciate chef Gerry Manley's fresh, frill-and-fad-free seafood. Watch the sun set across the water from the bar window, or better still, book one of the sought-after rooms at the front. ⊠ *10 The Strand, Portaferry, Co. Down BT22 1PE,* ☎ *028/4272–8231,* ℻ *028/4272–8999. 12 double rooms with bath; 2 single rooms with bath. Restaurant, bar. AE, DC, MC, V.*

$$ ✕⌗ **Dufferin Arms Coaching Inn.** Next door to Killyleagh Castle, this lively 1803 inn is presided over by Stewart and Morris Crawford. The atmosphere of the beautiful Georgian building is that of a rustic pub; the comfortable decor includes luxurious bedrooms with four-poster beds. Downstairs, the original stables have been converted into the Kitchen Restaurant, a banquet hall with a long bar where medieval feasts and formal dinner parties often take place. Rustic Irish cooking—entrées such as poached salmon and roast duck in cherry sauce—is a specialty. One of the bars has snugs, another an open fire; diversions such as pub quizzes, traditional Irish storytelling, and Cajun and jazz music keep things lively. ⊠ *35 High St., Killyleagh, Co. Down BT30 9QF,* ☎ *028/4482–8229,* ℻ *028/4482–8755. 7 rooms with bath. Restaurant, 3 bars, meeting room. AE, MC, V.*

$$ ⌗ **Killyleagh Castle Towers.** Killyleagh, a pretty though somewhat
★ rundown little port on the east shore of Strangford Lough, is home to this splendidly Baroque edifice. Hans Sloane (1660–1753), physician to George II and the man who founded the British Museum, was a village boy encouraged to educate himself in the castle's library. Travelers can rent three self-catering apartments with room for four; two are in the 17th-century turrets and a larger one is in a Victorian-style turret over the gateway. Royalty-watchers, take note: Fergie, the ex-wife of Prince Andrew, has ancestral links here. ⊠ *Lieut. Col. Rowan Hamilton, Killyleagh Castle, Killyleagh, Co. Down BT30 9QA,* ☎ ℻ *028/4482–8261. 3 apartments. Pool. No credit cards.*

Mount Stewart

40 *21 km (13 mi) north from Portaferry.*

Mount Stewart is the grand, 19th-century family home of the Marquesses of Londonderry, who also built one of London's most sumptuous residences on Park Lane. It was constructed in two stages, where an earlier house stood: George Dance designed the west facade (1804–5), and William Vitruvius Morrison designed the neoclassic main part of the building. The landscaped gardens are populated with surprising stone carvings of rare and extinct creatures. The house contains one of George Stubbs's most famous portraits, that of the celebrated racehorse Hambletonian, after he had won one of the most celebrated contests of the 18th century. The octagonal Temple of the Winds is a copy of a similar structure in Athens, and there's also a remarkable bathhouse and pool at the end of the wooded peninsula just before the entrance to the grounds. ✉ *Newtownards,* ☎ *028/4278–8387.* ✑ *U.K.£3.50.* ☉ *May–Sept., Wed.–Mon. 1–6; Apr. and Oct., weekends 1–6.*

Dining and Lodging

$$$ ✕▢ **The Old Inn.** On the outside, this 1614 coaching inn, which is reputedly Ireland's oldest, looks the part: It's pure 17th-century old-world England, with a sculpted thatched roof, half doors, and leaded windows. Inside there are roaring open fires in winter. Some of the bedrooms have four-poster beds and sitting rooms. The Churn Bistro's menu is solidly Irish, the staff jovial, and the locals inquisitive. Crawfordsburn is 16 km (10 mi) from Belfast. ✉ *15 Main St., Crawfordsburn, Co. Down, BT19 1JH,* ☎ *028/9185–3255,* ℻ *028/9185–2775. 33 rooms with bath. Restaurant, 2 bars. AE, DC, MC, V.*

NORTHERN IRELAND A TO Z

Arriving and Departing

By Bus

Northern Ireland's bus company, **Ulsterbus** (☎ 028/9033–3000), and the Republic's **Bus Éireann** (☎ 01/836–6111 in Dublin) both run direct services to and from Dublin. Buses arrive and depart from the Europa Buscentre; the ride takes 3 hours. Buses to Belfast also run from London and from Birmingham, making the Stranraer ferry (☎ 01776/702262) crossing.

By Car

Many roads from the Irish Republic into Northern Ireland were once closed for security reasons, but all are now reinstated, leaving drivers with a choice of legitimate crossing points. Army checkpoints at all approved frontier posts are rare, and few customs formalities are observed. The fast N1/A1 road connects Belfast to Dublin in 160 km (100 mi) with an average driving time of just over 2 hours.

By Ferry

Norse Irish Ferries (✉ Victoria Terminal 2, West Bank Rd., ☎ 028/9077–9090) has 11-hour, overnight car ferries that connect Belfast with the English west-coast port of Liverpool every other night. **P&O European Ferries** (☎ 0990/980980) has a 1-hour sailing to Larne from Cairnryan, Scotland; infrequent trains take passengers on to Belfast. You can also cross on the **SeaCat** (☎ 0990/523523) or the **StenaLine's HSS** (☎ 0990/204204), both fast catamarans that carry cars and passengers from Stranraer directly into Belfast in just 1½ hours. **SeaCat** also sails from Belfast to Heysham on the west coast of England, taking 4 hours. The **Argyll and Antrim Steam Packet Company** (☎ 0990/523523) is a

3-hour car-ferry service on the MV *Claymore* linking Campbeltown in Scotland with Ballycastle in County Antrim; it runs July–October. The **Isle of Man Steam Packet Company** (☎ 0990/523523) runs summer services to and from the Isle of Man and Belfast.

By Plane

Belfast International Airport at Aldergove (☎ 028/9042–2888) is the North's principal air arrival point, 30½ km (19 mi) from Belfast. **Belfast City Airport** (☎ 028/9045–7745) is the second airport, 6½ km (4 mi) from the city. It receives flights from U.K. provincial airports, from London Gatwick and Heathrow, and from Stanstead and Luton (both near London). **Aer Lingus** (☎ 028/9024–5151) flies once daily on Monday, Thursday, Saturday, and Sunday from New York's JFK directly to Belfast. Other scheduled services from the United States and Canada are routed through Dublin, Glasgow, London, or Manchester. Charter operators, including **American Trans Air** (☎ 01293/50237), run summer services directly into Belfast International.

Frequent services to Belfast's two airports are scheduled throughout the day from London Heathrow, London Gatwick, Luton, and Stanstead (all of which have fast coordinated subway or rail connections to central London), from 17 other U.K. airports and from Cork in the Republic of Ireland. Flights take about 1¼ hours from London. **British Airways and BA Express** (both ☎ 0345/222111), **British Midland Airways** (☎ 0345/554554), and **Jersey European Airways** (☎ 0345/676676) operate the majority of flights into Belfast. Direct flights from Amsterdam on **Air UK** (☎ 0345/666777) also arrive in Belfast.

City of Derry Airport (☎ 028/7181–0784) is 8 km (5 mi) from Derry and receives flights from Glasgow and Manchester.

BETWEEN THE AIRPORTS AND THE CITIES

Belfast. Ulsterbus (☎ 028/9033–3000) operates a shuttle bus every half hour (one-way U.K.£3.70, round-trip U.K.£6.40) between the International Airport and Belfast city center. From Belfast City Airport, you can travel into Belfast by train from Sydenham Halt to Central Station (✉ East Bridge St.) or catch a taxi from the airport to your hotel.

Derry. If you arrive at Eglinton Airport, 8 km (5 mi) from Derry, you may need to call a taxi (☎ 028/7181–1231 or 028/7126–3905) to get to your destination.

By Train

The Dublin–Belfast Express train, operated by both **Northern Ireland Railways** (☎ 028/9089–9411) and **Iarnród Éireann** (☎ 01/855–4477), travels between the two cities in about 2 hours. Six trains (check timetables, as some trains are much slower) run daily in both directions (three on Sunday) to and from Belfast's misnamed **Central Station** (✉ East Bridge St., ☎ 028/9089–9411). However, a free shuttle bus service will drop you off at City Hall or Ulsterbus's city-center **Europa Buscentre** (☎ 028/9033–3000), or you can change trains for the de facto city-center **Great Victoria Street Station** (✉ Great Victoria St., ☎ 028/9023–0671), which is adjacent both to the Europa Buscentre and the Europa Hotel.

Getting Around

By Bus

Visitors can take advantage of frequent and inexpensive Ulsterbus links between all Northern Ireland towns. The main bus stations in Belfast are the **Europa Buscentre** (✉ Glengall St., ☎ 028/9033–3000), which is easiest to find using its Great Victoria Street entrance to the left of the Europa Hotel, and the **Laganside Buscentre** (⊠ Donegall Quay, ☎ 028/9032–0111), around the corner from the Albert Clock and about 1 km (½ mi) from Central Station.

If you want to tour the North by bus, a **Freedom of Northern Ireland Ticket** allows unlimited travel on bus or train (U.K.£9 per day, U.K.£28 per week). An **Irish Rover** ticket from Ulsterbus covers Ireland, north and south, and costs U.K.£36 for three days, U.K.£85 for eight. For specific fares and schedules, call **Ulsterbus** (☎ 028/9033–3000). Within Belfast, visitors have access to good city-bus service. All routes start from Donegall Square; you'll find a kiosk there where you can pick up a timetable. Another contact is **Citybus** (☎ 028/9024–6485).

By Car

In general, drivers will find roads here are in much better shape and signposted more clearly than in the Irish Republic. Bad rush-hour delays can occur on the West Link joining M1 (heading south or west) and M2 (heading east or north). But on the whole, driving is quicker and easier in the North than in areas south of the border.

PARKING

Belfast has many parking garages, as well as street meter-ticket parking. Before parking on the street, check the posted regulations: During rush hours many spots become no-parking.

By Train

Northern Ireland Railways runs only four rail routes from Belfast's **Central Station** (⊠ E. Bridge St., ☎ 028/9089–9411)—which is not, in fact, that centrally located: northwest to **Derry** via Coleraine and the Causeway Coast; east to **Bangor** along the shore of Belfast Lough; northeast to **Larne** (for the P&O European ferry to Scotland [☞ *above*]); and south to **Dublin.** There are frequent connections to Central Station from the much more central Great Victoria Street Station (☞ Arriving and Departing, *above*) and from Botanic Station (⊠ Botanic Ave., ☎ 028/9089–9411) in the university area. **Rail Runabout** tickets allow seven days' unlimited travel from April to October only (U.K.£30). **Freedom of Northern Ireland** tickets also apply to trains (☞ *above*). For more information contact **Northern Ireland Railways** (⊠ 28 Wellington Pl., Belfast, ☎ 028/9089–9411).

Contacts and Resources

Banks and Money Exchange

The North uses British currency. Irish *punts,* or pounds, are not accepted. Rates change rapidly, but the British pound is generally worth slightly more than the Irish (☞ Money *in* Smart Travel Tips A to Z). You'll sometimes be given bank notes, drawn on Ulster banks, that are valid only in Northern Ireland; be sure not to get stuck with a lot of these when you leave, because they will be difficult to change at banks back home. Main banks are open weekdays 9:30–4:30, smaller branches weekdays 10:30–3:30. Changing money outside banking hours is possible at **Thomas Cook** branches. ⊠ *Belfast Airport,* ☎ 028/9442–2536. ☉ *Weekdays 7 AM–8 PM, weekends 7 AM–10 PM;* ⊠ *11 Donegall Pl.,* ☎ *028/9055–4455* ☉ *Mon.–Wed. and Fri.–Sat. 9–5:30, Thurs. 10–5:30;* ⊠ *22 Lombard Pl.,* ☎ *028/9023–6044.* ☉ *Mon.–Wed. and Fri.–Sat. 9–5:30; Thurs. 10–5:30.*

Car Rentals

Visitors can choose among several local rental companies, but car rental isn't cheap. A compact car costs U.K.£150 to U.K.£210 per week (including taxes, insurance, and unlimited mileage). If you're planning to take a rental car across the border into the Republic, inform the company and check its insurance procedures. Following are some of the main rental offices.

Avis (⊠ Belfast International Airport, ☏ 028/9442–2333; ⊠ Belfast City Airport, ☏ 028/9045–2017; ⊠ Great Victoria St., ☏ 028/9024–0404). **Dan Dooley** (⊠ Belfast International Airport, ☏ 028/9445–2522). **Europcar** (⊠ Belfast International Airport, ☏ 028/9442–3444). **Hertz** (⊠ Belfast International Airport, ☏ 028/9442–2533). **Europcar** (⊠ Belfast City Airport, ☏ 028/9045–0904). **Hertz** (⊠ Belfast City Airport, ☏ 028/9073–2451).

Ford (⊠ Desmond Motors, City of Derry Airport, ☏ 028/7181–0832); a £180 security deposit is required here.

Emergencies

Police, fire, ambulance or **coast guard** (☏ 999). **Belfast's main police station** (⊠ 6–10 N. Queen St., ☏ 028/9065–0222).

Belfast: Belfast City Hospital (⊠ Lisburn Rd., ☏ 028/9032–9241) is one of two main hospitals in the city with an emergency room. The **Royal Victoria Hospital** (⊠ Grosvenor Rd., ☏ 028/9024–0503) is the other.

Derry: Altnagelvin Hospital (⊠ Belfast Rd., ☏ 028/7134–5171) has an emergency room.

Guided Tours

Citybus (⊠ Milewater Rd., ☏ 028/9045–8484) offers a Belfast City Tour that takes in the shipyards and heads out from the city center as far as Stormont, 9½ km (6 mi) east, and Belfast Castle on Cave Hill to the north. The cost is U.K.£8, including afternoon tea. The City Tour leaves Castle Place June–September, Wednesday and Saturday at 1 PM. Other Citybus tours include "Lagan Experience," "A Look At Linen," and "Titanic: A Tour to Remember."

Ulsterbus (⊠ Milewater Rd., ☏ 028/9033–3000) operates half-day or full-day trips June through September from Belfast to the Glens of Antrim, the Giant's Causeway, the Fermanagh lakes, Lough Neagh, the Mourne Mountains, and the Ards Peninsula.

Erne Tours (☏ 028/6632–2882) operates *Kestrel*, a 63-seat water bus, which it leaves Round O pier at Enniskillen during the summer at 10:30, 2:15, 4:15, and 7:15 on Tuesday, Thursday, and Sunday for a 2-hour trip on beautiful Lough Erne. On weekdays the boat makes a ½-hour stop at Devenish Island (☞ *above*). From May to June there are Sunday trips at 2:30, and occasionally tours run at other times of the year.

Ulsterbus has also teamed up with the Old Bushmills Distillery to run the **Bushmills Bus,** an open-top tour bus running from Coleraine to the Giant's Causeway via the coast resorts; you also visit Bushmills to observe whiskey making. A bus leaves Coleraine daily at 9:20, 11:30, 2:10, 4, and 6. Call Ulsterbus (☏ 028/9033–3000 or 028/7034–3334) for prices.

Outdoor Activities and Sports

Rentals cost around U.K.£7 a day, U.K.£30 a week; local TIOs can offer suggestions for good cycling routes (☞ Visitor Information, *below*). In Belfast rent from **McConvrey Cycles** (⊠ 467 Ormeau Rd.,

☎ 028/9049–1163). **ReCycle** (✉ 1 Albert Sq., ☎ 028/9031–3113) is another good place to rent in Belfast.

Murphy's Wildlife Tours (✉ 12 Belvoir [pronounced beaver] Close, Belvoir Park, Belfast, ☎ 028/9069–3232) leads tours in all seasons, though if you're an advanced birder, you may want to concentrate on wintering wildfowl and waders that have migrated all the way from North America to the shores of Loughs Foyle, Neagh, and Strangford. For information, ideas, and details of field-study groups, contact Northern Ireland TIOs (☞ Visitor Information, *below*) and the **Royal Society for the Protection of Birds** (✉ Belvoir Park Forest, ☎ 028/9049–1547).

FISHING

Northern Ireland's system of pricing and administrating fishing licenses and permits can seem anachronistic, unnecessarily complex, and bewildering. No license is needed for sea fishing, but to catch freshwater fish, whether coarse or game, you need a rod license from the **Fisheries Conservancy Board** (✉ 1 Mahon Rd., Portadown, ☎ 028/3833–4666); another license from the **Foyle Fisheries Commission** (✉ 8 Victoria Rd., Derry, ☎ 028/7134–2100), depending on the area in which you're fishing; and probably need a local permit. The good news is that all licenses and Department of Agriculture and Fisheries permits are available from the **Northern Ireland Visitor Information Centre** (☞ Visitor Information, *below*) as well as from a number of TIOs and tackle shops around the province.

In the main angling areas, the following are useful contacts: **Moyle Outdoor Angling** (✉ 17 Castle St., Ballycastle, ☎ 028/2076–9521), **Joseph Braddell** (✉ 11 North St., Belfast, ☎ 028/9032–0525), **Tommy McCutcheon** (✉ 114 Sandy Row, Belfast, ☎ 028/9024–9509), **Carlton Park Fishing Centre** (✉ Belleek, ☎ 028/6865–8181), **Lakeland Tackle & Guns** (✉ Sligo Rd., Enniskillen, ☎ 028/6632–3774), **Albert Atkins** (✉ 67 Coleraine Rd., Garvagh, ☎ 028/2955–8555), **Hook, Line & Sinker** (✉ 43 South St., Newtownards, ☎ 028/9181–1671), **Joe Mullan** (✉ 74 Main St., Portrush, ☎ 028/7082–2209).

GOLF

All golf courses and clubs are listed in the Northern Ireland Tourist Board information guide No. 17, "Golf—Where to Play," available from main tourist offices. ☞ Northern Ireland *in* Chapter 9.

HIKING AND WALKING

More than 100 places to stay along the Ulster Way are listed in the Northern Ireland Tourist Board information guide *Accommodation for Walkers on the Ulster Way.* The **Sports Council for Northern Ireland** (✉ House of Sport, Upper Malone Rd., Belfast BT9 5LA, ☎ 028/9038–1222) can also give advice about the Ulster Way; it sells books covering each section of the route. Tougher walks in the hills are outlined in the informative handbook in the Irish Walks series, No. 4, *The North East,* by Richard Rogers, published by **Gill & Macmillan** (✉ 15–17 Eden Quay, Dublin, 01, ☎ 01/453–1005), which is available in local book and sporting goods stores in Northern Ireland; it gives precise details of 45 hill walks, complete with descriptions of the wildflowers you'll see along the way. For hikes in the Mountains of Mourne, you can obtain maps and details of suggested routes from the **Mourne Countryside Centre** (✉ 91 Central Promenade, Newcastle, Co. Down, ☎ 028/4372–4059). **Celtic Journeys** (✉ 111 Whitepark Rd., Ballycastle, ☎ 012657/69651) arranges wildlife and cultural walks.

HORSEBACK RIDING/PONY TREKKING

About 3¼ km (2 mi) south of center-city Belfast, the **Lagan Valley Equestrian Centre** runs pony treks and offers lessons—both group and private. ⊠ *170 Upper Malone Rd., Belfast,* ☎ *028/9061–4853.* 🎟 *Group lessons and trekking U.K.£8 hourly; private lessons U.K.£14.* ☉ *Weekdays 10–9, Sat. 10–3:30.*

Student Travel

For details on youth hostels in Belfast and elsewhere, contact **Y.H.A.N.I.** at the Belfast International Youth Hostel (⊠ 22 Donegall Rd., Belfast BT12 5JN, ☎ 028/9032–4733, ℻ 028/9043–9699). This modern and comfortable hostel has 128 beds.

Visitor Information

The **Northern Ireland Tourist Board Information Centre** in Belfast is the main TIO for the whole of the North (☞ Exploring Belfast, *above*). ⊠ *Donegall Sq.,* ☎ *028/9024–6609,* ℻ *028/9031–2424.* ☉ *Sept.–June, Mon. 9:30–5:15, Tues.–Sat. 9–5:15; July–Aug., Mon. 9:30–7, Tues.–Sat. 9–7, Sun. noon–4.*

Year-round local offices are also at these locations: **Armagh** (⊠ 40 English St., ☎ 028/3752–1800). **Ballycastle** (⊠ 7 Mary St., ☎ 028/2076–2024). **Bangor** (⊠ Quay St., ☎ 028/3727–0069). **Carrickfergus** (⊠ Heritage Plaza, ☎ 01960/366455). **Coleraine** (⊠ Railway Rd., 028/7034–4723). **Derry** (⊠ Foyle St., ☎ 028/7126–7284 or 028/7137–7577). **Downpatrick** (⊠ 74 Market St., ☎ 028/4461–2233). **Enniskillen** (⊠ Lakeland Visitor Centre, Shore Rd., ☎ 028/6632–3110). **Giant's Causeway** (⊠ Visitor Centre, ☎ 028/2073–1855). **Killymaddy** (⊠ Ballygally Rd., ☎ 01868/767259). **Larne** (⊠ Narrow Gauge Rd., ☎ 028/2826–0088). **Limavady** (⊠ Connell St., ☎ 028/7772–2226). **Lisburn** (⊠ Market Sq., ☎ 028/9266–0038). **Newcastle** (⊠ Central Promenade, ☎ 028/4372–2222). **Newtownards** (⊠ Regent St., ☎ 028/9182–6846). **Newry** (⊠ Town Hall, Bank Parade, ☎ 028/3026–8877). During June through August, many more towns and villages open TIOs.

Weather

Call **Weathercall** (☎ 0891/500427) or **Marine Call** (☎ 0891/505365) for a Northern Ireland weather forecast.

9 IRISH GREENS
GOLFING IN IRELAND

If you come to Ireland to golf, you may hear the story about Mick O'Loughlin, a County Clare butcher who spent more time playing at the Lahinch Golf Club than standing behind his meat counter. "He can't be making much money," a visitor remarked, upon hearing where Mick could usually be found. Came the reply: "Maybe not. But he's sure making plenty of friends." In the last 10 years, Ireland has invested nearly $400 million in a gambit to become Europe's premier golf destination. While its you-know-who neighbor to the northeast still has more courses, Ireland's 390—and counting—are gorgeously scenic and designed by golf's greatest.

ASK MOST GOLFERS WHERE TO FIND the golf vacation of a lifetime—a variety of breathtaking courses, beautiful settings, history seeping into every shot—and they'll probably point you in the direction of Scotland. Unless, of course, they've been to Ireland.

By Jonathan
Abrahams

Updated by
Dermot
Gilleece

Indeed, Ireland's neighbor to the northeast gets more world attention when it comes to golf. It plays host to most of the British Open championships and in many circles is considered the birthplace of the game. But Ireland doesn't lag far behind when it comes to golf history. Its oldest course dates back to 1881, and with more than 380 quality layouts, the Emerald Isle is second only to Scotland in the amount of golf it can offer per square mile. If you ask a local how Ireland's courses stack up against Scotland's, he'll fix you with a steely stare before defending his homeland on his life. Then he very well may buy you a pint of the local stout. But you don't have to be a native to have such passion for the golf courses of Ireland (not to mention the stout). Golfers the world over who are "in the know" have long sung the praises of Irish golf. Tom Watson, winner of five British Opens, lists as his favorite not any Scottish course but Ballybunion, as does the legendary writer Herbert Warren Wind, who, from an American standpoint, is credited with putting Irish golf on the map when he penned, "To put it simply, Ballybunion revealed itself to be nothing less than the finest seaside course I have ever seen." And although Ballybunion is generally considered the prize jewel of the Emerald Isle, it is reflective of the quality of courses found throughout the country.

So what makes Irish golf great? Architecture, perhaps the essence of a golfing experience, is one appropriate place to begin. Connoisseurs of golf in America hold such courses as Cypress Point and Pebble Beach in the highest regard because their designers used the spectacular lay of the land to create a beautiful, challenging, but fair layout. In Ireland, however, there are many such courses. Of the estimated 150 top-quality links courses in the world, 39 of them are in Ireland. Most of the leading courses in Ireland were designed by celebrated British architects, such as Tom Morris, James Braid, Harry Colt, and Alister Mackenzie, who happened to have as their raw material a spectacular landscape: Ireland is one of those remarkable places where mountains and sea meet, so there is no need to manipulate the land. Nature—the scraggly coast of a links-land or rolling hills of heather—dominates the courses here, not the other way around.

There is also something to be said for the sense of history that comes with playing golf on a land that is, most assuredly, "old world." Only 40 minutes from the airport in Shannon is the charming 18-hole course at Adare, complete with a green nestled in the ruins of a 14th-century abbey. Every step you take on an Irish golf course is a step back in history. Where in America can you find something comparable to the "Mass Hole" at Waterville, a par-3 built over a large hollow where Catholic priests used to hold services in secret, because praying was a capital offense at the time?

The Weather Factor. Pack heavy. You see all different kinds of weather in Ireland, from high winds to rain and sleet to beautiful sunshine, and you may see it all in one round. There are no rain checks here. You play unless it's lightning, so pack your sweaters and rain gear, especially if you're planning your trip for the off-season months of the spring and fall.

The Sunday Bag Factor. If you don't have a golf bag that's light enough for you to carry for 18 holes, invest in one before your trip. Electric carts are generally available only at the leading venues in Ireland, so you usually have the option of a using a caddy or caddy car (pull cart) or carrying your own bag. Many courses have caddies but will not guarantee their availability since they're not employed by the course directly, so it's conceivable that you may be left with only one option: toting your bag yourself. To be safe, make sure you have a carryall, or Sunday bag.

The Private Club Factor. Unlike America, most private golf clubs in Ireland are happy to let visitors play their course and use their facilities. It's important to remember, however, that the course is indeed there for the members first, and the majority of the club's concerns lie with them. Preferred days for visitors are listed below, but it's always a good idea to call in advance and make sure that the club will make time for you.

The Northern Ireland Factor. Some of the best and most beautiful courses are in Northern Ireland, where the leading venues are far less remote than in the Republic. The signing of a peace agreement in April 1998 only enhanced the region's attraction. But keep in mind that this part of the island is under British rule, so all currency is in U.K. pounds, though the Irish pound, or punt, is always welcome.

And finally, a reality check. Ireland's best courses rank with the best of the world, but after that there's a bit of a drop-off. Of the 390-odd courses, only about 30 are worth crossing an ocean to play. Others are good, but nothing you can't find at home. Of that 30, all are happy to have visitors play, except Royal Belfast, in Northern Ireland. It's the oldest club in Ireland, and it's exclusive: If you belong to a club in America, they must write a letter of introduction to Royal Belfast to secure your playing privilege. The remaining courses are listed below.

North of Dublin

County Louth Golf Club. Like many other Irish courses, County Louth is better known as its hometown, Baltray, a village sandwiched by the Boyne Estuary to the west and the Irish Sea to the east. Long hitters will love the atypical layout, a par-73 that features five par-5s, but beware the well-protected, undulating greens. ⊠ *Baltray, Drogheda, Co. Louth,* ☎ *041/22329. 18 holes. Yardage: 6,783. Par 73.* ☒ *Fees: weekdays, £45; weekends, £55.* ☉ *Visitors: Mon. and Wed.–Fri. Practice area, caddies (reserve in advance), caddy carts, catering.*

Island Golf Club. Talk about exclusive: Until 1960, the only way to reach this club was by boat. It was about as remote as you could get and still be only 24 km (15) mi from Dublin, but things have changed. The Island has opened its doors and revealed a fine links course that rolls in and around sandhills, with small, challenging greens. ⊠ *Corballis, Donabate, Co. Dublin,* ☎ *01/843–6205. 18 holes. Yardage: 6,625. Par 71.* ☒ *Fees: weekdays, £50; weekends, £60.* ☉ *Visitors: Mon., Tues., and Fri. Practice area, catering.*

★ **Portmarnock Golf Club.** Across an estuary from the easternmost point of Ireland, Portmarnock is perhaps the most famous of Ireland's "Big Four" (Ballybunion, Royal County Down, and Royal Portrush are the others). Largely because of its proximity to Dublin, this links course has hosted numerous major championships, most recently the 1997 European Men's Amateur Championship. Known for its flat fairways and greens, it provides a fair test for any golfer who can keep it out of the heavy rough. ⊠ *Portmarnock, Co. Dublin,* ☎ *01/846–2968. 27 holes. Yardage: 7,051, 3,449. Par 72, 36.* ☒ *Fees: weekdays, £70; week-*

ends, £90. ⊙ Visitors: Mon., Tues., and Fri. Practice area, caddies (reserve in advance), caddy carts, catering.

Royal Dublin Golf Club. Generally, links courses are in remote, even desolate areas (therein the charm), but this equally captivating one is only 6 km (4 mi) from the center of Dublin, on Bull Island, a bird sanctuary. It's the second-oldest club in Ireland and is routed in the old tradition of seaside links: The front 9 goes out in a line (wind helping), and the back 9 comes back in a line (wind against). Don't expect to make a comeback on the way home if you've struggled going out. ⊠ *Dollymount, Clontarf, Dublin 3, ☎ 01/833–6346. 18 holes. Yardage: 6,763. Par 72. ▦ Fees: weekdays, £60; weekends, £70. ⊙ Visitors: Mon., Tues., Thurs., and Fri. Practice area, caddies, caddy carts, catering.*

St. Margaret's Golf and Country Club. Not all of the worthwhile golf in Ireland is played on links courses that are a century old. St. Margaret's is a parkland (inland) course that opened in 1992 and immediately received high praise from Ireland's golfing inner circle. If, after getting blown around on the seaside links, you long for a taste of Western golf, this is your haven. ⊠ *St. Margaret's, Co. Dublin, ☎ 01/864–0400. 18 holes. Yardage: 6,965. Par 72. ▦ Fees: weekdays, £45; weekends and holidays, £40. ⊙ Visitors: daily. Practice area, caddies, caddy carts, club rental, catering.*

South of Dublin and the Southeast

Gleann na Drioite (Druids Glen) Golf Club. Owner Hugo Flinn presented designers Pat Ruddy and Tom Craddock with the brief "Build me the finest parkland course in Ireland, whatever the cost." After an outlay of more than $16 million their handiwork was opened to the public in September 1995. Only a few months later, it had been chosen as the venue for the 1996 Murphy's Irish Open and hosted it again in 1998 for a fourth time. Ruddy unashamedly admits to having copied some key elements of Augusta National—particularly the extensive use of water—in the layout. In any event, the course, situated about 40 km (25 mi) south of Dublin in County Wicklow, is remarkably beautiful, particularly around the glen from which its name derives. It is essentially an American-style target course incorporating some delightful changes in elevation, and its forbidding, par-3 17th has an island green, like the corresponding hole at TPC Sawgrass. ⊠ *Newtownmountkennedy, Co. Wicklow, ☎ 01/287–3600. 18 holes. Yardage: 7,058. Par 72. ▦ Fees: weekdays and weekends, £80. Practice area, caddies, caddy carts, catering.*

★ **The K Club.** At just 27 km (17 mi) west of Dublin, this 18-hole, Arnold Palmer–designed parkland course, one of the newest additions to the Irish golf scene, offers a round of golf in lush, wooded surroundings bordered by the River Liffey and was recently selected as the venue for the 2005 Ryder Cup. The generous fairways and immaculate greens are offset by formidable length, which makes it one of the most demanding courses in the Dublin vicinity. Additional stress is presented by negotiating the numerous doglegs, water obstacles, and sand bunkers. Facilities on the premises are of the highest standard, allowing a wide choice of sporting and nonsporting activities. ⊠ *Kildare Country Club, Straffan, Co. Kildare, ☎ 01/627–3333. 18 holes. Yardage: 7,171. Par 72. ▦ Fees: £130 (residents £70). ⊙ Visitors: daily except Mon.–Fri. 1:30–2:30, Sat. 9–1. Practice area, caddies, caddy carts, club rental, shoe rental, catering.*

Southwest

Adare Manor Golf Course. Situated in the ancestral estate of the Earl of Dunraven, this charming parkland stretch was officially opened for play in 1996. Its immediate success was virtually guaranteed by the international profile of its designer, Robert Trent Jones. The "grand old man" of golf-course architects seemed far more comfortable with the wooded terrain than he was when designing the second links at Ballybunion. As a result, he delivered a course with the potential to play host to events of the highest caliber. The front 9 is dominated by an artificial 14-acre lake with a $500,000 polyethylene base. It is in play at the 3rd, 5th, 6th, and 7th holes. By way of contrast, the dominant hazards on the homeward journey are the River Mague and the majestic trees. Both combine to make the par-5 18th one of the most testing finishing holes imaginable. ⊠ *Adare, Co. Limerick,* ☎ *061/ 395044. 18 holes. Yardage: 7,138. Par 72.* 🗺 *Fees: weekdays and weekends, £50. Practice area, caddies, caddy carts, catering.*

★ **Ballybunion Golf Club.** Simply stated, this is one of the finest courses in the world. The Old Course was a virtual unknown until Herbert Warren Wind sang its praises in 1968, and today Ballybunion is universally regarded as one of golf's holiest grounds. On the shore of the Atlantic next to the southern entrance of the Shannon, it has the huge dunes of Lahinch without the blind shots. No pushover, but every hole is a pleasurable experience. Watch out for "Mrs. Simpson," a double fairway bunker on the 1st hole, named after the wife of Tom Simpson, the architect who remodeled the course in 1937. The New Course, which opened in 1985, was designed by Robert Trent Jones. ⊠ *Sandhill Rd., Ballybunion, Co. Kerry,* ☎ *068/27611. 36 holes. Yardage: 6,593 (Old), 6,216 (New). Par 71, 72.* 🗺 *Fees: £60 (Old), £35 (New), £75 (both on same day).* ☉ *Visitors: weekdays. Practice area, caddies, caddy carts, catering.*

Cork Golf Club. If you know golf-course architecture, you're familiar with the name Alister Mackenzie, who designed Cypress Point in California and Augusta National in Georgia. One of his few designs in Ireland is Cork, better known as Little Island. There's water on this parkland course, but it's not the temperamental ocean; instead, Little Island is in Cork Harbour, a gentle bay of the Irish Sea. The course is little known but one of the Emerald Isle's best. ⊠ *Little Island, Co. Cork,* ☎ *021/353451. 18 holes. Yardage: 6,687. Par 72.* 🗺 *Fees: weekdays, £40; weekends, £45.* ☉ *Visitors: Mon.–Wed. and Fri. Practice area, caddies, caddy carts, club rental, catering.*

Dooks Golf Club. On the second tier of courses in Ireland's Southwest, Dooks doesn't quite measure up to the world-class tracks. It is, nonetheless, a completely worthwhile day of golf if you're touring the area. Built in the old tradition of seaside links, it's shorter and a bit gentler, although the greens are small and tricky. It's an excellent way to take a breath. ⊠ *Dooks, Glenbeigh, Co. Kerry,* ☎ *066/68205. 18 holes. Yardage: 6,010. Par 70.* 🗺 *Fees: £25.* ☉ *Visitors: weekdays. Caddy carts, catering.*

Killarney Golf and Fishing Club. Freshwater fishing is the sport here, for Killarney is an inland town, set among a stunning mixture of mountains, lakes, and forests. There are two golf courses, the Killeen Course, host of the 1992 Irish Open, and Mahony's Point, set along the shores of Lough Leane. Killeen is longer; Mahony's places a premium on accuracy. Despite the abundance of seaside links, many well-traveled golfers name Killarney as their favorite place to play in Ireland. ⊠ *Mahony's Point Demesne, Killarney, Co. Kerry,* ☎ *064/31034. 36 holes. Yardage: 7,056 (Killeen), 6,705 (Mahony's). Par 73, 72.* 🗺 *Fees: £40.* ☉ *Visitors: Mon.–Sat. Practice area, caddies, caddy carts, catering.*

★ **Mount Juliet Golf Course.** The championship parkland course, 19 km (11 mi) from Kilkenny Town, was designed by Jack Nicklaus and includes practice greens, a driving range, and, for those who feel a little rusty, a David Leadbetter golf academy. The heavily forested course has 8 holes that play over water, including the three signature par-3s. The back 9 presents a series of difficult bunker shots. A sporting day out comes to a welcome end in the Hunter's Yard or Rose Garden lodge, which cater to both the thirsty and the hungry. Greens fees are above average, and although visitors are always welcome, a weekday round is better than a weekend one, as tees can be crowded with members flocking to the course at week's end. ⊠ *Mount Juliet Estate, Thomastown, Co. Kilkenny,* ☎ *056/24455. Yardage 7,172. Par 72.* 🖹 *Fees: weekdays, £75, weekends £85.* ⊘ *Visitors: daily. Practice area, driving range, caddies, caddy carts, club rental, lessons, catering.*

Old Head of Kinsale. Opened in 1997, this is the latest Irish golfing delight. Situated on a celebrated, 215-acre County Cork peninsula, which juts out into the wild Atlantic nearly 300 ft below, it is an awe-inspiring spectacle that defies comparison. The only golfing stretches that could be likened to it are the 16th and 17th holes at Cypress Point and small, Pacific sections of Pebble Beach, from the 7th to the 10th and the long 18th. Even if the visitor's golf is moderate, pulses are certain to race at the stunning views and wonderful wildlife on this 18-hole course. ⊠ *Kinsale, Co. Cork,* ☎ *021/778444. Yardage 7,100. Par 72.* 🖹 *Fees: weekdays and weekends, £90.* ⊘ *Visitors: daily. Practice area, caddies (reserve in advance), caddy carts, catering.*

Tralee Golf Club. Tralee is perhaps what all modern-golf-course architects *wish* they could do in the States: find unspoiled, seaside links and route a course on it that's designed for the modern game. This is an Arnold Palmer–Ed Seay design that opened in 1984, and the setting is as classic as it gets, with plenty of cliffs, craters, dunes, and the gale-blowing ocean. Don't let the flat front 9 lull you to sleep—the back 9 can be a ferocious wake-up call. ⊠ *West Barrow, Ardfert, Co. Kerry,* ☎ *066/36379. 18 holes. Yardage: 6,738. Par 71.* 🖹 *Fees: weekdays, £45; weekends, £45.* ⊘ *Visitors: weekdays. Practice area, caddies, catering.*

Waterville Golf Links. Here's what you should know about Waterville before you play: The 1st hole of this course is aptly named "Last Easy." At 7,184 yards from the tips, Waterville is the longest course in Ireland or Britain, and it is generally regarded as their toughest test. Now the good news: The scenery is so majestic you may not care that your score is approaching the yardage. Six holes run along the cliffs by the sea, surrounding the other 12, which have a tranquil, if not soft, feel to them. ⊠ *Waterville, Co. Kerry,* ☎ *066/74102. 18 holes. Yardage: 7,184. Par 72.* 🖹 *Fees: £60.* ⊘ *Visitors: weekdays. Practice area, caddies, caddy carts, buggies, catering.*

West

Lahinch Golf Club. The original course at Lahinch was designed by Old Tom Morris, who, upon the unveiling in 1892, called it "as fine a natural course as it has ever been my good fortune to play over." That was when blind shots (those taken when you can't see your target) were in vogue, and there are many here, where towering sandhills dominate every hole. Only a course with as much charm as this one could get away with that in today's modern game. ⊠ *Lahinch, Co. Clare,* ☎ *065/81003. 18 holes. Yardage: 6,613. Par 72.* 🖹 *Fees: £50.* ⊘ *Visitors: daily. Practice area, caddies, caddy carts, catering.*

Connemara Golf Club. The local club for the small town of Clifden, Connemara is a links course where you can get carried away not only by the golf but by the surrounding scenery as well. The Atlantic Ocean and Ballyconneely Bay are immediately to the west, and the Twelve Bens Mountains are to the east. The course starts flat, then rises into the hills for the final, challenging 6 holes. ⊠ *Ballyconneely, Clifden, Co. Galway,* ☎ *095/23502. 18 holes. Yardage: 7,174. Par 72.* ▦ *Fees: £30.* ◷ *Visitors: Mon.–Sat. Practice area, caddies, caddy carts, catering.*

Westport Golf Club. Twice the host of the Irish Amateur Championship, this inland course lies in the shadows of religious history. Rising 2,500 ft above Clew Bay, with its hundreds of islands, is Croagh Patrick, a mountain that legend connects with St. Patrick. The mountain is considered sacred, and it attracts multitudes of worshipers to its summit every year. All the prayers might pay off at the 15th, where your drive has to carry the ball over 200 yards of ocean. ⊠ *Carrowholly, Co. Mayo,* ☎ *098/25113. 18 holes. Yardage: 6,667. Par 73.* ▦ *Fees: weekdays, £19; weekends, £24.* ◷ *Visitors: weekdays. Practice area, caddies, caddy carts, catering.*

Northwest

Carn Golf Links. This is a newer, Eddie Hackett–designed links course that takes advantage of its location, far to the west on the shores of Blacksod Bay. From the elevated tees and greens you have a view of a string of Atlantic islands: Inishkea, Inishglora, and Achill. ⊠ *Carn, Belmullet, Co. Mayo,* ☎ *097/82292. 18 holes. Yardage: 6,608. Par 72.* ▦ *Fees: £22.* ◷ *Visitors: daily. Practice area, caddies, caddy carts, catering.*

County Sligo Golf Club. A century old in 1997, the course at Sligo is one of the grand old venues of Ireland, having hosted most of the country's major championships. At 6,565 yards, this links course isn't particularly long; however, it still manages to have seven par-4s of 400 yards or more. Typical of Ireland's hidden jewels, Rosses Point clings to cliffs above the Atlantic. The third tee offers views of the ocean, the hills, and the unusual mountain Benbulben, which looks like a giant Irish arroyo. ⊠ *Rosses Point, Co. Sligo,* ☎ *071/77186. 18 holes. Yardage: 6,565. Par 71.* ▦ *Fees: weekdays, £32; weekends, £40.* ◷ *Visitors: Mon., Tues., Thurs., and Fri. Practice area, caddies (summer only), caddy carts, club rental, catering.*

Donegal Golf Club. On the shores of Donegal Bay and approached through a forest, the windswept links are shadowed by the Blue Stack Mountains, with the Atlantic Ocean as a backdrop. The greens are large, but the rough is deep and penal, and there's a constant battle against erosion by the sea. Legendary golf writer Peter Dobereiner called it "hauntingly beautiful," perhaps recalling his experience on the par-3 fifth, fittingly called "The Valley of Tears." ⊠ *Murvagh, Laghey, Co. Donegal,* ☎ *073/34054. 18 holes. Yardage: 7,153. Par 73.* ▦ *Fees: weekdays, £20; weekends, £27.* ◷ *Visitors: daily. Practice area, caddies, caddy carts, catering.*

Enniscrone Golf Club. Eddie Hackett designed this course on the shores of another bay, this time Killala. Hackett may be the Pete Dye of Ireland, due in part to the fact that he's blessed with wonderful land: Enniscrone's setting is a natural for good golf—a combination of flatlands, foothills, and, of course, the Atlantic. It's not overly long on the scorecard, but the persistent winds can add yards to almost every hole. It's among the small number of clubs in Ireland with electric carts, or, as they call them here, buggies. ⊠ *Enniscrone, Co. Sligo,* ☎ *96/36297. 18 holes. Yardage: 6,682. Par 72.* ▦ *Fees: weekdays, £25; weekends, £34.* ◷ *Visitors: weekdays, weekends by appointment. Practice area, caddies (weekends and holidays), caddy carts, buggies, club rental.*

Northern Ireland

Ballycastle Golf Club. Pleasure comes first here, with challenge as an afterthought: It's beautiful (5 holes wind around the remains of a

13th-century friary), short (less than 6,000 yards), and conveniently located right next to Bushmills, the world's oldest distillery, at nearly 400 years. ⊠ *2 Cushendall Rd., Ballycastle BT54 6QP, Co. Antrim,* ☎ *028/2076–2536. 18 holes. Yardage: 5,882. Par 71.* 🍴 *Fees: weekdays, U.K.£18; weekends, U.K.£25.* ☽ *Visitors: daily. Practice area, caddy cars, catering.*

Castlerock Golf Club. Where else in the world can you play a hole called "Leg o' Mutton"? Not in America, that's for sure. It's a 200-yard par-3 with railway tracks to the right and a burn to the left— just one of several unusual holes at this course, which claims, year-round, to have the best greens in Ireland. True or not, the finish is spectacular: from the elevated 17th tee, where you can see the shores of Scotland, to the majestic 18th, which plays uphill to a plateau green. ⊠ *65 Circular Rd., Castlerock BT51 4TJ, Co. Londonderry,* ☎ *028/7084–8314. 27 holes. Yardage: 6,499, 2,678. Par 73, 35.* 🍴 *Fees: weekdays, U.K.£30, U.K.£7; weekends, U.K.£35, U.K.£10.* ☽ *Visitors: Mon.–Thurs. Practice area, caddies (reserve in advance), caddy cars, catering.*

Malone Golf Club. Fishermen may find the 22-acre lake at the center of this parkland layout distracting: It's filled with trout. The golf, however, is just as well stocked; large trees and well-manicured, undulating greens combine to provide one of the most challenging inland tests in Ireland. Bring your power game—there are only three par-5s, but they're all more than 520 yards. ⊠ *240 Upper Malone Rd., Dunmurry, Belfast, BT17 9LB,* ☎ *028/9061–2758. 27 holes. Yardage: 6,642, 3,138. Par 71, 36.* 🍴 *Fees: Mon., Tues, Thurs., Fri. U.K.£33 (men), £21 (women); Wed. and weekends, U.K.£38 (men), £29 (women).* ☽ *Visitors: Mon., Thurs., and Fri. Practice area, catering.*

Portstewart Golf Club. A century old in 1994, Portstewart may scare you with its opening hole, generally regarded as the toughest starter in Ireland. Picture a 425-yard par-4 that descends from an elevated tee to a small green tucked between the dunes. The greens are known for uniformity and speed, and seven of the holes have recently been redesigned to toughen the course. Also, if you want a break from the grand scale of championship links, there's the Old Course 18 and the Riverside 9, 27 holes of downsize, executive-style golf. ⊠ *117 Strand Rd., Portstewart BT55 7PT, Co. Londonderry,* ☎ *028/7083–2015. 45 holes. Yardage: 6,784 (Championship), 4,733 (Old Course), 2,662 (Riverside). Par 72, 64, 32.* 🍴 *Fees: weekdays, U.K.£45 (Championship), U.K.£8 (Old Course), U.K.£10 (Riverside); weekends, U.K.£65 (Championship), U.K.£12 (Old Course), U.K.£15 (Riverside).* ☽ *Visitors: Mon., Tues., and Fri. Practice area, caddies, caddy cars, catering.*

★ **Royal County Down.** This is perhaps the most beautiful course in Ireland. Catch it on the right day at the right time and you may think you're on the moon; Royal County Down is a links course with a sea of craterlike bunkers and small dunes. Actually, for better players, every day is the right one. Harry Vardon labeled it the toughest course on the Emerald Isle, and if you can't hit your driver long and straight, you might find it the toughest course in the world. It's a true masterpiece. ⊠ *Golf Links Rd., Newcastle BT33 0AN, Co. Down,* ☎ *028/4372–2419. 36 holes. Yardage: 6,969 (Championship), 4,087 (No. 2). Par 71, 65.* 🍴 *Fees: weekdays, U.K.£65; weekends, U.K.£75.* ☽ *Visitors: Tues., Thurs., and Fri. Practice area, caddies, caddy cars, catering.*

★ **Royal Portrush.** The only club outside Scotland and England to have hosted a British Open, Portrush is perhaps the most understated of Ireland's "Big Four." The championship Dunluce course is named for the ruins of a nearby castle and is a sea of sandhills and curving fairways. The Valley course is a less-exposed, tamer track. Both are conspicuous for their lack of bunkers. The Dunlucee, in a poll of Irish golf legends, was voted the best in Ireland. ✉ *Dunluce Rd., Portrush BT56 8JQ, Co. Antrim,* ☏ *028/7082–2311. 36 holes. Yardage: 6,530 (Dunluce), 6,054 (Valley). Par 72, 70.* ▣ *Fees: weekdays, U.K.£60 (Dunluce), U.K.£22 (Valley); weekends, U.K.£70 (Dunluce), U.K.£30 (Valley).* ☷ *Visitors: weekdays. Practice area, catering.*

10 BACKGROUND AND ESSENTIALS

Books and Videos

Chronology

Smart Travel Tips A to Z

WHAT TO READ AND WATCH BEFORE YOU GO

Autobiography

Since it was published in September 1996, *Angela's Ashes,* Frank McCourt's enormously affecting memoir of growing up desperately poor in Limerick, has garnered every major American literary accolade, from the Pulitzer Prize to the National Book Critics Circle Award, and has become a fixture at the top of American best-seller lists. In *An Only Child* and *My Father's Son* (1969), Frank O'Connor, known primarily for his fiction and short stories, recounts his years as an Irish revolutionary and later as an intellectual in Dublin during the 1920s. Christy Brown's *My Left Foot* is the autobiographical account of a Dublin artist stricken with cerebral palsy (☞ Movies and Videos, *below*).

Guidebooks and Travel Literature

Exploring Ireland (2nd ed.), published by Fodor's, is a full-color guide packed with photographs; it is an excellent companion guide to this edition.

Peter Somerville-Large's *Dublin* is filled with anecdotes relating to the famed Irish city. *Georgian Dublin,* by Desmond Guinness, the founder of the Irish Georgian Society, explores the city's architecture, with photographs and plans of Dublin's most admirable buildings. The most up-to-date work on the Aran Islands is Tim Robinson's award-winning *The Stones of Aran: Pilgrimage.* Robinson has also written a long introduction to the Penguin edition of J. M. Synge's 1907 classic, *The Aran Islands.* Tomas Ó Crohán's *The Islandman* provides a good background on Dingle and the Blasket Islands.

In *Round Ireland in Low Gear* (1988), famed British travel writer Eric Newby breezily pens the story of his bicycle journey with his wife around the wet Emerald Isle. Fifty years older but no less fresh is H. V. Morton's *In Search of Ireland* (1938). Rebecca Solnit uses Ireland as a sounding board for her meditations on travel in *A Book of Migrations: Some Passages in Ireland* (1997).

History and Current Affairs

For two intriguing studies of Irish culture and history, consult Constantine FitzGibbon's *The Irish in Ireland* and Sean O'Faolain's *The Irish: A Character Study,* which traces the history of Ireland from Celtic times. J. C. Beckett's *The Making of Modern Ireland,* a concise introduction to Irish history, covers the years between 1603 and 1923. *Modern Ireland,* by R. F. Foster, spans the years between 1600 and 1972. Thomas Cahill's *How the Irish Saved Civilization* is a best-selling, lively look at how Irish scholars kept the written word and culture alive in the so-called Dark Ages. For an acclaimed history of Irish nationalism, try Robert Kee's *The Green Flag.* Peter De Rosa's *Rebels: The Irish Rising of 1916* is a popular, novelistic take on the defining event of modern Irish history. Irish country-house devotees should read *Aristocrats: Caroline, Emily, Louisa and Sarah Lennox, 1740–1832,* by Stella Tillyard; Louisa was the force behind Castletown House.

John Ardagh's *Ireland and the Irish: Portrait of a Changing Society* (1997) is the best current sociological and economic analysis of modern Ireland. *"We Wrecked the Place": Contemplating an End to the Northern Irish Troubles* (1996) by Belfast-based journalist Jonathan Stevenson is the best recent book on the subject. John Conroy's *Belfast Diary: War as a Way of Life* (1995) was reissued with a new afterword on the cease-fire.

Literature

Ulysses (1922) is the linguistically innovative masterpiece by James Joyce, one of the titans of 20th-century literature. Emulating the structure of *The Odyssey,* and using an unprecedented stream-of-consciousness technique, Joyce follows Leopold and Molly Bloom and Stephen Daedalus through the course of a single day—June 16, 1904—around Dublin. (Joyce set *Ulysses* on the day he and his future wife, Nora Barnacle, had their first date.) More accessible introductions to Joyce's writing include *A Portrait of the Artist as a Young Man* (1916) and *Dubliners* (1914), a collection of short stories (its most accomplished story, "The Dead," was made into a movie starring Angelica Huston in 1988). Joyce aficionados may want to tackle his final, gigantic work, *Finnegan's Wake* (1939), which takes the linguistic experimentation of *Ulysses* to an almost incomprehensible level. Arguably the greatest literary challenge of the 20th century, its pages include word plays and phonetic metaphors in more than 100 languages. To prepare you for reading Joyce, you might seek out audio recordings in which he reads in his inimitable lilting tenor voice.

Samuel Beckett fills his story collection *More Pricks than Kicks* with Dublin characters; if you enjoy literary gamesmanship, you may also want to try Beckett's trilogy—*Molloy* (1951), *Malone Dies* (1951), and *The Unnameable* (1953).

If you're drawn to tales of unrequited love, turn to Elizabeth Bowen's stories and her novel *The Last September* (1929), set in Ireland during the Irish Civil War. If you prefer reading more magical novels, take a look at James Stephens's *A Crock of Gold* (1912), a charming and wise fairy tale written for adults, and Flann O'Brien's *At Swim-Two-Birds* (1939), a surrealistic tale full of Irish folklore.

One of Ireland's foremost fiction writers working today, Edna O'Brien began her career with the comic novel *The Country Girls* (1960) and has published 17 books since, most recently *House of Splendid Isolation* (1994) and *Down by the River* (1997). Like many of her compatriots, she is a superb short-story writer. Her collection *A Fanatic Heart* (1985) is one of her best.

Thomas Flanagan's *The Year of the French* is a historical novel about the people of County Mayo, who revolted in 1798 with the help of French revolutionaries. *A Nest of Simple Folk,* by Sean O'Faolain, follows three generations of an Irish family between 1854 and 1916. Leon Uris's *Trinity* covers the years 1840–1916, as seen through the eyes of British, Irish Catholic, and Ulster Protestant families. In *No Country for Young Men,* Julia O'Faolain writes of two Irish families struggling to overcome the effects of the Irish Civil War. In John McGahern's prizewinning novel *Amongst Women,* modern-day Ireland attempts to reconcile itself to the upheavals of the early years of this century. For a more contemporary look at life in urban Ireland, try the phenomenally successful Roddy Doyle: All three works from his "Barrytown Trilogy"—*The Snapper, The Commitments,* and *The Van*—have all been made into films; *Paddy Clarke Ha Ha Ha,* another success, is sure to follow.

Movies and Videos

A plethora of movies have been made in or about Ireland, and the number of Irish characters on screen is legion (the most numerous being priests, drunks, New York cops, and Old Mother Riley). *Juno and the Paycock* (known in the United States as *The Shame of Mary Boyle*) and *The Plough and the Stars* (1936), about the months leading up to the Easter Uprising, are early screen adaptations of Sean O'Casey's theatrical masterpieces. John Ford's superb *The Informer* (1935) is a full-blooded and highly stylized tale of an IRA leader's betrayal during the struggle for independence by a simpleminded hanger-on who wants to emigrate to the United States. Ford's boisterous comedy *The Quiet Man* (1952) is an Irish-village version of *The Taming of the Shrew,* with John Wayne playing a boxer who returns to his ancestor's village in the west of Ireland to claim local beauty Maureen O'Hara, and Barry Fitzgerald. David Lean's epic *Ryan's Daughter* (1970) is a four-hour pastoral melodrama of a village schoolmaster's wife falling for a British officer in the troubled Ireland of 1916; the film was a critical and commercial disaster for Lean, who didn't make another film for 14 years.

Daniel Day Lewis and Brenda Fricker give Oscar-winning performances in Jim Sheridan's *My Left Foot* (1989), a biography of Christy Brown, the Irish writer and painter crippled from birth by cerebral palsy. Alan Parker's *The Commitments* (1991), from Roddy Doyle's best-seller, humorously recounts the efforts of a group of young, working-class northside Dubliners trying to make it as a soul band. In *A Man of No Importance* (1994), Albert Finney plays a sexually repressed bus conductor whose passion for poetry leads him to stage Wilde's *Salomé*. John Sayles hooked up with acclaimed cinematographer Haskell Wexler to make *The Secret of Roan Inish* (1996), a magical realist fable about a Selkie—a creature from Celtic folklore who is a seal in the water and a woman on land—and the fisherman's family whose lives she changes. *I Went Down* (1998) is an uproarious comedy about a couple of petty-thieves from Dublin on the lamb.

Some of the best movies made in Ireland deal with the Troubles that have afflicted Northern Ireland. *Four Days in July* (1984), directed by Mike Leigh in classic *cinema verité* style, is a poignant and compelling portrayal of the sectarian divide in working-class Belfast. Helen Mirren stars as the widow of an executed Protestant policeman in *Cal* (1984), based on Bernard MacLaverty's masterful novel about the troubles. Daniel Day Lewis was nominated for an Academy Award for his portrayal of Gerry Conlon, the wrongfully imprisoned Irish youth, in Jim Sheridan's *In the Name of the Father* (1993); Sheridan's latest film is *Some Mother's Son* (1997). Neil Jordan's *Michael Collins* (1996) depicts the turbulent life of the heroic commander in chief of the Irish Republican Army from the Easter Uprising in 1916, when Collins was 25, until his assassination in West Cork six years later; it went on to become the highest-grossing film ever in Ireland.

Periodical

Billing itself as "A magazine for the Irish diaspora: An ongoing celebration of Ireland and the Irish around the world," *The World of Hibernia* (issued quarterly; US [$50], Canada [$60 U.S.], and rest of the world [$80 U.S.]: ✉ 340 Madison Ave., Suite 411, New York, NY 10164-2920; Ireland and Britain [£32]: 22 Crofton Rd., Dun Laoghaire, Co. Dublin) has savvy, solid editorial coverage. Its production values are also high (on par with the finest art magazines), making it a magazine you're likely to keep on your coffee table months after the issue date.

Poetry

The poems of William Butler Yeats, Ireland's most celebrated poet, often describe the Irish landscape, including the Sligo and Coole countryside. A favorite poet among the Irish is Patrick Kavanagh, whose distinguished career was devoted to writing exceptionally about ordinary lives. Winner of the *Irish Times*–Aer Lingus Literary prize in 1993, Derek Mahon is the author of *Selected Poems* (1992) and many other books. Northern Ireland serves as the setting for many of Seamus Heaney's poems. *Selected Poems 1996–1987* (1990) and *The Spirit Level* (1996), his first collection published since he won the Nobel Prize in Literature in 1995, are both highly recommended introductions to his work. Though not as well known outside Ireland as Heaney, Paul Muldoon is another major Irish poet. His *Selected Poems: 1968–1986* (1987) and his most recent volume, *The Annals of Chile* (1994), are both good places to start. Eavan Boland is widely regarded as among the top tier of Irish poets and the finest woman writing poetry in Ireland today. *Object Lessons: The Life of the Woman and the Poet in Our Time* (1995) and *An Origin Like Water: Collected Poems 1957–*

1987 (1996) are two of her recent books.

Theater

Ireland's playwrights are as distinguished as its novelists and short-story writers. Samuel Beckett, who moved from Ireland to Paris and began writing in French, is the author of the comic modernist masterpiece *Waiting for Godot* (1952), among many other plays. Oscar Wilde's finest plays, *The Importance of Being Earnest* and *An Ideal Husband* (both 1895), were playing to packed audiences in London when he was charged by his lover's father as a sodomite, setting in motion the trials that lead to his downfall. Among the many plays of George Bernard Shaw, who grew up in Dublin, are *Arms and the Man* (1894), *Major Barbara* (1905), *Pygmalion* (1913), and *Saint Joan* (1923).

The history of Irish theater includes a number of controversial plays, such as J. M. Synge's *The Playboy of the Western World,* which was considered morally outrageous at the time of its opening in 1907 ("Playboy riots" took place in Dublin when the play was produced at the Abbey Theatre) but is appreciated today for its poetic language. Sean O'Casey wrote passionately about social injustice and working-class characters around the time of the Irish Civil War in such plays as *The Plough and the Stars* (1926) and *Juno and the Paycock* (1924). *The Quare Fellow* (1956), by Brendan Behan, challenged accepted mores in the 1950s and at the time could only be produced in London. Behan is also well known for his play *The Hostage* and for *Borstal Boy* (1958), his memoirs. Two more recently recognized playwrights are Hugh Leonard (*Da* and *A Life*) and Brian Friel (*Philadelphia, Here I Come!, The Faith Healer,* and *Dancing at Lughnasa*), whose work often illuminates Irish small-town life. A new wave of young, brash Irish playwrights has taken London and Broadway by storm. Martin MacDonagh's *The Beauty Queen of Linane* and Conor McPherson's *The Weir* have won awards on both sides of the Atlantic.

IRELAND AT A GLANCE

ca. 3500 BC Neolithic (new Stone Age) settlers (origins uncertain) bring agriculture, pottery, and weaving. They also build massive megaliths—stone monuments with counterparts in England (Stonehenge), Brittany (Carnac), and elsewhere in Europe.

ca. 700 BC Celtic tribes begin to arrive via Britain and France; they divide Ireland into "fifths," or provinces, including Ulster, Leinster, Connaught, Meath, and Munster.

ca. AD 100 Ireland becomes the center of Celtic culture and trade without being settled by the Romans.

432 Traditional date for the arrival of St. Patrick and Christianity; in fact, Irish conversion to Christianity began at least a century earlier.

ca. 500–800 Golden age of Irish monasticism; as many as 3,000 study at Clonard (Meath). Irish missionaries carry the faith to barbarian Europe; art (exemplified by the Book of Kells, ca. 700) and Gaelic poetry flourish.

795 First Scandinavian Viking invasion; raids continue for the next 200 years. Viking towns founded include Dublin, Waterford, Wexford, Cork, and Limerick.

1014 Vikings decisively defeated at Clontarf by Irish troops under King Brian Boru of Munster. His murder cuts short hopes of a unified Ireland.

1172 Pope Alexander III confirms Henry II, king of England, as feudal lord of Ireland. Over the next two centuries, Anglo-Norman nobles establish estates, intermarry with the native population, and act in a manner similar to that of the neighboring Celtic chieftains. Actual control by the English crown is confined to a small area known as "the land of peace," or "the Pale," around Dublin.

1366 Statutes of Kilkenny attempt belatedly to enforce ethnic divisions by prohibiting the expression of Irish language and culture and intermarriage between the Irish and English, but Gaelic culture prevails and the Pale continues to contract. Constant warfare among the great landowners keeps Ireland poor, divided, and isolated from the rest of Europe.

1534–40 Henry VIII's break with the Catholic Church leads to insurrection in Ireland, led by Garret Mor's grandson Lord Offaly ("Silken Thomas"). He is executed with five of his brothers.

1558–1603 Reign of Queen Elizabeth I; her fear of Irish intrigue with Catholic enemies of England leads to expansion of English power.

1580–88 Edmund Spenser, an administrator for the Crown in Ireland, writes *The Faerie Queene*.

1591 Trinity College, Dublin, is founded.

1607 The Flight of the Earls and the beginning of the end of Gaelic Ireland. The earl of Tyrone and his ally Tyrconnell flee to Rome; their lands in Ulster are confiscated and opened to Protestant settlers, mostly Scots.

1641 Charles I's policies provoke insurrection in Ulster and, soon after, civil war in England.

1649 August: British leader Oliver Cromwell, having defeated Charles and witnessed his execution, invades Ireland, determined to crush Catholic opposition. Massacres at Drogheda and Wexford.

1652 Act of Settlement—lands of Cromwell's opponents are confiscated, and owners are forced across the Shannon to Connaught. Never fully carried out, this policy nonetheless establishes Protestant ascendancy.

1690 Battle of the Boyne—William of Orange lands in England and Catholic James II flees to Ireland to rally opposition. William pursues him with a large army and defeats him on the banks of the River Boyne in County Meath.

1775 American War of Independence begins, precipitating Irish unrest. Henry Grattan (1746–1820), a Protestant barrister, enters the Irish Parliament.

1782 Grattan's Parliament—Grattan asserts independence of Irish Parliament from Britain. Britain agrees, but independence is easier to declare than to sustain.

1823 Daniel O'Connell (1775–1847), "the Liberator," founds the Catholic Association to campaign for Catholic Emancipation.

1828 O'Connell's election to Parliament (illegal, because he was a Catholic) leads to passage of Catholic Emancipation Act in 1829; later, he works unsuccessfully for repeal of the Union.

1845–49 Failure of potato crop leads to famine; more than a million die, others migrate.

1856 Birth of George Bernard Shaw, playwright (d. 1950).

1858 Fenian Brotherhood founded in New York by Irish immigrants with the aim of overthrowing British rule. A revolt in 1867 fails, but it compels Gladstone, the British prime minister, to disestablish the Anglican Church (1869) and reform landholding (1870) in Ireland.

1865 Birth of William Butler Yeats, the great Irish poet (d. 1939).

1871 Isaac Butts founds parliamentary Home Rule Party, soon dominated by Charles Stewart Parnell (1846–91), descendant of English Protestants), who tries to force the issue by obstructing parliamentary business.

1890 Parnell is named corespondent in the divorce case of Kitty O'Shea; his career is ruined.

1893 Second Home Rule Bill passes Commons but is defeated by Lords. Subsequent policy is to "kill Home Rule with kindness" with land reform, but cultural nationalism revives with founding of Gaelic League to promote Irish language. Yeats, John Synge (1871–1909), and other writers find inspiration in Gaelic past.

1898 On the anniversary of Wolfe Tone's rebellion, Arthur Griffith (1872–1922) founds the Dublin newspaper the *United Irishman,* preaching *sinn féin* ("we ourselves")— secession from Britain; Sinn Fein party founded 1905. Socialist James Connolly (executed 1916) founds the *Workers' Republic.*

1904 William Butler Yeats and Lady Gregory found the Abbey Theatre in Dublin.

1914 Despite fierce opposition the Third Home Rule Bill passes the Commons and the Lords but is suspended due to the outbreak of World War I.

1916 Easter Uprising—Irish Republican Brotherhood (IRB) stages insurrection in Dublin and declares independence; the uprising fails, but the execution of 15 leaders by the British turns public opinion in favor of the insurgents. Yeats writes "a terrible beauty is born."

1919 January: Irish Parliamentarians meet as the Dail Éireann (Irish Assembly) and declare independence. September: Dail suppressed; Sinn Féin made illegal.

1920–21 War breaks out between Britain and Ireland: the "Black and Tans" versus the Irish Republican Army (IRA). Government of Ireland Act declares separate parliaments for north and south and continued ties to Britain. Elections follow, but the Sinn Féin majority in the south again declare themselves the Dail Éireann under Eamon de Valera (1882–1975), rejecting British authority. December 1921: Anglo-Irish Treaty grants the south dominion status as the Irish Free State, allowing the north to remain under Britain.

1922 De Valera and his Republican followers reject the treaty; civil war results. The Irish Free State adopts a constitution; William T. Cosgrave becomes president. Michael Collins, chairman of the Irish Free State and commander in chief of the army, is shot dead in County Cork, not far from where he was born. In Paris, James Joyce's *Ulysses* is published.

1923 De Valera is arrested and the civil war ends, but Republican agitation and terrorism continue. William Butler Yeats is the first Irish writer to be awarded the Nobel Prize in Literature; he also takes a seat in the first Irish Parliament.

1938 New constitution creates Republic of Ireland with no ties to Britain.

1939–1945 Despite strong pressure from Britain and the U.S., Ireland remains neutral throughout World War II.

1959 Eamon de Valera resigns as Taoiseach (prime minister) and is later elected president.

1963 John F. Kennedy, the first Irish-American President of the United States, visits Ireland.

1972 Republic of Ireland admitted to European Economic Community. Troubles continue in the north: In Derry on January 30, British troops shoot 13 unarmed demonstrators on "Bloody Sunday." Stormont (the Northern Parliament) is suspended and direct rule from London is imposed. Acts of terrorism on both sides lead to draconian law enforcement by the British. "The Troubles," as the conflict is dubbed, will last 26 years and claim more than 3,000 lives.

1991 Mary Robinson becomes the first female President of the Republic of Ireland. Peace talks begin between the British and Irish governments and the main political parties of the North, excepting Sinn Féin.

1992 Ireland approves European Union. Sixty-two percent of the Irish vote in a referendum in favor of allowing pregnant women to seek an abortion abroad.

1994 The IRA, in response to advances made by the Irish, British, and U.S. governments, announces a complete cessation of activities. Protestant paramilitary groups follow suit one month later. Gerry Adams, the leader of Sinn Féin, speaks on British TV and radio.

1996 The IRA, frustrated by the slow progress of the peace talks, explodes bombs on the British mainland, throwing the whole peace process into doubt. But violence has not returned to the province, and all parties say they are committed to peace.

1997 The Republic of Ireland legalizes divorce. Newly elected British prime minister Tony Blair apologizes for the British government's policies during Ireland's Great Famine, acknowledging that his predecessors' policies prolonged "a massive human tragedy." The IRA reestablishes its cease-fire.

1998 On Good Friday 1998, all sides in the conflict agree on an agreement for sharing power that guarantees the rights of the Catholic minority. Referenda in the North and the Republic show overwhelming support for the agreement. A splinter IRA group opposed to the agreement explodes a bomb in Omagh, killing more than 20 people. Catholic leader John Hume and Protestant David Trimble share the Nobel Peace Prize.

1999 Preparations for a new executive branch of government are delayed over disagreements on decommissioning of weapons. Sporadic violence by splinter loyalist groups keeps tensions high.

Chronology

Antrim
Lynch
McDonnell
McNeill
O'Hara
O'Neill
Quinn

Armagh
Hanlon
McCann

Carlow
Kinsella
Nolan
O'Neill

Cavan
Boylan
Lynch
McCabe
McGovern
McGowan
McNally
O'Reilly
Sheridan

Clare
Aherne
Boland
Clancy
Daly
Lynch
McGrath
McInerney
McMahon
McNamara
Molon(e)y
O'Brien
O'Dea
O'Grady
O'Halloran
O'Loughlin

Cork
Barry
Callaghan
Cullinane
Donovan
Driscoll
Flynn
Hennessey
Hogan
Lynch
McCarthy
McSweeney
Murphy
Nugent
O'Casey
O'Cullane
(Collins)

O'Keefe
O'Leary
O'Mahony
O'Riordan
Roche
Scanlon
Sheridan

Derry
Cahan
Hegarty
Kelly
McLaughlin

Donegal
Boyle
Clery
Doherty
Friel
Gallagher
Gormley
McGrath
McLoughlin
McSweeney
Mooney
O'Donnell

Down
Lynch
McGuinness
O'Neil
White

Dublin
Hennessey
O'Casey
Plunkett

Fermanagh
Cassidy
Connolly
Corrigan
Flanagan
Maguire
McManus

Galway
Blake
Burke
Clery
Fah(e)y
French
Jennings
Joyce
Kelly
Kenny
Kirwan
Lynch
Madden
Moran
O'Flaherty
O'Halloran

Kerry
Connor
Fitzgerald
Galvin
McCarthy
Moriarty
O'Connell
O'Donoghue
O'Shea
O'Sullivan

Kildare
Cullen
Fitzgerald
O'Byrne
White

Kilkenny
Butler
Fitzpatrick
O'Carroll
Tobin

Laois
Dempsey
Doran
Dunn(e)
Kelly
Moore

Leitrim
Clancy
O'Rourke

Limerick
Fitzgerald
Fitzgibbon
McKeough
O'Brien
O'Cullane
(Collins)
O'Grady
Woulfe

Longford
O'Farrell
Quinn

Louth
O'Carroll
Plunkett

Mayo
Burke
Costello
Dugan
Gormley
Horan
Jennings
Jordan
Kelly
Madden
O'Malley

Meath
Coffey
Connolly
Cusack
Dillon
Hayes
Hennessey
Plunkett
Quinlan

Monaghan
Boylan
Connolly
Hanratty
McKenna
McMahon
McNally

Offaly
Coghlan
Dempsey
Fallon
(Maher)
Malone
Meagher
Molloy
O'Carroll
Sheridan

Roscommon
Fallon
Flanagan
Flynn
Hanley
McDermot
McKeogh
McManus
Molloy
Murphy

Sligo
Boland
Higgins
McDonagh
O'Dowd
O'Hara
Rafferty

Tipperary
Butler
Fogarty
Kennedy
Lynch
Meagher
(Maher)
O'Carroll
O'Dwyer
O'Meara
Purcell
Ryan

Tyrone
Cahan
Donnelly
Gormley
Hagan
Murphy
O'Neill
Quinn

Waterford
Keane
McGrath
O'Brien
Phelan
Power

Westmeath
Coffey
Dalton
Daly
Dillon
Sheridan

Wexford
Doran
Doyle
Hartley
Kavanagh
Keating
Kinsella
McKeogh
Redmond
Walsh

Wicklow
Cullen
Kelly
McKeogh
O'Byrne
O'Toole

ESSENTIAL INFORMATION

AIR TRAVEL

From North America and the U.K., Aer Lingus is the main carrier to Ireland. Indirect flights from the U.S. and Canada fly via London and then switch to Aer Lingus or Ryan Air for the final leg to Dublin. There are no direct flights from Australia or New Zealand.

BOOKING YOUR FLIGHT

When you book **look for nonstop flights** and **remember that "direct" flights stop at least once.** Try to avoid connecting flights, which require a change of plane.

CARRIERS

When flying internationally, you must usually choose between a domestic carrier, the national flag carrier of the country you are visiting, and a foreign carrier from a third country. National flag carriers have the greatest number of nonstops. Domestic carriers may have better connections to your home town and serve a greater number of gateway cities. Third-party carriers may have a price advantage.

Aer Lingus is the major air carrier to Ireland, with regularly scheduled flights to Shannon and Dublin from JFK, Newark, Boston's Logan, Chicago's O'Hare, and LAX. Delta jointly operates with Aer Lingus's JFK flights and also has a daily departure from Atlanta that flies first to Dublin and on to Shannon. Continental flies daily direct to Dublin and Shannon, departing from Newark Airport in New Jersey. Aeroflot flies twice weekly from Miami, three times weekly from Washington, DC (Dulles), and once a week from Chicago.

➤ AIRLINES & CONTACTS: **Aer Lingus** (☎ 800/223–6537). **Aeroflot** (☎ 888/340–6400). **Continental** (☎ 800/231–0856). **Delta** (☎ 800/241–4141).

CHECK-IN & BOARDING

Assuming that not everyone with a ticket will show up, airlines routinely overbook planes. When that happens, airlines ask for volunteers to give up their seats. In return these volunteers usually get a certificate for a free flight and are rebooked on the next flight out. If there are not enough volunteers, the airline must choose who will be denied boarding. The first to get bumped are passengers who checked in late and those flying on discounted tickets, so **get to the gate and check in as early as possible,** especially during peak periods.

Always **bring a government-issued photo ID to the airport.** You may be asked to show it before you are allowed to check in.

CUTTING COSTS

The least-expensive airfares to Ireland must usually be purchased in advance and are non-refundable. It's smart to **call a number of airlines, and when you are quoted a good price, book it on the spot**—the same fare may not be available the next day. Always **check different routings** and look into using different airports. Travel agents, especially low-fare specialists (☞ Discounts & Deals, *below*), are helpful.

Consolidators are another good source. They buy tickets for scheduled international flights at reduced rates from the airlines, then sell them at prices that beat the best fare available directly from the airlines, usually without restrictions. Sometimes you can even get your money back if you need to return the ticket. Carefully read the fine print detailing penalties for changes and cancellations, and **confirm your consolidator reservation with the airline.**

When you **fly as a courier** you trade your checked-luggage space for a ticket deeply subsidized by a courier service. There are restrictions on when you can book and how long you can stay.

Charter carriers such as **Scepter Charters** offer flights to Dublin and Shannon from various U.S. cities. **Air Canada Vacations** and **Regent Holidays** fly from Canada. Note that in certain seasons, usually fall and winter, their charter deals include mandatory hotel and car-rental packages.

To save money on flights from the United Kingdom and back, **look into an APEX or Super-PEX ticket.** APEX tickets must be booked in advance and have certain restrictions. Super-PEX tickets can be purchased at the airport on the day of departure—subject to availability.

➤ CONSOLIDATORS: **Cheap Tickets** (☎ 800/377–1000). **Up & Away Travel** (☎ 212/889–2345). **Discount Airline Ticket Service** (☎ 800/576–1600). **Unitravel** (☎ 800/325–2222). **World Travel Network** (☎ 800/409–6753).

➤ COURIERS: **New Voyager** ☎ 212/431–1616.

➤ CHARTERS: **Scepter Charters** (☎ 516/255–9800). **Air Canada Vacations** (☎ 800/263–0882). **Regent Holidays** (☎ 800/387–4860).

ENJOYING THE FLIGHT

For more legroom **request an emergency-aisle seat.** Don't sit in the row in front of the emergency aisle or in front of a bulkhead, where seats may not recline. If you have dietary concerns, **ask for special meals when booking.** These can be vegetarian, low-cholesterol, or kosher, for example. On long flights, try to maintain a normal routine, to help fight jet lag. At night **get some sleep.** By day **eat light meals, drink water** (not alcohol), and **move around the cabin** to stretch your legs.

FLYING TIMES

Flying time to Ireland is 6½ hours from New York, 7½ hours from Chicago, and 10 hours from L.A.

HOW TO COMPLAIN

If your baggage goes astray or your flight goes awry, complain right away.

Most carriers require that you **file a claim immediately.**

➤ AIRLINE COMPLAINTS: U.S. Department of Transportation **Aviation Consumer Protection Division** (✉ C-75, Room 4107, Washington, DC 20590, ☎ 202/366–2220). **Federal Aviation Administration Consumer Hotline** (☎ 800/322–7873).

RECONFIRMING

Even if an airline says there's no need to reconfirm, it's best to do so anyway 12–14 hours before your flight to ensure that your seat is held; you can also check to see if the flight schedule has changed.

AIRPORTS

The major gateways to Ireland are Dublin Airport, 10 km (6 mi) north of the city center, and Shannon Airport on the west coast, 25½ km (16 mi) west of Limerick. Two airports serve Belfast: Belfast International Airport at Aldergrove, 24 km (15 mi) from the city, which handles local and U.K. flights. In addition, the City of Derry Airport receives flights from Manchester, Birmingham, and Glasgow in the U.K. and Scotland.

➤ AIRPORT INFORMATION: **Shannon Airport** (☎ 061/471444). **Dublin Airport** (☎ 01/844–4900). **Belfast International Airport at Aldergrove** (☎ 01849/422888). **Belfast City Airport** (☎ 01232/457745).

BIKE TRAVEL

Ireland is a cyclist's paradise. The scenery is phenomenal, the roads are flat and uncrowded, and the distance from one village to the next is rarely more the 16 km (10 mi). On the down side, though, foul weather and rough roads are all too common, so raingear and spare parts are a must.

There are plenty of bike rental shops in the country. Most offer 12- to 18-gear mountain bikes with index gears and rear carriers for about £8 per day or £35 per week. A refundable deposit of £40 is often required. For a fee of £12 or so, you can rent a bike at one location and drop it off at another.

BIKE RENTALS

Raleigh International, Ltd. (☎ 01/6261333).

BIKES IN TRANSIT

Most airlines accommodate bikes as luggage, provided they are dismantled and boxed. For bike boxes, often free at bike shops, you'll pay about $5 (at least $100 for bike bags) from airlines. International travelers can sometimes substitute a bike for a piece of checked luggage at no charge; otherwise, the cost is about $100. Domestic and Canadian airlines charge $25–$50. Most ferries will transport your bicycle for free. If there's room, Irish buses and Irish Rail will transport bikes for a small fee.

BOAT & FERRY TRAVEL

There are two principal ferry routes to the Irish Republic: to Dublin from Holyhead on the Isle of Anglesea, and to Rosslare from Fishguard or Pembroke in Wales. Two companies sail the Dublin route: Irish Ferries from Dublin port and Stena Sealink, whose ferries go both to Dublin port and Dun Laoghaire, 4 km (2½ mi) south of the city center. SeaCat Ferries have also started service to Dublin from Liverpool. The trip takes about 4 hours. Prices and departure times vary according to season, so call either company to confirm. In summer, reservations are strongly recommended. Dozens of taxis wait to take you into town from both ports, or you can take DART or a bus to the city center.

Irish Ferries operates the Pembroke–Rosslare route; Stena Sealink operates the Fishguard–Rosslare route. To connect with the Fishguard sailings, take one of the many direct trains from London (Paddington). A connecting train at Rosslare will get you to Waterford by about 8:30 PM, to Cork by about midnight. For the Pembroke sailings, you have to change at Swansea. Sailing time for both routes is 4½ hours.

Swansea Cork Ferries operate a service between Swansea and Cork from mid March to early January. The crossing takes 12 hours, but easy access by road to both ports make this longer sea route a good choice for motorists heading for the Southwest. They also sail from Stranraer, Scotland to Belfast and Larne.

The cost of your trip can vary substantially, so **spend time with a travel agent and compare prices carefully**; flying is sometimes cheaper, and fares to Dublin are cheapest. **Book well in advance at peak periods.** Students and others under 26 should take advantage of the cheap fares offered by Eurotrain.

Car ferries run to Northern Ireland from the Scottish port of Stranraer. Trains leave London (Euston) for Stranraer Harbour several times a day. Sealink Ferries crosses the water to the port of Larne, where you pick up a train to Belfast. The whole trip is around 13 hours. Much faster and more convenient is the SeaCat, a huge, car-ferry catamaran that crosses from Stranraer right into Belfast in just 1½ hours. There is also a 9-hour crossing from Liverpool to Belfast, operated by Belfast Ferries. Trains leave London (Euston) for Liverpool throughout the day.

If you're traveling from County Kerry to County Clare and the West of Ireland, you can take the ferry from Tarbert (in County Kerry), leaving every hour on the half hour. Going the other way, ferries leave from Killimer (in County Clare) every hour on the hour. The 30-minute journey across the Shannon Estuary costs £7 per car, £2 for foot passengers.

A 10-minute car ferry crosses the River Suir between Ballyhack in County Wexford and Passage East in County Waterford. It saves you a boring drive through New Ross on the N25 and also introduces you to two pretty fishing villages, Ballyhack and Arthurstown. The ferry operates continuously during daylight hours and costs £3.50 per car, 80p for foot passengers.

The Cork Harbour crossing is a scenic route that allows those traveling from west Cork or Kinsale to Cobh and the east coast to bypass the city center. The five-minute car ferry runs from Glenbrook (near Ringaskiddy) in the west to Carrigaloe (near Cobh) in the east and operates continuously from 7:15 AM to 12:45 AM daily. It costs £3 per car, 60p for foot passengers.

You can reach many, but not all, of Ireland's offshore islands by ferry. There are regular services to the Aran Islands from Galway City, Rossaveal in County Galway, and Doolin in County Clare. Ferries also sail to Inishbofin off the Galway coast and Arranmore off the Donegal coast, and to Bere, Sherkin, and Cape Clear islands off the coast of County Cork. The islands are all small enough to explore on foot, so the ferries are for foot passengers and bicycles only. Other islands—the Blaskets and the Skelligs in Kerry, Rathlin, and Tory off the Donegal coast—can be reached by private arrangements with local boatmen (☞ relevant regional chapters). Full details on ferries to the islands are available in a publication from the ITB (☞ Visitor Information, *below*).

You can purchase tickets, with a credit card if you like, from the offices listed below. You can also pick them up at Dublin Tourism offices and from any major travel agent in Ireland or the UK.

➤ BOAT & FERRY INFORMATION: **Irish Ferries** (✉ Merrion Row, ☎ 01/661–0511). **Stena Sealink** (✉ Ferryport, Dun Laoghaire, ☎ 01/204–7777 or 204–7700). **Cork Swansea Ferries** (✉ 52 South Mall Street, Cork, ☎ 021/271–166).

SeaCat (✉ Donegal Quay, Belfast, ☎ 028/9031–2301).

BUS TRAVEL

IN THE REPUBLIC OF IRELAND

Buses are a cheap, flexible way to explore the countryside. Expressway bus services, with the most modern buses, cover the country's major routes. Outside the peak season, services are limited, and some routes (e.g., Killarney–Dingle) disappear altogether. There is often only one service a day on the express routes— and one a week to some of the more remote villages!

Long-distance bus services are operated by Bus Éireann, which also provides local services in Cork, Galway, Limerick, and Waterford. To ensure that your proposed bus journey is feasible, **buy a copy of Bus Éireann's timetable**—80p from any bus terminal.

Many of the destination indicators on bus routes are in Irish, so **make sure you get on the right bus.** Asking someone to translate is often the best way to avoid a mishap.

IN NORTHERN IRELAND

In Northern Ireland, all buses are operated by the state-owned Ulsterbus. Service is generally good, with particularly useful links to those towns not served by train. Ulsterbus also offers tours. (For details ☞ Northern Ireland A to Z *in* Chapter 9.)

FROM THE U.K.

Numerous bus services run between Britain and the Irish Republic, but **be ready for long hours on the road and possible delays.** All buses to the Republic use either the Holyhead– Dublin or Fishguard/Pembroke– Rosslare ferry routes. National Express, a consortium of bus companies, has Supabus (as its buses are known) services from all major British cities to more than 90 Irish destinations. Slattery's, an Irish company, has services from London, Manchester, Liverpool, Oxford, Birmingham, Leeds, and North Wales to over 100 Irish destinations.

Buses to Belfast run from London and from Birmingham, making the Stranraer–Larne crossing. Contact National Express (☞ below). The numbers listed are in London, so be sure to add the 44 country code and drop the 0 from the area code when dialing from abroad.

CLASSES

Buses have only one class, and prices are similar for all seats.

CUTTING COSTS

A Freedom of Northern Ireland ticket costs U.K.£32 for seven days' unlimited travel. A one-day ticket costs U.K.£9. Several passes offer discounts on both the bus and rail system in the Irish Republic, including the **Irish Explorer Rail & Bus Pass,** the **Go as You Please Rambler Card,** and the **Emerald Isle Card** (☞ Discount Passes *in* Train Travel, *below*).

➤ DISCOUNT PASSES: Bus Éireann and Ulsterbus offer discount passes.

PAYING

You can buy tickets at the main tourist offices, at the bus station, or on the bus (cash only for the latter option).

RESERVATIONS

Check the bus office to see if reservations are accepted for your route; if not, show up early to get a seat. Note: Pre-paid tickets don't apply to a particular bus time, just a route, so if one vehicle is full you can try another.

TICKETS & SCHEDULES

Pick up a timetable at any bus station or call the numbers below for a schedule. It's best to avoid Friday evening and Sunday morning travel, as this is when throngs of workers from the country return to and depart from Dublin on the weekends.

Bus Information: **BUS ÉIREANN** (☎ 01/836–6111).

National Express (☎ 020/7724–0741). **Slattery's** (☎ 020/7482–1604).

Ulsterbus (☎ 028/9033–3000).

BUSINESS HOURS

Business hours are generally from 9–5, sometimes alter in the larger towns. In smaller towns, stores often close from 1–2 for lunch. If a holiday falls on a weekend, most businesses are closed on Monday as well.

BANKS & OFFICES

Banks are open 10–4, Monday–Friday. In small towns they may close from 12:30–1:30. They remain open until 5 one afternoon per week; again, the day of week varies, although it's usually Thursday. Post offices are open weekdays 9–5 and Saturdays 9–1; some of the smaller country offices close for lunch.

In Northern Ireland bank hours are weekdays 9:30–4:30. Post offices are open weekdays 9–5:30, Saturday 9–1. Some close for an hour at lunch.

GAS STATIONS

There are some 24-hour gas stations along the highways; otherwise, hours vary from morning rush hour to late evenings.

MUSEUMS & SIGHTS

Museum and sights are generally open Tuesday–Saturday 10–5 and Sunday 2–5.

SHOPS

Most shops are open 9–5:30 or 6, Monday–Saturday. Once a week— normally Wednesday, Thursday, or Saturday—they shut at 1 for the afternoon. These times do *not* apply to Dublin, and they can vary from region to region, so it's best to check locally. Larger shopping malls usually stay open late once a week—generally until 9 on Thursday or Friday.

Shops in Belfast are open 9–5:30, Monday–Friday, with a late closing on Thursday, usually at 9. Elsewhere, shops close for the afternoon once a week, usually Wednesday or Thursday; check locally. In addition, most smaller shops close for an hour or so at lunch.

CAMERAS & PHOTOGRAPHY

EQUIPMENT PRECAUTIONS

Always **keep your film and tape out of the sun.** Carry an extra supply of batteries, and **be prepared to turn on your camera or camcorder** to prove to security personnel that the device is real. Always **ask for hand inspection of film,** which becomes clouded after successive exposures to airport X-ray machines, and **keep videotapes away from metal detectors.**

FILM & DEVELOPING

Major brands of film are available throughout Ireland, although 24-hour developing is found only in larger cities. Videotape is also widely available.

➤ PHOTO HELP: **Kodak Information Center** (☎ 800/242–2424). *Kodak Guide to Shooting Great Travel Pictures,* available in bookstores or from Fodor's Travel Publications (☎ 800/533–6478; $16.50 plus $4 shipping).

CAR RENTAL

If you are renting a car in the Irish Republic and intend to visit Northern Ireland (or vice versa), make this clear when you get your car, and check that the rental insurance applies when you cross the border.

Renting a car in Ireland is far more expensive than organizing a rental before you leave the U.S. Rates in Dublin for an economy car with a manual transmission, and unlimited mileage begin at $40 a day/$200 a week (January–April and November–December 15); $45 a day/$250 a week (May–June and September–October); and $60 a day/$320 a week (July–August and December 16–31). This includes the Republic's 12½% tax on car rentals.

Rates in Belfast begin at $42 a day/$210 a week (January–June, September–December 15) and $45 a day/$300 a week (July–August and December 16–31). This does not include the 17½% tax on car rentals in the North.

➤ MAJOR AGENCIES: **Alamo** (☎ 800/522–9696; 0181/759–6200 in the U.K.). **Avis** (☎ 800/331–1084; 800/879–2847 in Canada; 02/9353–9000 in Australia; 09/525–1982 in New Zealand). **Budget** (☎ 800/527–0700; 0144/227–6266 in the U.K.). **Dollar** (☎ 800/800–6000; 0181/897–0811 in the U.K., where it is known as Eurodollar; 02/9223–1444 in Australia). **Hertz** (☎ 800/654–3001; 800/263–0600 in Canada; 0181/897–2072 in the U.K.; 02/9669–2444 in Australia; 03/358–6777 in New Zealand). **National InterRent** (☎ 800/227–3876; 0345/222525 in the U.K., where it is known as Europcar InterRent).

CUTTING COSTS

To get the best deal **book through a travel agent who will shop around.** Also **price local car-rental companies,** although the service and maintenance may not be as good as those of a major player. Remember to ask about required deposits, cancellation penalties, and drop-off charges if you're planning to pick up the car in one city and leave it in another. If you're traveling during a holiday period, also make sure that a confirmed reservation guarantees you a car.

Do **look into wholesalers,** companies that do not own fleets but rent in bulk from those that do and often offer better rates than traditional car-rental operations. Payment must be made before you leave home.

➤ LOCAL AGENCIES: **Argus** (☎ 01/490–4444 in Dublin). **Dan Dooley** (☎ 800/331–9301 in the U.S., 081/994–2512 or 0800/282–189 in the U.K., 01/677–2723 in Dublin). **ECL Chauffeur Drive** (☎ 01/704–4062) offers chauffeur-driven Mercedes sedans, minivans, and coaches for a journey or daily rate.

➤ WHOLESALERS: **Auto Europe** (☎ 207/842–2000 or 800/223–5555, FAX 800–235–6321). **Europe by Car** (☎ 212/581–3040 or 800/223–1516, FAX 212/246–1458). **DER Travel Services** (✉ 9501 W. Devon Ave., Rosemont, IL 60018, ☎ 800/782–2424, FAX 800/282–7474 for information; 800/860–9944 for brochures). **Kemwel Holiday Autos** (☎ 914/835–3000 or 800/678–0678, FAX 914/835–5126).

INSURANCE

When driving a rented car you are generally responsible for any damage to or loss of the vehicle. Before you rent see what coverage your personal auto-insurance policy and credit cards already provide.

Collision policies that car-rental companies sell for European rentals usually do not include stolen-vehicle coverage. Before you buy it, check your existing policies—you may already be covered.

REQUIREMENTS & RESTRICTIONS

In Ireland your own driver's license is acceptable. An International Driver's Permit is a good idea; it's available from the American or Canadian automobile association, and, in the United Kingdom, from the Automobile Association or Royal Automobile Club. These international permits are universally recognized, and having one in your wallet may save you a problem with the local authorities.

SURCHARGES

Before you pick up a car in one city and leave it in another **ask about drop-off charges or one-way service fees,** which can be substantial. Note, too, that some rental agencies charge extra if you return the car before the time specified in your contract. To avoid a hefty refueling fee **fill the tank just before you turn in the car,** but be aware that gas stations near the rental outlet may overcharge.

CAR TRAVEL

A car journey on Ireland's many back roads and byways is the ideal way to explore the country's predominantly rural attractions. Roads are generally good, although four-lane, two-way roads are the exception rather than the rule. Most National Primary Routes (designated by the letter N) have two lanes with generous shoulders on which to pass. Brand-new divided highways, or motorways—designated by blue signs and the letter M—take the place of some N roads. They are the fastest way to get from one point to another, but use caution: They sometimes end as abruptly as they begin. In general, traffic is light, especially off the national routes, although Dublin is always very congested in rush hour and on weekend evenings. It's also wise to **slow down on the smaller, often twisty roads** and **watch out for cattle and sheep**; they may be just around the next bend. Speed limits are 96 kph (60 mph) on the open road, 112 kph (70 mph) on the motorways, and 48 kph (30 mph) in urban areas.

Road signs are generally in both Irish (Gaelic) and English; in the northwest and Connemara, most are in Irish only, so **make sure you have a good road map.** On the new green signposts distances are in kilometers; on the old white signposts they're given in miles. Because of the coexistence of both old and new signs, the route number is not always referred to on the signpost, particularly on National Secondary Roads (N-numbered routes) and Regional roads (R-numbered routes). On such roads, knowing the name of the next town on your itinerary is more important than knowing the route number: Neither the small local signposts nor the local people refer to roads by official numbers. At unmarked intersections, a good rule of thumb is to **keep going straight if there's no sign directing you to do otherwise.**

Traffic signs are the same as in the rest of Europe, and roadway markings are standard. Note especially that a continuous white line down the center of the road prohibits passing. Barred markings on the road and flashing yellow beacons indicate a crossing, where pedestrians have right of way. At a junction of two roads of equal importance, the driver to the right has right of way.

The road network in Northern Ireland is excellent and, outside Belfast, uncrowded. Road signs and traffic regulations conform to the British system. Speed limits are 48 kph (30 mph) in towns, 96 kph (60 mph) on country roads, and 112 kph (70 mph) on two-lane roads and motorways.

All ferries on *both* principal routes to the Irish Republic—Holyhead–Dublin and Fishguard/Pembroke–Rosslare— take cars. Fishguard and Pembroke are relatively easy to reach by road. The car trip to Holyhead, on the other hand, is sometimes difficult: Delays on the A55 North Wales coastal road are not unusual.

Car ferries to Belfast leave from the Scottish port of Stranraer and the English city of Liverpool; those to Larne leave from Stranraer and Cairnryan.

For reservations and information, ☞ Boat & Ferry Travel, *above*.

AUTO CLUBS

➤ IN AUSTRALIA: **Australian Automobile Association** (☎ 02/6247–7311).

➤ IN CANADA: **Canadian Automobile Association** (CAA, ☎ 613/247–0117).

➤ IN NEW ZEALAND: **New Zealand Automobile Association** (☎ 09/377–4660).

➤ IN THE U.K.: **Automobile Association** (AA, ☎ 0990/500–600). **Royal Automobile Club** (RAC, ☎ 0990/722–722 for membership; 0345/121–345 for insurance).

➤ IN THE U.S.: **American Automobile Association** (☎ 800/564–6222).

GASOLINE

You'll find gas stations along most roads, self-service is the norm in the larger establishments. Major credit cards and traveler's checks are usually accepted.

PARKING

Despite the relatively light traffic, parking in towns can be a problem. Signs with the letter *P* indicate that parking is permitted; a stroke through the *P* warns you to stay away or you'll be liable for a fine of £15 to £50; however, if you get towed, the fine is £150. In Dublin and Cork, parking lots are your best bet, but check the rate first in Dublin; they can vary wildly.

In Northern Ireland there are plenty of parking lots in the towns (usually free except in Belfast), and you should use them. In Belfast, you cannot park your car in some parts of the city center, more because of congestion than security problems.

ROAD CONDITIONS

Most roads are paved and make for easy travel. Watch for traffic at rush hours in Dublin, Cork, Limerick, Belfast, and Galway.

ROAD MAPS

Road maps can be found at most gas stations and bookstores.

RULES OF THE ROAD

The Irish, like the British, **drive on the left-hand side of the road.** Safety belts must be worn by the driver and front passenger, and children under 12 must travel in the back. It is compulsory for motorcyclists and their passengers to wear helmets.

Drunk-driving laws are strict. Ireland has a Breathalyzer test, which the police can administer anytime. If you refuse to take it, the odds are you'll be prosecuted anyway. As always, the best advice is **don't drink if you plan to drive.**

Army checkpoints are a thing of the past between the North and the South, though there are some border checkpoints for cattle (in an effort to contain BSE-contaminated livestock).

CHILDREN IN IRELAND

The Irish love children and will go to great lengths to make them welcome. Many hotels offer baby-sitting services, and most will supply a cot if given advance notice. Hotel and pub restaurants often have a children's menu and can supply a high chair if necessary. Unlike Great Britain, Irish licensing laws allow children under 14 into pubs—although they may not consume alcohol on the premises until they are 18, and they are expected to leave by about 5:30 PM (although they may be allowed to stay until 7 PM, depending on how busy the pub gets. This is a boon if you are touring by car because pubs are perfect for lunch or tea stops.

While most attractions and bus and rail journeys offer a rate of half-price or less for children, **look for "family tickets,"** which may be cheaper and usually cover two adults and up to four children. The Irish Tourist Board (ITB) publishes "A Tour of Favorite Kids' Places," that covers a week's worth of sights around the country.

Be sure to plan ahead and **involve your youngsters** as you outline your trip. When packing, include things to keep them busy en route. On sightseeing days try to schedule activities of special interest to your children. Most hotels in Ireland allow children under a certain age to stay in their parents' room at no extra charge, but others charge them as extra adults; be sure to **ask about the cutoff age for children's discounts.**

If you are renting a car don't forget to **arrange for a car seat** when you reserve.

LODGING

Most hotels in Ireland allow children under a certain age to stay in their parents' room at no extra charge, but others charge for them as extra adults; be sure to **find out the cutoff age for children's discounts.**

SIGHTS & ATTRACTIONS

Places that are especially good for children are indicated by a rubber duckie icon in the margin.

SUPPLIES & EQUIPMENT

Items for babies and children are available in every town and village; check the supermarket or family grocery store.

TRANSPORTATION

When flying, if your children are two or older **ask about children's airfares.** As a general rule, infants under two not occupying a seat fly at greatly reduced fares or even for free. When booking **confirm carry-on allowances** if you're traveling with infants. In general, for babies charged 10% of the adult fare, you are allowed one carry-on bag and a collapsible stroller; if the flight is full the stroller may have to be checked or you may be limited to less.

Experts agree that it's a good idea to use safety seats aloft for children weighing less than 40 pounds. Airlines set their own policies: U.S. carriers usually require that the child be ticketed, even if he or she is young enough to ride free, since the seats must be strapped into regular seats. Do **check your airline's policy about using safety seats during takeoff and landing.** And since safety seats are not allowed everywhere in the plane, get your seat assignments early.

When reserving, **request children's meals or a freestanding bassinet** if you need them. But note that bulkhead seats, where you must sit to use the bassinet, may lack an overhead bin or storage space on the floor.

CONSUMER PROTECTION

Whenever shopping or buying travel services in Ireland, **pay with a major credit card** so you can cancel payment or get reimbursed if there's a problem. If you're doing business with a particular company for the first time, **contact your local Better Business Bureau and the attorney general's offices** in your state and the company's home state, as well. Have any complaints been filed? Finally, if you're buying a package or tour, always **consider travel insurance** that includes default coverage (☞ Insurance, *below*).

➤ LOCAL BBBs: **Council of Better Business Bureaus** (✉ 4200 Wilson Blvd., Suite 800, Arlington, VA 22203, ☎ 703/276–0100, 𝔽𝔸𝕏 703/ 525–8277).

CUSTOMS & DUTIES

When shopping, **keep receipts** for all purchases. Upon reentering the country, **be ready to show customs officials what you've bought.** If you feel a duty is incorrect or object to the way your clearance was handled, note the inspector's badge number and ask to see a supervisor. If the problem isn't resolved, write to the appropriate authorities, beginning with the port director at your point of entry.

IN IRELAND

Moves are underway to abolish duty-free shopping in the EU, but for the moment two categories of duty-free allowance exist for travelers entering both the Republic of Ireland and Northern Ireland: one for goods obtained outside the European Union (EU), on a ship or aircraft, or in a duty-free store within the EU; and the other for goods bought in the EU with duty and tax paid.

Of the first category, you may import duty-free: (1) 200 cigarettes or 100 cigarillos or 50 cigars or 250 grams of smoking tobacco; (2) 2 liters of wine, and either 1 liter of alcoholic drink over 22% volume or 2 liters of alcoholic drink under 22% volume (sparkling or fortified wine included); (3) 50 grams of perfume and ¼ liter of toilet water; and (4) other goods to a value of £142 per person (£73 per person for travelers under 15 years of age).

Of the second category, you may import duty-free a considerable amount of liquor and tobacco—800 cigarettes, 400 cigarillos, 200 cigars, 1 kilogram of pipe tobacco, 10 liters of spirits, 45 liters of wine, 25 liters of port/sherry and 55 liters of beer. You'll need a truck!

Goods that cannot be freely imported to the Irish Republic include firearms, ammunition, explosives, illegal drugs, indecent or obscene books and pictures, oral smokeless tobacco products, meat and meat products, poultry and poultry products, plants and plant products (including shrubs, vegetables, fruit, bulbs, and seeds), domestic cats and dogs from outside the United Kingdom, and live animals from outside Northern Ireland.

No animals or pets of any kind may be brought into Northern Ireland without a six-month quarantine.

Other items that may not be imported include fresh meats, plants and vegetables, controlled drugs, and firearms and ammunition.

IN AUSTRALIA

Australia residents who are 18 or older may bring home $A400 worth of souvenirs and gifts (including jewelry), 250 cigarettes or 250 grams of tobacco, and 1,125 ml of alcohol (including wine, beer, and spirits). Residents under 18 may bring back $A200 worth of goods. Prohibited items include meat products. Seeds, plants, and fruits need to be declared upon arrival.

➤ INFORMATION: **Australian Customs Service** (Regional Director, ⊠ Box 8, Sydney, NSW 2001, ☎ 02/9213–2000, ℻ 02/9213–4000).

IN CANADA

Canadian residents who have been out of Canada for at least 7 days may bring home C$500 worth of goods duty-free. If you've been away less than 7 days but more than 48 hours, the duty-free allowance drops to C$200; if your trip lasts 24–48 hours, the allowance is C$50. You may not pool allowances with family members. Goods claimed under the C$500 exemption may follow you by mail; those claimed under the lesser exemptions must accompany you. Alcohol and tobacco products may be included in the 7-day and 48-hour exemptions but not in the 24-hour exemption. If you meet the age requirements of the province or territory through which you reenter Canada, you may bring in, duty-free, 1.14 liters (40 imperial ounces) of wine or liquor or 24 12-ounce cans or bottles of beer or ale. If you are 16 or older you may bring in, duty-free, 200 cigarettes and 50 cigars. Check ahead of time with Revenue Canada or the Department of Agriculture for policies regarding meat products, seeds, plants, and fruits.

You may send an unlimited number of gifts worth up to C$60 each duty-free to Canada. Label the package UNSOLICITED GIFT—VALUE UNDER $60. Alcohol and tobacco are excluded.

➤ INFORMATION: **Revenue Canada** (⊠ 2265 St. Laurent Blvd. S, Ottawa, Ontario K1G 4K3, ☎ 613/993–0534; 800/461–9999 in Canada).

IN NEW ZEALAND

Homeward-bound residents 17 or older may bring back $700 worth of souvenirs and gifts. Your duty-free allowance also includes 4.5 liters of wine or beer; one 1,125-ml bottle of spirits; and either 200 cigarettes, 250 grams of tobacco, 50 cigars, or a combination of the three up to 250 grams. Prohibited items include meat products, seeds, plants, and fruits.

➤ INFORMATION: **New Zealand Customs** (Custom House, ⊠ 50 Anzac Ave., Box 29, Auckland, New Zealand, ☎ 09/359–6655, ℻ 09/359–6732).

IN THE U.K.

If you are a U.K. resident and your journey was wholly within the European Union (EU), you won't have to pass through customs when you return to the United Kingdom. If you plan to bring back large quantities of alcohol or tobacco, check EU limits beforehand.

➤ INFORMATION: **HM Customs and Excise** (⊠ Dorset House, Stamford St., Bromley Kent BR1 1XX, ☎ 020/7202–4227).

IN THE U.S.

U.S. residents who have been out of the country for at least 48 hours (and who have not used the $400 allowance or any part of it in the past 30 days) may bring home $400 worth of foreign goods duty-free.

U.S. residents 21 and older may bring back 1 liter of alcohol duty-free. In addition, regardless of your age, you are allowed 200 cigarettes and 100 non-Cuban cigars. Antiques, which the U.S. Customs Service defines as objects more than 100 years old, enter duty-free, as do original works of art done entirely by hand, including paintings, drawings, and sculptures.

You may also send packages home duty-free: up to $200 worth of goods for personal use, with a limit of one parcel per addressee per day (and no alcohol or tobacco products or perfume worth more than $5); label the package PERSONAL USE and attach a list of its contents and their retail value. Do not label the package UNSOLICITED GIFT or your duty-free exemption will drop to $100. Mailed items do not affect your duty-free allowance on your return.

➤ INFORMATION: **U.S. Customs Service** (inquiries, ⊠ 1300 Pennsylvania Ave. NW, Washington, DC 20229, ☎ 202/927–6724; complaints, ⊠ Office of Regulations and Rulings, 1300 Pennsylvania Ave. NW, Washington, DC 20229; registration of equipment, ⊠ Resource Management, 1300 Pennsylvania Ave. NW, Washington, DC 20229, ☎ 202/927–0540).

DINING

The restaurants we list are the cream of the crop in each price category. For information about restaurants beyond those reviewed in our guide, look for *Dining in Ireland* (free in the U.S.; £2.50 otherwise), an illustrated guide in which establishments are organized by region with accompanying price brackets. It's available from Bord Fáilte offices. *Where to Eat* (U.K.£2.50), published by the Northern Ireland Tourist Board (NITB), contains lists many Northern Irish restaurants in the middle to lower price ranges.

CATEGORY	THE REPUBLIC*	NORTHERN IRELAND*
$$$$	over £25	over UK£25
$$$	£20–£25	UK£15–£UK25
$$	under £20	UK£10–£UK15
$	under £15	under UK£15

*All prices are per person for a first course, a main course, and dessert, including sales tax, excluding wine or tip.

MEALS

A typical Irish breakfast includes fried eggs, bacon, black-and-white pudding, sausage, and a pot of tea. A typical lunch might feature a hearty sandwich or smoked salmon on brown bread; dinner meals usually include meant and two vegetables. Some of the best food is found at family Bed & Breakfasts and in inexpensive cafés.

MEALTIMES

Breakfast is served from 7–10, lunch runs from 1–2:30, and dinners are usually mid-evening occasions.

Pubs are open Monday–Saturday 10:30 AM–11:30 PM May–September, closing at 11 the rest of the year. The famous Holy Hour, which required city pubs to close from 2:30 to 3:30, was abolished in 1988, and afternoon opening is now at the discretion of the owner or manager; few bother to close. On Sunday, pubs are open 12:30–2 and 4–11. All pubs close on Christmas Day and Good Friday, but hotel bars are open for guests.

Pubs in Northern Ireland are open 11:30 AM–11 PM Monday–Saturday and 12:30 PM–2:30 PM and 7 PM–10 PM on Sunday. Sunday opening is at the owner's or manager's discretion.

PAYING

Traveler's checks and credit cards are widely accepted, although it's cash-only at smaller pubs and take-out restaurants.

RESERVATIONS & DRESS

Reservations are always a good idea: we mention them only when they're essential or are not accepted. Book as far ahead as you can, and reconfirm as soon as you arrive. We mention dress only when men are required to wear a jacket or a jacket and tie.

WINE, BEER & SPIRITS

All types of alcoholic beverages are available in Ireland. Beer and wine are sold in shops and supermarkets, and you can get drinks "to go" at some bars, although at inflated prices. Stout (Guiness, Murphy's, Beamish) is the Irish beer; whiskey comes in many brands and is smoother and more blended than Scotch. Most pubs serve until 11:30 PM in the summer and until 11 the rest of the year. In the cities, many bars now stay open until 1 AM, and many small-town pubs ignore closing times and stay open as late as their clientele wish.

DISABILITIES & ACCESSIBILITY

Ireland has only recently begun to provide facilities such as ramps and accessible toilets for people with disabilities. Public transportation also lags behind. However, visitors with disabilities will often find that the helpfulness of the Irish often makes up for the lack of amenities.

➤ LOCAL RESOURCES: **National Rehabilitation Board** (44 N. Great George's St., Dublin, ☎ 01/874–7503). Disability Action (2 Annadale Ave., Belfast, ☎ 028/9249–1011.

LODGING

When discussing accessibility with an operator or reservations agent **ask hard questions.** Are there any stairs, inside *or* out? Are there grab bars next to the toilet *and* in the shower/tub? How wide is the doorway to the room? To the bathroom? For the most extensive facilities meeting the latest legal specifications **opt for newer accommodations.**

➤ COMPLAINTS: **Disability Rights Section** (✉ U.S. Department of Justice, Civil Rights Division, Box 66738, Washington, DC 20035-6738, ☎ 202/514–0301; 800/514–0301; 202/514–0301 TTY; 800/514–0301 TTY, 𝔽𝔸𝕏 202/307–1198) for general complaints. **Aviation Consumer Protection Division** (☞ Air Travel, *above*) for airline-related problems. **Civil Rights Office** (✉ U.S. Department of Transportation, Departmental Office of Civil Rights, S-30, 400 7th St. SW, Room 10215, Washington, DC 20590, ☎ 202/366–4648, 𝔽𝔸𝕏 202/366–9371) for problems with surface transportation.

TRAVEL AGENCIES & TOUR OPERATORS

In the United States, although the Americans with Disabilities Act requires that travel firms serve the needs of all travelers, some agencies specialize in working with people with disabilities.

➤ TRAVELERS WITH MOBILITY PROBLEMS: **Access Adventures** (✉ 206 Chestnut Ridge Rd., Rochester, NY 14624, ☎ 716/889–9096), run by a former physical-rehabilitation counselor. **Accessible Vans of the Rockies, Activity and Travel Agency** (✉ 2040 W. Hamilton Pl., Sheridan, CO 80110, ☎ 303/806–5047 or 888/837–0065, 𝔽𝔸𝕏 303/781–2329). **Care-Vacations** (✉ 5-5110 50th Ave.,

Leduc, Alberta T9E 6V4, ☎ 780/986–6404 or 780/986–8332) has group tours and is especially helpful with cruise vacations. **Flying Wheels Travel** (✉ 143 W. Bridge St., Box 382, Owatonna, MN 55060, ☎ 507/451–5005 or 800/535–6790, 𝔽𝔸𝕏 507/451–1685). **Hinsdale Travel Service** (✉ 201 E. Ogden Ave., Suite 100, Hinsdale, IL 60521, ☎ 630/325–1335).

DISCOUNTS & DEALS

Be a smart shopper and **compare all your options** before making decisions. A plane ticket bought with a promotional coupon from travel clubs, coupon books, and direct-mail offers may not be cheaper than the least expensive fare from a discount ticket agency. And always keep in mind that what you get is just as important as what you save.

DISCOUNT RESERVATIONS

To save money **look into discount-reservations services** with toll-free numbers, which use their buying power to get a better price on hotels, airline tickets, even car rentals. When booking a room, always **call the hotel's local toll-free number** (if one is available) rather than the central reservations number—you'll often get a better price. Always ask about special packages or corporate rates.

When shopping for the best deal on hotels and car rentals **look for guaranteed exchange rates,** which protect you against a falling dollar. With your rate locked in, you won't pay more, even if the price goes up in the local currency.

➤ AIRLINE TICKETS: ☎ **800/FLY–4–LESS.** ☎ **800/FLY–ASAP.**

➤ HOTEL ROOMS: **RMC Travel** (☎ 800/245–5738). **Steigenberger Reservation Service** (☎ 800/223–5652). **Travel Interlink** (☎ 800/888–5898).

PACKAGE DEALS

Don't confuse packages and guided tours. When you buy a package, you travel on your own, just as though you had planned the trip yourself. Fly/drive packages, which combine airfare and car rental, are often a good deal. If you **buy a rail/drive pass** you may save on train tickets and car rentals. All Eurail- and Europass holders get a discount on Eurostar fares through the Channel Tunnel.

ELECTRICITY

To use your U.S.-purchased electric-powered equipment **bring a converter and adapter.** If your appliances are dual-voltage you'll need only an adapter. Don't use 110-volt outlets, marked FOR SHAVERS ONLY, for high-wattage appliances such as hair dryers. Most laptops operate equally well on 110 and 220 volts and so require only an adapter.

EMBASSIES

➤ AUSTRALIAN: (✉ Fitzwilton House, Wilton Terr., ☎ 01/676–1517).

➤ BRITISH: (✉ 29 Merrion Rd., ☎ 01/205–3700).

➤ CANADIAN: (✉ 65 St. Stephen's Green, ☎ 01/4787–1988).

➤ U.S.: (✉ 42 Elgin Rd., ☎ 01/668–8777).

EMERGENCIES

For all emergencies, call 999.

ENGLISH-LANGUAGE MEDIA

English is the first, and often, the only, language spoken in Ireland. All major media, including television and newspapers, is broadcast or printed in English.

ETIQUETTE & BEHAVIOR

The Irish are a casual, comfortable lot who aren't too particular about points of etiquette. Handshakes are more common than hugs although public displays of affection—in moderation—are often seen. Two things to note, though, are the great respect of the younger Irish for their elders and the great respect of all churchgoers for the sermon (hence, no talking during the service.

GAY & LESBIAN TRAVEL

In 1993 the Republic of Ireland began to replace virulently homophobic laws (inherited from British rule and enforced up to the 1970s) with some of the most gay-progressive statutes in the EU. Homosexual acts have been decriminalized and hate crimes and discrimination in the workplace and

public accommodation are now illegal. Leading these efforts was Ireland's progressive president, Mary Robinson, the first woman to hold this office. (She was named United Nations High Commissioner for Human Rights in June 1997.)

This enlightened legal environment, however, doesn't readily translate into the same public lesbian and gay presence you find in U.S. and European cities. Outside the Republic's major cities—Dublin, Cork, and Galway—signs of gay life can be difficult to find, and even in these cities you're likely to find them only in small pockets: a pub here, a café there. If you do encounter any difficulties as a gay traveler, it's likely to be with lodging establishments. Proprietors at even some of most upscale places may resist letting a room with one bed to same-sex couples; at other establishments, no one may so much as raise an eyebrow. Test the waters in advance: Be explicit about what you want when you make your reservation.

CORK

Ireland's second-largest city has the country's only lesbian and gay community center and a decade-old gay bar. The Cork Film Festival (☞ Festivals and Seasonal Events *in* Chapter 1), held in October, incorporates the Irish Lesbian and Gay Film Festival.

➤ CORK CONTACTS: **Lesbian and Gay Line** (☎ 021/271087) operates Wednesday 7 PM–9 PM and Saturday 3 PM–5 PM; it functions as a lesbian hot line Thursday 8 PM–10 PM. **Loafers** (✉ 26 Douglas St., ☎ 021/311612) is Cork's main gay bar. **The Other Place** (✉ 8 S. Main St., ☎ 021/278745), the lesbian and gay community center, houses a bookstore and café and hosts Friday- and Saturday-night dances.

DUBLIN

By far, Dublin has more accessible lesbian and gay life than any other city in Ireland. Consult the *Gay Community News,* Ireland's free monthly lesbian and gay newspaper, and *In Dublin* for current information about what's going on in the community. The Gay Switchboard Dublin operates Sunday–Friday 8 PM–10 PM and Saturday 3:30 PM–6 PM.

➤ DUBLIN CONTACTS: *Gay Community News* (GCN; ☎ 01/671–9076 or 01/671–0939). **Gay Switchboard Dublin** (☎ 01/872–1055). **The George** (✉ 89 S. Great George's St., ☎ 01/478–2983). **Out on the Liffey** (✉ 27 Ormond Quay, ☎ 01/872–2480).

GALWAY

A young populace, a progressive university, and a few outstanding theater companies help make Ireland's bohemian left-coast city one of the country's most gay-friendly places. Neither Le Graal nor Neachtain's are specifically gay, but they are among the gay-friendlier places in town.

➤ GALWAY CONTACTS: **Galway Gay Helpline** (☎ 091/566134) operates Tuesday 8 PM–10 PM. **Galway Lesbian Helpline** (☎ 091/564611) operates Wednesday 8 PM–10 PM and Saturday noon–2 PM. **Le Graal** (✉ 38 Lower Dominick St., ☎ 091/567614). **Neachtain's** (✉ 17 Cross St., ☎ 091/561720).

➤ GAY- AND LESBIAN-FRIENDLY TRAVEL AGENCIES: **Different Roads Travel** (✉ 8383 Wilshire Blvd., Suite 902, Beverly Hills, CA 90211, ☎ 323/651–5557 or 800/429–8747, FAX 323/651–3678). **Kennedy Travel** (✉ 314 Jericho Turnpike, Floral Park, NY 11001, ☎ 516/352–4888 or 800/237–7433, FAX 516/354–8849). **Now Voyager** (✉ 4406 18th St., San Francisco, CA 94114, ☎ 415/626–1169 or 800/255–6951, FAX 415/626–8626). **Yellowbrick Road** (✉ 1500 W. Balmoral Ave., Chicago, IL 60640, ☎ 773/561–1800 or 800/642–2488, FAX 773/561–4497). **Skylink Travel and Tour** (✉ 1006 Mendocino Ave., Santa Rosa, CA 95401, ☎ 707/546–9888 or 800/225–5759, FAX 707/546–9891), serving lesbian travelers.

HEALTH

Ireland is a very safe country for travel, with virtually no risk of health problems from food, drink, or insects. The weather, however, is another story; be sure to dress for the cold and rain or you may find yourself plagued by a constant cough and sniffles.

HOLIDAYS

Irish national holidays are as follows: January 1 (New Year's); March 17 (St. Patrick's Day); April 21, 2000 (Good Friday); April 24, 2000 (Easter Monday); May 1 (May Day); June 7 and August 2, 2000 (Summer Bank Holidays); October 25, 2000 (Autumn Bank Holiday); and December 25–26 (Christmas and St. Stephen's Day). If you plan to visit at Easter, remember that theaters and cinemas are closed for the last three days of the preceding week.

INSURANCE

The most useful travel insurance plan is a comprehensive policy that includes coverage for trip cancellation and interruption, default, trip delay, and medical expenses (with a waiver for preexisting conditions).

Without insurance you will lose all or most of your money if you cancel your trip, regardless of the reason. Default insurance covers you if your tour operator, airline, or cruise line goes out of business. Trip-delay covers expenses that arise because of bad weather or mechanical delays. Study the fine print when comparing policies.

If you're traveling internationally, a key component of travel insurance is coverage for medical bills incurred if you get sick on the road. Such expenses are not generally covered by Medicare or private policies. U.K. residents can buy a travel-insurance policy valid for most vacations taken during the year in which it's purchased (but check pre-existing-condition coverage). British and Australian citizens need extra medical coverage when traveling overseas.

Always **buy travel policies directly from the insurance company**; if you buy it from a cruise line, airline, or tour operator that goes out of business you probably will not be covered for the agency or operator's default, a major risk. Before you make any purchase **review your existing health and home-owner's policies** to find what they cover away from home.

➤ TRAVEL INSURERS: In the U.S. **Access America** (✉ 6600 W. Broad St., Richmond, VA 23230, ☎ 804/285–3300 or 800/284–8300), **Travel Guard International** (✉ 1145 Clark St., Stevens Point, WI 54481, ☎ 715/345–0505 or 800/826–1300). In Canada **Voyager Insurance** (✉ 44 Peel Center Dr., Brampton, Ontario L6T 4M8, ☎ 905/791–8700; 800/668–4342 in Canada).

➤ INSURANCE INFORMATION: In the U.K. the **Association of British Insurers** (✉ 51–55 Gresham St., London EC2V 7HQ, ☎ 020/7600–3333, FAX 020/7696–8999). In Australia the **Insurance Council of Australia** (☎ 03/9614–1077, FAX 03/9614–7924).

LANGUAGE

Irish (also known as Gaelic)—a Celtic language related to Scots Gaelic, Breton, and Welsh—is the official national language. Though English is technically the second language of the country, it is, in fact, the everyday tongue of 95% of the population. Nowadays all Irish speakers are fluent in English.

Irish-speaking communities are found mainly in sparsely populated rural areas along the western seaboard, on some but not all offshore islands, and in pockets in West Cork and County Waterford. Irish-speaking areas are known as Gaeltacht (pronounced *gale*-taukt). While most road signs in Ireland are given in both English and Irish, within Gaeltacht areas the signs are often in Irish only. A good touring map will give both Irish and English names to places within the Gaeltacht. You really need only know two Irish words: *Fir* (men) and *mná* (women)—useful vocabulary for a trip to a public toilet.

LODGING

Accommodations in Ireland range from deluxe renovated castles and stately homes to thatched cottages and farmhouses. Room standards are rising all the time, especially in the middle and lower price ranges. Pressure on hotel space reaches a peak from June to September, but it's always a good idea to **reserve in advance.** Many Irish hotels can be booked directly from the United States. Ask your travel agent.

The ITB has an official grading system and publishes a list of "approved accommodations," which includes hotels, guest houses, bed-and-breakfasts, farmhouses, hostels, and camping parks. For each accommodation, the list gives a maximum charge that no hotel may exceed without special authorization. Prices must be displayed in every room, so if the hotel oversteps its limit, do not hesitate to complain to the hotel manager and/or the ITB.

Ideally, visitors should **sample a range of accommodations.** The very expensive country-house hotels and renovated castles offer a unique combination of luxury and history. Less impressive, but equally charming, are the provincial inns and country hotels with simple but adequate facilities. Many visitors, seeking to meet a wide cross section of Irish people, prefer a different B&B every night. Others enjoy the simplicity of self-catering for a week or two in a thatched cottage. ITB-approved guest houses and B&Bs display a green shamrock outside and are usually considered more reputable than those without. Hotels and other accommodations in Northern Ireland are similar to those in the Republic of Ireland.

The lodgings we list are the cream of the crop in each price category. We always list the facilities that are available—but we don't specify whether they cost extra: When pricing accommodations, always ask what's included and what costs extra. Properties indicated by an ✕🍽 are lodging establishments whose restaurant warrants a special trip. Assume that hotels operate on the European Plan (EP, with no meals) unless we specify that they use the Continental Plan (CP, with a Continental breakfast daily), Modified American Plan (MAP, with breakfast and dinner daily), or the Full American Plan (FAP, with all meals).

CATEGORY	DUBLIN*	ELSEWHERE IN THE REPUBLIC*
$$$$	over £180	over £140
$$$	£140–£180	£100–£140
$$	£100–£140	£80–£100
$	under £100	under £80

*All prices are for two people in a double room, including 12.5% local sales tax (VAT) and a service charge (often applied in larger hotels).

➤ PUBLICATIONS: The NITB publishes a complete list—called *Where to Stay* (U.K.£3.99)—of hotels, guest houses, farmhouses, bed-and-breakfasts, self-catering accommodations, youth hostels, and camping and trailer parks; prices and full information are included. The ITB and NITB also distribute five accommodation guides produced under separate auspices; all are free if obtained in the U.S.: *Be Our Guest* (£2) covers hotels and guest houses; *Bed & Breakfast Ireland* (£3) covers thousands of B&Bs; *Ireland's Blue Book* (free) includes 37 prestigious country houses and restaurants; *Friendly Homes of Ireland,* (£1) covers family homes and small hotels; *Self Catering Guide* (£4) covers family homes and holiday cottages on short-term lettings.

➤ RESERVATIONS: Bord Fáilte (☎ 011800/668–96866 and **Dublin Tourism** ☎ 01/605–7777, FAX 01/605–7787; ☎ 01/602–4129, FAX 01/475–8046 for non–credit card accommodation inquiries) operate a credit card central reservations service for hotels and other accommodations, including guest houses and B&Bs throughout Ireland. There's a booking fee of £3 plus a charge of 10% of the cost of the accommodations.

APARTMENT & VILLA RENTALS

If you want a home base that's roomy enough for a family and comes with cooking facilities **consider a furnished rental.** These can save you money, especially if you're traveling with a group. Home-exchange directories sometimes list rentals as well as exchanges.

➤ INTERNATIONAL AGENTS: **At Home Abroad** (✉ 405 E. 56th St., Suite 6H, New York, NY 10022, ☎ 212/421–9165, FAX 212/752–1591). **Drawbridge to Europe** (✉ 5456 Adams Rd., Talent, OR 97540, ☎ 541/512–8927 or 888/268–1148, FAX 541/512–0978). **Europa-Let/Tropical Inn-Let** (✉ 92 N. Main St., Ashland, OR 97520, ☎ 541/482–5806 or 800/462–4486, FAX 541/482–0660). **Rent-a-Home International** (✉ 7200 34th Ave. NW, Seattle, WA 98117, ☎ 206/789–9377, FAX 206/789–9379). **Vacation Home Rentals Worldwide** (✉ 235 Kensington Ave., Norwood, NJ 07648, ☎ 201/767–9393 or 800/633–3284, FAX 201/767–5510). **Villas and Apartments Abroad** (✉ 420 Madison Ave., Suite 1003, New York, NY 10017, ☎ 212/759–1025 or 800/433–3020, FAX 212/755–8316). **Villas International** (✉ 950 Northgate Dr., Suite 206, San Rafael, CA 94903, ☎ 415/499–9490 or 800/221–2260, FAX 415/499–9491). **Hideaways International** (✉ 767 Islington St., Portsmouth, NH 03801, ☎ 603/430–4433 or 800/843–4433, FAX 603/430–4444; membership $99).

B&BS

B&Bs are classified by the ITB as either town homes, country homes, or farmhouses. Town and country B&Bs are listed in the ITB's "Quality Approved Irish Homes Accommodation Guide." Many now have at least one bedroom with a bathroom, but don't expect this as a matter of course. B&Bs often charge an extra 50p–£1 for a bath or shower. If this is taken in the family bathroom, you should ask first whether you can use the facility. Many travelers do not bother booking a B&B in advance. They are so plentiful in rural areas that it's often more fun to leave the decision open, allowing yourself a choice of final destinations for the night.

➤ RESERVATION SERVICES: **Bord Fáilte** (☎ 1850/230330). **Dublin Tourism** (☎ 01/605–7799).

CAMPING

This is the cheapest way of seeing the country, and facilities for campers and caravaners are improving steadily. An abundance of coastal campsites compensates for the shortage of inland ones. All are listed in *Caravan and Camping Ireland* available from the ITB. Rates start at about £4 per tent, £6 per caravan overnight.

COTTAGES

In more than 100 locations there are clusters of holiday cottages for rent. Although often built in the traditional style, they have central heating and all the other modern conveniences. A three-bedroom cottage equipped for six adults is around £250 per week in mid-season. It is essential to reserve in advance. The ITB's publication *Self-Catering* lists individual properties and clusters of traditional cottages available by the week. For information on booking, contact the ITB (☞ Visitor Information, *below*).

FARM VACATIONS

Many Irish farms offer holidays with part board or full board on a weekly basis. These are listed in the ITB's illustrated publication *Farmhouse Accommodation*. You will notice at once from the booklet that very few are picturesque: They are more likely to be modern bungalows or undistinguished, two-story houses than creeper-clad, Georgian mansions—though exceptions do exist. Room and part board—breakfast and an evening meal—costs from £170 per week.

GUEST HOUSES

To qualify as a guest house, an establishment must have at least five bedrooms, but in major cities they often have many more. Some guest houses are above a bar or restaurant; others are part of a family home. As a rule, they're cheaper (some include an optional evening meal) and offer fewer amenities than hotels. But often that's where the differences end. Most have high standards of cleanliness and hospitality. Some even have a bathroom, a TV, and a direct-dial phone in each room.

HOME EXCHANGES

If you would like to exchange your home for someone else's **join a home-exchange organization,** which will send you its updated listings of available exchanges for a year and will include your own listing in at least one of them. It's up to you to make specific arrangements.

➤ EXCHANGE CLUBS: **HomeLink International** (✉ Box 650, Key West, FL 33041, ☎ 305/294–7766 or 800/ 638–3841, ℻ 305/294–1448; $88 per year). **Intervac U.S.** (✉ Box 590504, San Francisco, CA 94159, ☎ 800/756–4663, ℻ 415/435–7440; $83 per year).

HOSTELS

No matter what your age you can **save on lodging costs by staying at hostels.** In some 5,000 locations in more than 70 countries around the world, Hostelling International (HI), the umbrella group for a number of national youth-hostel associations, offers single-sex, dorm-style beds and, at many hostels, couples rooms and family accommodations. Membership in any HI national hostel association, open to travelers of all ages, allows you to stay in HI-affiliated hostels at member rates (one-year membership is about $25 for adults; hostels run about $10–$25 per night). Members also have priority if the hostel is full; they're eligible for discounts around the world, even on rail and bus travel in some countries.

➤ ORGANIZATIONS: **Australian Youth Hostel Association** (✉ 10 Mallett St., Camperdown, NSW 2050, ☎ 02/ 9565–1699, ℻ 02/9565–1325). **Hostelling International—American Youth Hostels** (✉ 733 15th St. NW, Suite 840, Washington, DC 20005, ☎ 202/783–6161, ℻ 202/783–6171). **Hostelling International—Canada** (✉ 400–205 Catherine St., Ottawa, Ontario K2P 1C3, ☎ 613/ 237–7884, ℻ 613/237–7868). **Youth Hostel Association of England and Wales** (✉ Trevelyan House, 8 St. Stephen's Hill, St. Albans, Hertfordshire AL1 2DY, ☎ 01727/855215 or 01727/845047, ℻ 01727/844126). **Youth Hostels Association of New Zealand** (✉ Box 436, Christchurch, New Zealand, ☎ 03/379–9970, ℻ 03/365–4476). Membership in the U.S. $25, in Canada C$26.75, in the U.K. £9.30, in Australia $44, in New Zealand $24.

HOTELS

All hotels listed have private bath unless otherwise noted.

➤ TOLL-FREE NUMBERS: **Adam's Mark** (☎ 800/444–2326). **Baymont Inns** (☎ 800/428–3438). **Best Western** (☎

800/528–1234). **Choice** (☎ 800/221–2222). **Clarion** (☎ 800/252–7466). **Colony** (☎ 800/777–1700). **Comfort** (☎ 800/228–5150). **Days Inn** (☎ 800/325–2525). **Doubletree and Red Lion Hotels** (☎ 800/222–8733). **Embassy Suites** (☎ 800/362–2779). **Fairfield Inn** (☎ 800/228–2800). **Forte** (☎ 800/225–5843). **Four Seasons** (☎ 800/332–3442). **Hilton** (☎ 800/445–8667). **Holiday Inn** (☎ 800/465–4329). **Howard Johnson** (☎ 800/654–4656). **Hyatt Hotels & Resorts** (☎ 800/233–1234). **Inter-Continental** (☎ 800/327–0200). **La Quinta** (☎ 800/531–5900). **Marriott** (☎ 800/228–9290). **Le Meridien** (☎ 800/543–4300). **Nikko Hotels International** (☎ 800/645–5687). **Omni** (☎ 800/843–6664). **Quality Inn** (☎ 800/228–5151). **Radisson** (☎ 800/333–3333). **Ramada** (☎ 800/228–2828). **Renaissance Hotels & Resorts** (☎ 800/468–3571). **Ritz-Carlton** (☎ 800/341–3333). **ITT Sheraton** (☎ 800/325–3535). **Sleep Inn** (☎ 800/221–2222). **Westin Hotels & Resorts** (☎ 800/228–3000). **Wyndham Hotels & Resorts** (☎ 800/822–4200).

MAIL & SHIPPING

Letters take a week to 10 days to reach the U.S. and Canada, 3 to 5 days to reach the U.K.

POSTAL RATES

Airmail rates to the United States and Canada from the Irish Republic are 45p for letters and postcards. Mail to all European countries goes by air automatically, so airmail stickers or envelopes are not required. Rates are 32p for letters and postcards.

Rates from Northern Ireland are 43p for letters and 37p for postcards (not over 10 grams). To the rest of the United Kingdom and the Irish Republic, rates are 26p for first-class letters and 20p for second class.

RECEIVING MAIL

Mail can be held for collection at any post office free of charge for up to three months. It should be addressed to the recipient "c/o Poste Restante." In Dublin, use the **General Post Office** (✉ O'Connell St., Dublin 1, ☎ 01/7057000).

MEDIA

NEWSPAPERS & MAGAZINES

In Ireland, there are three national daily broadsheet newspapers, *The Irish Times* and *The Irish Independent*—both Dublin based—and *The Examiner* (formerly the *Cork Examiner*), which is published in Cork. *The Irish Times* is the most authoritative and esteemed of the three, *The Irish Independent* is the most popular, and the *Examiner* is widely read in the southern counties. The British *Daily Star* and *The Sun* also have Irish editions.

The Evening Herald is the only nationwide evening newspaper. The *Evening Echo* is published by the Examiner group and sold in the Cork region. There are four Irish Sunday newspapers: the very popular and opinion-focused *Sunday Independent,* the more intellectual *Sunday Tribune,* the business-oriented *Sunday Business Post,* the popular tabloid, *Sunday World,* and the new *Ireland on Sunday.* Regional weekly newspapers are published in almost every county. Up in Northern Ireland, the main dailies are the *Belfast Telegraph* and the *Belfast Newsletter.* The British broadsheet and tabloid dailies and Sunday newspapers are widely available throughout Ireland.

RADIO & TELEVISION

Radio Telefis Eireann (RTE) is Ireland's national television and radio network. There are two television channels—RTE 1, which concentrates on news and documentaries, and Network 2. which carries more feature films and light entertainment shows. *TV3 is a new, private channel with a lot of American and British soaps and situation comedies. TnaG (Telifis na Gaeilge) is an Irish-language channel (with English subtitles). The British television channels (BBC 1, BBC 2, UTV, Channel 4) and many satellite channels—including SkyNews, SkyMovies, SkySports, CNN, MTV, and TV5 Europe are also widely available.

There are two 24-hour national radio stations in Ireland—Radio 1 (mainly talk shows) and the popular music-dominated station, 2FM. FM3 is a classical music station which is broadcast in the early mornings and evenings on the same wavelength as the daytime Irish-language radio station, Raidio Na Gaeltachta. There are more than 25 local commercial radio stations whose broadcasting standards vary from county to county. All the BBC radio channels are also available.

MONEY MATTERS

A modest hotel in Dublin costs about £100 a night for two; this figure can be reduced to under £70 by staying in a registered guest house or inn, and reduced to less than £35 by staying in a suburban B&B. Lunch, consisting of a good one-dish plate of bar food at a pub, costs around £6; a sandwich at the same pub, about £2. In Dublin's better restaurants, dinner will run around £20 per person, excluding drinks and tip. Theater and entertainment in most places are inexpensive—about £14 for a good seat, and double that for a big-name, pop-music concert. For the price of a few drinks and (in Dublin and Killarney) a small entrance fee of about £1.50, you can spend a memorable evening at a *seisún* (pronounced *say-shoon*) in a music pub. Entrance to most public galleries is free, but stately homes and similar attractions normally charge about £3 per person. Just about everything is more expensive in Dublin, so add at least 10% to these sample prices: cup of coffee, 80p; pint of beer, £2.20; soda, £1; and 2-km/1-mi taxi ride, £4.

Hotels and meals in Northern Ireland are less expensive than in the United Kingdom and the Republic of Ireland. Also, the lower level of taxation makes dutiable goods such as gasoline, alcoholic drinks, and tobacco cheaper.

Prices throughout this guide are given for adults. Substantially reduced fees are almost always available for children, students, and senior citizens. For information on taxes, *see* Taxes, *below.*

ATMS

ATMs are found in all major towns. Most major banks are connected to CIRRUS or PLUS systems; there is a four-digit maximum for PIN numbers.

CREDIT CARDS

Throughout this guide, the following abbreviations are used: **AE,** American Express; **DC,** Diner's Club; **MC,** Master Card; and **V,** Visa. The Discover card is not honored in Ireland.

➤ REPORTING LOST CARDS: **American Express** (☎ 0353/1205–5111). **Diners Club** (☎ 0353/661–1800). **Master Card** (☎ 0353/679–8436). **Visa** (☎ 0353/668–5500).

CURRENCY

The unit of currency in the Irish Republic is the pound or punt, pronounced *poont.* It is divided into 100 pence (abbreviated 100p). In this guide, the £ sign refers to the Irish pound; the British pound is referred to as the pound sterling and is written U.K.£.

Irish notes come in denominations of £100, £50, £20, £10, and £5. Coins are available as £1, 50p, 20p, 10p, 5p, 2p, and 1p, and they are not exchangeable outside the Republic of Ireland.

Ireland is now a member of the European Monetary Fund (EMU) and as of January 1, 1999 all prices should be quoted in pounds and Euros. Noncash transactions, including credit card payments, can be quoted in Euros. January 2002 will see the introduction of the Euro coins and notes, as well as the gradual withdrawal of the local currency.

CURRENCY EXCHANGE

For the most favorable rates, **change money through banks.** Although ATM transaction fees may be higher abroad than at home, ATM rates are excellent because they are based on wholesale rates offered only by major banks. You won't do as well at exchange booths in airports or rail and bus stations, in hotels, in restaurants, or in stores. To avoid lines at airport exchange booths **get a bit of local currency before you leave home.** Dollars and British pounds are accepted only in large hotels and shops geared to tourists. Elsewhere you will be expected to use Irish currency.

At press time (summer 1999), the punt stood at around US$1.44, Canadian $2.20, and U.K.£.87; however, these rates will inevitably change both before and during 2000; keep a sharp eye on the exchange rate.

➤ EXCHANGE SERVICES: **International Currency Express** (☎ 888/842–0880 on East Coast; 888/278–6628 on West Coast). **Thomas Cook Currency Services** (☎ 800/287–7362 for telephone orders and retail locations).

TRAVELER'S CHECKS

Traveler's checks are widely accepted in restaurants, hotels, shops, and stores, throughout Ireland. However, if you're going to rural areas and small towns, go with cash; traveler's checks are best used in cities. Lost or stolen checks can usually be replaced within 24 hours. To ensure a speedy refund, buy your own traveler's checks—don't let someone else pay for them: irregularities like this can cause delays. The person who bought the checks should make the call to request a refund.

OUTDOORS & SPORTS

FISHING

The salmon season is normally from January 1 to September 30, but dates vary from one district to another. The best period for sea trout is from June to late September. Permits are necessary on privately owned waters or club waters: the latter will cost £5–£15 a day for salmon, £2–£10 for trout. There is no closed season for coarse angling. Besides the permit for the use of a certain stretch of water, those who wish to fish for salmon and sea trout by rod and line must also have a state license. No license is required for brown trout, rainbow trout, or coarse fish, including pike. Sea angling is available on rocks and piers around the coast.

Licenses for salmon and sea-trout fishing by rod and line in the Irish Republic (£25 annually, or £10 for 21 days) are available in some tackle shops or from the Central Fisheries Board. To game fish in Northern Ireland, you need a rod license; Foyle Fisheries Commission distributes licenses for game fishing in the Foyle area and the Fisheries Conservancy

Board handles all other regions. A license costs approximately U.K.£10 for 8 days. You must also obtain a permit from the owner of the waters in which you plan to fish.

Most of the waters are owned by the Department of Agriculture, which charges about U.K.£15 for an eight-day permit, U.K.£3.50 for a daily one. If you plan to fish outside the jurisdiction of the Department of Agriculture, you must obtain a permit from one of the local clubs. For more information, and for Department of Agriculture permits and FFC and FCB rod licenses, contact the NITB (☞ Visitor Information, *below*).

➤ INFORMATION: **Central Fisheries Board** (⊠ Balngowan House, Mobhi Boreen, Glasnevin, Dublin 9, ☎ 01/837–9206). **Department of Agriculture** (⊠ Fisheries Division, Stormont, Belfast BT4 3PW, ☎ 028/9052–3431). **Fisheries Conservancy Board** (⊠ FCB, 1 Mahon Rd., Portadown, Craigavon, Co. Armagh BT62 3EE, ☎ 028/3833–4666). **Foyle Fisheries Commission** (⊠ FFC, 8 Victoria Rd., Derry BT47 2AB, ☎ 028/714–2100).

PACKING

In Ireland you can experience all four seasons in one day, so pack accordingly. Even in July and August, the hottest months of the year, a heavy sweater and a good waterproof coat or umbrella are essential. You should **bring at least two pairs of walking shoes**: It can and does rain at any time of the year, and shoes can get soaked in minutes.

The Irish are generally informal about clothes. In the more expensive hotels and restaurants most people dress formally for dinner, and a jacket and tie may be required in bars after 7 PM, but very few places operate a strict dress policy. Younger travelers should note that old or tattered blue jeans are forbidden in certain bars and dance clubs.

In your carry-on luggage **bring an extra pair of eyeglasses or contact lenses** and **enough of any medication you take** to last the entire trip. You may also want your doctor to write a spare prescription using the drug's generic name, since brand names may vary from country to country. In luggage to be checked, **never pack prescription drugs or valuables.** To avoid customs delays, carry medications in their original packaging. And don't forget to copy down and carry addresses of offices that handle refunds of lost traveler's checks.

CHECKING LUGGAGE

How many carry-on bags you can bring with you is up to the airline. Most allow two, but not always, so make sure that everything you carry aboard will fit under your seat, and get to the gate early. Note that if you have a seat at the back of the plane, you'll probably board first, while the overhead bins are still empty.

If you are flying internationally, note that baggage allowances may be determined not by piece but by weight—generally 88 pounds (40 kilograms) in first class, 66 pounds (30 kilograms) in business class, and 44 pounds (20 kilograms) in economy.

Airline liability for baggage is limited to $1,250 per person on flights within the United States. On international flights it amounts to $9.07 per pound or $20 per kilogram for checked baggage (roughly $640 per 70-pound bag) and $400 per passenger for unchecked baggage. You can buy additional coverage at check-in for about $10 per $1,000 of coverage, but it excludes a rather extensive list of items, shown on your airline ticket.

Before departure **itemize your bags' contents** and their worth, and label the bags with your name, address, and phone number. (If you use your home address, cover it so that potential thieves can't see it readily.) Inside each bag **pack a copy of your itinerary.** At check-in **make sure that each bag is correctly tagged** with the destination airport's three-letter code. If your bags arrive damaged or fail to arrive at all, file a written report with the airline before leaving the airport.

PASSPORTS & VISAS

When traveling internationally **carry a passport even if you don't need one** (it's always the best form of ID), and **make two photocopies of the data page** (one for someone at home and another for you, carried separately from your passport). If you lose your passport promptly call the nearest embassy or consulate and the local police.

ENTERING IRELAND

All U.S., Canadian, Australian, and New Zealand citizens, even infants, need a valid passport to enter Ireland for stays of up to 90 days. Citizens of the United Kingdom, when traveling on flights departing from Great Britain, do not need a passport to enter Ireland. Passport requirements for Northern Ireland are the same as for the Republic.

PASSPORT OFFICES

The best time to apply for a passport or to renew is during the fall and winter. Before any trip, check your passport's expiration date, and, if necessary, renew it as soon as possible.

➤ AUSTRALIAN CITIZENS: **Australian Passport Office** (☎ 131–232).

➤ CANADIAN CITIZENS: **Passport Office** (☎ 819/994–3500 or 800/ 567–6868).

➤ NEW ZEALAND CITIZENS: **New Zealand Passport Office** (☎ 04/494– 0700 for information on how to apply; 04/474–8000 or 0800/225– 050 in New Zealand for information on applications already submitted).

➤ U.K. CITIZENS: **London Passport Office** (☎ 0990/210–410) for fees and documentation requirements and to request an emergency passport.

➤ U.S. CITIZENS: **National Passport Information Center** (☎ 900/225– 5674; calls are 35¢ per minute for automated service, $1.05 per minute for operator service).

SAFETY

The theft of car radios, mobile phones, cameras, video recorders, and other items of value from cars is common in Dublin and other major cities and towns. Never leave any valuable items on car seats or in the foot space between the back and front seats or in the glove compartments. In fact, never leave anything whatsoever in sight in your car—even if you're leaving it for only a short time. You should also think twice about leaving valuables in your car while visiting tourist attractions anywhere in the country.

SENIOR-CITIZEN TRAVEL

To qualify for age-related discounts **mention your senior-citizen status up front** when booking hotel reservations (not when checking out) and before you're seated in restaurants (not when paying the bill). When renting a car ask about promotional car-rental discounts, which can be cheaper than senior-citizen rates.

➤ EDUCATIONAL PROGRAMS: **Elderhostel** (⊠ 75 Federal St., 3rd fl., Boston, MA 02110, ☎ 877/426–8056, ℻ 877/426–2166). **Interhostel** (⊠ University of New Hampshire, 6 Garrison Ave., Durham, NH 03824, ☎ 603/862–1147 or 800/733–9753, ℻ 603/862–1113).

STUDENTS IN IRELAND

To save money, **look into deals available through student-oriented travel agencies.** To qualify you'll need a bona fide student ID card. Members of international student groups are also eligible.

➤ STUDENT IDs & SERVICES: **Council on International Educational Exchange** (CIEE, ⊠ 205 E. 42nd St., 14th fl., New York, NY 10017, ☎ 212/822–2600 or 888/268–6245, ℻ 212/822–2699) for mail orders only, in the U.S. **Travel Cuts** (⊠ 187 College St., Toronto, Ontario M5T 1P7, ☎ 416/979–2406 or 800/667–2887) in Canada.

TAXES

VALUE-ADDED TAX (VAT)

When leaving the Irish Republic, U.S. and Canadian visitors **get a refund** of the value-added tax (VAT), which currently accounts for a hefty 21% of the purchase price of many goods and 12.5% of those that fall outside the luxury category. Apart from clothing, most items of interest to visitors, right down to ordinary toilet soap, are rated at 21%. Most crafts outlets and department stores operate a system called Cashback, which enables U.S. and Canadian visitors to collect VAT rebates in the currency of their choice at Dublin or Shannon Airport on departure. Otherwise, refunds can be claimed from individual stores after returning home. Forms for the refunds must be picked up at the time of purchase, and the form must be stamped by customs before leaving Ireland (including Northern Ireland). Most major stores deduct VAT at the time of sale if goods are to be shipped overseas; however, there is a shipping charge. VAT is not refundable on accommodation, car rental, meals or any other form of personal services received on holiday.

When leaving Northern Ireland, U.S. and Canadian visitors can also get a refund of the 17.5% VAT by the over-the-counter and the direct-export methods. Most larger stores provide these services upon request and will handle the paperwork. For the over-the-counter method, you must spend more than £75 in one store. Ask the store for Form VAT 407 (you must have identification—passports are best), to be given to customs when you leave the country. The refund will be forwarded to you in about eight weeks (minus a small service charge) either in the form of a sterling check or as a credit to your charge card. The direct-export method, where the goods are shipped directly to your home, is more cumbersome. VAT Form 704/1/93 must be certified by customs, police, or a notary public when you get home and then sent back to the store, which will refund your money.

Europe Tax-Free Shopping is a VAT. refund service that makes getting your money back hassle-free. ETS is Europe-wide and has 90,000 affiliated stores. In participating stores, **ask for the ETS refund form** (called a Shopping Cheque). As is true for all customs forms, when leaving the European Union you get them stamped by the customs official. Then you take them to the ETS counter and they will refund your money right there in cash, by check, or a refund to your credit card. All that convenience will cost you 20%—but then it's done.

➤ VAT REFUNDS: **Europe Tax-Free Shopping** (⊠ 233 S. Wacker Dr., Suite 9700, Chicago, IL 60606-6502, ☎ 312/382–1101).

TELEPHONES

Ireland's telephone system is up to the standards of the U.K. and the U.S. Direct-dialing is common; local phone numbers have five to seven digits. You can make international calls from most phones, and some cell phones also work here, depending on the carrier.

Do not make calls from your hotel room unless it's absolutely necessary. Practically all hotels add 200% to 300% to the cost of a call.

COUNTRY & AREA CODES

The country code for Ireland is 353; for Northern Ireland, 44. When dialing an Irish number from abroad, drop the initial 0 from the local area code. The country code is 1 for the U.S. and Canada, 61 for Australia, 64 for New Zealand, and 44 for the U.K.

DIRECTORY & OPERATOR INFORMATION

If the operator has to connect your call, it will cost at least one-third more than direct dial.

➤ REPUBLIC OF IRELAND: Call 1190 for directory inquiries within the Republic and Northern Ireland, call 1197 for U.K. numbers, and call 1198 for international numbers. Call 114 for operator assistance with international calls and 10 for operator assistance for calls within Ireland and the U.K.

➤ NORTHERN IRELAND AND THE U.K.: Call 192 for directory inquiries within Northern Ireland and the U.K., call 153 for international directory inquiries, which includes the Republic, call 155 for the international operator, call 100 for operator assistance for calls within the U.K. and Northern Ireland.

INTERNATIONAL CALLS

International dialing codes can be found in all telephone directories. The international prefix from Ireland is 00. For calls to Great Britain, dial 0044 before the exchange code, and drop the initial zero of the local code. For the U.S. dial 001.

LOCAL CALLS

To make a local call just dial the number direct.

LONG-DISTANCE CALLS

To make a long-distance call, just dial the area code, then the number.

If you are dialing Northern Ireland from the Republic, place 08 before the local code (e.g., Belfast is 08/ 01232, Derry is 08/01504, and Armagh is 08/01861).

LONG-DISTANCE SERVICES

AT&T, MCI, and Sprint access codes make calling long distance relatively convenient, but you may find the local access number blocked in many hotel rooms. First ask the hotel operator to connect you. If the hotel operator balks ask for an international operator, or dial the international operator yourself. One way to improve your odds of getting connected to your long-distance carrier is to travel with more than one company's calling card (a hotel may block Sprint, for example, but not MCI). If all else fails call from a pay phone.

➤ ACCESS CODES: **AT&T USADirect** (☎ 1800/550000 from the Republic of Ireland, 0800/0130011 from Northern Ireland). **MCI Call USA** (☎ 1800/5551001 from the Republic of Ireland, 0800/890222 from Northern Ireland using BT, or 0500/890222 using Mercury). **Sprint Express** (☎ 1800/552001 from the Republic of Ireland, 0800/890877 from Northern Ireland using BT, or 0500/890877 using Mercury).

PHONE CARDS

"Callcards" are sold in all post offices and at most newsagents. These come in denominations of 10, 20, and 50 units, and range in price from £2. for 10 to £16 for 100. Card phones are now more popular than coin phones.

PUBLIC PHONES

Public pay phones are in all towns and villages. They can be found in street booths and in bars and shops, some of which display a sign saying YOU CAN PHONE FROM HERE. There are currently at least three different models of pay phones in operation; read the instructions or ask for assistance. A local call costs 20p for three minutes; long-distance calls within Ireland are around 80p for three minutes.

Northern Ireland is part of the United Kingdom telephone system. A local call costs 10p.

TIME

Dublin is 5 hours ahead of New York, 8 hours ahead of Los Angeles and Vancouver, 9 hours ahead of Auckland, and 10 hours ahead of Sydney and Melbourne.

TIPPING

In some hotels and restaurants a service charge of around 10%—rising to 15% in a few plush spots—is added to the bill. If in doubt, ask whether service is included. In places where it is included, tipping is not necessary unless you have received particularly good service. But if there is no service charge, add a minimum of 10% to the total.

Tip taxi drivers about 10% of the fare displayed by the meter. Hackney cabs, who make the trip for a prearranged sum, do not expect tips. There are few porters and plenty of baggage trolleys at airports, so tipping is usually not an issue; if you use a porter, 50p is the minimum. Tip hotel porters about 50p per large suitcase. Hairdressers normally expect about £1. You don't tip in pubs, but for waiter service in a bar, a hotel lounge, or a Dublin lounge bar, leave about 50p.

TOURS & PACKAGES

On a prepackaged tour or independent vacation everything is prearranged so you'll spend less time planning—and often get it all at a good price.

BOOKING WITH AN AGENT

Travel agents are excellent resources. But it's a good idea to collect brochures from several agencies because some agents' suggestions may be influenced by relationships with tour and package firms that reward them for volume sales. If you have a special interest **find an agent with expertise in that area**; ASTA (☞ Travel Agencies, *below*) has a database of specialists worldwide.

Make sure your travel agent knows the accommodations and other services of the place they're recommending. Ask about the hotel's location,

room size, beds, and whether it has a pool, room service, or programs for children, if you care about these. Has your agent been there in person or sent others whom you can contact?

Do some homework on your own, too: Local tourism boards can provide information about lesser-known and small-niche operators, some of which may sell only direct.

BUYER BEWARE

Each year consumers are stranded or lose their money when tour operators—even large ones with excellent reputations—go out of business. So **check out the operator**. Ask several travel agents about its reputation, and try to **book with a company that has a consumer-protection program**. (Look for information in the company's brochure.) In the United States, members of the National Tour Association and United States Tour Operators Association are required to set aside funds to cover your payments and travel arrangements in case the company defaults. It's also a good idea to choose a company that participates in the American Society of Travel Agent's Tour Operator Program (TOP); ASTA will act as mediator in any disputes between you and your tour operator.

Remember that the more your package or tour includes the better you can predict the ultimate cost of your vacation. Make sure you know exactly what is covered, and **beware of hidden costs**. Are taxes, tips, and transfers included? Entertainment and excursions? These can add up.

➤ TOUR-OPERATOR RECOMMENDATIONS: **American Society of Travel Agents** (☞ Travel Agencies, *below*). **National Tour Association** (NTA, ✉ 546 E. Main St., Lexington, KY 40508, ☎ 606/226–4444 or 800/682–8886). **United States Tour Operators Association** (USTOA, ✉ 342 Madison Ave., Suite 1522, New York, NY 10173, ☎ 212/599–6599 or 800/468–7862, ℻ 212/599–6744).

TRAIN TRAVEL

The Irish Republic's train services are generally reliable, reasonably priced, and comfortable. All the principal towns are easily reached from Dublin, though services between provincial cities are roundabout. To reach Cork City from Wexford, for example, you have to go via Limerick Junction. It is often quicker, though perhaps less comfortable, to take a bus. Most mainline trains have two classes: standard and superstandard. Round-trip tickets are usually cheapest.

In Northern Ireland, Northern Ireland Railways has three main rail routes, all operating out of Belfast's **Central Station** (☎ 01232/899400). These are north to Derry, via Ballymena and Coleraine; east to Bangor along the shores of Belfast Lough; and south to Dublin and the Irish Republic. Note that **Eurailpasses are not valid in Northern Ireland.**

DISCOUNTS & PASSES

To save money **look into rail passes.** But be aware that if you don't plan to cover many miles, you may come out ahead by buying individual tickets.

Ireland (excluding Northern Ireland) is one of 17 countries in which you can **use Eurailpasses,** which provide unlimited first-class rail travel, in all of the participating countries, for the duration of the pass. If you plan to rack up the miles, get a standard pass. These are available for 15 days ($554), 21 days ($718), one month ($890), two months ($1,260), and three months ($1,558). If your plans call for only limited train travel, **look into a Europass,** which costs less money than a EurailPass. Unlike with Eurailpasses, however, you get a limited number of travel days, in a limited number of countries, during a specified time period. For example, a two-month pass ($348) allows 5 days of rail travel but costs $200 less than the least expensive EurailPass; 15 days of travel in two months costs $728. Keep in mind, however, that the Europass is good only in France, Germany, Italy, Spain, and Switzerland, and the number of countries you can visit is further limited by the type of pass you buy. For example, the basic two-month pass allows you to visit only three of the five participating countries.

In addition to standard Eurailpasses, **ask about special rail-pass plans.**

Among these are the Eurail Youth-pass (for those under age 26), the Eurail Saverpass (which gives a discount for two or more people traveling together), a Eurail Flexipass (which allows a certain number of travel days within a set period), the Euraildrive Pass and the Europass Drive (which combines travel by train and rental car). Whichever pass you choose, remember that you must **purchase your pass before you leave** for Europe.

The **Irish Explorer Rail & Bus Pass,** for use on Ireland's railroads, bus system, or both, covers all the state-run and federal railways and bus lines throughout the Republic of Ireland. It does not apply to the North or to transportation within the cities. An 8-day ticket for use on buses *and* trains during a 15-day period is $100. Contact Irish Rail International for details.

The **Emerald Isle Card** offers unlimited bus and train travel anywhere in Ireland and Northern Ireland, valid within cities as well. An 8-day pass gives you eight days of travel over a 15-day period; it costs $115, $56 for children. A pass for 15 days of travel over a 30-day period costs $200, $100 for children. Irish Rail International provides details on this card as well.

In Northern Ireland, **Rail Runabout** tickets, entitling you to seven days' unlimited travel on scheduled rail services April–October, are available from main Northern Ireland Railway stations. They cost U.K.£35 for adults, U.K.£18 for children under 16 and senior citizens. Interrail tickets are also valid in Northern Ireland.

RESERVATIONS

Many travelers assume that rail passes guarantee them seats on the trains they wish to ride. Not so. You need to **book seats ahead even if you are using a rail pass**; seat reservations are required on some European trains, particularly high-speed trains, and are a good idea on trains that may be crowded—particularly in summer on popular routes. You will also need a reservation if you purchase sleeping accommodations.

TICKETS & SCHEDULES

➤ TRAIN INFORMATION: In the Irish Republic: **Irish Rail** (Iarnrod Éireann; ☎ 01/836–6222), the rail division of CIE. In Northern Ireland: **Northern Ireland Railways** (☎ 028/9089–9411).

➤ INFORMATION AND PASSES: **BritRail Travel International** (✉ 1500 Broadway, New York, NY 10036, ☎ 212/575–2667, FAX 212/575–2542). **CIT Tours Corp.** (✉ 15 W. 44th St., 10th Floor, New York, NY 10036, ☎ 212/730–2400 or 800/248–7245 in the U.S., 800/387–0711 or 800/361–7799 in Canada). **DER Travel Services** (✉ 9501 W. Devon Ave., Rosemont, IL 60018, ☎ 800/782–2424, FAX 800/282–7474 for information or 800/860–9944 for brochures). **Irish Rail International** (✉ 108 Ridgedale Ave., Morristown, NJ 07960, ☎ 800/243–7687). **Rail Europe** (✉ 500 Mamaroneck Ave., Harrison, NY 10528, ☎ 914/682–5172 or 800/438–7245, FAX 800/432–1329; ✉ 2087 Dundas E, Suite 106, Mississauga, Ontario L4X 1M2, ☎ 800/361–7245, FAX 905/602–4198).

TRAVEL AGENCIES

A good travel agent puts your needs first. Look for an agency that has been in business at least five years, emphasizes customer service, and has someone on staff who specializes in your destination. In addition **make sure the agency belongs to a professional trade organization.** The American Society of Travel Agents (ASTA), with 27,0000 agents in some 170 countries, is the largest and most influential in the field. Operating under the motto "Integrity in Travel," it maintains and enforces a strict code of ethics and will step in to help mediate any agent-client disputes. ASTA also maintains a Web site that includes a directory of agents. (Note that if a travel agency is also acting as your tour operator, ☞ Buyer Beware *in* Tours & Packages, *above.*

➤ LOCAL AGENT REFERRALS: **American Society of Travel Agents** (ASTA, ☎ 800/965–2782 24-hr hot line, FAX 703/684–8319, www.astanet.com). **Association of British Travel Agents** (✉ 55–57 Newman St., London W1P 4AH, ☎ 020/7637–2444, FAX 020/7637–0713). **Association of Canadian**

Travel Agents (✉ 1729 Bank St., Suite 201, Ottawa, Ontario K1V 7Z5, ☎ 613/521–0474, FAX 613/521–0805). **Australian Federation of Travel Agents** (✉ Level 3, 309 Pitt St., Sydney 2000, ☎ 02/9264–3299, FAX 02/9264–1085). **Travel Agents' Association of New Zealand** (✉ Box 1888, Wellington 10033, ☎ 04/499–0104, FAX 04/499–0786).

VISITOR INFORMATION

For information on travel in the Irish Republic, contact the **Irish Tourist Board** (ITB), known as Bord Fáilte (pronounced Board Falcha). Information on travel in the North is available from the **Northern Ireland Tourist Board** (NITB) office.

➤ TOURIST INFORMATION ITB: **U.S.** (✉ 345 Park Ave., New York, NY 10154, ☎ 212/418–0800 or 800/223–6470, FAX 212/371–9052). **Canada** (✉ 160 Bloor St. E, Suite 1150, Toronto, Ontario M4W 1B9, ☎ 416/929–2779, FAX 416/929–6783). **U.K.** (✉ Ireland House, 150 New Bond St., London W1Y 0AQ, ☎ 020/7493–3201, FAX 020/7493–9065).

➤ NITB: **U.S.** (✉ 551 5th Ave., Suite 701, New York, NY 10176, ☎ 212/922–0101 or 800/326–0036, FAX 212/922–0099). **Canada** (✉ 111 Avenue Rd., Suite 450, Toronto, Ontario M5R 3J8, ☎ 416/925–6368, FAX 416/961–2175). **U.K.** ✉ 4–12 Lower Regent St., London BW1Y 4PQ, ☎ 020/7839–8417).

➤ U.S. GOVERNMENT ADVISORIES: **U.S. Department of State** (✉ Overseas Citizens Services Office, Room 4811 N.S., 2201 C St. NW, Washington, DC 20520; ☎ 202/647–5225 for interactive hot line; 301/946–4400 for computer bulletin board; FAX 202/647–3000 for interactive hot line); enclose a self-addressed, stamped, business-size envelope.

WEB SITES

Do check out the World Wide Web when you're planning your trip. You'll find everything from up-to-date weather forecasts to virtual tours of famous cities. Fodor's Web site, **www.fodors.com**, is a great place to start your on-line travels. For a comprehensive directory of sites on Ireland, visit **www. paddynet.com**. Some of the most popular sites (note that their log-on addresses are subject to change) are: **Irish Tourism Board** (www.ireland.travel.ie); **Northern Ireland Tourist Board** (www.ni-tourism.com); **Best of Ireland** (www.iol.ie/-discover/welcome.htm); and **Every Celtic Thing on the Web** (www.mi.net/users/ang/angris.html). In addition, many of the leading newspapers of Ireland (☞ Media, *above*) have their own Web sites, which can be mines of timely information about special events, the latest restaurants, and newest cultural happenings. Track down these newspaper Web sites using a search engine.

WHEN TO GO

Summer remains the most popular time to visit Ireland, and for good reason. The weather is pleasant, the days are long (daylight lasts until after 10 in late June and July), and the countryside is green and beautiful. But there will be crowds in popular holiday spots, and prices for accommodations are at their peak. As British and Irish school vacations overlap from late-June to mid-September, families, backpacking students, and other vacationers descend on popular coastal resorts in the South, West, and East. Unless you are determined to enjoy the short (July and August) swimming season, you would be well advised to **take your vacation in Ireland outside peak travel months.**

Fall and spring are good times to travel (late September can often be dry and warm, although the weather can be unpredictable. Seasonal hotels, restaurants, and accommodations

usually close from early- or mid-November until mid-March or Easter. During this off-season, prices are considerably lower than in summer, but your selection of hotels and restaurants is limited, and many minor attractions also close. St. Patrick's Week in March gives a focal point to a spring visit, but some American visitors may find the saint's-day celebrations a little less enthusiastic than the ones back home. Dublin, however, welcomes American visitors on March 17 with a weekend-long series of activities, including a parade and the Lord Mayor's Ball. If you're planning an Easter visit, don't forget that most theaters close from Thursday to Sunday of Holy Week (the week preceding Easter), and all bars and restaurants, except those serving hotel residents, close on Good Friday.

If you want to feel like the only tourist in town, **try a winter visit.** Many hotels arrange special Christmas packages with entertainment and outdoor activities. Horse races and hunting trips abound, although mid-November to mid-February is either too cold or too wet for all but the keenest golfers, and some of the coastal links courses are playable in almost any weather. There are cheerful open fires in almost all hotels and bars, and, with extra time on their hands, people tend to take an added interest in visitors.

CLIMATE

What follows are average daily maximum and minimum temperatures for some major cities in Ireland.

➤ FORECASTS: **Weather Channel Connection** (☎ 900/932–8437), 95¢ per minute from a Touch-Tone phone.

DUBLIN

Jan.	47F	8C	May	59F	15C	Sept.	63F	17C
	34	1		43	6		49	9
Feb.	47F	8C	June	65F	18C	Oct.	58F	14C
	36	2		49	9		43	6
Mar.	50F	10C	July	68F	20C	Nov.	50F	10C
	38	3		52	11		40	4
Apr.	56F	13C	Aug.	67F	20C	Dec.	47F	8C
	40	4		52	11		38	3

CORK

Jan.	49F	9C	May	61F	16C	Sept.	65F	18C
	36	2		45	7		50	10
Feb.	49F	9C	June	67F	19C	Oct.	58F	14C
	38	3		50	10		45	7
Mar.	52F	11C	July	68F	20C	Nov.	52F	11C
	40	4		54	12		40	4
Apr.	56F	13C	Aug.	68F	20C	Dec.	49F	9C
	41	5		54	12		38	3

BELFAST

Jan.	43F	6C	May	59F	15C	Sept.	61F	16C
	36	2		43	6		49	9
Feb.	45F	7C	June	65F	18C	Oct.	56F	13C
	36	2		49	9		45	7
Mar.	49F	9C	July	65F	18C	Nov.	49F	9C
	38	3		52	11		40	4
Apr.	54F	12C	Aug.	65F	18C	Dec.	45F	7C
	50	4		52	11		38	3

INDEX

L@@king
@ FOR A
great place to go?

We know just the place. In fact, it attracts more than 125,000 visitors a day, making it one of the world's most popular travel destinations. It's previewtravel.com, the Web's comprehensive resource for travelers. It gives you access to over 500 airlines, 25,000 hotels, rental cars, cruises, vacation packages and support from travel experts 24 hours a day. Plus great information from Fodor's travel guides and travelers just like you. All of which makes previewtravel.com quite a find.

Preview Travel has everything you need to plan & book your next trip.

air, car & hotel reservations

vacation packages & cruises

destination planning & travel tips

24-hour customer service

previewtravel.com

preview travel

aol keyword: previewtravel
www.previewtravel.com

FODOR'S IRELAND 2000

EDITOR: Holly S. Smith

Editorial Contributors: Dermot Gilleece, Geoff Hill, Alannah Hopkin, Anthony Howard, Vincent Jamison, Natasha Lesser, Helayne Schiff

Editorial Production: Stacey Kulig

Maps: David Lindroth, *cartographer;* Bob Blake, *map editor*

Design: Fabrizio La Rocca, *creative director;* Guido Caroti, *art director;* Jolie Novak, *photo editor;* Melanie Marin, *photo researcher*

Cover Design: Pentagram

Production/Manufacturing: Mike Costa

ISBN 0-679-00359-2

ISSN 0071-6464

SPECIAL SALES
Fodor's Travel Publications are available at special discounts for bulk purchases for sales promotions or premiums. Special editions, including personalized covers, excerpts of existing guides, and corporate imprints, can be created in large quantities for special needs. For more information, contact your local bookseller or write to Special Markets, Fodor's Travel Publications, 201 East 50th Street, New York, NY 10022. Inquiries from Canada should be directed to your local Canadian bookseller or sent to Random House of Canada, Ltd., Marketing Dept., 2775 Matheson Boulevard East, Mississauga, Ontario L4W 4P7. Inquiries from the United Kingdom should be sent to Fodor's Travel Publications, 20 Vauxhall Bridge Road, London SW1V 2SA, England.

PRINTED IN THE UNITED STATES OF AMERICA

10 9 8 7 6 5 4 3 2 1

IMPORTANT TIP
Although all prices, opening times, and other details in this book are based on information supplied to us at press time, changes occur all the time in the travel world, and Fodor's cannot accept responsibility for facts that become outdated or for inadvertent erros or omissions. So **always confirm information when it matters,** especially if you're making a detour to visit a specific place.

PHOTOGRAPHY
Wendy Carlson, *cover.*

Ballymaloe House: *Melanie Eclaire, 30C.*

Jan Butchofsky-Houser, *18G.*

Corbis: *7 bottom right, 18F. Michael St. Maur Sheil, 22C.*

Cork Kerry Tourism, *2 top right, 2 bottom center, 27C, 30B.*

Dublin Castle Conference Centre, *26A.*

Dúchas The Heritage Service, *26B, 30H, 30J.*

Dave G. Houser, *15C.*

Randall Hyman, *17D.*

The Image Bank: *Alan Becker, 1. Walter Bibikow, 7C, 9H. Michael Melford, 25C. Andrea Pistolesi, 10B, 28D. Stefano Scatá, 6B, 30A, 30D. John Vachon, 30F.*

Irish Tourist Board, *22B, 28E.*

Catherine Karnow, *8F, 8G, 11D, 19I.*

The Kildare Hotel & Country Club, *2 bottom left.*

James Lemass, *6A, 9J, 32.*

Longueville House, *30I.*

Mayo Naturally, *2 bottom right, 21 bottom right.*

Paul McCarthy, *21E.*

Northern Ireland Tourist Board, *24A, 29F, 29G.*

Jolie Novak, *20B.*

The Old Rectory Country House & Restaurant, *30E.*

Park Hotel Kenmare, *30G.*

PhotoDisc, *18E.*

Powerscourt Estate, *3 top right.*

Restaurant Patrick Gilbaud, *8E.*

Shannon Development, *3 top left, 3 bottom left, 3 bottom right, 20C.*

The Slide File, *4–5, 7D, 9I, 10A, 10C, 11E, 11F, 12A, 12B, 13C, 13D, 13E, 14A, 15B, 16A, 17B, 19H, 19J, 21D, 22A, 23D, 23E, 23F, 24B, 25D, 25E.*

Tim Thompson, *20A.*

Wexford Tourism, *2 top left, 15D.*

Nik Wheeler, *17C.*

ABOUT OUR WRITERS

Every Y2K trip is a significant trip. So if there was ever a time you needed excellent travel information, it's now. Acutely aware of that fact, we've pulled out all stops in preparing *Fodor's Ireland 2000*. To help you zero in on what to see in Ireland, we've gathered some great color photos of the key sights in every region. To show you how to put it all together, we've created great itineraries and neighborhood walks. And to direct you to the places that are truly worth your time and money in this important year, we've rallied the team of endearingly picky know-it-alls we're pleased to call our writers. Having seen all corners of the regions they cover for us, they're real experts. If you knew them, you'd poll them for tips yourself.

The updater of our golf chapter is Dublin native and resident **Dermot Gilleece,** the golf correspondent for the *Irish Times* and author of several books on golf, including a biography of Harry Bradshaw. In the course of his work he reports on all of the game's leading events, including the U.S. Masters, U.S. Open, British Open, and the U.S.P.G.A. Championships.

Geoff Hill is the travel editor of the *News Letter,* Northern Ireland's main morning newspaper. He writes regularly for the travel sections of the *Independent* and the Sunday and daily *Telegraph* in London, and has won six U.K. travel writing awards in the past six years.

A full-time freelance writer who lives near the sea in County Cork, **Alannah Hopkin,** our valued veteran contributor, has worked on the guide since 1985. This year she covered the Midlands, Southeast, Southwest, and the West of Ireland. Alannah has published an acclaimed book on the cult of St. Patrick, a book-length guide to County Cork, two novels, and several short stories. She writes on the arts for the London *Sunday Times* and contributes regularly to the *Cork Examiner.*

Anto Howard is a Northside Dublin native who studied at Trinity College before acquiring his U.S. green card. He moved to New York, where he is currently a travel writer, editor, and playwright. He has written numerous articles on Ireland, Central America, Russia, and the U.S.

Our Dublin restaurant coverage is the handiwork of **Vincent Jamison.** He is the food and wine critic for *The Sunday Business Post,* Ireland's leading business publication, a college lecturer in journalism, and coauthor of the books *Writing for the Media* and *The Media Primer.* Vincent brings his broad travel experience and wide-ranging interest in exotic cuisines and wines from the New World and the Old to many of the reviews in our Dublin dining section.

Don't Forget to Write

We love feedback—positive and negative—and follow up on all suggestions. So contact the Ireland editor at editors@fodors.com or c/o Fodor's, 201 East 50th Street, New York, NY 10022. Have a wonderful trip!

Karen Cure

Karen Cure
Editorial Director